CAMBRIDGE LIBRARY C

Books of enduring scholarly ι

Classics

From the Renaissance to the nineteenth century, Latin and Greek were compulsory subjects in almost all European universities, and most early modern scholars published their research and conducted international correspondence in Latin. Latin had continued in use in Western Europe long after the fall of the Roman empire as the lingua franca of the educated classes and of law, diplomacy, religion and university teaching. The flight of Greek scholars to the West after the fall of Constantinople in 1453 gave impetus to the study of ancient Greek literature and the Greek New Testament. Eventually, just as nineteenth-century reforms of university curricula were beginning to erode this ascendancy, developments in textual criticism and linguistic analysis, and new ways of studying ancient societies, especially archaeology, led to renewed enthusiasm for the Classics. This collection offers works of criticism, interpretation and synthesis by the outstanding scholars of the nineteenth century.

History of Greece

This vast study, first published between 1784 and 1818, and written on an unprecedentedly large historical scale, was begun at the urging of the author's friend Edward Gibbon. William Mitford (1744–1827), a scholar of private means, a magistrate and an MP, was concerned for the preservation of national and military stability, and he in part used his work to draw parallels between the rise of Athenian democracy and the contemporary status of the British constitution. This stance drew some criticism initially, but Mitford's approach was later praised in the wake of the French Revolution. The *History*, therefore, offers fascinating insights into its own time as well as a study of ancient Greece. The four volumes reissued here are from the uniform edition of 1808. The second volume takes the story of events in Greece from the Thirty Years' Truce to 404 BCE and the end of the Peloponnesian War.

Cambridge University Press has long been a pioneer in the reissuing of out-of-print titles from its own backlist, producing digital reprints of books that are still sought after by scholars and students but could not be reprinted economically using traditional technology. The Cambridge Library Collection extends this activity to a wider range of books which are still of importance to researchers and professionals, either for the source material they contain, or as landmarks in the history of their academic discipline.

Drawing from the world-renowned collections in the Cambridge University Library, and guided by the advice of experts in each subject area, Cambridge University Press is using state-of-the-art scanning machines in its own Printing House to capture the content of each book selected for inclusion. The files are processed to give a consistently clear, crisp image, and the books finished to the high quality standard for which the Press is recognised around the world. The latest print-on-demand technology ensures that the books will remain available indefinitely, and that orders for single or multiple copies can quickly be supplied.

The Cambridge Library Collection will bring back to life books of enduring scholarly value (including out-of-copyright works originally issued by other publishers) across a wide range of disciplines in the humanities and social sciences and in science and technology.

History of Greece

VOLUME 2

WILLIAM MITFORD

CAMBRIDGE
UNIVERSITY PRESS

CAMBRIDGE UNIVERSITY PRESS

Cambridge, New York, Melbourne, Madrid, Cape Town, Singapore,
São Paolo, Delhi, Dubai, Tokyo

Published in the United States of America by Cambridge University Press, New York

www.cambridge.org
Information on this title: www.cambridge.org/9781108011051

© in this compilation Cambridge University Press 2010

This edition first published 1808
This digitally printed version 2010

ISBN 978-1-108-01105-1 Paperback

THE

HISTORY

OF

GREECE.

By WILLIAM MITFORD, Esq.

———————

THE SECOND VOLUME.

———————

LONDON:

Printed by Luke Hansard & Sons, near Lincoln's-Inn Fields,

FOR T. CADELL AND W. DAVIES, IN THE STRAND.

1808.

CONTENTS

OF THE

SECOND VOLUME.

——————

CHAPTER XIII.

Affairs of GREECE, from the Thirty-Years Truce to that commonly called the PELOPONNESIAN WAR; with a summary view of the history of MACEDONIA, from the earliest accounts.

CHAPTER XIV.

Of the PELOPONNESIAN WAR, from its Commencement to the Death of PERICLES, with a summary view of the History of THRACE.

CHAPTER XV.

Of the PELOPONNESIAN WAR, from the Death of PERICLES, in the third Year, to the Application for PEACE from LACEDÆMON in the seventh.

CHAPTER XVI.

Of the PELOPONNESIAN WAR, from the Application for PEACE from LACEDÆMON, in the seventh Year, to the Conclusion of PEACE between LACEDÆMON and ATHENS in the tenth Year.

Macedonia,

CHAPTER XVII.

Of the PELOPONNESIAN WAR, during the PEACE between LACEDÆMON and ATHENS.

SECT.

CHAPTER XVIII.

Of the Affairs of SICILY, and of the ATHENIAN Expedition into SICILY.

Sect.

CHAPTER XIX.

Affairs of GREECE, from the Conclusion of the SICILIAN Expedition, till the Return of ALCIBIADES to ATHENS, in the Twenty-fourth Year of the PELOPONNESIAN WAR.

ment

viii CONTENTS.

CHAPTER XX.

Affairs of GREECE, from the Return of ALCIBIADES to ATHENS, till the Conclusion of the PELOPONNESIAN WAR.

THE

THE

H-I S T O R Y

OF

G R E E C E.

CHAPTER XIII.

Affairs of GREECE from the Thirty-Years Truce to that commonly called the PELOPONNESIAN WAR; with a summary View of the History of MACEDONIA from the earliest Accounts.

SECTION I.

Administration of Pericles: Science, Arts, and fine Taste at Athens. Change in the Condition of Women in Greece: Aspasia. Popular Licentiousness at Athens. The Athenian Empire asserted and extended. Project for Union of Greece.

ATHENS now rested six years, uningaged in any hostilities; a longer interval of perfect peace than she had before known in above forty years, elapsed since she rose from her ashes after the Persian invasion. It is a wonderful and singular phenomenon in the history of mankind, too little accounted for by anything recorded by antient, or imagined by modern writers, that, during this period of turbulence, in a commonwealth whose whole population in free subjects amounted scarcely to thirty thousand families, art, science, fine taste, and politeness, should have risen to that perfection which has made Athens the mistress of the world, through all succeeding ages. Some sciences indeed have been carried higher in modern times, and art has put forth new branches, of which some have given new helps to science: but Athens, in that age, reached a perfection of taste that no country hath since surpassed; but on the contrary all have looked up to, as a polar star, by which, after sinking in the deepest barbarism, taste has been guided in its restoration to splendor, and the observation of which will probably ever be the surest preservative against its future corruption and decay.

Much of these circumstances of glory to Athens, and of improvement, since so extensively spred over the world, was owing to Pericles. Peisistratus had nourished the infancy of Attic genius; Pericles brought it to maturity. In the age of Peisistratus books were scarcely known, science was vague, and art still rude. But during the turbulent period which intervened, things had been so wonderfully prepared, that, in the age of Pericles, science and every polite art waited, as it were, only his magic touch to exhibit them to the world in meridian splendor. The philosopher Anaxagoras of Clazomenë, whose force of understanding and extent of science acquired him the appellation of the Intellect, had been the tutor of the youth of Pericles, and remained the friend of his riper years. Among those with whom Pericles chiefly conversed was also the Athenian Pheidias, in whom, with a capacity for every science, was united the sublimest genius for the fine arts, which he professed; and Damon, who, professing only music, was esteemed the ablest speculative politician that the world had yet produced. Nor must the celebrated Aspasia be omitted in the enumeration of those to whom Pericles was indebted for the cultivation of his mind; since we have it on the authority of Plato, that Socrates himself acknowleged to have profited from the instruction of that extraordinary woman.

Plat. Alcib. 1. p. 118. t. 2. Plut. vit. Peric.

Plat. Menex.

It will not be the place here to inlarge upon the manners any more than upon the arts and knowlege, of the age of Pericles; yet it may be requisite to advert to one point, in which a great change had taken

place

place since the age which Homer has described.   The political circumstances of Greece, and especially of Athens, had contributed much to
exclude women of rank from general society.   The turbulence to which
every commonwealth was continually liable, from the contentions of
faction, made it often unsafe, or at least unpleasant for them to go
abroad.   But in democracies their situation was peculiarly untoward.
That form of government compelled the men to associate all with all.
The general assembly necessarily called all together; and the vote of
the meanest citizen being there of equal value with that of the highest,
the more numerous body of the poor was always formidable to the
wealthy few.   Hence followed the utmost condescension, or something
more than condescension, from the rich to the multitude; and not to
the collected multitude only, nor to the best among the multitude, but
principally to the most turbulent, illmannered, and worthless.   Not
those alone who sought honors or commands, but all who desired security for their property, must not only meet these men upon a footing
of equality in the general assembly, but associate with them in the
gymnasia and porticoes, flatter them, and sometimes cringe to them.
The ladies, to avoid a society which their fathers and husbands could
not avoid, lived with their female slaves, in a secluded part of the
house; associating little with oneanother, and scarcely at all with the
men, even their nearest relations; and seldom appearing in public, but
at those religious festivals in which antient custom required the women
to bear a part, and sacerdotal authority could insure decency of conduct
toward them.   Hence the education of the Grecian ladies in general,
and particularly the Athenian, was scarcely above that of their slaves;
and, as we find them exhibited in lively picture, in the little treatise   See also
upon domestic economy remaining to us from Xenophon, they were   Lysias
                                                                                                against
equally of uninstructed minds, and unformed manners.   Diogeiton.

   To the deficiencies to which women of rank were thus condemned,
by custom which the new political circumstances of the country had
superinduced upon the better manners of the heroic ages, was owing
that comparative superiority, through which some of the Grecian
courtezans attained extraordinary renown.   Carefully instructed in
every elegant accomplishment, and, from early years, accustomed to

converse among men, and men of the highest rank and most improved talents, if they possessed understanding it became cultivated; and to their houses men resorted, not meerly in the low pursuit of sensual pleasure, but to injoy, often in the most polished company, the charms of female conversation, which, with women of rank and character, was totally forbidden.   Hence, at the time of the invasion under Xerxes, more than one Grecian city is said to have been ingaged in the Persian interest through the influence of Thargelia, a Milesian courtezan, who was afterward raised to the throne of Thessaly.

Plut. vit. Peric.

Aspasia was also a Milesian, the daughter of Axiochus; for her celebrity has preserved her father's name.   With uncommon beauty were joined in Aspasia still more uncommon talents; and, with a mind the most cultivated, manners so decent, that, in her more advanced years, not only Socrates professed to have learned eloquence from her; but, as Plutarch relates, the ladies of Athens used to accompany their husbands to her house for the instruction of her conversation.   Pericles became her passionate admirer, and she attached herself to him during his life: according to Plutarch he divorced his wife, with whom he had lived on ill terms, to marry her.   We are informed, on higher authority, that he was not fortunate in his family, his sons being mentioned by Plato as youths of mean understanding.   After he was once firmly established at the head of the Athenian administration, he passed his little leisure from public business mostly in company with Aspasia and a few select friends; avoiding that extensive society in which the Athenians in general delighted, and seldom seen by the people, but in the exercise of some public office, or speaking in the general assembly: a reserve perhaps as advantageous to him, as the contrary conduct was necessary to the ambitious who were yet but aspiring at greatness, or to the wealthy without power, who desired security to their property.

Plat. Menon. p. 94. t. 2. & Alcib. 1. p. 118. t. 2.

Policy united with natural inclination to induce Pericles to patronize the arts, and call forth their finest productions for the admiration and delight of the Athenian people.   The Athenian people were the despotic soverein; Pericles the favorite and minister, whose business it was to indulge the soverein's caprices that he might direct their measures; and he had the skill often to direct even their caprices.   That fine taste
which

which he possessed eminently, was in some degree general among the Athenians; and the gratification of that fine taste was one mean by which he retained his influence. Works were undertaken, according to the expression of Plutarch, in whose time they still remained perfect, of stupendous magnitude, and in form and grace inimitable; all calculated for the accommodation, or in some way for the gratification, of the multitude. Pheidias was superintendant of the works: under him many architects and artists were employed, whose merit intitled them to fame with posterity, and of whose labors (such is the hardness of the Attic marble, their principal material, and the mildness of the Attic atmosphere) relics which have escaped the violence of men, still after the lapse of more than two thousand years, exhibit all the perfection of design, and even of workmanship, which earned that fame.

Meanwhile Pheidias himself was executing works of statuary which were, while they lasted, the admiration of succeeding times. Nor does the testimony to these works, which are now totally, or almost totally lost, rest meerly upon Grecian report; for the Romans, when in possession of all the most exquisite productions of Grecian art, scanty relics of which have excited the wonder and formed the taste of modern ages, were at a loss to express their admiration of the sublimity of the works of Pheidias. When such was the perfection of the art of sculpture, it were a solecism to suppose that the sister art of painting could be mean, since the names of Panænus, kinsman of Pheidias, and Zeuxis and Parrhasius, cotemporaries, remained always among the most celebrated of the Grecian school. At the same time the chaste sublimity of the great tragic poets Æschylus, Sophocles, and Euripides, and that extraordinary mixture of the most elegant satire with the grossest buffoonery, the old comedy, as it is called, were alternately exhibited in immense theaters, at the public expence, and for the amusement of the whole people.

Thus captivating the Athenians by their relish for matters of taste and their passion for amusement, Pericles confirmed his authority principally by that great instrument for the management of a people, his eloquence: but this was supported by unremitted assiduity in public business, and evident superiority of capacity for the conduct of

it ;

it; and, above all, by an ostentatious integrity. The whole Athenian

Apud Plut.
in vit. Peric.
Plat.Alcib.1.
Alcib. 1.
p. 104. t. 2.

commonwealth thus, with all its appurtenances, or, in the words of cotemporary authors, revenues, armies, fleets, ilands, the sea, friendships and alliances with kings and various potentates, and influence that commanded several Grecian states and many barbarous nations, all were in a manner his possession. Plutarch says that, while thus, during fifteen years, ruling the Athenian empire, so strict and scrupulous was his economy in his private affairs, that he neither increased nor diminished his paternal estate by a single drachma : but, according to

Isocr. de
pace, p. 254.
t. 2. ed.
Auger.

the more probable assertion, and higher authority of Isocrates, his private estate suffered in maintaining his public importance, so that he left it less to his sons than he had received it from his father.

But the political power of Pericles resting on the patronage, which he professed, of democracy, he was obliged to allow much, and even to bear much, that a better constitution would have put under more restraint. Such, under his administration, was the popular licentious-

Plut. vit.
Peric.

ness, that the comic poets did not fear to vent, in the public theaters, the grossest jokes upon his person, the severest invectives against his administration, and even the most abominable calumnies upon his character. His connection with Aspasia was not likely to escape their satire. She was called, on the public stage, the Omphalë of her time, the Deïaneira, and even the Juno. Many circumstances of the administration of Pericles were malevolently attributed to her influence, and much gross abuse and much improbable calumny was vented against both of them. It would indeed be scarcely possible to distinguish almost any truth amid the licentiousness of wit, and the violence, not to say the atrociousness, of party-spirit at Athens, had we not generally, for this interesting period of history, the guidance of a cotemporary author, Thucydides son of Olorus ; of uncommon abilities and still more uncommon impartiality, and whose ample fortune, great connections, and high situation in the commonwealth, opened to him superior means of information. For what is omitted in the concise review of Grecian affairs, which he has prefixed to his history of the Peloponnesian war, we have sometimes some testimony from Xenophon, Plato, Aristotle, Isocrates, or the orators. To later writers, when not in some

degree

degree supported by these, it is seldom safe to trust. Sometimes they have adopted reports carelessly ; and often, as we find Plutarch frequently acknowleging, they have been unable to unravel truth amid contradiction and improbability. Indeed Plutarch, tho often extremely negligent, is yet often, and especially for the life of Pericles, our best assistant. He frequently quotes his authorities ; and where unbiassed by some evident prejudice, he is generally impartial.

We may then trust the united authorities of Thucydides, Isocrates, and Plutarch, notwithstanding the vague accusations reported by Diodorus and others, that the clear integrity of Pericles, not less than the wisdom of his public conduct, was his shield against the scurrility of the comic poets, so adapted to make impression on the popular mind, as well as against every effort of the opposing orators [1]. One great point however of his policy was to keep the people always either amused or employed. During peace an exercising squadron of sixty trireme gallies was sent out for eight months in every year. Nor was this without a farther use than meerly ingaging the attention of the people, and maintaining the navy in vigor. Himself occasionally took the command ; and sailing among the distant dependencies of the empire, settled disputes between them, and confirmed the power and extended the influence of Athens. The Ægean and the Propontis did not bound his voyages : he penetrated into the Euxine ; and finding the distant Grecian settlement of Sinopë divided between Timesileos, who affected the tyranny, and an opposing party, he left there Lamachus with thirteen ships, and a body of landforces, with whose assistance to the popular side the tyrant and those of his faction were expelled. Their houses and property, apportioned into six hundred lots, were offered to so many Athenian citizens ; and volunteers were not wanting to go upon such conditions to settle at Sinopë. To disburthen the government at home, by providing advantageous establishments, in distant parts, for the poor and discontented among the soverein citizens of Athens, was a policy often resorted to by Pericles.

[1] The expression of Thucydides is of that forcible kind which is almost peculiar to him, and to which his character gives an additional weight that it would hardly have from any other writer: Περικλῆς —— δυνατὸς ὢν τῷ τι αξιώματι καὶ τῇ γνώμῃ χρημάτων τι διαφανῶς ἀδωρότατ⊙ γενόμεν⊙. Thucyd. l. 2. c. 65..

We

Ch. 12. s. 4.
of this Hist.

Diod. l. 12.
c. 9, & seq.
Ch. 2. s. 2.
of this Hist.

We have already seen him conducting a colony to the Thracian Chersonese; and it was during his administration, in the same year, according to Diodorus, in which the thirty years truce was concluded, that the deputation came from the Thessalian adventurers, who had been expelled by the Crotoniats from their attempted establishment in the deserted territory of Sybaris, in consequence of which the colony was established, under his patronage, with which Herodotus and Lysias settled at Thurium.

Plutarch has attributed to Pericles a noble project, unnoticed by any earlier extant author, but worthy of his capacious mind, and otherwise also bearing some characters of authenticity and truth. It was no less than to unite all Greece under one great federal government, of which Athens should be the capital. But the immediate and direct avowal of such a purpose would be likely to raise jealousies so numerous and extensive, as to form insuperable obstacles to the execution. The religion of the nation, tho even in this every town, and almost every family claimed something peculiar to itself, was yet that alone in which the Grecian people universally claimed a clear common interest. In the vehemence of public alarm, during the Persian invasion, vows had been in some places made to the gods, for sacrifices, to an extent beyond what the votaries, when blessed with deliverance beyond hope, were able to perform; and some temples, destroyed by the invaders, probably also from the scantiness of means of those in whose territories they had stood, were not yet restored. Taking these circumstances then for his ground, Pericles proposed that a congress of deputies from every republic of the nation should be assembled at Athens, for the purpose first, of inquiring concerning vows for the safety of Greece yet unperformed, and temples, injured by the barbarians, not yet restored; and then of proceeding to concert measures for the lasting security of navigation in the Grecian seas, and for the preservation of peace by land also between all the states composing the Greek nation. The naval question, but still more the ruin which, in the Persian invasion, had befallen Northern Greece, and especially Attica, while Peloponnesus had felt nothing of its evils, gave pretension for Athens to take the lead in the business. On the motion of Pericles, a decree of the Athenian people directed the appointment

of

of ministers, to invite every Grecian state to send its deputies. Plutarch, rarely attentive to political information, has not at all indicated what attention was shown, or what participation proposed, for Lacedæmon. His prejudices indeed we find very generally adverse to the Lacedæmonian government, and favoring the Athenian democracy. But, judging from the friendship which, according to the authentic information of Thucydides, subsisted between Pericles and Archidamus, king of Lacédæmon, through life, it is little likely that, in putting forward the project for the peace of Greece, Pericles would have proposed anything derogatory to the just weight and dignity of Sparta; which would indeed have been, with the pretence of the purpose of peace, only to have put forward a project of contest. Pericles, when he formed his coälition with Cimon, seems to have entered heartily into the inlarged views of that great man, and with the hope that, through their coälition, both the oligarchal and the democratical powers in Athens might be held justly balanced, had early in view to establish the peace of Greece on a union between Athens and Lacedæmon. It is however evident, from the narrative of Thucydides, that Archidamus rarely could direct the measures of the Lacedæmonian government. On a view of all information then it seems most probable that the project of Pericles was concerted with Archidamus; and that the opposition of those in Lacedæmon of an adverse faction, concurred with opposition from those in Athens, who apprehended injury to their interest from a new coälition with the aristocratical party, to compel the great projector to abandon his magnificent and beneficent purpose in a stage so early, that it was no object for the notice of the able and accurate cotemporary historian, in that valuable abridgement of early Grecian history which precedes his narrative of the Peloponnesian war.

SECTION II.

War between Samos and Miletus: Interference of Athens: Armament under Pericles: Samos taken. Funeral Solemnity at Athens in honor of the Slain in their Country's Service.

PEACE between Lacedæmon and Athens was indispensable toward the quiet of the rest of the nation, but, in the want of such a union as Pericles had projected, was unfortunately far from insuring it; and when war began anywhere, tho among the most distant settlements of the Grecian people, how far it might extend was not to be foreseen. A dispute between two Asiatic states, of the Athenian confederacy, led Athens into a war, which greatly indangered the
B. C. 440.
Ol. 84. 4.
Thucyd. l. 1.
c. 115.
truce made for thirty years, when it had scarcely lasted six. Miletus and Samos, claiming each the sovereinty of Priënë, itself originally a free Grecian commonwealth, asserted their respective pretensions by arms. The Milesians, not till they were suffering under defeat, applied to Athens for redress, as of a flagrant injury done them. The usual feuds within every Grecian state furnished assistance to their clamor; for, the aristocracy prevailing at that time in Samos, the leaders of the democratical party joined the enemies of their country, in accusing the proceedings of its government before the
Plut. vit.
Peric.
Athenian people. The opposition at Athens maliciously imputed the measures, which followed, to the weak compliance of Pericles with the solicitations of Aspasia, in favor of her native city; but it appears clearly from Thucydides, that no such motive was necessary: the Athenian government would of course take connisance of the cause; and such a requisition as might be expected, was accordingly sent to the Samian administration, to answer by deputies at Athens to the charges urged against them. The Samians, unwilling to submit their claim to the arbitration of those who they knew were always systematically adverse to the aristocratical interest, refused to send any

deputies.

deputies. A fleet of forty trireme gallies, however, brought them to immediate submission; their government was changed to a democracy, in which those who had headed the opposition of course took the lead ; and to insure permanent acquiescence from the aristocratical party, fifty men and fifty boys, of the first families of the iland, were taken as hostages, and placed under an Athenian guard in the iland of Lemnos.

What Herodotus mentions, as an observation applicable generally, we may readily believe was on this occasion experienced in Samos, ' that the lower people were most unpleasant associates to the nobles[a]. A number of these, unable to support the oppression to which they found themselves exposed, quitted the iland, and applied to Pissuthnes, satrap of Sardis, from whom they found a favorable reception.   At the same time.they maintained a correspondence with those of their party remaining in Samos, and they ingaged in their interest the city of Byzantium, itself a subject-ally of Athens.   Collecting then about seven hundred auxiliary soldiers, they crossed by night the narrow channel which separates Samos from the continent, and being joined by their friends, they surprized and overpowered the new administration. Without delay they proceeded to Lemnos, and so well conducted their enterprize, that they carried off their hostages; together with the Athenian guard set over them.   To win more effectually the favor of the satrap, the Athenian prisoners were presented to him. Receiving then assurance of assistance from Byzantium, and being not without hopes from Lacedæmon, they prepared to prosecute their success by immediately undertaking an expedition against Miletus.

Information of these transactions arriving quickly at Athens, Pericles, with nine others, according to the antient military constitution, joined with him in command, hastened to Samos with a fleet of sixty trireme galleys. Sixteen of these were detached, some to Chios and Lesbos, to require the assistance of the squadrons of those ilands, the rest to the Carian coast, to look out for a Phenician fleet in the Persian service, which was expected to support the Samians. Pericles with the remaining forty-four ships met the Samian fleet of seventy, returning from Miletus, and defeated it. Being soon after joined by forty more

Thucyd. l. 1. c. 116, 117.

[a] Συνοίκημα ἀχαριτώτατον. Herod. l. 7. c. 156.

c 2   gallies

gallies from Athens, and twenty-five from Chios and Lesbos, he debarked his infantry on the iland of Samos, and laid siege to the city of the same name, by land and sea.   Intelligence meanwhile arriving that the fleet from Phenicia was approaching, Pericles went with sixty of his gallies to Caunus in Caria; apparently apprehensive for his small squadron there.   The Samians, under the conduct of the able Melissus, (who, as was not unusual in that age, united the characters of philosopher and military commander) hastened to profit from his absence.   Issuing unexpectedly from the harbor with their fleet, they attacked the Athenian naval camp, which was unfortified, destroyed the ships stationed as an advanced guard [3], and then defeated the rest of the fleet, hastily formed for action against them.   Becoming thus masters of the sea, during fourteen days they had all opportunity for carrying supplies into the town.

Thucyd. l. 1. c. 41.

Meanwhile an assembly of deputies from the states of the Peloponnesian confederacy was held at Sparta, to consider whether the aristocratical party in Samos should be protected in what, according to Grecian political tenets extensively held in that age, was rebellion [4]. The Corinthians, yet weak from the consequences of their last war with Athens, principally decided the assembly to the rejection of the proposal.   Indeed, unless an invasion of Attica by land might have been effectual, the confederacy had not means to carry it into execution ; for its naval strength was very unequal to a contention with that of Athens.

The Samians, thus disappointed of assistance from Peloponnesus, were weakly supported by the satrap, and the promised succour from Byzantium was delayed.   The return of Pericles therefore compelled them to confine themselves within their harbor: and shortly a reïnforcement arrived to him, which might have inabled a less skilful

[3] Τὰς προφυλακίδας ναῦς: for which may be consulted Scheffer's treatise de Militiâ Navali, l. 3. c. 4. p. 108. tho he is not very satisfactory. 1 would not however undervalue his laborious compilation, which may often guard against the supposition of what was not, where it fails to inform what was.

[4] Ministers from Corinth, afterward giving an account to the Athenian assembly of what had passed at Sparta upon the occasion mentioned in the text, affirmed that their deputies had asserted the right of every leading city to PUNISH its allies: τοὺς σφετέρους ξυμμάχους αυτόν τινα κολάζειν. Thucyd. l. 1. c. 43.

commander

commander to overbear opposition; forty gallies from Attica, under Thucydides[5], Agnon, and Phormion, were followed by twenty more under Tlepolemus and Anticles, while thirty came from Chios and Lesbos. The Samians made one vain attempt to cut off a part of this formidable naval force; and then, in the ninth month from the commencement of the siege, they capitulated: their ships of war were surrendered, their fortifications were destroyed, they bound themselves to the payment of a sum of money by installment for the expences of the war, and they gave hostages as pledges of their fidelity to the soverein commonwealth of Athens. The Byzantines, not waiting the approach of the coërcing fleet, sent their request to be reädmitted to their former terms of subjection, which was granted.

This rebellion, alarming and troublesome at the time to the administration of Athens, otherwise little disturbed the internal peace of the commonwealth; and in the event contributed rather to strengthen its command over its dependencies. Pericles took occasion from it to acquire fresh popularity. On the return of the armament to Athens, the accustomed solemnities in honor of those who had fallen in the war were performed with new splendor; and in speaking the funeral oration, he exerted the powers of his eloquence very highly to the gratification of the people. As he descended from the bema, even the women presented him with chaplets; an ideä derived from the ceremonies of the public games, where the crowning with a chaplet was the distinction of the victors, and, as something approaching to divine honor, was held among the highest tokens of admiration, esteem, and respect.

[5] The historian not having distinguished the Thucydides here spoken of, by the mention of his father's name, it remains in doubt who he was. Some have supposed him the historian himself; others, the son of Melesias, once the opponent of Pericles, now reconciled to him; while others have imagined a third person of the name, nowhere else mentioned in history. No certainty can be had, and the matter is not important; but the first supposition appears to me far the most probable. Agnon and Phormion become, in the course of the history, farther known to us.

SECTION   III.

Affairs of Corcyra : Sedition at Epidamnus : War between Corcyra
and Corinth : Defect of the antient Ships of War : deficient Naval
Skill of the Peloponnesians : Sea-Fight off Actium : Accession of
the Corcyræans to the Athenian Confederacy : Sea-fight off Sybota :
Infraction of the Thirty-Years Truce.

THE threatened renewal of general war in Greece having been obviated,
by the determination of the Peloponnesian congress not to interfere
between the Athenians and their Asiatic allies, peace prevailed during
the next three years after the submission of the Samians; or, if hostilities occurred anywhere, they were of so little importance that no
account of them remains.   A fatal spark then, raising fire in a
corner of the country, hitherto little within the notice of history, the
blaze rapidly spred over the whole, with inextinguishable fury; insomuch that the further history of Greece, with some splendid episodes,
is chiefly a tale of calamities, which the nation, in ceaseless exertions
of misdirected valor and genius, brought upon itself.

The iland of Corcyra, occupied in an early age by a colony from
Corinth, became, in process of time, too powerful to remain a dependency, and, becoming independent, was too near a neighbor, and too
much ingaged in the same course of maritime commerce, not to be the
rival and the enemy of its metropolis.   It was common for the Grecian
colonies, even when they acknowleged no political subjection, to pay
a reverential regard to the mother-country; holding themselves bound

Thucyd. l. 1. by a kind of religious superiority.   At all public sacrifices and festivals,
c. 25.
          the citizens of the mother-country were complimented with the pre-
c. 24. cedency; and, if a colony was to be sent out, it was usual to desire a
citizen of the mother-country for the leader.   Thus, it was supposed,
the gods of their forefathers would still be their gods, would favor
the enterprize, and extend their lasting protection to the settlement.

Corcyra, already populous, had not yet intirely broken its connection with Corinth, when the resolution was taken by its gover-
ment to settle a colony on the Illyrian coast.   An embassy was therefore

fore sent, in due form, to desire a Corinthian for the leader.   Phalius, of a family boasting its descent from Hercules, was accordingly appointed to that honor: some Corinthians, and others of Dorian race, accompanied him; and Phalius thus became the nominal founder of Epidamnus, which was however considerd as a Corcyræan, not a Corinthian colony.

But in process of time, Epidamnus, growing populous and wealthy, followed the example of its mother-country, asserted independency, and maintained the claim.   Like most other Grecian cities, it was then, during many years, torn by sedition; and a war supervening with the neighboring barbarians, it fell much from its former florishing state. But the spirit of faction remaining, in spite of misfortnne, untamed, the commonalty at length expelled all the higher citizens.   These, finding refuge among the Illyrians, ingaged with them in a predatory war, which was unremittingly carried on against the city by land and sea.   Unable thus to rest, and nearly deprived of means even to subsist, the Epidamnians in possession resolved to request assistance from Corcyra.   Conscious however that their state had no claim of merit with the mother-country, those deputed on this business, when they landed on the iland, instead of presenting themselves with the confidence of public ministers, put on the usual habit of suppliants, and betaking themselves to the temple of Juno, thence addressed their petition.   The government of Corcyra appears to have been at this time aristocratical; and hence arose, with the Epidamnian ministers, the greater doubt of a favorable reception.   In their petition, therefore, they ventured to desire nothing more than the mediation of their metropolis with their expelled fellowcitizens, and protection against the barbarians; but even this humble supplication was totally rejected.

On the return of their ministers, the Epidamnians, in great distress, determined to recur to the antient resource of desponding states, the Delphian oracle.   Sending a solemn deputation to Delphi, they put the question to the god, ' Whether it would be proper for them to ' endevor to obtain protection from Corinth, by acknowleging that city ' as their metropolis, and submitting themselves accordingly to its

Thucd. l. 1.
c. 25.

' authority?'

' authority?' The response directed them, in clear terms, to do so ; and a deputation was in consequence immediately sent to Corinth[6].

The Corinthians were upon no friendly terms with Corcyra. The people of that iland, now among the richest and most powerful of Greece, had not only shaken off all political dependence upon them, but denied them all those honors and compliments usually paid by Grecian colonies to their parent states. Animosity therefore stimulating, the oracle incouraging, and the appearance of a fair claim seeming moreover to justify the opportunity for making an acquisition of dominion, the Corinthians accepted the proposal of the Epidamnians. A number of adventurers was collected to strengthen the colony ; and a body of Corinthian troops, with some Ambraciot and Leucadian auxiliaries, was appointed to convoy them. Fearful however of the naval force of Corcyra, which far exceeded that of Corinth, they passed by land to Apollonia, and, there imbarking, proceeded by sea to Epidamnus.

B.C. 436.
Ol. 86. 1.

No sooner was it known at Corcyra that the Corinthians had thus taken possession of a colony in whose affairs the Corcyræans themselves had refused to interfere, than the affair was taken up with warm resentment. Twenty-five triremes were immediately dispatched, with a requisition to the Epidamnians to receive their expelled fellowcitizens (for these had now been supplicating protection from Corcyra) and to dismiss the Corinthian colonists and garrison. This being refused, a reinforcement was sent to the squadron, which, in conjunction with the expelled Epidamnians and the neighboring Illyrians, laid siege to the town.

Thucyd.
l. 1. c. 27.

The Corinthian government was prepared to expect such measures.

---

[6] —— Εἰ παραδοῖεν Κορινθίοις τὴν πόλιν, ὡς οἰκιςαῖς;——Ὁ δ'αὐτοῖς ἀνεῖλε παραδῶναι, καὶ ἡγεμόνας ποιεῖσθαι. Thucyd. l. 1. c.25. In Thucydides's account of the disputes between Corinth, Corcyra, and Epidamnus, and of that which followed about Potidæa, we have more authentic information concerning the proper connection between a Grecian colony and its metropolis, than is perhaps elsewhere to be found ; but we are without means of determining the exact import of the expressions παραδῶναι τὴν πόλιν ὡς οἰκιςαῖς, and ἡγεμόνας ποιεῖσθαι, and we are equally uninformed of the proper authority of those Corinthian magistrates whom we find, in the sequel, annually sent to the colony of Potidæa in Thrace.

As

As soon therefore as intelligence of them was received, a proclamation was published, offering the privileges of a citizen of Epidamnus to any who would go immediately to settle there, and also to any who, chusing to avoid the dangers of the present circumstances, would pay fifty drachmas toward the expense of the expedition. What the advantages annexed to the citizenship of Epidamnus were we are not informed, but an allotment of land would probably make a part, and the sum to be risked was small. Corinth abounded with rich men and poor; and many were found to ingage personally in the adventure, and many to pay for the chance of profit from the event. But Corinth had at this time only thirty ships of war, whereas Corcyra was able to put to sea near four times the number; being, next to Athens, the most powerful maritime state of Greece. Application was therefore made to the republics, with which Corinth was most bound in friendship, for naval assistance. Eight ships were thus obtained from Megara, four from the Paleans of Cephallenia, five from Epidaurus, one from Hermionë, two from Trœzen, ten from Leucas, eight from Ambracia, and the Eleians lent some unmanned. Loans of money were moreover obtained from the Eleians, Phliasians, and Thebans. *Thucyd. l. 1. c. 27. & c. 30.*

It had been the settled policy of the Corcyræans, ilanders and strong at sea, to ingage in no alliances. They had avoided both the Peloponnesian and the Athenian confederacy; and with this policy they had hitherto prospered. But, alarmed now at the combination formed against them, and fearing it might still be extended, they sent ambassadors to Lacedæmon and Sicyon; who prevailed so far that ministers from those two states accompanied them to Corinth, as mediators in the existing differences. In presence of these the Corcyræan ambassadors proposed, to the Corinthian government, to submit the matters in dispute to the arbitration of any Peloponnesian states, on which they could agree; or to the Delphian oracle, which the Corinthians had supposed already favorable to them.. The Corinthians however, now prepared for war, and apparently persuaded that neither Lacedæmon nor Sicyon would take any active part against them, refused to treat upon any equal terms, and the Corcyræan ambassadors departed. *c. 32. & seq.* *c. 28.*

The Corinthians then hastened to use the force they had collected. The

The troops were already imbarked, when they sent a herald to Corcyra formally to declare war; a ceremony required by custom, which, throughout Greece, was held sacred.   But tho they would not omit this, they would delay it, till it might in the least possible degree answer its proper purpose.   The armament, consisting of seventy-five triremes, with two thousand heavy-armed infantry, under the command of Aristeus son of Pellicus, then proceeded for Epidamnus.   Off Actium in the Anactorian territory, at the entrance of the Ambracian gulph, where, as the cotemporary historian describes it, the temple of Apollo, stands (a place destined to be in after-times the scene of more important action) a vessel came to them with a herald from Corcyra, deprecating hostilities.   The Corcyræans had manned those of their ships which were already equipped, and hastily prepared some of those less in readiness, when their herald returned, bearing no friendly answer. With eighty galleys they then quitted their port, met the enemy, and gained a complete victory, destroying fifteen ships.   Returning to Corcyra, they erected their trophy on the headland of Leucimnë, and they immediately put to death all their prisoners, except the Corinthians, whom they kept in bonds.   Epidamnus surrendered to their forces on the same day.

The opportunities now open, for both revenge and profit, were not neglected by the Corcyræans.   They first plundered the territory of Leucas, a Corinthian colony, still connected with the mother-country: then going to the coast of Peloponnesus, they burnt Cyllenë, the naval arsenal of Elis.   Continuing nearly a year unopposed on the sea, there was scarcely an intermission of their smaller enterprizes; by some of which they gained booty, by others only gave alarm, but by all together greatly distressed the Corinthians and their allies.   It was not till late in the following spring that the Corinthians sent a fleet and some troops to Actium, to observe the motions of the enemy, and give protection to their friends, wherever occasion might require.   All the insuing summer the rival armaments watched one another without coming to action, and on the approach of winter, both retired within their respective ports.

B. C. 434.
Ol. 87. ⅔.

But, since their misfortune off Actium, the Corinthians had been unremittingly assiduous in repairing their loss, and in preparing to revenge it.

Thucyd. l. 1.
c. 31.

it. Triremes were built, all necessaries for a fleet were largely collected, rowers were ingaged throughout Peloponnesus, and where else they could be obtained for hire in any part of Greece. The Corcyræans, informed of these measures, were uneasy, notwithstanding their past success, with the consideration that their commonwealth stood single, while their enemies were members of an extensive confederacy; of which, tho a part only had yet been induced to act, more powerful exertions were nevertheless to be apprehended. In this state of things it appeared necessary to abandon their antient policy, and to seek alliances. Thucydides gives us to understand that they would have preferred the Peloponnesian to the Athenian confederacy; induced, apparently, both by their kindred origin, and their kindred form of government. But they were precluded from it by the circumstances of the existing war, Corinth being one of its most considerable members; and there was no hope that Lacedæmon could be ingaged in measures hostile to so old and useful an ally. It was therefore determined to send an embassy to negotiate alliance with Athens. *Thucyd. l. 1. c. 28.* *c. 31.*

A measure of this kind, among the antient commonwealths, if they had any mixture of democracy, was unavoidably public; and this is one among the circumstances favorable to antient history, which counterbalance the want of some advantages open to the historians of modern ages. Gazettes were then unknown; records and state writings were comparatively few; party-intrigues indeed abounded; but public measures were publicly decided; and some of the principal historians were statesmen and generals, bred to a knowlege of politics and war, and possessing means, through their rank and situation, of knowing also the facts which they related. Such particularly was Thucydides, son of Olorus, who has transmitted to us the transactions of the times with which we are now ingaged. No sooner then, as we learn from him, was the purpose of the Corcyræans known at Corinth, than ambassadors were sent thence also to Athens, to remonstrate against it.

The Athenian people were assembled to receive the two embassies, each of which, in presence of the other, made its proposition in a formal oration. The point to be determined was highly critical for Athens. A truce

existed

existed, but not a peace, with a confederacy, inferior indeed in naval force, but far superior by land ; and Attica, a continental territory, was

Thucyd. l.1.
c. 40. & 43.

open to attack by land.　That recent circumstance in the Samian war, the assembling of a congress at Sparta, for the purpose of considering whether the Samians, an Ionian people, a colony from Athens, and members of the Athenian alliance, should not be supported in war against their metropolis, the head of their confederacy, could but weigh in the minds of the Athenian people.　The meer summoning of such an assembly, to discuss such a question, strongly indicated the disposition of a powerful party at least in the Lacedæmonian confederacy ; and the determination of the question, in the negative, demonstrated a present unreadiness, principally among the Corinthians for the renewal of hostilities, from which they had lately suffered, rather than any friendly disposition to Athens.　The security of Athens rested principally on her maritime superiority.　But Corcyra was, next to Athens, the most powerful by sea of the Grecian republics ; and to prevent the accession of its maritime strength, through alliance, or through conquest, to the Peloponnesian confederacy, was highly important.　In the articles of the truce, moreover, it was expressly stipulated, that

c. 35. & 40.

any Grecian state, not yet a member of either confederacy, might at pleasure be admitted to either.　But, notwithstanding this, it was little

c. 44.

less than certain, that, in the present circumstances, an alliance with Corcyra must lead to a rupture with the Peloponnesians ; and this consideration occasioned much suspence in the minds of the Athenians. Twice the assembly was held to debate the question.　On the first day, the arguments of the Corinthian ambassadors had so far effect that nothing was decided: on the second, the question was carried for the alliance with Corcyra.

Thucydides gives no information what part Pericles took in this important and difficult conjuncture.　If it was impoffible, as it seems to have been, to establish secure peace with Lacedæmon, it would become the leader of the affairs of Athens to provide for maintaining future war; for strengthening the Athenian, and obviating accession of strength to the Lacedæmonian confederacy.　But we are enough informed that Pericles would be further pressed by other circumstances.

cumstances.   The difficulty of keeping civil order in a community of lordly beggars, such as the Athenian people were, which had driven Cimon, in advanced years, to end his life in distant enterprize, we shall find, in the sequel, a difficulty for which, even in speculation, the wisest politicians were unable to propose any remedy, beyond finding the fittest objects for restless ambition.   It is therefore everyway likely that Plutarch had ground for asserting, that the eloquence of Pericles was employed to promote the decision to which the people came.   The character of the measure taken, in pursuance of the decision, may seem to indicate the wisdom of Pericles, guiding the business: with all other states of the confederacy. the alliance was offensive and defensive; with Corcyra it was for defence only.   Meanwhile the earnestness with which the Corinthians persevered in their purpose of prosecuting the war against the Corcyræans, now to be supported by the power of Athens, appears to mark confidence in support, on their side, from the Lacedæmonian confederacy; some members of which indeed were evidently of ready zeal.   The Corinthians increased their own trireme galleys to ninety. The Eleians, resenting the burning of Cyllenë, had exerted themselves in naval preparation, and sent ten triremes completely manned to join them.   Assistance from Megara, Leucas, and Ambracia, made their whole fleet a hundred and fifty: the crews would hardly be less than forty thousand men.   With this large force they sailed to Cheimerion, a port of Thesprotia, overagainst Corcyra, where, according to the practice of the Greeks, they formed their naval camp.

Thucyd.
l.1. c.46.

The Athenian government, meanwhile, desirous to confirm their new alliance, yet still anxious to avoid a rupture with the Peloponnesian confederacy, had sent ten triremes to Corcyra, under the command of Lacedæmonius son of Cimon; but with orders not to fight, unless a descent should be made on the iland, or any of its towns should be attacked.   The Corcyræans, on receiving intelligence that the enemy was approaching, put to sea with a hundred and ten triremes, exclusive of the Athenian, and formed their naval camp on one of the small ilets called Sybota, the Sowleas or Sowpastures, between their own iland and the main.   Their landforces at the same time, with a thousand

l.1. c.45.

l.1. c.47.

sand auxilliaries from Zacynths, incamped on the headland of Lucimne in Corcyra, to be prepared against invasion; while the barbarians of the continent, long since friendly to Corinth, assembled in large numbers on the opposite coast.

The necessity among the antients for debarking continually to incamp their crews, arose from the make of their ships of war. To obtain that most valuable property for their manner of naval action, swiftness in rowing, burden was excluded: insomuch that not only they

Thucyd. 1. 4. c. 26.
l. 1. c. 44.

could not carry any stock of provisions, but the numerous crews could neither sleep nor even eat conveniently aboard. When the Corinthians quitted the port of Cheimerion, with the purpose of bringing the Corcyræan fleet to action, they took three days provision; which Thucydides seems to have thought a circumstance for notice, because

l. 7. c. 39, 40.

it appears to have been the practice of the Athenians, when action was expected, hardly to incumber themselves with a meal. Moving in the night, the Corinthians, with the dawn, perceived the Corcyræan fleet approaching. Both prepared immediately to ingage. So great a

l. 1. c. 48.

number of ships had never before met in any action between Greeks and Greeks. The onset was vigorous; and the battle was maintained,

c. 50.

on either side, with much courage but little skill. Both Corcyræan

c. 49.

and Corinthian ships were equipped in the antient manner, very inartificially. The decks were crouded with soldiers, some heavy-armed, some with missile weapons; and the action, in the eye of the Athenians, trained in the discipline of Themistocles, resembled a battle of infantry rather than a sea-fight. Once ingaged, the number and throng of the vessels made free motion impossible: nor was there any attempt at the rapid evolution of the diëcplus, as it was called, for piercing the enemy's line and dashing away his oars, the great objects of the improved naval tactics; but the event depended, as of old, chiefly upon the heavy-armed soldiers who fought on the decks. Tumult and confusion thus prevailing everywhere, Lacedæmonius, restrained by his orders from fighting, gave yet some assistance to the Corcyræans, by showing himself wherever he saw them particularly pressed, and alarming their enemies. The Corcyræans were, in the left of their line, successful: twenty of their ships put to flight the Megarians and Ambraciots who

were

were oppoted to them, pursued to the shore, and, debarking, plundered and burnt the naval camp.　But the Corinthians, in the other wing, had meanwhile been gaining an advantage, which became decisive through the imprudent forwardness of the victorious Corcyræans.　The Athenians now endevored, by more effectual assistance to their allies, to prevent a total rout: but disorder was already too prevalent, and advantage of numbers too great against them.　The Corinthians pressed their success; the Corcyræans fled, the Athenians became mingled among them; and in the confusion of a running fight, acts of hostility unavoidably passed between the Athenians and Corinthians. The defeated however soon reached their own shore, whither the conquerors did not think proper to follow.

In the action several galleys had been sunk; most by the Corinthians, but some by the victorious part of the Corcyræan fleet.　The crews had recourse, as usual, to their boats; and it was common for the conquerors, when they could seize any of these, to take them in tow and make the men prisoners: but the Corinthians, in the first moment of success, gave no quarter; and, unaware of the disaster of the right of their fleet, in the hurry and confusion of the occasion, not easily distinguishing between Greeks and Greeks, inadvertently destroyed many of their unfortunate friends.　When the pursuit ceased, and they had collected whatever they could recover of the wrecks and of their dead, they carried them to a desert harbour, not distant, on the Thesprotian coast, called, like the neighboring ilets, Sybota; and depositing them under the care of their barbarian allies, who were there incamped, they returned, on the afternoon of the same day, with the purpose of renewing attack upon the Corcyræan fleet.

Thucyd. l. 1. c. 50.

The Corcyræans meanwhile had been considering the probable consequences of leaving the enemy masters of the sea.　They dreaded descents upon their iland, and the ravage of their lands. The return of their victorious squadron gave them new spirits : Lacedæmonius incouraged them with assurance that, since hostilities had already passed, he would no longer scruple to afford them his utmost support; and they resolved upon the bold measure of quitting their port, and tho, evening was already approaching, again giving the enemy battle.　Instantly
they

they proceeded to put this in execution. The pæan, the song of battle, was already sung, when the Corinthians began suddenly to retreat. The Corcyræans were at a loss immediately to account for this; but presently they discovered a squadron coming round a headland, which had concealed it longer from them than from the enemy. Still uncertain whether it might be friendly or hostile, they also retreated into their port; but shortly, to their great joy, twenty triremes under Glaucon and Andocides, sent from Attica in the apprehension that the small force under Lacedæmonius might be unequal to the occurring exigencies, took their station by them.

Next day the Corcyræans did not hesitate, with the thirty Athenian ships, for none of those under Lacedæmonius had suffered materially in the action, to show themselves off the harbour of Sybota, where the enemy lay, and offer battle. The Corinthians came out of the harbour, formed for action, and so rested. They were not desirous of risking an ingagement against the increased strength of the enemy, but they could not remain conveniently in the station they had occupied, a desert shore, where they could neither refit their injured ships, nor recruit their stock of provisions; and they were incumbered with more than a thousand prisoners; a very inconvenient addition to the crowded complements of their galleys. Their object therefore was to return home: but they were apprehensive that the Athenians, holding the truce as broken by the action of the preceding day, would not allow an unmolested passage. It was therefore determined to try their disposition, by sending a small vessel, with a message to the Athenian commanders, without the formality of a herald. This was a service not without danger; for those of the Corcyræans, who were near enough to observe what passed, exclaimed, in the vehemence of their animosity, ' that the bearers should be put to death;' which, considering them as enemies, would have been within the law of war of the Greeks. The Athenian commanders, however, thought proper to hold a different conduct. To the message delivered, which accused them of breaking the truce by obstructing the passage to Corcyra, they replied, ' that it was not their purpose to break the truce, but only to ' protect their allies. Wherever else the Corinthians chose to go, they

' might

Thucyd.
l. 1. c. 51.

c. 52.

c. 53.

' might go without interruption from them; but any attempt against
' Corcyra, or any of its possessions, would be resisted by the Athenians
' to the utmost of their power.'

Upon receiving this answer, the Corinthians, after erecting a trophy
at Sybota on the continent, sailed homeward.   In their way, they took
by stratagem Anactorium, a town at the mouth of the Ambracian
gulph, which had formerly been held in common by their commonwealth and the Corcyræans; and leaving a garrison there, proceeded
to Corinth.   Of their prisoners they found near eight hundred had
been slaves, and these they sold.   The remainder, about two hundred
and fifty, were strictly guarded, but otherwise treated with the utmost
kindness.   Among them were some of the first men of Corcyra; and
through these the Corinthians hoped, at some future opportunity, to
recover their antient interest and authority in the iland.

Thucyd. l. 1. c. 54, 55.

The Corcyræans, meanwhile, had gratified themselves with the
erection of a trophy on the iland Sybota, as a claim of victory, in
opposition to the Corinthian trophy on the continent.   The Athenian
fleet returned home; and thus ended, without any treaty, that series of
action which is distinguished by the name of the Corcyræan, or, sometimes, the Corinthian war.

SECTION IV.

Summary View of the History of Macedonia.   War of Athens with
*   Macedonia :   Enmity of Corinth to Athens :   Revolt of Athenian*
*   Dependencies in Thrace : Battle and Siege of Potidæa.*

THE cotemporary historian has strongly marked the difficulties of those
who might have desired to guide the soverein people of Athens in the
paths of peace and moderation.   The Corcyræan war was far too small
an object for their glowing minds: the view toward Sicily and the
adjacent Italian shores were fondly looked to for new enterprize.   Nor
was it intended to stop there.   Where spoil allured no difficulty daunted;
and the wild vision of conquest was extended from Calabria to Tus-

c. 44.
l. 6. c. 90.
Plut. vit.
Pericl.

cany, and from Sicily to Carthage.　Pericles endevored to repress this
extravagant and dishonest ambition; and his view was assisted by
circumstances which necessarily ingaged attention nearer home.

The towns which the Athenians held under their dependency on the
northern shores of the Ægean, some highly valuable for their mines of
gold and silver, others furnishing the principal supplies of naval timber,
and all paying some tribute, gave Athens a near interest in the affairs
of MACEDONIA.　That country, peopled by the same Pelasgian race
which principally gave origin to the Greeks, and brought afterward
under the dominion of a Grecian colony, claimed always to be a part
of Greece.　Its history however, as that of most other Grecian states,
is almost only known through connection with Athenian history.
Thucydides, who must have had superior opportunity, appears to have
been able to discover little more than the geneälogy of its kings, downward from Perdiccas, who was ancestor in the seventh degree to Alexander son of Amyntas, the reigning prince at the time of the invasion
of Greece under Xerxes.

Thucydides and Herodotus agree in ascribing the foundation of the
Macedonian monarchy to Perdiccas; but later writers have given the
honor to a prince whom they call Caranus, and whose grandson they
reckon Perdiccas.　We cannot but doubt this addition to the pedigree
of the Macedonian kings, when opposed by the united authority of
Herodotus and Thucydides, almost within whose memory that pedigree
had been judicially discussed at the Olympian meeting[7].　Three
brothers, according to Herodotus, Heracleids of the branch of Temenus,
of whom Gavanes was the eldest, and Perdiccas the youngest, passed
from Argos into Macedonia, where the latter acquired the sovereinty;
and it seems not improbable that the ingenuity of chronologers, with a
little alteration of the name, has converted the elder brother into the
grandfather[8].　The founder of the Macedonian royal family however
was, according to every account, an Argian, descended from Temenus.

[7] Thus the learned and generally judicious
Henry Dodwell: Tres illos reges *Eusebianos*
rescindendos arbitror.　Annal. Thucyd. ad.
ann. A. C. 454.

[8] According to the chronologers Caranus
began to reign 814 years before the Christian
æra, and 36 before the first Olympiad; Perdiccas 729 years before the Christian æra,
in the fourth year of the 12th Olympiad.

the

the Heracleid, whence the princes of that family were commonly called
Temenids.   By a series of adventures, of which romantic reports only Herod. l. 8.
c. 137.
remain, he acquired command among the Macedonians; a Pelasgian
clan, who held the inland province of Æmathia, otherwise called
Macedonia proper, to the north of Thessaly, and then esteemed a part
of Thrace.

The Macedonian name, according to fable, fabricated however, Schol. ad
v. 226. l. 14.
apparently, in a late age, had its origin from Macedon, son of Jupiter Iliad.
and Æthria.   How the followers of Perdiccas came to assume it, and
by what wars or what policy they acquired extensive dominion, we have
no precise information; but circumstances are not wanting whence to
deduce some probable conjecture.   The innumerable clans who shared
that extensive continent, being in a state of perpetual warfare among
oneanother, the situation of the Macedonians, when the Argive adventurers arrived among them, might be such as to make them glad to
associate strangers, whose skill in arms and general knowlege were
superior to their own.   While civil and military preëminence were
therefore yielded to the new comers, and royalty became established in
the family of their chief, the name of the antient inhabitants, as the
more numerous, remained.   In the course of six or seven reigns the
Macedonians extended their dominion over the neighboring provinces
of Pieria, Bottiæa, Mygdonia, part of Pæonia, Eordia, Almopia, Anthe- Thucyd. l. 2.
c. 99.
mous, Grestonia, and Bisaltia; all, together with Æmathia or Mace-
donia proper, forming what acquired the name of Lower Macedonia,
which extended from mount Olympus to the river Strymon.   The people
of some of these provinces were exterminated, of some extirpated;
some were admitted to the condition of subjects, and some probably
reduced to slavery.   The expelled Pierians established themselves in
Thrace, at the foot of mount Pangæus; the Bottiæans found a settlement nearer their former home, in a tract on the borders of Chalcidicë,
which Thucydides distinguishes by the name of Bottica.   Lyncestis c. 101.
and Eleimiotis, with some other inland and mountainous provinces, c. 99.
each retaining its own prince, yet acknowleging the sovereinty of the
Macedonian kings, became known by the name of Upper Macedonia.

While wars almost unceasing with savage neighbors, and frequent

rebellions

rebellions of conquered subjects, prevented the progress of civilization among the Macedonians, the weakness of the prince and the wants of the people concurred to incorage Grecian establishments on the coast; of which however the principal, those of Chalcidicë and the three peninsulas, had been made probably before the Macedonian kingdom had acquired any considerable extent.   But in so little estimation was Macedonia held by the Greeks at the time of the Persian wars, that when, in his father's lifetime, Alexander son of Amyntas offered himself as a competitor for the prize of the stadion at the Olympian games, it was objected to him that he was a barbarian.   The prince however proving himself not only a Greek, but a Heracleid of the race of Temenus, was admitted by the Hellanodics, with the approbation of the assembly; and that illustrious origin of the royal family of Macedonia, fully acknowleged by both Herodotus and Thucydides, was, among all the invectives of the Grecian orators in aftertimes, never disputed[9].   The marriage of Gygæa sister of Alexander with Bubaris, a Persian of high rank, contributed to the security of the Macedonian kingdom, when Xerxes invaded Greece.   Alexander was a prince of considerable abilities, improved by communication both with Greeks and Persians; but after the retreat of Xerxes, he had so many wars to sustain against the neigboring barbarians, that, tho generally successful, he had little leisure for attending to the advancement of arts and knowlege among his people.

Long before the establishment of the Athenian sovereinty over the ilands and coasts of the Ægean, there had been a friendly connection between the commonwealth and the Macedonian kings; in consequence of which, at the time of the Persian invasion, Alexander son of Amyntas was esteemed the hereditary guest of Athens.   While he lived, the friendly connection seems not to have been interrupted or impaired, by any acquisition of sovereinty to the commonwealth, extending over towns which might be esteemed within Macedonia.

Herod. l. 5.
c. 22. &
l. 9. c. 45.
Thucyd. l. 2.
c. 99. &
l. 5. c. 80.
Herod. l. 5.
c. 21. &
l. 8. c. 136.
Justin. l. 7.
c. 3.

Herod. l. 8.
c. 136.

[9] Demosthenes, among other illiberal language, adapted to excite his audience against the great Philip, would call that prince a barbarian. Æschines called Demosthenes a barbarian, and showed his ground for it; but Demosthenes has not ventured an attempt to show any: he has meerly thrown out the ugly nickname to the Athenian populace, for the chance of the vogue it might obtain, and the effect it might produce.

His

His son and successor Perdiccas was honored with adoption to the citizenship of Athens, for his merit with the Greek nation, in defeating a body of the Persian forces, in their retreat from Greece; and the alliance passed to him as an inheritance.   But differences afterward arose.   One of the principalities of Upper Macedonia was the appanage of Philip younger brother of Perdiccas, and another was the inheritance of Derdas, a prince more distantly related to the royal family.   About the time of the Corcyræan war, Perdiccas proposing to deprive both his brother and his cousin of their territories, the Athenian administration thought proper to take those princes under its protection, and support them against the intended injury.   Perdiccas resented this as a breach of the antient alliance, and perhaps he was not without reason jealous of the ambition of the Athenian people.   The authority and influence of the two princes, however, were so considerable, that to attack them, while they could be supported by the power of the Athenian commonwealth, would have been hazardous : but the circumstances of the times offered a resource suited to the genius of the Macedonian king, who, without his father's virtues, was not without abilities.   The Athenians had just taken a decided part in the Corcyræan war.   The hostile disposition of Corinth toward them was in consequence avowed; that prevailing in Lacedæmon was well known to Perdiccas ; and an opportunity for intrigue, which would probably involve the Athenian commonwealth in war, with Corinth immediately, and ultimately with Lacedæmon, occurred in his very neighborhood.   Thus invited, Perdiccas, ambitious, active, crafty, and unrestrained by any principle of integrity, determined to persevere in his purpose.

Thucyd. l. 2. c. 100.

The town of Potidæa, critically situated on the isthmus which connects the fruitful peninsula of Pallenë with the confines of Thrace and Macedonia, was a Corinthian colony; so far still dependent upon the mother-country as to receive magistrates annually thence, yet nevertheless among the tributary allies of Athens.   Perdiccas sent an offer to Corinth to assist in recovering Potidæa from the Athenian dominion. He sent at the same time to Lacedæmon to propose alliance with that state, or to become a member of the Peloponnesian confederacy : and he negotiated not only with the Potidæans but also with the Chalcidians

dians and Bottiæans, subjects of Athens in his neighborhood, to induce them to revolt.

The Athenian government, informed of these transactions, and aware of the hostile disposition of Corinth, judged immediate precaution necessary to the preservation of their command on the northern shores of the Ægean. A squadron of thirty ships of war was already preparing in the port of Peiræus, to be accompanied by a thousand heavy-armed infantry, for the support of the Macedonian princes Philip and Derdas. According to that despotic authority then which the Athenian people assumed over the Grecian states of their alliance, peremptory orders were sent to the Potidæans, to demolish their fortifications on the side of Pallenë, to give hostages for security of their fidelity, and to send away their Corinthian magistrates and receive no more. The Potidæans very averse to obey, yet afraid to dispute these commands, sent ministers to Athens to solicit a recall or a mitigation of them; but at the same time they communicated privately, in common with the Corinthians, at Sparta, to solicit protection, if the Athenians should persevere in their requisition. The petition to Athens proving ineffectual, and the leading men in the Spartan administration [10] promising that a Peloponnesian army should invade Attica, if the Athenians attempted to inforce their commands by arms, the Potidæans communicated with the Chalcidians and Bottiæans, a league was formed and ratified in the usual manner by oaths, and all revolted together.

We have ample assurance that the command of the Athenian people over their subject states, always arbitrary, was often very oppressive; but as scarcely any accounts of the times have been preserved but through Athenian writers, few particulars have been transmitted to us. It is then from an Athenian writer we have information of the measure next resorted to by the Chalcidians; and, under the foreseen necessity for such a measure, it must apparently have been a galling oppression that could induce a people to revolt. The lands of their rich peninsula would be open to ravage from the superiority of the Athenian fleet, and its produce not only would be lost to them, but would assist the enemy to carry on the war against them. To obviate this evil

Thucyd. l. 2. c. 56 & 57.

c. 58.

[10] Τὰ τέλη τῶν Λακεδαιμονίων.

as far as might be; Perdiccas proposed to the Chalcidians, that they should themselves destroy all their sea-port towns, and abandon their lands; that Olynthus should be made their one strong place; and that all their people, beyond what the defence of that city would require, should remove, with their families, to a territory which he would assign them about the lake of Bolbë in Mygdonia; by the cultivation of which they might subsist till the war should be over. This proposal, severe as the sacrifice on the part of the Chalcidians must be, was accepted, and the measure, at least in great part, executed.

These transactions were yet unknown at Athens, when the armament intended for Macedonia sailed under the command of Archestratus. His instructions directed him to go first to Potidæa, and see the orders of the Athenian government executed there; then to take any measures that might appear expedient for preventing revolt in any other towns of the dominion of Athens in that neighborhood; and not till these were secured, to prosecute the proposed operations in Macedonia. On his arrival in Chalcidicë, finding the revolt already complete, he judged his force insufficient for any effectual measures there, and he therefore turned immediately toward Macedonia, to favor a projected invasion of the inland frontier of that kingdom by Philip. Thucyd. l. 2. c. 57 & 59.

Meanwhile the Corinthians, who had dissuaded war when the common cause of their confederacy only had instigated, became vehement in the call to arms when the particular interest of their own state was infringed. No negotiation was proposed, no desire to have differences accommodated according to the stipulations of the existing treaty was mentioned; but, while their ministers were everywhere assiduously endevoring to excite alarm and indignation among their allies, they prepared themselves immediately to assert their cause by force. Sixteen hundred heavy-armed and four hundred light-armed roops, partly volunteers of Corinth, partly ingaged for hire among the other states of Peloponnesus, were sent to Potidæa, under Aristeus son of Adeimantus, who had particular connections with that colony, and was esteemed there: and so much diligence was used in the equipment, that it was only the fortieth day after the revolt when they arrived. c. 40 & 60. c. 69. 71. & 78.

The Athenian government, on receiving intelligence of these proceedings c. 61.

ceedings of the Corinthians, sent Callias son of Calliades with forty triremes and two thousand heavy-armed to join the little army under Archestratus.   That army, with the assistance of its Macedonian confederates, had already taken Thermë and was besieging Pydna, when Callias arrived.   The business of the revolted colonies being deemed of more importance than the prosecution of hostilities, however successful, against Perdiccas, proposals were made to that prince.   He was not scrupulous, and perhaps reasonably enough had little confidence in any treaty with any of the republics.   A treaty however, not of peace only but alliance with him, was hastily concluded, in which some care apparently was taken of the interests of his brother and the other revolted princes; for so the clear interest of the Athenian people would require; and then the whole Athenian force, with a considerable body of allied infantry, and six hundred Macedonian horse from Philip, marched for Potidæa.

Thucyd. l. 2. c. 62.

Perdiccas held his ingagement with the Athenians no longer than to serve some present purpose, and then immediately sent two hundred horse to join the army of the Corinthians and their allies.   In this confederate army it was necessary to establish, by common consent, some system of command.   By election, therefore, Aristeus, general of the Corinthian forces, was appointed commander-in-chief of the infantry, and Perdiccas of the cavalry.   A compliment seems to have been intended to the Macedonian monarch.   Whether he esteemed the appointment such, we are not informed; but he deputed his general Iolaüs to execute the office.   The Athenian army soon after approaching, an action insued, in which Aristeus, with a chosen body, performing the duty more of a brave soldier than of an able general, broke and pursued a part of the enemy's line, while the rest completely routed his

c. 63.

remaining army, and drove the survivors for refuge within the walls of Potidæa.   Callias, the Athenian general, was killed; but Aristeus, returning from pursuit, not without difficulty and loss, by a hazardous effort, joined his defeated troops in the town.   The Athenian army sat

c. 64.

down before it, and being soon after reïnforced with sixteen hundred men under Phormion, they blockaded it by land and sea.

c. 65.

Aristeus, who, notwithstanding his error in the battle, appears to

2   have

have been a man of considerable abilities, as well as of daring courage and indefatigable activity, having regulated things within the place in the best manner for sustaining the siege, found means to slip out of the harbor, unnoticed by the Athenian guardships. Going himself to Olynthus, to take the command of the allied forces there, he hastened dispatches to Peloponnesus with information of what had passed, and pressing for a reïnforcement, without which Potidæa, he said, could not be saved : for Phormion was now so superior, that, after having completed a contravallation against the place, he could spare a part of his army to ravage Chalcidicë and the Bottiæan territory, and he took some smaller towns.

SECTION V.

Assembly of Deputies of the Peloponnesian Confederacy at Lacedæmon: The Thirty-years Truce declared broken. Second Assembly : War with Athens resolved. Embassies from Lacedæmon to Athens. Final Rejection of the Proposals from Lacedæmon by the Athenians.

Iᴛ is from the account, remaining from Thucydides, of that complicated and lasting war, to which the affairs just related immediately led, that we derive our best knowlege of the political and military state of Greece, with much collateral information concerning science, arts, and manners, during the period when those circumstances are most interesting; that remarkable period, when the leading Grecian commonwealths had a political importance, in the affairs of the world, beyond all proportion to their natural strength, and when science and art arose among them to a splendor totally unknown in preceding ages, and never in all points equalled since. If therefore, in following the steps of that able writer, we meet with circumstances which on first view appear little ; if armies ingaged are not numerous ; if the affairs of single towns, and sometimes of small ones, occupy some space in narration ; it must not be concluded that the subject is trifling, since those apparently little matters are connected with consequences among the most important that occur in the history of mankind.

Among those Greeks who were not held in subjection, the Corinthians appear to have been most affected by the rising power of Athens: their commerce was checked, and their colonial dependencies, not absolutely taken from them, were however compelled to acknowlege a degree of sovereinty in the Athenian people, and to pay a tribute; nominally for the common purposes of Greece, but more reälly for the particular benefit of Athens. The irritation excited by the check given to their ambition in former wars, and particularly by the loss of friends and relations in the unfortunate action in which Myronides commanded against them, was thus kept alive, and the Corinthians nourished the sharpest animosity against the Athenians. When therefore intelligence came from Aristeus of the transactions in Chalcidicë, far from abating of their ardor for war, they applied themselves with increased sedulity to excite their whole confederacy, and especially Lacedæmon, to take up their cause: ' The truce,' they exclaimed, '·was already broken, and Peloponnesus insulted and injured.' At the same time the Æginetans, who bore most impatiently their subjection to Athens, yet feared to make any open demonstration of a disposition to revolt, complained, by secret negotiation among the Peloponnesian states, of the dependency in which they were held, contrary, as they contended, to the treaty; and they redoubled their instances as they found a growing disposition to hostility. Thus instigated, the Lacedæmonians at length convoked the usual assembly of deputies from the states of their confederacy; and they invited the attendance of ministers from any other Grecian republics which might have any complaint to prefer against Athens.

The debates and negotiations which followed, afford, in the detail given by Thucydides, so much insight into the politics, the political manners, and the temper of Greece at the time, that, with the risk of some appearance of uncouthness to the modern reader, I shall venture to report the more material parts without abridgement, and with the least deviation that may be from the expression of the original. The

*Thucyd. l. 1.
c. 67.*

deputies

deputies of the confederacy, or a large proportion of them (for it appears Thucyd. l. 1. to have been not a full meeting) being arrived at Sparta, the general c. 87. assembly of the Lacedæmonian people was convened.   There happened to be present at the time ministers from Athens, commissioned on some c. 72. other public business; and these were allowed to attend the audience, with the deputies of the confederacy.   All being met, proclamation was c. 67. made, according to the custom of the Grecian assemblies, declaring permission for those to speak who had anything to advance.   Many came forward exhibiting various complaints against the Athenian government, mostly little important or dubiously founded, excepting those of the Megarians and Corinthians.   The Megarians urged that, contrary to existing treaty, they were, by a decree of the Athenian people, prohibited all commercial intercourse by land with Attica, and excluded from all ports within the Athenian dominion.   The Corinthians reserved themselves, till the others should have prepared the minds of the Lacedæmonian people for warmer instigation, and then spoke nearly thus:

'That strict faith, Lacedæmonians, which characterizes your con- c. 68.
'duct in public and in private affairs, inclines you to disregard accu-
'sations against others; and hence indeed you obtain the just praise
'of moderation and equity, but you remain ignorant of the transactions
'of forein states.   Often we have forewarned you of the wrongs which
'the Athenians were preparing for us; but not till we had already
'suffered, and hostilities were commenced, would you summon this
'assembly of our confederacy; in which we have perhaps more cause
'than others to come forward, injured as we have been by the Athe-
'nians, and neglected by you.   Not that we alone are interested: all
'Greece is concerned; many states being already reduced to subjec-
'tion, and others notoriously threatened; among which some have,
'from treaties of alliance, especial claim to our protection.   Corcyra,
'capable of furnishing a fleet superior to that of any republic of our
'confederacy, is already taken from us; and Potidæa, our most
'important post for holding dominion or carrying on commerce in
'Thrace, is at this time besieged.

'Nor can we avoid saying that these injuries, which we have thus

'suffered,

Thucyd. l. 1.
c. 69.

' suffered, are in great measure to be imputed to you. After the Persian
' war, you permitted the Athenians to fortify their city; then to build
' their long walls; and still you have continued to look on, tho boast-
' ing to be vindicators of the freedom of Greece, while they have
' deprived of freedom, not only their own, but our confederates. Even
' now the convention of this assembly has been with difficulty obtained;
' and even now we meet apparently not for the purpose which ought
' to be the object of our consideration. For is this a time to inquire
' whether we have been injured? No, rather how we shall repel injury.
' You have the reputation of being provident and circumspect; but
' facts do not justify the opinion. The Persians, we know, came
' against Peloponnesus from the farthest parts of the earth, before you
' had made any adequate preparation for defence; and now you are
' equally remiss against the Athenians in your neighborhood. Thus,
' as the barbarian failed principally through his own misconduct, so
' their errors, and not your support, have inabled us hitherto to main-
' tain ourselves against the Athenians. Let it not however be imagined
' that this expostulation is prompted by resentment; we expostulate
' with our friends who err; we criminate our enemies who injure us.

c. 70.   ' But you seem unaware what kind of people the Athenians are, and
' how totally they differ from you. They are restless and scheming,
' and quick to execute their schemes. You are ever bent upon the
' preservation of what you possess; averse to projects; and in execu-
' tion, even of necessary measures, deficient. They, again, are daring
' above their strength, adventurous even beyond their own opinion of
' prudence, and full of hope in the midst of misfortune. It is your
' disposition always to do less than your power admits, to hesitate even
' when acting on the surest grounds, and to think yourselves never
' free from danger. They are quick, you dilatory; they fond of roam-
' ing, you more than all others attached to your home; they eager to
' make acquisitions in any distant parts, you fearful, in seeking more,
' to injure what you already possess. They push victory to the utmost,
' and are least of all men dejected by defeat; exposing their bodies for
' their country, as if they had no interest in them, yet applying their
' minds in the public service, as if that and their private interest were
' one.

'one.   Disappointment of a proposed acquisition they consider as loss
'of what already belonged to them; success in any pursuit they
'esteem only as a step toward farther advantages; and, defeated in
'any attempt, they turn immediately to some new project by which to
'make themselves amends: insomuch that through their celerity in
'executing whatever they propose, they seem to have the peculiar
'faculty of at the same time hoping and possessing.   Thus they con-
'tinue ever, amid labors and dangers, injoying nothing, through sedu-
'lity to acquire; esteeming that only a time of festival, in which they
'are prosecuting their projects; and holding rest as a greater evil than
'the most laborious business.   To sum up their character, it may be
'truly said, that they were born neither to injoy quiet themselves, nor
'to suffer others to injoy it.

'When such a commonwealth is adverse to you, Lacedæmonians,
'you still delay.   You will consider those only as your enemies who
'avow hostility; thinking to preserve peace through your antiquated
'maxims of policy and equity, defending yourselves but offending
'none, which are no longer fit for these times.   It has been by other
'maxims, by new arts, and by a policy refined through modern expe-
'rience, that Athens has risen to a greatness which now threatens us
'all.   Let this then be the term of your dilatoriness: give at length
'that assistance to your allies which, by the stipulations of our con-
'federacy, you owe them, and relieve the distressed Potidæans.   This
'can no longer be effectually done but by an immediate invasion of
'Attica; which is the measure necessarily to be taken, unless you
'would leave a friendly and kindred people a prey to your most deter-
'mined enemies; and compel us, disposed by every consideration of
'interest, affection, and habit, to maintain our connection with you,
'through despair, to seek some new alliance.   Consult then your own
'interest, and do not diminish that supremacy in Peloponnesus which
'your forefathers have transmitted to you.'

The Athenian ministers judged it consonant neither to the dignity Thucyd. l. 1.
of their commonwealth, nor to the commission under which they acted, c. 72.
to answer particularly to the charges thus urged by the deputies of the
Peloponnesian confederacy before the Lacedæmonian people; yet they
thought

thought it not proper, on such an occasion, to be intirely silent. They
applied therefore to the ephors for leave to address the assembly, which

Thucyd. l. 1.
c. 73.

was allowed them [10], and they spoke to the following purpose : ' They
' considered themselves,' they said, ' not at all in presence of those who
' had any right to assume connizance of the conduct of the Athenian
' commonwealth or of its allies; yet as they had been so publicly
' witnesses to so virulent an invective against those in whose service
' they were commissioned, they thought it proper to admonish the
' assembly not to determine lightly and hastily concerning a matter of

c.73 & 74.

' very great moment.' Having then mentioned the merit of the Athenian people with all Greece in the two Persian invasions, and the sense
which the Lacedæmonians themselves at the time expressed of it, they

c. 75.

proceeded to observe, ' That the command of the Athenian people
' among the Grecian states had been acquired, not by violence, but by
' the dereliction of the Lacedæmonians, and by the consent, and even
' at the solicitation of the subordinate republics : that they had a fair
' interest in so glorious a possession, so honorably earned, which their
' reputation, not less than the advantages of command, would urge
' them to maintain ; and that even their just apprehensions forbad
' them to relinquish it, since the jealousy of the Lacedæmonians, long
' apparent, and now especially evident in the transaction of the present
' day, amply demonstrated what would be their danger in surrendering

c. 76 & 77.

' the smallest portion of their present power.' They then endevored
to palliate, but they were indeed equally unable to deny as to justify,
the general despotism of the Athenian people over their subject states,
and the particular measures of severity which had been taken against

c. 78.

some of them. In conclusion they asserted, that the truce was not
broken by them, neither had they yet to complain that the Lacedæmonians had broken it. They exhorted therefore perseverance in peaceful
measures ; they claimed for their commonwealth the justice to which
it was intitled by the stipulations of the existing treaty, which directed
a mode of judicial proceeding for the determination of disputes that

---

[10] Προσελθόντες ἐν τοῖς Λακεδαιμονίοις, ἔφασαν
βούλεσθαι καὶ αὐτοὶ ἐς τὸ πλῆθος αὐτῶν εἰπεῖν.
Cum igitur ad Lacedæmoniorum *magistra-* tus accessissent.—This translation is justified by the context, and by other passages
of the author.

might

might arise; and they declared themselves, in the name of their commonwealth, ready to abide judgement accordingly. ' Should the
' Lacedæmonians determine to refuse such justice, they submitted
' their cause to the gods, who had been invoked to attest the treaty,
' and their commonwealth would defend itself and its just command
' to the utmost.'

When the Athenians had concluded, the forein ministers were Thucyd. l. 1.
required to withdraw, and it remained for the Lacedæmonians to debate c. 79.
and to decide upon the question.   Thucydides, in his exile, as himself
informs us, had opportunities, not open to many foreiners, for acquiring l. 5. c. 26.
information concerning the internal transactions of the Lacedæmonian
state.   After the greater number of speakers, he proceeds to relate, had l. 1. c.79.
declared their opinion that the Athenians had already broken the truce,
and that war should be immediately commenced, Archidamus came
forward; the prince who, above thirty years before, had deserved so well
of his country by his conduct in the Helot rebellion.   In advanced age
now, he maintained the reputation of a wise and temporate man [12], and
he addressed the assembly thus: ' I, Lacedæmonians, have had experi- c. 80.
' ence of many wars, and I see those among you, my equals in age, who
' will not, as happens to many through inexperience, urge war as in
' itself desirable, or in its consequences certain.   Within Peloponnesus
' indeed, against bordering states, when hostilities arise, decision
' may be quick; and, the forces on both sides being the same in
' kind, the preponderancy of one or the other may be a subject
' of calculation.   But the war now proposed is widely different:
' operations are to be carried far from our frontier, against those whose
' fleets command the seas, who are superior to every Grecian state in
' wealth, population, and forces, cavalry as well as infantry, and who
' besides have under their dominion many tributary allies.   In our
' present unprepared situation, to what do we trust for success in
' attacking such an enemy? To our fleet? No; we are too inferior.
' To our riches? Far less; neither our public treasure nor our private
' wealth can bear any comparison with theirs.   We are superior, it is
' said, in the force of infantry of our confederacy, and we will ravage c. 81.

[12] 'Ανὴρ καὶ ξυνετὸς δοκῶν εἶναι καὶ σώφρων.

' their

' their country. But they have large possessions, far beyond the reach
' of your infantry, and a fleet that will come and go with the produce,
' undisturbed by any force that you can oppose to it; while your
' irresistible infantry will starve amid the devastation itself has made.
' Instead therefore of bringing your enemy immediately to terms by
' such measures, I rather fear you will leave the war as an inheritance
' to your posterity.

Thucyd. l. 1.　' Let it not however be imagined that I advise to suffer tamely the
c. 82.　' oppression of our allies, or to leave designs against ourselves unnoticed
' till the moment of execution.   Let us, on the contrary, prepare for
' war; let us endevor to extend our alliances, even among barbarous
' nations, if either naval or pecuniary assistance can be obtained from
' them; let us also contribute liberally from our private properties to
' form a public fund equal to the probable need.   But in the mean
' time let an embassy be sent to Athens; and, if our reasonable demands
' are complied with, our business will thus have its best conclusion.
' In all events however, till we are fully prepared for war, let their
' country remain unhurt.   It is a pledge always ready to our hands,
' the value of which we should not wantonly diminish.

c. 83.　' Nor let it be supposed that the delay, which I advise, will mark
' any pusillanimity.   War is a business less of arms than of expence,
' which alone can make arms efficacious[13]; especially in the contest
' of a continental with a maritime people.   Money therefore must in
c. 84, 85.　' the first place be provided.   As for that slowness and dilatoriness,
' with which you have heard yourselves upbraided, they flow from
' those institutions of our ancestors, which teach us, in public as in
' private life, to be modest, prudent, and just.   Hence it is our cha-
' racter to be, less than all others, either elated by prosperity or
' dejected by misfortune: hence we are neither to be allured by the
' flattery which we have been hearing, nor irritated by the reproach:
' hence we are at the same time warlike and circumspect; and hence
' we shall not be disposed to utter sounding words against our enemies,
' when we are unable to follow them up by deeds.'
' Let us not then wander from those maxims and institutions of

---

[13] Ἐστιν ὁ πόλεμος ὐχ ὅπλων τοπλέον, ἀλλὰ δαπάνης, δι'ἣν τὰ ὅπλα ὠφελεῖ. c. 83.

' our

‘ our forefathers, through which our state has long florished great and
‘ free, and beyond all others glorious : nor let us hurry, in one short
‘ portion of a day, to a decision, which must involve with it the lives
‘ of many individuals, the fortunes of many families, the fate of many
‘ cities, and our own glory.   Other states may be under necessity of
‘ taking measures hastily : our strength gives us the option of leisure.
‘ Since then the Athenians profess themselves ready to submit the
‘ subjects of complaint to a legal decision, it appears little consonant
‘ to justice to proceed against those as decidedly criminal, who offer
‘ themselves for trial.   Let your determination therefore be to send
‘ an embassy to Athens, but in the meantime to prepare for war.   Thus,
‘ more than by any other measure, you will be formidable to your
‘ adversaries ; and thus you will best consult both your advantage and
‘ your honqr.’

The effect which this sensible and dispassionate discourse should   Thucyd. l. 1.
have had, was obviated by the following blunt speech of the ephor   c. 86.
Sthenelaïdas : ‘ The verbose oratory of the Athenians I do not com-
‘ prehend.   They have been large in their own praise, but their inju-
‘ rious conduct toward our allies, and toward Peloponnesus, they have
‘ not denied.   If their behavior formerly against the Persians was
‘ praiseworthy, and is now against us the reverse, they deserve double
‘ punishment ; for ceasing to be meritorious, and for becoming culpable.
‘ We have not yet changed our conduct ; and, if we are wise, we shall
‘ not now overlook the wrong done to our allies, nor delay to revenge
‘ it.   Others have money, and ships, and horses : we have good allies,
‘ who ought not to be abandoned to the Athenians.   Nor are such
‘ disputes to be determined by words and legal process.   It has not
‘ been by words that they have been injured. We must therefore avenge
‘ them quickly, and with our utmost force ; nor let any one persuade
‘ that when we are injured we ought to deliberate.   Those rather
‘ ought to take long time for deliberation who mean to commit injury.
‘ Let your determination therefore, Lacedæmonians, be, as becomes
‘ the dignity of Sparta, for war; nor suffer the Athenians to increase
‘ in power, nor betray your allies, but, with the help of the gods, let us
‘ march against those who wrong us.’

VOL. II.   G   Sthenelaïdas,

Thucyd. l.1.
c. 87.

Sthenelaïdas, having thus spoken, proceeded, in the function of his office, to put the question to the assembly. A clamor being raised on each side (for in the Lacedæmonian assembly votes were given by the voice, and not, as at Athens, by silently holding up hands, or by the perfect secrecy of a ballot) the presiding ephor declared he could not distinguish which had the majority. Thinking therefore, as Thucydides supposes, that the necessity of manifesting more openly his party, would urge every one the rather to vote for war, he put the question again thus: 'Whoever is of opinion that the truce is broken, and that the ' Athenians have been the aggressors, let him go to that side; whoever ' is of the contrary opinion, to the other side.' Upon the division a large majority appeared for the affirmative. The deputies of the allies being then called, were informed of the determination; and farther told, that it was the wish of the Lacedæmonians to have another meeting of deputies from all the states of the confederacy, who should come authorized and prepared to decide, both concerning peace and war, and how the war, if resolved upon, should be carried on. With this the congress broke up: the deputies of the allies hastened to their several homes: the Athenian ministers waited to finish the business of their mission, and then returned to Athens.

c. 88.

The Lacedæmonian government was now determined for war; not so much, according to the historian of the times, influenced by the representations of their allies, as by their own apprehensions of the growing power of the rival state. The Athenian dominion, within Greece, had indeed been greatly contracted by the conditions of the Thirty-years truce, and by the losses which led to it; but the remaining empire had been gaining consistency, during fourteen years which had since elapsed under the able administration of Pericles; its force

c. 122.

was now such that no single state of Greece could undertake to cope with it; and even the extensive confederacy over which Lacedæmon presided, was, at the instant, far from being in condition to begin hostilities. To acquire a sanction therefore to their undertaking, which

c. 118.

might spread incouragement among those ingaged in it, they sent a solemn deputation to Delphi, to inquire of the god if they might hope for success. According to report (so Thucydides expresses himself)

ɪ

the

the god assured them, 'That, if they carried on the war with becoming 'vigor, they would be victorious; and that his favor should attend 'them invoked or uninvoked.'

Meanwhile the Corinthians were sedulous in canvassing the several states of the confederacy separately; endevoring to alarm their fears and excite their indignation, and to promote by every possible method the resolution for war.   Accordingly when the congress met again at Lacedæmon, and the great question was proposed, most of the deputies were vehement in accusation of the Athenians, and in requisition of the immediate commencement of hostilities.   The Corinthians, in pursuance of their former policy, reserved themselves to the last, and then spoke thus:

'We no longer, confederates, blame the Lacedæmonians, who, having 'now resolved on war, have summoned this assembly to desire its con-'currence in the resolution.   Presiding over the confederacy, the 'general prosperity requires that they should pay due attention to 'their own particular situation and circumstances; and hence arose 'their past delay: while the honors we pay them, and the command 'with which they are invested, impose on them the duty of constantly 'consulting the welfare of the whole; and hence flows their present 'determination.   It were needless, we are indeed persuaded, to admo-'nish any of you, who have had any experience of the Athenians, how 'much it behoves us to be upon our guard against them; but we will 'observe that it imports the people of the inland commonwealths to 'reflect, that, unless they support the maritime states, not only they 'will be deprived of the many advantages which accrue, even to 'them, from maritime commerce, but if they look on till we are sub-'dued, their subjection must follow.   Ultimately thus we are all 'equally interested in the matter on which we are going to decide; 'differing more in regard to the time when we may expect the evil to 'fall upon us, than the degree in which it will affect us.

'It is then to repel and to prevent injuries, and not with any ambi-'tious view, that we are earnest for war.   Our cause of complaint 'against the Athenians is ample: but when we have redressed our 'wrongs, peace will be our object.   Nor have we reason to doubt of

G 2   'success.

Thucyd. l. 1. c. 119.

c. 120.

c. 121.

' success. Our landforce is greater than theirs, and in military skill
' we excel them ; and surely a more unanimous zeal may be expected
' in our confederacy than in theirs. They are strong at sea : but if
' we duly employ the means which we severally possess, and add the
' wealth which we may borrow from Delphi [13] and Olympia, we can
' equal them even on that element. The offer of greater pay would
' intice the people of their alliance from their service : for it is to be
' remembered, that the power of Athens consists more in a purchased
' than a native force ; whereas ours depends less upon our riches than
' upon ourselves. One naval victory would therefore probably com-
' plete our business. Should that not immediately be obtained, yet
' their maritime skill will soon cease to give them any advantage,
' because ours will of course improve with increased experience. But
' even without a superiority at sea, we possess abundant means to dis-
' tress them ; among which we may reckon, as very important, the easy
' possibility of gaining their allies.

' It is however not our purpose to persuade you that the dispute
' before us resembles those, which, for ages, have been common within
' Greece, of each republic with its neighbor, of nearly equal force, con-
' cerning the limits of their respective territories. On the contrary,
' it deserves your most serious consideration, that the Athenians have
' attained a degree of power to inable them to contend with us alto-
' gether : and, what is disgraceful to Peloponnesus even to mention,
' the question is, whether we shall remain independent, or become their
' subjects. Our fathers were the vindicators of the freedom of Greece.
' We fall short indeed of their worth, if we cannot maintain our own
' freedom ; and while we anxiously oppose the establishment of
' monarchy in any state, yet suffer an ambitious commonwealth to be
' tyrant over all [14].

' To

[13] It appears from this passage and some following ones (l. 1. c. 143. and l. 2. c. 9.) that through some revolution not particularly mentioned by Thucydides, but probably a consequence of the thirty-years truce, not only Delphi was again brought under Lacedæmonian influence, but the Phocian people were gained to the Lacedæmonian interest ; or, which would operate to the same purpose, were put under oligarchal government.

[14] Τύραννον δὲ ἰῶμεν ἐγκαθεςάναι πόλιν. Thucydides afterward puts a similar expression into the mouths both of Pericles and of Cleon,

' To undergo any labor and risk any danger, in a virtuous cause, hath Thucyd. l. 1.
c. 123.
' been transmitted to us as an hereditary rule of conduct.   Ill would it
' become us now to deviate from it ; and, so much richer and more
' powerful as we are than our forefathers, to lose in the midst of
' abundance what they gained in penury.   Let us therefore cheerfully
' ingage in a war which the god himself hath recommended, with even
' a promise of his favor in it.   All Greece will be with us ; and right is
' on our side ; as not only notorious facts prove, but the god has
' testified.   Nor let there be delay ; for be it remembered that the
' Potidæans, Dorians, and our kinsmen, are at this time besieged by
' an Ionian army.   Let us therefore immediately take measures to
' reduce that proud republic, which is aiming at the tyranny of Greece ;
' that we may ourselves live in peace and independency, and that we
' may restore freedom to those Grecian states, which are now so inju-
' riously held in subjection.'

This speech concluding the debate, the question was put, and war c. 125.
was the determination of the majority.   Notwithstanding, however, the
clamor for hastening hostilities, and notwithstanding even the danger
of delay after such a resolution so publicly taken, it was presently
found, so deficiently prepared yet was the confederacy, that delay was
unavoidable.   The leading men therefore recurred to negotiation, in
which they had three distinct purposes ; to induce the Athenians to
suspend hostilities, while their own preparations should be advancing ;
to strengthen their own cause among the Grecian states, by making the
Athenians the refusers of offered peace ; and to sow dissention among
the Athenians themselves.

With these objects in view, ministers were sent to Athens, commis- c. 126.
sioned to make representations concerning a matter wholly forein to
everything that had yet been in dispute between the two republics, and
of no importance but what Grecian superstition might give.   Complete
atonement, it was pretended, had never been made for the sacrilege
committed, near a century before, when, under the direction of the
archon Megacles, the partizans of Cylon were taken from the altars to

Cleon, when speaking to the Athenian as-   different from reproach, b. 2. c. 63. and b. 3.
sembly, and having in view something very   c. 37. Τυραννίδα ἔχιτι τὴν ἀρχήν.

be

be executed.   Many who now injoyed the privileges of Athenian citizens, it was urged, stood affected by that pollution; which, according to the prevailing ideäs of the age, adhered to all the descendants of the sacrilegious.   Lest therefore the contamination should bring down the vengeance of the gods of Greece in some general calamity, the Lacedæmonians, as assertors of the common welfare, required that all such persons should be banished, and the pollution completely expiated.   This was intended as a blow principally against Pericles, who,

Thucyd. l. 1. c. 127.

by his mother, was descended from Megacles: not however with the expectation that the requisition would produce his banishment; but with the hope that, through alarm to the popular mind, some embarrassment might be created for the administration.

Pericles was however not at a loss for a measure to oppose to this. Two sacrilegious pollutions were recollected, in which many of the principal families of Lacedæmon were involved; the death of Pausanias, who had been starved in the temple of Minerva Chalcicæca, and the execution of some Helots who had been dragged from the sanctuary of Neptune on mount Tænarus.   The latter was esteemed a profanation so grossly impious, that popular superstition attributed to it that tremendous calamity the great earthquake of Sparta.   It was therefore required of the Lacedæmonian government to set the example of regard for the welfare of Greece and respect for the gods its protectors, by removing all those who were contaminated through either of those sacrileges.   With an answer to this purpose, the Lacedæmonian ministers returned to Sparta.

c. 139.

A second embassy arrived at Athens soon after, very differently instructed.   As preliminaries to a general peace, these ministers urged, that the siege of Potidæa ought to be raised and Ægina restored to independency; but chiefly they insisted, that the prohibitory decree against Megara should be revoked; and, that only being done, they pledged themselves that Lacedæmon would not commence hostilities. The two first propositions, little insisted on, were with little ceremony rejected.   To the third it was answered, 'That the Megarians had ' made themselves obnoxious to gods and men, by cultivating the ' extralimitary land between the boundaries of Attica and Megaris, 'which

' which was consecrated to the Eleusinian goddesses [15]; and that they
' received and incouraged runaway Athenian slaves.' With this answer
the second embassy returned to Sparta ; and soon after arrived a third,
of three members, Rhamphias, Melesippus, and Agesander, probably
men of more eminence than the former ministers, as Thucydides
distinguishes these alone by name.   In their representations they
noticed none of the requisitions of their predecessors, but they demanded, as the one condition of peace, that all Grecian states held in
subjection by Athens be restored to independency.   An assembly of
the people was then convened, and it was proposed to consider of a
decisive and final answer.   Many spoke, some urging war, some contending for peace, and particularly insisting that the offensive decree
against Megara ought not to remain an obstacle.   At length Pericles
ascending the bema, declared himself thus :

' My opinion, Athenians, has always been, that we ought not to   Thucyd. l. 1.
' submit to the Peloponnesians, and it remains yet the same ; sensible,   c. 140.
' as I am, that men seldom support a war throughout with the same
' animation with which they ordinarily begin it, but that, in disasters,
' even such as must in the course of things be expected, their spirits
' droop, and their opinions change.   Beforehand therefore I claim,
' from those who agree with me in opinion now, to concur with me in
' effort, whenever misfortune may arise ; or else, at once to renounce
' all pretension to merit, should success attend our endevors.

' With regard to the grounds of my opinion, the insidious designs
' of the Lacedæmonians against this commonwealth have long been
' obvious, and are now more than ever manifest.   For notwithstanding
' that the articles of the existing treaty point out the manner in which
' disputes between the two states should be adjusted, and declare that,
' in the mean time, each party should hold what it possesses, yet not
' only they have not desired such adjustment, but they refuse to admit
' it.   They are, in short, evidently enough determined to support their

---

[15] Ἐπικαλοῦντες ἐπ' ἐργασίαν τοῖς Μεγαρεῦσι
τῆς γῆς τῆς ἱερᾶς καὶ τῆς ἀορίσυ. Megarensibus
crimini dantes quod sacrum, nullisque limi-
tibus finitum solum colerent.—' Land that
' was sacred ; land not marked out for cul-

' ture.' Smith.—These interpretations are
totally unsatisfactory. The scholiast, who
has not equally evaded the difficulty, seems
to warrant the sense ventured in the text ;
but the matter is not of consequence.

' allegations

' allegations against us, not by argument, but by arms: they come to
' us, not accusing, but commanding: they require imperiously, that
' the siege of Potidæa shall be raised; that Ægina shall be indepen-
' dent; that the decree against Megara shall be annulled; and, now
' at last, that we shall renounce our command over all Grecian states.
' Let it not however be imagined that even the Megarian decree is too
' light a matter to be supported as a cause of war. That comparatively
' little matter has been thrown out as an ultimate object, meerly to try
' your steddiness. Were you to yield that point, a greater trial would
' quickly be imposed upon you: resisting that, you give them to under-
' stand, that they must treat with you as equals, not command you as
' subjects.

Thucyd. l. 1.
c. 141.   ' It behoves you therefore at once to resolve, either to submit to a
' state of dependency, without uselessly incurring the unavoidable evils
' of resistance, or, what appears to me far preferable, to take arms with
' a determination to yield to no command, whether concerning a
' matter in itself of great or of little moment, nor, at any rate, to hold
' what you possess in fear and under controul. For the moment you
' give up your right of judgement, and yield obedience to a command,
' however unimportant the object of that command, your subjection
' is decided.

' If then we cast our view upon the means of each party, we shall
' find ours not the unfavorable prospect. The funds of the Pelopon-
' nesians must be drawn from the produce of Peloponnesus: for they
' have no forein dependencies capable of affording considerable sup-
' plies; and in Peloponnesus neither private nor public wealth abounds [16].
' In protracted war, and in maritime war, they are equally unexperi-
' enced; for their poverty has always disabled them, for both. They
' cannot equip fleets; nor can they send armies often, or maintain
' them long from home. For, in the scantiness of their public revenue,
' every man must subsist on service from his private means; and by
' long absence from their domestic affairs, even those means must be

---

[16] We find this observation repeated more than once in the speeches reported by Thucydides, without any exception for the Corinthians, who were commercial and rich, and had colonies: but their wealth bore but small proportion either to the resources of Athens, or to the wants of Peloponnesus.

' ruined.

' ruined.   A superfluity of wealth alone, and not the strained contri-
' butions of a people barely above want, can support lengthened and
' distant hostilities.   Such a people are commonly readier to make war
' with their persons than with their purses: they hope that those will
' finally escape; but these may be completely drained and the business
' yet unfinished.   For a single battle indeed, the Peloponnesians, with
' their allies, might be equal to all the rest of Greece.   But for protracted
' war, beside their want of money, which is their great and insuperable
' deficiency, wanting one common administration, each state having
' its equal voice for the decision of measures, and each its separate
' interest[18], each anxious for its own particular concerns, the general
' good will be sometimes thwarted, often neglected, and no great
' design can be steddily pursued.

'   Hence you need neither fear that posts will be occupied and for-   Thucyd. l. 1.
' tified within your country, with which some would alarm you, nor   c. 142.
' that a formidable navy can be raised against you.   Since the Persian
' war, now above fifty years, you have been assiduously applying to
' naval affairs, and even your proficiency is yet far below perfection.
' Naval science, and the skill of experienced seamen are not to be
' acquired by a people when they please, and in moments of leisure;
' on the contrary they require practice, to the exclusion of almost all
' leisure.   Nor, should the Peloponnesians seize the Olympic or Del-   c. 143.
' phian treasures, will even that avail them, to the degree that some
' seem to suppose.   They cannot, with these, form naval commanders
' and seamen, such as we possess among our own citizens, more and
' abler than all Greece besides: nor is it to be supposed that the seamen
' of our allies, for a temporary increase of pay, will banish themselves
' from their country, and join the party which has the worse prospect
' of final success.

'   Such then are the deficiencies under which the Peloponnesians
' labor, while we not only are free from these, but possess advantages
' peculiar to ourselves.   If they are strong enough to invade our
' country by land, we are equally able to harass them by sea; and
' should we waste but a small part of Peloponnesus, and they even the
' whole of Attica, the distress would be far greater to them than to us:
' for they have no other country whence to obtain supplies; while we

[18] Ἰσόψηφοι ὄντες καὶ ἐχ ὁμόφυλοι.

' have our choice among ilands and continents. The command of the
' sea is indeed a most important possession. Consider then : were we
' ilanders, who would be so secure against all hostile attempts ? What
' therefore should be now our aim but to put ourselves as nearly as
' possible into the situation of ilanders? Our lands and their apperte-
' nances within Attica should be totally given up: no vain attempt
' should be made to protect them against the superior landforce of the
' enemy: our whole attention should be directed to the safety of the
' city and the command of the sea. Could we gain a battle, fresh and
' perhaps greater forces would be brought against us. But should we
' lose one, the revolt of our allies, the sources of our wealth and strength,
' would follow; for they will no longer rest under their present subjec-
' tion, than while we have power to compel them. Not the loss of
' lands and houses therefore, but the loss of valuable lives, whenever it
' may happen, is to be deplored ; for lands cannot produce men: but
' let us keep ourselves strong in men, and we shall not want for lands.
' If therefore I thought I could persuade you, I would propose that
' you should yourselves go forth and waste Attica ; to show the Pelo-
' ponnesians how vain their expectation is, that the fear of such an evil
' may induce you to surrender your independency.

Thucyd. l. 1,   ' I have indeed many other grounds for clear hope of success, pro-
c. 144.   ' vided our own impatience and rashness, and the wild desire of conquest,
' when defence should be our object, injure us not more than the
' strength or policy of our enemies. On these topics, however,
' admonition may be better reserved for the circumstances when
' they arise. The answer now to be returned to Lacedæmon
' should be this: 'Our ports and markets shall be open to the
" Megarians, provided the Lacedæmonians will abrogate their pro-
" hibitions of the residence of strangers within their territory, as far as
" regards us and our allies: for the treaty of truce leaves these matters
" equally open to both parties [19]. We will give independency to those
" states

[19] The rough manner in which the Lacedæmonians executed their decrees for the
expulsion of strangers is noticed by Aristophanes in his comedy of the Birds.
  Meton. Τί δ᾽ ἐςὶ δεινὸν; Peisthetærus. ῞Ωσπερ ἐν Λακεδαίμονι,
      Ξενηλατοῦνlαι, καὶ κεκίνηνlαί τινες
      Πληγαὶ συχναὶ κατ᾽ ἄςυ.—v. 1114.
Vhere it seems also implied that Lacedæmon afforded temptation for strangers to go
                                                  thither,

" states of our alliance, which were independent when the truce was
" concluded, whenever the Lacedæmonians will allow to the states of
" their alliance free agency in whatever concerns their several govern-
" ments, and will no longer inforce among them a constitution and a
" mode of administration, which, under the show of independency,
" keep them in effectual subjection to Lacedæmon [20]. Finally, we are
" ready to submit any disputed points to a judicial determination
" according to the terms of the treaty; and we will not begin war, but
" we will defend ourselves to the utmost." Such an answer will be
' just, will be honorable, will be consonant to the renown and to the
' wisdom of our ancestors, who raised this empire, which we ought not
' to transmit diminished to our posterity.'

The assembly assented to the opinion of Pericles, and an answer was
accordingly delivered to the Lacedæmonian ambassadors nearly in the
terms of his speech; concluding with the declaration, ' That the Athe-
' nian commonwealth would obey the commands of no power upon
' earth, but would readily abide the event of a judicial determination,
' conducted upon a footing of equality between the parties, in the mode
' directed by the existing treaty [21].'

Thucyd. l. 1.
c. 145.

With this answer the Lacedæmonians returned home, and no more
embassies were sent. Hitherto the people of the two states had communicated, as in peace, without the intervention of a herald, tho not
without caution and suspicion: for, since the affairs of Corcyra and
Potidæa, the truce was considered on both sides as broken, and war as
impending. But now, tho no hostilities immediately insued, yet
communication was ventured on neither side, without the same for-
malities as if war had been declared.

l. 2. c. l.

thither, probably for gain by sale or exchange of commodities. In the difficulties made
for commerce by the Lacedæmonian laws, especially the prohibition of money, the trader
would always have advantage over the exchanger, not a professional trader.

[20] Ὅταν κἀκεῖνοι ταῖς ἑαυτῶν ἀποδῶσι πόλεσι
μὴ σφίσι τοῖς Λακεδαιμονίοις ἐπιτηδείως αὐτονο-
μεῖσθαι, κ. τ. ι. To turn this into modern
language, or perhaps into any language, long
circumlocution is necessary.

[21] We want information from Thucydides
what that Δίκη κατὰ τὰς ξυνθήκας, which he
so repeatedly mentions, was to have been.

SECTION VI.

Attempt of the Thebans against Platæa.

WHILE want of preparation still withheld the Peloponnesians, the Thebans, judging war to be now unavoidable, thought the moment of suspence advantageous for an attempt toward the more complete establishment of their own sovereinty over Bœotia : Lacedæmon must favor them ; Athens would fear to attack them.

The little town of Platæa, with a territory of scarcely half a dozen miles square, utterly unable by its own strength to subsist in independency, had nevertheless, for near a century, been resolutely resisting all controul from Thebes, whence it was less than nine miles distant. When, before the Persian war, Cleomenes king of Sparta was with an army in the neighborhood, the Platæans, to obtain the protection, had offered to put themselves under the dominion of Lacedæmon. The answer which, with his usual expressive simplicity, Herodotus attributes to the Lacedæmonians upon the occasion, strongly paints the state of Greece : ' We,' they said, ' live afar off, and ours would be a cold kind ' of assistance[22]; for you might be overpowered and sold for slaves, ' before any intelligence about you could reach us. We recommend to ' you therefore rather to put yourselves under the dominion of Athens[23], ' a bordering state, and able to protect you.' This advice, adds the historian, they gave, not through any goodwill to the Platæans, but with a view to create embarrassment to the Athenians by embroiling them with the Bœotians. The Platæans however followed the advice. The solemnity of the sacrifice to the twelve gods being chosen for the occasion, ambassadors were sent to Athens, but in the habit and character of suppliants. Placing themselves at the altar, according to the customary forms of supplication, these ministers thence urged their petition ' That their commonwealth might be taken under the sovereinty

The marginal references: Herod. l. 6. c. 108. Thucyd. l. 2. c. 5. Herod. ut sup. Thucyd. l. 3. c. 55.

[22] Τοιήδε τις γίνοιτ' ἂν ἐπικουρίη ψυχρή.
[23] The expression of Herodotus is very strong, Δεναι ὑμέας αὐτὺς, *to give yourselves.*

' and

' and protection of Athens [14].' The Athenian people acceded to the humble request.

The Thebans, upon the first intelligence of this transaction, marched against Platæa. An Athenian army moved at the same time to protect the new dependency of the commonwealth. The Corinthians however interfering, it was agreed to submit the matter to their arbitration. Actuated apparently by the spirit of justice and of liberty, and desirous to give as great extent as the nature of things would admit, to that dubious independency which could be injoyed by the smaller Grecian commonwealths, the Corinthians decided, ' That the ' Thebans were intitled to no sovereinty over any towns of Bœotia, ' whose people chose to renounce the advantages of that Bœotian ' confederacy of which they had made themselves the chiefs.' The business being thus apparently settled, the Athenian army moved homeward ; but the Thebans, irritated by a decision so adverse to their views, followed and attacked them on their march. They were defeated; and then the Athenians took upon themselves to dictate terms : extending the limits which had been prescribed by the Corinthians for the Platæan territory, and taking the neighboring little town of Hysiæ also under their protection, they made the river Asopus the boundary of the Thebaïd, both against the Platæan and the Hysian lands.

Thenceforward Platæa, more than ever averse to Thebes, became warm in political attachment to Athens. The whole force of the little commonwealth was exerted on the glorious day of Marathon, in the honor of which the Platæans alone partook with the Athenians. In the not less memorable action of Salamis, they had their share, tho an inland people, aboard the Athenian fleet; and they had distinguished themselves, under the command of Aristeides, in that great and decisive battle, fought near their town, which, beyond all other circumstances, hath given celebrity to its name. Under the patronage of Athens, democracy of course prevailed at Platæa. But as Athens itself was not without an aristocratical party, so there were in Platæa persons to whom democratical government, sometimes perhaps partially oppressive, and always an obstacle to their ambition, would be dissatisfactory. Their cause being hopeless under the dominion of Athens,

[14] Ἐδίδοσαν σφίας αὐτὰς.

Thebes

Thebes was the protecting power to which they looked for an alteration in their favor.

Thucyd. l. 2. c. 2.
In these circumstances a plot was concerted between Naucleides, the leading man of the aristocratical Platæans, and Eurymachus, who held the greatest influence in Thebes. The official directors of the Theban government were gained to it; and, in the fifteenth year of the Thirty-years truce, when Chrysis was in the forty-eighth year of her priest-hood at Argos, Ænesias ephor at Sparta, and two months were yet

P. C. 431.
Ol. 87. ½.
7th May,
Ann. Thu.
but more
likely 8th
April [25].
wanting to complete the archonship of Pythodorus at Athens, in the sixth month after the battle of Potidæa, the spring then beginning, (thus, in the want of a readier and more perfect method, Thucydides has marked the date) an armed body, of somewhat more than three hundred Thebans, reached Platæa about the first sleep. The Bœotarcs Pythangelus and Diemporus commanded, and they were accompanied by Eurymachus. Through confidence in the existing peace, no guard was kept in so small a city, which scarcely had a public revenue; the gates only were shut at night; and being now opened by the party friendly to the enterprize, the Thebans entered unresisted. Naucleides and the Platæans about him, in the too commonly atrocious spirit of Greek sedition, would have completed the business by the immediate massacre of the principal of their fellowtownsmen of the opposite party. But Eurymachus and the Bœotarcs, not equally stimulated by the passions either of fear or resentment, refused to concur in any such proposal. Reckoning themselves already masters of the place, and depending upon the ready support of a body of troops, which was to follow from Thebes, they lodged their arms in the agora; and sending heralds around the town, with a conciliating proclamation, they invited all who were disposed to accede to the confederacy of the Bœotian people, to come and place their arms by theirs.

Thucyd. l. 2. c. 3.
The Platæans, hastily and in great alarm assembling, were, in the moment, rejoiced to find a disposition so far friendly, among those who seemed to have them, their families, and their whole state com-

---

[25] Eighty days after, according to Thucydides (b. 2. c. 19.) the corn of Attica was nearly ripe. Eighty days from the eighth of April would be the twenty-seventh of June, rather a late harvest-season in Attica. Eighty days after the seventh of May, namely the twenty-sixth of July, wheat is often ripe in the south of England.

pletely

pletely at mercy.   They showed therefore a ready disposition to accede to the terms proposed,   But in the course of the communication that insued, having opportunity to discover, amid the darkness, how few the Thebans were, they began to observe to oneanother that they were abundantly able to overpower those who had thus insidiously surprized them; and the resolution was quickly taken to make the attempt. That they might not be noticed in preparation, they broke ways through the partition-walls of houses, and they formed a barricade of carts and waggons, from behind which they might make their assault.   Waiting then till just before daybreak, while darkness might yet at the same time give them the greater advantage from their intimate knowlege of the place, and increase the alarm and uncertainty of the enemy, they began the attack.   Twice or thrice they were repulsed; but they returned to the charge, the women and slaves at the same time throwing stones and tiles from the house-tops, with an unceasing clamor which increased the confusion, while a heavy rain made the obscurity more complete.   The Thebans thus unable to hear commands or see commanders, were incapable of acting in concert, and at length fled, each as he could find a passage, in darkness and in dirt, mostly ignorant of the ways, while their pursuers were acquainted with every turn.   A Platæan had shut the gate of the town by which they had entered, and which alone had been open; and for want of other means at hand, fastened it by thrusting the head of a javelin into the catch of the lock. Checked thus in their hope of flight, some of the Thebans mounted the rampart, and throwing themselves down on the outside, mostly perished: some, finding a gate unguarded, obtained an axe from a woman, with which they forced the lock, and a few thus escaped.   Many were killed, scattered about the town; but the greater part, who had kept more in a body, entered a large building adjoining the rampart, whose door, which stood open, they mistook for the town-gate.   This was observed by the Platæans, who took immediate measures to prevent their egress.   It was then proposed to set fire to the building and burn those in it; but upon their offering to surrender themselves, they were received as prisoners at discretion; and shortly after, all the rest, who remained alive within the town, came and delivered their arms.

The

The march of the troops which should have supported the enterprize had been retarded by the rain. Upon their arrival at the Asopus, they found it so swelled that it was with difficulty forded; and before they could reach Platæa, the miscarriage of those who had entered the place was complete. As soon as they were aware of this, they determined to plunder the Platæan lands and villages, and to seize all the people they could find, that they might have hostages for the security of their own people, if any should be prisoners in Platæa. But the Platæans, expecting such a measure, sent a herald to them, threatening immediate death to the prisoners if any farther attempt was made against the persons or effects of the people of Platæa, but promising to restore them if the Thebans would immediately quit their territory. The agreement was presently made and ratified by oath, and the Theban army retired accordingly. Such, says Thucydides, is the Theban account: but the Platæans deny that any oaths passed, and that any promise was given for the restoration of the prisoners, except on condition that a treaty should be concluded between the two states. The Platæans, however, allowed no opportunity for farther treaty. Hastening the removal of their effects from the country within their fortifications, they put to death all their prisoners, to the number of a hundred and eighty, among whom was Eurymachus, the author of the enterprize.

Such was the inauspicious prelude to the Peloponnesian war. The execution of the unhappy prisoners, supposing no compact to forbid it, seems indeed to have been in strict conformity to what may be called the national law of the Greeks; upon the same principle as spies, traitors, and pirates, are liable to capital punishment by the law of nations in modern Europe. The bodies. as the Grecian law of humanity

required, were restored, through the intervention of heralds. But the Platæans, aware that the Thebans would feel upon the occasion, and perhaps reason, differently from themselves, prepared for resisting that revenge which was to be expected. Immediately upon discovery that the town was surprized, a messenger had been dispatched to Athens with the intelligence; and another as soon as the Thebans were made prisoners. Upon receiving the first news, the Athenian administration issued orders for seizing all Bœotians within Attica: in return to the

second,

second, directions were sent to keep the prisoners made in Platæa in safe custody, till the Athenian government should determine what farther was to be done.   Unfortunately, such was the ill-considered haste of the Platæans, the fatal execution had taken place before the messenger with this order arrived.   So severe a measure, even supposing no breach of faith, plighted or implied, would, by its operation upon the passions, preclude negotiation.   An Athenian army was therefore sent with a convoy of provisions to Platæa; a small body was left to strengthen the place; and the women, children, and whatever else would be useless in a siege, were brought away.

CHAPTER XIV.

Of the PELOPONNESIAN WAR, from its Commencement to the Death of PERICLES, with a summary View of the History of THRACE.

SECTION I.

State of the Athenian and Peloponnesian Confederacies. Invasion and Ravage of Attica by the Peloponnesians. Operations of the Athenian Fleet in the Western Seas under Carcinus: Gallant Action of the Spartan Brasidas: Ravage of the Peloponnesian Coast, and Acquisition of Cephallenia to the Athenian Confederacy. Operations of the Athenian Fleet in the Eastern Seas under Cleopompus. Measures for the Security of Athens: Remarkable Decree: Extermination of the Æginetans. Invasion and Ravage of Megaris by the Athenians.

Thucyd. l. 2.
c. 7.

THIS unfortunate transaction between two inferior republics, which no prudence in the leading states could prevent or foresee, made accommodation more than ever impracticable; and both parties prepared for hostilities with the most serious diligence. At this time,

c. 8.

says Thucydides, who was a living witness, Greece abounded with youth, through inexperience, ardent for war; while, among those of more sober age, many things contributed to stimulate passion, or excite apprehension. Many oracular responses were circulated, many signs and wonders were reported; and some phenomena reälly occurred, of a kind to affect the imaginations of men in a superstitious age; to raise hope or inspire alarm. Among these, what most ingaged attention was an earthquake that shook the sacred iland of Delos; which never, within the reach of tradition, had before been so affected. Amid this universal irritation of men's minds, a very general disposition prevailed, as the candid Athenian in the most explicit terms avows, to favor the Lacedæmonian cause, as the cause of liberty and independency: while

animosity

animosity and indignation were the sentiments excited by that arbitrary and oppressive command, which a large portion of the Grecian people experienced, and the rest dreaded, from the soverein Many of Athens.

The two confederacies, now upon the point of ingaging in war, were very differently composed, but the force of the Greek nation was very equally divided between them. With the Lacedæmonians all the Peloponnesian states joined, except the Argians, who remained neuter, and the Achaians; of whom the Pellenians only took part in the beginning of the war. Of northern Greece, the Megarians, Bœotians, Locrians, Phocians, Ambraciots, Leucadians, and Anactorians, joined the Peloponnesian alliance. The navy was to be formed by the Lacedæmonians, Corinthians, Sicyonians, Pellenians, Eleians, Megarians, Ambraciots, and Leucadians. The Bœotians, Phocians, and Locrians furnished cavalry; the other states infantry only. It was proposed to raise no less than five hundred trireme galleys within the confederacy; its proportion being assessed upon every maritime state; and contributions in money were required from all. Ministers were sent to endevor to form alliances among forein nations; and the great king, as the king of Persia was called, or oftener simply the King, was not neglected; but for external assistance the principal expectation was from the Italian and Sicilian Greeks, who possessed considerable maritime force, and mostly favored the Peloponnesian interest. *Thucyd. l. 2. c. 9.* *c. 9. Diod. l. 12. c. 41.*

Athens had few allies, properly so called. On the continent of Greece the principal were the Thessalians and the Acarnanians; the former little ingaged by interest or inclination, but bound by a treaty of long standing: most of the Acarnanian towns, tho some were adverse, joined with more zeal in the Athenian cause. The Platæans are besides named, and the Messenians of Naupactus: the republic of the former however, except the meer garrison of their town, existing only within the walls of Athens; and that of the latter never capable of existence but under Athenian protection. Of the ilands, Corcyra, Zacynthus, Chios, and Lesbos, are alone properly reckoned among the allies of Athens. Corcyra assisted in fixing Zacynthus, before disposed to the Athenian interest. Chios and the republics of Lesbos were still treated with respect by the Athenian government, as inde- *Thucyd. l. 2. c. 22.* *c. 9.*

I 2   pendent

pendent states; and they still possessed their own fleets.   All the other
ilands of the Ægean sea, except the Lacedæmonian colonies of Melos
and Thera, all the numerous and wealthy Grecian cities of Asia Minor,
of the Hellespont, and of Thrace, were tributary subjects of the Athenian people; not allowed to possess ships of war, but dependent upon
Athens for protection, and liable to every kind and degree of controul
from that imperial state.

Thucyd..l. 2.
c. 10.   News of the transactions at Platæa, arriving at Lacedæmon, hastened
the measure, before in some degree resolved upon, to invade Attica.
Summons were sent through the confederacy, in pursuance of which
two-thirds of the whole land-force of the Peloponnesian states met the
Lacedæmonian army, on an appointed day, at the Corinthian isthmus.
The command-in-chief was not denied to the venerable king Archidamus, notwithstanding his known disapprobation of the war, nor did
he scruple, in that command, to show his steddiness in the principles
he had always professed.   Before he would lead his forces out of Peloponnesus, he sent a herald, to make one more trial whether the threatening storm, now ready to burst, might have produced any disposition in
the Athenians to relax.   Thucydides has left no room to doubt either
that his purpose was liberal and generous, or that his influence to guide
the counsels of the confederacy in the way of liberality and generosity,
the way that he thought the common good of Greece, and the good of
Lacædemon and all Peloponnesus, as inseparable from the common good
of Greece, required, was very deficient.   In this persuasion apparently
of the Athenian administration, probably under the direction of Pericles,
an answer was returned, importing that, if the Peloponnesians would
communicate with the Athenians, they must first withdraw their army,
and send the troops of the several states to their respective homes: the
herald was required to leave Athens the same day, and conducted by a
guard to the Attic border.   Upon this Archidamus proceeded on his
march.   The Thebans, marching to join him, detached a part of their
infantry to waste the Platæan lands.   With the remainder, and all their
cavalry, they reached him in the Megarian territory.

c. 13.   While the Peloponnesian troops were assembling, Pericles was
ingaged in the arduous office of preparing the minds of the Athenian
                                                        people

people for what was to follow; obviating the clamors of faction, the discontent which would arise from the unavoidable calamities of a defensive war, and the jealousies to which his own situation of first-minister of the commonwealth would now more than ever expose him. He had been elected, according to the ordinary military establishment of Athens, with nine collegues, to command the Athenian forces. But since the first Persian invasion, the practice seems to have gained to appoint one of the ten, by popular election, to be perpetual chief, with the title of general of the commonwealth, and with the sole power to convoke, at his discretion, extraordinary assemblies of the people. Pericles was now so elected. But Pericles had lived in habits of friendship with the Spartan king Archidamus: they were ingaged together in the sacred league of hospitality. Possibly Archidamus, in kindness to Pericles, might, amid the general ravage of Attica, procure favor to his estates: possibly, to excite envy and jealousy against him, the Lacedæmonians most hostile to him might procure ostentation of such a mark of good-will from the enemies of his country. To prevent ill consequences, Pericles declared, in the assembly of the people, his apprehension of such circumstances; and he added that, if any of his estates should be more spared than those around them, they should be no longer his own but the public property. He took opportunity at the same time for repeating his exhortation to the people, to disregard the waste of their possessions in Attica, and by all means to avoid any general ingagement by land, directing their utmost attention to their navy. This alone, he said, could maintain their dominion over their invaluable transmarine possessions and dependencies, and only those could insure them that final success, which superiority of revenue, under the direction of wise counsels, must always give. He proceeded then to a display of the means which the commonwealth possessed. The annual tribute from transmarine dependencies, exclusively of other sources of revenue, he observed amounted now to six hundred talents, about one hundred and fifty thousand pounds sterling. But there were actually in the treasury, in coined money, no less than six thousand talents, or one million five hundred thousand pounds sterling. The uncoined gold and silver which might be employed, should the neces-

sities

sities of the commonwealth require, offerings public and private, sacred vases used in processions and public festivals, Persian spoils, and a variety of smaller articles, would amount to not less than five hundred talents. Beside all this, the pure gold about the single statue of Minerva in the acropolis was of the weight of forty talents; precisely, according to Arbuthnot, a ton averdupois, and in value about a hundred and fifty thousand pounds sterling [1]; and this quantity of gold had been so adapted by Pheidias that the whole might be taken off without injury to the statue; and whenever returning public wealth in settled peace afforded means, it might be replaced. The military force of the commonwealth was at the same time truly formidable. The native heavy-armed foot were no less than twenty-nine thousand men. Sixteen thousand of these sufficed for guards and garrisons; and the eldest and the youngest of the citizens were competent for that service; so that there remained thirteen thousand, the flower of the Athenian youth, to be employed in annoying the enemy wherever opportunity might offer. The cavalry, including the horse-bowmen, were twelve hundred; the foot-bowmen were sixteen hundred; and the whole native force of the commonwealth thus amounted to near thirty-two thousand men, exclusively of the numerous light-armed slaves always attendant upon Grecian armies. What should be added for the forces which might be raised among the allies and subjects of the state, the historian has not informed us, and we have no means for calculation. The fleet consisted of three hundred trireme galleys. The crews would be more than fifty thousand men. How far slaves were employed, and how far the citizens of subject states, we have no precise information. But every Athenian was more or less a seaman: even the heavy-armed sometimes worked at the oar; and, upon occasion, all the seamen equally served by land. But the meer sailor was commonly of the lowest order of citizens, carried only light armour, and was esteemed of inferior mili-

Thucyd. l. 6. c. 91. & al.

---

[1] A ton weight appears an enormous quantity of gold to be so employed; yet the account seems not to have excited suspicion among commentators, antient or modern. Indeed when a quantity of gold was collected, means to make interest of it were not, in those days, ready; and to secure it against democratical extravagance, for a resource in calamity, no method was so effectual as dedicating it in a temple.

tary

tary rank to the heavy-armed and perhaps even to the middle-armed Xen. Hal. l. 1. c. 2. s. 1, 2. soldier.

Persuaded, says Thucydides, by these, and other arguments which Thucyd. l. 2. c. 14. Pericles was accustomed to urge, the Attic people applied themselves to the ungrateful task of stripping their whole country, and fixing themselves with their families within that space, ample of its kind, which the walls surrounding and connecting Athens and its ports inclosed. All their furniture they brought with them; and many even the frames of their houses; valuable in a country where the materials for building were wood and marble; the former scarce; the latter, tho plentiful, yet in workmanship costly. Their cattle, great and small, and attending slaves, were transported to the neighboring ilands, principally to Eubœa. This measure however was not resolved on, even upon conviction of the pressure of necessity, without extreme reluctance; for the Attic people, continues the cotemporary writer, were, beyond all other Greeks, attached to their country possessions and a country life. The ravages of the Persian war were now repaired, with large improvement upon the antient state of things; most of the houses were newly built; some lately completed, and elegantly and expensively Isocr. Areiop p. 130, t. 2. furnished, so that, according to Isocrates, they were superior to the houses in the city. The temples also in the several borough towns, destroyed in the Persian war, had been zealously restored; and the people were warmly attached to those which they esteemed their own inherited religious rites, peculiar to that town which had been the town of their ancestors, before Theseus concentrated their religion, government, and jurisprudence of the country in Athens.

Beside the prejudices thus to be violated and imaginary evils to be supported, the real inconveniencies, unavoidably attending the measure, were great. While their improvements were to be demolished, and the revenues from their estates to cease, only a few of the more opulent could obtain houses for the habitation of their families; and but a small proportion could be received into those of their friends. The numerous temples of Athens afforded an incommodious shelter to many: all were occupied, excepting those within the citadel, and the magnificent and highly venerated Eleusinium, the fane of the mysterious

4   Ceres,

Ceres, with one or two others, which were firmly locked. Even the superstition which had taught to dread the roof of the temple called the Pelasgic, as under a curse from the deïty, yielded to the pressing necessity of the times. Those who, in the actual circumstances, took the lead in public business, had certainly a difficult and hazardous office: it was of urgent necessity for them to be cautious of pressing upon a larger portion of the soverein multitude in favor of a smaller; and hence perhaps the distressed individuals from the country were not objects, as apparently they ought to have been, of the care of government, but were left almost intirely to their own means and their own discretion. When the temples were all occupied, the turrets of the city-walls were resorted to for private residence. But neither buildings nor space within the city sufficed for the multitude. Many families formed for themselves the best shelter they were able, on the vacant ground inclosed within the long walls and about the port of Peiræus. In this space, could the administration have used the foresight and diligence which it seems to have possessed, all or the greater part, best both for themselves and for the public, perhaps might have been accommodated. Measures against the enemy showed ability and energy. The most effectual steps were taken for applying the force of the allies; and a fleet of a hundred triremes was prepared for an expedition against Peloponnesus.

Thucyd. l. 2. c. 18.   The Peloponnesian army meanwhile entered Attica by the way of Œnoë, and the first operation was the siege of that town, critically situated for the defence of the border against Bœotia, and therefore strongly fortified and well provided. The reluctance of the Athenians to abandon their estates had been such, that much of their effects might have been the prey of the invaders, if the delay occasioned by the siege of Œnoë had not given opportunity to complete the removal. Complaint was in consequence loud against Archidamus. That worthy prince had scarcely now given up all hope that some disposition to concession on the part of the Athenians might afford opportunity to open a treaty, and save Greece from the ruin threatened by the exertion of its whole force so equally divided against itself. But when the

c. 19.   siege had been pressed for several days, with the machines then in use,

and

and in all the known ways of attack upon fortifications[2], and little progress was made, discontent spreading and growing more vehement through the army, and no symptom appearing of a disposition among the Athenians to treat, Archidamus yielded to the wishes of his troops. About eighty days after the attempt upon Platæa, when the corn was 26th June. nearly ripe, being joined by the Theban infantry, he raised the siege of Œnoë, and advanced into Attica with an army, according to Plutarch, of Plut. vit. sixty thousand men. The Eleusinian and Thriasian plains were immedi- Peric. ately ravaged: a body of Athenian horse was defeated near Rheiti; and the army, keeping mount Ægaleon on the right, passed by the way of Cecropia to Acharnæ, the largest and richest borough of Attica, situate within eight miles of Athens.

Archidamus had expected that the Athenian people, strong in num- Thucyd. l. 2. bers, naturally high-spirited and impatient, and prepared for war as c. 20. they had never before been, would not have borne, without opposition, the waste of the Eleusinian and Thriasian lands; but he depended still more upon the ruin now hanging over Acharnæ. The people of that borough formed no fewer than three thousand heavy-armed foot; they could not but have great weight in the Athenian assembly; and Archidamus thought it probable that their impatience, under the destruction of their property, would influence the whole people to require that they should be led out to battle: or otherwise, that when the Acharnians saw their own estates ruined, they would with little zeal ingage in the defence of those of others, and thus he might proceed with more security to ravage all the rest of the country. What passed in Athens proved the justness of his judgement. From the time of the c. 21. Persian war, now remembered only by a few of the oldest citizens, Attica, except a small part of the border, had never felt the ravage of an enemy. The Eleusinian and Thriasian plains had been plundered about fourteen years before by the army under Pleistoanax; and so much was supported now as matter to be expected. But when the Peloponnesian army incamped within sight of Athens, and the rich Acharnian vale was to be the next object of devastation, the whole city was in uproar. Some were vehement for marching out to defend

[2] Μηχαναῖς τι καὶ ἄλλῳ τρόπῳ.

their property; others as warmly opposed a measure which would so indanger the commonwealth; but on all sides there was an outcry against Pericles; who, whether as advising the war, or refusing the means of ingaging the enemy, was reproached as the principal author of the present evils.

Thucyd. l. 2.
c. 22.
Amid all the vehemence of clamor, the intrigues of faction, and the threats of popular animosity, Pericles remained immoveable. Leaving the ferment to evaporate in altercation among individuals, he would convene no assembly; he would hold no council; but while he gave his own attention, he directed also that of others as much as possible to what, in any moment of sober reflection, all would admit to be of the first importance, the guard of the city and the preservation of good order. Meantime he was frequently sending out parties of cavalry to cut off stragglers and prevent the extension of ravage to any distance from the Peloponnesian camp. Expectation thus raised, and an interest created for the public mind, popular passion was diverted, popular combination dissipated, and ruinous resolutions were prevented. In an action with the Bœotian horse, the Athenian and Thessalian had the advantage, till a body of Peloponnesian foot coming up, compelled them to retreat. They so far however vindicated the honor of their arms as, on the same day, to carry off their dead, without a truce, which the defeated usually solicited for the purpose; and it was not till the next day that the Peloponnesians, in claim of victory, erected a trophy on the field. After some time, provisions beginning to fail in

c. 23.
the Peloponnesian camp, and every provocation appearing ineffectual against the resolution of the Athenians not to risk a general ingagement, the army moved from Acharnæ. Ravaging the lands between the mountains Parnes and Brilessus, they proceeded by Oropus, whose territory they also ravaged, into Bœotia, and having thus traversed Attica from west to east, they returned into Peloponnesus, and dispersed to their several homes.

While such were the sufferings of Attica in this first summer of the war, a fleet of a hundred trireme galleys, with a thousand heavy foot and four hundred bowmen, was sent from Peiræus, under Carcinus, Proteas, and Socrates son of Antigenes, to retaliate devastation upon

Peloponnesus.

Peloponnesus. Fifty galleys from Corcyra, and a few from some of the other allies, joined this armament.   A descent was made first on the Messenian coast, and the troops marched toward Methonë; a town then ill fortified, and without a garrison.   As it was known that there was no considerable military force in the neighborhood, they incamped, scattered around the place, at the same time to prevent valuables from being carried out, and to collect booty from the country.   But Brasidas, who commanded the district, with only a hundred Lacedæmonians, piercing their camp, got into Methonë; and by the order which he established among the inhabitants, together with the small force which he brought (for the Spartans were all bred to be either soldiers or officers as occasion might require) secured the place against an assault[3]. The Athenian commanders, finding their design thus frustrated, for it was not at all their purpose to ingage in a siege, reïmbarked their forces. By this bold and successful effort, Brasidas gained great credit in Sparta, and became considered as an officer superiorly qualified for commands which might require activity and daring exertion.

The Peloponnesians early found that a navy was not to be created so rapidly as some of their warmer politicians had promised them. A wide extent of coast remained, and was likely to remain, open to the attacks of the Athenian fleet.   The land-force was again debarked near the Eleïan town of Pheia, which was taken; the neighboring country was ravaged, and the Eleians, assembled in haste to protect their property, were defeated.   To keep Pheia being however no object to the Athenian commanders, the Eleians were no sooner collected in force sufficient to oppose them, than they reïmbarked their troops, and proceeding northward along the coast, continued their depredations wherever they found most temptation and least danger.   They took Solium, a small town on the Ætolian coast belonging to the Corinthians, and gave it to the Acarnanians of Palira.   They took Astacus in Acarnania, and, expelling its tyrant Evarchus, they committed the

Thucyd. l. 2. c. 25.

c. 30.

---

[3] Ἀθρώπων ἐκ ἐνόἶων, is the phrase used by Thucydides in first speaking of Methonë. In the very next sentence he says that Bra sidas ἐζοήθει τοῖς ἐν τῷ χωρίῳ. His meaning therefore was, that there were no Lacedæmonians in the place, and consequently no soldiers; the inhabitants being all unarmed Messenians and Helots.

K 2   supreme

supreme power to the popular assembly, and the city became a member of the Athenian confederacy. They proceeded then to Cephallenia, which was at that time divided between no less than four republics, Palë, Cranë, Samë, and Pronë. The particularity with which Thucydides describes its situation and circumstances implies that, in his time, those western ilands were little generally known among the Greeks. Without any act of hostility, the whole of Cephallenia was induced to accede to the Athenian alliance. After these considerable services, the armament returned to Attica.

Thucyd. l. 2. c. 26.

While the war was thus carried into the western seas of Greece, a squadron of thirty galleys, under Cleopompus, sailed eastward and northward, to protect Eubœa, and to annoy the hostile states in its neighborhood, especially Locris. Some of the lands on the Locrian coast were ravaged ; the town of Thronium, capitulating, gave hostages to insure the performance of some compact, probably for payment of a subsidy and abstaining from hostilities, and the Locrians of the other towns, taking the field to relieve Thronium, were defeated at Alopë.

c. 32.

To prevent depredations which the Opuntian Locrians were accustomed to make, on the Eubœan coast, the little iland of Atalanta, near the coast of Locris, was fortified, and a small naval force was stationed there.

Within Attica, meanwhile, after the departure of the Peloponnesian army, the counsels of the administration were diligently directed to provide the best security for the country that its exposed situation and the inferiority of its landforce would admit : posts were occupied on the frontier, and guard-ships were stationed on different parts of the coast. A measure followed, which, taking place at the time when Thucydides wrote and Pericles spoke, and while Pericles held the principal influence in the administration, strongly marks both the inherent weakness and the indelible barbarism of democratical government. A decree of the people directed that a thousand talents should be set apart in the treasury in the citadel, as a deposit, not to be touched unless the enemy should attack the city by sea; a circumstance which implied the prior ruin of the Atherian fleet, and the only one, it was supposed, which could superinduce the ruin of the commonwealth.

But

But so little confidence was placed in a decree so important, sanctioned only by the present will of that giddy tyrant the multitude of Athens, against whose caprices since the depression of the court of Areiopagus, no balancing power remained, the denunciation of capital punishment was added against whosoever should propose, and whosoever should concur in, any decree for the disposal of that money to any other purpose, or in any other circumstances. It was at the same time ordered, by the same authority, that a hundred triremes should be yearly selected, the best of the fleet, to be employed on the same occasion only.

Another measure, of no small actual severity, was thought justifiable by public expediency, and by the right and the duty of obviating public danger. It was judged unsafe to permit a people so invete- *Thucyd. l. 2.*
rately inimical as the Æginetans, and known to have been active in *c. 27.*
exciting the war, any longer to hold, tho under the controul of an Athenian garrison, that iland which had been emphatically termed the Eyesore of Peiræus. It was desirable at the same time to disincumber the city of a part of the multitude which so inconveniently crouded it. The Æginetans were therefore expelled from their iland, and a colony of Athenians took possession of their lands and houses. A garrison was thus maintained without public expence, and the government was relieved of some portion of the care incumbent on it, to provide for those citizens who were unable to provide for themselves. A distribu- *Plut. vit.*
tion of money from the public treasury alleviated the present wants of *Peric.*
the remaining poor in Athens. No provision seems to have been made or proposed by the Athenian government for the exterminated Ægi- netans. Instances indeed are so familiar, in Grecian history, of an obnoxious people, a Grecian people, reduced to slavery by a Grecian people, that it might perhaps be thought an act of clemency to allow them to migrate. The Lacedæmonians however gave them the *Thucyd. ut*
Thyreatis, a small territory on the confines of Laconia and Argolis, a *sup.*
situation probably inconvenient enough, from the constant enmity of Argos to Lacedæmon. A few only of the exiles found more desirable establishments among their friends in other parts of Greece. Thucy- dides mentions, among the events of this summer, a nearly total

eclipse

eclipse of the sun, beginning soon after midday, which ascertains the chronology.

Toward the close of autumn the whole force of Athens marched, under the command of Pericles, to retaliate the vengeance and reap the profit of ravage, where it could be done most readily, and now with complete security, in the bordering territory of Megara. The fleet under Carcinus, just returned from the western sea, was lying at Ægina. Proceeding to the Megarian coast, its landforce joined that under Pericles. Thus was formed, according to Thucydides, the largest Athenian army ever assembled in the course of the war. The Athenians were not less than ten thousand, and the Metics, those denizens of Athens who had not the privileges of Athenian citizens, were four thousand heavy-armed foot: the number of light-armed he does not state, but he says they were a large body. When plunder and waste had been carried as far as circumstances allowed, the whole armament returned to Peiræus and Athens.

SECTION II.

Summary View of the History of Thrace: Alliance negotiated by Athens with Sitalces King of Thrace and Perdiccas King of Macedonia. Public Funeral at Athens in honor of the Slain in their Country's Service. Expedition of the Corinthians against Acarnania and Cephallenia.

SUCH were the military transactions of the first summer of the war. Meanwhile negotiations had been diligently prosecuted; with the purpose chiefly of providing security for that revenue, arising in tribute from transmarine Grecian states, which inabled Athens to maintain the most powerful navy then in the world, and to withstand the superior land-force of the Peloponnesian confederacy. The enmity of the king of Macedonia threatened inconvenience; and, especially to obviate this, an improvement of friendly connection with the extensive monarchy of Thrace was desirable.

Thrace, as we have formerly observed, appears to have been occupied in early times by the same Pelasgian hords who principally gave origin to
the

the Grecian people. But instead of advancing with the Greeks in knowlege and civilization, those glimmerings of science which, according to
the oldest Grecian traditions, beamed upon their country before they
reached Greece, were totally lost ; and two prejudices, perhaps brought
by hords from the mountains of the interior, who overwhelmed the
civilized inhabitants of the coast, becoming leading principles
over the whole nation, made the Thracians incorrigibly barbarous:
' To live by war and rapine,' says Herodotus, ' is their delight   Herod. 1. 5.
' and their glory; and nothing they esteem so dishonorable as   c. 6.
' agriculture.' A most indispensable ornament of their persons was
to have the skin punctured in various figures; a whimsical practice
of barbarians, remarkable for its universality ; found antiently among
our ancestors the Britons, in the extreme of the old world, and lately
among their antipodes in the little ilands of the Pacific ocean ; who,
but for the wonderful improvements of modern European navigation,
must have remained ever equally unknown to the people of the old
world, and of what has been called the new.   Between mount Hæmus
and the Danube lived the Getes, by some supposed the founders of the
Gothic name ; according to Thucydides a Thracian people, but still more   Thucyd. 1. 2.
barbarous than the other Thracians ; resembling in manners the Scythi-   c. 96, 97.
ans, who wandered to an unknown extent, over the vast continent
to the northward and northeastward of the Danube and the Euxine.

Under the reign of Darius, the whole of the Thracian country had
been brought to acknowlege the Persian dominion. The retreat of the
Persians out of Europe, after the defeat of Xerxes, appears to have
given opportunity for forming, among its people, an empire such
as had been before unknown. What wars or what policy led to it we
are uninformed ; but Teres, chief of the Odrysian clan, became soverein   c. 29.
of all the Thracians, from the Ægean sea to the Danube, and from the
Euxine to the Strymon ; a country considerably larger than all Greece.
Some mountaineers of the borders, and some clans of the plains, in the
central part of the continent beyond the Strymon, alone maintained
themselves in independency. The Grecian towns on the coast, all
paying tribute to Athens to have safety for their commerce, found it
convenient also to pay tribute to the Thracian prince, to have safety
for their lands and towns. So far then owning subjection, and contri-
buting

buting to the strength and splendor of the monarchy, they were not
objects of jealousy and oppression, but rather of protection and incouragement: for the Thracians, wealthy by the possession of ample and
fruitful territory, by the produce of mines of the richest metals, and
by the command of numerous tributaries, but despising agriculture
and commerce, did not despise conveniencies, or even luxuries, which
only agriculture and commerce can give.

On the death of Teres the extensive monarchy of Thrace devolved
to his son Sitalces, who had married the sister of Nymphodorus, a
citizen of the Grecian town of Abdera, one of the subject dependencies
of Athens. An advantageous opening was thus offered to the Athenian
government for improving their interest with the Thracian king.
Through Nymphodorus an alliance was formed with Sitalces: and
such was the ascendancy which the little republics of Greece had
acquired among forein nations, Sadocus, the eldest son of the powerful
monarch of Thrace, accepted, as a valuable honor, his admission to the
name and privileges of one of the Athenian people. The brother-in-
law of Sitalces then undertook to be mediator between the king of
Macedonia and the Athenian commonwealth; and, for the town of
Thermë, Perdiccas joined the Thracian prince in the Athenian
alliance.

Winter setting in, and military operations being suspended, Pericles
did not neglect the means which established custom offered, for
animating the Athenian people in the cause in which they were
ingaged, and converting even the calamities of war into an occasion
of triumph. The funeral of those who had fallen in their country's
service was publicly solemnized; and the manner of it remains
particularly described by Thucydides. Three days before the ceremony of burial, the bones, collected from the bodies previously
burnt, according to the ordinary practice of the Greeks, were arranged under an ample awning. While thus, according to the
modern phrase, they lay in state, it was usual for the relations to
visit them, and throw on anything that fancy or superstition gave
to imagine a grateful offering to the spirits of the deceased, or honorable to their memory among the living. The day of the burial being
arrived, the bones were placed in ten chests of cypress-wood, raised

Thucyd. l. 2.
c. 34.

on

on carriages, one for each ward of Attica, and an eleventh carriage
bore an empty bier with a pall, in honor of those whose bodies could
not be recovered.   Procession was then made in solemn march to the   Thucyd. l. 2.
public tomb in the Cerameicus, the most beautiful suburb of the city ;   & Not. ed.
the female relations of the deceased attending, and, according to the   Duk.
Grecian custom, venting their lamentations aloud.   From the institu-   Thucyd. l. 2.
tion of the ceremony, the tomb in the Cerameicus had been the recep-   c. 34.
tacle of all who had been honored with a public funeral, excepting
those who had fallen at Marathon; who, for the supereminence of their
merit, and the singular glory of the action, had been buried in the field
of battle, where their peculiar monument was raised over them.   Some
person of superior dignity and eminent abilities was always appointed
by the people to speak the funeral panegyric.   On the present occasion
every circumstance directed the public choice to Pericles.   When
therefore the ceremony of intombing was over, Pericles passed through
the croud to a lofty stand raised for the occasion, so that he might be
heard by the attending multitude the most extensively possible ; and
thence delivered that oration, the heads of which at least Thucydides,   l. 1. c. 22.
who was probably present, has, it is from his own professions to be pre-   l. 1. c. 35 &
sumed, faithfully collected, preserving in a great degree even the   46.
manner in which it was spoken.   It remains, in its original language,
a finished model of the simple and severe sublime in oratory, which has
been the admiration of all succeeding ages; but which must sink in
any translation, denies abridgement, and defies either imitation or
paraphrase, perhaps beyond any composition that ever was committed
to writing.

The winter was not for all parts of Greece, as for Athens, a season   l. 2. c. 33.
of repose.   Evarchus, the expelled tyrant of Astacus in Acarnania,
applied to Corinth for assistance to restore him to his little dominion.
The antients seldom ventured upon maritime expeditions in short days
and stormy seasons; the narrowness of their seas, the height and
rockiness of their coast, the frequency of sudden squalls, and the want
of a guide in cloudy weather, rendering it far more dangerous than
where the ocean is at hand, and where in a stout vessel, under guidance

Vol. II.   L   of

of the compass, distance from land is safety. The zeal of Corinth
however was not to be deterred.   Forty ships of war and fifteen hundred
heavy foot, under Euphamidas, with some auxiliary mercenaries raised
by Evarchus, recovered Astacus.   Attempts were made upon some
other towns of Acarnania, but without success.   The Corinthians then
moving homeward, debarked in Cephallenia, on the Cranæan lands.
The Cranæans, amusing them with the pretence of a disposition to
capitulate, attacked them unawares, and forced them to reimbark with
loss; upon which, without attempting anything further, they returned
to Corinth.

SECTION III.

*Second Invasion of Attica by the Peloponnesians. Pestilence at Athens.
Operations of the Athenian Fleet on the Peloponnesian Coast under
Pericles; and on the Macedonian Coast under Agnon. Effects of
popular Discontent at Athens. First Effort of the Peloponnesian
Fleet. Attempt of the Peloponnesians to send an Embassy into
Persia. Barbarity of the Grecian System of War. An Athenian
Squadron stationed in the Western Sea. Surrender of Potidæa to
the Athenians. Death of Pericles.*

THE events of the first campain justify the wisdom both of Pericles
and of Archidamus, in the counsels they respectively gave before the
commencement of hostilities.   The Peloponnesians were evidently not
prepared to wage offensive war against Athens with any advantage.   A
considerable part of Attica had been ravaged; the harvest had been
consumed, carried off, or destroyed.   But Athens could support that
loss; and the Athenian fleets had meanwhile, with less expence and
inconvenience, and probably with more profit, been dealing destruction
and gathering spoil in various parts of Peloponnesus and its confederate
states.   At the same time negotiations had been concluded which promised great access of strength to Athens for the campains to insue;
while the Peloponnesians, who had proposed to extend their alliances,
had brought nothing of the kind to effect.

4

In

In the second year the Peloponnesian army was again assembled in spring; and toward the beginning of summer, still under the command of Archidamus, again entered and ravaged Attica.   But a natural calamity, far more terrible than the swords of their enemies, now attacked the Athenians; a pestilential fever, in many points nearly resembling that scourge which, under the name of the plague, has been, in modern times, continually desolating the fine climates of the east; yet, according to the accurate Thucydides, differing in some essential circumstances.   It was then new to the Greeks.   Like the modern plague, it was supposed to have originated in Ethiopia; whence, passing into Egypt, it was quickly communicated over the greater part of the Persian empire.   Among the Greeks it was first observed in some towns of the Asian coast, and of the neighboring ilands, particularly Lemnos.   Its first appearance among the Athenians was in Peiræus; and they were so little aware how it came, or what it was, that a fancy arose, and gained some credit among them, that the wells had been poisoned by the Peloponnesians.   Quickly it made its way into the upper town, as Athens was often called, and then the mortality increased rapidly.   What was the cause of this malady, says Thucydides, I will leave to others to investigate; but I will describe its effects, which I can undertake to do exactly; having both experienced them in my own person, and seen numbers of others under the same affliction.

The year, it is universally acknowleged, was remarkably healthy, till Thucyd. l. 2. the pestilence appeared; and then every existing sickness seemed to c. 49. change into that one, or lost its symptoms in the violence of the supervening disorder.   Persons, apparently in perfect health, were suddenly seized, first with extreme heat in the head, attended with particular redness and inflammation of the eyes; then quickly the tongue and throat assumed a bloody appearance, the breath became fetid, frequent sneezing followed, with hoarseness of the voice; and before long the breast labored, and a violent cough came on.   The stomach was then affected; evacuations in all ways followed, attended with excessive colicky pains, and often with violent hiccoughs and spasms.   The flesh meanwhile, not externally hot to the touch, appeared reddish and livid, and broke out in pustules and ulcers.   But the internal fever was such

L 2   that

that the patient could scarcely bear the lightest covering ; and what
the affection of the moment gave to imagine as the most agreeable
relief, was to plunge into cold water.   Many of the poorer sort, ill
attended, ran to the wells, and there indulged, to extreme, the immediate calls of immoderate thirst.   Through the whole of the disorder
to sleep was impossible ; yet considering the violence of the symptoms,
the sufferers were less weakened than might have been expected.   The
fever was mostly spent by the seventh, or, at farthest, by the ninth day ;
and if the patient resisted so long, he was generally left not without
some strength to combat what was to follow.   But the ulceration of
the bowels, which then took place, and the flux, its consequence,
destroyed numbers.   For the disease, beginning with the head, pervaded the whole body, and finally fixed upon the extremities : so that
some, who had supported all the vehemence of its attack upon the
vital parts, survived at last, not without the loss of their hands, their
feet, their privy members, or their eyes.   Some were totally deprived of
memory ; on their recovery not knowing their nearest friends, nor even
Thucyd. l. 2. themselves.   The extreme and singular virulence of the disorder
c. 50. appeared also remarkably in the refusal of animals of prey to touch
the corpses, which lay in numbers unburied, and in the death which
insued to the more ravenous few which fed on them.   Of birds of
prey indeed there was a very remarkable scarcity, almost a dereliction of the country, so that the effect was principally observed
in dogs.

c. 51.   For this terrible disease, the skill of physicians was found utterly
vain, and all attempted remedies were either useless or totally uncertain ; what seemed to relieve some patients appearing even injurious to
others.   Nor did any strength of constitution avail ; but the robust
and the infirm were nearly equally affected.   Among the first symptoms,
and the most grievous, an extreme dejection of spirits was almost universal ; the patient lost the ability even to struggle for life ; and this
despondency was rendered the more fatal by the infectious nature of
the disorder, which either deterred assistance, or quickly involved the
attendants upon the sick in the same evil and the same inability with
those whom they served, or to whom their charity was afforded.

Many

Many therefore died wholly unattended: while others received little advantage from every assistance that could be given.   One only comfortable circumstance appeared to alleviate this dreadful calamity: different from the modern plague, the disease was among those which, through some inscrutable management of Providence, the human frame is incapable of receiving more than once; or, at least, if not perfectly secured, by once suffering, against all future injury from the virulence of the infectious matter, yet incapable of receiving twice the full force of the disorder.   Of those who had recovered from the Athenian pestilence, none were again so infected, by any communication with the diseased, as to appear in any danger of their lives.   Thus hope first shone upon the sick, upon those yet in health, and upon those who had borne the disease; thus alarm first ceased to be universal, and thus the Athenian people seemed at length warranted against that utter extinction which the effects of the disorder had appeared to threaten.

The mortality was however tremendous; and the misery was greatly inhanced by the increase of multitude in the city, which the war had occasioned.   The want of sewers, a convenience unknown in Grecian towns, and of which the Romans appear to have given the first example, would also be severely felt upon this occasion [4].   It was the hot season; and not only every house was fully occupied, but very many families of the poorer people were crouded together in stifling huts, where they died in heaps.   To bury all regularly was impossible: corpses were rolled out into the streets, and there left; and numbers were to be found dead and dying about every fountain, whither intolerable thirst impelled them to seek relief.   What would before have been esteemed a portentous pollution, became now familiar; the temples of the gods, occupied as the habitations of men, were filled with dead bodies. Funeral rites were not less profaned, and a singular kind of robbery

Marginal notes: Thucyd. l. 2. c. 52.   Strab. l. 5. p. 235.

[4] The necessity of a drain for the marshy soil, as well as of a vent for the filth which accumulated, in the hollow between the Palatine hill and the Capitoline, seems to have given occasion to that wonderful structure the cloaca maxima at Rome, perhaps the first and the greatest of its kind.   Sewers are seen among the ruins of Carthage, or were so when Shaw visited the site of that city, in the beginning of the past century; but whether Carthaginian works or Roman does not appear.   Shaw's Travels, p. 151. ed. fol. 1738.

became

became common.   When those who had means of burning the bodies
of their deceased friends, according to the established practice, had
formed their funeral pile, others would put on their dead, and immediately set fire to it.   With less scruple, of course, where a pile was
found burning, many, without ceremony, would throw on it a corpse,
and go their way.

   The moral effects of this extraordinary visitation, reported by that
judicious eye-witness to whom we owe this whole detail, deserve our
notice.   Wherever the doctrine of retribution in a life to come, for
good and evil deeds in this world, has taken any hold on the minds of
men, a general calamity strongly tends to check the passions, to inspire
serious thought, to direct attention toward that future existence, and
to make both hope and fear converge to the great Author of nature, the
all-powerful, all-wise, and all-just God, who can recompense the sufferings of the good with endless blessings, and convert to lasting misery
any short-lived joys that can arise from the perpetration of evil.   But
in Athens, where the deity was looked to very generally and very
anxiously for the dispensation of temporal good and evil only, it was
otherwise[5].   The fear of the divine power, says Thucydides, ceased;
for it was observed, that to worship or not to worship the gods, to obey
or not to obey those laws of morality which have always been held
most sacred among men, availed nothing.   All died alike; or, if there
was a difference, the virtuous, the charitable, the generous, exposing
themselves beyond others, were the first and the surest to suffer.   An
inordinate, and before unknown, licentiousness of manners followed.
Let us injoy ourselves, let us, if possible, drown thought in pleasure
today, for tomorrow we die, was the prevailing maxim.   No crime,
therefore, that could give the means of any injoyment was scrupled;
for such were the ravages of the disease, that for perpetrator, accuser,
and judges, all to survive, so that an offender could be convicted in
regular course of law, was supposed against all chance.   The final
consummation already impending over equally the criminal and the

   [5] Anaxagoras, the preceptor of Pericles,   allowed, which was afterward propagated
seems to have been the first who taught   by Socrates and his disciples, and he was
that better religion, if the term may be   persecuted for it as an atheist.

                                                        innocent,

innocent, by the decree of fate or of the gods, any punishment that human laws could decree, was little regarded. How most to injoy life while life remained, became the only consideration; and this relaxation, almost to a dissolution of all moral principle, is lamented by Thucydides as a lasting effect of the pestilence of Athens.

The Peloponnesian army had already begun the ravage of Attica when the pestilence was first publicly observed. They wasted all the vale of Athens, and then proceeded through the seaside country, more fruitful and better cultivated than the inland hills, toward the silver-mines of mount Laureium. The firm mind of Pericles meanwhile was not to be depressed by all the calamities which surrounded him, nor by all the terrors which threatened, from the war, from the pestilence, and, above all, from the irritation and despair of the despotic people whose minister he was. Steddily persevering in his former policy, of avoiding any decisive action with the landforce of the enemy, he prosecuted offensive operations by sea, as if Athens was under no affliction; thinking, probably, in some degree to divert the public mind from brooding over domestic misfortune, and to suspend any rising acrimony against himself. He took the command of the armament destined against Peloponnesus, consisting of a fleet of a hundred Athenian and fifty Chian and Lesbian triremes, with an army of four thousand foot and three hundred horse. It appears from Thucydides, that this was the first instance of cavalry being sent by any Grecian state on an expedition by sea; tho the practice was not new to the Asiatics, since the Persians had, sixty years before, sent a large force of horse across the Ægean, under Datis and Artaphernes. Vessels were ordinarily built, or, at least, fitted, for the purpose, with the name of hippagogi, horse-transports. For the present occasion some old triremes were converted under the direction of Pericles. The first descent was made on the Epidaurian territory, the greater part of which was ravaged. The operations of waste and plunder were then continued along the coast, through the Trœzenian, Halian, and Hermionian lands. The troops being then reïmbarked, the fleet passed the Argian coast, and a second descent was made in Laconia, near the town of Prasiæ, which was taken. After ravage had been extended through the neighboring country,

Thucyd. l. 2. c. 47, 54.

c. 56

country, as far as circumstances permitted, the whole armament
returned to Peiræus and Athens. They found the country then clear
of an enemy. The Peloponnesians, alarmed by the accounts given by
deserters, probably slaves, of the rapid progress of the pestilence, and
of its fatal effects in Athens, and seeing themselves the frequent
blazing of funeral piles, had hastened their retreat homeward, about
the fortieth day from their entering Attica.

Thucyd. l. 2.
c. 58.

The Athenian armament soon sailed again under Agnon son of
Nicias, and Cleopompus son of Cleinias, two of the nine collegues of
Pericles in the supreme military command. The purpose was to press
the siege of Potidæa, which remained still blockaded by Phormion.
This was apparently an ill-judged, and certainly an unfortunate
measure. The fresh troops, carrying with them the pestilential disorder from Athens, not only fell down themselves in great numbers,
but communicated the infection to Phormion's army, which had before
been healthy. After losing, within forty days, no fewer than fifteen

Ibid. et
l. 3. c. 17.

hundred of his four thousand foot, Agnon sailed with the remainder to
Attica. Phormion, with about three thousand, continued the blockade
of Potidæa.

l. 2. c. 59.

Accumulated evils, public and private, at length irritated beyond
sufferance the minds of the Athenian people. Popular discontent will
find an object on which to vent itself, and that object now was Pericles.
Such was the depression of the public spirit that ambassadors were sent
to Lacedæmon, to try the temper of the Peloponnesians, and endevor
to negotiate a peace; but as the Athenians drooped, the Lacedæmonians and their allies became arrogant, and the negotiation failed. The
shame of disappointment, and increased apprehension from the failure,
added to former feelings, raised such a ferment, that Pericles found it
necessary to take active measures for calming it. In his capacity of
general of the commonwealth, or first of the board of war, if we may
so express it, he had a right to summon the general assembly, whenever
he thought proper. The people met, and he mounted the speaker's
stand. He began his oration with urging a maxim applicable to all
states, but the force of which would be more particularly sensible in

l. 2. c. 60.

the little Grecian republics, 'That every individual has a deeper
                                                        ' interest

'· interest in the public than in his privatė prosperity ; for the decay of
' private affluence must ever be involved with the country's ruin : but
' while the country flourishes, opportunity will be open for the recovery
' of private fortune.' He proceeded then to assert, with manly confidence, his own claim to the merit of integrity above suspicion, and to
reproach the people with that want of firmness, which disposed them
to impute, as a crime to him, a public misfortune, impossible equally to
be prevented and to be foreseen ; and which could reasonably be ascribed
only to the inscrutable will of the deïty. 'So far then,' he added,
' from having just cause for that despondency which infected them,
' they were still in full possession of what, well used, would give them
' certain superiority over all their enemies.   No potentate upon earth
' possessed such a navy as theirs, nor could any one prescribe bounds to
' the empire which they might acquire by it.   Such an opinion he never
'·had declared before ; and, but for the universal depression of the
' public mind, he would not now have uttered a truth too flattering to
' them, and too alarming to all the world besides.   What then were
'·their houses and fields, the momentary loss of which they deplored, in
' comparison with such a possession ? To others indeed necessaries ;
' but to them meerly incidental decorations of high fortune ; or, at
'·most, luxuries and superfluous conveniencies, with which they could
' well, for a time, dispense.   Their fleet, on the contrary, was truly
' essential ; not only to their command, but to their independency ;
' not only to their prosperity, but to their safety against the revenge
' which that invidious empire, that tyranny which they had long
' extensively held, could not fail to excite[6].   What we suffer from the
' gods,' continued Pericles, ' we should bear with patience ; what from
' our enemies, with manly firmness ; and such were the maxims of our
' forefathers.   From unshaken fortitude in misfortune hath arisen the
' present power of this commonwealth, together with that glory, which,
' if our empire, according to the lot of all earthly things, decay, shall
' still survive to all posterity.   Let no more begging embassies then be
' sent to Lacedæmon, nor let it any way appear that you are sinking

[6] Ὡς Τυραννίδα γὰρ ἔχετε αὐτὴν (τὴν ἀρχὴν).—Thucyd. l. 2. c. 63.

' under your misfortunes; but be assured that the steddiest resistance
' will bring our troubles to their best conclusion.'

Thucyd. l. 2.
c. 65.
     This speech had not all the effect which Pericles hoped from it. So
far he prevailed, that it was determined no more to take any measure
bearing the appearance of suing for peace from Sparta. But the acrimony excited among the people, by their private sufferings, was not to
be immediately appeased: many of the poor were reduced to total want,
while the rich bore with extreme uneasiness the loss of revenue from
their estates in Attica, the destruction of their country-houses, their
favorite residences, and the waste of all the expence bestowed on them.
But what now, says Thucydides, principally affected all, was, that
instead of peace they had war; not, as often formerly, war far from
home, but all the present evils of war at their doors, and apprehension
of consequences which could not be considered without shuddering.
The ferment did not subside till Pericles was deposed from his military
command, and mulcted in a heavy fine[7].

At the same time with this public disgrace, Pericles was suffering
under the severest domestic misfortunes. Several of his children, some
in this year, some in the former, had died of the pestilence; which,
with the return of warm weather, had broken out again in Athens.
The same cruel disorder had deprived him of others of his nearest relations, together with some of those invaluable friends in whose assistance
he could best confide for the administration of public affairs. During
these successive and complicated scenes of private woe, rendered more
distracting by the public calamity, and the pressure of that popular
discontent which arose from it, the firmness of his mind was the admiration of all around him. That philosophy, then new in Greece, which
had been the favorite study of his leisure, inculcated rather the pride
of disdaining to complain, and of being above the feelings of humanity,
than a just resignation to the will of a supreme being, infinitely wise

[7] Thucydides, in mentioning the fine, does not name the sum. According to Diodorus, if we may trust our copies, it was no less than eighty talents, about nineteen thousand pounds sterling. (Diod. l. 12. c. 45.) But Plutarch says, that among various accounts extant in his time, none made it exceed fifty talents, about twelve thousand five hundred pounds; whereas some asserted it to have been no more than fifteen, less than four thousand pounds ster-ling.

                                         and

and good; tho such a being it acknowleged for the author and pre-
server of nature.　No complaint was heard from the disciple of Anaxagoras, no change of countenance or manner was perceptible in him, till
he lost his favorite son Paralus.　Even then he would not seem to feel
the anguish which oppressed him.　But when, according to custom, in
the funeral ceremony, he approached the bier to put the chaplet on the
head of the deceased youth, the sight overcame him, and he burst into
a flood of tears[8].　In this accumulation of distress, to retire from public
business was, in the moment, a relief.

Plut. vit. Pericl.

But the people had no sooner vented their anger than they repented
of what they had done: the keen sensation of distress in their private
affairs, says the cotemporary historian, abated, while, upon reflection,
they became aware that no other man was qualified, like Pericles, for
the supreme direction of public business.　First, or equal to any, in
birth, clearly superior in abilities, eminent in tried integrity, in all
together he had not a second.　None of the other orators therefore,
with all the support of faction they were able to muster, could satisfy
the multitude.　With loud and anxious voices Pericles was called for
to mount the bema, as the stand whence orations delivered to the people
was called, and declare his opinion of public affairs, what was the
situation of things, and what measures, in his judgement, ought to be
taken.　He did not refuse to obey the honorable summons; and quickly
a strong reflux of popular favor restored him to the situation of commander-in-chief and prime minister, if we may use the term, the nearest
which modern language affords, but inadequate to express the plenitude
of that power, which absolute possession of the favor of the people gave
him over the Athenian empire[9].

While Athens, weakened by the pestilence, and laboring with internal
discord and the depression of public spirit, was in some degree disabled
for exertion, the Peloponnesians, for the first time, ventured upon a
naval expedition.　A hundred triremes, with a thousand heavy-armed

Thucyd. l. 2. c. 66.

[8] According to Plutarch, Pericles lost all his legitimate sons by the pestilence, one of his own name, who survived him, being ille-gitimate.　But Xenophon mentions Pericles son of Pericles, without noticing any irre-gularity of his birth; (Xen. Mem. Socr. l. 3. c. 5.) and it appears that he long survived his father.　Plato also speaks of a son or sons of Pericles, and as surviving him, and not as illegitimate.

[9] Στρατηγὸν εἵλοντο καὶ πάντα τὰ πράγματα ἐπέτρεψαν.—Thucyd. l. 2. c. 65.

M 2　　　　　　　　　　　　　　　　Lacedæmonians,

Lacedæmonians, sailed to Zacynthus; an Achaian colony, but of the Athenian confederacy. The troops debarked, and ravaged great part of the open country; but the fortified places all either deterred or resisted their efforts : the people could neither by threats nor promises be induced to treat, and the armament returned home.

Thucyd. l. 2. c. 67.
Herod. l. 7. c. 137.

Toward the end of the summer a measure was taken in another line, from which more important advantages were expected. An embassy was appointed to go to the Persian court, with a view to negotiate an alliance, and particularly, to obtain pecuniary assistance. It consisted of three Lacedæmonians, Aneristus, Nicolaüs and Pratodemus, with the Corinthian Aristeus, Timagoras of Tegea, and Polis, an Argian, who went unauthorized by his own commonwealth; a circumstance which indicates that he was of the party in opposition to the ruling party there. But means to make their journey to Susa were not obvious; for the Athenians commanded all the western coast of Asia minor with the Hellespont; and the hazards that might attend the unusual passage by the way of Phœnicia, were many, to their knowlege, and probably many which they could not know. It was therefore determined to go first to the court of Sitalces, king of Thrace; whose alliance with Athens did not bind him to be the enemy of Lacedæmon. On the contrary, hopes were entertained of detaching him from the Athenian interest; and his protection was depended upon for the journey through his dominion to the satrapy of Pharnaces, on the Asiatic side of the Hellespont, whence the progress to Susa, tho long, would be secure. The ambassadors accordingly fonnd a courteous reception from the Thracian prince, tho two Athenian ministers, Leärchus and Ameiniades, were with him. Their endevors however to withdraw him from the Athenian alliance not succeeding, they proceeded on their journey. The Athenian ministers were equally unable to ingage Sitalces in all their views; but they found the zeal of an Athenian citizen in Sadocus his eldest son. That prince took upon himself to send a party, under the orders of Leärchus and Ameiniades, in pursuit of the Peloponnesian ministers; who were seized before they could imbark to cross the Hellespont, put aboard a ship, and conveyed to Athens, where a decree of the people, without a trial, consigned them all to the executioner. Thucydides acknowleges the most illiberal policy in his fellowcountry-

11   men

men as, in part at least, instigating this measure: they dreaded the enterprizing abilities of the Corinthian Aristeus, which had been conspicuous in operations against them in Chalcidicë and Macedonia. The law of retaliation was however alledged in justification of it; and such was the illiberal and cruel spirit of war among the antients, that the law of retaliation might generally be pleaded to justify almost any atrocity: from the beginning of the war, the Lacedæmonians, wherever they met with merchant-ships of the Athenians or their allies, or even of the neutral Greeks, had usually put the crews to death.   Thucyd. l. 2. c. 67.

Such were the transactions of the summer.   In the beginning of winter circumstances arose, in the north-western parts of Greece, to call the attention of the Athenian administration; in consequence of which Phormion, recalled from his command in Chalcidicë, was sent, with a squadron of twenty ships, to block the Corinthian gulph. Meanwhile, tho the Peloponnesians had no fleet at sea, yet their priva-teers[10], harbouring on the coasts of Caria and Lycia, had been annoy-ing the Athenian trade with Asia minor, and with the eastern parts of the Mediterranean.   A squadron of six triremes was thought sufficient both to prevent such depredations, and to collect the tributes due from the dependent states in those parts.   But Melisander, who commanded, being induced to undertake an expedition up the country of Lycia, with the troops of his little squadron and some auxiliaries which he collected, was overpowered in an action in which he lost his life.   c. 68, 69.

The winter was not far advanced when the Potidæans, so pressed by famine that they had begun to eat oneanother, and hopeless of succour, desired to capitulate.   Xenophon son of Euripides, who with two other generals now commanded the besieging army, taking into consideration what their troops must suffer in winter operations, and what expence the commonwealth had already incurred by the siege, which was not less than two thousand talents, about five hundred thousand pounds sterling was induced to treat.   The garrison and people were allowed to quit the place; the men each with one garment, the women with two; and both with a small specified sum of money, which might inable them to travel to such retreats as they could find in Chalcidicë,   c. 70.

[10] Τὸ Λησικὸν τῶν Πελοποννησίων.—Thucyd. l. 2. c. 69.

or

or elsewhere in the neighboring country.   Xenophon and his collegues did not escape censure from their soverein the Athenian people, for granting, without first consulting them, terms, even such terms to those who were considered as meriting vengeance, and who, it was found after the surrender, were incapable of longer resistance.   Thus however the Athenians, unable, in their full strength, to defend their own country, yet nevertheless persevering amid affliction and resisting weakness, gained that distant object of contention which had given immediate rise to the war.

Pericles lived probably to know the success of the Athenian arms against Potidæa, and it was not long after that he fell a victim to that calamity, the endemial disorder, which had already carried off so many of his nearest relations, and most valued friends.   He survived however the violence of the fever, and died, in full possession of his senses, of a lingering ilness which it superinduced.

Plut. vit. Pericl.

No man seems to have been held in such estimation, by most of the ablest writers of Greece and Rome, for universal superiority of talents, as Pericles.   The accounts remaining of his actions hardly support his renown; which was yet perhaps more fairly earned than that of many, the merit of whose atchievements has been in a great degree due to others acting under them, whose very names have perished.   The philosophy of Pericles taught him not to be vainglorious, but to rest his fame upon essentially great and good, rather than upon brilliant actions. It is observed by Plutarch that, often as he commanded the Athenian forces, he never was defeated; yet, tho he won many trophies, he never gained a splendid victory.   A battle, according to a great modern authority, is the resource of ignorant generals: when they know not what to do, they fight a battle.   It was almost universally the resource of the age of Pericles: little conception was entertained of military operations, beyond ravage and a battle.   His genius led him to a superior system, which the wealth of his country inabled him to carry into practice.   His favorite maxim was to spare the lives of his soldiers; and scarcely any general ever gained so many important advantages with so little bloodshed.   It is said to have been his consolation and his boast, in his dying hours, that he never was the cause that a fellow-citizen

Saxe's Memoirs.

citizen wore mourning: a glorious and perhaps a singular subject of exultation for a head of a party in Greece; where, in the struggles of faction, secret assassinations, numerous public executions, and bloody contests in arms, were so ordinary.   Pericles might almost equally have made it his boast as general of the commonwealth: for when his soldiers fell, they fell victims to the necessity of their country's service, and not to the incapacity, rashness, or vanity of the commander.   Had he been less a patriot, less a philosopher, less humane, his atchievements might have been more brilliant, but he would not equally have earned, from the mouth of Socrates, and the report of Plato, the praise of super-eminence in whatever was wise, great, and becoming [11].

This splendid character however perhaps may seem to receive some tarnish from the political conduct of Pericles; the concurrence, at last, which is imputed to him in depraving the Athenian constitution, to favor that popular power by which he ruled, and the revival and confirmation of that pernicious hostility between the democratical and aristocratical interests, first in Athens, and then by the Peloponnesian war, throughout the nation   But it is remarkable that Thucydides and Xenophon, both suffering banishment, one for twenty years, the other for life, from that democratical power with which both express themselves abundantly dissatisfied, nevertheless always speak with the highest respect of Pericles. The testimony of Isocrates will also deserve consideration.   Complaining of the depraved state of the Athenian constitution in his own time, that patriotic statesman says, ' Pericles ' found the constitution less perfect than it had been, but still tolerably ' good; yet he did not use his extraordinary power for his own profit, ' but leaving his private fortune less than he had received it from his ' father, he carried into the treasury eight thousand talents (near ' two millions sterling) over and above the proceeds of the sacred ' revenue.' This concurrence of three such men, in successive ages (of whom, Thucydides, probably had personal acquaintance) all

Isocr. de Pace. p. 254.

[11] Περικλία, ὅτω μεγαλοπρεπῶς σοφὸν ἄνδρα, is a phrase which Plato puts into the mouth of Socrates, immediately after the mention of Themistocles and Aristeides. Plat. Menon. p. 94. t. 2.   The force and elegance of the Greek, expressing in one compound adverb the great and the becoming, cannot be given perhaps in any other language.

friendly

friendly to the aristocratical interest, and all anxious for concord with Lacedæmon, strongly indicates that what may appear exceptionable in his conduct was, in their opinion, the result not of choice but of neces- sity; a necessity produced by the violence of a party in opposition to him at home, together with the violence of a party in Peloponnesus, adverse to the politics of his friend the king of Lacedæmon, Archi- damus. By no other conduct probably the independency of Athens could have been preserved; and however the power of Athens, unless it might be moderated and modelled by an extraordinary union of political wisdom and moral rectitude in the leaders, was threatening to the liberty of every other Grecian state, yet the independency of Athens, as the event showed, was indispensable for the liberty of Greece. On such a view of things those three great writers may seem to have formed their judgement of the political conduct of Pericles, and to have reckoned that on his wisdom, his probity and his influence, had his life been lengthened, would have rested the best chance for an advantageous settlement of the singularly troubled state of the Greek nation.

CHAPTER XV.

Of the PELOPONNESIAN WAR, from the Death of PERICLES, in the third Year, to the Application for PEACE from LACE-DÆMON in the seventh.

SECTION I.

Siege of Platæa by the Peloponnesians.

IN the third spring of the war, the Peloponnesians changed their plan of offence. By the invasion and ravage of Attica for two following summers, tho much injury had been done to the Athenians, little advantage had accrued to themselves: the booty was far from paying the expence of the expedition; the enemy, it was found, could not be provoked to risk a battle, and the great purpose of the war was little forwarded. The Peloponnesians were yet very unequal to attempt naval operations of any consequence. Of the continental dependencies of Athens none was so open to their attacks, none so completely excluded from naval protection, none so likely by its danger to superinduce that war of the field which they wished, as Platæa. Against that town therefore it was determined to direct the principal effort; and success was more reasonably expected, as, at Athens, public councils were no longer directed, and popular passion no longer restrained, by the wisdom and the influence of Pericles.

Under the command still of Archidamus, the confederate army accordingly entered the Platæid, and ravage was immediately begun. The Platæans sent ministers to deprecate hostilities; urging the antient merit of their commonwealth in the Persian wars, and the privileges solemnly granted to it, when, after the glorious battle in their territory, Pausanias sacrificed to Jupiter the deliverer, in the agora of their city. Archidamus was not disposed to harsh measures, and he offered them neutrality.

B. C. 429.
Ol. 87 ¾.
P. W. 3.
Thucyd. l. 2.
c. 71.

c. 72.

neutrality.   The Platæans professed that, if they could chuse for themselves, they should willingly accept his offer; but without the consent
of the Athenians, in whose power their wives and children were, they
could decide nothing.   Besides, should they lose the protection of
Athens, they could never be secure against the superior power of the
Thebans, their most bitter enemies, longer than while a Peloponnesian army remained in the neighborhood.   To obviate the latter
objection, Archidamus made this remarkable proposal: ' If such are
' your fears, deliver your city, your lands, and all your immoveable
' property in trust to the Lacedæmonians.   Show us the boundaries of
' your territory, number your fruit-trees, and take an exact account of
' whatever else admits numeration or description.   Go then yourselves
' wherever you can find the most convenient residence while the war
' shall last; and we will provide that your lands shall be duly culti-
' vated; we will ingage that subsistence shall be regularly remitted to
' you; and, when the war is over, everything shall be restored.'   The
Platæan deputies returned with this answer, and proposing it to the
assembled people, or rather garrison, it was agreed to accept the conditions, provided the consent of the Athenian government could be
obtained.   Leave was readily granted by the Spartan prince to send to
Athens, and deputies were dispatched; but they brought back a requisition that the Platæans should abide by the terms of their confederacy
with Athens, accompanied with assurance of every assistance.   The
c. 74.   Platæans in consequence resolved to remain firm to the Athenian
alliance; and, without sending to the Peloponnesian camp, they
declared, from their ramparts, 'That it was impossible for them to
' comply with the demands of the Lacedæmonians.'   Archidamus then
made this solemn address to the deïties of the country: ' Ye gods and
' heroes, who preside over Platæa, be witnesses, that not till the Pla-
' tæans have renounced the sworn terms of the general confederacy of
' the Greeks, we act hostilely against this land, in which our fathers,
' after due invocation to you, vanquished the Persians, you rendering
' it propitious to their arms.   We have made liberal offers, which have
' been rejected.   Grant therefore that they may receive that punish-
' ment

' ment which breach of faith deserves, and that we may obtain the
' success to which a righteous cause intitles.'

Then immediately was begun that siege, the first of which any con-   Thucyd. l. 2.
nected detail remains in the annals of mankind. The town was small,   c. 75.
as may be judged from the very small force which sufficed for an effectual garrison; only four hundred Platæans, with eighty Athenians.   c. 78.
There were besides in the place a hundred and ten women to prepare
provisions, and no other person free or slave. The besieging army,
composed of the flower of the Peloponnesian youth, was numerous.
The first operation was to surround the town with a palisade, which   c. 75.
might prevent any ready egress; the neighboring forest of Cithæron
supplying materials. Then, in a chosen spot, ground was broken,
according to the modern phrase, for making approaches. The business
was to fill the town-ditch, and against the wall to form a mound, on
which a force sufficient for assault might ascend. For this operation
also the woods of Cithæron were highly serviceable. Either extremity
of the mound was made firm with interwoven piles, and the interval
was filled with wood, stones, earth, anything that came readiest to hand.
Seventy days were employed unintermittingly on this work; reliefs
being established through the army, and Lacedæmonian officers always
superintending; those appointed to the allies bearing the peculiar title
of Xenage.

Such was at that time the inartificial process of a siege. Thucydides
appears to have been well aware that it did no credit to the science of
his age. The principal dependence of the besieging army, he says, was
on the disproportionate superiority of its numbers. To oppose this
mode of attack, the first measure of the besieged was to raise, on that
part of their wall against which the mound was forming, a strong
wooden frame, covered in front with leather and hides; and, within this,
to build a rampart, with bricks from the neighboring houses. The
wooden frame bound the whole, and kept it firm to a considerable
height: the covering of hides protected both work and workmen
against weapons discharged against them, especially fiery arrows. But
the mound still rising as the superstructure on the wall rose, and this
superstructure becoming unavoidably weaker with increasing height,

N 2   while

while the mound was liable to no counterbalancing defect, it was necessary for the besieged to devise other opposition. Accordingly they
broke through the bottom of their wall, where the mound bore against
it, and brought in the earth.   The Peloponnesians, soon aware of this,
instead of loose earth, repaired their mound with clay or mud inclosed
in baskets. This requiring more labor to remove, the besieged under-
mined the mound ; and thus, for a long time unperceived, prevented it
from gaining height.   Still however, fearing that the efforts of their
scanty numbers would be overborne by the multitude of hands which
the besiegers could employ, they had recourse to another device.
Within their town-wall they built, in a semilunar form, a second wall,
connected with the first at the extremities.   These extended, on either
side, beyond the mound ; so that, should the enemy possess themselves
of the outer wall, their work would be to be renewed in a far less favorable situation.

Machines for battering walls were already known among the Greeks.
According to the historian Ephorus, as Plutarch informs us, tho he
says it was disputed by other writers, they were first used by Pericles at
the siege of Samos, under the direction of a lame engineer named
Artemon ; who being commonly carried among his works in a litter [1],
had thence the surname of Periphoretus. Battering-rams were certainly
of much earlier date in the east ; and indeed Thucydides would scarcely
have left unmentioned the first introduction of so remarkable a military
engine among the Greeks, had it happened within his own memory.
The Peloponnesians were not without it at the siege of Platæa, but they
seem to have been unskilful in its use ; and probably the machine itself
was far less adapted to its purpose than, through various improvements,
it afterward became. A ram, advanced upon the Peloponnesian mound,
battered the superstructure on the Platæan rampart, and shook it
violently ; to the great alarm of the garrison, but with little farther
effect. Other machines of the same kind were employed against
different parts of the wall itself, but to yet less purpose. The Platæans,
letting down ropes from the rampart, dragged some out of their direction ; others they broke by dropping on them weighty beams suspended

[1] Φορείῳ.

with

with chains. No means however were neglected by the besiegers that either approved practice suggested, or their ingenuity could devise, to promote their purpose : yet, after much of the summer consumed, they found every effort of their numerous forces so completely baffled by the vigilance, activity, and resolution of the little garrison, that they began to despair of succeeding by assault. Before however they would recur to the tedious method of blockade, they determined to try one more experiment, for which their numbers, and the neighboring woods of Cithæron, gave them more than ordinary facility. Preparing a very great quantity of faggots, they filled with them the town-ditch in the parts adjoining to their mound, and disposed piles in other parts around the place, wherever ground or any other circumstance gave most advantage. On the faggots they put sulphur and pitch, and then set all on-fire. The conflagrationwas such as was never before known, says Thucydides, to have been prepared and made by the hands of men, tho, in mountain-forests, the friction of dry wood, by the agitation of the wind, may sometimes have produced greater. Had the wind favored, it must have had all the effect that the besiegers desired : great part of the town actually became unapproachable. But fortunately for the garrison, a heavy rain, brought on by a thunder-storm without wind, extinguished the fire, and relieved them from an attack far more formidable than any they had before experienced.

This attempt failing, the Peloponnesians determined immediately to reduce the siege to a blockade; which, tho slow and consequently expensive, would in the end be sure. To the palisade, which already surrounded the town, a contravallation was added ; with a double ditch, one without, and one within. A sufficient body of troops being then appointed to the guard of these works, the Bœotians undertaking one half, the other was allotted to detachments drafted from the troops of every state of the confederacy, and, a little after the middle of September, the rest of the army was dismissed for the winter.

Thucyd. l. 2. c. 78. 6 July.

Sept. 19.

SECTION II.

Operations of the Athenians on the Northern Coast of the Ægean.
Affairs of the Western Parts of Greece : Assistance sent by Pelo-
ponnesus to the Ambraciots against the Amphilochian Argians and
Acarnanians: Battle near Stratus: Sea-fight between the Pelopon-
nesian Fleet under the Corinthian Machon, and the Athenian Fleet
under Phormion: Sea-fight between the Peloponnesian Fleet under
the Spartan Cnemus, and the Athenian Fleet under Phormion.
Attempt to surprize Peiræus. Success of Phormion in Acarnania.
Invasion of Macedonia by Sitalces king of Thrace.

B. C. 429. WHILE the Peloponnesians were thus bending their whole strength,
Ol. 87. 4. and hitherto so vainly, against the little town of Platæa, offensive ope-
P. W. 3.
Thucyd. l. 2. rations were not neglected by the Athenians.   Xenophon son of
c. 79. Euripides, who had commanded the Athenian forces at the taking of
Potidæa, was sent again into Chalcidicë, with a body of two thousand
heavy foot, and two hundred horse.   A little before harvest he entered
Bottiæa, and ravaged the country about Spartolus.   Often in the wars
of the Greeks among oneanother, the intrigues of faction did more
than arms.   Through such intrigue the Athenian general entertained
hope of acquiring Spartolus; but timely support, which the party in
opposition to the Athenian interest obtained from the neighboring city
of Olynthus, disappointed him.   A battle insuing, the superiority of
the enemy in cavalry prevailed against the superior discipline of the
Athenian heavy foot: Xenophon, with two general officers his collegues, and above four hundred of their heavy-armed, were killed ; and
the remainder, who found an immediate refuge in Potidæa, too weak to
prosecute offensive operations, returned to Athens.

Through this extensive war, upon which the Athenians fixed the
name of the Peloponnesian, we become in some degree acquainted with
c. 63. the history of some parts of Greece, which would otherwise have
remained totally unknown.   The Amphilochian Argos, a city on the
4   border

border of Acarnania against Epirus, was founded, according to Thucydides, by Amphilochus, son of that Amphiaraüs who is celebrated among the heroes of the war of Thebes.   Amphilochus himself fought at Troy.   On his return to the Peloponnesian Argos, his native city, little satisfied with the state of things under the usurpation of Ægistheus, he departed with such as chose to follow his fortune, and settled his colony at the bottom of that gulph antiently called the Amphilochian, but afterward the Ambracian.   To the town which he built there he gave the name of that from which he had migrated; and the same partiality fixed upon the river, near whose mouth it stood, the name of the Peloponnesian stream of Inachus.   The epithet Amphilochian was added to the town for the convenience of distinction.   Situate among barbarians, at the extremity of Greece, the city of Amphilochus florished; the inferiority, in arts and knowlege, of the neighboring clans, to whom the Amphilochian name was communicated, but who, according to Thucydides, were barbarian, being perhaps a principal cause of its prosperity.   Afterward, through various misfortunes, its strength was so reduced that it was scarcely able to support itself as an independent commonwealth; and to obviate other evils, its people recurred to a dangerous expedient for weak states, that of associating a number of families from the neighboring Corinthian colony of Ambracia.   Disputes arose between the two people, and in the end the Ambraciots expelled the Argians from their own city.   These applied to the neighboring people of Acarnania, and the Acarnanians to the Athenians; who, a little before the beginning of the Peloponnesian war, sent Phormion with thirty triremes to their assistance.   Through the abilities of that officer, and the superior discipline of the very small body of Athenians which he commanded, Argos was taken by assault. The city and territory were restored to the Argians, with whom some Acarnanians were associated; and according to the barbarous practice not unusual with the most polished of the Greeks, the Ambracian inhabitants and garrison were condemned to slavery.   Hence followed the alliance of both Acarnania and the Amphilochian Argos with Athens, which has been mentioned as subsisting when the Peloponnesian war began.

In

In the second summer of that war, while the pestilence was raging at Athens, the Ambraciots, incensed against the Argians by the treatment of their captive fellowcitizens, determined to attempt revenge. Associating the Chaonian and some other barbarous clans of their neighborhood, they overran the territory of Argos, but, after some vain efforts against the city, returned home. In the following year, that of the siege of Platæa, they proposed not only to take Argos, but to conquer all Acarnania. With this view they applied to Lacedæmon; promising that, if they might have such support, naval and military, as they desired, not only they would reduce their particular enemies the Acarnanians, but they would bring over the neighboring ilands of Zacynthus and Cephallenia to the Peloponnesian confederacy, and they hoped also to take Naupactus. Thus the Athenians would be deprived of what principally inabled them to carry expeditions around Peloponnesus, and keep a fleet in the western seas. The project was alluring: the Corinthians instantly and zealously ingaged in it; incited by their enmity to Athens, their connection with Ambracia, the desire of revenge against Corcyra, and the hope of recovering their power in that iland, to which any success in the proposed measures would be at least a step; and they induced the Lacedæmonians to concur.

Thucyd. l. 2. c. 80.

The Athenian administration, receiving intelligence of these motions and preparations, and judging Phormion, apparently on account of his experience of the western people and western seas, most proper for the command there, recalled him from Chalcidicë, and sent him, as we have seen, with twenty triremes to Naupactus. In the following summer, in pursuance of the measures concerted with the Peloponnesians, the naval force of the Leucadians, Anactorians, and Ambraciots, was assembled at Leucas; and the Spartan admiral Cnemus had the good fortune to join them from Cyllenë, with a small squadron and a thousand heavy-armed Peloponnesian infantry, undiscovered in his passage by the Athenians. The Corinthians and Sicyonians were preparing their naval force, but could not so readily escape out of their own gulph. Cnemus therefore, without waiting for them, determined to begin operations, by marching directly for Stratus, the largest town of Acarnania, in the hope that he might carry it by assault; by which he expected

so to break the force of the province that it would become an easy
conquest.

The Acarnanians, meanwhile, informed that beside the formidable Thucyd. l. 2. c. 81.
army already in their country, a fleet was expected, which might chuse
its points of attack upon their coast, resolved to remain within their
respective towns, and attempt the protection of their fields only so far as,
with their strength, and opportunities offering, might be prudent. The
Athenian admiral at Naupactus, to whom they sent a request for assistance, gave them to understand that he could spare no part of his scanty
force from attendance upon the Peloponnesian fleet, in the Corinthian
gulph, which was ready to sail. The allied army therefore marched
unopposed from Leucas, through the Argian territory, into Acarnania.
It was disposed in three columns ; the Peloponnesians and Ambraciots
forming the left, the Leucadians, Anactorians and some other Greeks the
right, and the barbarian Epirots the center. The Greeks kept their columns
regularly formed, and chose their camps carefully ; which, according
to their usual practice, in an enemy's country, they constantly fortified.
But the Epirots, and particularly the Chaonians, vain of their reputation
for superior prowess among the clans of that part of the continent,
disdained the trouble and delay of nice choice of ground ; and pressed
forward, in confidence that the town would yield to their first assault,
and the glory would be all their own. Intelligence of these circumstances being carried to the Stratians by their scouts, they planted an
ambush, into which the imprudent Epirots fell. The forces from the
town sallied ; the Epirots, partly through surprize, partly through the
vigor of the attack, were instantly put to flight, a great number were
killed, and the rest were pursued till they reached the Grecian camps.
The Stratians would neither make any attempt upon these, nor risk any
close ingagement against the superior discipline of the Peloponnesians;
but they gave unceasing annoyance from a distance with their slings ;
in the use of which the Acarnanians universally excelled.

Information of the important success obtained by the Stratians, was
rapidly forwarded through all the Acarnanian towns, accompanied with
exhortation to assemble the force of the country, and drive out a half-
conquered enemy. Cnemus meanwhile found his measures so broken

by the defeat of the Epirots, that in the insuing night he retreated to the river Anapus, ten miles from Stratus.   Thence he sent a herald to desire a truce for the burial of the slain; and, soon after, falling back to Œneiadæ, he dismissed the allies, and imbarked himself for Peloponnesus.   Acarnania thus was completely freed from so alarming an invasion.

Thucyd. l. 2.
c. 83.
During these transactions by land, the allied fleet, consisting of forty-séven trireme galleys, under the Corinthian admirals Machon, Isocrates, and Agatharchidas, sailed out of the gulph.   It was the purpose of Phormion, who, with only twenty, watched them from Chalcis and the river Eveñus, on the Ætolian coast, to let them pass the straits, and attack them in the more open sea.   The Corinthians, strong in men as well as in ships, but less confident in naval skill, hugged, according to the sea-phrase, the southern shore as far as Patræ; and thence, in the night, pushed across for the Acarnanian coast; their object being less to ingage the Athenians, than to join their allies in the prosecution of the preconcerted purposes of the campain.   The daring vigilance of Phormion surprized them in the middle of the passage.   Tho it was night, yet being perfectly clear and calm, they perceived his approach at some distance.   Immediately they formed their fleet in a circle, the largest they could, so as not to give opportunity for that evolution of piercing the line, called the diëcplus, in which the Athenians excelled, and which their enemies dreaded. The prows of course were on all sides outward; the transports[2], with a reserve of five of the swiftest triremes, were stationed in the center; and thus in posture of defence, as if to oppose an enemy who outnumbered them, forty-seven triremes remained to receive the attack of the twenty under Phormion, if, which they could not readily believe, he should be bold enough to attack them.

c. 84.
But the Athenian admiral, confident in his own abilities and experience, and in the practised skill of his people, and observing the order of the enemy to be very readily susceptible of confusion, bore immediately upon them with his line of battle formed a-head, and rowed around them; having first directed his captains to threaten as near as

[2] Τὰ λιπτὰ πλοῖα.

possible

possible so as to avoid ingaging, till they should have the signal from him. He well knew that when the breeze from the gulph sprung up, which seldom failed about daybreak, the enemy's circle could not long remain perfect; and his purpose was, by alarming, to hasten and in-, hance the confusion. It happened precisely as he foresaw: the first of the breeze drove the windward ships against the transports in the center: confusion immediately arose; clamor, with expostulation from ship to ship, insued; orders were no longer heard; signals remained unobserved; the attention of the crews was wholly ingaged in obviating the continually threatened shock of one ship against another, or of many against one; and the swell, that quickly arose, sufficed to prevent any effectual use of oars by rowers so little skilful. Phormion seized the critical moment for giving the signal of attack. In the first onset one of the Corinthian admirals was sunk; several other ships were quickly disabled; and such was the confusion that resistance was scarcely attempted, but the first effort of the Peloponnesians was to fly toward the friendly ports of Patræ and Dymë. The Athenians took twelve triremes, the greater part of whose crews they put to the sword. Having pursued as far as was judged convenient, they returned with their prizes to the Ætolian coast; according to the usual practice, which landlocked and stormy seas, the want of the compass, and the deficiency of accommodation in the antient ships of war, made necessary. On the headland of Rhium they raised a trophy, and dedicated to Neptune one of the captive triremes, after which ceremonies they returned to their station at Naupactus. Then the defeated Peloponnesians moved, from the places of their first refuge, to the Eleian port of Cyllenë, where Cnemus, with the forces from Acarnania, soon after joined them.

This action of Phormion, tho the forces employed on either side were too small for the consequences to be very important, yet for the boldness of the attempt, the ability displayed in the execution, and the completeness of the success, has been deservedly reckoned by Plutarch among the most brilliant atchievements of the war[1]. It appears to Thucyd. l. 2. have disturbed, not a little, the Peloponnesians, and particularly the c. 85.

[1] We find a compliment to Phormion, which seems to mark the popularity of his character, in the comedy of Aristophanes, called The Knights, v. 551.

O 2   Lacedæmonians.

Lacedæmonians. Those who directed the administration of their government, unversed in naval affairs, could not readily conceive a superiority of science among the Athenian commanders, and of skill among their seamen, that should give the advantage against more than double their numbers, without great misbehavior on the part of their own people; especially as in land-war the superiority of the Peloponnesians, to all the world besides, was held incontestable. The unwise practice of dividing military command, ordinary with most of the other Greeks, was little usual with the Lacedæmonians; but now, in some indignation that the Peloponnesian navy should, by a squadron of only twenty ships, be excluded from the western seas, which were esteemed more peculiarly their own, three Spartan officers, Timocrates, Brasidas, and Lycophron, were sent to be of council with Cnemus in his command. The ships damaged in the late action were diligently repaired; a reïnforcement was required from the maritime states of Peloponnesus; and a fleet of seventy-seven triremes was thus collected, which proceeded from Cyllenë to Panormus on the Achaian coast; where a land-army, in the antient manner of naval war generally capable of advantageous coöperation with a fleet, was also assembled.

Thucyd. l. 2. c. 86.

c. 85.

Phormion, informed of these preparations, had sent intelligence of them to Athens, and desired a reïnforcement. Twenty triremes were in consequence ordered to join him. It is upon this occasion that we first discover in history the importance of the loss of Pericles, and the want of those superior abilities for the direction of public affairs, which had hitherto, in so great a degree, obviated misfortune and commanded success. Nicias, a Cretan of Gortynium, having in view to advance his own power, proposed to the Athenian government the reduction of Cydonia in Crete, a member of the Peloponnesian confederacy. It would be an easy conquest, he said, for the fleet which was ready to sail for Naupactus, and with the assistance to be readily procured within the iland, could occasion little delay. The Athenian people were ill-advised enough to decree as he desired. The armament went to Crete, and ravaged without opposition the Cydonian lands; but the town was found so strong, and its people so determined, that there appeared no probability of taking it without the tedious process of a

siege,

siege, or perhaps a blockade. The commanders would have then hastened their voyage to Naupactus, but contrary winds detained them long in Crete.

Meantime Phormion was left to exert his abilities and his vigilance against an enemy who too much outnumbered him.   Yet tho they had nearly four times his strength, so confident was he in superior skill, that Thucyd. l. 2. not only he did not refuse, but he appears to have been desirous to c. 86. meet them wherever he could have sea-room.   Moving therefore from Naupactus, he took a station just without the gulph, near the headland of the Molycrian or northern Rhium; and a small army, composed c. 90. chiefly of Naupactian Messenians, joined his naval camp on the shore, to assist in case of any attempt from a superior force upon the fleet in its station.   This movement was not without danger, as the event proved; but the apprehension that the squadron expected from Attica might be intercepted and overpowered by the Peloponnesian fleet, appears to have been his motive for quitting the security of his station at Naupactus, before that assistance arrived.

The Peloponnesians however, with all their advantage of numbers, with all the pride of reputed preëminence in arms, and all the zeal of the Lacedæmonian commanders to incite them, so felt their inferiority in naval action, from the event of the late ingagement, that they perseveringly avoided the open, and directed their endevors to draw the Athenians into the narrow sea.   From Panormus, which is a little within the gulph, and nearly opposite Naupactus, they moved to the Achaian or southern Rhium, overagainst the station of the Athenians. The two headlands, forming the mouth of the gulph, are less than a mile asunder: the stations of the two fleets would be something more.

During six or seven days they watched oneanother without c. 86. moving. The Peloponnesians then practised a stratagem, apparently well imagined, for forcing the Athenian admiral to action within the gulph. The town of Naupactus, while its youth were in the army attending the Athenian fleet, was left almost without defence. At daybreak the Peloponnesians moved eastward, along the Achaian coast, in a column with four triremes abreast; twenty of the swiftest forming

an

an advanced guard. Phormion was immediately in alarm for Naupactus. With all haste he got his people aboard from his naval camp,
and proceeded eastward by the northern coast of the gulph, with his
line of battle formed ahead; the Messenians at the same time pressing
their march along the shore toward their town. This was precisely
what the Peloponnesians wished. They no sooner saw the Athenian
fleet irrecoverably ingaged within the straits, than, trusting to the
advanced guard for preventing its escape into the harbour of Naupactus, they formed for action in line of battle abreast, and pushed
across the gulph. The eleven headmost ships of the Athenian line,
through superior swiftness, outstretching the right wing of the Peloponnesians, escaped attack: the nine others were intercepted, overpowered, and forced ashore. One was taken with its whole crew: all
fell into the hands of the Peloponnesians ; but, of their people, many
escaped by swimming; the rest were mostly put to the sword. What
followed, reported by the authoritative pen of Thucydides, proves how
important, in the antient system of naval war, the coöperation of an
army might be to a fleet. The brave Messenians, zealous in hereditary
enmity to Lacedæmon, arriving on the beach, dashed completely armed
through the surf, boarded the stranded galleys, and driving out the
conquerors, recovered all : tho some were already taken in tow.

Thucyd. l. 2.
c. 91. Meanwhile the twenty galleys of the Peloponnesian advanced guard
were pursuing the eleven Athenian which had overstretched the main
body. Ten of these reached the harbour of Naupactus: and forming
against the shore, prepared to resist any attack that might be attempted
c. 92. against them. A Leucadian trireme, the swiftest of the allied fleet, in
which was Timocrates, the first of the Lacedæmonian commissioners
appointed to be of council with the admiral, pursued the eleventh, and
gained upon her so fast, that to escape into the harbour of Naupactus
c. 91. seemed impossible. It happened that a large merchant-ship was lying
at anchor off the harbour's mouth. The Athenian captain having
passed this vessel, turned close round it, and judged his time so well,
and managed the evolution with such combined rapidity and exactness,
that with his beak he struck the galley of the amazed Leucadians
amidship, and with such force that she presently sunk. Timocrates,

in

in a fit of passionate despair, stabbed himself; and his gored body, floating into the harbour of Naupactus, was afterward taken up there. The rest of the advanced squadron was at this time following in a disorderly manner, the crews singing the song of triumph, as if already completely conquerors[4]. The catastrophe of their comrades, happening within sight of all, astonished and alarmed them. Some rested on their oars to await the main body of their fleet, but the main body of their fleet was far off, and the enemy near. Some, through ignorance of the coast, struck upon shoals. Their hesitation and distress were as a signal to the Athenians in the harbour. The Athenians, quickly aware of all circumstances, advanced in good order against the enemy yet in confusion. The contest was not long: the Peloponnesians fled for their port of Panormus, on the opposite coast of the gulph, distant about seven miles, losing six triremes taken by the Athenians. The main body of their fleet, too distant to give any considerable support, and apparently fearful of passing the night on a hostile coast with which they were imperfectly acquainted, also sought the security of the port[5]. The success of the Athenians was altogether extraordinary: they took six of the enemy's triremes; they sunk one: they recovered all their own which had been taken or forced ashore, excepting only that which had fallen into the enemy's hands with its crew aboard; they collected the wreck and their own slain; they restored the slain of the enemy only through the customary ceremony of a truce solicited for the purpose; and erecting their trophy, which was the easiest part of the business, they vindicated to themselves, against a force so superior, every ordinary mark of decided victory. The Peloponnesians also erected a trophy at the Achaian Rhium, on pretence of their success in

---

[4] The song of battle and the song of victory, both hymns to the gods, one a prayer before battle, and at the same time a signal for ingaging, the other a thanksgiving for success were equally called Pæan; but Thucydides distinguishes that it was the song of triumph which was sung upon this occasion ;—Ἐπαιώνιζον τι ἅμα πλίοντες, ὡς νενικηκότες.

[5] Thucydides does not, with his usual accuracy, account for the inefficiency of the main body of the Peloponnesian fleet in the latter part of the day. Perhaps there was among them something of that mismanagement frequently incident to confederate armaments, of which he was not himself perfectly informed.

the

the early part of the day, and placed by it the single captured ship which had not been retaken, as an offering to the god of the sea.

If the event of the former action against Phormion had excited indignation at Lacedæmon, that of the recent battle would give Cnemus, and his two surviving coadjutors, to apprehend no very favorable reception on their return thither. A project therefore occurring, while the fleet remained yet assembled on the Corinthian coast, for attempting an important stroke against the enemy before they dispersed for the winter, was received, particularly by the enterprizing Brasidas, with eager joy. It was known to the Megarians that the Athenian government, secure in naval superiority, left their harbour of Peiræus without an adequate guard. That most important place therefore it was proposed to surprize. A select body of seamen were marched by land to Megara, each carrying his oar, his cushion, and his thong[6]. Arriving in the evening, they with all haste launched forty triremes which had been laid up in the port of Nisæa, and putting immediately to sea, made for the Attic coast. A contrary wind, presently arising, gave them to apprehend that they should not be able to reach Peiræus in time to accomplish a surprize. Doubtful therefore of the possibility of executing their original plan, they determined upon a smaller enterprize, which was clearly within their power. Instead of pushing for

Thucyd. l. 2. c. 93.

---

[6] Τὴν κώπην καὶ τὸ ὑπηρέσιον, καὶ τὸν τροπωτῆρα.—*Cum singulis remis, & singulis pulvinis, quos sibi remigantibus substernerent, & cum singulis scalmis.* The thong, or loop, to fasten the oar to the rowlock, is not unknown with us, and I have seen the cushion used by Thames wherrymen ; yet that the cushion should have been so indispensable an implement as the account in the text would make it appear, we do not readily conceive. Tho therefore the scholiast gives the explanation, which the Latin translator has followed, ὑπηρέσιον ἐςὶ τὸ κῶας ᾧ ἐπικάθηνται οἱ ἐρέσσονλες, διὰ τὸ μὴ συνξρίξεσθαι αὐτῶν τὰς πυγὰς, I cannot help having some suspicion that it meant another thing. A

marble fragment, which, before the spoliations of the French, was in the Vatican museum at Rome, has been mentioned in a former note, (24. s. 4. ch. 8.) as the most satisfactory representation known of an antient ship of war. In that curious monument, the oars project from the side of the vessel through apertures, like the rowports of our small ships of war; but at the aperture every oar has a bag about it, whose purpose apparently has been to prevent the waves from flowing in. I leave it for those who have leisure for the inquiry to decide whether the ὑπηρέσιον of Thucydides may have been such a case or bag, rather than a cushion to sit upon.

eiræus,

Peiræus, they debarked on Salamis.   Notice communicated to Athens
by fire-beacons, raised an alarm there, says Thucydides, equal to anything experienced in the course of the war.   The immediate apprehension
was, that the enemy were already in Peiræus: the inhabitants of that
place supposed that the Peloponnesians were at least masters of the
town of Salamis, and that the attack would reach them without delay.
At daybreak the whole strength of Athens moved down to the port;
and the galleys were hastily launched and manned, while a strong garrison was appointed to Peiræus.   The danger however was over almost
as soon as known.   The Peloponnesians, after collecting some booty,
making some defenceless people prisoners, and seizing three triremes
from which the crews had fled, hastened back to Nisæa, not without
apprehension that their leaky vessels might founder before they reached
that port.   Had the Peloponnesians persevered, says Thucydides, in
their first design, supposing no hindrance from the wind, they might
easily have succeeded.   The event therefore was salutary to Athens, by
the admonition it gave.   A proper guard was thenceforward kept in
Peiræus, the mouth of the harbour was shut with a chain, and all due
precaution was observed against surprizes.

As soon as the Peloponnesian seamen returned to their fleet, the ships
were sent to their several homes, and laid up for the winter.   But the
active Phormion did not let the severe season pass unemployed.   A
party adverse to that which favored the Athenian alliance was strong   Thucyd. l. 2.
in some of the Acarnanian towns.   As soon as certain intelligence   c. 102.
arrived that the Peloponnesian fleet was dispersed, nothing remaining
to be feared for Naupactus, he sailed to Astacus.   Debarking there
four hundred heavy-armed Athenians and as many Messenians, he
marched through Acarnania, and concerting measures with the
friendly at Stratus, Coronta, and other principal towns, he banished
the obnoxious.   Œneiadæ, strongly situated among marshes near the
mouth of the Acheloüs, alone of all the Acarnanian cities, maintained
its alliance with the Peloponnesians.   Reïmbarking then with his escort,
he returned to Naupactus.   In spring he proceeded to Athens, taking
with him the captured ships, and the prisoners; of whom the freemen

Vol. II.   P   were

were shortly exchanged for so many Athenians, prisoners with the Peloponnesians.

During these transactions in the western part of Greece, while, in Lacedæmon and Athens, war seemed to sleep for the winter, far more alarming movements occurred on the northern borders. Philip, brother of Perdiccas king of Macedonia, dying, his son Amyntas claimed the succession to the principality which he had held in Upper Macedonia. Perdiccas, who had proposed to deprive his brother of that little subordinate sovereignty, seized it on his death. What the Macedonian law on the subject may have been, we have no information, and perhaps it was not very well defined. Amyntas however resorted to the neighboring powerful soverein of Thrace, Sitalces. This prince, by his recent alliance with Athens, for what advantages in return, is not said, had ingaged to compel the revolted dependencies of Athens in Chalcidicë to return to their obedience. Ready therefore with his army, he took Amyntas under his patronage; and, Perdiccas refusing to reïnstate that prince in the principality which had been held by his father, he resolved to dethrone Perdiccas, and make Amyntas king of Macedonia.

Winter was approaching, but winter warfare, we find, was more common with the Thracians than with the Greeks. The forces of Sitalces, unlike the little armies of the Grecian republics, almost rivalled in numbers the hosts of Asia: but, far alien from Asiatic effeminacy, Thrace was held by the Greeks themselves to be the favorite residence of Ares and Enyo, or, as the Romans named them, Mars and Bellona, the deïties of war. Sitalces put himself at the head of a hundred thousand foot and fifty thousand horse; and, taking with him the Macedonian prince, marched toward that inland district of the Macedonian kingdom, which had been his father's appanage. Here Amyntas had still friends, and the towns of Gortynia and Atalanta readily opened their gates to his protector. Perdiccas, tho of no mean talents, and commanding a considerable dominion, yet weakened by civil war with the princes of his family, was utterly unequal to meet the Thracian army in battle. With his cavalry only he attended upon its motions, while his people sought refuge, some in the fortified

towns;

Thucyd. l. 2. c. 95.

Ch. 13. s. 4. of this Hist.

Xen. Hel. l. 7.

Thucyd. l. 2. c. 98.

c. 100.

towns; but as these in Macedonia, a country yet little improved, were few and small, the greater part fled to the mountains, woods, and marshes.

The first opposition that Sitalces met was from the town of Eidomenë, which he took by assault.   He next attacked Europus; but unskilled in sieges, and unprovided for them, he there failed.   Meanwhile the Macedonian horse, armed for defence in the Grecian manner, did not fear to meet superior numbers; and it was found that against the most numerous body of Thracians, wherever they made a charge, they made an impression.   Being nevertheless constantly in the end overpowered, and continually liable to be surrounded, they soon desisted from efforts which were found unavailing.   All the open country therefore was at the mercy of the Thracian prince: the provinces of Mygdonia, Grestonia, Anthemous, and Æmathia, were wasted.   It had been concerted with the Athenian government, that an Athenian fleet should coöperate with the Thracian army; but it was so little expected that Sitalces would perform his ingagement at that season, that the fleet was never sent.   As soon as it was known that he had actually entered Macedonia, an embassy was dispatched to apologize for the omission, carrying presents, as the Thracian custom required.   Sitalces, in some degree gratified, sent a part of his army into Chalcidicë; and the ravage of that country was added to the destruction made through so many other provinces.   The people however found security in their towns: for against a Grecian town, moderately fortified, unless by surprize or by the slow operation of a blockade, all the force of Thrace was little efficacious.

The apprehensions excited by the fame of the vast army of Sitalces, were not confined to Macedonia.   All the Greeks as far as Thermopylæ were in alarm, and took measures for resisting the storm, should it reach them.   The various clans of free Thracians, north of the Strymon, were not less apprehensive and not less in motion.   But want and the rigor of the season began soon to press severely upon such a multitude, so unprovided as the army of Sitalces[7].   The able Perdiccas

Thucyd. l. 2. c. 101.

[7] There is remarkable resemblance between this expedition of the king of Thrace, as compendiously related by Thucydides, and that of the Khan of Crim Tartary, described at large by baron Tott, who accompanied the Tartar prince in his winter campain, in war between Russia and Turkey.

used the opportunity for negotiation.   He found means,.through confidential persons, to communicate with Seuthes, nephew and principal
favorite of the Thracian monarch.   Stratonicë, sister of Perdiccas, was
offered him in marriage, with a large portion.   The intrigue succeeded:
the restoration of Amyntas to his father's principality was of course
allowed; and, after a month spent in wasting Macedonia and Chalci-
dice, but no farther purpose of the expedition accomplished, Sitalces led
his forces home.   A treaty of amity followed between the two monarchs,
and the Macedonian princess gave her hand to Seuthes.

SECTION III.

*Fourth Campain: Third Invasion of Attica.   Revolt of Mitylenë.
Flight of Part of the Garrison of Platæa.   Siege of Mitylenë by
Paches.   Distress and Exertions of Athens.   Transactions under
the Lacedæmonian Alcidas, and the Athenian Paches on the Ionian
Coast.*

Thucyd. l. 3.   In the former summer, as we have seen, invasion of Attica was inter-
c. 1.
B. C. 428.   mitted by the Peloponnesians; but in the year to whose transactions
Ol. $\frac{87}{88}$. $\frac{4}{1}$.   we now proceed, the fourth of the war, they entered that country for
P. W. 4.   the third time, still under the command of the Spartan king Archi-
damus.   They chose as usual the season just before harvest, and
extensive waste followed: but the Athenian cavalry was successful in
desultory attacks, and repressed the excursions of the Peloponnesian
light troops beyond the protection of their heavy-armed, so that the
lands immediately around Athens were little infested.   After no long
stay, the Peloponnesian army, having consumed the small stores
brought with it, and what could be collected in Attica, returned home
and was disbanded.

    But new troubles were preparing for Athens, the more dangerous as
they had their source in the defective constitution of the empire.
Among its most valuable and most powerful dependencies was the iland
of Lesbos, about forty miles long only and ten wide, yet divided

between six republics, which claimed their separate and equal independency. In population and power, however, Mitylenë and Methymnë were far superior to the others. The consideration of their Æolian extraction tended to dispose all the people of Lesbos to the Lacedæmonian alliance; but more especially to the Bœotian, rather than to the Athenian, to which the course of events, the naval superiority of Athens, and their own situation as ilanders, had led them. But the momentary interest of faction, too commonly among the Greeks, overwhelmed all other considerations; deadened all feeling for the ties of blood, and blinded to all views of inlarged policy. In Methymnë the democratical party was decidedly superior, and its people held close alliance with those of the neighboring iland of Tenedos, who were influenced by the same political principles. The Methymnæans and Tenedians were therefore warmly attached to Athens. But in Mitylenë the aristocratical party was powerful; and an aristocratical party, if not oppressed, must be always insecure, where Athenian influence prevailed. Nor could men of observation and foresight consider, without great apprehension, what had already befallen other states of the Athenian confederacy; all of which, except those of Lesbos and Chios, were deprived of their marine, forbidden even fortifications for their defence, and reduced to complete subjection under the despotic will of the Athenian multitude.

Thucyd. l. 3. c. 2.

Accordingly, before the war broke out between Athens and Lacedæmon, the principal Mitylenæans had sent offers to the Lacedæmonian administration to renounce the Athenian, and reünite themselves with the Peloponnesian confederacy. Their views indeed extended farther than the meer change of their domestic constitution and forein connections: they proposed to reduce the rival republic of Methymnë, or at least to repress the democracy there; they had already a secure influence in the four inferior commonwealths; and thus the whole iland would be brought under one dominion, in which they would have the principal if not the sole authority. The Lacedæmonians, however, seem to have judged far better on the occasion than the Mitylenæans: aware that they were utterly incapable of protecting an ally, across the Ægean, against the Athenian navy, they declined the proposal.

c. 5.

proposal. The same sentiments nevertheless continuing to animate the Mitylenæans, when they saw the Athenians, between invasion and pestilence, in deep distress, they thought the season favorable for the execution of their project : they built ships of war ; they strengthened the walls of their town ; they took measures for giving security to their harbour ; they imported corn from the Euxine to form magazines ; and they increased their military force by hiring archers from the same parts.

Thucyd. l. 3.
c. 3.

In the dejection of the public mind at Athens, under severe and complicated calamity, there was great unwillingness to credit the information of these transactions at Mitylenë, and of the prevailing political sentiments there ; which was repeatedly given by the Methymnæans, by the Tenedians, and by the democratical party in Mitylenë itself. At length commissioners of inquiry and inspection were sent, with a requisition for the Mitylenæans to desist from measures which gave alarm to the neighboring commonwealth of Methymnë, and umbrage to Athens. The Mitylenæans nevertheless continued active in preparation. On the return of the commissioners therefore it was determined to use every exertion for checking, in its beginning, an evil which, in its progress, might involve the ruin of the commonwealth.

The Peloponnesian army had now quitted Attica.; and the news of the extraordinary successes of Phormion, manifesting a decided superiority in the Athenian marine, had somewhat reänimated administration and people. A squadron of forty triremes, under the command of Cleïppides, was ready to sail on an expedition against the Peloponnesian coast. It was recollected, by the Athenian administration, that the festival of the Maloeian Apollo was approaching, in the celebration of which the whole Mitylenæan people would go in procession out of the city. Cleïppides was ordered with his squadron to surprize them in the performance of this ceremony ; but apparently a vote of the general assembly was deemed necessary to authorize the measure. To prevent the communication of intelligence therefore, ten Lesbian triremes, then in the ports of Attica as auxiliaries to the Athenian fleet, were stopped, and their crews put into safe custody. A private Lesbian nevertheless carried the intelligence: hastening to Geræstus in Eubœa, and procuring a small vessel, he reached Mitylenë on the third day
from

from his leaving Athens. The Mitylenæans in consequence kept within their walls, and prepared for defence. Cleïppides arriving shortly after, and finding the intended surprize frustrated, demanded the surrender of all ships of war, and the demolition of the fortifications of the city; informing the Mitylenæans that his instructions required him, in case of refusal, to denounce war against them, and immediately to begin operations. The Mitylenæans, yet incompletely prepared, endevored to gain time by negotiation; and Cleïppides, thinking his force insufficient for the reduction of the place, permitted them to send a deputation to Athens. The deputies were directed to assure the Athenian people that no defection from their political ingagements had been intended by the Mitylenæans; and, to give some color to the assertion, one of the persons who had sent intelligence to Athens, but who had been gained over to the ruling party in Mitylenë, was appointed of the deputation. Looking however only for the relief of delay from this measure, the Mitylenæans at the same time privately dispatched a trireme with ministers to Lacedæmon, to report the state of things, and again urge solicitation for assistance.

Thucyd. l. 3.
c. 4.

The Mitylenæan deputies returning from Athens, as was expected, without procuring any relaxation of the terms required, both parties prepared for hostilities. All Lesbos declared for the Mitylenæans, except Methymnë, whose whole force joined the Athenian armament, which was farther strengthened from Imbrus, Lemnos, and other places. The Mitylenæans at first endevored to gain credit to their cause, by making a parade of their strength in taking the field against the Athenians; but after an action in which, tho not defeated, no advantage was obtained, they retired within their fortifications. Then the Athenian general sent with more confidence to require assistance from the other allies; who came in with readier zeal as they began to conceive a worse opinion of the Mitylenæan affairs; and the siege of Mitylenë was regularly formed.

c. 5.

The Mitylenæan ministers arriving at Sparta, found no very earnest disposition to ingage in their cause. The Lacedæmonian government would neither of itself undertake it, nor call a congress of the confederacy. The Mitylenæans were coldly told, that the season of the Olympian festival was at hand: they might go to Olympia, where they would

c. 8.
Ol. 88.
B. C. 428.
July.

would find some principal persons of every state of the Lacedæmonian alliance, and so they might have opportunity to learn how each was disposed. Going accordingly, they found readier favor among the subordinate than in the imperial government. After the conclusion of the festival, a meeting of deputies of the several states was held, in which it was determined to receive the Lesbians into alliance, and to make immediately a diversion in their favor by a fresh invasion of Attica. Summons were issued for two-thirds of the force of the confederacy to repair without delay to Corinth; and to give new efficacy to the invasion, frames were prepared, on which to drag the triremes, which lay in the Corinthian gulph, across the isthmus, that a fleet might coöperate with the army: for weakened as the Athenians were by the pestilence, by the repeated waste of their territory, and by the distraction of their forces, it was supposed impossible that they could make any considerable opposition by sea, without withdrawing their squadrons employed in the siege of Lesbos and on the coast of Thrace, and exposing their maritime dependencies.

This new crisis roused the spirit of the Athenian administration and people. It was indeed become of the utmost importance to show that they had still resolution to dare, and still strength to execute. The formidable state of their navy at this time, which inabled so small a commonwealth to command such extensive dominion, and to resist such a powerful confederacy, is indeed truly wonderful, and does the highest honor to the foresight and exertions of Themistocles, by whom it was first raised, and of Pericles, by whom principally it was maintained and improved. Forty triremes were employed at Lesbos, ten on the Thracian coast; thirty under Asopius son of Phormion were circumnavigating and ravaging Peloponnesus; and there were guardships stationed in various parts of the coasts of Attica and Eubœa. None were called in. A hundred ready for service remained in the harbour of Peiræus, and these it was determined immediately to use. Every Athenian was in some degree a seaman. Excepting only those of the highest orders, distinguished by the titles of knights and penta cosiomedimnians, to whom, with the superannuated and the minors, the charge of the city was left, all within the age for forein service, resident foreiners as well as Athenians, went aboard. The fleet moved

Thucyd. l. 3. c. 15.

c. 16, 17.

moved immediately for the isthmus, and displayed its strength in August. sight of the Peloponnesians; who remained in their ports motionless. Debarkations were made at pleasure, on various parts of the Peloponnesian coast, and a watch was kept on the movements of the Peloponnesian army.

The Lacedæmonian leaders were astonished and distressed by this well-judged and successful bravado.   They had confided in the Thucyd. l. 3. report of the weakness of Athens, which the Lesbians were led by c. 16. their interest to exaggerate.   They had depended upon the compliance of their allies with the summons for their proportions of c. 15. troops for the invasion of Attica, and there too they were not less disappointed. Where the people are at the same time cultivators and soldiers, they cannot be always ready to go on distant expeditions, and leave the care of their domestic affairs to women and slaves.   The Peloponnesians were now busy with their harvest; they were already wearied with fruitless invasions of Attica, and they delayed to obey the call to arms.   Meanwhile intelligence arrived that the armament under Asopius was ravaging Laconia; upon which, without more delay, the projected invasion of Attica was abandoned, and the Lacedæmonian forces marched home.   Then the Athenian fleet also retired within its ports.

The purpose of preventing the immediate pressure of the siege of c. 18. Mitylenë had nevertheless been in some degree fulfilled. The Athenian force in Lesbos was so little equal to its object, that the Mitylenæans, holding intelligence with the aristocratical faction in Methymnë, marched to that place, in hope of having it betrayed to them.   They were disappointed; but in their return they regulated, at leisure, the affairs of the subordinate republics of Antissa, Pyra, and Eresus, and, without any effectual opposition from Cleïppides, returned into Mitylenë. Upon receiving intelligence of this, the Athenian government sent Paches son of Epicurus, with a reinforcement of a thousand Beginn. heavy-armed Athenians, to take the command in Lesbos.   This Octob. sufficed to insure superiority; and, by the beginning of winter, a contravallation was completed, and Mitylenë was blockaded by land and sea.

Thucyd. l. 3.
c. 17.
The expences of the war however had been so great to Athens, that its treasury, wealthy as it had been at the beginning, was now exhausted. The daily pay of every Athenian foot-soldier on distant service (Thucydides mentions particularly those employed in the siege of Potidæa) was no less than two Attic drachmas, about twenty pence English; one drachma for his own subsistence, the other for a slave-servant. The pay of the fleet was the same. Thucydides does not indeed specify that the seamen had their servants aboard, but, what may imply the contrary, the thousand soldiers, who went with Paches to Lesbos, themselves rowed the vessels which carried them. Upon other occasions also we find Athenian soldiers doing duties that would seem to be rather the business of servants, if any were attending; and as none are mentioned by the historian, we must suppose the indulgence was not always allowed. Sieges were the most expensive military operations of the age, and generally lasting. Extraordinary measures were therefore necessary to provide means for prosecuting the siege of Mitylenë; and accordingly now, for the first time, a contribution, apparently in the
c. 19.
way of a free gift, was collected from the Athenian citizens, to the amount of two hundred talents. This manner of taxation became afterward, as was likely in a government where the multitude was despotic, a source of intolerable oppression upon the higher ranks. A reduction of pay to the soldiers and seamen seems to have taken place, as a correspondent tax upon the lower; for we learn from Thucydides, that the pay was afterward considerably below what he states it to have been till this time. Exactions from the subject cities supplied the farther wants of the commonwealth.

c. 20.
While the vengeance of Athens was thus directed against the seceders from its confederacy, its faithful allies of the little republic of Platæa seem to have been forgotten. Closely blockaded now for above a year and a half, distress was coming fast upon them. It was already winter: they had nearly consumed their stores, relief was despaired of, to hold out much longer was impossible, and from their besiegers no mercy was expected. In this situation of their affairs the commander of the garrison, Eupolpidas, incouraged by his friend Theænetus, who was, either by reputation or by office, a prophet, proposed to attempt escape,

by

by forcing their passage across the enemy's lines. The proposal was at first joyfully accepted by the whole garrison, and preparation was zealously commenced for the execution: but on the nearer view of so hazardous an undertaking, full half retracted. About two hundred and twenty however persevered with the commander. Ladders were prepared, equal to the height of the enemy's wall, which was calculated by counting the rows of bricks. The interval between the walls of circumvallation and contravallation, to use terms the nearest to the purpose that our language possesses, was sixteen feet. This space, being roofed, formed barracks for the besieging army, the appearance being that of one thick wall, with a parapet and battlements on each side. At the interval of every ten battlements were towers, of equal width with the space inclosed by the walls: in these towers the guards were kept, and, in bad weather, the sentries sheltered. *Thucyd. l. 3. c. 21.*

It was midwinter when all was ready for the undertaking. A dark, stormy night was chosen, with rain and sleet falling. The adventurers were all compactly armed; and, that they might tread more surely on the slippery soil, with the right foot bare. Observing distance, to avoid the clashing of arms, they directed their way to the middle of the interval between two towers. Having passed the ditch unperceived, ladders were placed, and twelve light-armed, with only a short sword and a breastplate, mounted under the command of Ammeas son of Corœbus, who himself led. On reaching the top they divided, six toward each tower, and waited. Others, meanwhile, hastened to support them, light-armed, with small spears; their shields, that they might climb more nimbly, being borne by those who followed. Many were already mounted, while the din of the storm and the extreme darkness of the night prevented discovery, when a tile, accidentally thrown from a battlement, fell with so much noise as to alarm the guard in the neighboring tower. The call to arms was immediate, and the whole besieging army was presently in motion. The remaining garrison, according to the plan concerted with them, attentive to this, sallied from the opposite part of the town, and made a feigned attack upon the contravallation. The besieging army being thus distracted, and in darkness and tempest unable to discover what were the real *B. C. 427. after 25th Jan. Thucyd. l. 3. c. 22.*

Q 2　　　　　　　circumstances,

circumstances, none dared quit his post: a body of three hundred only, appointed as a picket-guard to move whithersoever emergency might require, went without the wall of circumvallation, directing their march by the clamor. Fire-signals were raised to give notice to Thebes; but, to render these unintelligible, the garrison formed similar signals in various parts of the town.

Meanwhile those Platæans, who first mounted the wall, had forced the towers on each side, put the guards to the sword, and proceeding by their ladders on the tops of the towers, from that height discharged missile weapons, with advantage, against those who approached to disturb the passage of their comrades. The parapet between the towers, to make the passing easier, was then thrown down; ladders were placed on the outside, and every one, as soon as over the outer ditch, formed on the counterscarp; whence, with arrows and darts, he coöperated with those on the towers in protecting the rest. To cross the ditch, however, was not easy; for there was much water in it, frozen, but not so as to bear; and before those from the tower-tops, who were the last to descend, could effect it, the enemy's picket-guard approached. But the torches which these carried, of little use to themselves, inabled the Platæans to direct missile weapons against them, so efficaciously as to give opportunity for the last of their own people to get over the ditch; which was no sooner done than they hastened off, and, leaving the temple of the hero Androcrates on the right, so Thucydides describes their march, struck directly into the Theban road, as that which they would least be expected to take. The stratagem was completely successful: they could plainly perceive the Peloponnesians, with their torches, pursuing along the Athenian road, by Dryocephalæ toward mount Cithæron. Having themselves followed the Theban road about three quarters of a mile, they turned short to the right, and passing by Erythræ and Hysiæ, soon gained the mountains, whence they proceeded securely to Athens.

Of those who ingaged in this hazardous but well-planned and ably-executed enterprize, two hundred and twelve thus profited from its success: none were killed; one only was taken on the counterscarp of the circumvallation; five or six returned into the town without

attempting

attempting to scale the wall.   These told the garrison that their comrades, who persevered, were all cut off.   Next morning therefore a herald was sent to solicit the dead for burial, and by his return the success of the undertaking was first known in the town.

The relief of Mitylenë meanwhile was not forgotten at Lacedæmon. Requisitions were sent to the several maritime states of the confederacy to furnish their proportion of a fleet of forty ships of war; and toward spring, while these were preparing, Salæthus was forwarded with a single trireme to inspect the state of things, and direct what might be necessary.   Salæthus, landing at Pyrrha, found means, through some defect in the contravallation, where it crossed a deep watercourse, to enter Mitylenë.   The people, pressed by the able and vigorous conduct of Paches in the command of the besieging armament, were already talking of capitulation; but the exhortations of Salæthus, with assurance of speedy succour, encouraged them to persevere in defence.   Early in summer the fleet, which the zeal of the confederacy had increased to forty-two ships of war, sailed for Mitylenë under the command of Alcidas; and, shortly after, the Peloponnesian army, commanded by Cleomenes, as regent for his minor nephew Pausanias, son of the banished king Pleistoanax, invaded Attica.   Not only the produce of the earth was destroyed, wherever cultivation had been attempted in the tract formerly ravaged, but parts of the country before untouched were now laid waste; so that, excepting that of the second year of the war, this was the most destructive inroad that Attica had experienced.

Meanwhile, Alcidas loitering long on the coast of Peloponnesus, and then not pressing his voyage across the Ægean, the Mitylenæans, distressed by scarcity of provisions, began to despair of timely succour. Salæthus himself at length grew hopeless of that assistance of which he had brought the promise; but he thought he saw a resource in the yet unexerted strength of the garrison.   The oligarchal party in Mitylenë, according to a policy common in the Grecian commonwealths, reserved to themselves exclusively the complete armour and efficacious weapons of the heavy-armed, and allowed the lower people the use of the inferior arms, and the practice of the inferior discipline, of the light-armed

Marginal notes:

Thucyd. l. 3. c. 16.

c. 25.

After 23d Feb.

B. C. 427. P. W. 5. Thucyd. l. 3. c. 26.

c. 29.

c. 27.

armed only. Salæthus, who, in an oligarchy supported by the extra-ordinary institutions of Lycurgus, was accustomed to see all the citizens, without inconvenience, equally intrusted with the completest armour, and trained in the completest discipline, thought nothing was wanting to inable the Mitylenæans, instead of starving within their walls, to meet Paches in the field, but to distribute among the lower people the arms lying in their stores. The experiment was made under his authority, but the event was very wide of his hope. The lower people were no sooner vested with this new military importance, than they assumed civil controul: they held their own assemblies; they would no longer obey the magistrates; but they required that the remaining stock of provisions should be open to public inspection, and distributed equally to the people of all ranks; and they threatened, in case of refusal, to make immediately their own terms with the Athe-nians. In this state of things, the leading men thought no time was to be lost: they proposed at once to the people to treat for a capitula-tion, in which all should be included. This was approved: a herald was sent to the Athenian general, and the following hard terms were accepted: That the Mitylenæans should surrender themselves to the pleasure of the Athenian people: That the Athenian army should be immediately admitted into the city: That the Mitylenæans should send deputies to Athens to plead their cause: That, before the return of these, the Athenian general should neither put to death, reduce to slavery, nor imprison any Mitylenæan. The concluding stipulation was intended particularly for the security of those of the aristocratical party, who had been active in the negotiation with Lacedæmon. Many of them, nevertheless, whether doubtful of Athenian faith, or apprehensive of vengeance from their fellowcitizens, who through their means chiefly had been led to their present diasterous situation, took refuge at the altars. Paches removed them under a guard to the iland of Tenedos, there to await the judgement of the Athenian people.

Alcidas, with the fleet which should have relieved Mitylenë, was no farther advanced than the ilands of Icarus and Myconus, when report of its surrender met him. Desirous of more authentic information, he proceeded to Embatus, a port of the Erythræan territory on the Ionian coast;

Thucyd. l. 3. c. 28.

c. 29.

coast; and there receiving assurance that the Athenian forces had been seven days in possession of Mitylenë, he summoned a council of war to concert measures.   In the fleet were some Ionian refugees, who proposed to excite a defection of Ionia, the richest dependency of Athens, the great source of that revenue which supported the war.   The people they affirmed would be found not averse: it would only be necessary, by a sudden and vigorous exertion, to get possession of some one Ionian city, or of Cuma in Æolis, for which the strength of the armament was more than sufficient, and the business would be done; and besides that a greater blow could scarcely be given to the Athenian power, it would lead of course to communication with the Persian satraps of the western provinces, who might probably be induced to form alliance with the Peloponnesians.   The assertions of the Ionians were corroborated, and the project recommended, by the Mitylenæan ministers, who returned with the fleet from Peloponnesus.   But Alcidas was not enterprizing : all proposals for vigorous exertion were rejected, and he was most inclined to return immediately home.   Weakness indeed seems to mark equally what was blameable and what was praiseworthy in his conduct.   He proceeded at length eastward along the coast, as far as appears, without any decided object, unless to make prize of merchant-ships, of which he took numbers; for since he had been in those seas none had avoided him, some rather making toward his fleet, supposing it Athenian; being without suspicion that a Peloponnesian fleet could show itself on the Asiatic coast.   At Myonnesus, in the Teian territory, he put to death the greater part of the prisoners thus made.   Alarm spred in consequence, and, as he proceeded toward Ephesus, deputies from Samos came to him, deprecating such barbarities.   Convinced by their representations, at least of the impolicy of his proceeding, he dismissed many of his surviving prisoners, particularly the Chians, and he made no more such executions.

Meanwhile intelligence brought to Paches, that the Peloponnesian fleet was on the Ionian coast, occasioned no small uneasiness; for there was little or no Athenian force in Asia Minor, and most of the towns were unfortified ; having been rendered purposely incapable of defence, that they might be the less capable of revolt.   Paches therefore hastened

Thucyd. l.3. c. 31.

c. 30.

c. 32.

c. 33.

hastened thither with his fleet; but the cautious Alcidas had put himself beyond his reach in the way to Peloponnesus, before he could
arrive.   Paches followed as far as Latmos, when, finding pursuit vain,

he turned toward Ionia, where opportunity offered to do a service to his
country; but by an act of united treachery and cruelty, which, through
the impartial justice of the admirable historian his cotemporary and
fellowcountryman, has marred with a blot of eternal infamy a character
otherwise of some glory, not without extending a stain to that of the
Athenian government and people, who approved and profited from the
deed.

Colophon, once famous for the wealth of its citizens, being torn by
contending factions, about three years before the time we are treating of, one party, obtaining assistance from Itamanes, a Persian officer,
expelled all their opponents.   Thus far we have only an ordinary
occurrence among the Grecian republics.   What followed is marked
by more singularity.   The fugitives possessed themselves of Notium,
the seaport of Colophon, and became there a separate commonwealth.
But faction shortly arose among them also, to such a point, that one
party applied to the satrap Pissuthnes, under whose authority Itamanes
had acted in expelling them from their antient city.   Pissuthnes ordered
some Arcadian mercenaries in his service, together with some barbarian
troops, to their assistance.   Their opponents were in consequence
expelled; but they were themselves forced to submit to the government of their most inveterate enemies, their fellow citizens in possession
of Colophon, who had preöccupied the satrap's favor.   Such was the state
of things when Paches came with his fleet into the neighborhood.   To
him then the new fugitives from Notium applied; claiming his protection, and that of the Athenian commonwealth, to which, they asserted,
they had been faithful against barbarians and rebels, by whom they were
oppressed.   Paches, going accordingly to Notium, and landing his
forces, desired a conference with Hippias, the commander of the Arcadian troops.   Hippias, trusting in a safe-conduct, went into his camp,
but was immediately arrested; and Paches advancing with his forces
to Notium, where no such attempt was apprehended, took it, and put
all the Arcadian and Persian troops to the sword.   Not satisfied with
                                                          this

this efficacious treachery, as if in mockery of good faith, conducting Hippias unhurt into the town, and claiming so to have complied with the terms of his ingagement, he ordered that deluded officer to execution.   The Colophonians of the party adverse to the Persian interest were then put in possession of Notium, and Paches returned to Mitylenë.   Notium was soon after strengthened by a colony of Athenians ; the antient constitution was superseded by the Athenian law, and the town was made an immediate appendage of Attica.

The measure which followed, on the return of Paches to Mitylenë, seems to have been as little consistent with his plighted faith as his treatment of the unfortunate Hippias.   All those Mitylenæans remaining in the city who had been active in the revolt, that is, all the aristocratical party, were apprehended ; and, together with those who had been lodged in Tenedos, were sent to Athens.   The Lacedæmonian Salæthus, who had been discovered in conce lment during the absence of Paches, was sent prisoner with them.   This measure seems to have been hastened that another might safely follow, which was probably required by the Athenian government, and which the state of its finances would make necessary ; the greater part of the forces were sent home : with the rest the general remained to administer the affairs of the iland.

SECTION IV.

State of the Athenian Government after the Death of Pericles. Nicias : Cleon. Inhuman Decree against the Mitylenæan : Death of Paches. Platæa taken.

THE supreme direction of the Athenian affairs had now passed into very different hands from those whose extraordinary abilities had raised the commonwealth to its present power.   After the abolition of royalty, and even after the establishment of the constitution of Solon, which reduced the aristocracy, while democratical sway was gradually advancing, illustrious birth had still been greatly considered among the

Athenian people, and was almost necessary for rising to high political situations. For, little as the Athenians were willing to allow superiority of rank, superiority of political situation was indispensably to be given to some; and they submitted to it less impatiently in families which they had been accustomed for ages to respect, than in new men, yesterday their equals or inferiors. Themistocles and Aristeides seem to have been the first whom the most extraordinary advantages of ability and character could raise, from even middle rank, to that eminence which inabled them to take a decisive lead in public affairs. After them, in Cimon, and again in Pericles, superior talents met with illustrious birth. But even the constitution of Solon had contributed to transfer to riches, that respect which was formerly paid to high ancestry. Other circumstances afterward assisted to give immoderate influence to the possession of wealth. The great Cimon set the injurious example, to probably not the first example, of bribing the people from his private purse. The great Pericles set the still more ruinous example of bribing the people from the public treasure. After his death no man was found capable of wielding a democracy as he had wielded it; commanding, with little interruption, for fifteen years, a people, every individual of whom claimed equality with himself, as if he had, by the most undisputed claim, been their legal soverein. But a constant succession of men possessing superior abilities, with disposition and constitution to exert them in public business, is not to be expected among the mall numbers who compose the highest rank in any state. Nicias, son of Niceratus, to whom the principal families, and sober men in general, now looked as the fittest person to lead the councils of the commonwealth, was a man of high merit, but unfortunately not, like the great men who had preceded him, born for the peculiar circumstances of the situation for which he was wanted. His abilities, political and military, were considerable. Integrity, piety, generosity, a pleasant complying temper, and an elegant taste, were conspicuous in him. Decidedly adverse to democratical power, he was nevertheless so clear a friend to public welfare, so ready and so judicious in the employment of his large fortune in gratifications for the multitude, so humane and liberal in relieving the distressed and promoting the

advantages

advantages of individuals, that he was in no small degree a favorite of the people. But he was bashful and diffident: of clear courage in the field, in, the assembly of the people he was a coward; while a reserve, the effect of bashfulness, injured him as if it had been the effect of pride. It was said of him, that his generosity was a revenue to the deserving, and his fearfulness to the undeserving. Under a better government, his character might have been splendid; but his diffidence and want of firmness, amid the civil turbulence in which it was his fate to live, gave it sometimes the appearance even of weakness [8].

In opposition to Nicias stood a man such as never before was known to sway the Athenian assembly. Cleon seems to have been as remarkably born for the depression of Athens as Miltiades, Themistocles, Aristeides, Cimon, and Pericles for its exaltation. Bred among the lowest of the people, the son of a tanner, and said himself to have exercised that trade, he was the opposite of Nicias in character as in political interest. Of extraordinary impudence and little courage, slack in the field but forward and noisy in the assembly, corrupt in practice as in principle, but boastful of integrity, and supported by a coarse but ready eloquence, he had gained such consideration, by flattering the lower people, and railing at the higher, that he stood in the situation of head of a party [9].

Such was the state of things, when the unhappy Mitylenæans surrendered their lives and fortunes to the pleasure of the Athenian people. On the arrival of the prisoners, the Lacedæmonian Salæthus was ordered, by the assembled people, for immediate execution. To obtain a respite he made large offers, and, among other things, undertook to procure the raising of the siege of Platæa; but he was not heard. The assembly then deliberated concerning the punishment to be inflicted upon the Mitylenæans; and sentiments of anger, inflamed by the boisterous eloquence of Cleon, prevailing, the inhuman decree passed for putting

B. C. 427.
Ol. 87. ¾.
P. W. 5.
Thucyd. l. 3.
c. 36.

---

[8] Plato certainly esteemed Nicias an able statesman and general. See the dialogue Laches, throughout, but particularly p. 198. v. 2. ed. Serran. Plutarch is large upon his defects.

[9] ' Xerxes himself did not suffer more by ' the flattery of his courtiers than the Athe- ' nians by that of their orators.' Lord Lyttelton's dialogue of Pericles and Cosmo de' Medici.

every

every man to death, and reducing the women and children of all ranks to slavery. Such was the right which the Athenian people claimed over Greeks whom they called allies, and who had every pretension so to consider themselves; and such the punishment for renouncing that alliance, to connect themselves with other Greeks. The assembly was no sooner dismissed than a trireme was dispatched, with orders for Paches to carry the decree into immediate execution.

But the Athenians were not universally of a temper to sleep upon such a deed without remorse. The very next morning extensive repentance became evident; and many of the principal men joined the Mitylenæan deputies, in pressing the summoning of a second assembly, for the purpose of reconsidering the decree; and they prevailed. The people were hastily called together, and various opinions were delivered. The mild Nicias was a weak opponent to the insolent Cleon, who harangued with vehemence in support of the measure already taken.

Thucyd. l. 3. c. 37, 38,39, 40.

' What folly,' he said, ' to rescind, on one day, what had been, on due ' deliberation, resolved but on the preceding! Without more stability ' in measures, there was an end of government. With regard to the ' purport of the decree complained of, example was become absolutely ' necessary; and a more just example than the Mitylenæans never ' could be found. They had always been treated by Athens, not only ' with justice but with kindness, not only without offence but with ' cautious respect. And as nothing could be more unprovoked than ' the revolt, so nothing could be less defended upon any plea of neces- ' sity. The Mitylenæans could not be compelled to the part they had ' taken: being ilanders, attack could hardly reach them; possessing ' ships and fortifications, they could have repelled it. Injoying then ' these advantages, they had before their eyes the example of others, ' who, having revolted against Athens, had been punished by depriva- ' tion of their marine, demolition of their fortifications, and reduction ' under a strict subjection. Nevertheless, unsatisfied with possessed ' felicity, undeterred by obvious example, they not barely renounced ' their political connection, but they united themselves with those ' whose professed purpose was the destruction of Athens. Such being ' the case, it would be weakness to let sentiments of mercy prevail;
' and

'and it would be folly even to delay that decision which wisdom
'required, but which, if the present anger of the people cooled, they
'would want resolution to make.' These were the principal arguments
in support of the inhuman sentence. But Cleon would inforce argument by menaces; and knowing that he could not use a more effectual
weapon against the timid Nicias, impudently imputing corrupt motives
to any who should dare to oppose him, he threatened criminal prosecution before that wild judicature the assembled people.

The assertor of the cause of humanity, upon this occasion, was
Diodotus son of Eucrates. He must have deserved to be better known,
but upon this occasion only we find him mentioned in history [10].   In
the debate of the preceding day he had been the principal opponent of
Cleon; and he now again came forward with firmness, with zeal, and   Thucyd. I. 3.
at the same time with prudence, to plead a cause which, he insisted, was   c. 43.
not more that of humanity than of political wisdom.   Such was the
ferment of men's minds, and so much passion entered into the decision
of political questions at Athens, that he would not venture to attribute   c. 42—48.
injustice to the decree; he would not venture to affirm that the Athenians might not, in strict right, condemn the whole Mitylenæan people
to death; but he desired them to consider, 'that the lower Mityle-
'næans had no sooner had the power, in consequence of having arms
'put into their hands, than they compelled the aristocratical party to
'treat with the Athenian general. Setting aside however the question
'of right and justice, he would consider the matter at issue upon the
'point of expediency only. The terror of capital punishment, it was
'notorious, did not prevent the commission of crimes: it was the
'business therefore of a wise policy, by attentive precaution, to pre-
'vent revolt, and not to inhance evils, to which negligence or misrule
'might give occasion, by making the situation of those ingaged in
'revolt completely desperate: it was the business of a wise policy to
'draw profit from conquest, and not to convert a city, capable of paying
'large tribute, into a heap of ruins, and a cultivated country to a desert.

[10] A brother of Nicias was named Eucrates, (Lys. or. pro. fil. Eucr.) and the
manner in which family-names were usually
distributed among the Greeks, would favor
the supposition that the father of Diodotus
may have been brother of Niceratus, the
father of Nicias.

'The

' The lower people, he observed, even in the subject-states, were in
' general attached to Athens.   Even were it just, therefore, nothing
' could be more impolitic than, by an act of extreme severity, to alie-
' nate, in every subject-state, that party which alone was, or ever
' would be, well-disposed to them.'   He concluded with recommending, ' that those who had been selected by Paches as most involved in
' the guilt of revolt, should be, not condemned in haste and in anger,
' but judged at leisure with dispassionate deliberation, and that the rest
' of the Mitylenæan people should have a free pardon.'

Thucyd. l. 3.   The speeches being concluded, the question was put, and Diodotus
c. 49.
prevailed; but the influence of Cleon was such that he prevailed but
by a very small majority.   It was, after all, very much feared that
notice of the second decree could not be conveyed to Mitylenë in time
to prevent the execution of the first; orders for which had been forwarded near twenty-four hours.   A trireme was in all haste dispatched,
with no small promises to the crew for arriving in time.   They rowed
incessantly, refreshing themselves with a preparation of meal, wine,
and oil, which they could take without quitting their labor, and sleeping
by reliefs.   Fortunately no adverse wind impeded; and the trireme
with the first decree, going on an odious errand, did not press its way.
It arrived however first; the general had opened the dispatches, and
was taking measures for executing the horrid order, when the second
trireme arrived with the happy countermand.

c. 50.   The case of those whom Paches had sent to Athens, as principal
actors in the revolt, seems to have been hopeless, since Diodotus himself had not ventured to offer a word in their favor, farther than to
claim for them a dispassionate trial.   They were more than a thousand,
and all were put to death.   Nor were those saved from the executioner
treated with the generosity which Diodotus recommended.   All the
ships of war of the Mitylenæan commonwealth were confiscated to the
use of the Athenian people; the fortifications of the city were demolished, and the lands were disposed of in a manner which appears to
have been new.   According to the genius of democracy, it was calculated rather for private emolument than public advantage, being either
required by the soverein people, as an indulgence which they wished

11   and

and could command, or proposed by some leading men as a bribe to obtain popular favor.   The whole iland of Lesbos, except the territory of Methymnë, was divided into three thousand portions.   Three hundred of these were dedicated to the gods; for it was supposed the deïty might be thus bribed, not only to pardon, but even to favor the most atrocious inhumanity.   The remainder was divided by lot among the Athenian citizens, who were however not to have possession of the lands: that was to remain with the Lesbians, who, for each portion, were to pay a yearly rent, in the nature of our quitrents, of two mines, nearly eight guineas.   A territory belonging to the Lesbians, on the neigboring continent, was disposed of in the same manner.   Both the insular and the continental territory were reduced under complete and immediate subjection to the sovereinty of the Athenian people.   But the gratification of individuals only was provided for, the public treasury derived nothing from the arrangement.

A very remarkable fact, unnoticed by Thucydides, may, on the authority of Plutarch, require mention here.   The conduct of Paches, throughout his command, appears to have been able, and his services were certainly important.   On his return to his country he expected honor and respect, suitable to those services; but he found himself called upon to answer a charge of peculation before the assembled people.   The orators who conducted the accusation were virulent: their harangues had evident effect upon the multitude; and the indignation of Paches, perhaps less an orator than a soldier, was so raised that, in presence of the assembly, he stabbed himself to the heart.

After proceeding thus far in Greeian history, we become so familiarized with instances of slaughter committed in cold blood, generally not without at least a claim of sanction from lawful authority, and a pretence to the execution of justice, that the horror lessens, and we are prepared for the tragedy which closed the siege of Platæa.   We find Thucydides. so often giving due measure of censure to his fellow-countrymen, that it seems reasonable to suppose they would not have escaped his animadversion for neglecting all endevor to succour the brave little garrison of that place, had there been any prospect of success from any attempt within their power.   We may conceive, indeed,
that

that the pestilence first, and then the revolt of Lesbos, would greatly weaken their means; not only reducing their ability for exertion, but making all risk doubly dangerous. The besieging army however alone would scarcely deter them; but the force of Bœotia was at hand, equally to support the besieging army, or to take advantage of the absence of the Athenian forces from Attica, and to intercept their return; and the loss of a battle, in the critical circumstances of that time, might have indangered all the dependencies of Athens, and even Athens itself.

Thucyd. l. 3. c. 52. Such being the inability of the Athenians to relieve Platæa, in the course of the summer, the third of the siege, the garrison began to be severely pressed by famine. The first proposal for a capitulation was nevertheless made by the Lacedæmonian general, in pursuance of instructions, the result of an illiberal and even treacherous policy, which we should deem more unworthy of Sparta, were there fewer instances of it upon record to her shame. The success of the Peloponnesians in the war, not having been so great and so rapid as they had promised themselves, it was foreseen that, to restore places taken on both sides, might probably become a necessary condition of any peace. But it was an object with the Lacedæmonian government, in compliment to Thebes, not to restore Platæa. As soon therefore as it was known that the garrison were in extremity of want, the general sent a herald with the proposal, ' that if they would voluntarily submit ' themselves to the Lacedæmonians, and take them for their judges, ' the guilty only should be punished, and none without trial.' The Platæans, utterly unable to struggle for better terms, acceded to these, and surrendered their town and themselves to the Lacedæmonians.

Commissioners shortly arrived from Sparta, authorized to pronounce the doom of the unfortunate garrison, which seems to have been already determined; for the mode of trial promised nothing equitable. No accusation was preferred, but the simple question was put to the Platæans, ' Whether, in the existing war, they had done any service to ' the Lacedæmonians or their allies?' Startled at such a proceeding, the Platæans requested that they might be permitted to speak more largely for themselves than meerly to answer that question. This being not denied,

denied, Astymachus and Lacon, the latter connected by hospitality with Sparta, were appointed to speak for the whole body. After urging their confidence in the justice of the Lacedæmonians, and the expectation of a different kind of trial, which had induced them to surrender themselves, they pleaded the acknowleged merit of their commonwealth with Lacedæmon and with all Greece in the Persian wars; and they mentioned their service to Sparta in particular in the Helot rebellion. They stated the refusal of the Lacedæmonians to undertake the protection of their commonwealth against the oppression of Thebes, which above ninety years before had given origin to their alliance with Athens : and they expatiated on the extreme hardship of their case, if they were to be punished for fidelity to that alliance, which they could not have deserted without the basest ingratitude and the foulest dishonor. They expostulated on the proposed desolation of those temples, where thanksgiving had been offered to the gods, for blessing Greece with liberty, through the glorious success obtained against the Persians, and on the abolition, which, from the destruction of their commonwealth, would insue to those solemn rites then appointed, by the grateful voice of Greece united, to be performed by the Platæan people. Finally, adjuring the Lacedæmonians by the sepulchers of their ancestors, to which the Platæans paid annual honors, they deprecated, beyond all things, being delivered to their inveterate enemies the Thebans, whose insidious attempts against them, they said, after having successfully resisted, they had justly punished; and they required rather to be restored to the possession of their town, to which, by the terms of the capitulation, they were equitably intitled, there to have the choice of their mode of perishing : but on the mercy of the Lacedæmonians they would willingly throw themselves.

The Thebans, with exasperation, not abated by time, but rather increased by the difficulties they had undergone in obtaining means to revenge their friends and relations, murdered, according to their sentiment, by the Platæans, undertook to reply. They began with asserting Thucyd. l. 3. their claim to sovereinty over Platæa, derived from their ancestors, c. 61. founders of all the municipal governments of Bœotia, when they conquered the country. They would allow no merit to the Platæans for their exertions in the Persian war: to which they were led, it was insisted, not by any inlarged spirit of patriotism, not by any liberal regard for the common cause of Grecian freedom, but meerly by an attachment to Athens, founded on the separate interest, not even of

Thucyd. l. 3. c. 63.

their city, but only of a faction in their city. No connection with Athens however could excuse their defection from the general confederacy of the Greek nation, under the presidency of Lacedæmon, of which Athens itself had been a member. On the contrary, if it was dishonorable to betray any ingagement, into which they had unguardedly entered with Athens, much more dishonorable and more criminal was it to betray the common cause of Greece, by supporting the Athenians in their endevors to subdue the whole nation, against the Lacedæmonians and their allies, whose only purpose was to protect its

c. 64.

liberties. Thus, among others, the Æginetans, whose commonwealth had been a member of the general confederacy, were already reduced to a state of subjection: and yet, notwithstanding these offences, liberal offers had been made to the Platæans before the siege, and had been rejected.

c. 65.

'With regard then,' continued the Theban orator, 'to the attempt ' to surprize your city during an existing truce, which is so vehemently ' objected to us, had it been a measure of our own, or had we come ' hostilely against you, ravaged your lands and attacked your persons, ' you might indeed reasonably have accused us. But the leaders in ' that business were the best of your own citizens: they invited us; ' they opened your gates to us; under their authority, who had the ' best title to authority among you, we acted: nothing hostile was ' done, nothing intended; but the sole purpose was the salutary one of ' withdrawing you from a forein connection, and reüniting you to the

c. 66.

' body of the Bœotian people. Nevertheless the death of those of our ' fellowcitizens who fell in arms, we are willing to pass over; but for ' the assassination of those others, who submitted themselves to your ' mercy, whom in the moment you spared, and for whose safety you

c. 68.

' pledged yourselves to us, how can it be excused? Shall then, Lace- ' dæmonians, their lamentations and prayers for mercy avail them? ' The fathers of those gallant youths, who have been thus murdered,

'were

' were the very men who, by their deeds in the field of Coroneia,
' rescued Bœotia from the Attic yoke, and restored it to the Grecian
' confederacy.   Some of them fell there; some, now in old age, living
' to bewail the treacherous massacre of their sons and the orbitude of
' their families, are with far better plea your suppliants for revenge.
' We therefore demand of you, Lacedæmonians, in the punishment of
' these men, that justice to which the laws and customs of Greece, so
' nefariously violated by them, intitle us.'

Thucydides, cautious almost to extreme of offending against that
impartiality so valuable and so uncommon in a cotemporary historian,
avoids declaring any sentiment as his own upon this extraordinary
transaction ; the more important to be related in some detail, because
it was afterward but too much drawn into precedent, and because the
circumstances, and the speeches commenting upon them, tend much to
explain both the nature of the Grecian confederacy, and the ideäs,
prevailing at the time, concerning the laws of nature and of nations.
It is not indeed likely that the speeches made upon the occasion would
come very exactly reported even to Thucydides.   In what that historian therefore has given us for those speeches, as well as in what he
attributes to the Lacedæmonian commissioners as the ground of their
proceeding, he seems rather to have stated the arguments publicly
circulated by the friends of the several parties.   It appears to have been
very generally held among the Greeks of that age, that men were
bound by no duties to each other without some express compact.   The
property of foreiners might be anywhere seized, and themselves reduced
to slavery, or even put to death, without the breach of any human law ;
and not only without the breach of any divine law, but prayers were
addressed to the gods-for favor and assistance in the commission of
such violences.   Those connected with them by political or social
compact the Greeks described by a term peculiar to themselves,
ENSPONDI; meaning, originally, persons with whom they had poured
wine to the gods, or with whom they had made a compact, sanctified
by the ceremony of pouring wine to the gods : those who were bound
to them by no compact, or who had forfeited their claim to the benefit
of a compact once existing, they called ECSPONDI, out of compact, or

outlaws.

outlaws. The Lacedæmonian commissioners, upon the present occasion, determined that the Platæan people, in consequence of their renuntiation of the Lacedæmonian confederacy, and of their refusal of equitable terms offered them immediately before the siege, were ecspondi; and not only so, but they were ecspondi who had treated the Lacedæmonians and their allies injuriously. It was therefore resolved that the sentence should rest upon the answer that could be given, and supported, to the simple question first proposed. Accordingly the Platæans were again called upon, one by one, to say, ' Whether in ' the present war they had done any service to the Lacedæmonians or ' their allies ?' All answering in the negative, they were severally led aside and immediately put to death, to the number of not fewer than two hundred Platæans, and twenty-five Athenians; to whom probably this severity was extended with the less hesitation, in consequence of the late execution of the Spartan, Salæthus, at Athens. The women were condemned to slavery; the town and territory were given to the Thebans. A few Platæan refugees of the aristocratical party, together with some Megarians, whom faction had also driven from their own city, were permitted to inhabit Platæa during one year. Afterward, the lands were confiscated to the public use of the Theban state, and let to Theban citizens on leases for ten years; the town was levelled with the ground, the temples however being carefully preserved; and, adjoining to the temple of Juno, an inn two hundred feet square, something like the modern caravanserais of the East, was built with the materials. In the spirit of Grecian piety, with which revenge was congenial, and no vice absolutely inconsistent, furniture for the inn, made of the iron and brass found in the town, was dedicated to Juno; and a new temple, a hundred feet long, was erected to the same goddess. Such was the fate of Platæa in the ninety-third year from its first alliance with Athens.

SECTION V.

Sedition of Corcyra ; Operations of the Athenian Fleets under Nico-
stratus and Eurymedon, and of the Peloponnesian under Alcidas.

FROM this scene of bloodshed and desolation, such is the tenor of
Grecian history, we proceed to another still more shocking, whence
we should willingly avert our eyes, but for the more than curious information, the valuable instruction which, as from a well-imagined tragic
fable, may be derived from it.   In the iland of Corcyra, since its connection with Athens, the democratical had been the prevailing interest.
In the sea-fight with the Corinthians off Sybota, a number of Corcy-   Ch. 13. s. 3.
ræans of rank had, as we have seen, been made prisoners ; and it became   of this Hist.
immediately the policy of the Corinthian government to conciliate
these, in the hope, through them, to bring over Corcyra to the Peloponnesian confederacy, which would of course restore some portion at
least of the antient influence and authority of Corinth in the iland.
The Corcyræan nobles readily acceded to the first idea ; and possibly a   Thucyd. l. 3.
less reward than the change from a dungeon, with daily fear of death,   c. 70.
to liberty, affluence, and power, might have induced them to accede to
the second ; for to be masters of their iland, under the sovereinty of
Corinth, was likely to be for them far preferable to living under the
rod of democratical rule in the hands of their fellowcitizens.   They
were however set at liberty.   It was given out that they were bound by
sufficient pledges to pay a large sum for their ransom, but the real
ransom appeared in the sequel.   Every Corcyræan was canvassed separately for his support, in the general assembly, to a question for
renouncing the Athenian alliance, and renewing the antient connection
of Corcyra with Corinth its mother-city.   Success in this intrigue was
various ; but party soon became warm, and the whole iland was in
commotion.   The democratical leaders, in alarm, sent information to
Athens, and the Athenian government dispatched ministers to watch
over the interests of the commonwealth in Corcyra.   It happened that
ministers

ministers from Corinth arrived nearly at the same time.   An assembly
of the Corcyræan people was held in presence of both; the question
concerning the alliance was discussed; and the Corinthians so far prevailed, that, tho it was resolved to maintain the alliance with Athens, it
was nevertheless resolved to maintain peace with Peloponnesus.

How far it might have been possible for the aristocratical party to
stop there, and preserve quiet, we have not means to judge; but that
no discreet zeal directed their following measures amply appears.   A
prosecution was commenced against Peithias, chief of the democratical
party, the most powerful individual of the iland, warm in the Athenian
interest, and a public guest of the Athenian commonwealth.   The vague
accusation urged against him was, 'that he had subjected, or endevored
' to subject his country to Athens.'   The aristocratical party had so
ill considered their strength, or so ill concerted their measures, that he
was acquitted.   It was then perhaps necessary for him to ruin those
who would ruin him; and the interest which had inabled him to repel
the attack, would be likely to give him means of revenge.   He accused
five of the wealthiest of the aristocratical party of cutting stakes in the
sacred groves of Jupiter and Alcinoüs.   Superstition furnished the
crime, and party-spirit would decide upon the fact.   We have difficulty
indeed to imagine an inducement for men of wealth and rank to risk
the penalty, which was a stater, about a guinea, for every stake.   The
five were all condemned in fines, to an amount that would reduce them
to indigence.   Immediate payment or imprisonment were the alternative, to be avoided only by flight, if indeed that were now practicable,
or by taking refuge at the altars.   They chose the latter expedient,
hoping that their friends might yet obtain for them a mitigation of the
penalty.   The interest of Peithias however prevented; and, more
master in the supreme council in consequence of the absence of the
five, he procured a resolution for proposing to the people an alliance
offensive as well as defensive with Athens.   The suppliants, looking
upon their ruin and that of their party as complete if this should be
carried, in the rage of despair, quitted the altars, collected some of their
adherents, armed themselves with daggers, and rushing into the
council-hall, killed Peithias, with others, some counsellors, some private
persons,

persons, to the number of sixty. Those counsellors of the democratical party, who avoided the massacre, fled for refuge to the Athenian trireme, which lay in the harbour.

The five were no sooner thus masters of the council than they sum- Thucyd. l, 3. c. 71. moned an assembly of the people, acknowleged what they had done, and claimed merit from it, as what alone could save the commonwealth from subjection to Athens; and then immediately proposed a decree for maintaining a strict neutrality, for refusing to admit more than one ship of war at a time belonging to either of the belligerent powers, and for declaring any attempt to introduce more into any port of Corcyra an act of hostility. Their own influence was extensive, their opponents were intimidated and without a head, the decree, moderate in its purposes, was well calculated to gain in the instant the approbation of all who were not violent in party, and it was carried. Ministers were then dispatched to Athens to apologize, as far as might be, to the Athenian government for what had passed, as a measure, without forethought, produced by the crisis of the moment, and to effect a reconciliation, if possible, with the Corcyræans who had fled thither, in apprehension of the efficacy of their endevors otherwise to ingage the Athenians to interfere. Instead however of being received, at Athens, as deputed by due authority, they were apprehended as rebels, and sent in custody to Ægina.

Meanwhile the aristocratical party in Corcyra were far from being decidedly masters of the government. Incouraged by the arrival of a Corinthian ship, with ministers from Lacedæmon, they attacked, and in the moment overpowered their opponents; who however not only held the citadel, but maintained themselves in some of the higher parts of the town. Collecting then their strength, they took possession of one of the ports of the city, called the Hyllaïe. The aristocratical party held the agora and the principal port. Next day both sent detach- c. 73. ments into the country, to invite the peasant-slaves to their assistance, with promises of freedom. In this the democratical party had the greater success. The nobles on the other hand obtained eight hundred Epirot auxiliaries from the continent. In the course of the day light skirmishes passed with missile weapons.

On

On the next day but one matters were brought to a crisis. System was now in some degree restored in the conduct of the affairs of the democratical party; and leaders were become settled in command and influence, in the room of those who had been assassinated: they were superior in numbers, and, within the city, they possessed the more commanding situations. With these advantages, issuing from their quarters they attacked their opponents; and, such was the effect of party-spirit, the women took a zealous part in the action, throwing bricks and tiles from the house-tops, and supporting the tumult of battle, says Thucydides, with a resolution beyond their nature. Late in the evening the aristocratical party were compelled to yield; and fearing that their opponents, pressing upon them in their retreat, might become masters of the naval arsenal and the port, their last refuge, they set fire to all the buildings about the agora, sparing neither their own houses (for there the principal men mostly had their residence) nor those of others; so that, beside dwellings, many warehouses full of valuable merchandize were consumed; and had any wind blown toward the city, the whole would have been destroyed. The conflagration effectually checked pursuit, and prevented that immediate destruction which the aristocratical party had apprehended; but their affairs nevertheless suffered from the defection of their friends. In the night not only the greater part of the Epirot auxiliaries made their escape to the continent, but the commander of the Corinthian trireme consulted his safety by sailing away.

At the beginning of this civil war, the democratical party had sent intelligence to Naupactus, where Nicostratus son of Deïtrephes commanded the Athenian squadron. On the next day after the departure of the Epirot troops and the Corinthian ship, Nicostratus arrived in the harbour of Corcyra with twelve triremes and five hundred heavy-armed Messenians. His purpose of course was to support the democratical, which was the Athenian party; but in the present circumstances, his arrival perhaps gave greater joy to the defeated nobles, who dreaded nothing so much as the unrestrained revenge of their fellowcitizens. Nor did he deceive their expectation: proposing a.

11   treaty,

treaty, he succeeded in mediating an agreement, by which it was determined that ten only, who were named as the most guilty of the nobles, should be brought to trial, and that the rest should retain all their rights as citizens, under a democratical government. He provided then that even the selected ten should have opportunity to escape; and thus a sedition, begun with the most outrageous violence, was composed in a manner little heard of in Grecian annals, totally without bloodshed. The proposal for a league offensive and defensive with Athens was carried, as in the present circumstances might be expected, without opposition.

Nicostratus would then have returned with his whole squadron to Naupactus; but, the more completely to insure the continuance of quiet so happily restored, the democratical leaders requested that he would leave five of his ships; undertaking to supply him with as many of their own, completely manned. The magistrates, whose office it was to appoint citizens for this service, thought to gain farther security against fresh commotion by selecting many of the aristocratical party. Unfortunately a suspicion arose among these, that the pretence of service was only a feint: that the purpose was to send them to Athens; where, from the soverein people, they expected no favorable measure. Under this persuasion they betook themselves, as suppliants, to the temple of Castor and Pollux, which no assurances from Nicostratus could persuade them to quit. This extreme, and apparently weak, mistrust excited suspicion among the democratical party. Arming themselves, they broke into the houses of the nobles to seize their arms; and they would have proceeded to bloodshed, if Nicostratus had not prevented. The alarm of the aristocratical party then became universal, and four hundred took sanctuary in the temple of Juno. All the labors of Nicostratus to restore peace and harmony were thus frustrated; for mutual jealousy prevented the possibility of accommodation. While the suppliants of Juno feared assassination should they quit their sanctuary, and starving if they remained, their opponents were apprehensive of some sudden blow meditated by them. To prevent this, therefore, they proposed to remove them to a small iland not far from the shore, near which the temple stood, promising not only safety, but regular supplies of pro-

visions. The utter inability of the suppliants in any way to help
themselves, induced them to consent. The same confidence earlier
given to the oaths of their adversaries, and to the faith of the generous
Nicostratus, might have prevented the miseries that followed.

Thucyd. l. 3.
c. 76.

c. 69.

In this state things had rested four or five days, when a Peloponnesian fleet of fifty-three ships of war appeared in sight. It was commanded by Alcidas, who, on arriving at Cyllenë, with the fleet intended
for the relief of Lesbos, had found orders to go immediately to Corcyra, with thirteen additional ships, taking Brasidas for his collegue in
command. Consternation and tumult immediately spred through the
town, the party now triumphant scarcely knowing whether most to
dread the Peloponnesian armament or their own fellowcitizens. They
however obeyed Nicostratus, who, with his little squadron, quitting the
port to meet the Peloponnesian fleet, directed the Corcyræans to support him as they could get their triremes ready. Sixty were immediately launched; but they were manned with so little selection, that
as they advanced, scattered, toward the enemy, two deserted; and, in
some others, the crews went to blows among themselves. The Peloponnesians, observing their confusion, detached twenty triremes against
them, retaining thirty-five, including the deserters, to oppose the
Athenian squadron. Nicostratus showed himself not less able in
military, than prudent and humane in civil command. By superiority
in evolution, avoiding the enemy's center, he attacked one wing, and
sunk a ship. The Peloponnesians then, as in the ingagement with
Phormion off Rhium, formed in a circle. Nicostratus, as Phormion
had done, rowed round them. With twelve triremes he was thus acting
with advantage against thirty-five, when the detached squadron, which
had obtained more decisive advantage against the Corcyræan fleet,
returned to support their own. Nicostratus then retreated toward the
port, in such order as to inable the distracted Corcyræans also to reach it
without farther loss; but thirteen of their ships had been already taken.

c.77.

c.78.

c. 79.

It was now evening, and nothing could exceed the alarm and confusion in Corcyra. An immediate attack was expected from the
victorious fleet, while it was scarcely possible to be secure against the
domestic foe. The suppliants of Juno were however removed from the
iland to their former situation in the temple, more out of reach of the

Peloponnesians,

Peloponnesians, and such measures for defence of the town were taken as, in the tumult of the moment, were judged proper. But the inability of the Spartan commander-in-chief, and apparently his cowardice, uncommon as that defect was in a Spartan, were their best security. After his naval victory, instead of immediately pushing his success and profiting from the consternation of the enemy, he retired with his prizes to the harbour of Sybota. Even on the next day, the active zeal of Brasidas in vain exhorted attack upon the city; Alcidas would carry his exertion no farther than to debark some troops on the headland of Leucimnë, and ravage the adjacent fields. The democratical Corcy- Thucyd. l. 3. ræans nevertheless remained in the most anxious suspence. Their c. 80. domestic opponents were indeed completely in their power, but a superior enemy might severely revenge any severity exercised against them. It was therefore resolved to try, in a conference, to make some arrangement for mutual benefit. The body of the aristocratical party still refused all confidence to their opponents: but some, both of those who had, and of those who had not, taken refuge in the temples, less fearful, consented to serve in the fleet; and thirty triremes were manned with mixed crews, those of the aristocratical party being distributed, so as best to obviate danger from their disaffection. Alcidas however attempted no attack: about noon he reïmbarked his ravaging troops, and returned to his harbour of Sybota, where, in the evening, he received intelligence, by fire-signals, that a fleet of sixty Athenian ships of war was approaching. Immediately he got under c. 81. way; and hastening his course close under shore, as far as Leucadia, would not double the cape of that peninsula, but dragged his gallies across the isthmus, and so passed undiscovered to Peloponnesus.

No sooner were the Corcyræan people assured of the approach of the Athenian fleet and the flight of the Peloponnesian, than every dark passion mixed itself with the joy which instantly superseded their fears; and measures were deliberately taken for perpetrating one of the most horrid massacres recorded in history. The Messenians, hitherto incamped without, to oppose the forein enemy, were now introduced within the walls. The fleet was then directed to pass from the town port to the Hyllaïc port. In the way, all of the aristocratical

party

party among the crews were thrown overboard, and in the same instant massacre began in the city.   The suppliants only in the temple of Juno remained protected by that superstitious dread, which so generally possessed the Greeks, of temporal evil from the vengeance of the gods for affronts to themselves, while no apprehension was entertained for the grossest violation of every moral duty.   The fear of starving nevertheless induced about fifty of them, on the persuasion of their opponents, to quit their situation and submit to a trial.   They were all summarily condemned and instantly executed.   Their miserable friends in the sanctuary, informed of their fate, yielded to extreme despair: some killed oneanother within the temple; some hanged themselves on the trees of the adjoining sacred grove; all, in some way, put a hasty end to their wretchedness.

In the city, and through the iland, the scene of murder was not so quickly closed.   For seven days the democratical party continued hunting out their opponents, and massacring wherever they could find them.   Some had taken sanctuary in the temple of Bacchus.   Superstitious fear prevented any direct violence there, but a wall was built around the temple, and they were starved to death.   Nor was difference of political principles and political connections the only criterion of capital offence.   Opportunities for private revenge, or private avarice, were in many instances used.   Debtors cancelled their debts by the murder of their creditors; the nearest relations fell by each-other's hands; audaciousness in crime went so far that some were forced from the temples to be murdered; and some even murdered in them ; and every enormity, says the historian, usual in seditions, was practised, and even more.

The Athenian admiral, Eurymedon son of Thucles, lay in the harbour with his powerful fleet, the quiet and apparently approving spectator of these disgraceful transactions; and not till the democratical Corcyræans had carried revenge to the utmost, sailed away.   The impolicy of his conduct seems to have been equal to the inhumanity.   Nicostratus, interfering as a generous mediator, had put Corcyra into a situation to be a valuable ally to Athens.   The licence which Eurymedon gave, to massacre all who were supposed adverse to the

Thucyd. l. 3. c. 85.

Athenian

Athenian interest, had a very different effect[11]. About five hundred had escaped; some aboard the triremes which had deserted to the Peloponnesians, some on other occasions. They took possession of some forts and lands, which had belonged to the Corcyræan people, on the continent opposite to their iland; and thence, with all the activity that the spirit of revenge, the thirst of plunder, and the desire of recovering their antient possessions, united could excite, they carried on hostilities against Corcyra; seizing ships, making descents on the coast, living by depredation, and wasting whatever they could not carry off. After this experience of the weakness of their adversaries, they determined to attempt the recovery of the iland; and having in vain solicited assistance from the Lacedæmonians and Corinthians, who would no more risk their fleet against the naval force of Athens, they, with a few auxiliaries, who made their whole number only six hundred, debarked on Corcyra. The conduct of these undoubtedly brave, but apparently ill-judging men, misled by passion, remarkably supports an observation which Strabo, who lived in an age to see and to advert at leisure to the consequences, has made upon the conduct and character of his fellowcountrymen. The warmth of temper, which perpetually ingaged their whole souls in party disputes and petty quarrels, disabled them for great objects : insomuch that they were continually employing, for mutual destruction, abilities and courage, which, with more political union, might have inabled them to defend their independency for ever, against Romé, and against the world. The aristocratical Corcyræans, had they directed their views to their establishment on the soil where they had found refuge, might probably have raised a powerful city

[11] Thucydides in his manner of marking the different characters and different merits of the two Athenian commanders, offers an admirable model for writers of cotemporary history. Without any offensive remark, meerly stating facts in the simplest manner, he gives the reader fully to discover which deserved the highest praise, and which disgraced himself and his country. Nicostratus, arriving in the very height of the sedition, with only a small force, with which he had soon to cope with a very superior enemy, interfered as a generous mediator, and so efficaciously as to prevent all outrage. Eurymedon came commanding a fleet of sixty ships of war, a force that deterred opposition : he stayed seven days, during which all the enormities were committed, and he went away. This is absolutely all that the historian says of Eurymedon : but that so short a tale, with so few circumstances marked, might not escape the reader's notice, with a slight variation of words, he repeats it.

there.

there. But passion, to an extraordinary degree, still directed their measures. Immediately on landing in Corcyra, determined to maintain themselves or die, they burnt those vessels by which they had hitherto been successful and even powerful. They then occupied and fortified mount Istonë, which was certainly a prudent step; and, from that advantageous post, issuing as opportunity offered, they compelled their adversaries to confinement within their walls, and themselves commanded the country. The calamities which followed, being connected with Athenian history, will be for notice hereafter.

SECTION VI.

An Athenian Squadron sent to Sicily under Laches. End of the Pestilence at Athens. Sixth Year of the War: Operations of the Athenians, under Nicias on the Eastern Side of Greece, and under Demosthenes on the Western: State of Ætolia: Defeat of Demosthenes near Ægitium: A Peloponnesian Army sent into the Western Provinces; Ozolian Locris acquired to the Peloponnesian Confederacy: Demosthenes elected General of the Acarnanians; Battle of Olpæ; Battle of Idomenë: Important Successes of Demosthenes: Peace between the Acarnanians and Ambraciots.

The Sicilian Greeks, mostly well-disposed to the Peloponnesians, and ingaged in alliance with them, but distracted by a variety of political interests within their iland, had given no assistance in operation. War had now broken out among themselves; and toward the end of summer, after the return of Eurymedon from Corcyra, the Athenians sent a squadron of twenty ships, under Laches son of Melanopus, to assist the Leontines, an Ionian people, against the Syracusans, who were of Dorian race. The consequences did not become immediately very important; and it may be most convenient to defer all farther account of Sicilian affairs till the period when Sicily became the principal scene of military operation.

B. C. 427.
Ol. 88. 2.
P. W. 5.
Thucyd. l. 3.
c. 86.

c. 87.

In the beginning of the insuing winter, the pestilence again broke

out

out in Athens.   It had never yet intirely ceased, tho after the two first
years there had been a remission: but in the renewal of its fury it
seems to have worn itself out, and we hear of it no more.   In its whole
course it carried off not less than four thousand four hundred of those
Athenians in the prime of life who were inrolled among the heavy-
armed, and three hundred men of the higher rank who served in the
cavalry.   Of the multitude of other persons who perished by it, no
means existed for ascertaining the number.

Archidamus king of Sparta did not long outlive the friend of his
youth, whom in old age he was destined to oppose in arms, the illustrious citizen, who with more than regal sway had directed the affairs
of the Athenian democracy.   Pericles died about the beginning of the
third campain of the war.   Archidamus commanded the Peloponnesian
army which invaded Attica in the following spring; and it is the last
occasion upon which the cotemporary historian mentions him.   In the
fifth year Cleomenes, regent for the minor king of the other reigning
family, had the office of general of the confederacy; and now, in the
sixth spring, the command was given to Agis, son of Archidamus.
The forces were assembled at the Corinthian isthmus for a proposed
invasion of Attica, when the terrors of repeated earthquakes, which
affected various parts of Greece with uncommon violence, checked the
design, and the troops were dismissed.

B. C. 486.
Ol. 88 ⅔.
P. W. 6.
Thucyd. l. 3.
c. 89.

As the war drew out in length, every circumstance tended more and
more to justify the counsels which led the Athenians to ingage in it.
Notwithstanding that calamity, beyond human prudence to foresee,
which had so reduced the strength of the commonwealth; notwithstanding the loss of those talents which had prepared its resources
during peace, and directed them during the two first years of hostility;
Athens was advancing toward a superiority which promised, under able
conduct in the administration, to be decisive.   Indeed the energy of
the Athenian government, directed for near a century by a succession
of men of uncommon abilities, was so put into train, that notwithstanding the inferiority of the present leaders, it was scarcely perceived
to slacken.   Democracy, tho a wretched regulator, is a powerful
spring.   The highest offices in Athens were now open to the lowest
people.

people. Great competition of course arose; and one consequence was, that men of rank and education, however unambitious, were forced to put themselves forward in public business, that they might avoid being trodden upon by their inferiors. Thus Nicias seems to have been rather compelled by circumstances, than induced by his own inclination, to accept the situation in which he was placed. He had succeeded Pericles in the office of commander-in-chief. Plutarch says, that his cautious temper led him always to chuse commands where success might be certain, tho the glory would be small; not from any defect of personal, but of political courage; he was less afraid of the swords of enemies than of the voices of fellowcitizens. After the reduction of Lesbos he had conducted the Athenian forces against a fortified ilet, called Minoa, at the mouth of the harbour of Nisæa, the sea port of Megara. It was without much difficulty taken, and a garrison was left in it. The purpose was to prevent any future surprize, like that lately attempted upon Peiræus, and to curb more effectually the Megarian privateers; which, notwithstanding the lookout from Salamis, annoyed the Athenian trade.

In the present summer it was determined to send out two expeditions. Having recovered the principal of those dependencies in Thrace, whose revolt had given rise to the war, having checked defection in Asia by the severe punishment of the Lesbians, having learnt to despise the ravage of Attica, and, safe within their walls, possessing a navy that commanded the seas, the Athenians had leisure and means to prosecute offensive operations. Nicias, with a fleet of sixty triremes, went to the iland of Melos; whose people, a Lacedæmonian colony, tho through dread of the naval force of Athens they had avoided acting with the Peloponnesians, yet rejected the Athenian alliance, and refused to pay tribute. It was expected that the waste of their lands would have brought them to submission; but the Melians shutting themselves within their walls, with a declared determination not to treat, the tedious business of a siege was postponed for another enterprize, which had been concerted before the fleet left Attica. Passing to Oropus, on the confines of Bœotia, Nicias landed his forces by night, and marched immediately to Tanagra, where he was met by

the

the whole strength of Athens, under Hipponicus son of Callias, and
Eurymedon son of Thucles, whose conduct at Corcyra, it appears,
had not displeased the people his soverein.   The day was spent in
ravaging the Tanagræan lands.   On the following day, the Tanagræans,
reïnforced by a small body of Thebans, ventured an action, but were
defeated.   Erecting then their trophy, the forces under Hipponicus and
Eurymedon marched back for Athens, and the others to their ships.
Nicias proceeded with the fleet to the Locrian coast, plundered and
wasted what was readily within reach, and then he also returned home.
The expedition indeed seems to have had no great object. Apparently,
the principal purpose was to acquire a little popularity to the leaders,
and obviate clamor against them, by retaliating the evils of invasion
on those of their enemies who were most within reach, and by holding
out the recompense of pillage to gratify the vulgar mind.

The purpose of the other expedition was to·support the allies, and
extend the influence of Athens, in the western parts of Greece; a service
on which a squadron had been employed every summer from the
beginning of the war.   Phormion, during his command on that
station, had so indeared himself to the Acarnanians, that they particularly requested his son, or at least some relation, for his successor.   A
petition so honorable to so deserving an officer was not denied.   In the
fourth year of the war, Asopius son of Phormion was appointed to the
command of a squadron of thirty ships.   With thèse he successfully
ravaged the coast of Laconia, and then, according to his orders, sending home the greater part, proceeded with twelve to his station at
Naupactus.   Anxious, on his arrival there, to show himself worthy of
the preference given to a son of Phormion, he seems to have undertaken what his force was unequal to ; and after an unsuccessful attempt
against Œniadæ, he lost his life in an attack upon Leucas.   In the
next year we find the command committed to Nicostratus, who, with
only twelve triremes had distinguished himself so advantageously in
the Corcyræan sedition, and in action with the Peloponnesian fleet.
Thirty were now sent to Naupactus, under Demosthenes son of Alcisthenes.

Demosthenes began operations by the surprize of Ellomenus, a port

Margin notes: Thucyd. l.3. c. 91.   c. 7.   c. 91.   c. 94.

of the Leucadian territory, whose garrison he put to the sword; and then, collecting the allies of those parts, Acarnanians, Zacynthians, and Cephallenians, in addition to the Naupactian Messenians, who were in effect Athenian subjects, and obtaining fifteen triremes from Corcyra, he proceeded against Leucas itself. The Leucadians, unable to resist such a force in the field, abandoned their territory to its ravages, and confined themselves within their walls. The Acarnanians were highly desirous to reduce a city perpetually hostile to them, and situate in a manner within their country. But, before the siege could be formed, Demosthenes was allured by a more splendid, tho far more hazardous project, suggested by the Naupactian Messenians.

Ætolia was a much more formidable foe to Naupactus than Leucas to Acarnania. Always numbered among the members of the Greek nation, yet even in that age, when science and art were approaching meridian splendor in Attica, scarcely sixty miles from their borders, the Ætolians were a most rude people. Since the Trojan war, barbarism rather than civilization seems to have gained among them. They lived scattered in unfortified villages: they spoke a dialect scarcely intelligible to the other Greeks; and one clan of Thucyd. l. 3. them at least, the Eurytanian, was said to feed on raw flesh: they used c. 95. only light arms; yet their warlike character was high. The Messenians urged, that this hostile people might be subdued with the force now collected; and then nothing would remain, in that part of the continent, able to oppose the confederate arms. Not only these arguments ingaged the attention of Demosthenes, but the view which they opened led him to form a more extensive plan. Having reduced Ætolia, he thought he should be able, without other forces than those within his command, to penetrate through the Ozolian Locris, and, keeping the impassable summits of Parnassus on the right, traverse the high lands as far as Cytinion in Doris. Hence the descent would be easy into Phocis, whose people he hoped, from of old friendly to Athens, would zealously join him with their forces; for they had been withheld from the Athenian confederacy only by their situation, surrounded by the allies of the Peloponnesians; and if a party adverse to the Athenian interest should now prevail among them, he could easily

restore

restore the superiority to its friends.   Arrived in Phocis, he should
be on the borders of Bœotia; and assisted by the Phocian forces, he
could make such a diversion on the northern or western frontier of
that powerful hostile province, that, with due coöperation from Athens,
and some assistance from a party favoring democracy, which was to
be found in every Grecian state, there was no degree of success against
the enemies of the commonwealth in the northern parts of Greece, to
which it might not lead.

In the opinion of Thucydides, if we may judge from the manner of
a writer so cautious of declaring an opinion, the enterprize was ably
projected; but obstacles occurred, against the projector's hopes.   The
Acarnanians, disappointed in their own views, and offended at the preference apparently given to the Messenians, refused to join in it.   The
Corcyræans, whose government, pressed by a domestic enemy, could
ill spare any part of its strength, took the opportunity of example
for returning home.   The Cephallenians, Zacynthians, and Messenians
remained; apparently all together no great force, and the Athenian
infantry were only three hundred; but the Ozolian Locrians of
Œneon, inveterate enemies of the Ætolians, were ready to join in any
attempt against them; and their intimate knowlege of the country,
and practice in war with the people, made their assistance particularly
valuable.   The Messenians moreover, who were best acquainted with
the strength of Ætolia, and were likely to be the greatest sufferers from
a miscarriage of the undertaking, persevered in recommending it; and
Demosthenes was unwilling to give up a favorite project, with opportunities which might not recur.   It was accordingly determined that
the siege of Leucas should be postponed, and that the forces under the
Athenian general should enter Ætolia by the nearest way from Œneon,
while the Œneonians took a circuit to meet him in the interior
country.

The army of Demosthenes was so little numerous, that the whole Thucyd. l. 3.
passed a night in the precinct of the temple of Nemeïan Jupiter, on the c. 96.
borders of Locris, where, according to report current in the country,
the poet Hesiod died.   Nevertheless, no force appearing in the field
capable of opposing him, the three towns of Potidanium, Crocylium,

and Tichium, were taken in as many days; and plunder was collected to such an amount as to influence the decision of future measures.   It was sent to Eupolium in Locris, while the army remained at Tichium.

Thucyd. l. 3.
c. 97.
As soon as it was safely lodged, pursuing still the advice of the Messenians, without waiting for the Locrians, who had not yet joined him, Demosthenes proceeded to Ægitium, which was abandoned on his approach, and he took possession of the empty town.

c. 97. & l. 4.
c. 30.

l. 3. c. 96.
He was now in a mountainous and woody country, full of defiles, with his little army consisting almost wholly of heavy-armed infantry. Meanwhile the Ætolians, who had early gathered his intention from his preparations, and who, by the time he passed their frontier, had already collected their forces from the most distant parts, arrived in the neighborhood of Ægitium. Well knowing their advantage, they would come to no regular ingagement; but occupying the heights around, made desultory attacks upon the allied army in various parts, running down the hills, throwing their darts, retiring whenever the enemy advanced, pursuing when they retired, and, both in pursuit and in retreat, possessing, with their light armour, certain advantage.

Demosthenes had now to regret that he had not waited the arrival of his Locrian allies, armed like the Ætolians, and accustomed to contend with them in their desultory mode of action. As long as
c. 98.
the few bowmen of his army had a supply of arrows, wherever they could give their assistance, their weapons, of longer flight, kept off the enemy, ill armed for defence. But when, at length, all were worn with long exertion, and their arrows were nearly spent, their commander received a mortal wound, and presently they dispersed, each to seek safety as he might. The heavy-armed then, unable to stand the darts of the Ætolians, whom, with their weapons, they could not reach, had no resource but in hasty retreat. Pursued by active men, practised in running among rocks and mountains, many were killed. A Messenian, on whom they had principally depended as their guide in this wild and rough country, was among those who early fell. Some then strayed into impassable dells, and, a considerable body entering a pathless wood, the Ætolians set fire to it, and all were destroyed. Order was ow totally lost, and every form of flight and of destruction, says the cotemporary historian, was experienced
rienced

rienced by the Athenians and their allies. Procles, the second in command, was killed, with a hundred and twenty of the three hundred heavy-armed Athenians; and of all the youth of Athens who fell in the whole war, continues the historian, those were the prime. Of the allies also a large proportion were slain. The survivors, with difficulty reaching the coast, at the distance of about ten miles from the place of action, proceeded to Œneon. The bodies of the dead being obtained for burial, through the usual ceremonies, those of the Athenians were carried to Athens by the returning fleet; but the unfortunate commander, fearing to meet the anger of his soverein the Athenian people, remained at Naupactus.

A circumstance which, in the eye of dispassionate reason, must tend to justify the attempt of Demosthenes, would perhaps inhance, at least in the moment, the indignation of an ill-informed public. The Ætolians had sent three ambassadors, one from each of their principal clans, to Corinth and Lacedæmon, to request assistance against the common enemy; proposing, as their particular object, to take Naupactus, which would deprive the Athenians of their best means for keeping a fleet in the western seas. The success obtained against Demosthenes appears to have obviated former scruples, and it was resolved to gratify the Ætolians; but whether the jealousy of the kings or of the people was the obstacle, there seems to have been always a difficulty in sending out a Lacedæmonian force otherwise than under royal command. The business of Ætolia not being thought of importance enough to require one of the kings of Sparta, no Lacedæmonian troops were sent: a body of three thousand of the allies only, were toward autumn assembled at Delphi; but these were placed under the orders of three Spartans, Eurylochus, Macarius, and Menedæus. *Thucyd. l. 3. c. 100.*

c. 101.

The Ozolian Locrians, whose country lay between Delphi and Ætolia, were then in alliance with Athens. But the people of Amphissa, one of the principal towns, alarmed at the prospect of attack from the Peloponnesian confederacy, and still more apprehensive of any interest which their neighbors and inveterate enemies, the Phocians, might acquire with the Lacedæmonian commanders, proposed to Eurylochus to ingage in alliance with Lacedæmon; and assured him that he might make a readier acquisition of all the Ozolian Locris,

Locris, so little firm was it in the Athenian interest, by negotiation than by arms. The proposal perfectly suiting the views of the Spartan general, he sent ministers through all the Locrian towns. The narrow territory of the Ozolian Locris was at this time divided between no less than thirteen republics. Urged at the same time by the Peloponnesian arms, ready to fall upon them, and by both the example and the persuasion of the Amphissians, eight of these acceded to the Peloponnesian confederacy. Of the remainder, the Olpæans gave hostages as pledges that they would commit no hostility against the Peloponnesians, but refused to ingage in offensive alliance against the Athenians. The Hyæans refused even to give hostages, till the Peloponnesian forces entered their territory and took one of their villages. The Œneonians and Eupolitans persevering in fidelity to their ingagements with Athens and with their neighbors of Naupactus, their towns were

Thucyd. l. 3.
c. 102.

attacked and taken. The hostages being then sent to Cytinion in Doris, and the Ætolian forces having joined the Peloponnesian, Eurylochus entered the Naupactian territory, ravaged the whole, and took the suburbs of Naupactus, which were unfortified. Postponing then the siege of the town, he proceeded to the easier conquest of the neighboring town of Molycreium, a Corinthian colony, but long since subject to Athens.

Demosthenes, living as a private individual at Naupactus, saw with the utmost anxiety these consequences of his rash enterprize. Uncommissioned he went into Acarnania; and, tho at first ill received, he persevered in apology, remonstrance, and solicitation, till he obtained a thousand heavy-armed Acarnanians, with whom he passed by sea to Naupactus. The principal hope of taking the place having been founded on the extent of the fortifications, and the disproportionate smallness of the garrison, this seasonable reïnforcement gave it security: for blockade by land would be nugatory against a town open to the sea, of which the Athenians were masters.

The disappointment on this occasion was lessened to Eurylochus by greater views offering in another quarter. Ministers from Ambracia had solicited his assistance for the conquest of the Amphilochian Argos. Success, they urged, would be attended with the immediate
submission

submission of all Amphilochia; Acarnania might then be attacked with advantage; and the consequence, reasonably to be hoped for, would be the acquisition of all that part of the continent to the Lacedæmonian confederacy. Eurylochus acceded to the proposal, and, withdrawing his forces into Ætolia, waited there, while the Ambraciots should prepare for the execution of their part of the undertaking.

Autumn was already advanced, when a body of three thousand Ambracian heavy-armed foot entered Argeia (so the territory of the Amphilochian Argos was called) and seized Olpæ, a strong fortress upon a hill close upon the gulph, belonging to the Acarnanians, but little more than three miles from Argos.   Intelligence was immediately communicated through Acarnania, and the force of the country was assembled : part marched to the assistance of Argos, part was stationed at Crenæ in Amphilochia, to watch the approach of Eurylochus, which the motions on all sides had given reason to expect.   At the same time dispatches were sent to Aristoteles son of Timocrates, then commanding the Athenian squadron in the western seas, requesting succour; but, such was the opinion which the Acarnanians held of Demosthenes, notwithstanding his defeat in Ætolia, notwithstanding the offence they had taken at him, and while he was yet afraid to meet the judgement of the despotic multitude in his own country, in this critical moment they sent him an invitation to take the office of commander-in-chief of the forces of all the Acarnanian republics.   This remarkable fact, highly honorable to Demosthenes, proves more than that he was personally respected among the Acarnanians. - Their country was nearly equal in extent to Attica, and perhaps proportionally populous in free subjects, tho not in slaves.; but being divided among a number of village republics, no man could have either the education of Athenians of rank, or that acquaintance with public business upon a great scale, which the Athenians in office acquired.   Hence, in a great measure, the admitted superiority of the Athenians and Lacedæmonians to the other Greeks; and hence the Acarnanians felt the want of a man better educated, and better initiated in public business than any among themselves, to take, in the present moment of danger, the supreme direction of their affairs.

Thucyd. l. 3. c. 105.

Eurylochus,

Thucyd. l. 3.
c. 106.
Eurylochus, upon receiving information of the movement of the Ambraciots, crossed the Acheloüs, and hastened through Acarnania. Avoiding the towns, he passed unnoticed through the country, now deserted, the men being with the army, the women in the fortified places, till he reached Agraïs, a detached district, occupied by an Strab. l. 8.
p. 338. Ætolian tribe. Thence proceeding over an uncultivated mountainous tract, and evading thus the body of Acarnanians appointed to watch his entrance into Amphilochia, he descended by night into Argeia, passed unperceived between the town of Argos and the Acarnanian camp, and joined the Ambraciots in Olpæ. Strong with this junction, he moved next morning, and chose a situation not far distant, where he incamped.

Thucyd. l. 3.
c. 107.
Aristoteles meanwhile, with his squadron of twenty ships, arrived in the Ambracian gulph, accompanied by Demosthenes, who brought a small reïnforcement to the land-force, two hundred heavy-armed Messenians, and sixty Athenian bowmen. The whole strength of Acarnania was already collected at Argos, with only a small body of Amphilochians, of whom the greater part, friendly to the Athenian interest, were withheld by the Ambraciots. Invited by the Acarnanians only, Demosthenes was now elected commander-in-chief of all the allied forces; and the resolution was taken, by common consent, to give the enemy battle. The army in consequence moved toward Olpæ, and Demosthenes incamped on ground divided only by a deep valley from the camp of Eurylochus.

c. 107, 108.
Thus situated, both armies rested five days, and on the sixth both prepared for battle. Demosthenes had observed that the enemy outnumbered him, and, to prevent being surrounded, he placed four hundred heavy and as many light-armed Acarnanians in a hollow covered with bushes, whence they would have opportunity to attack, in the rear, that extreme of the enemy's line which would overstretch his flank. The Messenians were placed in the right, with a few Athenians, apparently from the fleet, with whom he took post himself. The Amphilochians, who were not regular heavy-armed, but used javelins, were mixed with the Acarnanians in the rest of the line: the Argians are not mentioned, few of them probably being to be spared from the

garrison

garrison of their town.   On the other side Eurylochus, with a chosen
body, took the left of his line, against Demosthenes and the Messenians: the Mantineians were posted next to him; the other Peloponnesians were mixed with the Ambraciots; who, being a Corinthian
colony, preserved the Peloponnesian arms and discipline, and were
esteemed the best soldiers of that part of the continent.

The armies meeting, the Peloponnesian left outstretching the right
of the enemy, was wheeling to attack their flank, when they were themselves attacked in the rear by the Acarnanians from the ambush.
Eurylochus was killed; the Peloponnesians about him, panic-struck,
fled; and this immediate defeat of what was reputed the firmest part
of the army, spred dismay as far as the knowlege of it was communicated.   Demosthenes profited from the opportunity, the Messenians in
particular seconding him with a valor worthy of the fame of their
antient heroes; and quickly the left and center of the enemy were
completely routed, the Mantineians only retreating into Olpæ in some
order.   But in the mean time the Ambraciots and others, who held the
right of the Peloponnesian army, had defeated the Acarnanians opposed
to them, and pursued as far as Argos.   Here however the flying troops
found refuge, while the conquerors, returning toward the field of battle,
were attacked by superior numbers, and, not without considerable loss,
joined their defeated comrades in Olpæ.   The slaughter of the Peloponnesian army altogether was very great, and, of the three Spartan
generals, Menedæus only survived.

By the unforeseen train of circumstances which led to this battle,
and much by the activity and able conduct of Demosthenes, both in
previous measures and in the action itself, the face of things was now
completely changed in the western countries; the Athenian affairs
were at once restored, as if the disaster in Ætolia had never happened;
and instead of gaining Naupactus, lately considered as the last refuge
of the Athenian interest in those parts, the Peloponnesian cause was in
a far worse situation than before any force from Peloponnesus was sent
into the country.   Menedæus, with whom the command of the defeated   Thucyd. l. 3.
army remained, was at a loss for measures.   He had force indeed   c. 109.
sufficient to defend the fortress he held, but means were wanting to

subsist there. He had no stores, and by land a victorious army, by sea
the Athenian fleet, excluded supplies. On the day after the battle
therefore, when he applied for leave to bury the dead, he sent proposals
for surrendering Olpæ, upon condition of having safe passage for his
troops to their several homes. Leave to bury the dead was readily
granted ; the rest was openly refused ; but assurance was secretly given,
that the Peloponnesians might depart in safety, if they would go quietly
and quickly. In this Demosthenes and the Acarnanian chiefs had two
objects; to have the Ambraciots, and the mercenary troops in their
service, at mercy ; and to weaken the Peloponnesian interest in those
parts, by rendering the Peloponnesian name, and particularly the Lacedæmonian, odious for self-interestedness and treachery. Menedæus
did not scruple to accept the conditions : the dead were hastily buried ;
and then the Peloponnesians, of whom the Mantineians were the largest
surviving portion, went out in small parties, under pretence of gathering herbs and firewood. The Ambraciots and others, as soon as it was
observed that all the Peloponnesians had quitted the place, and were
already at a distance, in great alarm followed, in hope to overtake
them. The Acarnanians from their camp perceiving this, without
waiting for orders, immediately pursued equally Peloponnesians and
Ambraciots ; and when their commanders interfered, some went so far
as to throw darts at them, supposing the public interest betrayed. The
matter being however at length explained, the Peloponnesians, where
they could be with certainty distinguished, were permitted to pass
unmolested. But much doubt arose, and much contention, which
were Peloponnesians ; for the Ambraciots retained so nearly the armour,
habit, and speech of their mother-country, that the discrimination was
difficult. About two hundred were killed ; the rest reached Agraïs,
whose prince, Salynthius, gave them a kind reception.

Thucyd. l. 3.   The administration of Ambracia, on receiving intelligence that their
c. 110.   troops were possessed of Olpæ, had hastened to support them with their
whole remaining strength. Ignorant of what had since passed, they
had already entered Amphilochia, when information of their march
c. 112.   was brought to Demosthenes. Immediately that general sent a strong
detachment of Acarnanian troops to preöccupy the defiles of the high-

4   lands,

lands, which the enemy must cross to enter the plain of Argeia. A few miles from Olpæ were two lofty hills, called Idomenë, at the highest of which the detachment arrived by night, unperceived by the Ambraciots, who were incamped on the other hill. Demosthenes, after having made the remainder of his army take refreshment, marched in the evening in two divisions; one of which he led himself by the plain, the other he sent over the Amphilochian mountains. About daybreak both arrived at the camp of the Ambraciots, who were still at their rest. Demosthenes had formed his advanced guard of Messenians; who, speaking the Doric dialect, deceived the Ambraciot outguards, while it was yet too dark to see distinctly, so as to pass for their own people from Olpæ. The surprize was in consequence complete, and the rout immediate. Great slaughter was made on the spot; the fugitives sought the highlands: but the roads were preöccupied by the Acarnanians of the advanced detachment; and the light-armed Amphilochians, among their own mountains, were terrible in pursuit of the Ambraciots, ignorant of the country, and incumbered with their panoply. Some who had made toward the gulph, seeing the Athenian triremes close in with the shore, swam to them; in the urgency of the moment, says Thucydides, chusing to receive their death from Grecian foes, rather than from the barbarous, and most inveterately hostile Amphilochians. As if blushing to declare in express terms their catastrophë, the historian adds no more than that a very small portion only of the defeated army escaped to Ambracia.

Next day a herald arrived from the Ambraciots, who had escaped with the Peloponnesians from Olpæ into Agraïs, for leave to bury those who had been killed on that occasion. Ignorant of what had since passed, and astonished at the number of his slaughtered fellowcitizens, whom he saw lying scattered over the country, he was so overwhelmed with grief, on being informed of the extent of the calamity, that he returned without executing his commission. During the whole war, says Thucydides, no Grecian city suffered equally, within so short a time; and could Demosthenes have persuaded the Acarnanians and Amphilochians to march immediately to Ambracia, it must have yielded to the first assault. But a just jealousy in their chiefs prevented. While

Thucyd. l. 3. c. 113.

x 2   there

there were cities, in those parts, connected with the Peloponnesians, the Acarnanians would be necessary allies to the Athenians, and would be treated with deference; but when nothing remained adverse to the Athenian interest, they would not long avoid the fate of so many other states, once allies, but now subject to the despotic rule of the Athenian Thucyd. l. 3. people.   Winter was approaching, the season of rest from warfare; so, c. 114. after dividing the spoil, of which a third was allotted to Athens, they dispersed to their several homes.   Demosthenes, no longer fearing to meet his fellowcitizens, carried with him three hundred panoplies, selected from the spoil of the enemy, in pursuance of a vote of the army, as an honorable testimony to the merit of their general, which he dedicated in the temples of Athens.

After the departure of Demosthenes and the Athenian fleet, the conduct of the Acarnanians was directed by a wise and liberal policy, of which we cannot but wish that Grecian history afforded more examples. They permitted the refugees in Agraïs to pass, under assurance of safety, to Œneiadæ, and thence to their several homes; and soon after they concluded a treaty of alliance offensive and defensive, for a hundred years, with the Ambraciots, including in it the Amphilochians; with a condition, judiciously added, that neither the Ambraciots should be bound to act offensively with the Acarnanians against the Peloponnesians, nor the Acarnanians with the Ambraciots against the Athenians: and the only concessions required were, that whatever towns or lands the Ambraciots had taken from the Amphilochians should be restored, and that the Ambraciots should not assist Anactorium in the war in which it was ingaged with Acarnania.   This wise moderation of the Acarnanians was not without its reward.   It established for a long time, in their part of the continent, not perfect peace, but more quiet than was usual among the Grecian republics; and it tended to fix upon them that character of benevolence and uprightness, by which Polyb. l. 4. we find they were long honorably distinguished, and for which they p. 299. were respected throughout the Greek nation.

SECTION VII.

*Seventh Campain: Fifth Invasion of Attica. Conquest in Sicily pro-
jected by the Athenian Administration. Pylus occupied by Demosthenes: Blockade of Sphacteria: Negotiation of the Lacedæmonians
at Athens. Cleon appointed General of the Athenian Forces:
Sphacteria taken: Application for Peace from Lacedæmon to
Athens.*

THE Athenians were now so familiarized to the invasion and waste of
Attica, and to the inconvenience of confinement within their fortifications, which experience would teach to alleviate, that the eloquence
and authority of Pericles had ceased to be necessary for persuading to
bear them.   The want of his wisdom, and the want of his authority,
were however felt in the general conduct of affairs; an authority
capable of controuling every part of the administration, and of preserving concert and consistency throughout.   While Attica was, in the
seventh year of the war, a fifth time the prey of the Peloponnesian   B. C. 425.
forces, now commanded by Agis king of Lacedæmon, the Athenians,   Ol. 88 ⅔.
                                                                      P. W. 7.
contrary to the admonition of Pericles, were looking after forein con-   Thucyd. l. 4.
quest.   Instead of meerly inabling their Sicilian allies to support   c. 2.
themselves, and preventing naval assistance to Peloponnesus from their
Sicilian enemies, the experience of their naval power led them to covet
acquisition in that rich iland, and to imagine that they might reduce
the whole under subjection.   In the winter a fleet of forty triremes had   Thucyd. l. 3.
been preparing for that service.   Pythodorus was hastened off, with   c. 115.
those first ready, to supersede Laches in the command in Sicily; and
in spring the larger number followed, under Eurymedon son of Thucles   l. 4. c. 2.
and Sophocles son of Sostratidas.   Intelligence having been received
that the city of Corcyra was reduced to extreme famine by the expelled
Corcyræans, now masters of all the rest of the iland, Eurymedon and
Sophocles had orders to relieve it, in their way to Sicily.   Those officers,
and Pythodorus also, were apparently of the ten generals of the establishment.

lishment. Demosthenes was in no office military or civil; for under
the Athenian government no military rank seems to have been held
beyond the term for which the people specifically granted it.   But he
was now become a favorite of the people; and irregularities of all kinds
seem to have been growing familiar in the Athenian government.
Without any public character, and without any military rank[12], he was
authorized to imbark in the fleet with Eurymedon and Sophocles, and,
during the circumnavigation of Peloponnesus, to employ its force, tho
those officers were present, as he should think proper[13].

No opportunity for any service, within the plan of Demosthenes, had
occurred, when, off the Laconian shore, under which description
Thucydides commonly includes the Messenian, intelligence was met
that a Peloponnesian fleet of sixty triremes had sailed from Cyllenë,
and was already at Corcyra.   Eurymedon and Sophocles, probably
never well pleased with the unusual interference in their command,
thought themselves now justified in refusing to delay their voyage for
any operations on the coast of Peloponnesus.   Demosthenes on the
contrary, claiming the authority committed to him by the Athenian
people, insisted that they should stop at Pylus on the Messenian coast;
and when that service for which he was commissioned, and which the
interest of the commonwealth required, was performed there, it would
be time enough to proceed for Corcyra.   The admirals persisted in
refusal; but it happened that a storm compelled them to seek refuge in
the very port which Demosthenes desired to make.

Thucyd. l. 4.
c. 3. et al.
Strab. l. 7.
Descr. de
la Morée
par Bellin.

The harbour of Pylus, one of the best of Greece, was at this time
deserted: the ruins only of an old castle remained, and the bordering
country, to a considerable extent, was uninhabited; for the Lacedæmonians, in conquering Messenia, had acquired what, according to
their institutions, they could little use.   Here it was the purpose of
Demosthenes to fortify some advantageous post, and place in it a garrison of Messenians from Naupactus; whose zeal in vindicating a

[12] Ὄντι ἰδιώτη.
[13] We are not accurately informed of the
nature of the joint commands, so usual in
the Athenian and other Grecian services.
Thucydides sufficiently marks that there was
a gradation, tho the inferiors appear to have
had some controuling power. The commission given to Demosthenes was of a
different kind.

possession,

possession, which they esteemed of right their own, would second his views, and whose Doric speech would give them great advantage for incursion upon the Lacedæmonian lands. Unable however to persuade the generals at all to coöperate with him, he had recourse to a very dangerous expedient, for which democracy gave licence; he applied first to the soldiers and then to the officers, but still in vain. A regular system of military command, under a democratical government, was hardly possible; and indeed due subordination appears to have been, in this age, nowhere established by law among the Greeks, excepting only the Lacedæmonians.   But the military spirit of the Greek nation must have been great, when, with subordination so deficiently inforced, and in some cases so ill understood, a regularity of conduct so generally prevailed, that would do credit to troops under the severest discipline. It happened that foul weather, continuing, prevented the departure of the fleet from Pylus; and at length the soldiers, tired of inaction, took the inclination, for amusement, to construct the proposed fort. No preparation had been made for the work, no tools were brought for it.   Loose stones, found about the spot, were carried by hand, and laid in the most advantageous manner that their accidental form and size permitted: and the interstices were filled with mud, which, for want of better means, the soldiers bore on their backs; bending, and locking their hands behind them. The fancy, thus taken, grew into zeal; all diligence was used to render the place defensible before it should be attacked, and the greater part of the circuit was strong by nature.   In six days the rest was fortified, so far that, with the crews Thucyd. l. 4. of five triremes, which the generals now consented to leave at Pylus, c. 6. Demosthenes resolved to remain, while the fleet proceeded on its destination.

When the first intelligence of these transactions arrived at Lacedæ- c. 5. mon, the people were celebrating one of those religious festivals which so much ingaged the Greeks. The news gave little alarm, but rather excited ridicule: for, confident in the superiority of their landforce, yearly experienced in the unopposed invasion of Attica, the Lacedæmonians could not immediately believe that the Athenians, through any management, could become formidable by land in Peloponnesus;

and

and a fort raised in six days, they thought, could not cost the strength of Lacedæmon much time to take and destroy. The same intelligence, however, carried to the army in Attica, made a different impression.

Thucyd. l. 4. c. 6.

After middle of May.

The invasion there, moreover, having been made earlier than ever before, the corn of the country, commonly a considerable resource for subsistence, was yet green; provisions began to fail, and the weather, unusually stormy for the season, pressed them. After a stay therefore of only fifteen days in Attica, Agis hastened back into Peloponnesus.

Thucyd. l. 4. c. 8.

It was not long before the business of Pylus began to be more seriously considered also at Lacedæmon. A fortress on their coast, occupied by an enemy commanding the sea, and garrisoned by men connected by blood with their slaves, of whom they were, not without cause, ever apprehensive, might indeed give very reasonable alarm; and the measures immediately taken in consequence, would alone go far to justify what had been deemed at first, both by friends and foes, the improvident and extravagant project of Demosthenes. Beside promoting the evacuation of Attica, Corcyra was instantly relieved, the Peloponnesian fleet being in all haste recalled thence; and, to avoid observation and consequent attack from the Athenian fleet, it was again hauled across the Leucadian isthmus. Requisitions for auxiliary troops were at the same time dispatched to all the allies within Peloponnesus; and the Spartans of the city marched for Pylus, while the Lacedæmonians of the provincial towns, just returned from one expedition, required some time for preparation to proceed on another.

The situation of Demosthenes however was highly critical. Already part of the enemy's forces were arrived, to form the siege of his little garrison, when he descried their fleet also approaching. He just saved opportunity for sending two of his triremes with dispatches to Eurymedon at Zacynthus, and presently he was blockaded by land and sea.

It became immediately the object of the Lacedæmonians to push their assaults, so as to complete their business before the Athenian fleet could arrive; and this they hoped would not be difficult, against a fort so hastily constructed, and a garrison so small. At any rate, however, they wished to avoid a naval action, and yet to keep the command of the

the harbour; and then the fort, scantily provided, and cut off from supplies, could not hold long. The harbour of Pylus, now Navarino, is a spacious bason with two entrances, one at each end of an iland, then called Sphacteria, near two miles long, uncultivated and woody. The northern entrance, near which stood the Athenian fort, barely admitted two triremes abreast; the southern not more than eight or nine. This iland the Lacedæmonians occupied with a body of troops: other troops they disposed along the shore; and both entrances of the harbour they proposed to defend with triremes, moored with their prows toward the sea. Beyond the harbour's mouth the coast was rocky and without landing-place [14].

Thucyd. l. 4. c. 8. Descr. du Golfe de Venise par Bellin.

Meanwhile Demosthenes, to make the most of the small force under his command, hauled ashore the three triremes which remained to him, and formed of them a kind of outwork against the sea, under his fort. Two small Messenian privateers had accidentally put into Pylus; and with some shields, mostly of wicker, and other sorry armour which he found aboard them, he armed the sailors from his triremes [15]. Forty heavy-armed Messenians, who had formed part of the complement of the privateers, were a more valuable addition to his garrison. In the hasty construction of his fort, he had been most careful to strengthen it toward the land, as the side on which the Lacedæmonians were generally most to be apprehended. Toward the sea it was far weaker, but then on that side it could be approached only from the sea. To resist an army and a fleet moving in concert to attack him, he selected, from his whole force, sixty heavy-armed and a few bowmen, whom he posted upon the beach to oppose debarkation, and of whom he took himself the immediate command. The remainder he appointed to the defence of the walls.

Thucyd. l. 4. c. 9.

Where soldiers are members of that assembly in which soverein power legally resides, and where persuasion may with impunity be attempted to induce them to disobey their officers, incouraging speeches previous to action may be often necessary; and to such a little band

---

[14] Ἁλίμενα.

[15] Ναύτας. Those who constructed the fort were soldiers, ςρατιῶται, but the historian does not mention what proportion there was of each.

as that with which Demosthenes had ingaged in a very arduous under-

Thucyd. l. 4.
c. 10.

taking, they would be easily addressed. ' My fellow-soldiers, and
' companions in the chance of war,' said that able officer, ' let no man
' now think to show his wisdom, by computing the exact magnitude of
' the danger which threatens us, but rather let every one cheerfully
' resolve to exert himself to the utmost, as the one thing necessary to
' the safety of us all. Nevertheless, I think, notwithstanding the
' disproportion of numbers, the circumstances are in our favor, if we
' make the most of advantages in our possession. We Athenians,
' practised in naval war, well know that debarkation in the face of an
' enemy is no easy business, if opposed with firmness. Let the Pelo-
' ponnesians then, who have not the same experience, now try it; for,
' adding the difficulties of this rocky shore, which will fight for us, I
' have no doubt of success, if we are only true to ourselves.' This
simple oratory, adapted to excite, not the boiling spirit of enterprize,
which in the circumstances might have been even injurious, but the
deliberate valor which defence requires, had the desired effect, and the
Athenians waited in due preparation to receive the attack.

c. 11.

The Peloponnesian fleet consisted of forty-three triremes, mostly of
the allies, but commanded in chief by Thrasymelidas, a Spartan [16].
While the fort was threatened on all sides, by sea and land, the principal attack was made from the fleet, precisely where Demosthenes
expected. But a few triremes only could approach at a time, and those
not without risk from the rocks and the surf. The attack was therefore carried on by reliefs, and no exhortation was omitted to promote
exertion. Some of the captains and masters [17], nevertheless, hesitating
at the view of the dangers of the shore, the Spartan Brasidas, who commanded a trireme, became presently distinguished by the Athenians,
loud in expostulation: ' Ill it became them,' he said, ' to spare their
' timbers, when the enemy possessed a post in the country : the Lace-
' dæmonians deserved better things of their allies. Striking, splitting,
' landing anyhow, they should make themselves masters of the place,
' and of the men who held it.' Brasidas was not of a disposition thus

---

[16] Ναύαρχος.

[17] Τριηράρχοι καὶ κυβερνῆται, answering precisely to our terms captain and master.

to

to exhort others without setting the example himself. Having com- Thucyd. l. 4. c. 12.
pelled his master to lay his galley close to the shore, he was stepping
upon the gangboard [18], to lead the landing, when a number of the
enemy's missile weapons at once struck him; insomuch that he fainted,
and fell backward, fortunately into the ship, while his shield, which
among the antients it was highly disgraceful and even criminal to lose,
dropped into the sea. Notwithstanding this ill success of Brasidas,
the attempt to force a landing was repeated through the whole of that c. 13.
day, and part of the next, but was resisted so efficaciously that at length
the fleet drew off. Demosthenes then, for the incouragement of his c. 12.
people, and not without just claim of victory, erected his trophy, of
which the shield of Brasidas, taken up by the Athenians, became the
honorable ornament. No stain, however, could insue to the reputation
of the owner; but on the contrary, the story being related through
Greece, it was everywhere remarked, as a singular result of the incident, that what disgraced others brought glory to Brasidas.

The Lacedæmonian commanders, hopeless now of succeeding by
assault, prepared immediately to proceed to a regular siege, and with
that view sent some ships for timber to make battering-engines. Before
these could return, Eurymedon arrived with the Athenian fleet; which,
with the junction of four Chian ships, and a reïnforcement taken from
the station of Naupactus, consisted of forty triremes. Approaching
enough to observe that the harbour of Pylus was occupied by the
enemy's fleet, and the iland before it and the shore on each side by
their army, Eurymedon withdrew, and incamped for the night on the
small iland of Protë, at no great distance. On the morrow he pre- End of May.
pared for action, determined to attack the enemy in the harbour, if
they would not meet him in the open sea.

The Peloponnesian fleet seems to have been ill commanded: the
proposed blockade of the mouths of the harbour had been omitted, and
the resolution was taken to ingage within the bason; where the confined space, and the army surrounding, it was thought, would give
advantage. But the Athenian fleet was entering unopposed by both Thucyd. l. 4. c. 14.
the mouths, while the greater part of the Peloponnesian crews were

[18] Ἐπὶ τὴν ἀποβάθραν.

but

but quitting their camp to go aboard.   Others had gotten their ships already under way; but these, seeing they should not be supported, instantly fled to the shore.   Five triremes were taken ; the crews however escaping from all except one.   The Athenians then proceeded to attack the ships upon the beach, and to haul away those from which the crews had fled.   The Lacedæmonian landforces, mortified by the disaster of their fleet, but far more alarmed for their troops in the iland, pressed down to the shore.   A fierce ingagement insued, between the Athenians from their galleys, and the Lacedæmonians dashing into the water to defend theirs.   After much bloodshed on both sides, the Lacedæmonians secured all their ships except the five first taken. With these the Athenians drew off, masters also of the enemy's dead, which they restored on the usual application from the defeated.   Eurymedon erected his trophy, and then directed his care to keep a strict watch upon Sphacteria, looking upon the Lacedæmonians there as already his prisoners.   They were four hundred and twenty, drafted by lot from the several lochi of the army, with attending Helots, whose number the historian does not mention.   These indeed were little thought of; but among the others were some connected with most of the principal families of Lacedæmon.

Thucyd. I. 4.
c. 8.

The transactions, which followed, furnish very remarkable proof of the importance of a very few citizens to the most powerful of the little republics of Greece.   Those republics were all so constituted that they could bear neither diminution, nor any considerable increase of their citizens, without inconvenience.   It was not the loss of inhabitants to the country that would be felt, tho of a small republic, when four hundred men were killed or taken ; but it was the loss of those intimately connected with the ruling powers, by ties of blood, by religious prejudices, by political prejudices, and most of all if by party prejudices. Those who formed the strength of every Grecian state for every other purpose, the slaves, could not be trusted with arms.   But the military establishment was composed of all the freemen capable of bearing arms. Losses in war therefore could be recruited only by time, which would bring boys to manhood, and by fresh births; unless the invidious and hazardous resource were admitted, of associating foreiners, or of raising

slaves

slaves to be citizens.   Of the small proportion then of the inhabitants who filled the military function, four hundred lost would affect a great number of families; and hence private passion had such influence on public measures.

Intelligence of the transactions at Pylus filled Sparta with consternation.   The men in Sphacteria had not, like the Romans, whom, we are told, their country refused to ransom, disgraced themselves by flight or by the surrender of their arms; but placed in their present situation in the accidental turn of duty, with their honor clear, they were likely to become a sacrifice to the mismanagement, or deficient exertion of those who, by more effectually opposing the Athenian fleet, ought to have preserved them from such calamitous circumstances. The principal magistrates therefore of Lacedæmon, the leaders of the administration [19], came to the camp at Pylus to assure themselves of the exact state of things; and when they were satisfied that to rescue those in the iland was impossible, it was immediately determined to enter into negotiation with the enemy, with a view to a treaty of peace. A truce was accordingly agreed upon, of which these were the conditions: ' That, as a preliminary measure, all the Peloponnesian ships of ' war which had been in the late action, and all others then in any port ' of the Lacedæmonian territory, should be delivered as pledges to the ' Athenian admiral at Pylus: That Lacedæmonian ambassadors should ' be conveyed to Athens in an Athenian trireme, to treat concerning a ' peace; and brought back again by the same conveyance: That the ' truce should hold during their absence, and that, on their return, ' the ships delivered should be restored: That, in the mean time, the ' Lacedæmonians should be permitted to supply their people in the ' iland with provisions in specified quantities, under the inspection of ' Athenian officers: That the Athenians should still keep their naval ' guard over the iland, but not land upon it; and that the Lacedæmo-' nians should send no vessel thither, but in conformity to the terms of ' the truce: That a breach of any one article of the treaty should be ' esteemed an annihilation of the whole.'

[19] Τὰ Τέλη.

The

The Lacedæmonian ambassadors [20], arriving at Athens, had a business
to manage, in itself difficult, and rendered more so by the forms of
democratical administration, and the ready jealousy of a soverein multitude.   The distress which occasioned the negotiation was peculiar to
théir own state, but in any treaty their allies must be included ; the
discussion of whose interests, before the assembled Athenian people,
could scarcely be conducted so as to avoid offence.   Before the
assembled Athenian people, however, it was necessary that some declaration should be made of the purpose of their mission.   In their speech,
therefore, they simply proposed a treaty of peace, together with an
alliance offensive and defensive between Lacedæmon and Athens, each
party keeping what it possessed; and in return for the restoration of
their fellowcountrymen, in a manner prisoners in Sphacteria, they
offered simply the glory which would redound to Athens, from a peace
solicited by those who were heretofore in a situation rather to grant
conditions, together with gratitude for a generous deed, whence might
arise that mutual goodwill between the two republics, which alone
could make a peace lasting.

Thucyd. l. 4.
c. 21.
Aristoph.
Pax et
Acharn.

It was not without probable ground for supposing the proposal would
be welcome at Athens, that the Lacedæmonian administration had
determined thus to sue for peace.   They knew that a large portion of
the Athenian people had always been averse to the war; and that a
majority of them, since they had experienced its evils, had more than
once manifested great anxiety for a conclusion of it.   But, at this
time, the favor which Cleon had acquired with the lower people, proved
an obstacle of which they could not be intirely aware.   That turbulent
orator reminded the assembly, that the Megarian ports of Nisæa and
Pegæ had once belonged to the Athenian people ; that the Athenian
people had commanded the city of Trœzen ; that all Achaia had been
of their confederacy ; and that these possessions had been wrested from
them, not in war, but by a treaty ; to the hard terms of which a calamity, similar to that which now pressed the Lacedæmonians, had
compelled them to consent.   This therefore was the time for recovering

[20] The name of the chief of the embassy, Archeptolemus, not mentioned by Thucydides, is given by Aristophanes, Equit. v. 794.

those

those possessions. It should be insisted that the Lacedæmonians in Sphacteria should be brought prisoners to Athens; to be released as soon as Nisæa and Pegæ were surrendered to the Athenians, and the administrations of Achaia and Trœzen restored to the footing upon which they stood before the thirty years truce. Accordingly such were the terms which the soverein assembly of Athens required.

To debate before a whole people concerning propositions affecting to such a degree the interests of the allies of Lacedæmon, the Lacedæmonian ambassadors judged utterly imprudent. Instead therefore of giving any answer, they desired that commissioners might be appointed to discuss the several points at more leisure than the nature of a general assembly admitted. This proposal suited the views of Cleon, only as it afforded opportunity to infuse into the people a jealousy of the ambassadors, and of those who were disposed to favor their purpose, and an opinion of his own political sagacity. He exclaimed against it, accordingly, in a style of indecent passion: 'Well he knew before,' he said, 'that the Lacedæmonian ambassadors came with injurious 'views, and for clandestine purposes; but now their refusal to declare 'themselves before the people, and their requisition to treat with a 'small number of commissioners, must make it manifest to all. If 'they had anything just and honorable to propose, they need not 'hesitate to speak it publicly.' The ambassadors, highly desirous of an accommodation upon any moderate terms, yet seeing the Athenian people impracticable through the sway which Cleon held among them, and considering the probable ill consequences of publicly proposing conditions disagreeable to their allies, which might after all be rejected, immediately took their leave.

They arrived at Pylus about the twentieth day after their departure thence, and with their return the truce of course expired. The Lacedæmonians then demanded the restoration of their ships according to the treaty: but the Athenians refused; alledging some hostility committed against the garrison of the fort, and some other matters of little importance, contrary to the strict letter of the convention, but all together, in the opinion evidently of the impartial but cautious Thucydides, not warranting a procedure so contrary to the spirit of it.

Whether

Thucyd. l. 4. c. 22.

c. 23, & 39. End of June.

Whether Demosthenes or Eurymedon was the principal actor in this business, we are not informed; but in favor of either it may be observed, that to exercise any discretionary power was extremely hazardous, when responsibility was immediate to that despotic and wayward soverein the Athenian people, under the influence of Cleon. If Cleon, or any other turbulent orator, could persuade the people that their generals ought not to give up, of their own authority, any advantage that the letter of the treaty warranted, their utter ruin, even capital condemnation, might have been the consequence of a contrary conduct.

Both parties now prepared to prosecute hostilities with vigor. The Athenians directed their attention particularly to the guard of Sphacteria: two triremes were constantly circumnavigating it during day, and at night the whole fleet kept watch; in moderate weather all around the iland; but fresher winds induced the necessity of leaving the side toward the sea unguarded. A reinforcement of twenty triremes from Attica made the number of the fleet seventy.

The Peloponnesians meanwhile pushed the siege of the fort. But the object for which the Lacedæmonians were most anxious was to relieve their people in Sphacteria; and what they chiefly apprehended for them was famine. Large rewards were therefore offered, freedom to Helots, and money to any freemen, who would introduce provisions. Many were thus allured to the attempt; and tho some were taken, some succeeded; especially in blowing nights, when the Athenian triremes could not hold their station at the back of the iland. Some supply was also carried by divers, who swam under water across the port, rising occasionally only for air, and dragging after them skins filled with bruised linseed, or with poppyseed mixed with honey.

The blockade of the iland being thus protracted, the Athenians began to suffer those very wants through which they had hoped to compel the Lacedæmonians to surrender. In their fort was one small spring, ample for the garrison, but very inadequate to the supply of the whole armament; the greater part of which was reduced to the use of brackish water, obtained by digging in the sand under the fort. All the rest of the coast was possessed by the superior landforce of the Peloponnesians; and

Thucyd. l. 4. c. 26.

and the triremes, far from capable of carrying supplies for any length of time, had not convenient room even for their crews to sleep or to eat aboard; insomuch that Thucydides mentions it, among their hardships upon this occasion, that they went ashore by reliefs for their meals, living otherwise aboard their triremes at anchor.

The uneasiness hence arising in the fleet and army was ere long communicated to Athens, and reasonable apprehension arose that approaching winter would increase the difficulties; that it would become impossible to supply the armament with provisions by the navigation round the capes of Peloponnesus, which in summer they found could not be done in the requisite extent; and that, even if supplies could be obtained, the fleet could not remain, during the stormy season, on a coast where they possessed no port.   It was then farther considered, that, if the Lacedæmonians should recover their people from Sphacteria, not only an opportunity for making an advantageous peace was lost, but future opportunities were precluded : at least the first proposal must hereafter come from themselves; for the Lacedæmonians would scarcely risk the disgrace of a second refusal.

Thucyd. l. 4.
c. 27.

Public indignation was rising fast against Cleon, as the evil counsellor of the commonwealth, and author of the evils felt or apprehended. He found it necessary, for obviating popular clamor and disgust, to exert himself in the assembly; and in a very extraordinary train of circumstances that followed, his impudence and his fortune (if, in the want of another, we may use that term) wonderfully favored him.   He began with boldly insisting, ' that the circumstances of the fleet and ' army were not so adverse as they were reported.'   This assertion called forward the officers who brought the intelligence: they desired ' that, if they were thought unworthy of belief, proper persons might ' be sent to examine into the state of things.'   The assembly assented to this request, and Cleon himself was named among those to be commissioned for the purpose.   Pressed by this proposal, which he was aware would not answer his end, and anxious anyhow to throw the weight of the business upon others, he seems in the moment to have lost his guard.   ' It were idle waste of time,' he said, ' to send com- ' missioners to inquire, when they should rather send generals to

'execute. If those who directed the military affairs of the com-
'monwealth were men, it would be easy, with the force which they
'could at all times command, to subdue the little band in Sphacteria:
Thucyd. l. 4.
c. 28.
'were he in that station, he would ingage to effect it.' The unenter-
prizing Nicias, at this time commander-in-chief, being thus called
upon, in his anxiety to obviate crimination, miserably betrayed the
dignity of his high office. 'As far as depended upon him,' he said,
'Cleon might take what force he pleased, and make the attempt.'
Cleon immediately accepted the offer, thinking it not seriously made;
but Nicias persisting, Cleon would have retracted, saying, 'Nicias,
'not he, was general of the republic.' Nicias however, observing that
his proposal had not displeased the people, declared solemnly before the
assembly, that for the business of Pylus he waved his right to command. The more then Cleon appeared still anxious to withdraw, the
more the people, as the historian observes, in the usual temper of
mobs[21], insisted that he should make his words good; with clamor
requiring that Nicias should resign the command, and that Cleon
should take it. Thus appointed general, Cleon, tho alarmed with the
danger, was elated with the extravagant honor; and in the next
assembly held on the business[22], he resumed his arrogant manner: 'He
'did not fear the Lacedæmonians,' he said; 'and for the expedition
'to Pylus, he would desire no Athenian forces: he would only take
'the Lemnian and Imbrian heavy-armed, at that time in Attica, with
'the middle-armed of Ænus, and four hundred bowmen of the allies;
'and with that small addition to the armament then at Pylus, he
'would, within twenty days, either bring the Lacedæmonians in
'Sphacteria prisoners to Athens, or put them to the sword upon the
'spot.' Amid the many very serious considerations involved with the
business, this pompous boast excited a general laugh in the assembly:
yet even the graver men, says the historian, were upon the whole
pleased with the event, upon considering that of two good things
one must result; either an important advantage must be gained over

[21] Ὁῖον ὄχλος φιλῖ σοιεῖν. Thucyd. l. 4. c. 28.
[22] Thucydides does not specify that it was in a second assembly; but from the circumstances, and from the tenor of his narrative, it should seem that it must have been so.

the

the Lacedæmonians, or, what they rather expected, they should be finally delivered from the importunity of Cleon.

It however soon appeared, that tho, for a man, like Cleon, unversed in military command, the undertaking was rash and the bragging promise abundantly ridiculous, yet the business was not so desperate as it was in the moment generally imagined; and in fact the folly of the Athenian people, in committing such a trust to such a man, far exceeded that of the man himself, whose impudence seldom carried him beyond the controul of his cunning. He had received intelligence Thucyd. l. 4. that Demosthenes had already formed the plan, and was preparing for c. 29. the attempt, with the forces upon the spot or in the neighborhood. Hence his apparent moderation in his demand for troops; which he judiciously accommodated to the gratification of the Athenian people, by avoiding to require any Athenians. He further showed his judgement, when the decree was to be passed which was finally to direct the expedition, by a request, which was readily granted, that Demosthenes might be joined with him in the command.

The natural strength of Sphacteria, uneven, rocky, woody, together with ignorance of the enemy's force there, had long deterred Demosthenes from attempting any attack; and the more, because his misfortune in Ætolia had arisen from incautiously ingaging himself in a rough and wooded country, against unknown numbers. But it had happened that a fire, made by the Lacedæmonians for dressing their provisions, had accidentally caught the woods, and, the wind favoring, had burnt almost the whole. Their best defence being thus destroyed, Demosthenes, now inabled to see his enemy and his ground, no longer hesitated concerning measures. He had sent for such reïnforcements as might be obtained from the nearest allies, but before they could join him Cleon arrived.

Demosthenes himself had been appointed to an anomalous command, interfering with the authority of the regular generals of the commonwealth; and it does not appear that he made any difficulty of yielding to the wayward will of his soverein, and taking the second rank in the command with Cleon. When the new general arrived at Pylus with his reïnforcement, it was determined first to try if their business could

not

not be managed by negotiation; and a message was accordingly sent to the commander-in-chief of the Lacedæmonian army, proposing that the men in Sphacteria should surrender themselves prisoners, with the condition, that they should be liberally treated in confinement, till the two republics might come to some accommodation.

Thucyd. l. 4. c. 31.

This being refused, Cleon and Demosthenes prepared to use the force under their command. Giving one intire day of rest to their troops, on the next, at night, they imbarked all their heavy-armed, who were only eight hundred, and, a little before dawn, landed at the same time on both sides of Sphacteria, from the harbour and from the open sea. An advanced post of the Lacedæmonians was surprized, and the guard

c. 31—32.

put to the sword. As soon as day broke, the rest of the forces were landed, consisting of eight hundred bowmen, about as many middle-armed, a few Messenians and others from the garrison of the fort, and, except the rowers of the lowest bench, distinguished by the name of thalamians, all the seamen of the fleet; who, as the triremes were more than seventy, would be a large body. The force all together was not of the most regular kind, but it was ample against those who held Sphacteria; of whom the Lacedæmonians, the only regular troops, had been originally but four hundred and twenty, and thirty of those were killed in the outpost. Of the number of attendant slaves, and of those who, after landing provisions, may have remained in the iland, we are not informed. Epitadas, the commander, had posted himself, with his main body, in the central and plainest part, near the only spring the iland afforded. A small reserve he placed in an antient fort, of rude construction, but strong by situation, at the extremity next Pylus.

The Lacedæmonians, and indeed all the Peloponnesians, seem to have been absurdly attached, through a point of honor, to the exclusive use of weapons for close fight. Among the early Greeks, the first purpose of arms, after self-defence, was to defend their cattle: the second, when civilization advanced, to protect their harvest and cultivated fruits: the third, and not least important, to hold a secure superiority over their numerous slaves. Hence, as well as because of the more determined courage requisite for the use of them, and of their greater efficacy in the hands of brave and able men wherever they can

4   be

be used, arms for stationary fight in plains were deemed more honorable than missile weapons.   But as, under many circumstances, especially in mountainous countries, like the greatest part of Peloponnesus
and of all Greece, it was easy to evade the force of the heavy-armed,
and yet to give them annoyance, we find the Lacedæmonians often
suffering for want of light troops and missile weapons.   Epitadas chose,
with his little band, to meet an enemy who so outnumbered him, in
the levellest part of the iland ; not only because the fountain there was
necessary to him, but because there the weapons and the discipline of
his people would be most efficacious.   But among the Athenians, tho
the first honor was given to the panoply, yet the use of the bow was
cultivated ; and we find the Athenian archers frequently mentioned as
superior troops of their kind.   Demosthenes had been taught by misfortune both how to value light troops, and how to use them ; and
Cleon's prudence left him the direction of operations.   He placed
his light-armed in detached bodies of about two hundred each, on
the heights around the Lacedæmonian station, and then, advancing
with his heavy-armed within a certain distance of the front of it, he
halted.

Epitadas did not refuse to meet superior numbers; but, as he   Thucyd. l. 4.
advanced to attack Demosthenes, he was assailed on each flank and   c. 33.
in his rear with darts, arrows, and stones.   If he turned, those who thus
annoyed him instantly fled from his attack, and his heavy-armed would
in vain pursue them ; but the moment he resumed his march toward
Demosthenes, they renewed their annoyance.   Such was the character
of the Lacedæmonian heavy infantry at this time in Greece, that with
all the advantage of numbers on their side, the light-armed of the
Athenian army had not approached them without awe, and, as Thucydides expresses it, a kind of servile apprehension.   But, incouraged by
the effect which their first wary exertions derived from the able disposition of Demosthenes, and by the evident inability of the Lacedæmonians for efficacious pursuit, the light-armed pressed their attacks.
This desultory manner of action astonished the Lacedæmonians with
its novelty : the ashes and dust, formed by the late conflagration,
rising

rising and mingling their darkness with that of the constant flight of
missile weapons, disabled them from seeing their enemy, whom with
their arms they could not reach, if they could see; while the clamorous
noise of the irregular assailants drowned the voice of command.
Utterly at a loss for means of effectual opposition, when many were
already severely wounded, they retreated in a compact body toward
their reserve in the castle, which was not far distant. The light-armed
then pressed their assault with increased ardor: the Lacedæmonians
gained the fort, but not without loss.

Thucyd. l. 4.
c. 35.

The efficacy of the light troops being now obviated, Demosthenes
led his heavy-armed to the attack; but the Lacedæmonians having
great advantage of ground, as well as some defence from the old walls,
maintained an equal conflict against superior numbers. It was already
late in the day; both parties were suffering from heat, thirst and
fatigue, and neither had any prospect of decisive advantage, when the
commander of the Messenian troops coming to Cleon and Demosthenes,
told them he had discovered a way by which, with a party of light-
armed and bowmen, he thought he could scale the fort. The party he
desired being accordingly put under his orders, he led them, so as to
avoid being seen by the enemy, to a precipitous part of the rock,
where, through confidence in the natural strength of the place, no
guard was kept. Climbing with great difficulty, he made his way
good, and appeared suddenly on the summit. Effectual resistance was
now no longer possible for the Lacedæmonians, worn with incessant
action through a sultry day, and surrounded by superior numbers.
Cleon and Demosthenes therefore, desirous of carrying them prisoners
to Athens, checked their troops, who would shortly have put them to
the sword; and sent a herald to offer quarter, upon condition that they
should surrender themselves to the mercy of the Athenian people. It
was doubted whether, even in their hopeless situation, Lacedæmonians
would submit to become prisoners; but as soon as they saw the heralds
approaching, they grounded their shields and waved their hands, inti-
mating that they were disposed to hear proposals. Epitadas was no
more; Hippagretes, his second in command, had been so severely
wounded

c. 36.

c. 37.

wounded that he lay for lifeless among the slain; Styphon, on whom the command had thus devolved, desired permission to send a herald to the Lacedæmonian army on the continent for orders. This was refused, but the Athenian generals sent for a herald from the Lacedæmonian army; and after the interchange of two or three messages, a final answer came to the garrison of the iland in these terms : 'The 'Lacedæmonians permit you to consult your own safety, admitting nothing disgraceful [23].' After a short consultation, they then surrendered, according to the Greek expression, their arms and themselves.

On the morrow the commanders of the Lacedæmonian army on the continent sent a herald for their slain, and the Athenians erected their trophy. The killed were a hundred and twenty-eight Lacedæmonians, and the prisoners two hundred and ninety-two. Of the fate of the Helots and others, who were with the Lacedæmonians in Sphacteria, we have no information. The blockade, from the action in the harbour Thucyd. l. 4. to that in the iland, had continued seventy-two days, including the c. 39. truce of twenty days, during which the garrison was regularly served with provisions. For the rest of the time they had only had such casual supplies as could be introduced by stealth; yet, such had been the economy of Epitadas, provisions remained when the iland was taken. The Athenian commanders, leaving a sufficient garrison in Pylus, sailed away with the fleet; Eurymedon with his division for Corcyra and Sicily, and Cleon and Demosthenes for Attica: and the Toward the ingagement of Cleon was completely fulfilled; for they entered the end of August. port of Peiræus with their prisoners within twenty days after he had quitted it.

Nothing during the whole war, says Thucydides, happened so con- Thucyd. l. 4. trary to the general opinion and expectation of the Greeks as this c. 40. event; for it was supposed that neither hunger, nor the pressure of any other the severest necessity, would induce Lacedæmonians to surrender their arms; insomuch that among some it was doubted whether the prisoners were of the same race, or at least if they were of equal rank

[23] Μηδὲν αἰσχρὸν ποιεῦντας.

with

with their comrades who had been killed.   Hence an Athenian auxiliary, with more ill manners than wit, asked one of the prisoners,
Thucyd. l. 4.
c. 40.
' Whether those who fell in the iland were the men of superior rank
' and merit [24] ?' To which the Spartan coldly replied, ' An arrow
' would indeed be a valuable weapon, if it could distinguish rank and
' merit.'

The prisoners, being many of them connected with the first families
of Sparta, were considered by the Athenians as most valuable pledges.
c. 41.
It was determined, by a decree of the people, that they should be kept
in chains [25] till the two republics should come to some accommodation,
unless any invasion of Attica should be attempted by the Peloponnesians.   In that case the decree declared, in terror to the Lacedæmonian
public, that they should be put to death.   Such were at that time
the maxims of warfare among those who boasted to be the most
civilized, and indeed the only civilized people upon earth; and such
the motives for preferring death in the field to the condition so mild,
in modern Europe, except in France since the revolution, of a prisoner
of war.

By the event of the business of Pylus the Lacedæmonians were in a
state of distress totally new to them.   From the first establishment of
their ancestors in Peloponnesus, it was not known by tradition that
such a number of their citizens had fallen into the hands of an enemy;
and it was as little remembered that an enemy had ever possessed a
post within their country.   Pylus was now so fortified that, as long as
it was open to supplies by sea, no mode of attack by land, with which
the Lacedæmonians were acquainted, would be effectual against it:
a garrison of Messenians from Naupactus infested the neighboring
country with continual incursions; and the Helots, deserting in numbers, found sure protection.   In this situation of things, the Lacedæmonian government, anxiously desirous of peace, expected only insult
from the haughty temper of their enemy, should they send ministers
publicly to propose terms.   They made, however, repeated trials by

[24] Καλοί καγαθοί: a phrase which cannot be exactly translated.
[25] Δισμοῖς.

secret

fecret negotiation. The wiser and more moderate Athenians, and those of higher rank in general, would gladly have profited from present prosperity, to make an advantageous accommodation.   But the arrogance of the people, fed by success, and inflamed by the boisterous eloquence of Cleon, now the popular favorite, made all endevors for the salutary purpose fruitless.

CHAPTER XVI.

Of the PELOPONNESIAN WAR, from the Application for PEACE from LACEDÆMON in the seventh Year, to the Conclusion of PEACE between LACEDÆMON and ATHENS in the tenth Year.

SECTION I.

Expedition under Nicias to the Corinthian Coast. Conclusion of the Corcyræan Sedition. Embassy from Persia to Lacedæmon. Lacedæmonian iland of Cythera, and Æginetan Settlement at Thyrea, taken by the Athenians. Inhumanity of the Athenians.

IF, stopping for a moment at this point of Grecian history, we turn our view back to past transactions, as reported by the impartial pen of the cotemporary historian, we cannot but admire the able policy, the clear foresight, and the bold firmness of him who has by fome writers, antient and modern, been traduced as the wanton author of this, in the end, unfortunate war, the all-accomplished Pericles; and if we take any interest in the fate of Athens, or of Greece, we cannot but regret that he was not yet living to conduct to a conclusion the scene of bloodshed, through the opportunity which now offered, and to exert his capacious mind toward the establishment of a political union, which might have given stability to peace through the country. What might have been done, had Pericles and his virtuous and venerable friend the Spartan king Archidamus met in such a crisis, we might amuse ourselves, perhaps not unprofitably, with imagining, were we to take into the consideration all the circumstances of the times, as they remain reported by Thucydides, and illumined with no inconsiderable collateral light, by other cotemporary and nearly cotemporary writers. After the general abolition of kingly power, so fair an opportunity certainly never occurred for carrying into effect the noble

3   project,

project, said to have been conceived, and even attempted by Pericles, Plut. vit. Pericl. of a federal union of the Greek nation, which might prevent hostility within itself, and afford means of united exertion against forein enemies. But the desire simply of keeping peace at home, perhaps never led to such a union among any people: some pressure of a forein power is wanting; some overbearing neighbor, or a general superiority of force in surrounding states.   No such pressure at this time bore upon Greece.   Persia had ceased to give alarm: Macedonia was not yet formidable: Carthage had small inducement to turn her views to a country, where war was so well understood, and riches so little abounded: the name of Rome was scarcely known.   The little republics therefore of Lacedæmon and Athens, judging from experience of the past, for they were not always led by the capacious mind of a Pericles, vainly supposed themselves equal to resist any power ever likely to arise upon earth; an opinion indeed generally entertained, as the writings of Plato and Aristotle prove, even among the ablest politicians of the time; and tho Xenophon was aware of their error, yet he was not aware of any good remedy for the weakness of the antient republics, and the defects of the political system of Greece.

Under the controul of Cleon, the Athenian government was not likely to be distinguished for moderation; and the fortunate event of that adventurer's late presumptuous undertaking, increasing his favor with the people, would not lessen his own arrogance.   The conduct of the war moreover, on the part of the Athenians, was so far rendered easy, by the decided superiority which their fleet possessed, and by the pledges in their hands, which secured them from invasion, that they might chuse their measures.   Any very consistent plan, as in the present circumstances of their administration it was not very likely to be formed, so it was not absolutely necessary to success.   Passion seems to have dictated their next undertaking: they would take revenge on Thucyd. l. 4. c. 42. B. C. 425. Ol. 88. 4. P. W. 7, September. the Corinthians, the first instigators of the war, and, upon all occasions, the most zealous actors in it.   A fleet of eighty triremes was equipped, and a landforce imbarked, consisting of two thousand Athenian heavy-armed foot and two hundred horse, with the auxiliary troops of Miletus, Andrus, and Carystus.   Nicias commanded.   The armament, proceed-

ing

ing up the Saronic gulph, made the shore between Chersonesus and
Rheitus, scarcely eight miles from Corinth.   The Corinthians, apprized
of its destination by intelligence from Argos, had already assembled
the whole force of their Peloponnesian territory, except five hundred
men absent on garrison duty in Ambracia and Leucadia, and they
marched to oppose the expected debarkation.   But Nicias, moving in
the night unobserved, landed his troops near Chersonesus.   The Corin-

Thucyd. 1. 4.
c. 43.
thians, quickly informed by signals, hastened thither with half their
forces, leaving the other half at Cenchreæ, for the security of the
neighboring coast and country.   A very obstinate action insued, in

c. 44.
which, after various efforts, and some turns of fortune, the exertions of
the Athenian horse decided the event of the day.   The Corinthian
general being killed, with two hundred and twelve heavy-armed, the
rest of the army, distressed for want of cavalry to oppose the Athenian,
retreated, but in good order, to some strong ground in its rear.   The
Athenians stripped the enemy's dead, and erected their trophy.   The
honor of victory thus was clearly theirs, but the advantage gained was
otherwise small: they dared not await the junction of the forces from
Cenchreæ with the defeated army; and the less, as all the elders and
youths in Corinth were besides hastening to join it, and ere long the
neighboring allies would come in.   Nicias therefore reïmbarked his
forces in such haste, that he left behind him two of his dead, who had

Thucyd.
ibid.
Plut. vit.
Nic.
not been immediately found.   Apprehensive then of the clamor and
popular ill-will to which this might give occasion, he sent a herald to
the Corinthians to request the bodies; and thus, according to Grecian
maxims, surrendered the honor of the trophy, and all claim to the glory
of victory.

But the decided command of the sea, which the Athenians possessed,
gave them means to distress their enemies greatly, with little risk to
themselves.   The antient ships of war were singularly commodious for
operations upon a coast; moving any way in any wind, if not too fresh;
and for debarkation and reïmbarkation, wanting no intervention of

Thucyd. 1. 4.
c. 45.
boats.   While the Corinthians were assembling all their forces in the
neighborhood of Chersonesus, the Athenians moved to the coast beyond
Cenchreæ, now unguarded; and debarking near Crommyon, plundered
the

the adjacent country, incamped for the night, and reïmbarking early in the morning, were thus at once secure from the revenge of the Corinthian arms.   They then proceeded to the Epidaurian coast, and seizing Methonë, a town on a small peninsula between Epidaurus and Trœzen, they raised a fortification across the isthmus.   The fleet then returned home ; but a garrison, left in Methonë, carried depredation, as opportunity offered, through the Trœzenian, Epidaurian, and Halian lands.

The close of this summer brought the tragedy of the Corcyræan sedition to a conclusion.   Eurymedon and Sophocles, according to their instructions, making Corcyra in their way from Pylus to Sicily, debarked their forces, and, with the Corcyræans of the city, stormed the fort on mount Istonë, held by the aristocratical Corcyræans ; most of whom, nevertheless, escaped to a neighboring eminence, so difficult of approach that it was inexpugnable.   Being however without means to subsist there, they were soon obliged to surrender ; their auxiliaries to the discretion of the besieging army, and themselves to that of the Athenian people.   Eurymedon and Sophocles, unwilling to give to others the triumph of leading their prisoners into Athens, and to lose the popular favor which attaches strongly in the moment, but is presently diverted by new objects, placed them in the adjacent little iland of Ptychia, as on their parole ; with the condition, that if anyone should attempt escape, the benefit of the capitulation should be forfeited for all.   The atrociousness of what followed would be beyond belief, if it came attested by less authority than that of Thucydides [1].   The chiefs of the democratical Corcyræans feared that their fellow-citizens of superior rank, were the Athenian people to decree the doom, tho the Athenian people were not always remarkable for mercy, might yet escape death.   They devised therefore a fraud to seduce them to their own destruction.   Persons likely to find confidence were employed to infuse apprehension that the Athenian generals intended to deliver them to the Corcyræan people; offering at the same time to provide a vessel in which they might escape from what

[1] This was written before the transactions in France had beggared all ideas formerly conceived, among the modern European nations, on such subjects.   The reader who has met with information of what passed at Lyons, after its surrender to the republican arms, will be struck with the similarity of some principal circumstances.

they

Thucyd. l. 4.
c. 47. they so beyond all things abhorred. The prisoners gave into the snare, and were taken in the ship. The capitulation was undeniably broken, and the Athenian generals surrendered the wretched remains of the Corcyræan nobility, if we may use the term, to the pleasure of their people. These then resolved that their revenge should be completed, and that as far as might be consistent with public order, the utmost indulgence for that passion should be allowed to every individual among the soverein multitude. The prisoners were placed all in one large building. The people, in arms, formed a lane at the door. Twenty of their unfortunate adversaries, bound together, were brought out at a time. Men with scourges drove on any that hesitated, while the armed citizens selected for revenge those to whom they bore any ill-will, cutting and stabbing as the passion of the moment excited.

c. 48. Sixty had been thus killed, when the rest received intimation of what had been passing. Calling then aloud to the Athenians to put them to death, if such was their pleasure, they declared they would neither go out of the building, nor permit any to come in. The people, not to encounter their despair, got upon the roof, and taking off the covering, thence in safety discharged missile weapons. The prisoners endevored at first to defend themselves; but when night came on, no symptom appearing of any relaxation in the animosity of their enemies, they determined to put the finishing stroke to their own misery: some strangled themselves with the cords of some beds which were in the place, some with strips of their own clothes, some used the weapons which had been discharged at them. When day broke, all were found dead. The corpses, heaped upon waggons, were carried out of the city, and disposed of without any of those funeral ceremonies which, among the Greeks, were held of such sacred importance. Eurymedon, after the completion of this abominable scene of treachery and cruelty, prosecuted his voyage for Sicily.

c. 49. The taking of Anactorium finished the successes of the Athenian arms, and the operations of the war, for the summer. Being attacked by the Athenian force from Naupactus, in conjunction with the Acarnanians, it was betrayed into their hands. The inhabitants, a Corinthian colony, underwent no severer fate than expulsion from their settlement,

and

and the loss of all their property.   Their houses and lands were occupied by a new colony drawn from the several towns of Acarnania.

From the beginning of the war, intrigue had been carrying on by the Lacedæmonian government with the court of Persia; and that court, it appears, was not disposed to disdain negotiation with a little Grecian republic: but the distance, the difficulty and danger of communication, difference of manners, and contrariety in maxims of government, pride on both sides, and some apprehension, on that of Lacedæmon, of the superior weight of the Persian empire, had prevented any treaty from being brought to a conclusion.   In the autumn following the affairs of Pylus and Corcyra, while an Athenian squadron, sent under the command of Aristeides son of Archippus to collect tribute, lay at Eion upon the Strymon, Artaphernes, a Persian, was apprehended there; and, his writings being seized and translated, it appeared that he was commissioned by the king of Persia, Artaxerxes, as his minister to Lacedæmon; that the purpose, or at least the pretence of his mission, was to bring to effect a treaty of alliance with that state; and the reason was found alledged, that, of several ministers who had passed from Lacedæmon into Persia, no two had carried the same proposals. Apparently, however, the principal object of the Persian court was to examine into the state of things in Greece; for Artaphernes was not to conclude any treaty, but only to conduct into Persia ministers from Lacedæmon, sufficiently authorized to treat for their commonwealth. Aristeides immediately forwarded this important prisoner to Athens. The Athenians had not hitherto solicited any alliance with Persia; yet they were anxious not to embroil themselves with that powerful empire, while they were ingaged in war with Peloponnesus.   They would not however permit the minister to proceed to Lacedæmon.   He was conveyed to Ephesus, and ambassadors from the Athenian people were appointed to attend him to the Persian court.   But, on their arrival in Ionia, news of the death of Artaxerxes met them, and such troubles followed in the empire, that without proceeding farther, they returned to Athens.

Spring

Thucyd. l. 4.
c. 50.

After 24
Sept.
P. W. 7.
Ol. 88. 4.
B. C. 425.

B. C. 424.   Spring advancing, the Lacedæmonians, depressed by their misfor-
Ol. 88 4.   tunes, remained inactive ; but in Athens, while many were still desirous
P. W. 8.   of peace, the more restless and ardent spirits prevailed, and it was
determined to push success, and press the Peloponnesians on all sides.

Thucyd. l. 4.   The iland of Cythera was a very important appendage of the Lacedæ-
c. 53.   monian dominion ; the possession of it was particularly advantageous
for securing the Laconian and Messenian coast against piratical depredation ; and it was commodious for the purpose of such communication with the fertile regions of Africa, as the wants of Sparta might
occasionally require, and its institutions would permit. The lands
were all possessed by Lacedæmonians ; the government was administered by a magistracy sent annually from Sparta ; and a Spartan
garrison was constantly kept there. Against this iland an armament
of sixty triremes, with two thousand heavy-armed Athenian foot, a
small body of horse, and a considerable force of auxiliary troops, sailed
c. 54.   under the command of Nicias and Autocles. The garrison and inhabitants were quickly compelled to surrender, without any condition
but for their lives only.

c. 55.   The alarm which this event occasioned in Lacedæmon, and the
measures taken in consequence, mark, not so much the want of force
in the hands of the Lacedæmonian government, as the want of ability
to direct it. Descents upon the Lacedæmonian coast were expected,
but where they would be attempted could not be foreseen. Their great
legislator seems to have been well aware that a moving force may be
more effectual for the protection of a country than any fortifications,
since he forbad that Sparta itself should be fortified. In opposition to
this maxim, they now divided their strength in forts and strong posts,
through the length of their winding coast. The consequence was,
that the Athenians could land anywhere without risk ; they wasted
the lands at pleasure ; and having defeated the only small body of
troops that rashly ventured to oppose them, they erected their trophy,
and returned to Cythera. An Ionian trophy in Laconia was a thing
unknown before, since the establishment of the Dorians in the country ;
and tho the consequence of the defeat was otherwise trifling, the fame
of the event made a strong impression through Greece, and the Lace-
daemonians

dæmonians felt severely the injury to their reputation.   The Athenians Thucyd. l. 4. c. 56.
then sailing again from Cythera, after ravaging a part of the Epidau-
rian coast, proceeded to take their last revenge of the unfortunate
Æginetans, now established at Thyrea, within the territory and under
the immediate protection of Lacedæmon.   Thyrea was situated, like
most of the older maritime towns of Greece, not upon the shore, but
about a mile from it, on rising ground, fitter for defence.   But the
Æginetans, accustomed to affluence, derived, not from their lands, but
from their maritime commerce, still directed their views to the sea; and
were at this time busied in constructing a fort on the shore, for the
protection of their shipping.   On discovering the Athenian fleet they
hastily retired into Thyrea; which was however itself so deficiently
fortified, that a small band of Lacedæmonians of the bordering country,
who had been appointed by their government to assist in raising and
protecting the works, refused to share in the danger of its defence.
The Æginetans, nevertheless, resolved to attempt the protection of
the little property remaining to them.   But Nicias, landing his whole
force, quickly overpowered them; and all, who did not fall in the
assault, became prisoners at discretion, together with their Lacedæmonian governor, Tantalus, who had been wounded.   Thyrea, being
stripped of everything valuable, was burnt, and the armament returned,
with the booty and prisoners, to Athens.   A despotic multitude was
then to decide the fate of that miserable remnant of a Grecian people,
once declared by an oracle, and confessed by all Greece, the most
meritorious of the Greek nation, for their actions in its common defence
against the most formidable enemy that ever assailed it.   What few
individual tyrants could have thought of without horror, the Athenian
people directed by a deliberate decree.   The law indeed established by
the Lacedæmonians, and sealed with the blood of the unfortunate
Platæans, was but too closely followed, and the Æginetans were all
executed.   Tantalus was added to the number of living pledges,
obtained at Sphacteria, for the security of Attica.

Another decision then waited the pleasure of the Athenian people,
the fate of their new conquest of Cythera, and, particularly, that of
some of the principal inhabitants, whom the generals had thought it

VOL. II.   B b   unsafe

unsafe to leave there. These were distributed among the ilands of the Athenian dominion. The rest of the Cytherians, to whom the capitulation only assured their lives, were however left unmolested in their possessions; with a reserve only, from the whole iland, of four talents in yearly tribute to Athens.

SECTION II.

Effects of the Superiority gained by Athens in the War: Sedition of Megara: Distress of Lacedæmon: Movements in Thrace and Macedonia. Atrocious Conduct of the Lacedæmonian Government toward the Helots. Brasidas appointed to lead a Peloponnesian Army into Thrace: Lacedæmonian Interest secured at Megara.

B.C. 24. 4. THE superiority now acquired by the Athenians in the war, began to
Ol. 88 4.   appear decisive. Their fleets commanded the seas and the ilands,
P. W. 8.   without a prospect of successful opposition from any quarter: their
landforce was growing daily more formidable; while the Lacedæmonians, in a manner, imprisoned within Peloponnesus, and unable to defend even their own territory there, were yet more unable to extend protection to their still numerous allies beyond the peninsula. The extravagant views and wild presumption insuing among the Athenian people, which the vying flattery of interested orators contributed not a little to inflame, are marked by their own favorite poet, the admirable
Aristoph.   satirist of the age. 'A thousand cities,' says one, in his comedy of
Vesp. v. 705. The Wasps, 'pay tribute to Athens. Now were each ordered to
' furnish subsistence for only twenty Athenians, twenty thousand of
' us might live in all ease and luxury, in a manner worthy of the
' dignity of the republic, and of the trophy of Marathon.' In another
comedy, The Birds, the extravagance of their petulant and presump-
Aristoph.Av. tuous haughtiness is jeered: 'It is intolerable,' says one of them, that
v. 1,225.   ' we, an imperial people, commanding many cities, should be treated
' with an air of superiority by the gods, who ought to know how to
v. 1,023—   ' respect us as their betters.' And in the same piece, the inordinate
1,050.   craving

craving of their restless ambition is ludicrously noted : report being
spred of a new city founded in the air by the birds, the Athenians are
represented as immediately earnest to send thither their superintendants and their decrees [2]. Indignation, hatred, animated and obstinate
enmity became of course mixed with the fear which the prevalence of
their arms infused through a large portion of the Greek nation, and
hence arose a fermentation which principally gave birth to the transactions now requiring attention.

The circumstances of the little republic of Megara, the nearest
neighbor to Athens, were peculiar. Tho the government was democratical, and the chiefs of the aristocratical party, with a large portion
of their adherents, in exile, yet the antient animosity between Megara
and Athens did not cease. Fear of the tyranny of the Athenian people
kept even the democratical party connected with Lacedæmon. Meanwhile adversity inforcing moderation among the Lacedæmonians, against
their usual practice, they allowed the Megarians to chuse their form
of government, tho a Peloponnesian garrison, under a Lacedæmonian
governor, held their port of Nisæa, a mile only from the city, with
which, as Athens with Peiræus, it had a fortified communication. At
the same time the ilet of Minoa, taken, as we have seen, by Nicias,
close upon the mouth of the harbour, was occupied by an Athenian
garrison ; and twice in every year it had been as a rule for the Athenian forces to overrun and ravage the Megarian territory. Yet the
aristocratical exiles, having possessed themselves of Pegæ, the Megarian port on the Corinthian gulph, were enemies to those in the
city, exceeding the Athenians in animosity almost as much as they
were inferior in power : their watchfulness for every opportunity of
plunder, waste, and slaughter, was incessantly harrassing. The distress
which this complicated pressure brought upon Megara, rendering the
lower people dissatisfied with their leaders, imboldened the remaining
friends of aristocracy. Depending upon countenance from Lacedæmon, they ventured to propose a composition with the exiles, and to
urge it as of indispensable necessity, to prevent impending ruin. The

Thucyd. l. 4.
c. 66.

---

[2] The French, in the paroxysm of their democratical mania, seèm to have borrowed
from this antique joke their ideä of sending commissioners to fraternize all nations.

leaders

leaders of the democratical party, finding this proposal grow popular,
and fearing that the fall of their power, and perhaps the necessity of
seeking safety in exile, might follow, negotiated secretly with the
Athenian generals, Hippocrates son of Ariphron, and Demosthenes son
of Alcisthenes.   Terms being settled, it was proposed to put the Athenians in possession of the walls connecting the city with its port; and,
communication between the Peloponnesian party in the former, and the
Peloponnesian troops in the latter, being thus intercluded, both, it was
hoped, must quickly fall.

Thucyd. l. 4.   Matters then being prepared, Hippocrates conducted a squadron by
c. 67.
After 18   night to Minoa, while Demosthenes marched a sufficient landforce, and
July.   the long walls were mastered with little opposition.   The Megarian
conspirators had taken measures for introducing the Athenian army
into the city; but suspicion among the Peloponnesian party produced
Thucyd. l. 4. precautions that disappointed their purpose.   Intelligence of this being
c. 69.   communicated to the Athenian generals, they resolved to direct their
whole force immediately against Nisæa, which, they thought, might
thus be taken before any assistance could arrive from Peloponnesus;
and then Megara, a considerable party within its walls favoring them,
would probably not hold long.   The select force which they had first
led from Athens was joined by all the troops that could be spared from
the guard of the city, together with their usually attending slaves.   A
contravallation was immediately begun against Nisæa: those houses
of the suburbs which lay conveniently for the purpose, formed a part
of it; the others furnished materials for the rest; and the work was
prosecuted with such diligence, that in two days it was nearly completed from the long walls to the sea.   The garrison of Nisæa, totally
without magazines, had received subsistence daily from Megara.   Not
only they were now deprived of this, but all communication being
precluded, they supposed the city already in the power of the opposite
party.   Despairing therefore of being able to make any effectual
resistance, they capitulated.   The Athenian generals required all the
Lacedæmonians as prisoners at discretion: the others they agreed to
ransom at a specified price.

Lacedæmon, from the beginning of the war, far from having any

man

man capable of balancing the extraordinary abilities of a Pericles in the supreme direction of affairs, had produced none to equal the science and activity of a Phormion or a Demosthenes in the conduct of a campain.   At this time, as Thucydides assures us, a general and very unusual dejection prevailed in Sparta.   A series of misfortune and defeat was what the Lacedæmonians had not for ages experienced. In the regular course of their singular government they were accustomed to overbear opposition; insomuch that it seemed as if great abilities in a leader were superfluous: wisdom, communicated by education and practice to every individual of the state, appeared as sufficient, as it was always ready, for public purposes upon all occasions. But a new business was now undertaken, for which their great legislator not only had not provided, but which his institutions strongly forbad.   They had ingaged in a naval war, a complicated war, and unavoidably a protracted war.   To conduct this, other abilities and other management were necessary, than had sufficed for the simple warfare of former ages.   But, in seven campains, only one man among them had yet distinguished himself: he was still a young man; and the Spartan institutions were singularly unfavorable to eminence in youth.   The good fortune however of Brasidas, in his gallant opposition to the first descent of the Athenians on the Messenian coast, did not follow him in his succeeding attempts; he had been foiled in all.   But Brasidas could learn from misfortune, without being dejected by it.   Of a temper as persevering, and a genius as fruitful as his understanding was strong and his courage clear, he alone among the Lacedæmonians was looking around for opportunities of new enterprize, which might relieve his country from the evils which pressed it, from the humiliation into which it was fallen, and from the greater evils which threatened.

Some circumstances appeared favorable to his views, and particularly the alarm arising, on all sides, at the progress of the Athenian power; long since irresistible by sea, and now growing more and more formidable by land.   The terror of it had induced the Sicilian Greeks to Thucyd. l. 4. repress the animosities and accommodate the differences which had c. 58. long prevailed between the several cities of their iland.   Those who & seq.

had

had been friends to Athens would no farther promote its power; those who had been enemies would no farther irritate its vengeance: the determination was general to maintain peace within the iland, and a neutrality with regard to the differences of the mother-country. But Thucyd. 1. 4. the revolted cities in Thrace had not equally the means of chusing c. 79. their party. Expecting that the vengeance which had cut off the people of Ægina from the face of the earth, would next fall upon them, there was nothing which they were not ready to undertake in opposition to the power which gave them such apprehensions. Nor was the king of Macedonia easy in any confidence that he could place in his present alliance with the Athenian commonwealth, with which he had been so often at enmity: and while he was not without apprehension for the safety of what he already possessed, he was incited by views of ambition to which his connection with Athens was adverse; for he coveted the province of Lyncus, or Lyncestis, which the Athenian alliance in some degree guaranteed to its prince Arrhibæus.

These circumstances bringing the Macedonian monarch and the chiefs of the Chalcidian towns to a communication of counsels, they had carried on in common a secret negotiation at Lacedæmon. They c. 80. desired a body of Peloponnesian troops, for which they offered to provide all supplies; and, with such assistance, they ingaged, not only to maintain the Peloponnesian interest in the revolted towns, but to extend the revolt. The Lacedæmonian government gladly received a proposal to draw the war from their doors, where it now pressed them, and employ the Athenians in the defence of their distant possessions. But means to send the desired succour were not obvious; for by sea they could neither oppose, nor easily evade the Athenian fleets; and by land the march was long and difficult; through the territory, in part, of uncertain friends, if not of declared enemies. Brasidas was the man to put himself forward for the conduct of an undertaking, which to timidity and inertness appeared impossible, and to injudicious boldness would have been reälly so.

But the Lacedæmonian administration was composed of men far different from Brasidas. Tho they anxiously desired to carry the war to a distance, they feared to diminish their force at home;

where

where their own slaves, objects of jealousy now more than ever, since Pylus was held by Messenians, caused them greater apprehensions than their forein enemies. A more nefarious measure than that to which they resorted for obviating the danger, is not recorded in history, nor easily to be imagined. Proclamation was made, that any Helots, who thought themselves capable of meriting freedom and the dignity of Lacedæmonian citizens, by their actions in arms, might present themselves to the magistracy, and a number should be selected, to be put upon the honorable trial. This was supposed a ready and a safe method for discovering which among them would be most forward to revolt: for the same high spirit would incite to seek freedom and the rank of citizens, by deeds of danger, if opportunity offered, equally against Lacedæmon as against the enemies of Lacedæmon. About two thousand were accordingly chosen; and, being crowned with chaplets, were marched in solemn procession around the temples. Thus, as they were given to expect, they were to receive freedom by being admitted to communicate in religious rites with the free. Soon after they disappeared, and the massacre was managed with such careful secresy, that in what manner any one of them perished was never known.

Thucyd. l. 4. c. 80. & Diod. l. 12. c. 67.

After this shocking and dastardly precaution, the Spartan ministry less scrupled to send a part of their force on a forein expedition. Still however they would allow no more than seven hundred Lacedæmonians [3] for the hazardous attempt to march by land as far as Thrace. But the reputation of Brasidas for prudent and ingaging conduct among the allies of Lacedæmon, as well as for ability and activity in military command, had reached Chalcidicë; and the leading men, in the

Thucyd. l. 4. c. 81.

[3] αὐτῶν—which Rollin and some of the commentators have understood to mean Helots. But Smith, with his usual caution, translating literally and explaining nothing, must be understood to mean Lacedæmonians; and I think Thucydides meant to be so understood. In the 34th chapter of his fifth book we learn that the Helots who fought under Brasidas were presented with their freedom, but they were removed from Laconia, and established as a colony in Lepreum. But in the 67th chapter of the same book we find the Brasidian soldiers, Βρασίδιοι ϛρατιῶται, holding apparently a post of honor in the line of the Lacedæmonian army; and they are there distinguished from the Νεοδαμώδεις, the newly admitted citizens. They are mentioned again in the 71st, 72d, and 74th chapters.

revolted

revolted towns, had solicited his appointment to the command of the armament intended for their support. Their solicitation met the wishes of Brasidas; and the Lacedæmonian ministry did not refuse him an honor for which there seems to have been no competitor. He was to increase the scanty force assigned him, as he could, by interest, or by hire, among the Peloponnesian states.

Thucyd. l. 4. c. 80.

c. 70.

It happened that he was preparing in Sicyon and Corinth for his march northward, when he received information of the measures of the Athenians against Megara. Brasidas thought no business not his, in which he could serve his country. The allies of the immediate neighborhood felt as he did for the safety of Megara, and of the Peloponnesian garrison in Nisæa. In addition therefore to the troops collected for the Thracian expedition, two thousand seven hundred Corinthians, and a thousand Sicyonians and Phliasians, put themselves under his command; and a requisition was dispatched into Bœotia for the force of that country to meet him at Tripodiscus, a village of Megaris, situate under mount Geraneia. On his march, intelligence met him, that Nisæa was already taken; upon which, leaving his army at Tripodiscus, he hastened, in the night, with three hundred chosen men, to Megara, and arrived under its walls, undiscovered by the Athenians. Meanwhile a singular kind of concord, between the factions in Megara, had been produced by mutual fear. The democratical chiefs apprehended, that the admission of a Lacedæmonian general would be immediately followed by the restoration of the exiles, and their own banishment; the aristocratical party not less feared, that the consequence of any alarm to the popular mind would be a prevailing resolution to admit the Athenians, which would produce their own inevitable ruin. A momentary compromise was therefore followed by a unanimous resolution not to admit Brasidas. Both parties expected a battle between the Athenian and Peloponnesian armies; and, when the event of that was decided, they might chuse their measures, they thought, more safely. Brasidas therefore, after having in vain attempted to remove the apprehensions of both, withdrew to Tripodiscus.

c. 71.

c. 72.

Before the arrival of the messenger from Corinth, the Bœotians, in alarm

alarm for their allies of Megara, had been assembling their forces; and by daybreak Brasidas was joined at Tripodiscus by two thousand two hundred of their heavy-armed foot, with the very important addition of six hundred horse.   The whole of his heavy-armed foot amounting thus to six thousand, a force superior to the regular troops of the Athenian army before Megara, he marched immediately for that place.   The Bœotian horse presently put to flight the Athenian light troops, scattered over the plain.   The Athenian cavalry advancing to protect them, a sharp action insued, in which the commander of the Bœotian horse was killed, with little advantage otherwise gained on either side.   The measures of Brasidas mark the judicious commander, who knew when to refrain, as well as how to dare.   It was notorious, that the Megarians watched the event to decide their measures.   Brasidas therefore chose for his camp an advantageous situation, very near Megara, and waited there.   The Athenian generals, having already carried their purpose in a great degree, deemed it utterly unadvisable, for what remained, to risk the army they commanded, under disadvantageous circumstances, against a superior force.   As soon then as the Megarians of the oligarchal party were convinced that the Athenians would not venture a battle, they no longer hesitated to introduce Brasidas; upon which the Athenian generals, leaving a garrison in Nisæa, withdrew to Athens. Brasidas, after a very essential service to his country and its allies, thus effected without hazard, except to his own person, returned to Corinth.

Thucyd. l. 4. c. 73.

c. 74.

What followed, in Megara, seems to have been among the instances of depravity in Grecian manners, to which Thucydides has in general terms adverted, imputing it in some degree to the example set in the Corcyræan sedition.   Those Megarians of the democratical party, who had been most forward in the Athenian interest, fearing apparently the concurrence of the enmity of Lacedæmon with that of their fellow-citizens, avoided worse consequences by a voluntary exile.   Those who had been less violent in party-measures, thought they might then make a composition with the aristocratical party.   A conference was accordingly held for the purpose.   What the democratical leaders most feared was the return of those aristocratical chiefs who were in exile at Pegæ. Their restoration however was not to be obviated, but it was agreed

Thucyd. l. 3. c. 82.

l. 4. c. 74.

that a complete amnesty for all past transactions should be solemnly sworn to by all. The exiles accepted the condition, and took the oath. They were presently raised to the principal offices of their little state. Taking then the opportunity of a general review of arms, for which the people of the Grecian towns were usually from time to time assembled, they apprehended a hundred of those whom they considered as having been most their enemies; preferred an accusation of treason against them before the assembled people ; and, condemnation being pronounced, all were executed. The superiority of the oligarchal party being thus rendered decisive, the supreme power in Megara, says Thucydides, remained long vested in very few hands.

SECTION III.

Sedition in Bœotia and Phocis : Attempts of the Athenians against Bœotia : Battle of Delium : Siege of Delium.

B. C. 424.
Ol. $\frac{88}{19}$?.
P. W. 8.

Thucyd. l. 4.
c. 76.

THE advantage gained by Athens in the war continued to extend its effects. The partizans of democracy in all the oligarchal republics, but with still more eagerness the numerous democratical exiles, were everywhere watching for opportunities to profit from the turn in the affairs of Greece. In this state of things a plan was concerted for a revolution in Bœotia. Ptœodorus, a Theban exile, was at the head of the business ; some banished Orchomenians were among the most zealous and active in it ; and a party in Phocis was prepared to join them on the first favorable occasion. The Orchomenians undertook to ingage mercenary troops in Peloponnesus : for persons either by principle or by circumstances disposed to favor democracy, or open to the persuasion of bribery, were to be found under all oligarchal governments. Ptœodorus meanwhile communicated with the Athenian generals Hippocrates and Demosthenes, and a project was formed for betraying Siphæ and Chæronæa into their hands ; the former a small seaport of the Thespian territory on the Corinthian gulph ; the other, an inland town of the Orchomenian territory, on the borders of Phocis. The Athenians were at the same time to seize and fortify Delium, a

temple

temple of Apollo in the Tanagræan district, near the coast overagainst Eubœa; and the intention being that these attempts on distant points should take place on the same day, it was expected the distraction would prevent effectual opposition anywhere.   If then the democratical party in Bœotia should not be imboldened everywhere immediately to rise, yet those posts being securely occupied, and inroads made from them as opportunity offered, with due incouragement given to the revolted and to those disposed to revolt, the whole of Bœotia would quickly be brought under democratical sway, and of course into the alliance and under the protection, which would be, in a great degree, to be under the dominion of Athens.

Such was the project: for the execution, while Hippocrates kept the force in Attica prepared, Demosthenes conducted a fleet of forty triremes around Peloponnesus to Naupactus; and, to prevent suspicion of the principal design, began operations against the enemies of the Athenian confederacy in the western provinces.   On his arrival, he found Œniadæ, so long the thorn of Aoarnania, already reduced by his allies of that province.   Being joined by those allies, he marched against Salynthius, prince of Agraïs in Ætolia, who was quickly compelled to submit to his terms.   After then reducing some hostile towns or clans of inferior note, and settling the affairs of those parts to his satisfaction, he returned to Naupactus, to prepare for the execution of the greater enterprize concerted at Athens. *Thueyd. 1. 4. c. 77.*

In the autumn, having collected a considerable force of Acarnanians and other allies of the western provinces, he sailed for Siphæ; but on his arrival he had the mortification to find the place strongly garrisoned, and well provided, and the whole strength of Bœotia prepared to oppose him.   It appeared afterward that not only the design had been betrayed to the enemy, but through mistake of the day on which it was to be executed, Hippocrates had not moved from Athens to make the expected diversion in the east of Bœotia.   To attempt anything at Siphæ therefore appearing useless, Demosthenes, after an unsuccessful descent upon the Sicyonian coast, reconducted his armament to Naupactus. *c. 89. After 13th Octob.* *c. 101.*

The Bœotians, in giving security to Siphæ, seem not to have been *c. 90.*

C C 2   aware

aware of what was intended against the opposite side of their country. Hippocrates therefore, marching with the whole force of Attica, citizens, metics, and foreiners [*], to Delium, on what he conceived to be the appointed day, found nothing there to oppose him. The object was to fortify the post in all haste, so as to render it tenable by a garrison. A ditch was therefore excavated, and a wall of earth raised, with wooden towers at intervals. The antient manner of fortification requiring height and perpendicularity, the wall was strengthened with piles, formed of the timbers of some neighboring houses, and faced with interwoven vine-branches, cut near the spot. The work was begun on the morning of the third day after the army marched from Athens; and being nearly finished by noon of the fifth, the general then ordered the army to move homeward, while he should give final directions to the garrison, for the disposition of their guards and the completion of the works. The irregulars and all the light-troops immediately pressed their march: the heavy-armed halted, a little more than a mile from the place, to wait for the general.

Thucyd. l. 4. c. 91.

In consequence, meanwhile, of intelligence communicated through Bœotia, the forces of all the towns of the province had been assembled, under the eleven Bœotarcs, at Tanagra. There information came to them that the Athenian army had begun its march homeward; upon which a council of war was held, and the majority determined not to seek a battle. Pagondas, however, one of the two Theban Bœotarcs, whose turn of command it was for the day, dissatisfied with the determination of the council, addressed his eloquence to the troops, and so efficaciously, that he excited a general ardor for ingaging. Having thus provided for obedience to his orders, in opposition to his collegues in office, tho it was already late in the day, he would not lose the opportunity, but immediately led the army against the Athenians.

c. 93.

[*] —'Αθηναίους πανδημεί, αυτὸς, καὶ τὰς μετοίκους καὶ ξίνων ὅσοι παρῆσαν——Omni Atheniensium populo, civibus, incolis, et peregrinis quotquot aderant. Duker.—The whole force of Athens, as well citizens as so-journers, not excepting even the foreiners who chanced at that time to be there. Smith. These translations are not satisfactory; and we find no assistance from notes. The precise distinction, however, betweeu μίτοικος and ξίνος, tho we should be glad to know what it was, is not particularly important. here.

Where

Where an intervening hill prevented them from seeing him, while the distance was small, he halted to form his order of battle; and then marching up the hill, rested upon the top.

Hippocrates was yet at Delium, when information was brought of the unexpected approach of the Bœotians. Leaving a body of three hundred horse, who attended him, to watch an opportunity for attacking the enemy in the rear, he proceeded himself with all speed to join the main body of his army. When he arrived it was already formed for action. He rode along the line, making a short speech of incouragement; but scarcely had' reached the center when the Bœotians moved down the hill, giving the shout of battle. Upon this he ordered immediately to advance, according to the usual practice of the age, it being esteemed disadvantageous to remain stationary and receive the onset. *Thucyd. l. 4. c. 96.*

The heavy foot on each side were about six thousand. The Bœotians had, besides, a thousand horse, five hundred targeteers, and above ten thousand light-armed. The Athenian light-armed, whose march, it appears, had been stopped in time, were more numerous, but less disciplined and worse appointed, the regular light-troops of the republic being mostly on forein service. The Thebans of the Bœotian army, if we may trust and can understand our copies of Thucydides, were formed no less than twenty-five deep; the other Bœotians variously, according to the practice of the several towns, or the opinions of the commanders. The Athenian army was disposed in files of eight men. The horse of both armies were placed in the wings. The extremes, however, of neither could come into action, being prevented by the intervention of deep water-gullies. The field was well disputed between the rest; in action so close, that they joined opposing shields; and where weapons could not avail against the compact arrangement of defensive armour, they endevored to break each other's line by force of pushing. With their right wing the Athenians obtained the advantage, so that the extremity of the enemy's left retreated toward their own right. Next in the Bœotian line to the troops which gave way, were the Thespians, whose left flank being thus exposed, they were surrounded, and suffered greatly. But in this evolution the conquerors fell into disorder, and, *c. 94.*

meeting

meeting in action, ingaged one another. Meanwhile Pagondas, with
the Thebans, in the right of the Bœotian line, was gaining advantage
against the Athenian left. Information reaching him of the distress
of his own left, he sent two squadrons[s] of horse around the hill, who
came unawares upon the victorious wing of the Athenians, while they
were yet in the confusion which they had themselves created. Panic
seized them, and they fled: the rest of their line, already severely
pressed, finding themselves thus deserted, quickly joined in the flight,
and the rout became complete: some made toward Delium, some to the
port of Oropus, some to mount Parnes, others variously as hope of safety
pointed the way.

A reïnforcement of Locrian troops joined the Bœotian army in the
moment of victory. Being comparatively fresh, they undertook pursuit, together with the Bœotian cavalry; and the event would have
been very fatal to the Athenians, if approaching night had not favored
their escape. It was upon this occasion that the philosopher Socrates,
who served among the Athenian infantry, pressed by the pursuing
enemy, was in imminent danger of being put to the sword, when his
pupil Alcibiades, coming up with a body of cavalry, gave such effectual
protection, that Socrates, with those about him, made good their
retreat[6]. Near a thousand, however, of the Athenian heavy-armed
fell, with Hippocrates, the commanding general, and a much greater
number of the light-armed and irregulars. When pursuit had been
pushed as far as circumstances would permit, Pagondas raised his
trophy, collected the spoil, and, leaving a strong guard over the
enemy's dead, retired with the main body of his army to Tanagra.

Next day a herald was sent by the surviving commanders of the
Athenian troops, to request the accustomed leave for burying the slain.
On his way he met a Bœotian herald, who assured him that his labor

Plat. Laches,
p. 181. t. 2.
& Conviv,
p. 221. t. 3.
Plut. vit.

Thucyd. l. 4.
c. 101.

c. 97.

[s] Δύω Τέλη.
[6] Strabo relates that Socrates saved his
pupil Xenophon in this battle. Athenæus,
as is observed by Casaubon, in his note on
the passage, has shown that this could not
be (Athen. l. 5. c. 15.) and he deduces his
proof from Plato. Yet Barthelemi, in his

Anacharsis, not only tells the story from
Strabo, but has been so careless as to refer
to Plato for authority for it. In the passage
of Plato to which he refers (Conviv. p. 221.
t. 3.) not a syllable is to be found to the
purpose.

                                              would

would be vain, and that he would do best to accompany him back to
the Athenian camp, whither he was going. The Athenian complied;
and audience being given to the Bœotian herald by the principal
officers, he represented, ' that the Athenians had violated the common
' law of the Greeks, by which it was established, that, in any invasion
' of each other's territories, no temple should be profaned: that in for-
' tifying Delium, they had made the sacred precinct a habitation for
' men, and whatever men usually do in a profane place yas done there;
' particularly the water, which the Bœotians had always held it unlaw-
' ful for themselves to touch but for holy ablution[7], was drawn for all
' common uses: that the Bœotians therefore, in their own name and in
' that of the god, invoking the gods of the country and Apollo, warned
' them to quit the temple, and clear it of whatever belonged to them.'
Amid the most serious political concerns, with the utmost disregard of
all moral obligations, we find such matters of meer religious ceremony
often deeply ingaging the attention of the Greeks. The Athenians, in Thucyd. l. 4.
return, sent their own herald to the Bœotian camp, who represented, c. 98.
' that the Athenians neither had profaned the temple, nor would inten-
' tionally do so: that, by the common law of the Greeks, with the
' possession of territory the possession of temples always passed: that
' the Bœotians themselves, who had acquired their present country by
' conquest, had taken possession of the temples of other people, which
' they had ever since held as their own: that if, in the necessity to
' which the Athenians were impelled by the unjust violence of the
' Bœotians and their other enemies, to use extraordinary means for
' securing their country against invasion, they had disturbed the sacred
' fountain, they depended upon the indulgence of the god for the
' transgression, if it was one, where no offence was intended: that, on
' the contrary, the refusal of the Bœotians to restore the Athenian
' slain, was an impiety without excuse: finally, that the Athenians
' considered Delium as theirs by conquest, and would not evacuate it;
' but they nevertheless demanded that their dead should be restored,
' according to the laws and customs of all the Greeks, transmitted from
' their forefathers.' The Bœotians appear to have felt the imputation

[7] Πρὸς τὰ ἱερὰ χέρνιβι χρῆσθαι.

of

Thucyd. l. 4,
c. 99.
of impiety and contravention of the institutions of their forefathers, for they endevored to obviate it by an evasion. They said, that, if Oropia, the district in which the battle was fought and Delium stood, was a Bœotian territory, the Athenians ought to quit what was not theirs, and then their dead should be restored ; but if it was an Athenian territory, to ask permission of others for anything to be done there was superfluous. With this the negotiation ended, and the Bœotians prepared immediately to besiege Delium.

We learn, from the details of sieges remaining from Thucydides, that the Greeks of his age were not only very deficient in the art of attacking fortifications, but that their mechanics were defective, to a degree that we could not readily suppose of those who had carried the arts of masonry and sculpture so high. Fortunate for the people of the age, in the inefficacy of governments to give security to their subjects, that it was so, and that thus, those who could find subsistence within a fortification might generally withstand assault. The Bœotians were far from thinking the army, with which they had defeated the whole strength of Attica, sufficient for the reduction of a fort of earth and

c. 100.
wood, constructed in three days, and hopeless of relief. Two thousand Corinthians, a body of Megarians, and part of the Peloponnesian garrison which had escaped from Nisæa, joined them after the battle. Still they thought themselves deficient in troops practised in the use of missile weapons, and they sent for some dartmen and slingers from the Malian bay. After all perhaps they would have been foiled, but for an engine invented for the occasion. A large tree, in the want of instruments for boring, was sawed in two, lengthways ; and the parts, being excavated, were rejoined, so as to form a pipe, at one end of which, protected by iron plates, was suspended by chains a large cauldron, into which, from the end of the wooden pipe, a tube of iron projected. On the seventeenth day after the battle, the preparations were com-

Novem.
plete. The machine, being raised on wheels, was moved to that part of the fort where vine-branches and wood appeared to have been most used in the construction. The cauldron was then filled with sulphur, pitch, and burning charcoal ; large bellows were applied to the opposite end of the cylinder ; and a fire was thus raised that rendered it impossible

4

sible

sible for any living being to remain in the adjoining part of the fort. During the confusion thus created, the besiegers, chusing their moment for assault, carried the place.   A considerable part of the garrison nevertheless found opportunity for flight, and saved themselves by getting aboard an Athenian squadron which lay off the neighboring coast: some however were killed, and, what was most important, about two hundred were made prisoners.   Presently after, but while the event was yet unknown at Athens, a herald arriving to demand again the bodies of the slain in the late battle, obtained them without difficulty.

S E C T I O N   IV.

March of Brasidas into Thrace.   Transactions in Macedonia and Thrace.

Tʜᴇsᴇ transactions protracted the campain in Greece to a late season. Meanwhile Brasidas, having put Megara into a state of security, returned to Corinth, and while summer was not yet far advanced, had set forward on his difficult and hazardous march toward Thrace.   He had collected a thousand heavy-armed Peloponnesians in addition to his seven hundred Lacedæmonians.   As far as the new Lacedæmonian colony of the Trachinian Heracleia, he passed through friendly territories; but there he arrived on the border of a country, not indeed at declared enmity with Sparta, but allied to Athens; and across the Thessalian plains, in defiance of the Thessalian cavalry, with his small band, which, including the light-armed and slaves, would scarcely exceed four thousand men, he could not attempt to force his way.   The greatest part of Thessaly was nominally under democratical government, and the democratical party was zealous in the Athenian alliance; yet, in most of the towns, the interest of a few powerful men principally decided public measures.   This facilitated negotiation, and Brasidas was not less able in negotiation than in arms.   Employing sometimes the interest of the king of Macedonia, sometimes that of other allies, and never neglecting the moment of opportunity for

B. C. 424.
Ol. 89. 1.
P. W. 8.
Thucyd. l. 4.
c. 78.
July.

Vᴏʟ. II.   D ᴅ   gaining

gaining a step, he obtained free passage as far as the river Enipeus.
There he found a body in arms, whose leaders declared their resolution
to oppose his farther progress, and expressed, in reproaches to his
Thessalian guides, their resentment at the permission and assistance so
far given to an army of strangers passing through the country, unauthorized by the general consent of the Thessalian people. Fair words,
discreetly used, nevertheless softened them; and, after no long treaty,
Thucyd. l. 4. Brasidas obtained unmolested passage.   Through the remainder of
c. 79.   Thessaly, dubiously disposed to him, but unprepared for immediate
opposition, he made his way by forced marches till he reached Perrhæ-
bia; among whose people, subjects of the Thessalians, he had provided,
by previous negotiation, for a favorable reception. The difficult passage over mount Olympus, which was next to be undertaken, made
the friendship of the Perrhæbians particularly important. Under their
guidance he arrived with his force intire at Dium, on the northern side
of Olympus, where he was within the dominion of his ally the king of
Macedonia.

Here the difficulties of his march ended, but difficulties of another
kind arose. A common interest in opposing Athens had united the
king of Macedonia with Lacedæmon, and with the allies of Lacedæmon in his neighborhood; but their interests were otherwise different, and their views, in some points, opposite. The principal object
of Perdiccas was to subdue the province called Lyncus, or Lyncestis,
among the mountains on the western frontier of Macedonia, and far
from the Grecian colonies. This was a measure by no means calculated to promote the interest of Lacedæmon; which rather required
that alliances should be extended on all sides, and that the confederacy
should have no enemy but Athens. Eight years before, Perdiccas had
been chosen, by the confederate Grecian army, to the secondary command of general of the cavalry, while a citizen of Corinth was appointed
commander-in-chief. He seems to have been then little pleased with
such a compliment, and apparently it was his purpose now to preclude
the means for a repetition of it. Joining his forces with those of
Brasidas, he assumed command, and directed the march of the combined army toward Lyncestis.

11   The

The prince of Lyncestis, Arrhibæus, little able to withstand the
united forces of Macedonia and Lacedæmon, had sent to Brasidas to
request his mediation with Perdiccas. The Spartan general therefore,
not immediately refusing to march, stopped however on the Lyncestian
frontier; and representing that the apprehension of so great a force,
ready to fall upon his country, would probably induce the Lyncestian
prince to a reasonable accommodation, he declared that, for the Lacedæmonians, he judged it neither expedient nor just to proceed hostilely,
till the trial had been made. Accordingly a negotiation was opened,
and shortly a treaty was concluded, by which Arrhibæus became numbered among the allies of Sparta. Perdiccas, unable to prevent this
measure, was however highly dissatisfied; and he showed his resentment by declaring that, instead of furnishing, as heretofore, half the
provisions for an army so little disposed to promote his interest, he
would in future furnish a third only.

The accommodation nevertheless would be upon the whole satisfactory to Brasidas and his Grecian allies. The dominion of Arrhibæus
preserved, might become a valuable weight in the balance against the
growing power of so uncertain a friend as Perdiccas; and the arms of
the confederacy would now of course be directed to the object which
the confederate Greeks desired, the reduction of the power of Athens.
Their first attempt was against Acanthus. Some of the principal men Thucyd. l. 4.
there had been always disposed to join with the Chalcidians in renounc- c. 84.
End of
ing the Athenian dominion. The democratical party was zealous in August or
the Athenian interest, but, being unable to oppose the approaching beginn. of
Sept.
enemy in the field, they were in alarm for their property, and especially
for their vintage, now ready to gather. Upon a knowlege of these
circumstances measures were taken. They were summoned, not as
enemies, but as those who ought to be friends, to join the confederacy.
After some conciliatory negotiation, the Acanthians conceded so far
as to agree that Brasidas should be admitted into the town alone; and
allowed to declare his proposals before the general assembly.

Brasidas, for a Lacedæmonian, says Thucydides, was eloquent: he
was besides politic; and, tho not strictly scrupulous of truth, he was
highly liberal in his policy. He began with assuring the Acanthians, Thucyd. l. 4,
c. 85.

D D 2 'that

' that the great object of the Lacedæmonians in the war was to give
' liberty to Greece. It was therefore matter of wonder to him that
' the Acanthians did not at once receive him joyfully ; that they hesi-
' tated to join the confederacy ; that they entertained an idea of
' opposing their own deliverance, and that of Greece, from Athenian
' subjection.   Nothing in reason could hold them to such a purpose,
' but apprehension of the power of Athens ; and how vain that appre-
' hension was, he had himself had the good fortune to prove to the
' world, when, before the walls of Megara, the whole force of Athens
' feared to ingage that small band of Peloponnesians which he now
' commanded in Thrace.'   This politic boast, tho totally false, for he
commanded at Megara more than triple the force that he led into
Thrace, nevertheless passed with the Acanthians, ill informed of transactions in Greece, and had considerable effect.   He proceeded then to

Thucyd. l. 4. tell his audience, ' that he had received assurances from the principal
c. 85.   ' magistrates of Lacedæmon, confirmed by the most solemn oaths, that
' whatever cities, through negotiation with him, might accede to the
' Peloponnesian confederacy, should be subject to no claims of autho-
' rity from the Lacedæmonians, but should be perfectly independent.
' From himself he assured them, that none need fear for person, pro-
' perty, or civil rights, on account of any political principles they had
' held, or any political conduct they had followed ; for he was deter-
' mined to support no faction, but, with his best power, to establish,
' wherever he might have influence, that equal liberty for all ranks,
' which formed the boast and the happiness of his own country.   If,
c. 87.   ' then, refusing conditions not only perfectly equitable but highly
' advantageous, they would persist in their connection with Athens,
' and, tho only by the tribute which they paid, promote the subjection
' of other Grecian states, he should think himself not only justified,
' but bound, to consider them as enemies, and to begin immediately,
' the waste of their lands.   He trusted however they would save him
' the necessity of a measure so opposite to his inclination, and would
' rather be zealous in setting an example to the other cities of Thrace
' for the recovery of independency.'

The eloquence of Brasidas, powerfully seconded by his army at their
gates,

gates, had its full effect upon the Acanthians; and the suffrages of the assembly being taken secretly, that none might be afterward individually criminated for the vote given, a majority was found for revolting from Athens.   The city of Acanthus thus became a member of the Lacedæmonian confederacy ; and before the end of the summer, the example was followed by the neighboring city of Stageirus.

Of the ten generals of the regular establishment of Athens, it should seem that two were usually appointed to the Thracian command. Eucles and Thucydides, the historian, son of Olorus, now held that station.   Eucles commanded in Amphipolis: Thucydides was at the iland of Thasus, with the squadron of the station, consisting of only seven triremes.   It was to be expected that in spring the Athenians would send powerful reinforcements.   It behoved Brasidas, therefore, to make every use of opportunities yet open to him ; and the severe season was rather favorable for some of the enterprizes which he meditated. Thucyd. l. 4. c. 108.

Amphipolis was the most important place held by the Athenians in Thrace.   It lay upon a noble river, which it commanded, and whose banks, with the neighboring hills, bore a growth scarcely exhaustible of excellent ship-timber.   The country around was a rich plain, and the invironing mountains had mines of silver and gold : the port of Eion, at the mouth of the river, was but an appendage, yet a valuable appendage of Amphipolis.   This advantageous spot had been colonized, first from Miletus by the unfortunate Aristagoras, and afterward from Athens by Cimon; whose colony, also unfortunate, was destroyed, as we have seen, by the Thracians.   During the administration of Pericles, and thirteen years only, according to Diodorus, before the campain of Brasidas in Thrace, a new colony passed from Athens, under the conduct of Agnon, an Athenian of rank, and of very popular character.   The place was already populous and flourishing; but the inhabitants were a mixt multitude from various Grecian cities; some connected, by blood, or by habit and intercourse, with the revolted Chalcidians; some, by interest, with the king of Macedonia. Ch. 12. s. 3. of this Hist. Diod. l. 12. c. 32. Thucyd. l. 4. c. 103.

On these circumstances Brasidas founded a project for gaining Amphipolis to the Lacedæmonian confederacy.   Communication c. 102.

was

was managed with some of the inhabitants, and a plan concerted with them.   Collecting then all the force he could obtain from his allies, on a dark stormy evening, with sleet falling (the weather which he preferred for the attempt) he arrived at Aulon and Bromiscus, where the waters of the lake of Bolbë discharge themselves into the sea; and, halting there only while his army took refreshment, he proceeded in the night to Argilus.   The people of that little town, always disaffected to Athens, were prepared to receive him.   Its territory was divided from the Amphipolitan only by the river Strymon.   Near Argilus was a bridge, which, as an important pass, was protected by a constant guard; but no attempt being at present apprehended, the guard was small.   Under the guidance of the Argilians, and favored by the storm, Brasidas surprized the guard.   Becoming thus master of the bridge,

the Amphipolitan territory was open to him.   Extreme alarm and confusion immediately insued among the Amphipolitans; who, as a heterogeneous people, collected from various parts, were almost wholly without confidence each man in his neighbor; and if, instead of plundering the country, Brasidas had led his forces directly against the town, he would have become master of it, probably as soon as he arrived at the gates.   This, however, might perhaps be more than his authority could effect.   After gratifying his troops, therefore, with the spoil of the country, he waited in expectation that, from so populous a place, with an Athenian general commanding, something would be attempted against him; and in any action in open field he promised himself success, which would not fail to incourage his friends in the town, and promote his measures.

The inactivity of Eucles disappointed Brasidas.   No movement was made from the town; and it was to be apprehended that the arrival of Thucydides, with the squadron from Thasus, would utterly defeat the enterprize: for beside the force he would bring, having large property and antient family connections in the neighborhood, Thucydides had great influence among both Greeks and Thracians; and his presence would not only confirm the Amphipolitans in the Athenian interest, but assist much toward the collection of a powerful landforce for opposing the Peloponnesians.   Measures that might be quickly decisive were therefore

fore necessary to Brasidas.   Thucydides imputes expressly no blame to Thucyd. l. 4. c. 105. his collegue; but the conduct of Eucles appears evidently to have been deficient either in judgement or in vigor, or rather in both.   Brasidas found means to send assurance into Amphipolis, ' that it was not his ' purpose to deprive any person in the city, not even the Athenians, of ' either property or civil rights: that all the inhabitants might chuse ' whether they would remain upon the footing of free citizens, or ' depart with their effects; only, if the latter was their choice, they c. 106. ' must go within five days.'   This proposal had immediate efficacy: the Athenians, a small proportion only of the inhabitants, little confident, evidently, in their general, and highly diffident of their fellow-colonists, had supposed their persons, their properties, and their families, in the most imminent danger of the worst that could befall them: the terms were incomparably more favorable than, from the common practice and policy of Grecian commanders, was to be expected; and in their present circumstances, hopeless of timely succour, they could hardly wish for more.   Such being the sentiments of the Athenians, the other multitude were still readier to rejoice in the offer, generous as it appeared, of the Spartan general.   The promoters of the revolt, therefore, boldly stepped forward; the interposition of Eucles was disregarded; the people in assembly decreed that the terms should be accepted; and Brasidas, with his forces, was immediately admitted into the city.   That active officer, then, without a moment's loss of time, proceeded to take measures for possessing himself of Eion, distant about three miles, and so excluding the Athenian fleet from the river. But late in the evening of the same day on which Amphipolis surrendered, Thucydides, having made unexpected haste from Thasus, entered the harbour with his squadron.   Eion was thus secured, but Amphipolis was beyond the power of Thucydides to recover.

To the loss of that city from the Athenian dominion, we seem principally to owe our best information concerning the history of the times with which we are ingaged, and almost our only means for any accucurate acquaintance with the Grecian republics, in that period in which their history is most interesting.   The news of the successes of Brasidas c. 108. in Thrace, but particularly of the surrender of Amphipolis, made great

impression

impression at Athens; and the more, as the public mind was sore with
the recent calamity at Delium, the greatest experienced from the hands
of the enemy in the course of the war.   Those distant dependencies,
from whose wealth the republic principally derived its power, had been
esteemed hitherto secure under the guard of the Athenian navy, with
which no potentate upon earth could contend : but now, through the
adventurous and able conduct of Brasidas, they were laid open to the
superior landforce of the Peloponnesians; which, if the Thessalians
should not oppose, might be poured in upon them to any amount.
Dwelling upon these considerations, and irritated more than instructed
by misfortune, the Athenian people vented against their best friends
that revenge which they knew not how to vent against their enemies.

Thucyd. l. 5. Thucydides, whose peculiar interest and influence in Thrace gave him
c. 26. singular means to serve them there, was deprived of his command, and
banished from Attica for twenty years.   Precluded thus from active
life in the service of his country, it was the gratification of his leisure
to compose that history which has been the delight and admiration of
all posterity.   The affairs of Athens continued to be known to him
through his numerous friends in high situations there.   His banishment,
as himself informs us, led to information concerning those of the Peloponnesians, which he could scarcely otherwise have acquired.

Brasidas then, thus successful through the inability or remissness of
Eucles at Amphipolis, and disappointed through the activity of Thucydides at Eion, had however done, with a very small force, very
important services for his country.   His sedulity to prosecute them
was unremitting, and he had now greatly increased his means.   The
Thucyd. l. 4. reputation of his unassuming and conciliating behaviour toward the
c. 108. allies whom he had gained, was communicated through the other
Grecian cities in Thrace.   His character passed for a specimen of the
character of his fellowcountrymen; and his constant declaration, that
the great purpose of his commission was to give perfect freedom and
independency to all Grecian cities, received such support from the wise
liberality of his conduct, that it found general credit.   Perdiccas, a
prince of much policy and little honor, forgetting his resentment, was
desirous of profiting from his connection with such an ally as Brasidas,
and

and condescended to visit him for the purpose of concerting measures for prosecuting the common interest of the confederacy.   Meanwhile the fame of the late defeat of the Athenians in Bœotia, now spred over the country, assisted to promote the disposition to revolt: it tended to establish the credit of the politic tho untrue assertion of Brasidas, that, with only the small force of Peloponnesians which he commanded in Thrace, he had defied the whole strength of Athens under the walls of Megara; and the vaunt had its effect.   The naval power of Athens became less an object of fear, when it was supposed that protection against it might always be obtained by land.   Shortly Myrcinus, Gapselus, and Œsymë revolted to the confederates; while several other towns, fearful yet to declare themselves, intimated privately their desire to be freed from subjection to Athens.

Such success and such prospects incouraged Brasidas, in sending to Sparta an account of them, to request a reïnforcement, which might inable him to pursue his advantages, and attempt still greater things. A man who so united talents for military and civil command, who could conquer, as occasion required, either by force or by persuasion, and who had knowlege and temper to maintain his acquisitions, Lacedæmon had not yet presented to the notice of history.   But talents so superior, in a man not of royal race, not qualified by age for superiority, and distinguished only by his spirit of enterprize, his daring courage, his indefatigable activity, his uncommon prudence, his noble liberality, his amiable temper, and those ingaging manners which conciliated the affection of all with whom he conversed, excited envy and apprehension among the cautious elderhood of Sparta.   The reïnforcement was totally denied.   The Athenian people meanwhile, however illiberal, and capriciously rigorous to those who served them, were not so untrue to their own interest as to neglect the important possessions, with the loss of which they were threatened: some reïnforcements were sent during winter; more were to follow in spring.

No disappointment, however, nor any rigor of season, could abate the activity of Brasidas.   With the progress of his successes he inlarged his views; and, being now possessed of a country favorably situated, and producing materials in singular abundance, he formed the bold

Vᴏʟ. II.   E ᴇ   project

Thucyd. l. 4.
c. 109.
project of creäting a fleet at Amphipolis. Meanwhile, with his small force of Peloponnesians, and what allies he could collect, he marched into Actë, that part of the peninsula of Athos which lay within the king of Persia's canal. It contained the little towns of Sanë, Thryssus, Clæone, Acrothoœ, Olophyxus, and Dium, which were so many separate republics. The first only was a pure Grecian colony, from Andrus. The inhabitants of the others were a mixed people, a few Chalcidian Greeks, but the greater part Thracians; of that Tuscan people [8], says Thucydides, who formerly inhabited Lemnus and Athens. All were under the dominion of the Athenian commonwealth, but all presently acceded to the terms offered by Brasidas, except Sanë and Dium, whose territories he wasted.

c. 110, 112,.
113.
A more important object then offering in the neighboring peninsula of Sithonia, he led his forces thither. A small party in Toronë, one of the principal Chalcidian seaports, invited him to support them in revolt. A majority of the Toronæan people still favored the Athenian interest; fifty heavy-armed Athenians were in the place, and two Athenian triremes in the harbour. Nevertheless, through the able conduct of Brasidas, and the bold adventure of only seven men, introduced in the night by the party disposed to revolt, it was taken. The Athenians, except a few who were killed, and the greatest part of the Toronæans, c. 114, 115,
116. fled to the neighboring fortress of Lecythus. Brasidas summoned the place, offering permission for the Athenians to depart with their effects, and promising to the Toronæans the full enjoyment of their rights as citizens of Toronë, together with the restoration of whatever of their property had fallen into his possession or under his power. The terms were inviting to men in their perilous situation; yet the Athenians, having prevailed upon the Toronæans to adhere to them, refused to surrender, but requested a day of truce for the burial of the dead. What followed deserves notice, in the great scarcity of any inlarged patriotism among the Greeks, as an instance of the firmness with which they often adhered to party-principle. Brasidas granted two days, and used the opportunity for employing all his eloquence and all his address in the endevor to conciliate the Toronæans to

[8] Τυρσηνῶν.

his

his interest.   But the democratical party remained true to the Athenians; and not till machines were prepared, and a force was assembled,
scarcely possible for them to resist, nor then till an accident occasioned
a sudden panic, they quitted their fort of earth and wood, and most
of them, getting aboard vessels lying at hand, escaped across the
gulph into Pallenë. Such was the concluding event of the eighth year
of the war.

SECTION V.

*Negotiation for Peace between Athens and Lacedæmon.   Truce con-
cluded for a Year.   Transactions in Thrace.   War renewed.   Thespiæ
oppressed by Thebes.   War between Mantineia and Tegea.   Remarkable Instance of Athenian Superstition.*

INTELLIGENCE of the rapid successes of Brasidas, coïnciding with
the unfortunate event of the battle of Delium, and accompanied with
reasonable apprehension of spreading defection among the subject
cities, was of powerful effect to damp the wild ambition, and lower the
unruly haughtiness of the Athenian people.   It began again to be very
generally observed and regretted among them, that their leaders, those
in whom they most trusted, had advised them ill; and that so favorable an opportunity for making an advantageous peace, as that which
had been proudly rejected, might not again recur.   Fortunately for
them, at this time, no spirit of enterprize animated the Lacedæmonian
councils.   The successes of Brasidas, highly gratifying as far as they
tended to dispose the Athenians to peace, excited at the same time
some apprehension among the Lacedæmonian leaders, that their own
allies, and even the Lacedæmonian people, might be excited to desire
the continuance of the war, to which they were anxious to put a conclusion.   The great object of the principal families was to recover their
kinsmen and friends, prisoners in Athens; and while they dreaded a
reverse of fortune, that might renew the arrogance of their enemies,
they feared also such success as might too much elate their allies.

E E 2   Such

Such being the sentiments on both sides, negotiations for peace were opened, and, in the beginning of spring, a truce for a year was con-

Thucyd. l. 4. c. 118, 119.

cluded.   Each party retained what it possessed, but the Peloponnesians however conceded the intire command of the Grecian seas to Athens; excluding themselves totally from the use of long ships (the general term for ships of war) and of any vessel of the row-galley kind of above five hundred talents measurement, which, according to Arbuthnot, was sca cely more than twelve ton.   To this treaty the Lacedæmonians, Corinthians, Sicyonians, Epidaurians, and Megarians only were parties, on the side of the Peloponnesian confederacy; but they ingaged to·use their interest for persuading the Bœotians and Phocians to accede; and it was the professed purpose of the truce to give opportunity for negotiating a general and permanent peace.

While these measures were taking in Greece for putting an end to the ravages of war, circumstances arose in Thrace to disturb the effect of the negotiation, and to give new fewel to animosity.   The people

c. 120.

of Scionë, the principal town of the fruitful peninsula of Pallenë, reckoned themselves a Peloponnesian people; referring their origin to a colony of Achaians of Pellenë or Pallenë, in Peloponnesus, who had established themselves on the coast of Thrace in returning from the war of Troy.   This tradition tended to establish, among the Scionæans, a general partiality for the Peloponnesian connection, to which those of higher rank would otherwise incline; and a party among them communicated to Brasidas their desire to reject the dominion of Athens, and to be received under his protection.   To correspond concerning the proposal was not easy; for not only the Athenians commanded the sea, but, by the possession of Potidæa on the isthmus, they completely commanded also the communication by land.   Brasidas therefore, who chose always to depend upon his own address rather than that of any deputies, and who refused no danger in the prosecution of the great objects of his command, resolved to go himself to Scionë, and, in a small swift boat, escorted by one trireme, he arrived safe in the harbour.   He was so well assured of the strength of his party in the town, that he ventured immediately to assemble the people, and exert that eloquence which he had already found so useful.   He

began.

began with his usual declaration, which experience had proved no less politic than liberal, ' that no man should suffer in person, property, or ' privileges for past political conduct, or existing political connections.' He was then large in praise of the Scionæan people, ' who, notwith- ' standing the peculiar danger to which their situation, inclosed within ' a peninsula, exposed them, in revolting against that tyrannical power ' which at present commanded the seas, had nevertheless not waited ' till freedom should be forced upon them through the prevalence of ' the Peloponnesian arms, but had been forward to assert it ;' and he concluded with assurances ' of his readiness to give all protection, and ' his wish to do all honor, to a people who, he was confident, would ' prove themselves among the most meritorious allies of Lacedæmon.'

The rhetoric and the liberality of Brasidas had their desired effect. Many, even of those who before were adverse to the revolt, became now satisfied with it, and the whole people vied in paying honors, public and private, to the Spartan general. From the city he received a golden crown, which was in solemn ceremony placed on his head, as the deliverer of Greece; and individuals presented him with fillets, a usual mark of approving admiration to the conquerors in the public games; which, as something approaching to divine honor, was esteemed among the highest tokens of respect. Thucyd. l. 4. c. 121.

Scionë being thus gained, Brasidas was extending his views to Potidæa and Mendë, in both which places he held correspondence, when commissioners arrived, Aristonymus from Athens, and Athenæus from Lacedæmon, to announce the cessation of arms. The intelli- gence was joyful to the new allies of Lacedæmon in Thrace, as the terms of the treaty removed at once all the peril of the situation in which they had placed themselves. With regard to the Scionæans alone a dispute arose. Aristonymus, finding upon inquiry that the vote in assembly, by which they formally acceded to the Lacedæmo- nian alliance, had not passed till two days after the signing of the articles, declared them excluded from the benefit of the treaty. Bra- sidas, on the contrary, no way pleased with a truce that checked him in the full career of success, the first of any importance obtained by the Lacedæmonians in the war, and conceiving himself strongly pledged c. 122.

to

to preserve the Scionæans from Athenian vengeance, insisted that the revolt, truly considered, had taken place before the signing of the articles, and he refused to surrender the town. Aristonymus sent information of this to Athens, where preparation was immediately made to vindicate the claim of the commonwealth by arms. The Lacedæmonian government, disposed to support Brasidas, remonstrated; but the Athenian people, indignant, as Thucydides says, that not only their continental subjects, but now even those who were in the situation of ilanders, should so presume in the protection of the landforce of Peloponnesus, at the instigation of Cleon, made a decree, declaring that Scionë should be taken, and the people put to death.

At the very time when this passionate act of democratical despotism was passing, an event occurred, which might have taught the Athenians, if a mob could be taught, the superiority of the generous policy Thucyd. l. 4. of Brasidas to their illiberal and inhuman proceedings. Some of the c. 123. principal men of Mendë, an Eretrian colony, also within the peninsula of Pallenë, had already gone so far in measures for leading their city to revolt, that they dreaded beyond all things the scrutiny, and the consequent punishment, which were to be expected from the jealous tyranny of Athens. Accordingly, finding Brasidas, notwithstanding the truce, ready to receive them into the Lacedæmonian alliance, they thought it their safest way to prosecute the measure begun; and tho a majority of the lower people was adverse, they succeeded in their design. Brasidas justified himself, partly by urging counter-complaints of infraction of the treaty by the Athenians, partly by maintaining that nothing forbad his receiving any Grecian people into the Lacedæmonian alliance, when the measure on their part was voluntary, and on both sides without fraud or treachery. But the Athenians judged otherwise; they would not indeed deem the truce void, but they would proceed to inforce by arms their own sense of the conditions of it. Brasidas, expecting this, removed the families and effects of the Scionæans and Mendæans to Olynthus, strengthened the garrisons with five hundred heavy-armed Peloponnesians and three hundred middle-armed Chalcidians, and, having put everything in the best state for defence that time and circumstances would permit, he appointed Polydamidas,

3   apparently

apparently a Lacedæmonian, to the chief command, and returned himself to his army.

In the arduous and complex business in which Brasidas was ingaged,
in his quality of commander-in-chief of the Peloponnesian forces and
superintendant of the Peloponnesian affairs iñ Thrace, while among
Grecian towns his negotiations succeeded beyond hope, he found insuperable difficulty in managing his interests with the ambitious, crafty,
haughty, capricious, and faithless king of Macedonia. Whether
Arrhibæus had contravened or deserted his ingagements, or whether
Brasidas thought it of so much importance to preserve the friendship
of Perdiccas as to be induced himself to break with Arrhibæus, Thucydides does not inform us ; but the Spartan general and the Macedonian
king, with united forces, invaded Lyncestis.   Three thousand heavy- Thucyd. l. 4.
armed foot formed the principal strength of the former, and a thousand c. 124.
horse that of the latter, who was besides followed by a numerous body
of barbarian irregulars.   A battle was fought, in which the Lyncestians,
who were not without regular heavy-armed foot[9], were put to flight,
but the country being mountainous, they soon reached the heights,
where neither the Macedonian horse nor the Peloponnesian foot could,
with any hope of advantage, follow them.   Perdiccas proposed then to
overrun the plain country.   Brasidas was anxious for his new allies;
particularly those of Mendë, where the lower people were so generally
disposed to the Athenian interest, that should an Athenian force
approach the place in his absence, the citizens of higher rank, who had
effected the revolt, could not but be in the utmost peril.   Having
therefore so far served the king of Macedonia, he thought he might
reasonably withdraw his forces, to give necessary protection to their
common allies.   Perdiccas, however was dissatisfied that his wishes
were disputed ; and, while differences hence arising were yet unsettled,
intelligence arrived, that a large body of Illyrian mercenaries, expected c. 125.
to reïnforce the Macedonian army, had betrayed their ingagement, and
joined Arrhibæus.

This alarming information disposed Perdiccas to retreat with Brasidas ; but in consequence of their disagreement, measures were not

---

[9] The term ὁπλίτης always imports so much.

readily

readily concerted between them.   Night was approaching, and nothing
yet determined, when exaggerated reports of the Illyrian numbers
excited a panic through the Macedonian army, and the whole multitude of barbarian irregulars, with many of the Macedonians themselves,
took to sudden flight.   Already the evil was beyond remedy, before
Perdiccas was informed of it; and his camp was so distant from the
Peloponnesian, that it became necessary to follow his flying troops,
without waiting to communicate with the Spartan general.

When day broke, Brasidas found himself in a very perilous situation.
The superiority of the enemy's force, and his own want of means for
subsistence, left no choice but of hasty retreat.   He formed therefore
his heavy-armed in a hollow square: the light-armed he placed in the
center : he selected a small body of the youngest and most active men,
for a reserve, to assist in any point that might be most pressed ; and he
took upon himself the immediate command of the rear-guard, consisting
of three hundred chosen men.   Having then assured his people that
irregular barbarians, however alarming their numbers and their clamor
might appear, could never be reälly formidable to steddy troops, he
began his march.

Thucyd. L 4.
c. 126.

c. 127.   The Illyrians immediately pursued, with much vociferation and
tumult, as if already victors, and slaughter their only business.
They attacked : and, to their astonishment, were repulsed with loss:
they repeated the attempt with no better success ; and presently
deterred by the firm countenance of the retreating army, with its
readiness for efficacious resistance in every part, they drew off; but a
body of them pressed forward, with intention to occupy the defile of
the frontier mountains of Lyncestis, through which the Peloponnesians
must necessarily pass to enter Lower Macedonia.   Brasidas, aware of
this, detached his three hundred, with orders to proceed with all haste
to dislodge the enemy from the high ground, at least on one side of
the pass.   They succeeded in acquiring possession of one of the hills,
the enemy evacuated the other, and the army arrived on the same day
at Arnissa, the first town of the dominion of Perdiccas.

In the course of this well-conducted retreat, the Peloponnesians fell
in with much of the baggage and stores of the Macedonians, following,
as

as the conductors were able, scattered, and without a guard, the disorderly flight of their army. Irritated by the base desertion, as they esteemed it, of the Macedonians, the Peloponnesians seized whatever was most valuable and most portable; and then, loosing from their yokes the oxen employed in drawing the carriages, turned them wandering about the country. This ill-judged revenge, which the general probably could not prevent, completed the alienation of Perdiccas; who, that he might with less danger break with the Peloponnesians, began thenceforth to seek opportunity for renewing his alliance with Athens.

On returning into Thrace, Brasidas found reason to regret his unwilling absence from the protection of his new allies, and from the care of his interests in that country. An armament had arrived in Pallenë, under the command of Nicias and Nicostratus, consisting of forty Athenian and ten Chian triremes, with a thousand heavy-armed and six hundred bowmen of their national troops, a considerable body of middle-armed of their allies, and a thousand Thracian mercenaries. Proposing to direct their measures against the revolted cities of Mendë and Scionë, the Athenian generals began their operations with an attempt to force Polydamidas from a strong situation near the former, in which they narrowly escaped a total defeat. Reïmbarking however their troops, they went to Scionë, and took the suburbs on the first assault; but, unable to make any impression on the town, they proceeded to plunder the surrounding country. A party favoring them within the place, not powerful enough to put it into their hands, was nevertheless powerful enough to deter the ruling party from quitting their walls to protect their fields. Next day therefore the army was divided: half, under Nicias, ravaged the borders of the Scionæan and Mendian territories; while Nicostratus, with the other half, approached the town of Mendë [10].

Polydamidas, who had retired into that place with his Peloponne-

Thucyd. l. 4. c. 129.

---

[10] The text of Thucydides appears here evidently deficient, and neither the antient scholiast nor the modern annotators give any assistance. It is nevertheless pretty clear, from the context, that the sense here given, in which Smith's translation has been followed, is just. A note, however, which we do not find, to explain on what grounds his translation rested, would have added to our satisfaction.

sians, thought himself strong enough, if he could persuade the Mendians to zealous coöperation, to attack the Athenians in the field.   He
accordingly assembled the people, and proposed the measure; but he
was answered by one of the democratical party, ' that the Mendians
' would not march against the Athenians, and that no true interest of
' theirs had led them into their present ingagements with the Pelopon-
' nesians.'   Polydamidas, in pursuance of the rules of Spartan discipline, and of that authority which Lacedæmonians in command usually
everywhere assumed, rather than of the policy which his situation
required and the example of his general recommended, seized the man
with his own hands, and was proceeding to drag him out of the assembly.
This violent and arbitrary act so incensed the democratical party, that
they immediately assaulted his adherents.   These, imagining that measures had been concerted with the Athenian generals, now at the gates,
fled into the citadel, whither Polydamidas and the troops about him
also retired.   Meanwhile the gates were actually thrown open by some
of the democratical party; and the whole Athenian army, the forces of
Nicias having now joined those under Nicostratus, entered the town,
ignorant of what had passed within, and wondering why they were not
opposed.   The soldiers accordingly proceeded immediately to pillage,
and were with difficulty restrained even from putting the Mendians,
their friends, to the sword.   The tumult, however, being soon composed, the people were summoned to the agora.   The Athenian generals
then directed the restoration of the democratical form of government;
and, with a politic liberality, declared they would institute no inquiry
about the past, but would leave the Mendians to their own measures
concerning those, if any such remained among them, who had been
active in the revolt.

  Matters being thus settled in Mendë, and a part of the army left to
watch the citadel, the generals proceeded with the larger part against
Scionë.   Polydamidas had occupied a hill, the possession of which
would have prevented the surrounding of the town with a contravallation.   They dislodged him, and then immediately began to form
their lines.   Meanwhile the blockade of the citadel of Mendë had its
effect in reducing the place into the power of the Athenians; but the

garrison, by a bold effort, saved themselves. Sallying in the dusk of evening, they overcame the Athenian guard next the sea, and proceeding under cover of the night toward Scionë, broke through the Athenian camp there, and the greater part got safe into the town.

During these transactions, the negotiation for renewing the alliance between Athens and Macedonia, concerning which, presently after his retreat from Lyncestis, Perdiccas had begun to tamper with the Athenian generals, was brought to a conclusion; and the immediate consequence was of great importance. The party in Lacedæmon which favored Brasidas, had so far prevailed, that it was determined to send a body of forces, by the way of Thessaly, to strengthen his army. Intelligence of this being conveyed to Nicias and Nicostratus, they applied to their new ally, the king of Macedonia, to prevent the measure. Perdiccas had always maintained a strong interest in Thessaly, principally through personal communication in hospitality with the leading men. Being desirous to give proof of his sincerity in his revived ingagements with Athens, and otherwise little willing that his dominion should become a common road of communication for troops between Peloponnesus and Thrace, he prevailed with his Thessalian friends to interfere so effectually, that the Lacedæmonian government desisted from their purpose. Commissioners, however, were sent, of whom Ischagoras was chief, to inspect into the state of things in Thrace; and, contrary apparently to the ingagements of Brasidas, governors with the title of harmost, regulator, were sent with them from Sparta, to be constant guardians of the Lacedæmonian interests in the several towns. It is remarked by Thucydides, that all of these were under the age required by the Lacedæmonian institutions for forein command. Brasidas, deprived of the reïnforcement which he had long been soliciting, and which the Lacedæmonian government too late became disposed to grant him, toward the end of winter, nevertheless, made an attempt to surprize Potidæa; but, being discovered by the sentries, before he could apply scaling-ladders to the walls, he withdrew without effecting anything.

Thucyd. l. 4. c. 132.

c. 135.

During this year of nominal truce between Lacedæmon and Athens, while the interests of the two states were still prosecuted by arms in

Thrace, some circumstances for notice occurred in Greece. The

Thucyd. l. 4. c. 133.
Thebans accused the Thespians of the crime of Atticism, as they termed the inclination to an alliance with Athens. The Thespians, however, had been principal sufferers in the late battle with the Athenians, near Delium : but this very circumstance, which should have proved them not obnoxious to justice, rendered them unfortunately open to oppression ; and the Thebans, under the claim of that arbitrary authority which they asserted over all Bœotia, required that the fortifications of Thespiæ should be demolished, to which the people of that little city were obliged to submit.

c. 134.
A dispute between the Arcadian cities, in the want of a superintending authority, led to a petty war, and in the autumn of this year an obstinate battle was fought between the Mantineians and Tegeans. Each claimed the victory ; each raised its trophy ; and both being disabled for farther exertion immediately in the field, both endevored to gain the favor of the deïty, for future occasions, by presenting at

c. 133.
Delphi the spoil collected in the battle. About the same time, through some negligence of the antient priestess Chrysis, then in the fifty-fifth year of her sacred office, the celebrated temple of the Argian Juno was destroyed by fire. Chrysis, in dread of the judgement or the wrath of the Argian people, fled to Phlius.

Meanwhile the informed Athenians were offering a very remarkable instance of popular superstition. Ever looking up to a superior cause for the direction of the events of this world, they did not attribute the reverse of fortune, which they were beginning to experience, to the wretched constitution of their government, now so altered from that which Solon had established, nor to their own insufficiency for deciding on public measures, nor to the folly which, making them dupes to the boisterous eloquence of the ignoble and ignorant Cleon, led them to commit the administration of public affairs principally to his direction. Nor did they conceive themselves obnoxious to divine anger for all their unjust violence to their allies, and all their shocking cruelties to those whom they called rebellious subjects ; yet they did attribute

Thucyd. l. 5. c. 11. Diod. L. 12. c. 73.
their misfortunes to the indignation of the deïty. The fancy arose that the purification of the sacred iland of Delos had been deficiently performed,

performed, and it was proposed to secure the favor of the god by a new act of cruel injustice. The whole Delian people, subjects who had every right to protection from the Athenian government, were expelled from their iland, without having any other settlement provided for them. Those miserable Greeks, thus inhumanly treated by the most polished of their fellowcountrymen, found, however, charity from those whom they called barbarians: the Persian satrap Pharnaces gave them the territory of Atramytteium, on the Æolian coast, to cultivate for their subsistence.

SECTION VI.

State of Athens: Effect of Theatrical Satire: Cleon fined: Cleon appointed General in Thrace: Battle of Amphipolis.

AFTER the death of Pericles, there seems to have remained no man of rank in Athens, whose powers of elocution were of that superior kind, which, together with extraordinary talent for popularity, are necessary, in a democracy, for the guidance of public affairs. When all graver men were now tired of ineffectual opposition to the arrogance of the low and petulant Cleon in the general assembly, a poet undertook their cause, and attacked him on the public stage. The practice of the old comedy still subsisted in Athens: public characters were exhibited with the utmost freedom in the theater: masks, representing their countenances, being worn by the actors, who, in thus mimicking their persons, assumed, without any disguise, their names. This licence was of great political consequence; giving opportunity for those who could write, but who could not speak, to declare their sentiments, or to vent their spleen, on political topics: in the want of that art which now furnishes such ready means to multiply copies, a composition was thus at once communicated to a whole public; and stage exhibitions supplied the place of the political pamflets of modern times. The interest of a party thus might be promoted on the stage as in the agora; and those opinions might be propagated, and those passions excited, on one day

by

by theatrical exhibitions, which on the morrow might decide the measures of the general assembly.

Aristoph. Equit. v. 702.
It was after the affair of Pylus, when Cleon was in the height of his popularity, when, in pursuance of a decree of the people, he was honored with precedence at the public spectacles, and maintenance in the Prytaneium, that Aristophanes brought upon the stage of Athens that extraordinary comedy, which remains to us with the title of The Knights. Cleon is there represented in the most ludicrous and ignominious light; satire being at the same time not spared against the Athenian people, personated in their collective character by a single actor, with the name of Demus; as Swift, whose writings, by their extraordinary mixture of wit, elegance, buffoonery, and political acumen, approach beyond any other modern compositions to those of Aristophanes, has characterized the people of England under the appellation of John Bull. Such was the known influence of Cleon among the Athenian people, and such the dread of the intemperate use he
230.
might make of it, that no actor could be found bold enough to represent him on the stage, nor any artist to make a mask in his likeness. But Aristophanes would not be so disappointed: himself a man of rank, personally an enemy to Cleon, certain of support from all the first families of the republic, and trusting in his own powers to ingage the favor of the lower people, he undertook himself to act the part; and, for want of a proper mask, he disguised his face, after the manner of the strolling comedians of Thespis's time, with lees of wine.

The immediate effect of this extraordinary exhibition was great. The performance was relished and applauded; Cleon was ridiculed and reviled: in this temper of the people an accusation was preferred
Aristoph. Acharn. v. 6. & Nub. v. 559.
against him for imbezzeling public money: and, not finding his wonted support, he was condemned in a fine of five talents, above twelve hundred pounds sterling.

In such a government, however, as that of Athens, nothing was lasting but the capriciousness of the people. The reproach of a condemnation, against which the greatest and purest characters were scarcely more secure than the vilest, was not likely long to affect Cleon. Pericles himself had been condemned; and, within a few days,
the

the people anxiously invited him to take again the lead in public affairs.   Cleon wanted no such invitation; he did not, with his reputation, lose his impudence.   Continuing to cabal in the porticoes and vociferate in the assemblies, he loaded with vague accusation all the principal men cf the commonwealth.   The people gave him credit for abuse of their superiors, as they had given Aristophanes credit for abusing him.   In the general assembly the field thus became his own. Demosthenes son of Alcisthenes, an able officer, and apparently an able statesman, but unknown as a public speaker, seems to have yielded before him; the mild and timid Nicias feared to exert his abilities in the contest; and Cleon by degrees so reïngratiated himself with the people, as to become again the first man of the commonwealth, and to have its forces at his disposal.

His success at Pylus gave him to delude, not only the people but himself, with the imagination that he possessed military talents: he thought he could now command armies without the assistance of Demosthenes; and another fortunate expedition would drown the memory of what his reputation had suffered from the attack of Aristophanes, and inable him to overbear rivalship.   He therefore opposed, to his utmost, all proposals of a pacific tendency; urging continually that the tarnished glory of the commonwealth ought to be restored, and its losses repaired, by at least the recovery of what had been lately ravished from it.   His arguments were calculated to make impression on the passions of the multitude: and the truce was no sooner expired than a decree passed for sending a force into Thrace, to the command of which he was appointed.   The armament consisted of one thousand two hundred foot, and three hundred horse, of the flower of the Athenian youth, a considerable body of the allies, also select troops, and thirty trireme gallies.   The commission of commander-in-chief in Thrace gave power to increase his force from the auxiliaries of that country, and from the Athenian troops already there.

Thucyd. 1. 5. c. 2.

Thucyd. ibid. Aristoph. Nub. v. 581.

Thus vested with an important and extensive command, in the tenth spring of the war, Cleon took his departure from Peiræus with his armament.   Touching first in Pallenë, and reïnforcing himself with a part

B. C. 422. Ol. 89. 2. P. W. 10.

of

May.

of the army which was besieging Scionë, he proceeded to a place called the Colophonian port, not far from Toronë, in the neighboring peninsula of Sithonia.   He had been informed that, in pursuance of a plan of Brasidas, for extending the fortifications of Toronë, so as to include the suburbs, a part of the old wall had been taken down, and the new works were not yet completed.   Intelligence now came to him by

Thucyd. l. 5. c. 3.

deserters, that Brasidas was absent, and the garrison weak.   A sudden assault was in consequence attempted, which succeeded, and the governor, Pasitelidas, a Lacedæmonian, was made prisoner, with all those of the garrison and people who survived the first slaughter.

c. 6.

Elated with this easy success, Cleon determined to proceed against Amphipolis, the most important of all the places of which the valor and ability of Brasidas had deprived the Athenian empire.   Sailing therefore round Athos, and entering the Strymon, the armament anchored in the port of Eion.   This place Cleon chose for his central post.   Hence he made a fruitless attempt upon Stageirus, but he succeeded against Galepsus.   Meanwhile he applied to the king of Macedonia for the auxiliary force, which, according to treaty, he was to furnish, and endevored to obtain some mercenaries by negotiation with Polles, prince of the Odomantian Thracians.

c. 6.

Brasidas, who depended less upon any force he could with certainty command, than upon his own activity and address and the faults of his enemy, had hastened in vain to the relief of Toronë; tho when taken, he was already with a body of troops within five miles.   When Cleon moved toward the Strymon, Brasidas directed his attention to Amphipolis.   He could muster there, exclusively of the Amphipolitans, no more than two thousand regular heavy-armed foot, and one thousand middle-armed Thracian Greeks, with the valuable addition, however, of three hundred Grecian horse.   The strength of the Amphipolitans, to be relied upon, was uncertain, on account of the difference in political sentiments among so mixed a people.   The Edonian Thracians, however, voluntarily joined him with the whole force of their clan, horse and middle-armed foot, and he ingaged fifteen hundred Thracian mercenaries.   With a body of fifteen hundred

men,

men, selected from these various troops, he occupied Cerdylium, a lofty
and strong situation on the western bank of the Strymon, whence he
could observe the motions of the Athenian army incamped on the
opposite bank.   The remainder of his forces he left within the walls of
Amphipolis, under the command of Cleäridas.

This being the situation of the two armies, Cleon, whose business Thucyd. l. 5.
was offensive operation, rested some time in total inaction, through c. 7, 8, & 10.
meer ignorance, as Thucydides assures us, how to proceed.   The numbers on each side were nearly equal; but the Athenian army was far
superior in the kind of troops; those who were not Athenian citizens
being the flower of the Lemnian and Imbrian forces.   Confident in
their own ability, and from the first little satisfied with the command c. 7.
under which they were placed, they grew uneasy in inactivity; while
in their leisure they compared the known talents and courage of Brasidas with the evident deficiency of their own general. Cleon, informed
of the growing discontent, became apprehensive of the consequences.
It was his desire to await the reinforcements which he expected:
but, in the mean time, to hold out to his troops the appearance at least
of employment, and the expectation of something more intended, and
thinking, says Thucydides, to infuse an opinion of his military skill
by a movement similar to what, tho not his own, had gained him so
much credit at Pylus, he quitted his camp and approached Amphipolis.
His declared purpose was, not to attack the enemy, who, he trusted,
would feel their inferiority too much to venture to attack him:
but only to make observations, and when the expected reinforcements should arrive, he intended at once to surround and storm the
town.   He therefore occupied a lofty hill, which overlooked the place,
and commanded, on one side, a view of the Strymon expanding into a
lake as it approached the sea, on the other, of the varied ground
through which its waters flowed from the inland country.   Here he
formed his camp, confident of holding it in his option equally to remain
or retire, unmolested.   Meanwhile the gates of the town being kept
close, and no troops appearing upon the walls, he began to think he
had been deficient in not bringing machines, with the coöperation of

which, in the apparent weakness and timidity of the garrison, a brisk assault might, he imagined, have carried the place.

Thucyd. 1. 5. c. 8. Brasidas, aware of the inferiority of his own troops in arms and in discipline, but the more confident in the resources of his genius, as he knew the inability of the general opposed to him, was anxious to bring on a battle before the reïnforcement should arrive. As soon therefore as he saw Cleon in motion, he also moved from his post on Cerdylium into Amphipolis. Observing then the disorderly negligence of c. 9. the enemy, and their apparent confidence in security, he formed his plan accordingly. By a sudden attack, without that perfect order of battle to which the Greeks generally attached great importance, he expected to gain two points: first, to throw the enemy into a confusion, which might reduce their troops to a level with his own; and then to prevent the incouragement which they would derive from the observation, if he allowed them means for it, of the small proportion which his regular heavy-armed bore to his total numbers. He could not, however, prudently omit those ceremonies which Grecian religion required as indispensable preparatives for a battle; and the Athenians, from the height which they occupied, could plainly distinguish the sacrifice performing in Amphipolis, before the temple of Minerva, and c. 10. the bustle of preparation throughout the town. Thucydides adds, that the feet of horses and men in great numbers, as preparing to come out, so near might the antient fortifications be approached for the purpose of observation, could be discerned under the town-gates.

Cleon, receiving information of these circumstances, and then assuring himself of the truth of it with his own eyes, would not await attack from a force which he had affected to despise, but instantly commanded the retreat of his whole army to Eion. This the nature of the ground would permit only to be performed by files from the left; which, in the Greek system of tactics, was highly disadvantageous. To remedy the defect and obviate the consequent danger, Cleon thinking he should have leisure for it, as soon as the ground permitted, wheeled round his right. If he had been in concert with the enemy to expose his army to certain defeat, he could scarcely have taken

measures

measures more effectual for the purpose. The evolution not only broke, for the time, that compact arrangement whence arose the security and strength of the Grecian phalanx, but exposed the soldier's right side, unprotected by his shield, to the enemy's weapons. This was an advantage beyond what Brasidas had hoped for. Exulting he exclaimed, ' An army moving in that manner does not mean to stand its ' ground; the victory is already ours; open the gates for me;' and immediately at the head of a chosen band of only one hundred and fifty men, if our copies of Thucydides are right, he ran toward the center of the Athenian army, the part, at that instant, the most disordered. At the same time Cleäridas, at the head of the rest of the Peloponnesian forces, issuing out of that called the Thracian gate, with a more steddy pace, supported Brasidas, and attacked other parts of the Athenian line.

In this situation of things, the Athenian left, already some way advanced, punctually obeyed the orders received, to hasten the march toward Eion, and, breaking away from the center, was soon out of reach of the enemy. This conduct was justified by that of the general, whom nothing could divert from his first purpose, to retreat. Quitting his right, with intention to join his left in its security, he was intercepted by a Myrcinian targeteer, from whom he received the death he deserved, marked with the ignominy of flight.

The disordered center of the Athenian army having been defeated in the first moment of attack, while the left had withdrawn from the contest, Brasidas directed his efforts to the right; which, tho deserted by its general, had preserved its order; and regaining the high ground, resisted firmly. Exerting himself apparently too much as a private soldier, of which his uncommon strength and activity, perhaps, led him to be over-fond, Brasidas received a wound; and falling, unperceived by the Athenians, was carried off by his friends. The heavy-armed under Cleäridas, coming to support him, were repulsed more than once, and the Athenians maintained the contest till they were surrounded; the enemy's horse and middle-armed foot galling their rear and flanks, while the whole force of the heavy-armed pressed them in front. Compelled thus at length to give way, they retreated toward

the

the neighboring mountains, which they gained not without great difficulty and much loss; and then dispersing, fled, each as he best could,
to Eion.   Brasidas lived to be brought into Amphipolis, and to know
that his army was completely victorious, and soon after expired.

Scarcely any Spartan known in history, and indeed few men of any
nation, have shown themselves so indowed with talents to command
armies and to persuade citizens, to make and to maintain conquests, as
Brasidas. The estimation in which he was held, was remarkably testified
by the honors paid to his memory   His funeral was performed with the
utmost solemnity at the public expence; all the allies, as well as the
Peloponnesian forces, attending in arms.   A spot in front of the agora
of Amphipolis was chosen to receive his ashes, and, as sacred ground,
was inclosed with a fence, to prevent profane intrusion: a monument
was erected there to perpetuate his memory: every testimony to the
foundation of the colony by the Athenian Agnon, whether public
building or whatever else, was carefully destroyed; and it was ordained
by public decree, that, in future, Brasidas, the founder of the liberty of
Amphipolis, should be venerated as the true founder of the city; and to
conclude all, worship was decreed to him as a hero or demigod, and
public games, with sacrifices, were instituted, to be annually performed
to his honor[12].

Thucyd. 1. 4.
c. 11.

[12] Diodorus, and, after him, Plutarch,
relate, that ambassadors from the Thracian
Greeks to Sparta (and such a mission is
mentioned by Thucydides, l. 5. c. 21.) were
questioned by the mother of Brasidas, Argaleonis, concerning the death of her son.
In reply, speaking largely in his praise, they
said, that Brasidas had not left his equal
behind him. 'Strangers,' answered Argaleonis, ' you mistake: my son was a man
' of great merit, but there are many supe-
' rior to him in Sparta.' Diod. l. 12. c.74.
Plut. Apoph. Lacon. This anecdote is perfectly consonant to the spirit of patriotism,
which it was the purpose of the Spartan institutions to instil into every citizen of
either sex, and it may have had its foundation in fact: but according to every account

of the times, particularly that of Thucydides, Argaleonis, if the story is fairly told,
was more partial to her country than just
to her son, and tho the sentiment had
something noble, the assertion was not
true; for Brasidas did not leave his equal
behind him in Sparta, nor, apparently in all
Greece. The high reputation in which he
was held by his enemies, may be gathered
from an expression which Plato has put
into the mouth of Alcibiades, where, speaking of great characters, and of Socrates as
the only one without a parallel, he says
Brasidas was not so, for he might be compared to Achilles: Ὁιος γὰρ Αχιλλεὺς ἐγενέτο,
ἀπεικάσειεν ἄν τις καὶ Βρασίδαν. Conviv.
p. 221. t. 3.
This expression of Plato seems to mark
the

11

SECTION VII.

Passage through Thessaly denied to the Lacedæmonian Troops. Nego-
tiation for Peace resumed by Lacedæmon and Athens: A partial
Peace concluded.

Too late the envy of the leading men in the Spartan administration had   Thucyd. l. 5.
yielded to the pressing occasions of the commonwealth, which wanted   c. 12.
abilities like those of Brasidas, and a body of nine hundred heavy-
armed, under the command of Ramphias, Autocharidas, and Epicydides,
had been ordered to his assistance.   Toward the end of summer they   Mid. Sept.
arrived at Heracleia in Trachinia, and while they were settling the
deranged affairs of that colony, the action near Amphipolis happened.
They had already entered Thessaly, when intelligence of it reached   Thucyd. l. 5.
them; and about the same time a declaration was communicated to   c. 13.
them from the Thessalians, that their march through Thessaly would
be opposed.   The difficulty thus presented, the consciousness, as Thucydides adds, of their insufficiency for the prosecution of those designs
which had originated with Brasidas, the consideration that the necessity
for reïnforcing the Peloponnesian troops in Thrace was alleviated by
the advantages already gained there, and the knowlege that the leading men of their administration were more anxious for peace than
willing to risk farther the events of war, all together determined them
immediately to lead their little army home.

A concurrence of circumstances now contributed to induce the two   c. 14.
leading powers nearly equally to desire peace.   The Lacedæmonians

the superior strength and activity of Brasidas, and his disposition to personal exertion in battle.   Perhaps we might do him
an honor not less his due, by comparing
him with a soldier of our own country, not
particularly remarkable for those qualities.
The concluding part of his life, at least,
bore a strong resemblance to that of our
conqueror of Canada.   The obvious differences are, that Wolfe commanded the
smaller and more disciplined army against
the more numerous and less regular; that
his business was attack, that of Brasidas
defence; and that, instead of a Cleon, the
general opposed to him was a man of rank,
and of distinguished abilities, experience and
general worth.

                                        had

had originally ingaged in the war in confidence of decisive superiority,
and in full hope that the waste of Attica, with a battle, which they
expected would insue, and in which they had no doubt of being victorious, would bring the Athenians to their terms.   The event had everyway deceived their expectation.   The ravage of Attica had produced
no important consequence; they found themselves utterly unable to
raise that formidable navy which they had projected : on the contrary,
their allies had been exposed to continual danger, and suffered extensive injury, from the Athenian fleets; and at length the blow had fallen
severely on themselves.   Their loss in killed and prisoners at Pylus
was such as never within memory had happened to their state: the
enemy possessed a fortress within their country; a most galling circumstance, and still more strange to them : an iland was taken from
them, which commanded their coast; and from Pylus and from Cythera
their lands were infested, and depredation was spred, in a manner before
totally unexperienced.   Their slaves at the same time deserted in numbers, and the apprehension was continual, that confidence in forein
assistance would excite insurrection among the numerous remainder of
those oppressed men.   Anxiety was unceasing in the principal families,
for their friends and relations confined in the public prison of Athens;
and, to make the prospect more alarming, a truce, which had been concluded for thirty years between Lacedæmon and Argos, was on the
point of expiring, and the Argians refused to renew it but on terms to
which the Lacedæmonians were very unwilling to submit ; while at the
same time there appeared reason to apprehend that a breach with Argos
would make a schism in Peloponnesus, and that some of the principal
states of their alliance would side with the Argians against them.

So many and so weighty were the causes which still urged Lacedæmon, notwithstanding the late turn of fortune in her favor, to be solicitous for peace.   At the same time that turn of fortune had considerably lowered the haughty tone of Athens.   The defeats at Delium and
Amphipolis, the revolt of so many of their dependencies, and the fear
that others would follow a successful example, had checked the idea
before prevailing, that they could command the fortune of war, and
might dictate the terms of peace ; and there followed a very general
regret,

Thucyd. l. 5.
c. 15.

c. 14.

regret, that the favorable opportunity, procured by the success at Pylus, had been, in wanton haughtiness, thrown away.

With the inclination of the people, on both sides, it fortunately happened that the temper and interests of the leading men concurred. By the death of the turbulent Cleon, the mild Nicias was left undisputedly first minister of the Athenian commonwealth. While the innate temper of Nicias disposed him to peace, the inclination was heightened by the accidental circumstance of possessing a very large patrimony, which, in the insecurity of the scanty territory of a Grecian republic, peace only could inable to injoy; and even the desire of glory, to which he was not insensible, led him to seek the reputation of being the peace-maker for his country, while peace could yet be made with certain advantage. At the same time, among the Lacedæmonians, the interest of Pleistoanax, the reigning prince of the house of Eurysthenes, led him to be urgent for peace. Pleistoanax, as we have heretofore seen, in early youth, had been condemned to banishment, on suspicion of taking bribes from Pericles to lead the Peloponnesian army out of Attica. The Lacedæmonian ministry, it appears, whether in the necessity of complying with popular superstition, or desirous of finding a cover for their own inability and an excuse for miscarriages, frequently applied for advice to the Delphian oracle; and they were disturbed with the continual repetition of an exhortation annexed to every response, ' That the Lacedæmonians should bring back the demigod, ' son of Jupiter.' The friends of Pleistoanax interpreted this as a divine admonition to restore that prince, the descendant and representative of the demigods Hercules and Perseus, acknowleged by Grecian superstition as sons of Jupiter; and Pleistoanax was in consequence restored, after a banishment of nineteen years. But a report was circulated, and gained extensive credit, that the admonitory response had been procured by bribery to the Delphian priests; and the party in opposition did not fail to make advantage of that report, attributing every adversity that befel the Spartan arms, to the anger of the gods at the restoration of Pleistoanax, at any rate offensive to them, but doubly so, as having been procured by such impious collusion. Thus

it

Thucyd. l. 5. c. 16.

Ch 12. s. 5. of this Hist.

Thucyd. ut sup.

it became particularly an object with that prince to obviate the risk of
calamities from war.

Thucyd. l. 5.
c. 17. Such being the disposition on both sides, conferences were opened,
and they were continued through the winter. Toward spring the
negotiation was so little advanced, that the Lacedæmonians circulated
notices among their allies, to prepare, not only for a fresh invasion of
Attica, but for the establishment of a fortified post in the country.
Soon after, however, preliminaries were agreed upon ; the fundamental
principle of which was, that each party should restore what had been
taken in the war ; except that Nisæa was reserved to Athens, in consideration of the refusal of the Thebans to surrender Platæa. A convention of deputies from the states of the Lacedæmonian alliance was then
assembled, when the Bœotians, Corinthians, Eleians, and Megarians
protested against the proposed terms : but the other states, who formed
a majority of the assembly, approving them, the Lacedæmonian government proceeded to ratify the peace in the name of the whole confe-
c. 18. deracy. It ran nearly thus : ' That the common temples, the religious
' rites, and the oracles of the Greek nation, (those of Delphi particu-
' larly named) should be equally open to all, to pass to and from at all
' times in safety, by sea or by land ; and that the Delphian people
' should be independent, yielding obedience and paying tribute to
' none : That the treaty should remain in force for fifty years : That
' if any disputes should arise between the contracting powers, they
' should be determined by judicial process, the mode of which should
' be hereafter settled : That the cities to be restored by Lacedæmon,
' namely, Argilus, Stageirus, Acanthus, Scolus, Olynthus, Spartolus,
' together with those in the peninsula of Athos, should be free, paying
' only to Athens the tribute appointed by Aristeides : That those cities
' should not, by the operation of this treaty, be bound in confederacy
' with either party ; but that it should be permitted them, by their own
' act, if they should hereafter chuse it, to join the Athenian confede-
' racy : That Amphipolis, being an Athenian colony, should be
' restored unconditionally : and that the Lacedæmonians should pro-
' cure the restoration of the fortress of Panactum in Attica, taken by
                                                        ' the

' the Bœotians.   On the other side, that Coryphasium (the territory
' in which Pylus was situated) Cythera, Methonë, Pteleum, and Ata-
' lanta should be restored to Lacedæmon.   Prisoners were to be equally
' restored on both sides.   The Scionæans, now besieged, were left to
' the mercy of the Athenian people; the safe departure of the Pelo-
' ponnesians in garrison with them only being provided for.   It was
' then stipulated that every state acceding to the treaty should severally
' swear to the observation of it, by that oath which its own religious
' institutions made for itself most sacred and binding; that such oath
' should be repeated annually; and that columns, with the treaty
' inscribed, should be erected at Olympia, at Pytho (the name by
' which Homer calls Delphi, and which seems to have been continued
' in use as a more solemn and sacred appellation) at the isthmus, at
' Athens in the citadel, and at Lacedæmon in the Amyclæum: and,
' finally, that it should be lawful for the Athenians and Lacedæmo-
' nians, by mutual consent, to supply any omission, and, after due
' discussion, to make any alteration in these articles.'   The date is then   Thucyd. l. 5.
added thus : 'At the conclusion of the treaty presided the ephor Pleis-   c. 19.
' tolas, on the fourth day before the end of the Lacedæmonian month
' Artemisius, and the archon of Athens, Alcæus, on the sixth day before
' the end of the Athenian month Elaphebolion,' which our chronologers
make the tenth of April.   Fifteen Lacedæmonians and seventeen Athenians, as representatives of the two states, assisted at the sacrifices, and
took the oaths.   The name of the ephor Pleistolas stands at the head
of the Lacedæmonians, that of Lampon is first of the Athenians; among
whom we find those of Nicias, Laches, Agnon, Lamachus, Demosthenes, and others who had been in high situations in the government.

CHAPTER XVII.

Of the PELOPONNESIAN WAR, during the PEACE between LACEDÆMON and ATHENS.

SECTION I.

Difficulties in the Execution of the Articles of the Peace. Alliance between Lacedæmon and Athens. Intrigues of the Corinthians: New Confederacy in Peloponnesus: Dispute between Lacedæmon and Elis: Dispute between Lacedæmon and Mantineia. Tyranny of the Athenian People: Surrender of Scione: Superstition of the Athenian People.

THE treaty of peace thus concluded between the leading powers of the two confederacies, which had been contending, with little remission, now ten years in arms, was ill calculated to give general and permanent quiet to the nation. A want of able men in the administration of Lacedæmon, which had been manifested in the conduct of the affairs of that state through the whole of the war, above all showed itself in this treaty, and in the circumstances which followed. A narrow policy appeared in the treaty itself: the exclusive interest of Lacedæmon was considered: that of the allies, by whom Lacedæmon was powerful, and without whom she scarcely could be safe (such was the alteration since the simple age of her great legislator) were unpardonably neglected. The Lacedæmonians themselves were to recover all that had been taken from them; but their old and necessary allies the Corinthians were to remain deprived of their colonies of Soleium in Ætolia, and Anactorium in Acarnania: the Megarians were to put up with the much more distressing loss of Nisæa, their port, not a mile from the city; while the Eleians were suffering, not neglect, but what they imputed to Sparta as active injustice and oppression. With all this, the Lacedæmonian administration found themselves unable to

Thucyd. l. 5. c. 21.

4

carry

carry into effect some of the most important articles of their own
treaty.   It was to be decided by lot, which of the contracting parties Thucyd. l. 5.
should first perform its ingagement, for the restoration of prisoners and c. 21.
places taken, and the lot fell upon Lacedæmon.   Accordingly the
Athenian prisoners were immediately released; and Ischagoras, with
two other commissioners, was sent into Thrace, to direct the surrender
of Amphipolis, and to require compliance with the terms of the treaty,
from the towns which had been received into the Lacedæmonian
alliance.   But those towns refused; and Cleäridas, who had succeeded
Brasidas in the command in chief in Thrace, would not, pretending he
could not, in opposition to the Chalcidians, surrender Amphipolis.
Both the general, however, and the Chalcidian chiefs, became apprehensive of the consequences of this disobedience; and the former went
himself, the others sent deputies, to apologize for their conduct, but at
the same time with a view to procure an alteration of the articles, or
even to disturb the peace.   Cleäridas was hastily remanded, with orders
to bring away all the Peloponnesian forces, if compliance with the
terms of the treaty should be any longer delayed.

The congress of deputies of the confederacy remained still assembled c. 22.
in Lacedæmon, and the Lacedæmonian administration had been in
vain urging the dissentients to accede to the treaty.   They were
equally unsuccessful in the endevor to accommodate matters with
Argos; so that, with that state, a war seemed inevitable, in which,
according to all appearance, the greater part of Peloponnesus would be
against them.   Alarmed by these considerations, they proposed a c. 23.
defensive alliance with Athens, which was hastily concluded; and then
the Athenians released the prisoners taken in Sphacteria.   Meanwhile c. 24.
the congress of the Peloponnesian confederacy was dismissed, with a
disposition, among many of the members, far from friendly to the poli- c. 22. 27
tical quiet of Greece.

The complex intrigues that insued among the Grecian republics,
form, in the detail of them remaining to us from Thucydides, not
indeed the most splendid, but one of the most curious and instructive
portions of Grecian history.   Nothing gives to know so intimately
the political state of Greece in general, at the time, or the state of

H H 2   parties

parties in the principal republics; and nothing affords equal ground
for a just estimation of the value of that union, scarcely to be called a
federal union, but rather a connection founded on opinion, and supported principally by similarity of language, manners, and religious
belief; a connection subsisting unequally, uncertainly, and yet subsisting, among the numerous and scattered members of the Greek
nation. It may indeed be difficult, even with that able and exact
historian for our guide, to avoid some tediousness, and perhaps some
confusion in the narration; which must however be hazarded, rather
than evade an important part of the office of historian.

Thucyd. l. 5.   The Corinthians, irritated now against Lacedæmon, were not less
c. 27.   warm than at the beginning of the war in enmity to Athens. When
the convention of the confederacy was dismissed, their deputies, instead
of returning immediately home, went to Argos, where means of confidential communication with some of the leading men ' were open to
them. To these they urged, that ' since the Lacedæmonians, resign-
' ing their antient character, or rather their pretension to the character,
' of protectors of the liberty of Greece, had made not only peace, but
' a close alliance, with the Athenians, its most determined and dangerous
' enemies, it became the Argians to interfere, toward the preservation,
' at least, of Peloponnesus. The opportunity which present circum-
' stances offered,' they said, ' was inviting : for such was the disgust
' taken at the conduct of Lacedæmon, it would be only to declare, by
' a public decree, the readiness of the Argian people to enter into
' alliance with any independent Grecian cities, and they would quickly
' find themselves at the head of a powerful confederacy.' The Argian
chiefs were very well disposed to the measure thus recommended ; but
a difficulty occurred in the democratical form of their government.
In regular course, all negotiation with forein states must be transacted
with the assembly of the people. This would unavoidably make the
business more public than suited the views of the Corinthian deputies,
or could consist with the safety of the leading men in some of the
republics with which they meant to negotiate. The Corinthian ministers therefore advised to propose, in general terms only, to the Argian

' —— Τῶν ἰν τίλει.

people,

people, ' That alliances should be made with friendly Grecian states;' and when this proposition had received the sanction of a decree, it might be ventured farther to recommend, 'That the necessary nego- ' tiations should be intrusted to select commissioners.'

A concurrence of circumstances at this time favored the purpose of the Corinthians.   While the reputation of Lacedæmon had been con- siderably lowered in Greece by the events of the late war, Argos, keeping upon good terms with all the contending powers, had thriven in peace. Ambition grew with increasing wealth and strength, and the decay of Lacedæmon seemed to offer an opening for Argos, to recover its antient preëminence and command in Peloponnesus; which, far from an empty honor, would be a very important advantage, when, as at present, a war with that still powerful neighbor was impending.   Thus the Corinthian deputies succeeded with the Argian chiefs, and these with the people; and a committee of twelve men was appointed, with full power to conclude treaties of alliance, defensive and offensive, with any Grecian states, except Athens and Lacedæmon: if either of these should offer, it was required that the proposal should be laid before the Argian people. Thucyd. l. 5. c. 28.

Not any liberal view to an improvement of the federal union of Greece, but the separate interest of particular republics, brought the first accession to the proposed new confederacy under the presidency of Argos.   While the war with Athens had kept Lacedæmon fully ingaged, the Mantineians had compelled a part of Arcadia, before inde- pendent, to submit to their dominion; and they justly apprehended that, in the leisure of peace, however any generous regard for the com- mon welfare might be wanting, the consideration of their own interest would urge the Lacedæmonians to interfere, and prevent such exercise of sovereinty over any people within Peloponnesus.   The universal liberty of Greece had been held out as the first principle of the new confederacy; but to make a beginning toward collecting allies, was esteemed by the Argians of more importance than a strict adherence to any such principle.   The government of Mantineia, like their own, was democratical: which was a reason both for their union in oppo- sition to Lacedæmon, and for the allowance of some indulgence to c. 29.

Mantineia

Mantineia in the exercise of a tyrannical authority over other Grecian states.

This narrow and corrupt policy was, in the moment, not unattended with the proposed advantage. Great and general offence and alarm had been taken at that article in the treaty between Lacedæmon and Athens, which declared that the Lacedæmonians and Athenians, without mention of any other states of Greece, might in concurrence, at any time, make whatever alteration in the conditions to them should seem fit; which was little less than a declaration of authority, in those two states united, to give law to Greece. The accession of Mantineia to the new confederacy increased the ferment: for, while intelligence of the fact was circulated, the motives were not universally obvious; and it was very generally supposed, that the Mantineians, near neighbors to both Lacedæmon and Argos, knew more than was generally known, and that reasons which impelled them ought probably to weigh with all.

Thucyd. l. 5.   The Lacedæmonian administration, early informed of all these poli-
c. 30.   tical movements, were greatly alarmed. Ministers were dispatched to Corinth, which was understood to be the fountain-head of the intrigue, to inquire and remonstrate. By the terms of that confederacy of which Lacedæmon was the head, it was stipulated that the voice of a majority of the states should bind the whole; with an exception, however, required perhaps by Grecian superstition, but singularly adapted to political evasion, expressed in these terms, ' provided no hindrance ' occurred from the gods or heroes.' Whatever might be the views of some leading men among the Corinthians in desiring the continuance of the war, the cause of the general dissatisfaction of the Corinthian people with the terms of the peace, was well known, and was reasonable. The Lacedæmonians, in stipulating for the restoration of all places taken from themselves by the Athenians, had ceded the towns of Soleium and Anactorium, taken from the Corinthians. But this, however a real grievance and a just cause of dissatisfaction, could not properly be urged by the Corinthians as a cause for refusing accession to the treaty with Athens, which was a regular act of the confederacy. They resorted therefore to the gods for their pretence; alledging that
                                                                    they

they had bound themselves by oath to protect the Potidæans and their other allies in Thrace; whence arose a hindrance from the gods, such that they could not accede to the terms of the treaty.   To the complaints of the Lacedæmonians about the Argian confederacy, they replied, ' that they would consult their allies, and do nothing but what ' should be deemed proper and just.'   With these answers the Lacedæmonian ministers, unable to obtain any farther satisfaction, returned home.

In the disputes, difficult by any means to settle, to which the division of Peloponnesus into so many independent village states gave perpetual occasion, circumstances had arisen to set the Eleians, still more than the Corinthians, at variance with Lacedæmon.   Before the war, the people of the little town of Lepreum, oppressed by the united enmity of some neighboring Arcadian villages, had applied to Elis for protection, offering half their lands to obtain it.   The Eleians, accepting the condition, compelled the Arcadians to make peace, and then allowed the Lepreans still to occupy the ceded territory, paying only an acknowlegement of a talent yearly to Olympian Jupiter.   For anything that appears, the bargain was advantageous for a people so unable to defend their property, and maintain themselves in unconnected independency, as the Lepreans.   But when the war with Athens broke out, the Lepreans, as well as the Eleians, being members of the Lacedæmonian confederacy, urged the expence of expeditions into Attica, and other burthens of the war, as pretences for discontinuing the payment.   This however, the Eleians would not admit; upon which the Lepreans appealed to Lacedæmon: but the Eleians, apprehending that they should not have fair measure of justice there, waved the arbitration, and asserted their right by arms.   The Lacedæmonians nevertheless proceeded to give sentence in the cause, declaring the Eleians aggressors, and the Lepreans free; and upon the refusal of the Eleians to accept this decision, they had put a body of forces into Lepreum for its protection.

Irritated by this arbitrary, and, as they esteemed it, unjust proceeding, the Eleians were prepared for the opportunity which now offered for ingaging in a confederacy of Peloponnesian states, in oppo-

sition

Thucyd. l. 5. c. 31.

sition to Lacedæmon.   They sent ministers to Corinth, who concluded
a separate treaty of alliance with that state; and, proceeding to Argos,
pledged their commonwealth to the new confederacy.   Then the
Corinthians also acceded to that confederacy, and their influence
decided the Chalcidians of Thrace to the same measure.   The Bœotians
and Megarians were enough dissatisfied with Lacedæmon to declare
approbation of it, and an intention to concur.   But the consideration
that the presidency of a democratical government could scarcely fail
to jar with the interests of their oligarchal administrations, made them
hesitate to conclude.

Thucyd. l. 5.
c. 33.   While these intrigues were going forward, for the purpose of subverting the power of Lacedæmon, the administration of that state were
carrying into effect against the Mantineians, after their usual method,
by force of arms, that undefined and arbitrary kind of jurisdiction,
which the Peloponnesians seem, in some measure, by common consent
to have committed to them, and which, tho not often successfully, had
nevertheless been opposed almost as often as exercised.   A party at
Parrhasii in Arcadia, one of the townships which the Mantineians had
subjected, applied to Lacedæmon for relief.   The Mantineians were
not only obnoxious at Lacedæmon, for their new connection with
Argos, but still more particularly for having put a garrison into
Cypsela, a fortress in the Parrhasian territory, close upon the borders
of Laconia.   At the same time therefore to take Cypsela, and to relieve
the Parrhasians from their subjection to Mantineia, which would be
in effect to bring them under subjection to Lacedæmon, the whole
force of the commonwealth marched under the king Pleistoanax.

The resource of the Mantineians, not one of the smallest republics
of Greece, is among the strongest proofs of the miserably uncertain
state of government, law, property, and freedom, through the greatest
part of that country.   That they might exert their whole force in
defence of the Parrhasian territory, they committed their own city,
with their families, and indeed their all, except themselves and their
arms, to a garrison of Argians.   They were nevertheless unable to give
any effectual opposition to the Lacedæmonian army : Cypsela was
destroyed, and Parrhasii, as far as under Lacedæmonian protection
                                                        might

might be, became again an independent state. The fidelity of the Argians to their trust, however, cemented the new connection between their state and Mantineia.

In the course of the summer, Cleäridas returned to Lacedæmon, with the troops which had fought under Brasidas in Thrace; and the government rewarded the valor and zeal of the Helots of that army with the present of their liberty, giving them leave to settle themselves wherever they could find a livelihood. The present seems thus to have been of small value; for the Helots were little able to provide a settlement for themselves. But in Lacedæmon were some other Helots, who, to strengthen the state in its declining circumstances, had been admitted to the rights of citizens; and Spartan pride and Spartan jealousy, now peace was restored with Athens, would willingly see all those persons members of any state rather than of their own. The infranchised Helots therefore were all established in Lepreum, as an increase of force to that town against the enmity of Elis. ^{Thucyd. l. 5. c. 34.}

A measure of arbitrary severity, not indicating a good and firm constitution, was about the same time taken, on the plea of necessity for the security of the commonwealth, against the unfortunate men who had been just restored to their country, after so long languishing in Athenian prisons. Not only many of them were of high rank, but some were actually in high offices. They found themselves nevertheless exposed to frequent invective, for having done, what was esteemed, among the Lacedæmonians, so disgraceful and so illegal, and hitherto so unknown, as surrendering their arms to an enemy, tho, for the occasion, it had been specially warranted by the executive power. Some disturbance was apprehended in consequence; to prevent which, a decree of degradation was passed by the people against them, rendering them incapable of office, and, what appears extraordinary, whether as precaution or punishment, incapable of buying or selling. Some time after, however, tho what occasioned the change we are not informed, they were restored to their former rights and honors.

Peloponnesus thus, long esteemed the best-governed and the happiest portion of the Greek nation, might seem now to have sheathed the sword, drawn against external enemies, only to give the freer opportunity ^{Isoc ehid. & or. ad Philipp.}

tunity for internal convulsion.   Athens meanwhile, and her confederacy, were not better prepared for political quiet and civil order.   In
that state indeed of the Athenian constitution, which gave means for
Cleon to become first minister and general in chief, the fate of the subordinate republics, subjected to the arbitrary will of such a soverein as
the Athenian people, under the guidance of such a minister as Cleon,
could not but be wretched, or in the highest degree precarious.   That
tyranny over them, described and remonstrated against, especially by
Xenophon and Isocrates, appears to have been then at its greatest
height; nor could the mild benevolence of a Nicias go far toward its
restraint.   Not satisfied with the simple possession and exercise of absolute power, tho it sent those who offended to execution or slavery, by
thousands, the Athenian people would indulge in the pride and vanity
and ostentation of tyranny.   'So diligent,' says Isocrates, 'were they
'to discover how they might most earn the detestation of mankind,
'that, by a decree, they directed the tribute money to be exhibited,
'at the Dionysian festival, on the stage of the theater, divided into
'talents; thus making parade before their allies, numbers of whom
'would be present, of the property wrested from them to pay that
'very mercenary force, by which they were held in so degrading a sub-
'jection; and setting the other Greeks, of whom also many would at-
'tend, upon reckoning what orphans had been made, what calamities
'brought upon Grecian states, to collect that object of pride for the
'Athenian people.'

Isocr. de
Pace. p. 222.
t. 2. ed.
Auger.

Such was the character of the Athenian government, when the unfortunate Scionæans, all assistance being withdrawn from them, were
reduced to the dreadful necessity of surrendering themselves at discretion to the Athenian forces; and the Athenian people added, upon
the occasion, a shocking instance to the many that occur in history, of
the revengeful and unrelenting temper of democratical despotism.
Tho Cleon was no longer living to urge the execution of the decree, of
which he had been the proposer, it was nevertheless executed in full
strictness: every male of the Scionæans, arrived at manhood, was put
to death, and the women and children were all reduced to slavery : the
town and lands were given to the Platæans.

Thucyd. l. 5.
c. 32.

Amid such acts of extreme inhumanity, we have difficulty to discover
any

any value in that fear of the gods, and that care about the concerns of what they called religion, which we find ever lively in the minds of the Greeks. The late change in the fortune of war, and the losses sustained by the commonwealth, gave the Athenians to imagine that the gods had taken offence at something in their conduct; but they never looked beyond some vain ceremony; whether, in its concomitant and consequent circumstances, moral or most grossly immoral. The cruel removal of the Delians from their iland had been undertaken as a work of piety, necessary toward obtaining the favor of the deïty. The contrary imagination now gained, that the god's pleasure had been mistaken; and the Delians were restored to their possessions. Possibly some leading men found their ends in amusing the minds of the people with both these mockeries.

Thucyd. l. 5.
c. 32.

SECTION II.

Continuation of Obstacles to the Execution of the Articles of the
Peace. Change of Administration at Lacedæmon: Intrigues of the
new Administration; Treaty with Bœotia; Remarkable Treaty with
Argos; Resentment of Athens toward Lacedæmon.

THE peace restored free intercourse between Athens and those Pelo- ponnesian states which acceded to it; tho inability, on one side, com- pletely to perform the conditions, produced immediately, on the other, complaint, with jealousy and suspicion, which soon became mutual. The Peloponnesian troops were withdrawn from the protection of Amphipolis; but the place was left to the inhabitants, with arms in their hands. The other Thracian towns, which had joined the Pelo- ponnesian alliance, refused to acknowlege the authority of the treaty: for the conditions, tho favorable to the democratical, would have been ruinous to the oligarchal, which, through the connection with Lace- dæmon, was become the ruling party. In consequence of repeated remonstrances, a day was at length named, within which, if all those included in the treaty, as members of the Peloponnesian confede- racy, did not comply with the terms, Lacedæmon should hold them

c. 35.
B. C. 421.
Ol. 89 ¾.

I i 2   as

as enemies, and join Athens in her measures. The time passed, and the Lacedæmonians still made excuses. They had manifested their desire, they said, to fulfil their ingagements, by doing everything in their power: they had restored the Athenian prisoners, they had withdrawn their troops from Thrace; they still hoped, without so rigorous a measure, against antient allies, as compulsion by arms, to succeed to their desire with the Corinthians and Bœotians; and with regard to the prisoners in the hands of the latter, about whom the Athenians were particularly anxious, they had no doubt of obtaining their release. It therefore became the Athenians to show an equally good disposition by surrendering Pylus; or, if they would still detain that place as a pledge, they should however remove the Messenians and Helots, implacable and restless enemies of Lacedæmon, and garrison it with Athenians only, who would not contravene the terms of the peace. With the latter requisition the Athenians, after much altercation, complied; and the Messenians and Helots, removed from Pylus, were established in Cephallenia.

Thucyd. l. 5. c. 36. The change in the annual magistracies, in autumn, brought a change in the politics of Lacedæmon, which of course affected all Greece. Lacedæmon like other Grecian states, had its factions; and there was now an opposition, if we may use a modern term perfectly apposite, not only adverse to the peace, but holding constant correspondence with the Corinthians, Bœotians, and other seceders from the confederacy. The political power of the kings, which should have given stability to the measures of executive government, was nearly annihilated; while the ephors, in the name of the people, had been gradually acquiring, to their own office, a despotic controul over the whole administration; and, that office being annual, the Lacedæmonian councils became of course liable to much fluctuation. At the late change, two of the opposition, Cleobulus and Xenares, had been elected ephors. In the following winter a congress of deputies, from all the principal states of Greece, was assembled at Sparta, for the professed purpose of accommodating the numerous existing differences; but, after much altercation, they parted without settling anything. Cleobulus and Xenares then put forward an intrigue, apparently well

conceived,

conceived, for the purpose, at the same time, of serving their party, of relieving their country from evils actual or threatened, and of confirming and even extending its antient preëminence among the Grecian republics.   In Argos itself, the state most inimical to Lacedæmon, they held correspondence with a friendly party ; and they were upon good terms with the leading men of Corinth and Bœotia, which their predecessors had not been.   These circumstances formed the basis of their project.   Instead of opposing the new confederacy, they proposed, through the Corinthian and Bœotian deputies, who were friendly to their purpose, first, to promote the projected alliance of Bœotia with Argos, and then to endevor to ingage Argos itself in alliance with Lacedæmon.   That being effected, it would not be difficult to renew the connection with Bœotia, Corinth, Mantineia, and Elis; and thus Lacedæmon would find itself at the head of its whole antient confederacy, with the powerful and long inimical commonwealth of Argos added.

The plan, so laid, was communicated to the friendly party in Argos. Thucyd. l. 5. and the Bœotian and Corinthian deputies returned home.   The c. 37. Bœotarcs, being then sounded, were found perfectly disposed to the measure.   But the publicity required for all transactions of government, even in the aristocratical Grecian commonwealths, thwarted a project for which secrecy was indispensable.   It was necessary for the c. 38. Bœotarcs to obtain the assent of the four supreme councils.   They began with proposing alliance with Corinth; to which a majority in the councils would have had no repugnancy, could they have been assured of the concurrence of the Spartan administration; but being uninformed of what had passed between their deputies at Sparta and the ephors, they were alarmed at the proposal of a measure which would be apparently a declaration of enmity to the Lacedæmonians, with whom they chose to maintain their connection.   Ministers from Argos were already arrived at Thebes; but the leading proposal of an alliance with Corinth being rejected, the Bœotarcs did not venture any mention c. 37. of an alliance with Argos, and, for the present, the whole business dropped.

While this intrigue was going forward, another business from c. 39.

Lacedæmon

Lacedæmon was negotiated at Thebes. Nothing now pressed the Lacedæmonians so much as the retention of Pylus by the Athenians; and they knew that nothing pressed the Athenians so much as the retention of the Athenian prisoners, and the fortress of Panactum in Attica, by the Bœotians. The object of Lacedæmon therefore was to procure from the Bœotians the restoration of Panactum and the prisoners, so that they might obtain in return the surrender of Pylus from the Athenians. The difficulty was to find means of remuneration to Bœotia. The Bœotians would accept nothing but an alliance with Lacedæmon, upon precisely the same conditions with that lately concluded with the Athenians; but this was directly contrary to an article of the treaty between Lacedæmon and Athens, which positively declared that neither party should form any new alliance but in concurrence with the other. Through the interest nevertheless of the party in Lacedæmon, which desired a rupture with Athens, the treaty was concluded; and, after all, the Bœotians deceived the Lacedæmonians: for, to prevent the inconvenience, which might arise to themselves, from a fortress critically situated upon their borders, instead of surrendering Panactum they destroyed it.

Thucyd. l. 5. c. 40.

Report of the public circumstances of these transactions being quickly conveyed to Argos, without any information of the secret intrigue, occasioned great anxiety and alarm there. Not imagining the Lacedæmonian government would so immediately contravene their ingagements with Athens, after a treaty solemnly made, the terms of which were known, the Argian administration concluded that the alliance with Bœotia had been concerted with the Athenian government; that Athens of course was to be a party to the confederacy; that thus Argos would be precluded from any advantageous connection with Athens, which had always been looked to as a certain resource whenever necessity might press; and, instead of being the presiding power of a confederacy of the principal republics of the Greek nation, they should stand single to oppose Lacedæmon at the head of such a confederacy. Urged by this apprehension, they determined immediately to attempt an accommodation with Lacedæmon, and for negotiators they chose Eustrophus and Æson, the two men among them

1   who,

who, on account of their party-connections (for these, in every Grecian city, extended among neighboring states) were most likely to find confidence from the Lacedæmonians now in power.   The negotiation is remarkable for a circumstance, which proves how far the ideäs of the rude ages were still retained in those Grecian commonwealths, which had not taken a leading part in the affairs of the nation.   The object in dispute between Lacedæmon and Argos was the territory of Cynuria. Thucyd. l. 5. The Argians demanded that the question of right to this territory, c. 41. formerly theirs, but long since possessed by the Lacedæmonians, should be referred to the arbitration, either of some state, or of some individuals, who might be agreed upon by the two parties.   This was positively refused.   The Argians then, anxious for peace, but anxious also to maintain their claim, offered to make a truce for fifty years, without any other condition than a provision for the future discussion of the question, according to a mode of which the history of the two states furnished an example: they proposed that either party should be at liberty to call upon the other, when not ingaged in war nor afflicted with endemial sickness, to meet them in battle on the disputed lands, and the victory should finally decide the right of property; but, to prevent unnecessary slaughter, neither should pursue into the other's territory.   The Lacedæmonian government, practised in extensive political negotiation for near a century, while their state had presided over the affairs of a great confederacy, received this proposal, however countenanced by the practice of former ages, as something ridiculous.   But the Argian administration, probably not wholly unaware of the futility of such a provision, but expecting credit for it with the multitude their sovereign, persevered in the requisition; and the Lacedæmonians, not thinking the matter important enough to warrant the rejection of a proposal otherwise meeting their anxious wishes, at length assented; declaring however that they could not trust the ambassadors of a democracy, so far as to consider the peace as concluded, until it should be ratified by a public act of the Argian people.   This was obtained, and the peace thus completely made.

Meanwhile commissioners had been sent from Lacedæmon into c. 42. Bœotia, to receive the Athenian prisoners in the hands of the Bœotians,

together

together with the fort of Panactum. When they arrived, the fort was already destroyed; and, in excuse for this, it was pretended that, according to an antient compact between the Bœotians and Athenians, the territory of Panactum was to be the exclusive property of neither people, and cultivated by neither, but to remain a pasture for the common use of both. The prisoners were however delivered to the Lacedæmonians, who repaired with them to Athens; and, in restoring them, declared also the rasing of the fortifications of Panactum, and the retreat of the garrison, which they affected to consider as equivalent to a restitution of the place. But the Athenians, already informed of the treaty concluded by Lacedæmon with Bœotia, so repugnant to repeated professions made to Athens, were disposed to see the matter differently. Reproaches for these, and for many less important breaches or neglects of the treaty, were freely vented; the restoration of Pylus was refused; and the Lacedæmonian commissioners were obliged to return, without effecting any of the purposes of their mission.

SECTION III.

Alcibiades. A third Peloponnesian Confederacy; and Athens the leading Power.

Thucyd. l. 5.
c. 43.
WHILE such was the mutual dissatisfaction between Lacedæmon and Athens, there was in the latter, as well as in the former state, a party desirous of renewing the war; and at the head of that party a new character was coming forward, singularly formed to set the world in a flame. Alcibiades son of Cleinias was yet a youth, or at least in any other city, says Thucydides, would have been esteemed too young to be admitted to a leading public situation [a]; but high birth, great connections, and extraordinary talents gave him premature consequence. His family boasted their descent, as we learn from the words which

---

[a] Thus, I think with our translator Smith, the passage is to be understood; but Duker's note may be consulted.

Plato

Plato puts into the mouth of Alcibiades himself, from Eurysaces son of the Telamonian Ajax, and through him from Jupiter. His great-grandfather, named also Alcibiades, had been among the associates of Cleisthenes in expelling the Peisistratids, and restoring the commonwealth. His grandfather Cleinias had gained the honorable reward of the Aristeia, for his conduct in the first action with the fleet of Xerxes, off Artemisium, in a trireme which he had fitted at his own expence; and his father, called also Cleinias, fell in the service of his country, in the unfortunate battle of Coroneia, against the Bœotians. His mother, Deinomachë, was daughter of Megacles, head of the Alcmæonids, the first family of Athens; and by her he was nearly related to Pericles, who, on the death of his father, became his guardian. Unfortunately his connection with that great man did not bring those advantages of education, which might have been expected from a guardian, who so united the philosopher with the statesman, and, amid all the cares of his high situation, gave so much attention to science. Left therefore to himself, a very large patrimonial estate afforded Alcibiades means for that dissipation in pleasure, to which passions, constitutionally strong, impelled, and various circumstances contributed in an unusual degree to invite. The graces of his person are mentioned, by cotemporary writers, as very extraordinary. In the seclusion, in which the Athenian ladies lived, they could be little liable to the seduction of wit and ingaging behavior; but they were thence perhaps only the more alive to the impression of personal beauty, when sacrifices and processions afforded the scanty opportunity of mixing with the world, so far as to see, tho not to converse with, men. Alcibiades, as we are assured by Xenophon, was the object of passion and intrigue for many of the principal ladies of Athens[1]. The splendor of his fortune, and the power of those with whom he was connected, at the same time drew about him a croud of flatterers of the other sex: Athenian citizens, allies, subjects, and strangers, vied in paying court to him;

Plat. Alcib. 1. & Plut. vit. Alcib.

Isocrat. de bigis, p. 152. & p. 154. t. 3. Ch. 8. s. 4. of this Hist.

Plat. Alcib. 1. p. 112. t. 2.

Plat. Alcib. 1. p. 122.

Plat. Conviv. Xen. Mem. Socr. l. 1. c. 2. s. 24. Plut. vit. Alcib.

---

[1] Διὰ μὲν κάλλος ὑπὸ πολλῶν καὶ σεμνῶν γυναικῶν θηρώμενος. Xen. Mem. Socr. l. 1. c. 2. s. 24. The coarseness of this expression, of an elegant writer among a refined people, has been owing to the want of intercourse between the sexes, which alone can give manners their best polish.

and there was danger that the intoxicating powers of adulation might have destroyed, in the bud, all hope of any valuable fruit from the singular talents of his mind.

In this period of his life occurred the extraordinary addition to the rest of his extraordinary fortune, to become acquainted with the philosopher Socrates. That wonderful man, who had then for some time made it his business, as it was his pleasure, gratuitously to instruct the youth of Athens in those two points, which preceding professors of science had most neglected, the duty of men to men, and, as far as uninlightened reason could discover, the duty of men to God, justly considered Alcibiades as one who deserved his peculiar care; since he was certainly one whose virtues or vices might go very far to decide the future fortune of his country. Alcibiades was not of a temper to rest satisfied with ignorance. Ambition, but still more the love of distinction than the love of power, was the ruling passion of his mind.

Plat. Alcib. & Conviv.

To obtain instruction therefore, which might promote the gratification of that ruling passion, he submitted his other passions to the controul of the philosopher. Consciousness of superior abilities, and ambition inflamed by flattery, had inspired Alcibiades with the purpose of putting himself forward as a public speaker, before he had attained his twentieth year: but, tho he spurned at the remonstrances of his other friends, the authority and advice of Socrates diverted him from that extravagance. A singular friendship grew between them. They were companions in

Plat. Conviv. p. 219. t. 3. Isocrat. de bigis, p. 154. t. 3.

peace and in war. Socrates, who was indowed by nature with a constitution of body scarcely less remarkable for its firmness than that of his mind for its powers, served a campain in Thrace with Alcibiades, then in earliest manhood. The soldier-sage, yielding to none in courage in the day of battle, was the admiration of all for his patience, in want, fatigue, and the cold of that severe climate. Alcibiades was his most zealous emulator; but in action it was particularly

Ch. 15. s. 2. of this Hist.

Plut. vit. Alcib. Plat. Conviv. p. 220. t. 3.

his aim to outdo him. In a battle near Potidæa, apparently that in which the generals, Xenophon son of Euripides and his two collegues, were killed, he was severely wounded, and would have lost his life, but for the protection given him by Socrates, who fought by his side. The daring exertion of Alcibiades, which had led him into the danger,

was

was deemed by the principal officers of the army, perhaps a little partial, says Plutarch, to his high rank and high connections, to deserve the Aristeia. The generous youth, just to the superior merit of his master, declared they were much rather due to Socrates: but the philosopher, adding the authority of his voice to that of the officers, the reward was given as it was first decreed. Alcibiades returned the benefit, in the unfortunate battle of Delium, where he saved Socrates, as we have already seen, from the swords of the pursuing Bœotians.

Ch. 16. s. 3. of this Hist.

But the passions of Alcibiades were too strong for constant perseverance in submission to the advice of his incomparable friend. His predominant passion, the desire of preëminence in everything, was not to be subdued. No sooner had he acquired possession of his estate, than the splendor of his style of living became such, as in Athens had been utterly unknown. Much as things differed from those in our time and country, we may form some idëa of his extravagant magnificence from one circumstance, related by the authentic pen of Thucydides. It had before been esteemed a splendid exertion, for the greatest individual citizen, to send one chariot to contend in the races at the Olympian festival; it was reckoned creditable for a commonwealth to send one at the public expence. Alcibiades sent no less than seven to one meeting; where he won the first, second, and fourth honors. No commonwealth nor any prince had before done so much. In the same manner in all those public offices, which in his rank and circumstances were not to be avoided, presidencies of theatrical entertainments and athletic games, and the equipment and command of ships of war, his sumptuousness far exceeded what had been common. This ostentation, and the general splendor of his manner of living, while they attracted some friends and numerous followers, excited also much censure and many murmurs. They were considered, and with much indignation considered, by many, as repugnant to that moderation and equality, which ought to be maintained among the citizens of a democracy; while by others they were looked on with more complacency, as the most innocent way of evaporating that boiling spirit, and reducing those large means, which might otherwise have been more dangerously employed.

Thucyd. l. 6. c. 16. Isocrat. de bigis, p. 153. t. 3. Plut. vit. Alcib.

K K 2

In

In the midst of a career of dissipation and extravagance, that excited at the same time wonder, alarm, indignation, and admiration, the circumstances of the times, and even the wishes of many grave men, seem to have invited Alcibiades to put himself forward in public busi-

Aristoph.
Pax, v. 680,
690, 921,
1319.
Equit. v.
1300, 1313.
Nub. v. 1061,
1065.
Thucyd. l. 8.
c. 73.
Plut. vit.
Nic. & Alcib.

ness.   Nicias, who, since the death of Pericles, had stood at the head of the most respectable party in the commonwealth, was sinking under the turbulence of Hyperbolus, the friend of Cleon when Cleon was living, of similar birth, similar talents, similar character, and the successor to his influence among the lowest of the people.   In this situation of things, the nephew of Pericles seemed the person to whom to look for an associate to the successor of Pericles; and the gravity and mild dignity of Nicias, it was hoped, might temper the too vivacious spirit of Alcibiades.

But Alcibiades had not yet learnt the necessity of moderation in anything.   Young as he was, he would hold no second place.   With his influence, derived from inheritance and connection, and assisted by talents, wealth, and profusion, popularity was much in his power; and he had no sooner determined upon being a public man, than he would in the very outset be at the head of things.   It was generally important, for those who sought eminence in any Grecian commonwealth, to have political connections among the other states of Greece.   The family

Thucyd. l. 5.
c. 43.

l. 8. c. 6.

of Alcibiades were, from antient times, hereditary public guests of Lacedæmon, and they had been connected by private hospitality with some of the first Lacedæmonian families.   Alcibiades was a Laconic name; first given, among the Athenians to the great-grandfather of the pupil of Socrates, in compliment to a Spartan family, with which the Athenian was connected in close friendship.   But the interference

Ch. 5. s. 5.
& c. 7. s. 2.
of this Hist.

Thucyd. l. 5.
c. 43.

of the Lacedæmonians in favor of the Peisistratids, which we have heretofore had occasion to notice, would be likely to excite the indignation of an associate of Cleisthenes; and accordingly the elder Alcibiades, with those ceremonies which custom prescribed, as creditable among men and necessary to obviate the wrath of the gods, renounced the hereditary hospitality of his family with Sparta.   His great grandson resolved to seek a renewal of that antient connection; and, as a preparatory step, was assiduous in kind attention to the Lacedæmonian

11   prisoners

prisoners in Attica.　But the Lacedæmonian government, systematically indisposed to youth in political eminence, and not less systematically indisposed to the wild and luxurious extravagance of Alcibiades, slighted his advances ; and when business occurred with the Athenian commonwealth, as it was necessary to communicate with some leading men, they chose rather to address themselves to Nicias or Laches.

　This aversion, on the part of Lacedæmon, decided Alcibiades to a line of political conduct, adverse at the same time to Lacedæmon and to Nicias.　He was about his twenty-sixth or twenty-seventh year, when he first tried the powers of his eloquence in the general assembly[*]. The affair of Panactum was his topic: he inveyed against the faithlessness of Sparta, as if the demolition of that fortress had been concerted by the Bœotians with the Lacedæmonian government.　He was heard with ready attention by the Athenian people.　All the opponents of the aristocratical cause were not admirers of Hyperbolus.　Alcibiades, to carry his point against Nicias, professed zeal for the democratical interest ; and the experience of his abilities as a speaker, added to the weight he derived from birth, property, and connection, made him presently the head of a considerable party.　He continued his invective against Lacedæmon ; and the league hastily made by that state with Argos, afforded fresh matter.　Nothing, he said, but inimical intentions against Athens, could have induced the Lacedæmonians to form such a connection with such inveterate enemies as the Argians ; their purpose could be only to deprive Athens of a valuable ally, that so they might, with better hope, renew the war.　The people continued to listen with a favorable ear, and Alcibiades gained influence and authority daily.　Meanwhile he had been communicating among neighboring states; he had confidential intercourse with the leading men at Argos, of the party adverse to Lacedæmon ; and, finding circumstances on all sides favorable, he formed an extensive and extraordinary plan, which he began immediately to carry into execution.

Thucyd. l. 5. c. 43.

　[*] So we are told by Diodorus and Nepos; but Acacius has calculated, from several circumstances mentioned by Plato, that he must have been at least thirty. The reader who will take the pains to consult the note in the 343d page of Duker's Thucydides, will judge for himself how far to give credit to that calculation.

The

B. C. 470.
Ol. 89. 4.
P. W. 12.
Thucyd. l. 5.
c. 44.
The Argian people were no sooner undeceived concerning the circumstances of the alliance between Lacedæmon and Bœotia, and the supposed participation of Athens in that measure, than they became careless about peace with Lacedæmon, and inclined much rather to renew and improve their connection with Athens; an antient ally, and, what was an important consideration, of congenial government. Upon this disposition of the Argians, Alcibiades principally founded his project. He proposed to his friends in Argos, leaders of the democratical party there, to procure that ministers should be sent to Athens from their state, from Elis, and from Mantineia; and he would then ingage to make the Athenian commonwealth a member of the Argian confederacy. His Argian friends undertook the business; the Argian people were readily persuaded to concur in it: the influence of Argos prevailed with Elis and Mantineia; and shortly ministers from all those commonwealths met in Athens.

This unexpected stroke of the young Athenian politician alarmed the Lacedæmonian government. Not only the negotiation of Cleobulus and Xenares, from which such important advantages had been expected, was likely to be thwarted, but there was apparent danger that Athens might become the leading power of the very confederacy, at the head of which it was the direct purpose of that negotiation to establish Lacedæmon. Anxious to obviate this, they sent an embassy to Athens, carefully composed of persons the most likely to be well received there; of whom Endius was a hereditary friend and guest of the family of Alcibiades. The ambassadors were instructed to apologize for the treaty with Bœotia, as a measure neither in intention or effect injurious to Athens; to demand the surrender of Pylus in return for the evacuation of Panactum; and by all means to obviate any league of Athens with Argos.

c. 45.
Plut. vit.
Alcib. &
Nic.
On their arrival at Athens, having audience from the council of Five hundred, whose office, in time of war nearly superseded by that of general of the commonwealth, had now resumed its importance, they found reason to promise themselves a favorable issue to their negotiation. This would not only ruin the immediate project of Alcibiades, but would go far to establish the power of the opposite

party

party in Athens; and no common policy, nor perhaps any honorable
policy, could prevent such consequences. Alcibiades was ingenious,
and not scrupulous. He ingaged the Lacedæmonian ambassadors in a
private conference, in which he persuaded them by no means to
acknowlege, before the Athenian people, the fulness of the powers with
which they were vested : they would find, he said, the arrogance of
the multitude insupportable; and the only way to check the most
unreasonable demands would be to deny their plenipotentiary commission. If they would only take his advice in this matter, his opposition should cease, and he would even become the advocate of their
cause. The reasoning, in itself plausible, was urged in a manner so
plausible, and with such professions and protestations, that the Lacedæmonians implicitly assented to it.

Next day they had their audience of the assembled Athenian people.
After they had declared the purpose of their mission, Alcibiades put
the question to them, 'Whether they came with full powers or with
' limited?' and they answered, 'that they were limited by instruc-
' tions.' The members of the council, whom they had assured that
their commission was plenipotentiary, were astonished at this reply :
Nicias, with whom they had not had the precaution to communicate,
was astonished; but presently the ambassadors themselves were still
more astonished, when Alcibiades reproached them as guilty of gross and
shameful prevarication, and concluded a harangue, the most virulent
against Lacedæmon, and the most soothing and alluring to the Athenian people, with proposing the question for ingaging the Athenian
commonwealth in the Argian alliance. His daring and well-conducted
treachery would, in the opinion of Thucydides, have had full success
in the instant, but for an accident, which alarmed the superstition, at
the same time that it excited the natural fears, of the Athenian people.
The city was, in the moment, shaken by an earthquake; no mischief
followed; but the assembly was immediately adjourned.

The delay of a day thus gained, giving time for passion to cool and
reflection to take place, was advantageous to the views of Nicias. In
the assembly held on the morrow, urging that the people ought not to Thucyd. l. 5.
decide hastily, and in the midst of uncertainty, concerning a matter c. 46.

of

of very great importance, he prevailed so far against Alcibiades, that, instead of immediately concluding the alliance with Argos, it was determined first to send an embassy to Lacedæmon, of which Nicias himself was appointed chief. But the measure which Alcibiades could not prevent, he contrived to render ineffectual; or, rather, to convert to the promotion of his own purposes. The embassy to Lacedæmon being voted, instructions for the ambassadors were to be considered; and it was resolved, that the restoration of the fort of Panactum, the immediate delivery of Amphipolis into the power of the Athenian people, and a renunciation, on the part of Lacedæmon, of the alliance with Bœotia, or, instead of it, the accession of Bœotia to the terms of the late peace, should be preliminary conditions, without assent to which, in their fullest extent, nothing should be concluded. The year of magistracy of the ephor Xenares was yet unexpired, and the party of Xenares still prevailed. The Bœotian alliance had been the measure of that party: the requisition of a renuntiation of it was of course ill received; and Nicias and his collegues were obliged to return to Athens without obtaining, either for their commonwealth or for themselves, any one object of their mission.

Indignation would not unnaturally arise upon such an occasion among the Athenian people; and art was not wanting, and pains were not spared, to inflame it. The party of Alcibiades thus gained an accession of strength, which gave it a decided superiority in the assembly. The Argian and Eleian ministers were still at Athens, and a league offensive and defensive, for a hundred years, with their republics, the dependent allies of each contracting power (such nearly is the expression of Thucydides[5]) being included, was proposed and carried: it was agreed that pillars of marble, with the treaty ingraved, should be erected, at the separate expence of each republic, at Athens in the

Thucyd. l. 5. c. 47.

citadel, at Argos in the temple of Apollo in the agora, and at Mantineia in the temple of Jupiter; and that a brazen pillar, with the treaty also ingraved, should be placed, at the common expence of the confederacy, at Olympia. By this extraordinary stroke in politics, Athens, and no longer Lacedæmon, was the leading power even of the Dorian states, and head of the principal confederacy in Peloponnesus itself.

[5] Ξυμμάχων ὦν ἄρχουσιν,

SECTION IV.

*Implication of Interests of the principal Grecian Republics. Conti-
nuation of Dispute between Lacedæmon and Elis. Affairs of the
Lacedæmonian Colony of Heracleia. Alcibiades elected General;
Importance of the Office of General of the Athenian Commonwealth:
Influence of Alcibiades in Peloponnesus: War of Argos and Epi-
daurus. Inimical Conduct of Athens toward Lacedæmon.*

Bʏ the several treaties now lately made, the interests of the principal Thucyd. l. 5,
Grecian republics were strangely implicated. Inimical to Sparta as c. 48.
the late transaction of the Athenian commonwealth certainly was, and
not less in direct contravention of subsisting ingagements with Athens
as the treaty a little before concluded by Lacedæmon with Bœotia
appears, the alliance between Lacedæmon and Athens nevertheless
subsisted. At the same time Corinth, ingaged in confederacy with
Argos, Elis, and Mantineia, refused to concur with those states in the
Athenian alliance; inclining rather to renew its old connection with c. 49.
Lacedæmon, then at open hostility with Elis, and scarcely upon better
terms with the other states of the confederacy.

Meanwhile the Eleians, conceiving themselves grossly injured by
the Lacedæmonians in the affair of Lepreum, and unable to vindicate
their claim by arms, had recourse to the authority derived from their
sacred character and their presidency over the Olympian festival.
Before the Olympian tribunal, composed of their own principal
citizens, they accused the Lacedæmonians of prosecuting hostilities
after the commencement of the Olympian armistice; and sentence was
pronounced, according to the Olympian law, condemning the Lacedæmonian commonwealth in a fine of two thousand mines, between seven
and eight thousand pounds sterling; being two mines for every soldier
employed. The Lacedæmonian government, more anxious, on account
of the late turn in Grecian politics, to clear themselves of offence
against the common laws and common religion of Greece, declared

that they would submit to the penalty, had they or their officers been guilty of the crime; but they insisted that, when the hostilities complained of were committed, the armistice had not been made known to them by the customary proclamation. In the irregularity and uncertainty of the Grecian year, proclamation only could ascertain to each republic when the armistice was to begin. The Eleians maintained that, according to antient constant custom, it was proclaimed first within their own territory : that then they held themselves immediately bound to abstain from hostilities against others; and reason, not less than the Olympian law, required that they should then be exempt from injury by hostility from any member of the Greek nation. The Lacedæmonians still insisted that they ought not to be fined for an involuntary crime. The Eleians maintained that the sentence was just, and could not be reversed or altered; but, if the Lacedæmonians would restore Lepreum, which had been so injuriously and impiously seized, they would not only remit the portion of the fine due to themselves, but also pay for the Lacedæmonians that due to the god. The

Thucyd. l. 5.
c. 50.

Lacedæmonian government positively refusing both to restore Lepreum, and to pay the fine, the Eleians declared the whole Lacedæmonian people excluded, both from contending in the games at the approaching festival, and from partaking in the sacrifices; not however forbidding their attendance as spectators.

It was apprehended that the high spirit of the Lacedæmonian people, long accustomed to give law to Peloponnesus and to Greece, might not acquiesce under this decision, excluding them from the common religious solemnities of the Greek nation. To obviate violence, there-

Ol. 90.
After July 3.

fore, the whole youth of Elis attended during the festival in arms; and a thousand heavy-armed Argians, as many Mantineians, and a body of Athenian horse, came to assist in keeping the peace. Such a measure might alone indicate how hardly the peace of Greece was to be kept. But, with all this precaution, an occurrence at the games excited general apprehension. Leichas, a Lacedæmonian, had a chariot prepared for the race: and not to be disappointed, excluded as he was from entering it in his own name, he obtained permission to enter it in the name of the Bœotian people. As a public chariot of Bœotia, it

3

won.

won. But the vanity of Leichas was not to be so satisfied; to make it known to whom the victorious chariot reälly belonged, he stepped forward before the assembly, and placed a chaplet on the head of his charioteer. The rod-bearers, whose office it was to inforce order, as in the roughness of Grecian manners, amid republican equality, it seems they were authorized to do, without any consideration for the dignity of the man or of his city, struck Leichas in presence of the assembly [6]. Such an affront, however, to a Lacedæmonian citizen, it was feared might bring a Lacedæmonian army to Olympia: but the Lacedæmonian government, not subject to passionate counsels, overlooked the offence to an individual, and the affair had no immediate consequence.

After the conclusion of the festival, Corinth became the seat of political negotiation. The Argians sent ministers thither to press the accession of the Corinthian state to the new confederacy. The Lacedæmonian government, judging it necessary to counterwork the various intrigues carrying on to their disadvantage, sent also ministers to Corinth. After much negotiation through the summer, to little or no effect, the terrors of an earthquake, of which however no mischief is reported, occasioned the dissolution of the congress.

The affairs of the Lacedæmonian colony of Heracleia continue to ingage notice, as they contribute to characterize the state of Greece. The people of Trachinia and its neighborhood had never forgiven the gross trespass committed upon the rights and property of a Grecian people, by those who assumed the title of protectors of Grecian liberty, and they disturbed Heracleia with continual hostilities. Success had been various; but in this autumn the Heracleians were defeated in battle, with such loss, that the survivors scarcely sufficed for the defence of their walls and of the property necessary to their subsistence. In the next spring therefore the Bœotians, fearing that, while the Lacedæmonians were intent upon their nearer interests in Peloponnesus, the Athenians might seize Heracleia, took upon themselves to

Thucyd. l. 5. c. 51.

After 30 Sept.

Thucyd. l. 5. c. 52.
B. C. 419.
Ol. 90. ¼.
P. W. 13.

[6] It is sometimes difficult to estimate the exact value of words and phrases in a dead language, when it depends on laws and customs of which we are not exactly informed. The manner in which Lysias tells this story would rather give to suppose that Leichas was formally condemned to receive a public whipping, which was inflicted accordingly; and the phrase of Thucydides will bear that meaning.

L L 2   direct

direct its affairs, and to send away the Lacedæmonian governor Hegesippidas, as unfit for his command.   The Lacedæmonian government,
not a little dissatisfied with this species of kindness, had however too
much upon their hands to take immediately any active measures for
vindicating their dominion over their colony.

B. C. 419.   While these transactions ingaged some of the principal states,
Ol. 90. ¼.   Alcibiades had been prosecuting intrigue, ably and successfully, within
P. W. 13.   and without Attica.   His measures at home procured his election to
the high office of general in chief of the commonwealth; an occasional
office, created only in times of supposed emergency; but which, beside
the importance of the military command, carried with it, not nominally
indeed but effectually, greater civil power than any of the permanent
magistracies, or than all of them : for the general, having the right to
assemble the people at all times, had no occasion to consult any other
council; so that, as long as he could command a majority in the assembly, he was supreme and sole director of the executive government.
Nearly absolute soverein thus in Athens, he was hardly less so in
Argos, and his influence extended widely among other states in
Peloponnesus.   In the beginning of summer, having previously concerted matters with the leading men of the Argian administration, he went, with a small escort of heavy-armed and bowmen, to
Argos, whence, with an addition of Peloponnesian troops, he made a
progress through the cities of the confederacy within the peninsula;
and, with plenitude of assumed power, arranged matters everywhere so
as to give a decided superiority to the party which favored his views.
To confirm the democratical interest in the little city of Patræ in
Achaia, he persuaded the people to connect their town with their port
by fortifications, which would bring them more immediately within
the protection of the Athenian fleet.   A similar measure, proposed at
the Achaian Rhium, was prevented by the Sicyonians and Corinthians.

Among these turns in Grecian politics, the little republic of Epidaurus, a dismembered branch of the antient Argolic state, was firm in
the Lacedæmonian alliance.   Epidaurus, always obnoxious, would, in
the event of the expected war with Lacedæmon, be particularly annoy-
ing to Argos; being so situated that it would very much interrupt
                                                communication

communication with Athens : for if the Corinthians, who were now dubious, should become adverse, the passage could be made only by sea, round the Scyllæan promontory ; and this, in case of a serious attack from Lacedæmon, would make assistance from Athens to Argos slow and precarious.   A pretext, of whimsical appearance in modern times, was found for making war upon Epidaurus : it was the neglect to send a victim to a temple of the Pythian Apollo, in the Argian terri-tory, due as a quit-rent for some pastures held of Argos by the Epidau-rians.   On this ground it was proposed to subdue Epidaurus ; and mea-sures were concerted with Alcibiades for the purpose.

Meanwhile preparation was made by the Lacedæmonian government, as for some very important enterprize, the object of which was kept a profound secret.   Troops were required of the allies, without any inti-mation of the purpose.   Such requisitions are, more than once men-tioned by Thucydides ; and they strongly indicate the importance of that supremacy which subordinate states acknowleged in the head of their confederacy.   The whole force of Laconia marched, under the command of king Agis, to Leuctra, on the borders ; where, according to the constant practice of the Greeks, before they would move in arms beyond their own territory, the diabaterial or border-passing sacrifice was performed.   The symptoms of the victims being, on this occasion, declared by the priests unfavorable, after all the pomp and all the labor and expence of preparation, Agis immediately dismissed the allies and led the Lacedæmonian forces home.   The allies were however directed to hold themselves in readiness to march again, immediately after the conclusion of the approaching festival of Carneia. _{Thucyd. I. 5.}

The Argians, before restrained by the alarm of the great preparations made by Lacedæmon, determined to use the opportunity, now so unex-pectedly allowed them, for prosecuting their purpose against Epidaurus; for which the Carneian festival was particularly commodious.   The Carneian was a festival common to all the Dorians, and one of the prin-cipal of their calendar.   Its ceremonies were mostly military, and, for the celebration, which lasted many days, a camp was always formed. The Argians, tho they chose their time well, seem to have concerted their measures ill ; but the measures of their opponents were still more

defective,

defective, and tend, among numberless circumstances occurring in Grecian history, to show both the inconvenience of the Grecian religious festivals, and the inefficiency of league among the Grecian republics for preserving internal security and domestic quiet. Four

14 Aug.

days before the holidays, the Argians entered the Epidaurian lands in arms, and immediately commenced plunder. The Epidaurians sent to their allies for succour. Some excused themselves on account of the festival; which, as they affirmed, they were religiously bound to celebrate: some came as far as the Epidaurian borders and halted: none

Thucyd. l. 5. c. 55.

gave any effectual assistance. At this very time a convention of deputies of the several states of the Argian alliance was sitting at Mantineia, assembled at the requisition of the Athenian government, for the professed purpose of negotiating a general peace. Intelligence of the attack upon Epidaurus was quickly communicated there, and the Corinthian deputy (for Epidaurus was among the allies of Corinth) remonstrated warmly against it. The Argians in consequence withdrew their troops, but the convention separated soon after without concluding anything; and the Argians recommenced hostilities, which were continued, but with little effect, through the remainder of the summer.

c. 56.

A reinforcement of three hundred men, which passed by sea from Laconia to Epidaurus in the following winter, produced a very remarkable remonstrance from the Argian to the Athenian government. In the treaty of alliance between the two states, it was stipulated that neither should permit the enemies of the other to pass through its dominion. The Argian administration accused the Athenian of contravening this article, by permitting the Lacedæmonians to pass by sea to Epidaurus. This may seem to have been dictated by Alcibiades, and to mark the extraordinary extent of his influence in Argos; for, under the semblance of a remonstrance, it was reälly an acknowlegement that the Grecian seas, even to the very shores of Peloponnesus, were the dominion of Athens. The reparation which they required for this injury would appear, in modern times, scarcely less extraordinary than the accusation: it was, that the Athenians should withdraw the Athenian garrison from Pylus, and replace there the Messenians and Helots

who

who had been removed to Cephallenia.   Apparently this requisition
was concerted with Alcibiades, or perhaps suggested by him; for he
was the mover of the measures which followed in Athens.   A decree of
the people directed, that, on the column on which was ingraved the
late treaty with Lacedæmon, a clause should be added, declaring that
the Lacedæmonians had broken the treaty.   This being taken as the
ground, it was then commanded, by the same decree, that the Messenians and Helots, lately removed to Cranë in Cephallenia, should be
reëstablished in Pylus.

In the course of the winter many skirmishes passed between the
Argians and the Epidaurians, but no important action; and an attempt,
toward spring, to take Epidaurus by escalade, failed.

SECTION V.

*War of Lacedæmon and Argos: Battle near Mantineia: Siege of
Epidaurus.*

THE Lacedæmonians could not, without extreme uneasiness, consider   Thucyd. 1. 5.
the present state of things in Peloponnesus, not only as their own com-   c. 17.
mand and influence were diminished, but as what they had lost had
accrued to their rivals of Athens and Argos.   By midsummer of this
year, the continued pressure of the Argian arms, however defectively   B. C. 418.
conducted, had reduced the Epidaurians, old and still faithful allies of   Ol. 90. 3/7.
Lacedæmon, to great distress.   Some effort must be made, or all com-   P. W. 14.
mand and influence in Peloponnesus, beyond their own territory, would
be gone.   It was only to sound the trumpet, and the whole Lacedæmonian people were at any time assembled, ready for service.   The
allies yet remaining to the state were summoned; and the Lacedæmonian army, strengthened with the greatest force of Helots that could be
trusted, marched under the command of king Agis.   They were presently joined by the Tegeans, and all those other Arcadians who had
not, with the Mantineians, renounced the Lacedæmonian alliance:
Phlius was the appointed place of junction for the allies, equally those
within

within and those without Peloponnesus. No less than five thousand
heavy-armed, as many light, and five hundred horse, with a foot-
soldier attending every horseman, marched from Bœotia[7]; Corinth
sent two thousand heavy-armed; Sicyon, Pallenë, Epidaurus, and
Megara, all they could spare, and the Phliasians were prepared to join
with their whole strength.

Thucyd. l. 5.
c. 58.   The Argians, quickly informed of these movements, dispatched to
their allies urgent requisitions of assistance. Accordingly the Mantineians joined them with their whole force, the amount of which Thucydides does not specify: the Eleians sent three thousand heavy-armed.
Thus in consequence of the successful treachery of Alcibiades, Peloponnesus was divided at arms within itself; while Athens, preparing
indeed assistance for her ally, but risking little, looked on, and injoyed
the storm.

The Argians, being joined by the Mantineians and Eleians, proposed
to prevent the junction of the Lacedæmonians with their northern allies;
and with that view took a position near Methydrium in Arcadia. It
was evening when Agis incamped on a hill overagainst them, as if
intending to ingage next morning ; but moving silently in the night,
he passed on unperceived so as to secure his way to Phlius. The
Argians had then to expect the invasion of their country by the whole
combined force of the enemy. To prevent this, they moved to a position on the road of Nemea; the only way by which a numerous army
could conveniently pass the mountains, which divide Argolis from
Phliasia and Corinthia. Agis, by apparently a very able disposition,
rendered this measure fruitless. Leading the Lacedæmonians by a
rough and difficult mountain-road, he entered the Argian plain unopposed, and placed himself between the Argian army and Argos. The
Corinthians, Phliasians, and Pallenians, by another road, also difficult
and little practised, entered another part of the plain, equally unresisted.
The Bœotians, Megarians, and Sicyonians only were sent by the
Nemean road, with orders to avoid ingaging, unless the enemy should
move against either of the divisions in the plain. In that case the

[7] What those attending foot-soldiers were, whom Thucydides distinguishes by the name
of ἄμιππος, we are informed only by late writers, whose authority seems very doubtful.

Bœotian

Bœotian horse, more numerous than that of the enemy, if indeed the enemy had any, might find opportunity to attack with advantage.

These well-judged movements being all successfully executed, the Argian army was surrounded by a force so superior, that its destruction seemed inevitable.   Thrasyllus, one of the five generals of Argos, saw the peril of his situation: he communicated upon it with Alciphron, an Argian of rank, connected by hospitality with Lacedæmon, and they determined together upon a measure which would appear very extraordinary in itself, and scarcely credible in its success, if we were not already somewhat familiarized with Grecian politics.   They went privately to Agis, and, pledging themselves to lead their state to alliance with Lacedæmon, upon terms that should be satisfactory, they prevailed with him to grant upon the spot, of his sole authority, a truce for four months; and, to the astonishment of the Lacedæmonian army, orders were immediately issued for retreat. Thucyd. l. 5. c. 60.

By this negotiation, fortunate as it was bold, Thrasyllus and Alciphron hoped to acquire such favor among the Argian people as might inable them to promote at the same time their two objects, the oligarchal interest and the Lacedæmonian alliance.   They were, however, utterly disappointed.   The Argian people, and even their commanders, totally unpractised in war upon any extensive scale, were so unaware of the danger from which they had been rescued, that they imagined they had been deprived of a most favorable opportunity for crushing the Lacedæmonians; inclosed, they imagined inadvertently, between the allied army and the garrison of Argos.   The public indignation, stimulated apparently by the democratical leaders, rose so high, that Thrasyllus saved his life only through the protection of an altar to which he fled, and a decree of the people declared all his property confiscated.

Presently after the retreat of the Lacedæmonians, the auxiliary force from Athens arrived at Argos; a thousand Athenian heavy-armed and three hundred horse, commanded by Laches and Nicostratus.   The oligarchal party in Argos, tho unable to protect Thrasyllus against the momentary rage of the people, were nevertheless strong; and they would immediately have dismissed the Athenian forces, as no longer c. 61. After 11th July.

wanted in Peloponnesus for any purpose of the confederacy. But Alcibiades was too watchful a politician to suffer his purposes to be so baffled, and the important alliance of Argos to pass from him. Quickly informed of all circumstances, he went to Argos in quality of ambassador, and, in conjunction with the two generals, demanded an audience of the Argian people. The oligarchal Argians very unwillingly consented, and not without a degree of compulsion from their Mantineian and Eleian allies, who were still present. The eloquence of Alcibiades then prevailed. The Argian people felt his reproaches for breach of faith with Athens, gave credit to his representations of the strength of the confederacy, and of the circumstances now peculiarly favorable for prosecuting the war; and, a proposal being suggested for striking an important stroke with little risk, it was summarily resolved upon. Hostages had been taken by the Lacedæmonians from some Arcadian towns of their alliance, whose fidelity they doubted, and had been placed in custody of the Orchomenians, whom they thought firm. The allied army instantly marched to Orchomenus. The fortifications of that little city were weak; the people were alarmed by the greatness of the force preparing to attack them, and, apprehensive that they might be overpowered before succour could arrive, they insured present safety by an early capitulation. Surrendering the hostages committed to their charge, and giving hostages of their own people, they were admitted members of the Argian alliance.

Thucyd. l. 5. c. 62.   This stroke being thus rapidly struck, the question was agitated, to what object the allied army should next be directed. The Eleians were urgent for Lepreum; but the recovery of Lepreum, however desirable for the Eleians, little interested the other allies. The Mantineians therefore proposing the far more important acquisition of Tegea; and giving assurance that they had intelligence with a party in that city, which would favor the enterprize, the Argians and Athenians concurred with them. The Eleians were so dissatisfied with this preference of the great concerns of the confederacy to the particular interest of their state, that they marched home. The rest of the allied army prepared to go against Tegea.

c. 63.   The Lacedæmonians, more reasonably displeased with their prince than

than the Argians with their general, had been however more temperate in their anger. While peace was the apparent consequence of his measure, the public discontent vested itself only in expressions of disapprobation. But when, instead of breaking the force of Argos by one blow, or even taking the city, to which some thought the opportunity might have extended, they found, on the contrary, great advantage given to the enemy, an allied city of some importance lost, and their pledges for the fidelity of the rest of Arcadia taken from them, Agis was called to account, with a degree of passion not usual, says Thucydides, with the Lacedæmonians. He was upon the point of being judicially condemned in a fine amounting to more than four thousand pounds sterling[8], and moreover to suffer the indignity of, what was otherwise probably no very important loss, having his house levelled with the ground. But consideration for his former assiduity in service, with his unblameable deportment on all occasions, and respect for the blood of Hercules and the dignity of the Spartan government, at length prevailed. His intreaty to be allowed an opportunity of proving, by future conduct, that he had not deserved such severe censure, was granted, and he resumed the command of the army, but not without a limitation never before put upon Spartan kings: ten persons were appointed to be his military council, without whose concurrence he was not to lead the forces beyond the Lacedæmonian dominion. For the detail of military operation, however, he seems to have been intrusted with the usual authority.

Meanwhile intelligence arrived at Lacedæmon, from the party yet ruling in Tegea, that, if assistance was not quickly given, their opponents of the democratical interest would prevail, and that important city would be annexed to the Argian confederacy. The whole force of Laconia was in consequence assembled, with unexampled celerity, and marched immediately. The Arcadian allies were required to hasten to Tegea, and expresses were dispatched to Corinth, Bœotia, and as far as Phocis and Locris, for the forces of those provinces to meet the Lacedæmonian army before Mantineia. Tegea was quickly put into a state of security; and then the Lacedæmonians, with their Arcadian

Thucyd. l. 5.
c. 64.

---

[8] A hundred thousand drachmæ.

M M 2

allies,

allies, entered the Mantineian lands, and the usual ravage of Grecian armies followed.

Thucyd. l. 5.
c. 65.
The views of the confederates upon Tegea being th s checked, nothing remained for them but to retreat and leave their own country open to extensive waste, or to risk a battle.   They determined upon the latter, and, approaching the Lacedæmonian army, occupied some strong ground, where they formed.   Agis, eager to do away the disgrace he had incurred, took the earliest moment for leading his forces to action.   He was already within arrow's flight of the enemy, when one of the elder officers [9] called aloud to him, in the terms of a Greek proverb, ' that he was going to mend evil with evil [10] :' meaning that, to atone for his former ill-judged retreat, he was now rushing to an inconsiderate and ruinous attack.   Seeing presently the justness of the admonition, and incouraged by it to the measure which prudence required, tho rashness or acrimony might blame, Agis instantly gave orders to halt, and then drew off without ingaging.

Thucyd. l. 5.
c. 66.
Whatever, on the other hand, might have been the abilities of the Argian generals, and it appears they were considerable, the democratical weight in the Argian government would have rendered them of little avail.   The generals wished to hold their present advantageous ground : but the troops, little practised in military subordination, and impatient of rest and delay, grew tumultuous, and accused them of traitorously permitting a flying enemy to escape.   Unable otherwise to compose the disorder, they marched after the Spartan king.   This was precisely what Agis desired: and to provoke it, he had been employing his troops in diverting the course of a mountain-stream, so as to damage the Mantineian lands.   Being informed that the confederates nevertheless persevered in holding their strong post, he was returning, without due precaution, toward the hills, when he suddenly met them advancing in order of battle along the plain.   Never, says Thucydides, was such consternation known in a Lacedæmonian army. The excellence of the Lacedæmonian discipline, however, inabled the

[9] Τῶν πρεσβυτέρων τις, which might mean one of the council appointed to advise him, or possibly only one of the elder officers of his army.

[10] Κακὸν κακῷ ἰᾶσθαι.

king to form his order of battle in a shorter time than would have been possible with any other troops then in the known world; and, before the attack could be made, they were prepared to receive it.

The Argians and their allies, after a short exhortation from the several commanders, rushed forward with fury. The Lacedæmonians, continues the cotemporary historian, use speeches of exhortation less than any other Greeks; well knowing that discipline, long and carefully practised, gives more confidence to troops than any harangue, however fine and however ingeniously adapted to the occasion. To the astonishment of the confederates, who had observed with joy the tumult occasioned by the first alarm, they were seen presently in perfect order, silent and without hurry, stepping in exact time to the sound of numerous flutes, and thus preserving their front compact and even, without any breaking or floating, the seldom failing defects of extensive lines[11]. The numbers, on either side, Thucydides professes that he could not learn with certainty; thus teaching us what credit is due to writers incomparably farther removed from means of information, who pretend to state with precision the force of contending armies. The extent, however, of the Lacedæmonian front evinced their superiority; and the two armies were the most numerous that ever, within the bounds of tradition, had met in Peloponnesus. On the Argian side the Athenian, of the other army the Lacedæmonian, was the only cavalry. Indeed the Lacedæmonians seem to have been the only Peloponnesian people who, at this time, had any cavalry.

In all actions among the antients, the right, on both sides, commonly

Thucyd. l. 5. c. 69, 70.

c. 71.

---

[11] It is Thucydides' description of the march of the Lacedæmonian phalanx, upon this occasion, that Milton has imitated in the first book of the Paradise Lost:

———————————— Rose
A forest huge of spears; and thronging helms
Appear'd, and serried shields, in thick array,
Of depth immeasurable. Anon they move,
In perfect phalanx, to the Dorian mood
Of flutes and soft recorders; such as raised
To highth of noblest temper heroes old,
Arming to battel, and, instead of rage,
Deliberate valor breathed, firm, and unmoved
With dread of death to flight or foul retreat.

overstretched

overstretched the left of the opposing army. For, ingaging hand to hand, the shield, the principal defence, being borne on the left arm, was less a protection for the right side; and the soldier in the extreme of the right wing, to avoid exposing the undefended part of his body, would always rather incline to the right. The man then next on the left, and so every man in the line, would also press rather toward the right, to profit from the protection of his neighbor's shield. Thus, on the present occasion, it happened that before the armies met, the Mantineians, on the right of the Argian line, had considerably overstretched the Lacedæmonian left; and, on the other side, the Tegeans, on the right of the Lacedæmonian line (the Lacedæmonian front being of greater extent) had still more overstretched the Argian left. Agis, observing this, when the armies were only not ingaged, inconsiderately ordered a movement, with a view to remedy the inconvenience which he apprehended. The Skirite and Brasidian bands (by the latter name those soldiers were honorably distinguished who had fought under Brasidas in Thrace) forming the left of the Lacedæmonian line, were directed to break away from the main body, so far as to prevent the Mantineians from taking the army in flank; and two lochi of Lacedæmonians, under the polëmarcs Hipponoïdas and Aristocles, were commanded, from another part, to fill the interval. The Skirites and

Thucyd. l. 5. c. 72.

Brasidians instantly obeyed: but Hipponoïdas and Aristocles, whether the enemy were so near that it was impossible, or they thought the danger of the movement to the whole army would justify their disobedience, kept their former post. The Skirites and Brasidians therefore, being presently attacked by the whole force of the Mantineians, together with a thousand chosen Argians, were cut off from their main body, overpowered, compelled to retreat, and pursued to the baggage of their army.

Meanwhile the rest of the line of the Lacedæmonians had everywhere the advantage, and particularly in the center, where Agis himself took post. The Argian center scarcely came to action with him, but

c. 73.

fled the onset. The Athenians thus, who formed the left of the confederate line, were completely deserted; the center having fled, while the right was pursuing. Their total destruction must have followed,

but

but for the protection given to their retreat by their own cavalry, whose services on that day were eminent.   Even thus, however, they would scarcely have been inabled to save themselves, had not the defeat of the Skirites and Brasidians called the attention of the Lacedæmonian king.   The victorious Mantineians, when they found the rest of their army defeated, avoided his attack by hasty retreat.

Agis, true to the institutions of Lycurgus, pursued no farther than to make victory sure.   The killed therefore were not numerous in proportion to the numbers ingaged and the completeness of the success : seven hundred Argians, two hundred Mantineians, and two hundred Athenians, among whom both the generals fell, are the numbers of the confederates reported by Thucydides.   Of the Lacedæmonians about three hundred were killed, principally Brasidians and Skirites ; and of the allies of Lacedæmon a very small number, as they were little ingaged.   After collecting the spoil of the field and erecting their trophy, the Lacedæmonians carried their dead to Tegea, and intombed them ceremoniously.   The enemy's dead were restored, on the usual application from the vanquished.

The other Spartan king, Pleistoanax, had advanced as far as Tegea, Thucyd. l. 5. with an army composed of Lacedæmonians above and under the age c. 75. for forein service, to be ready, in case of misfortune, to support Agis. Immediately upon receiving information of the victory, he returned ; and at the same time messengers were dispatched to Corinth, and the more distant allies, to countermand the march of their troops.   The victorious army, after paying honorable attendance upon the obsequies of the slain, returned home, and the great Doric festival of the Carneia, whose period was at hand, ingrossed the public attention.

The event of this battle restored the Lacedæmonian character in Greece.   The advantage of numbers, indeed, had been on the side of the Lacedæmonians ; but the circumstances of the action proved their superiority in discipline, and in that valor which discipline infuses, by giving individuals to confide in the combined exertions of numbers with whom they act.   This discipline in the soldier, we find, was, in the late battle, of efficacy even to counterbalance defective precaution and defective judgement in the general ; while the want of it

in

in the confederate army rendered superior abilities in the commanders of no effect[12]. The misfortunes, the misconduct, and the apparent slackness of the Lacedæmonians, in the course of the war with Athens, were in consequence no longer attributed to any degeneracy in the people, but to the mismanagement of leaders, and the chance of war: a contempt, which had been gaining, for the Spartan institutions and discipline, as if hitherto respected above their worth, was done away; and the Spartan character resumed its wonted superiority.

But the Carneian festival occupied the Lacedæmonians at a very inconvenient season for a military people. Regulated, as all the Grecian festivals, by the revolutions of the moon, it began this year about the seventh of August. Its principal ceremonies lasted nine days: but the whole month, named among the Dorian Greeks the Carneian, was, in a degree, dedicated to religious festivity. In the rude ages of the Heracleids and of Lycurgus, this check to military enterprize might be salutary: but in days of more refined and extensive policy, when wars, not of choice, but of political necessity, might be to be maintained against states capable of supporting lasting hostilities, such avocations should no longer have been allowed to interrupt public business. The Lacedæmonians were, however, so attached to their antient institutions, that, till the period of the Carneia was completed, no

Dodw. Ann. Thu.

Thucyd. l. 4. c. 76.

---

[12] Thus much may be gathered from Thucydides' account of the battle. But his opinion is farther delivered in a remark upon it, in a manner sufficiently intelligible, tho in cautious and rather obscure terms: Ἀλλὰ μάλιϛα δὴ κατὰ πάντα τῇ ἐμπειρίᾳ Λακεδαιμόνιοι ἐλασσωθέντες τότι, τῇ ἀνδρείᾳ ἔδειξαν οὐκ ἧσσον περιγενόμενοι. Thucyd. l. 5. c. 72. ' But on this occasion, ' more remarkably than ever, the Lacedæ- ' monians, tho in all respects outdone in ' the military art, gave signal proofs of ' their superiority in true manly valor.' Thus Smith has translated, aiming to follow the letter, and certainly missing the sense. Thucydides could not mean here to speak disrespectfully of that military art and discipline of the Lacedæmonians, which, in the preface to his account of this very battle, he has taken occasion to describe, admirable in theory, and well supported by practice; and which, in his account of the battle itself, he shows to have been not less admirable in effect. Κατὰ πάντα must have been intended to relate to the circumstances of the battle, and not to any circumstances of the military art; and by ἐμπειρία has been meant the experience and science of the general, and not the skill of the soldier. A strong sense of delicacy, not less a characteristic of Thucydides than his scrupulous impartiality, has apparently prevented him from expressing his opinion on this occasion more openly.

military

military operations were prosecuted for profiting from the victory of Mantineia:

Soon after that event, the arrival of a thousand Athenian and three thousand Eleian heavy-armed to join the Argian army, inhanced the regret and indignation of all thinking men in the Argian confederacy, at that petulant impatience and unadvised rashness, inherent in democratical government, which had superinduced their defeat. So powerful a reïnforcement, seconding superior abilities in the generals, could those abilities have been effectually exerted, might have given the advantage over the ill-directed discipline of the Lacedæmonians. Offensive operations were immediately resumed; not indeed directly against Lacedæmon, but against their allies on the other side of the peninsula. The Epidaurians, objects hitherto of unjust ambition and oppressive policy, had now made themselves objects of revenge; entering the Argian territory, while its principal force was absent, wasted the country, and slaughtered the inferior troops appointed to its protection. The siege of Epidaurus was regularly formed, and while the Lacedæmonians were supinely intent upon their festival, a contravallation was completed. Winter then approaching, a sufficient force was appointed to guard the lines, and the rest of the troops dispersed to their several homes.

SECTION VI.

Change in the Administration of Argos: Peace and Alliance between Argos and Lacedæmon: Overthrow of the Athenian Influence, and of the Democratical Interest in Peloponnesus. Inertness of the Lacedæmonian Administration: Expulsion of the Oligarchal Party from Argos, and renewal of Alliance between Argos and Athens. Siege of Melos by the Athenians: Fresh Instance of atrocious Inhumanity in the Athenians. Feeble Conduct of the Lacedæmonians: Distress of the Oligarchal Argians. Transactions in Thrace. Conclusion of the Sixteenth Year of the War.

SCARCELY any disaster could befal a Grecian commonwealth that would not bring advantage to some considerable portion of its citizens. The unfortunate battle of Mantineia strengthened the oligarchal cause in Argos. The fear of such another blow, and of the usually dreadful consequences of unsuccessful war among the Greeks, brought the Argian people to a temper to bear advice about an accommodation with Lacedæmon; while the inconvenience of democratical sway unbalanced, which had been so severely experienced in the circumstances of the battle, disposed them to hear, with less impatience, of the necessity of trusting executive government to a few. On this turn, in the public mind, the oligarchal leaders founded a project to overset the present politics, not only of their own state, but of all Greece. They would first propose to the Argian people simply to make peace with Lacedæmon: that being effected, and the Athenian alliance in consequence no longer necessary, the people might probably be persuaded, for the sake of confirming the peace, to make alliance with Lacedæmon. Having thus far used the power of the people as the instrument of their measures, they would then turn those very measures against the power of the people: with assistance from Lacedæmon they would abolish the authority of the general assembly, and establish oligarchal government.

Such

Such was the scheme, and it appears to have been ably conducted. The Carneia gave opportunity for communication with Lacedæmon; and tho the watchful acuteness of Alcibiades led him to suspect the intrigue, insomuch that he passed to Argos purposely to counterwork it, yet the measures of the oligarchal party were so well taken, and the depression of the popular mind gave them in the moment such opportunity, that the vote for peace was carried. This leading step being gained, the oligarchal party proceeded to push their advantage. Matters had been prepared by secret negotiation, and articles were soon settled; according to which it was agreed, 'That all Peloponnesian Thucyd. l. 5. 'cities, small equally and great, should be independent, as in the times c. 77. 'and according to the customs of their forefathers[13]: That the hostages 'in the hands of the Argians should be restored to their friends: That 'the siege of Epidaurus should be raised: That, if the Athenians per- 'severed in prosecuting it, the Lacedæmonians and Argians should 'unitedly oppose them; and that they should equally oppose the 'interference of any forein armed force, upon any occasion, within the 'peninsula.'

This blow to the politics of Alcibiades and the interest of Athens, c. 78. was quickly followed by an alliance, defensive and offensive, between Lacedæmon and Argos, accompanied with a renunciation, on the part of Argos, of the alliance with Athens, Elis, and Mantineia. Among the articles which Thucydides has reported, in the Doric dialect in which they were written, and apparently at large, the following particularly deserve notice: 'All cities of the confederacy, those of the 'Lacedæmonian equally and of the Argian alliance, shall have the 'clear and independent injoyment of their own laws and their own 'polity, according to antient usage[14]. If city has difference with city, 'it shall be decided by judges to be duly appointed by both[15]; or it 'shall be lawful to refer the decision to any third city equally friendly

---

[13] Κατὰ τὰ πάτρια.

[14] Κατὰ τὰ πάτρια.

[15] I know not how more satisfactorily to paraphrase the single word of the original, διακριθῆμεν: translators and commentators give no assistance; and here, as for the dis-

pute between Athens and Lacedæmon before the war, we want information by what rule of law, by what process, and under what sanction, such litigation between state and state was to be managed.

'to

' to both.   Military command shall rest with the Lacedæmonians and
' Argians; who shall, by joint councils, direct, equitably and impar-
' tially, the military affairs of the whole confederacy.'

Thucyd. 1, 5. c. 80. As soon as this second treaty was concluded, a requisition was sent
to Athens, in the name of the united republics, for the immediate evacuation of the Epidaurian territory, with a declaration that neither
embassy nor herald from Athens would be received, while Athenian
troops remained in Peloponnesus.   The Athenian administration prudently yielded to the necessity of the moment, and Demosthenes was
sent to bring away the Athenian forces.   That officer showed his usual
ability in the execution of this ungrateful commission : he saved the
dignity of his republic by giving the affair the appearance of a favor
granted by Athens to both Epidaurus and Argos; and he more essentially served his republic by restoring, in some degree, a good correspondence with both those cities.

Success animated the administrations of the newly-allied states, and
they pushed it with a degree of vehemence.   Ambassadors were sent
to invite Perdiccas king of Macedonia to join their confederacy, with
orders at the same time to ratify by oath, in the name of the two states,
to the Chalcidian towns, the alliance, and ingagement for protection,
formerly made by Lacedæmon.   Contrary then to that spirit of equity,
moderation, and peace, which the terms of their confederacy appeared
to hold forth, commissioners, escorted by a thousand heavy-armed from
each state, went to Sicyon, and, by their assumed authority, subverting
the established democratical government there, committed the supreme
power to an oligarchy of their own selection.   This, however, they
would vindicate by asserting that the antient constitution of Sicyon
was oligarchal, and the democracy a usurpation.

Measures, which had been for some time preparing, toward a revolution of the same kind at Argos, were now thought mature.   Accordingly those leading men, who had conducted the negotiations with
Lacedæmon, and had since directed the administration of Argos, under
the nominal authority of the popular assembly, assumed to themselves
the supreme power of the state, and the authority of the popular
assembly was expressly abolished.   Meanwhile the Mantineians,
seeing

seeing that, instead of any longer receiving protection from Argos, they were to expect oppression from the union of that powerful state with Lacedæmon, yielded, very reluctantly, their command over the Arcadian towns which they had subjected, and made their peace with Lacedæmon upon such terms as they could obtain. The Lacedæmonians then took upon themselves to regulate the little republics of Achaia, so as to restore the Lacedæmonian influence, where it had been overpowered by a democratical party, and to confirm it, where it was tottering; and they found universal acquiescence. Thus, before the end of winter, all the effect of the treacherous policy of Alcibiades, which had been at first so threatening to Lacedæmon, was done away, and Peloponnesus was more completely than ever united, not immediately in war, but in politics, against Athens. *Thucyd. l. 5. c. 82.*

This important change seems to have been produced by springs, not within the power of human wisdom in the Athenian administration to controul. Its advantages were lost to Lacedæmon through the want of energy, which had so long been conspicuous in the administration of that state. Tho the democratical form of government was abolished in Argos, the democratical interest remained powerful; and, early in spring, a conspiracy was formed to overturn the oligarchy. The time chosen, for carrying it into effect, was the season of the Gymnopaideia, the Naked Games, at Sparta. But a democratical party could not easily keep a secret. Intelligence of the design was acquired by the Argian administration, and communicated to Sparta, with a request of precautionary assistance; yet, such was the infatuated attachment of the Lacedæmonians to those stated festivals, they would not stir. The discovery of the plot, and the knowlege that it was discovered, led the two parties in Argos to arms; and, intelligence of this being forwarded to Sparta, then at last it was thought proper to adjourn the celebration of the festival, and send an army to save so important an ally. But it was too late: the two parties had come to action in Argos, the oligarchal party was defeated, many had been killed, and most of the rest forced into exile. Some of the fugitives met the Lacedæmonian army at Tegea, and were the first to give information of their own misfortune. They expressed at the same time confident hope that their affairs might yet be restored: in the confusion unavoidable immediately on *B. C. 417. Ol. 90. ¾. P. W. 15. After 2d April.*

such

such a revolution, it would be easy, they said, for so powerful an army to become masters of the city; and to their remonstrances they added the most urgent intreaty.   But the chiefs of the Lacedæmonian army were not to be so persuaded; they led their forces immediately home, to conclude the celebration of their festival.   Had we not these circumstances from the authentic pen of Thucydides, we should scarcely conceive them possible of a people, who could sometimes conduct themselves with so much united dignity and policy as the Lacedæmonians.

The conscious weakness of the prevailing party in Argos, marked by one of their first measures, makes the conduct of the Lacedæmonians appear the more extraordinary and more inexcusable.   Confident neither in their own strength, nor in the expectation of assistance from Athens, the Argians sent a deputation to make their peace with Lacedæmon.   The exiles did not fail to send deputies to oppose them.   The Lacedæmonians, with ostentatious moderation, referred the matter to the general convention of deputies from the states of their confederacy.   Both parties were heard; but judgement was given, as might be expected, against the democratical party; and it was decreed that an army should be sent to carry it into effect.   The weak remissness of the Lacedæmonian government again showed itself, in delaying the execution of this decree; and the Argian administration, thus at the same time threatened and incouraged, recurred to Athens, where their application was gladly received, and the former connection of Athens and Argos was restored.

Those measures which the existing circumstances rendered advisable, were then taken by the Argians, for resisting the vengeance of Lacedæmon; which, instigated continually by their banished fellowcitizens, would scarcely fail at length to fall upon them.   The landforce of Lacedæmon would be decidedly superior to any they could expect to assemble: upon their walls therefore they must depend for protection, and upon the sea, if matters were pushed to extremity, for subsistence. Accordingly they applied, with the utmost sedulity, to secure the communication of their city with the sea, by long walls; such as connected Athens with its ports, and such as the policy of the Athenian govern-

4

ment

ment had recommended to many other Grecian towns, standing, according to the usual choice of situation among the early Greeks, near, but not on, the shore.   The Athenian government, under the influence of Alcibiades, gave large assistance, particularly furnishing builders, and artificers; and all the Argian citizens, all the slaves, and even the women, assisted in the work.   Those indeed were not likely to want zeal for such business, who had to apprehend the miseries which the Grecian practice of war usually brought upon a town taken.

It was not till the following autumn that the Lacedæmonians exerted themselves, so far as to undertake any military operation, in favor of those miserable families, the principal of Argos, who, confiding in the Lacedæmonian alliance, had ingaged in the measures through which, with the loss of all their property and many friends and relations, they now languished in exile.   Then at length the confederacy was called upon for the due proportions of troops, and the Laeedæmonian forces marched under Agis.   Some friends to the oligarchal interest yet remained in Argos: these had communicated with the exiles and with Lacedæmon; and it was hoped that the approach of the Lacedæmonian army would inable them to stir with effect.   The precaution however of the democratical leaders prevented this; and the Lacedæmonians were neither prepared nor disposed to undertake the siege of Argos.   They however destroyed the yet unfinished works of the long walls; they took Hysiæ, a small town of Argolis, and put all the freemen to the sword; and then returning home, dismissed their forces. The Argians used the opportunity thus left open for revenge.   Their fugitive nobles found favor and protection principally in Phlius, where most of them resided.   The Phliasians suffered for their charity, through the ravage of their lands by the Argian forces.

The restoration of Argos, in its present state, to the Athenian confederacy, was but a small step toward the recovery of that influence in Peloponnesus, which Athens had lately held, and a very deficient gratification for the ambition of Alcibiades.   That restless politician therefore looked around for other opportunities to promote his own power and consequence, through an extension of the empire of his

                                                    commonwealth;

Thucyd. l. 5. c. 83.

Ibid.
Plut. vit.
Alcib. &
Nic.

commonwealth; and particularly carried his views forward to a war, in which he would certainly command, and hoped to shine. An expedition had been prepared, under Nicias, for the reduction of the revolted cities of Thrace; but it became necessary to abandon the measure, in consequence of the neglect of Perdiccas king of Macedonia to send the troops which, according to treaty, he should have furnished. His alliance with Argos and Lacedæmon becoming also known, he was, for the two offences, declared an enemy to Athens, and the Athenian fleets stopped the maritime commerce of his dominions.

Thucyd. l. 5.
c. 84.
B. C. 416.
Ol. 90. 4.
P. W. 16.
Intrigues of the oligarchal party being still carried on, or suspected, in Argos, Alcibiades went thither in spring with twenty ships of war, and, with the support of the democratical party, seized no less than three hundred of those supposed most connected with the oligarchal interest, whom he placed in several ilands of the Ægean, under the Athenian dominion. This, among the usual violences of Grecian politics, may be esteemed a lenient measure. The next step of the Athenian democracy, said by Plutarch to have been also dictated by Alcibiades, was a much grosser and more shocking trespass upon the common rights of mankind, and much less defensible upon any plea of political necessity. Alcibiades would not recommend any direct hostility against Lacedæmon; policy forbad; but he recommended everything that might most provoke Lacedæmon to begin hostilities. The people of Melos, both irritated and incouraged by the failure of the attempt against them, in the sixth year of the war, under Nicias, became presently active in hostility against Athens. They were, however, of course included in the peace between Athens and Lacedæmon, and we are not informed of any offence they afterward gave; yet it was now determined by the Athenian people to subdue the iland. An armament was accordingly prepared, consisting of thirty Athenian, six Chian, and two Lesbian ships of war, twelve hundred heavy-armed, three hundred bowmen, and twenty horse-bowmen, all Athenians, and fifteen hundred heavy-armed of the allies.

This force, under the command of Cleomedes and Tisias, debarked in Melos without opposition. Before any ravage, a deputation was sent into the city to persuade the people to submit to the Athenian dominion,

dominion, without making violence necessary to their reduction; and it was supposed that, could the deputies have addressed their eloquence to the people at large, they might have succeeded; but this the chiefs would not permit. With the chiefs therefore only a conference was held, of which Thucydides has left an account in detail; meaning however, apparently, not to repeat exactly what passed, but only to give a methodized account of the general arguments, and perhaps to express his own opinion on some points, particularly the ungenerous inertness of the Lacedæmonian administration, in a less invidious way than if he had spoken in his own person. The claim of the strong to command the weak, with absolute authority, was so familiar among the Greeks, that it seems not to have shocked even Thucydides; who, on this occasion, makes the Athenian deputy assert it in the most unqualified manner; professing even his confidence in a continuance of that favor of the gods, which had already inabled the Athenian people to exercise so many cruelties, and reduce so many Grecian states to subjection.

The Melians however, in hope of assistance from Lacedæmon, refusing to submit, the blockade of their city was formed by sea and land. Their resistance was for some time vigorous. In the course of the summer they made a successful sally, upon that part of the contravallation where the Athenian magazine was, and carried a considerable supply of provisions into the town. In the winter they made another sally, attended with some success: but this occasioned a reinforcement from Athens to the besieging army. The town being then closely pressed, discontent arose among the lower people. The chiefs apprehending sedition, with a design to betray them to the enemy, and doubting their means of prevention, took the desperate resource of surrendering the place, with all in it, to the pleasure of the Athenian people.

After all we have gone through of Grecian history, we cannot but shudder at what followed. The Athenians had no pretence for any command over the Melians but that they were stronger. Connected by blood, by habit, and by their form of government, with Lacedæmon, those ilanders had nevertheless been cautiously inoffensive to

Thucyd. l. 5. c. 112. 114.

c. 115.

c. 116.

Athens, till forced to become enemies. The punishment for this involuntary crime, even to the lower people, supposed all along in some
degree friendly, when all were surrendered together to the mercy of
the Athenians, was no less than what the unfortunate Scionæans had
undergone, for that termed their rebellion. All the adult males were
put to death, and the women and children, of all ranks, were sold for
slaves. The iland was divided among five hundred Athenian families.
With the most unquestionable testimony to facts, which strike with
horror when perpetrated by a tribe of savages, we are at a loss to conceive how they could take place in the peculiar country and age of
philosophy and the fine arts; where Pericles had spoken and ruled,
where Thucydides was then writing, where Socrates was then teaching,
where Xenophon and Plato and Isocrates were receiving their education, and where the paintings of Parrhasius and Zeuxis, the sculpture
of Pheidias and Praxiteles, the architecture of Callicrates and Ictinus,
and the sublime and chaste dramas of Sophocles and Euripides formed
the delight of the people.

Tho the late battle near Mantineia had restored the tarnished glory
of the Lacedæmonian arms and the sullied character of the people, yet
the conduct of their administration continued to earn for them those
imputations of ill faith, illiberal policy, and inertness, which, in report-
ing the conference at Melos, Thucydides puts into the mouth of the
Athenian commissioner, and which, for their conduct toward Argos,
they had deserved. Their total abandonment of the faithful and unfortunate Melians was deeply disgraceful. Their Argian friends, wandering
up and down Peloponnesus, were, wherever they showed themselves or
were heard of, striking testimonies to their discredit. In the existing
tumult of Grecian politics, some exertion was unavoidable; but it was
generally feeble, irregular, and confined to little objects. No less
than thrice, since the beginning of hostilities with Argos, the Lacedæmonian army, after advancing to the frontier, was stopped by
unfavorable appearances in the border-passing sacrifice, and returned home; a circumstance little known when able and active
men directed public affairs. Once indeed we have this religious trick
politically accounted for. Incouragement from the friends of oligarchy

garchy in Argos induced the Lacedæmonian army to march, and intelligence that the plot was discovered occasioned the stop, which was imputed to forbidding tokens in the sacrifice. At times, however, party ran high in Lacedæmon itself; which might contribute to the visible feebleness and irregularity in the conduct of the administration at this period. Before the end of the winter in which Melos fell, an effort was made to relieve the Argian fugitives, and distress the Argians in possession; but, tho the preparations promised something great, what followed was little and inefficacious. The forces of all the Peloponnesian allies, except Corinth, were assembled, and the strength of Laconia joined them. But, from the first, the objects seem to have been no more than to carry off the plunder of the villages of Argolis, for which waggons attended the march of the army, and to establish the Argian fugitives in Orneæ, an Argolic town on the borders of Phliasia. Both were very incompletely executed. A small part of Argolis only was plundered; and the Lacedæmonian army was no sooner withdrawn, and, according to the practice of the Greeks, dispersed for the winter, than the Argians, with a small auxiliary force from Athens, marched against Orneæ, which was so ill provided for defence, that those who held it consulted their safety by immediate flight.

Thucyd. l. 6.
c. 7.

During these military transactions, the Lacedæmonian administration so far exerted themselves in negotiation, as to endevor to excite the Chalcidians of Thrace, whose present independency was a benefit derived from the arms of Lacedæmon, to join the king of Macedonia in hostilities against Athens. But the Chalcidians, no longer won and animated by the abilities, the activity, the popular manners, and the generous faith of a Brasidas, and probably both apprehensive of the power and distrustful of the character of Perdiccas, refused. While indeed they injoyed independency in peace, the small tribute assessed by Aristeides was apparently not an object for which to provoke the naval power of Athens; and it was rather their interest to see Perdiccas, after all his wiles, unquiet within his own government, as well as harrassed by a forein war. The troubles within Macedonia disabled him for any considerable exertion without; while Methonë, an Athe-

O o 2

nian

nian garrison on the borders, became an asylum for Macedonian refugees and malcontents; who, together with a body of Athenian horse stationed there, employed themselves in inroads wherever they could find most plunder and least resistance. Such were the transactions of the sixteenth winter of the war.

CHAPTER XVIII.

Of the Affairs of SICILY, and of the ATHENIAN Expedition into SICILY.

SECTION I.

Affairs of Sicily: Hieron King of Syracuse. Expulsion of the Family of Gelon, and Establishment of Independent Democracies in the Sicilian Cities: Agrarian Law. Ducetius King of the Sicels. Syracuse the Soverein City of Sicily. Accession of Syracuse to the Lacedæmonian Confederacy: War between the Dorian and Ionian Sicilians: First Interference of Athens in the Affairs of Sicily: Peace through Sicily procured by Hermocrates of Syracuse.

THE Athenian people, whose numbers were far below the name of a nation, being indeed a very small portion of the Greek nation, but whose men were all soldiers and seamen; possessing a fleet that no one state then on earth could resist, high discipline, military as well as naval, officers of extensive experience, a civil and political system upon the whole admirably arranged, with large revenue from mines and from tributary states; there is no foreseeing how far their tyrannous dominion might not have been extended over Greeks and among forein nations, but that the folly of democracy unrestrained would of course work its own ruin. The evident weakness in the political conduct of the only rival power, Lacedæmon, operated to the incouragement of chiefs and people; and in the same winter in which the inhabitants of the little iland of Melos were cut off from the face of the earth, the wild ambition of the people of Athens became eager in project for the conquest of another iland, many times larger, not only than Melos, but than Attica; ignorant at the same time, almost all of them, of its magnitude, its population, its value if conquered, and its means to resist conquest.

Thucyd. l. 6. c. 1. Plut. vit. Nic.

In

In the succinct history of Sicily formerly given, we have seen Gelon, from a private citizen of Gela, become king of that city and of Syracuse, and head of the Grecian interest in the iland. His dominion comprehended all the Grecian settlements on the eastern coast, the greatest part of those on the southern, with some on the northern, and extensive command over the inland barbarians. After an illustrious reign of only seven years, dying at no very advanced age, in the next year, if we can understand and may trust Diodorus, after the glorious battle of Himera, he was succeeded by his brother Hieron. The only considerable power besides in Sicily, was that of Theron prince of Agrigentum; who, like Gelon, had raised himself from a private station, and had also merited his advancement. He outlived Gelon, according to Diodorus, seven years, dying in the first of the seventy-seventh Olympiad, after a reign of only ten. His son Thrasydæus, who succeeded him, was of a different character: arrogant abroad, as tyrannical at home, he ingaged in war with Hieron. Being defeated, he lost the respect of his own people; and flying, for refuge from their animosity, to the Misæan Megarians, was by them put to death. His opponents made peace with the Syracusan prince, and a republican form of government was restored.

Arist. de
Rep. l. 5.
c. 12.
Diod. l. 11.
c. 38.
B. C. 479.

B. C. 472.

Gelon's reign was too short for completing a work of such complex difficulty as that of molding into one regular government, and well fixing in their several places, the many parts, little disposed to coalesce, of which his dominion consisted. His policy had made Syracuse a very large city. Probably before his accession its population was become too great to be contained within the limits of Ortygia, the original site. The narrow channel, separating that iland from the northern shore of the bay, was in part filled, and the town was extended upon the mainland. The increase of inhabitants under Gelon, however, required a very great addition of buildings. Among the advantages of the situation was an inexhaustible store of free-stone under the soil, of a kind easily wrought, yet, after exposure to the weather, sufficiently hard. On the northern side of the harbour, a hill composed intirely of such stone, was, in extent and form, commodious for the site of the new town Rising precipitous from the sea and from the

plain,

plain, so that slight fortifications would be strong defences, its hight was moderate, and its summit level; the western end only rising into lofty craggs.   The level part, ten or twelve miles in circuit, became intirely covered by the new town ; which was divided by fortifications into two parts, with the names of Achradina and Tychë; the former eastward against the sea, the other reaching westward toward the craggy hight; so that Syracuse consisted now of three towns, Achradina, Tychë, and Ortygia, capable of separate defence against a common enemy, or against each other.   Whether the fourth, with the name of Neapolis, Newtown, stretching along the shore of the great port, below Tychë, toward the river Anapus, had its beginning under Hieron, seems uncertain. The extraordinary extent and population how-ever, which Syracuse finally acquired, will be matter for future notice.

Hieron, as well as Gelon, was a man of superior character, but of a character less exactly fitted for the difficult situation to which, on his brother's death, he succeeded.   Learned and a munificent incourager of learning; splendid and of elegant taste; humane and of fine feel-ings; he was rather qualified to preside beneficially and with dignity over an established government, than to direct the affairs of a state so compounded as that of which Syracuse was the capital. He had talents for war, which he had displayed under his brother's reign.   After he came himself to the throne, no dispute with forein powers required his personal exertion in military command ; but his fleet relieved the Cumæans of Italy by a victory over the Tuscan fleet.   In peace there-fore his wealth inabled him, as his taste disposed him, to shine in the costly race of chariots on the Olympian course, and liberally to reward those who had talents for mixing his fame with the achievements of his coursers there.   Accordingly the poetical abilities of Pindar have been peculiarly dedicated to promote the renown of Hieron.   At the same time men of genius from various parts of Greece were entertained in his court; among whom the poets Æschylus, Simonides, and Bac-chilides, are principally mentioned.   Yet, if we may trust that elegant dialogue remaining from Xenophon, in which Hieron and Simoniues are the supposed speakers, he was utterly unable to accomplish his anxious wish for changing the nature of his government, and converting

Demetr. de eloc. s. 312.

Xenoph. Hieron.

Diod. l. 11. c. 51. Ol. 76. 3.

ing his tyranny into a constitutional monarchy. He there pathetically laments that, while his subjects could pass, as business or amusement led them, wherever they pleased, without fear, he could be free from apprehension nowhere; but must go, as tyrants it seems usually did, himself constantly armed, as well as surrounded by armed attendants; and he particularly regrets that his subjects (not all, nor, in any probability, a majority, but a party) were more to be dreaded by him than any forein enemy. Apparently Hieron had not the art, like Gelon, to mediate between the higher and lower ranks of citizens, and compose their jarring pretensions. His disposition led him to be more attentive to the splendor of his court, the conversation of men of genius and science, and perhaps the great business of fleets, armies, and forein connections, than to the detail of interior government, and the secret workings of political fermentation. It is not unlikely that, disgusted with petulance and illiberality, he might show himself indisposed to the democratical interest, more than political prudence would allow. For the lower people of the Greeks, unlike those of the freëst and most high-spirited nations of modern Europe, who are generally the most orderly as well as the most industrious, were, on the contrary, disdainful of labor, as the office of slaves, and, unless in military employment,

Xén. Hier.
Aristot. de
Rep. l. 5.
c. 12.
Diod. l. 11.
c. 66.
Ol. 78. 2.
B. C. 467. busy only in faction. Of particulars we are not informed, but we learn that to hold his high station, and support those who supported him, Hieron was reduced, against his nature, to use severities. He died nevertheless in peace, in the eleventh year of his reign, and was succeeded in his authority by his younger brother Thrasybulus.

The circumstances of the revolution, which quickly followed, are very deficiently reported. Thrasybulus is accused of cruel severity, and a conduct generally despotic. The democratical party were certainly strong throughout the cities of his dominion: they ingaged in

Diod. l. 11.
c. 67, 68. their cause those who held the principal sway in Agrigentum, Himera, Selinus, and some other towns, and then openly revolted. The people of higher rank, however, generally adhered to Thrasybulus; and the two parties divided the city itself of Syracuse between them; Thrasybulus maintaining himself in Ortygia and Achradina, while the rest was occupied by the insurgents. War was thus carried on for some

s   time:

time: but at length Thrasybulus, finding his force insufficient for any hope of final success, retired to Locri in Italy, where he passed the remainder of his days in private life.

Diodorus is, unfortunately, the only author from whom we have any account, with any attempt at connection, of these and the insuing events; which could not but abound in political matter, at the same time curious and instructive.   His concise narrative of the demolition of Gelon's fabric of empire, is little consistent with what we learn, from the more authentic pen of Herodotus, concerning its establishment, and as little consistent with the account given, even by himself, of Gelon s uncommon popularity while he lived, and of the high respect in which his memory continued for ages to be held.   It is a confused mass, injudiciously compounded of the contradictory reports, evidently, of contending factions.   Nevertheless, comparing that narrative, such as it is, with the purer tho more scanty sources of Herodotus and Thucydides, we may acquire no unsatisfactory general idea of the train and of the character of political events in Sicily.

On the expulsion of Thrasybulus, the democratical party everywhere predominating, and the democracy of Syracuse not being yet strong or settled enough to assert command, every town of the dominion of the tyrants assumed its separate independency.   But as the acquisition had been effected through communication among all, it was proposed still to secure it by friendly political intercourse; and for this purpose a congress was held, of deputies from the several towns.   The principal measures of this meeting, reported by Diodorus, strongly mark the democratical principle by which it was animated.   A festival was established, to be called the Eleutheria or Feast of Freedom, common for all the Sicilian cities, at whose common expence a colossal statue of the Eleutherian Jupiter was to be erected; and, on every return of the festival, four hundred and fifty oxen were to be sacrificed, whose carcases should regale the citizens intitled to partake in the rites.   At the same time it was resolved that no less than seven thousand citizens (if we may trust our copies of Diodorus,) including most of the principal families, should no longer be competent for the honors of magistracy in the commonwealth.   The historian, with much apparent reason, ascribes to this source the long troubles that followed.   Those injured men,

Diod. l. 11. c. 72. Ol. 79. 2. B. C. 463.

Diod. l. 11. c. 73.

refusing to acquiesce under the tyrannous decree, possessed themselves of two divisions of the city, Achradina and Ortygia, and carried on war by land and sea against their opponents. From similar causes troubles nearly similar arose, about the same time, in Agrigentum, Gela, Himera, Messena, and Catana. Everywhere the parties were nearly balanced; cultivation was interrupted; produce was destroyed; and the acquisition of freedom, as it was called, involved one of the most productive countries upon earth, after much ineffectual bloodshed, in universal want. This at length produced a general composition; and a retreat being provided for those who could not accommodate matters with the prevailing party in their respective towns, by allotting a portion of the Messinian territory for their possession, it was hoped tranquility might have been restored to the iland.

But thus, in every little state, lands were left to become public property, or to be assigned to new individual owners. Everywhere then that favorite measure of democracy, the equal division of all the lands of the state, was resolved upon ; a measure impossible to be perfectly executed ; impossible to be maintained as executed ; and of very doubtful advantage if it could be perfectly executed and perfectly maintained. The attempt produced neither the proposed quiet, nor any other public benefit, in Sicily. Private interest and party interest were everywhere busy and everywhere powerful. In the inscription of citizens, many, through favor of leading men, were admitted hastily and with little examination; others were arbitrarily rejected: many, even of those benefitted by acquisition of land, envied others with portions more fruitful or better situated; while many others, deprived of both property and municipal rights, which they had before possessed, were reduced to the condition of vagabonds and beggars. New and violent dissentions followed. In many towns the government, with the favorite name of democracy, was so unsteddy, that through the discontent of the lower people, sometimes arising from caprice, sometimes from oppression, temptation arose for the powerful and wealthy to aspire to tyranny. In Syracuse especially this occurred; but, of many adventurers none succeeded: Tyndarion lost his life in the attempt. It was however among the Greeks, so common to impute the purpose of tyranny, and even to give the title of tyrant,

to

Ol. 79. 4.
B. C. 461.

Diod. l. 11.
c. 85.

c. 86.

Ol. 81. 3.
B. C. 454.

to the leader of an adverse party, that the value of the terms, as we find them used by antient authors, is often very uncertain.

After the death of Tyndarion, Syracuse seems to have injoyed a short season of rest under democratical government; and in this period an exertion was made against a forein foe, which proved that, amid all the troubles, forein commerce had not ceased, and the marine of Syracuse was not totally decayed.   The Tuscans, long powerful pirates in the western parts of the Mediterranean, but repressed by the able and vigorous exertions of Gelon and Hieron, took advantage of the dissentions among the Sicilian commonwealths, to renew their depredations on the Grècian commerce and coasts.   The Syracusans fitted out a B. C. 453. fleet against them, of sixty triremes, which, under the command of Ol. 81. 4. Diod. l. 11. Apelles, spred terror through the Tuscan seas; and a debarkation being c. 67. made in Corsica, then chiefly under the Tuscan dominion, the coast was plundered, the town of Æthalia taken, and the fleet returned to Sicily laden with booty, particularly prisoners, who were made valuable as slaves.

Meanwhile the antient possessors of Sicily, called by the Greeks bar- c. 78. barians, who still held the inland parts, derived, from the long distraction of the Grecian interest, a respite from oppression. This was so ably used by a Sicel prince, Ducetius, that he became the principal potentate of the iland.   Long confined to strong holds among the hills, carrying thither from the vales whatever of their harvests they could save from the rapacity of the Greeks, and cultivating the vales only as they could snatch opportunity, at the risk of being carried off for slaves, the Sicels had maintained little connection among themselves, every village having its separate and independent polity.   Ducetius united all, c. 87. except the Hyblæans, under one dominion; and then he ventured to move his residence and the seat of his government from Neæ, among the mountains, to a new town which he founded, with the name of Palicë, in the vale beneath, by which he would of course acquire more complete command of that vale, and more effectually vindicate its produce.   Whether ambition or political necessity produced the measures which followed, we are without means to Diod. l. 2. know.   Ducetius, becoming ingaged in war with the Agrigentines, c. 90. Ol. 82. 1. took Motya, then held by an Agrigentine garrison; and, the Syracu- B. C. 452.

P P 2   sans

sans sending assistance to the Agrigentines, he defeated their united forces. Popular rage, at Syracuse, wreaked its illiberal vengeance against the unfortunate general who had commanded; he was condemned to suffer death as a traitor, and executed. But when passion subsiding gave room for reflection, wiser measures were adopted. The power, the proved abilities, and the various successes of Ducetius excited general apprehension among the Sicilian Greeks, unaccustomed to such a potentate within their iland. The Syracusans and Agrigentines taking together the lead, a large force was in the next summer collected; a battle was fought, and, after a very obstinate resistance, the Sicels were routed. The Agrigentines quickly retook Motya, and then rejoining the Syracusans, their united forces followed the motions of the Sicel prince.

Ducetius had not the resources of a settled government, or of the command of a civilized nation. Deserted by some of the troops who had attended his first flight, and upon the point of being betrayed by some of those who still accompanied him, he took a measure which the completest despair only could dictate. Mounting his horse by night, he rode alone into Syracuse, and placed himself at an altar in the agora. Early in the morning the circumstance became known, and the magistrates assembled the people, to receive their orders for measures to be taken with a suppliant of such importance. Diodorus, the warm advocate of the Sicilian Greeks, acknowleges that there were some among the Syracusans, who thought only of revenge against the unhappy prince, for what they had suffered from his able conduct in war against them; but the majority was decided by more generous sentiments, and probably a better policy. To permit him to remain in Sicily being judged inexpedient, he was conducted to Corinth, where he was liberally maintained at the public expence of the Syracusan commonwealth.

Diod. l. 11. c. 91.

The government of Syracuse, after a long course of troubles, appears at this time to have been settled into some consistency; and the city, large, populous, and wealthy, began to feel its weight in the scale of Sicilian politics. The people of the smaller towns were become sensible that they had been making themselves miserable for an independency which they could not maintain, that they were equally un-

2

able

able to coalesce in federal union, and that they must unavoidably lean upon a superior. The only competitor, with Syracuse, for superiority among the Sicilian towns, was Agrigentum; and while the competition remained, lasting peace could not easily subsist between them. The Syracusan chiefs brought back Ducetius from Corinth, appa- Diod. 1. 12. rently to make him instrumental to their own views for advancing the Ol. 83. 3. power of their commonwealth. They permitted, or rather incouraged B. C. 446. him to establish a colony of mixed people, Greeks and Sicels, at Calë Actë, on the northern coast of the iland. This was considered by the Agrigentines as a measure inimical to them : a war followed; and the Agrigentines, being defeated, were compelled to receive terms of peace from Syracuse. Thus the Syracusan democracy became decidedly the leading power among the Greeks of Sicily.

One Sicel town, Trinacia, among all the troubles of the iland, had Diod. 1. 12. always preserved independency; and its people, now alone within c. 26. Sicily, except the Carthaginian garrisons and perhaps the Elymian c. 29. towns, refused to acknowlege the sovereinty of the people of Syracuse. This was deemed a sufficient cause for war; and the wretched barba- Ol. 84. 4. rians, after a most gallant resistance, were compelled to yield. All the B. C. 441. principal men, of vigorous age, had first fallen in action; the elder, to avoid the ignominy and misery of servitude, or of massacre, from the hands of their implacable enemies, put themselves to death; the surviving inhabitants were made slaves, and the town was destroyed.

The Syracusans, having thus overborne opposition, proceeded to take Diod. 1. 12. measures for securing the dominion they had acquired. They exacted c. 30. tribute, and from time to time augmented the exaction, from all the cities of the iland. With the revenue thus arising they increased their navy and their establishment of cavalry ; and when the Peloponnesian war broke out, Syracuse, by its extent of dominion, and its naval force, Thucyd. was among the most powerful of the Grecian republics. Its alliance was therefore a great object for both the contending powers in Greece. As a Dorian people, the Syracusans were disposed to favor the Peloponnesians, and actually ingaged in their confederacy; but as democratical, they were not zealous in a cause which was in so great a degree the cause of oligarchy. Circumstances moreover quickly arose,

within

within their iland, to prevent them from giving that assistance which the Peloponnesians hoped, and which, strong as Syracuse was in marine, had its force been exerted while Athens was weak from pestilence and revolt, might have given a very different turn to the war.

Thucyd. l. 3. c. 86. Diod. l. 12. c. 53. B. C. 428[*]. Ol. 87. 4.

But the empire of democracy being of course oppressive, opportunity only was wanting for revolt against that of Syracuse. The Leontines, whether suffering more than others, or incouraged by better hope of forein assistance, were the first to resist. They were of Ionian origin, from Chalcis in Euboea, and their revolt was a signal for all the Ionian states in Sicily to take arms against Syracuse. The powerful city of Rhegium in Italy, whose people were also partly of Chalcidian race, joined them. Camarina moreover, originally a Dorian city (how re-peopled, after the removal of its inhabitants to Syracuse under Gelon, we are not informed), having however particular quarrel with Syracuse, joined the Ionian confederacy. But all the other Dorian cities, more numerous and powerful than the Ionian, adhered to the Syracusans; and the Epizephyrian Locrians of Italy concurred in their alliance.

B. C. 427.

In the fifth year of the Peloponnesian war, during the revolt of Lesbos and the sedition of Corcyra, the Syracusans, already undisputed masters of the field, blockaded Leontini by land and sea. The Ionian towns then all trembled for their fate: a subjection still more severe than that which had excited the revolt, would be the certain consequence of the fall of Leontini, which they were unable to relieve. In these circumstances, and under these apprehensions, they turned their thoughts to Athens, as the mother-state of the Ionian blood; and a deputation was sent thither to request assistance, urging the claim, not only of consanguinity, but of antient treaties of alliance.

The factions of Sicily, and the general prevalence of democracy, had promoted the cultivation of oratory. Gorgias of Leontini is reported to have been the first rhetorician who reduced his profession to an art, which he taught for pay, and he was at this time in high reputation. Gorgias, according to Diodorus, was placed at the head of the em-

---

[*] This date is gathered from the circumstances. Thucydides has not specified the time when the war began, and Diodorus is inaccurate.

bassy to Athens; and the novelty of his artificial and flowery eloquence, tho afterward justly reprobated by maturer Attic taste, is said to have then wonderfully captivated the Athenian people.   The season was, however, favorable for the effect of his talents: the rebellious Mitylenæans had recently yielded to the arms of Paches; and the Athenian interest triumphed in Corcyra, under the auspices of the Athenian admiral Eurymedon, through the horrid massacre of the oligarchal party there.   Nor were inducements wanting for the interference of the Athenian government in the affairs of Sicily.   The Peloponnesians derived thence supplies of corn, which, by a squadron in the Sicilian seas, or rather, according to the manner of cruizing among the antients, on the Sicilian coast, it was proposed to stop. Thucyd. l. 3. c. 86.

Hopes moreover were entertained that, under the name of alliance, the Athenian dominion might be extended in Sicily; which would bring, at the same time, increase of income to the state, increase of office and emolument for powerful men, and increase of importance, with opportunities for profit, regular and irregular, to every Athenian citizen. Thus incited, in opposition to the salutary advice left them as a legacy by their great minister Pericles, the Athenians ingaged in the affairs of Sicily.   A squadron of twenty ships of war, under Laches son of Melanopus, and Charœades son of Euphiletus, being in the autumn sent to assist the Leontines, took its station in the friendly port of Rhegium. B. C. 427. Ol. 88. ½. P. W. 5.

The immediate effect of this reïnforcement, as appears from the tenor of the narrative of Thucydides, was, that the blockade of Leontini by sea was given up or became ineffectual, and supplies could be introduced.   In the winter an expedition was undertaken by the Athenian commanders, against the Liparæan, called also the Æolian ilands, inhabited by a colony of Greeks from Cnidos.   The Liparæans held alliance with the Syracusans, and probably were troublesome to the Rhegians and their allies by maritime depredation.   The measures of the Athenians against them however failed.   In the following summer the relief of Leontini from the land blockade being attempted, Charœades fell in action.   Laches nevertheless, conducting the allied forces against Messena, took that city by capitulation, and then Thucyd. l. 3. c. 115. & l. 4. c. 25.

Thucyd. l. 3. c. 88.

B. C. 426. Ol. 88. ⅔. P. W. 6. Thucyd. l. 3. c. 90.

sailing

sailing to the Epizephyrian Locrian coast, ravaged the country, de-

Thucyd. l. 3.
c. 90.
feated the Locrians, who came out to protect it, and took the small town of Peripolium.

c. 103.
In the next winter an attempt was made against the citadel of Nessa in Sicily, held by a Syracusan garrison; but the allies were compelled to retire with loss. The Syracusans then, decidedly superior by land, but excluded by a squadron of only twenty triremes from their own seas, where they had long been accustomed to command, resolved to restore their marine, of late neglected, and give battle to the enemy's fleet. Intelligence of this was forwarded to Athens, with a request for reinforcement; and, the success already obtained incouraging the Athenian government, it was determined to send such a fleet as should at once give superiority beyond competition at sea, and, it was hoped, command speedy success in the final object of the war. Pythodorus son of Isolochus was forwarded immediately with a small squadron to supersede Laches in the command in chief, while triremes were preparing in the port of Peiræus, to follow in spring, under Eurymedon son of Theocles, and Sophocles son of Sostratidas, which should make the number of the relieving fleet sixty.

This change in the command seems not to have been advantageous. The conduct of Laches in Italy and Sicily had been apparently judicious and vigorous, and, for the force he commanded, successful; and the situations in which we afterward find him, prove that his estimation was not mean in Athens or in Greece. He was the person to whom, together with Nicias, the Lacedæmonian government always applied, when business was to be transacted with the government of Athens. When the truce for fifty years was made with Lacedæmon, he was the person appointed to the dignified office of pronouncing the prayer, that the event might be fortunate for the commonwealth: when the war broke out between Argos and Lacedæmon, he commanded the Athenian auxiliary forces in the army of the Argian confederacy; and he lost his life, as we have seen, in conducting the gallant, and, for the circumstances, successful retreat of those troops, from the unfortunate field of Mantineia. His successor in the Sicilian command began his

operations

operations inauspiciously : debarking his forces on the Locrian coast, Thucyd. l. 3.
near the town of Peripolium, which Laches had taken, he was attacked c. 103.
by the Locrians, and compelled to retire with loss.

The following spring was rendered remarkable by an eruption of c. 106.
mount Ætna, the third remembered among the Greeks, from their first
establishment in Sicily.   The boiling matter overflowed a part of the
Catanian territory, but did not affect the town.   In the beginning of
summer, faction disabling the Rhegian government, and the Athenian B. C. 426.
general being either weak or remiss in his command, the Syracusans, P. W. 6.
through intelligence in Messena, recovered that important place.   It Thucyd. l. 4.
was about this time that Demosthenes ingaged in his extraordinary c. 1.
attempt at Pylus, which ended so advantageously for Athens.   Intelligence arrived at Syracuse, that the fleet under Eurymedon and
Sophocles, destined to reinforce Pythodorus, instead of advancing from
Corcyra, was returned to the Peloponnesian coast, and likely to be
detained there.   The opportunity seemed favorable for the Syracusans
to try a naval action; but they could assemble, in the harbour of Messena, no more than thirty triremes.   Pythodorus however had only Thucyd. l. 5.
sixteen Athenian and eight Rhegian.   Coming to action, nevertheless, c. 25.
in that strait so celebrated for the poetical terrors of Charybdis and
Scylla, he gained the advantage, but it was not decisive.

The circumstances of Camarina then, sedition raging, and the Syracusan party nearly prevailing, induced him to lead his whole fleet
thither.   He saved Camarina, but the opportunity of his absence was
taken by the enemy, for marching against Naxus, a Chalcidian city,
of the Ionian confederacy, not far from Messena.   The Naxians however were fortunate in alliance with the Sicel barbarians, of their neighborhood; who no sooner heard of the distress of their friends, than
they came, in large force, to their relief.   The Sicels attacked the
besieging army: the Naxians sallied opportunely: of the Messenians and others, of the Dorian army, to the amount of more than
a thousand were killed upon the spot, and, of the rest, only a small
proportion escaped the hands of the pursuing barbarians.   The Syracusan fleet, deprived of a land-force on which it could depend for pro-

VOL. II.   Q q   tection,

tection, such was the antient marine, dared no longer await the return of the Athenian fleet to Messena. The Leontines, the blockade of their town by land having been already abandoned, then marched to coöperate with the Athenian fleet, in an attack upon Messena. The attempt however failed; and, the Athenian armament remaining inactive during the rest of the summer and all the following winter, tho hostilities were continued among the Sicilian Greeks, nothing important resulted.

Thucyd. 1. 5. c. 58, & seq.   Meanwhile the fame of the various successes of Athens, and of the general turn in the fortune of the war, contrary to the expectation of all Greece, in favor of that ambitious and restless republic, raised alarm among thinking men; and this was increased by the arrival of the fleet under Eurymedon and Sophocles in the Sicilian seas. During the winter, Camarina and Gela, neighbor-cities of Sicily, not actuated by any extensive view, but meerly considering the separate convenience of their own communities, concluded a peace between themselves, for themselves only; each city holding itself bound to the conditions of its former confederacy, for all purposes of war against other states. But the superior political importance of Syracuse gave larger views to its leaders; among whom Hermocrates son of Hermon was rising to eminence, for abilities, courage, activity, and, above all, for a disposition truly patriotic. The small beginning of peaceful measures made by the Camarinæans and Geloäns, appeared to Hermocrates a favorable opening for proposals for a general peace. He first prevailed with his own city, and then procured a congress of ministers, at Gela, from all the cities of the iland. A variety of clashing interests, among so many little states, made accommodation difficult; but the eloquence of Hermocrates displayed so forcibly the danger of forein interference, and particularly of Athenian interference, and urged so plausibly the evident disinterestedness of Syracuse, decidedly superior in the war, and no way pressed to promote peace but by the desire of benefits and the apprehension of evils which would involve all Sicily, that he finally prevailed. A general peace, was concluded, by the conditions of which every city retained what it held at the time, except

1   that,

that, for a stipulated sum, the Syracusans restored Morgantina to the Camarinæans.

The success of Hermocrates in this negotiation effectually checked the ambitious views of the Athenians upon Sicily. The commanders of the fleet, seeing no opportunity of farther service to their country, sailed home. Indignation however met them from their soverein the people, for permitting their allies to make peace: Pythodorus and Sophocles were punished with banishment. The services of Eury-, medon, at Corcyra and at Pylus, apparently saved him from so severe a sentence, but he was condemned in a fine.

SECTION II.

New Troubles in Sicily: New Interference of Athens; stopped by the Peace between Athens and Lacedæmon. Assistance solicited from Athens by Egesta against Selinus. Contention of Parties at Athens; Banishment of Hyperbolus. Assistance to Egesta voted by the Athenian Assembly: Nicias, Alcibiades, and Lamachus appointed to command. Mutilation of the Terms of Mercury: Completion of the Preparations for the Sicilian Expedition, and Departure of the Fleet.

HERMOCRATES, it appears, had no ideä, and, indeed, Thucydides seems to have had no ideä, of the possibility of molding all the Sicilian Greek municipal governments into one commonwealth, or even of establishing among them an effective federal union. The Sicilian patriot is represented, by the statesman-historian, admonishing the congress only to exclude forein interference, and such wars as might arise among themselves would have no very important ill consequences. Through such extreme deficiency in Grecian politics, new troubles quickly arose in Sicily. Time and various circumstances had greatly altered the state of property in all the Sicilian commonwealths, since that incomplete and iniquitous partition of lands, which had been

Thucyd. l. 5. c. 4.

Q Q 2   made,

made, on the general establishment of democratical government, after the expulsion of the family of Gelon. In other cities the poor rested under their lot; but in Leontini they were warm in project for a fresh and equal partition; and, to strengthen themselves against the party of the wealthy, they carried, in the general assembly, a decree for associating a number of new citizens. The landowners, thus, not only upon the point of being deprived of their patrimonies, but exposed to every kind and degree of oppression from democratical despotism, applied to Syracuse for protection; and, with assistance thence, expelled all the lower people. Whether it might have been possible, by any milder expedient, to have obtained any reasonable security for themselves, considering all we learn of the common temper of faction among the Greeks, must appear at least doubtful. It was however hardly possible that the violent measure adopted could place them at ease. Having only their slaves to divide offices with them, the business and the burden of arms must be exclusively their own, in circumstances requiring the most watchful attention of a garrison. For not only the worst evils that man can inflict on man were constantly to be apprehended from the vengeance of the expelled, but the produce of their fields could not be vindicated, and their subsistence insured, without, if not constant exertion, yet constant readiness for exertion, against plunderers. The Syracusans therefore carrying their liberal kindness so far as to offer all the Leontine landowners admission into the number of Syracusan citizens, all migrated to Syracuse, and Leontini was totally deserted.

What, in their new situation, offended or alarmed these men, apparently so generously relieved, we are not informed; but there seems ground for conjecture that it was some violence, committed or threatened, by the democratical party in Syracuse. A number of them quitted that city in disgust, and seizing a part of the town of Leontini, called Phoceæ, and a fort in the Leontine territory named Bricinniæ, they invited their own expelled lower people to join them. Many of these, who had been wandering about Sicily, mostly in sufficient distress, accepted the invitation; and predatory war upon the Leontine and Syracusan territories became the resource of all for subsistence.

Intelligence

Intelligence of the expulsion of all the commonalty from the principal Ionic city of Sicily would not be received with satisfaction at Athens.   It was quickly followed by information of the partial revival of the democracy of Leontini, through the establishments made in Phoceæ and Bricinniæ.   The resolution was then taken to send ministers to Sicily, to discover the strength of the Athenian interest throughout the iland, and to promote a league hostile to Syracuse.   Phæax son of B. C. 422. Erasistratus was sent, with two others, to manage this business; and Ol. 89. ⁷⁄₇. P. W. 10. he seems to have conducted it ably.   Urging, both in public harangue and in colloquial communication, the notorious oppression of the Leontine people, and the evident disposition of Syracuse to assume tyrannical sovereinty over all Sicily, he succeeded with the powerful states of Agrigentum and Camarina.   At Gela he failed; and finding no promising prospect in any other city, he passed through the country of the Sicels to Bricinniæ.   The garrison there however was greatly incouraged by his information of the alliances he had procured for them in Sicily, and by his assurances of assistance from Athens.   Returning then homeward by sea in the usual course, by the Italian coast, in his way he added to the Athenian interest in those parts by an advantageous treaty which he concluded with the Epizephyrian Locrians.

This prosperous beginning toward a restoration of Athenian influence in Sicily, through a revival of troubles among the Grecian colonies there, was early checked by the event of the battle of Amphipolis, which happened in the summer of the same year.   The negotiations for peace between Athens and Lacedæmon, begun in the succeeding autumn, were brought to a conclusion in the following spring.   The party of Nicias then predominated: the maxims of Pericles again swayed the Athenian councils; views of farther acquisition to the dominion of the commonwealth were rejected, and all interference in the affairs of Sicily dropped.

The interest of the principal states of Greece in Sicilian affairs thus ceasing, for near six years we have little information concerning them. But, in that interval, two small republics, toward the western end of the iland, Selinus and Egesta, became ingaged in that kind of domestic war, which, according to the political doctrine maintained by Hermocrates,

Thucyd. l. 6.
c. 6.
crates, in his speeches to the Sicilian congress, could have no important
ill consequences, were forein interference only excluded.   The Séli-
nuntines obtained assistance from Syracuse; which was within the
proposal of Hermocrates for insuring general safety and happiness to
Sicily.   But the Egestans found themselves thus effectually deprived
of their portion of safety and happiness among the Sicilian people; for
they were presently blockaded by séa and land.   It behooved them to
find, if possible, assistance equally powerful with that of Syracuse; but
within Sicily it was impossible.   Pressed therefore by the apprehension
of what usually befel a captured town from a Grecian enemy, they
determined to seek forein aid; and none appeared so likely to be
B. C. 416.
Ol. 90. 4.
P. W. 16.
obtained and to be effectual as that of Athens.   Ministers were accordingly sent, who urged arguments which might not unreasonably have
weight with the Athenian people.   ' The Syracusans,' they observed,
' had already exterminated the Leontines, a people connected with the
' Athenians, not only by antient alliance, but by blood.   If this passed
' with impunity, and not this only, but that domineering people were
' permitted to go on oppressing all the allies of Athens in Sicily, let
' it be considered what a force might accrue to the Peloponnesian con-
' federacy, in a future, nay, a now impending war.'   To these arguments assurances were added, that the Egestans wanted only troops,
their wealth being ample.

Athens was at this time more than usually agitated by faction.
Alcibiades, checked in his ambitious views by the event of the sedition of Argos, which had nearly annihilated his extraordinary
influence in Peloponnesus, was looking around for new opportunity
of enterprize, and his purpose to ingage the commonwealth in war
again was notorious.   The party of Nicias dreaded war on its
own account, but still more on account of the increase of influence
and authority which would insue to Alcibiades; and they vigilantly
opposed all his measures.   This contest was favorable to Hyperbolus,
who had still great weight, through the support of that body of the
citizens which had raised Cleon to greatness.   Hyperbolus had nearly
overborne Nicias by vehemence of railing and by threatening prosecutions; but he could not so overbear Alcibiades.   Against him
                                                    therefore

therefore he directed another kind of policy. The vast ambition of
Alcibiades, his splendid manner of living, and the superiority he   Plut. vit.
affected in everything, gave occasion for the suggestion, which was   Nic. &Alcib.
sedulously circulated among the people, that his power and influence
were greater than could be safe in a democracy, and that the
ostracism was necessary to bring men to a just level. Alcibiades and
his friends were alarmed at this idea, and at the readiness with which the
people appeared to receive it. They endeavored at first to counterwork
it by urging, that not Alcibiades, whose power rested intirely on the
favor of the people, but Nicias and the aristocratical party, were the
persons reälly to be feared; and the banishment of the head of that
party would best restore a just equilibrium in the commonwealth.
Hyperbolus used all his art to inflame the dispute, and at the same time
to set the people equally against both the leaders. His influence was
such, that it was evidently in his power to decide which of the two
should be banished. But he had a politician to incounter, such as
Cleon never met with. Alcibiades communicated with Nicias : an
assembly of the people was held; both collected their strength; and
Hyperbolus was named as a person, by his weight, influence, and seditious designs, dangerous to the commonwealth. The people were
surprized; for no man of his mean condition was ever before proposed
as a subject for the ostracism. But the Athenian people loved a joke;
and this appeared a good one : they would honor him by ranking him
with Miltiades, Aristeides, Themistocles, and Cimon. To the whim
of a thoughtless multitude was added all the weight of interest of
Alcibiades and Nicias, and the banishment of Hyperbolus was decided.

The coälition of parties, however, lasted no longer than to strike this
blow against a man whom both feared. One was still as earnest for
war as the other anxious to maintain peace. The embassy from Egesta
afforded an opportunity such as Alcibiades wished. As general of the
commonwealth, for he still held that office, he received the ministers in
the most favorable manner, and warmly recommended their cause to
the people. None of his measures seem to have been opposed with
more effort by the party of Nicias. For a time they prevented any
decision

decision in favor of the Egestans.   But at length the various arguments and repeated supplications, which the authority and influence
of the general gave opportunity to urge, in some degree prevailed
with the people.   In the autumn of the sixteenth year of the war,
while the Melians were still resisting the Athenian forces, and about
the time that the Lacedæmonians were so inefficiently employed in
establishing their Argian friends in Orneæ, commissioners were sent
into Sicily to gain information of the state of things, and particularly
to inquire whether the Egestans reälly possessed those funds, for supporting a large armament, which their ministers pretended.

B. C. 415.
Ol. 91. 1.
P. W. 17.
Thucyd. 1. 6.
c. 8.
In the following spring, the commissioners returned, accompanied
by new ministers from Egesta; who brought with them sixty talents
in silver, about fifteen thousand pounds sterling, as a month's pay in
advance for sixty triremes, which they were directed to request.   With
this specious voucher in their hands, they were introduced into the
Athenian assembly.   The commissioners, devoted to the party of
Alcibiades, concurred with them in every representation, true or false,
that might induce the people to vote the assistance desired; not
scrupling to add their testimony to the assertion, that the sum produced
bore but a small proportion to the resources of the treasury of Egesta
and the wealth of its temples.   This was found afterward to be a gross
imposition; but the assembly was persuaded, and the decree passed for
sending the sixty triremes.

The policy of Alcibiades upon this occasion, unnoticed by Plutarch
and all the later writers, is however not very defectively unfolded in the
simple and concise statement of facts by Thucydides.   Tho Nicias so
vehemently opposed the favorite measure of Alcibiades, yet Alcibiades
would not appear the opponent of Nicias: on the contrary, he would
use the weight and influence of Nicias against Nicias himself.   The
decree for sending a force to Sicily being carried, the commanders were
to be named.   The partizans of Alcibiades were still the proposers of
all measures, yet Nicias was named first in command; Alcibiades
Aristoph.
Acharn.
v. 597, 601,
615, et Pax,
v. 604.
second; and, for a third, Lamachus was chosen; a man of birth, who,
tho yet in the prime of life, had seen much service, but a soldier of
fortune, of a dissipated turn, and of no great weight, either by abilities

or

or property.   Instructions were then voted ; that the generals should use the force committed to them, first, to give security to Egesta against the Selinuntines; then to restore the commonwealth of Leontini ; and afterward to take any measures they might judge proper for promoting the Athenian interest in Sicily.   For carrying into effect these purposes, it was decreed that they should have discretionary powers.

Such rapid decision could not but be hazardous, where the measures of executive government were directed by a whole people.   But it was the object of Alcibiades and his party not to let popular passion cool. Four days only were allowed before a second assembly was held, to decide upon the detail of the armament, and to grant any requisition of the generals, for which a vote of the people might be necessary. Nicias, unprepared before to oppose a decree which had appointed him to a great command unsought, but disapproving the purpose, which he knew to be really the conquest of Sicily, now stepped forward to admonish the multitude his soverein.

' To urge to Athenian tempers,' he said, ' that in reason they should ' rather take measures to secure what they already possess, than ingage ' in wild projects for farther acquisition, I fear will be vain ; yet I ' think it my duty to endevor to show you how rash and unadvised your ' present purpose is.   Within Greece you seem to imagine yourselves ' at peace: yet some of the most powerful states, of the confederacy ' with which you have been at war, have not yet acceded to the treaty, ' and some of the articles are still controverted by all.   In short, it is ' not a peace, but meerly a dubious suspension of hostilities, prolonged ' by ten-day truces, which will hold only till some misfortune befall ' us, or till Lacedæmon give the word for war.   At the same time ' your antient subjects, the Chalcidians of Thrace, have been years in ' a rebellion which they are still maintaining ; and some others, whom ' you esteem dependent states, pay you but a precarious obedience. ' Is it not then extreme impolicy to incur needlessly new and great ' dangers, with the view to increase a dominion already so insecure ?

' As to the dominion which Syracuse may acquire in Sicily, which ' some desire to represent as highly alarming, far from an object of

VOL. II.   R R   ' apprehension,

' apprehension, it would rather give us security. For while Sicily is
' divided, each state will court the favor of the Lacedæmonians, who
' profess themselves the protectors of independency; but when once
' the Syracusans are masters of all, they will be less forward in
' connection with Lacedæmon, and more cautious of opposing the
' Athenians; whose cause is similar to theirs, and whose interest
' congenial.

 ' For myself,' continued Nicias, ' at my years, and after the long
' course of services in which my fellowcitizens have been witnesses of
' my conduct, I may venture to say that no man is less anxious for
' his personal safety. I have large property, through which my welfare
' is intimately connected with that of the commonwealth. But we
' owe both life and fortune to our country; and I hold that man to be
' a good citizen who is duly careful of both. If then there is among
' you a young man, born to great wealth and splendid situation, whose
' passion for distinction has nevertheless led him far to exceed, in
' magnificence, both what suited his means and what became his
' situation; if he is now appointed to a command above his years, but
' with which, at his years especially, a man is likely to be delighted;
' above all, if repairs are wanting to a wasted fortune, which may make
' such a command desirable to him, tho ruinous to his country, it
' behooves you to beware how you accede to the advice of such a coun-
' sellor. I dread indeed the warm passions of that crowd of youths,
' the followers and supporters of the person of whom I speak: and
' notwithstanding the decree of the last assembly, all men of sober
' judgement ought yet to interfere, and prevent rash undertakings, of
' a magnitude that may involve, with their failure, the downfall of the
' commonwealth. If therefore, honored as I am, by the voice of my
' country, with appointment to the chief command of the intended
' expedition, I may presume to advise, it shall be, that the expedition
' be not undertaken; that the Sicilians be left still divided by their
' seas from Athens; that the Egestans, as without communication with
' Athens they ingaged in war with the Selinuntines, so, without our
' interference they accommodate their differences; and that, in future,
' the Athenians ingage in no alliances with states which, in their own

1   ' distress,

' distress, will claim assistance, but, in the distress of Athens, could
' afford none.'

Alcibiades, thus particularly called upon, mounted the bema to reply.
He began with insisting upon his just pretension to the high command
to which he was raised, and with glorying in the extravagances of which
he was accused. ' My ancestors before me,' he said, ' have been
' honored for that very conduct which is now imputed to me as
' criminal.   I own, and it is my boast, that I have exceeded them all
' in magnificence, and I claim merit with my country for it.   The
' supposition had gained, throughout Greece, that Athens was ruined by
' the war.   I have shown that an individual of Athens could yet outdo
' what any prince or state had ever done.   I sent seven chariots to the
' Olympian festival, and gained the first, the second, and the fourth
' prizes : and the figure I maintained throughout, at that meeting of
' the whole Greek nation, did not disparage the splendor of my victory.
' Is this a crime ? On the contrary, it is held honorable by the customs
' of Greece, and reflects honor and renown, even on the country of
' those who exhibit such magnificence.   With regard then to my
' extravagance, as it has been called, at home, whether in public
' entertainments or in whatever else, perhaps I may have drawn on me
' the envy of some of our own citizens : but strangers are more just;
' and in my liberality and hospitality they admire the greatness of the
' commonwealth.

' If then even in these things, comparatively meer private concerns,
' I have deserved well of my country, let it be inquired what my public
' conduct has been.   Glory, I will own, I ardently desire; but how
' have I sought to acquire it, and what has been my success? Have I
' promoted rash enterprize ? Have I been forward, as it is said youth
' is apt to be, to ingage the commonwealth, wildly and without fore-
' sight, in hazardous war ? or was it I who, by negotiation, without
' either danger or expence to yourselves, brought all Peloponnesus to
' fight your battles for you against Lacedæmon, and reduced that
' long-dreaded rival state to risk its existence at Mantineia, in arms
' against its own antient allies ? If such have been my services, on

' first entering upon public business, you need not, I hope, fear but my
' greater experience will now be advantageous to you.

  ' With regard then to Nicias, who has long and honorably served
' you in the high situation of general of the commonwealth, tho he
' has been expressing himself acrimoniously against me, I readily
' acknowlege his merit, and have no objection to serve with him : on
' the contrary, I think it would become your wisdom to employ us
' together.   Nicias has the reputation of cautious prudence, and
' singular good fortune ; I am said to be more than prudently enter-
' prizing.   For want of enterprize his wisdom, and the good fortune
' with which the gods have been accustomed to bless it, will be una-
' vailing to the commonwealth : checked by his prudence, my dispo-
' sition to enterprize cannot be dangerous.

  ' To come then to the question more immediately before the assembly;
' the opportunity now offered to the commonwealth, for acquisition in
' Sicily, ought not to be neglected.   The power of the Sicilians, which
' some would teach you to fear, has been much exaggerated.   They are
' a mixed people, little attached to one another, little attached to a
' country which they consider as scarcely theirs, and little disposed to
' risk either person or fortune for it ; but always ready for any change,
' whether of political connection, or of local establishment, that may
' offer any advantage, or relieve from any distress.   Nor is their mili-
' tary force such as some have pretended ; several Grecian states and
' all the barbarians of the iland, will be immediately in your interest.
' Distracted then by faction, as it is well known the rest are, negotia-
' tion, well managed, may soon bring more to your party.

  ' But it is endevored to alarm you with apprehensions of invasion
' from Peloponnesus.   With regard to this, late experience has demon-
' strated what may suffice us to know.   The Peloponnesians are always
' able to overrun the open country of Attica, even when none of our
' force is absent on forein service ; and, should the expedition now
' proposed take place, they can do no more.   Ought we then to abandon
' allies, whom treaties ratified by oath bind us to protect ?   Is it a just
' reason for so failing in our ingagements, that those allies are unable

                                                              ' to

' to afford us mutual protection? It was surely not to obtain Egestan
' forces for the defence of Attica that the treaty was made; but to
' prevent our enemies in Sicily from injuring Attica, by finding them
' employment within their own iland.   It has been by readiness to
' ASSIST ALL, whether Greeks or barbarians, that OUR empire, and ALL
' empire, has been acquired.   Nor, let me add, is it now in our choice
' how far we will stretch our command; for, possessing empire, we
' must maintain it, and rather extend than permit any diminution of
' it; or we shall, more even than weaker states, risk our own subjection
' to a forein dominion.   I will then detain you no longer than to
' observe, that the command which we possess of the sea, and the
' party of which we are assured in Sicily, will sufficiently inable us to
' keep what we may acquire, and sufficiently insure means of retreat if
' we should fail of our purpose; so that, with much to hope, we have,
' from any event of the proposed expedition, little to fear.   I am
' therefore firmly of opinion that your decree for it ought not to be
' rescinded.'

This speech of Alcibiades was received with loud and extensive Thucyd. l. 6.
applause.   It was followed by speeches of the Egestan and Leontine c. 19.
ministers, imploring pity and urging the faith of treaties, which also
had their effect; and at length the disposition of a large majority of
the people to favor the purpose of Alcibiades became so evident, that
Nicias would not any longer directly oppose it.   But, as first of the
generals elect, it was his privilege to name the force that he judged
requisite for the enterprize; and he thought to damp the present ardor,
and excite a little reflection, by naming what, he expected, for the
Athenian commonwealth to send on distant service, would be deemed
extravagantly great.   While therefore he appeared to accede to the
general wish, he endevored to divert it from its object by reciting the
difficulties that would oppose its accomplishment.   'We have, at c. 20.
' present,' he said, ' for allies in Sicily, the Egestans, semibarbarians,
' and the Leontines, who scarcely exist as a people.   It is to be hoped
' that Naxus and Catana, on account of their connection by blood
' with the Leontines and with Athens, may be induced to join us: but
' there are, beside these, seven independent Grecian cities in Sicily, on
                                                                        ' whose

' whose opposition we may rely'; all of them possessing regular forces
' of land and sea, with funds to maintain them; and especially Selinus
' and Syracuse, the first objects of the war.   The Syracusans, in addi-
' tion to considerable wealth of their own, command tribute from the
' barbarians of the iland.   But the two points in which they will
' principally have advantage over us, are the possession of a numerous
' cavalry, and of the stores which a plentiful country affords; while
' we must depend upon precarious supplies by sea.   In addition there-
' fore to a powerful fleet, an army, such as we have been accustomed to
' send on forein service, will be very unequal to the object.   Unless
' we obtain other allies than the Egestans, such a force could not stir,
' in Sicily, for the cavalry alone of the enemy.   It must then be con-
' sidered that we shall not only be far from home, but far also from
' any territory under our command.   Supplies will therefore reach us,
' not without risk and difficulty at all times; but during the four
' winter months, scarcely an advice-boat can pass to us.   These things
' considered, it appears that, beside a large force of regular heavy-
' armed of our allies and subjects, in addition to what it may be
' advisable to send of our own, if we can obtain any for hire in
Thucyd. l. 6. ' Peloponnesus, it should be done.   Since moreover to transport so
c. 22.   ' far a body of cavalry capable of opposing the cavalry of the country
' is impossible, we must add a large force of bowmen and slingers,
' who may at least relieve our heavy-armed against the annoyance of
' the enemy's horse.   Our fleet must be superior beyond competition;
' otherwise we can have no certainty even of subsistence; and it will
' be proper to provide abundantly beforehand for so numerous an
' armament, to prevent the distress that might otherwise arise from
' accidents of winds and seas.   Beyond all things, however, we must
' be amply supplied with money; because what the Egestans talk of, I
' am confident they only talk of.   In a word, to begin our business
' with any prospect of success, we must, from the moment we land, be
' in every point superior to the enemy.   This is what the welfare of the
' commonwealth, I am fully persuaded, requires.   If any man can

         ' Syracuse, Selinus, Camarina, Gela, Agrigentum, Himera, Messena.

                                                          ' convince

' convince you that my opinion is unfounded, I am ready to resign my
' command to him.'

The simple prudence of the experienced Nicias was no match for
the versatile sagacity of the young politician with whom he had to
contend.   The friends of Alcibiades received this speech with the
highest approbation; affecting to consider it not at all as dissuading
or discouraging the undertaking, but, on the contrary, wisely and pro-
vidently recommending what would insure success.   The whole people
were infatuated with the spirit of enterprize.   Love of novelty and
change, with certainty of present pay, and hope of they knew not what
future acquisition, influenced the more thoughtless of all ranks; while
the past successes of Athens, and the evident weakness and inefficiency
of the Lacedæmonian administration, incouraged even the more experienced and prudent; insomuch that if any deeper thinkers disapproved,
a declaration of their sentiments might have subjected them to the
danger of being deemed disaffected to the commonwealth, and fined,
banished, or even capitally condemned, according to the momentary
caprice of the despotic soverein.

Such being the disposition of the people, Nicias was called upon to
declare what precisely was the force that he thought necessary.   He
would have declined in the moment, urging that he wished to consult
his collegues; but popular impatience would admit no delay, and, over-
come with importunity, he at length said, that less than a hundred
triremes and five thousand heavy-armed, with a due proportion of
bowmen and slingers (making, in the whole, at least thirty thousand
men, those in the sea-service included) would be insufficient; and that
stores and all necessaries should be plentifully provided to accompany
the fleet; which ought not to be left dependent upon precarious supplies.   Popular zeal did not confine itself to the meer grant of what was
thus demanded; but a vote was immediately passed, impowering the
generals to command, for the expedition, whatever they should judge
expedient for the prosperity and glory of the commonwealth.   The
ravage made by the pestilence, at the beginning of the war, was now
in a great degree repaired: the loss in battle had never been great;
and the revenue, far exceeding the ordinary expences of the common-
                                                                wealth,

Thucyd. l. 6.
c. 24.

c. 25.

wealth, which in peace were trifling, incouraged ambition. Preparation therefore, thus amply supplied, was made with a celerity proportioned to the zeal of the people.

During the equipment, and while the popular mind was bent with a singular degree of passion upon the proposed conquest, injoying already in ideä large acquisition of sovereinty, whence tribute would accrue, such as might give every Athenian citizen to be forever exempt from labor and from poverty, without occupation or profession but that of arms, everything was suddenly disturbed by a strange circumstance, to which Grecian superstition alone gave any importance. It was a custom among the Athenians, derived from very early times, when art was rude, to place an imperfect statue of Mercury, the head completely carved, the rest generally a block meerly squared, in front of every residence, whether of gods or men: this custom was still held sacred, and neither temple nor house at Athens was without one of those formless guardians. In one night the greatest part of them had the face mutilated by persons unknown. Alarm and indignation imme-diately filled the city: the matter was taken up most seriously by magistrates and people: however the act of ill-designing men, it was very generally considered as an omen foreboding ill to the proposed

Thucyd.

expedition; and great rewards were publicly offered to any, free or slave, who would discover the perpetrators. With regard to the offence in question, inquiry and temptation were equally ineffectual; not the

Andoc. de myst. p. 20. Thucyd. l. 6. c. 28.

least discovery was made; but indication was obtained concerning the mutilation of some statues, some time before, by young men heated with wine, and also of a profanation of the sacred mysteries, by a mock celebration of them in private houses; and in this accusation Alcibiades was involved.

Thucyd. Isocrat. pro Alcib. vel de bigis, p. 138. t. 3.

Of the party in opposition to Alcibiades were all who leaned to oligarchy, and most of the most powerful men of the commonwealth; who indignantly bore the superiority assumed by that young man, by whose abilities, assisted by the splendor of his birth, and the greatness of his fortune, and supported by the favor of the people, they found themselves so overwhelmed, that they had for some time past submitted in silence. But the present was an opportunity not to be neglected:
                                                            they

they set themselves instantly to take advantage from it to ruin him in the favor of the people, that foundation of sand on which all power in Athens must rest, and then the reins of the commonwealth would of course pass into their own hands. The report was sedulously propagated, that Alcibiades was the principal author of all the late outrages. Facts known, it was said, afforded sufficient presumption of what could not be directly proved; and the meer style of living of Alcibiades, so unbecoming the citizen of a commonwealth, and notorious to all, for it was displayed ostentatiously, demonstrated that he had no moderate purposes, and that nothing less than the tyranny of Athens was the ultimate object of his ambition.

Comparing the cautious account of Thucydides with the known circumstances of the times, the temper of party at Athens, and events preceding and following, we find strong reason to suspect, tho we cannot be certain, that, not Alcibiades, but the enemies of Alcibiades, were the authors of the profanation whence the disturbance arose. Alcibiades was known, in his revels, to have committed irregularities, which would give color to suspicion against him. But the mutilation of the Mercuries was no affair of a revel; it was evidently a concerted business, conducted with the most cautious secresy. Nothing could be more injurious, nothing more necessarily ruinous in its consequences to all the warmest wishes of Alcibiades, than such an event at such a time, and nothing could equally favor the purposes of his opponents: nothing therefore more without temptation for him, while the strongest motives might urge them to commit the deed in secret, with the hope of fixing upon him the suspicion. Accordingly, in no one circumstance of his public life does Alcibiades seem to have conducted himself more unexceptionably than under this accusation. He neither avoided inquiry, nor attempted to overbear it; but coming forward, with the decent confidence of innocence, he earnestly desired immediate trial, and deprecated only accusation in his absence. ' If guilty,' he said, ' he was ready to submit to the death which he should deserve: if ' innocent, he ought to be cleared of the shocking imputation; and as ' it would be unjust, so would it be in the highest degree imprudent to ' keep such a charge hanging over a man vested with so great a

Vᴏʟ. II.   S s   ' command.

' command.' But, as usual with all factions, what prudence would dictate for the benefit of the commonwealth was, with his opponents, but an inferior consideration ; what would advance the power of their party was the first. Dreading, therefore, his popularity with the army, fearing particularly the alienation of the Argian and Mantineian auxiliaries, whom his influence principally had obtained for the expedition, and apprehensive that blame thus might fall upon themselves, they determined neither immediately to accuse, nor wholly to give up accusation ; and they prevailed with the people to decree simply, that Alcibiades should hold his command, and proceed on the expedition [a].

Thucyd. 1.6.
c. 30.

This being determined, popular zeal returned to its former object, and by midsummer the preparations were completed. So great and so splendid an armament was never before sent by any Grecian state on

c. 31.

forein service. The importance of the armament itself, the importance and distance of its object, and the popular predilection with which it was favored, occasioned extraordinary. allowance for the equipment. Private zeal contended with public; the commanders of triremes not sparing their own purses, every one to have both his crew and his vessel completest, equally for show and for service. The daily pay of a drachma, tenpence sterling, was given by the public to every private sailor ; and the captains added extraordinary pay to able seamen, and to all the rowers of the upper bench, distinguished by the name of Thranites, whose situation was more exposed, and whose office both required more skill and was more laborious than that of the rowers of the lower benches. The heavy infantry, all chosen men, who, as usual in the Greek service, provided their own arms and appointments, vied with each other in the excellence and good appearance of both.

c. 30.
B. C.
Ol. 91. ¼.
P. W. 17.
After 8 June.

On the day named for imbarkation, the Athenian citizens inrolled for the expedition appeared on the parade at daybreak, together with those of the allied forces which were then at Athens. The whole city accompanied their march to Peiræus ; the natives, says the cotemporary

---

[a] This is Thucydides's account. According to an oration remaining from Isocrates, the accusers of Alcibiades were punished, which would imply an acquittal of himself. But apparently the orator has taken occa- sion, from a later transaction, to assert so much thus generally, leaving to his hearers to refer it to the time to which it belonged. Isocrat. de bigis, p. 133, 134. v. 3.

historian,

historian, divided between hope and fear, on seeing so great a proportion of the strength of the commonwealth, with some relations or friends of every family in it, committed to the rage of elements and the chance of war, at a distance which, for antient navigation, was so great[3]; while the numerous foreiners more calmly gratified their curiosity with so splendid and interesting a spectacle.   As soon as the imbarkation was completed, and everything prepared for getting under way, trumpets sounded for signal of silence, and prayers for success were put up to the gods with more than usual formality, heralds directing, and the whole armament uniting their voices.   Goblets of wine were then produced in every ship, and officers and privates together, out of gold and silver cups, poured libations and drank to the prosperity of the armament and of the commonwealth, the citizens and strangers on the beach joining in the ejaculation.   This ceremony being performed, the pæan was sung, and the whole fleet moved for Ægina, thence to take its departure for Corcyra.

SECTION III.

Defects of the Syracusan Constitution.   Force of the Athenian Armament.   Measures of the Athenian Armament.   Able Conduct of Alcibiades.   Intrigues, Tumult, popular Panic, and their Consequences at Athens.

INTELLIGENCE of the extraordinary magnitude of the Athenian preparations passed from various quarters to Syracuse ; and the destination, in a democratical government, could not remain a secret.   Nevertheless it was long before the news gained such credit, among the Syracusan people, as to produce any measure for obviating the threatened evil. It is not specified by historians, but the account of Thucydides makes it evident, that there had been a revolution in the government of

Thucyd. l. 6, c. 32.

---

[3] Thucydides calls it the most distant as well as the greatest expedition ever made by any Grecian state.   The coasting navi- gation of the antients therefore made Sicily, in his opinion, more distant than Egypt.

s s 2

Syracuse,

Syracuse, or at least a great change in the administration, since the oligarchal Leontines were admitted to the rights of Syracusan citizens. The democratical party now bore the sway ; and some jealousy toward the nobles, lest preparation for war should throw an increase of power into their hands, appears to have influenced the leaders of the day. At the same time the circumstances of Syracuse, considerably altered since the former interference of Athens in the affairs of Sicily, were such as would inflame the usual presumption of a democratical government. The Ionian interest, formerly, with the assistance of Camarina, nearly balancing the Dorian, was now suppressed ; Syracuse was the acknowleged head of the Grecian name in Sicily ; and the Syracusan people trusted that, excepting the semibarbarian Egestans and the Leontine freebooters, the Athenians would not find a friend in the iland, who would dare to own himself.

At length, however, accumulated accounts arriving, each more alarming than the former, it was thought proper to convene the general assembly. The patriotic and able Hermocrates, the peacemaker of Sicily when harassed by internal war, was among the foremost to pro-
Thucyd. l. 6.
c. 33. pose vigorous measures against forein attack. Representing the Athenian armament as really great and formidable, but dangerous to Syracuse only in proportion to its deficiency of exertion, he proposed to strengthen the Syracusan confederacy by conciliating the barbarians of the iland, and by extending alliance among the Italian Greeks : he would even make overtures to Carthage, the richest commonwealth upon earth, and therefore ablest to give that kind of assistance which was most desirable, as being most efficacious with least danger ; and it was reasonable to suppose, he said, that apprehension of the growing power and extravagant ambition of Athens would dispose the Carthaginians to the connection. Application ought also to be made to Corinth and Lacedæmon, whose favorable disposition could not be doubted. Such in general was the negotiation which, in his opinion, their circumstances required. With regard then to military operation, he was clear that they ought to meet invasion before it reached them : and, high as the reputation of the Athenian navy was, yet local circumstances gave them such advan-

5   tages,

tages, that a proper exertion of the naval force which the Sicilian states were able to raise, might make it impossible for the Athenians ever even to reach the Sicilian coast.   This idea was founded on the deficiencies of the antient marine; of which the words put into the mouth of Hermocrates, by the able cotemporary historian, give the clearest as well as the most authentic information.   ' The Tarentines,' said Hermocrates, ' are our allies ; and the Athenian fleet, to go from ' Corcyra, their known place of assembling, to Sicily, must first make ' the Iapygian coast, and cannot avoid passing Tarentum.   The harbor ' of Tarentum therefore should be the station for the greatest naval ' force that can be collected.   So numerous a fleet, as that of the enemy, ' cannot keep exact order in the long passage (for so, in Thucydides's ' narrative, Hermocrates terms it) across the Ionian gulph.   From the ' harbour of Tarentum, therefore, we may chuse our moment of attack, ' with certain advantage.   We shall go into action with our crews ' refreshed in a friendly port, and our galleys light; the Athenians ' fatigued with rowing and incumbered with stores : or, should they, ' at the expence of these, prepare for action, we may, if prudence ' require it, retire into our port, and wait for fresh advantages.   Nor ' can these fail to offer : for the enemy must then again incumber ' his gallies with stores, or risk to suffer from want, in the passage ' along a hostile coast.   Such being the inconveniencies and the ' hazards which he must have to incounter, I think, if the measure I ' propose were taken, he would scarcely venture at all to cross the ' gulph.'

This able advice, to a whole people in assembly directing executive government, did not find the attention it merited.   Many would not yet believe that the Athenians meant to invade Sicily with views of conquest: some even ridiculed the idea: various contradictory opinions were warmly maintained; and Athenagoras, chief of the democratical party, endevored to use the opportunity for carrying a point against the nobles.   ' It was rather to be wished than feared,' he said, ' that the Athenians would be so mad as to invade Sicily.   For himself, ' he thought them wiser.   Peloponnesus itself was not better able to ' resist them ; and the force of Syracuse alone was superior to double

Thucyd. l. 6. c. 35.

' the

' the armament whose approach was represented as so alarming. No
' cavalry, he well knew, was imbarked : within Sicily the Athenians
' could obtain none, except an inconsiderable force from Egesta ; and
' even their heavy-armed were inferior in number to the Syracusan.
' Such being their deficiency, if, instead of commencing operations,
' as they must, from their naval camp, with scarcely a friend within the
' iland, they possessed a neighboring city equal to Syracuse, even so
' their army, instead of making conquest, would hardly escape destruc-
Thucyd. l. 6. ' tion.'   Having declared his sentiments against the measures proposed
c. 38, 39, 40. by Hermocrates, he proceeded to invey against him and the whole
body of the nobles.   ' The ambition of young men,' he said, ' panted
' for military command ; but the city would not so impose a yoke upon
' itself.   On the contrary, prosecution should prevent the seditious
' purposes of those who would spred alarm ; and punishment should
c. 41.   ' not fail for such offences against the common welfare.'   He was proceeding thus in the endevor to excite popular passion, when one of the
generals (for the Syracusan constitution at this time divided the chief
military command between a board of fifteen) interfered with the
authority of office.   He strongly reprobated the attempt to check the
freedom of debate, and deter individuals from declaring their opinion
on public affairs :   ' When hostilities were threatened,' he said, ' the
' welfare of the commonwealth unquestionably required preparation in
' due proportion to the danger.   It should therefore be the care of the
' generals to acquire more certain intelligence, than seemed yet to have
' been obtained, and in the mean time to communicate with the allies
' of the commonwealth, and take all other proper precaution.' Without
putting any question to the vote, he then dismissed the assembly.
c. 42.   While such, through the defects in the constitution of the government, was the unprepared state of Syracuse, the whole of the Athenian
c. 43.   forces was already assembled at Corcyra.   The fleet consisted of a
hundred and thirty-four triremes, and two Rhodian penteconters.   Of
the triremes, a hundred were Athenian ; and of these, sixty were light
for action, forty carried soldiers.   The other thirty-four triremes were
of the allied states, principally Chian.   The heavy-armed were, in all,
five thousand one hundred ; of whom two thousand two hundred were
                                                    Athenian

Athenian citizens; and of these only seven hundred, appointed to the inferior service of marines [4], were of the Thetes, the other fifteen hundred. being of the higher orders.   The Argian auxiliary heavy-armed were five hundred ; the Mantineian, including a few Peloponnesian mercenaries, two hundred and fifty; the remainder of the heavy-armed were from the subject states.   The regular light-armed were four hundred Athenian and eighty Cretan bowmen, seven hundred Rhodian slingers, and a hundred and twenty Megarian refugees.   A single horse-transport carried thirty horse.   The storeships provided by the Athenian government, which carried also both sutlers and artificers, were thirty of large burden, of the kind called holcads, and a hundred smaller [5]; but many other vessels, belonging to individuals, followed, for the sake of profit from the market of so large an armament.

Through the rash precipitancy of one party in the administration, and the opposition by which the other was perplexed, so deficient had been the preparatory measures, that it was yet unknown to the generals what Italian or Sicilian cities would receive them.   Three triremes were therefore dispatched to inquire and to negotiate, with orders to meet the fleet as soon as possible with information.   The whole then moved from Corcyra, in three divisions; each of which separately might more readily find, in the Italian ports, those supplies which the antient ships of war could so scantily carry, and that shelter which they were so extremely liable to want.   All however together crossed the gulph, and made the Iapygian promontory, without misfortune.   Then they dispersed to seek supplies around the bay of Tarentum ; but not a single town would admit them within its walls, or even make a market for them.   Tarentum and Locri denied them water and the shelter of their ports.   At length the whole fleet reässembled, without disaster, at Rhegium, the first allied city in their course.   But even the Rhegians cautiously refused to admit them within their walls ; allotting them however commodious ground for incampment, and providing for them a plentiful market.

The Syracusans, at length, satisfied of the necessity of giving up private ease for public service, and no longer hesitating between party

Thucyd. 1. 6. c. 42.

---

[4] Επιβάται τῶν νιῶν.   [5] Πλοῖα.

interest

interest and general welfare, permitted their leaders to make serious preparation for meeting the coming evil.   Ministers were sent to conciliate some of the Sicel tribes; garrisons were placed in situations to controul others; arms and horses were examined; and troops marched to occupy some of the most critical posts for defending the Syracusan territory.

Meanwhile the three Athenian ships, dispatched from Corcyra, had been as far as the Egestan territory, and did not rejoin the fleet till it was arrived in the harbour of Rhegium.   They brought information, that the representations made by the Egestan ministers at Athens, of the wealth of their state, had been utterly false, and that the commissioners, sent by the Athenian government to inquire concerning it, had been grossly deceived.   The richest temple of the Egestan territory was that of Venus at Eryx; where indeed the collection of cups, flagons, censers, and other vessels of silver, was considerable.   After being conducted to a display of these sacred riches, the commissioners had been variously invited and entertained by the principal Egestans; and, wherever they went, not only all the gold and silver plate of the place was studiously collected, but whatever besides could be borrowed from neighboring towns, Phenician as well as Greek.   These commissioners had been appointed by the influence of Alcibiades and his party. Whether they were chosen for their ability or their folly may be difficult to guess; but they had either believed, or affected to believe, and reported to the Athenian people accordingly, that they could not sufficiently admire the wealth of Egesta.   The commissioners sent from Corcyra were, on the contrary, such as Nicias, the first in command, would approve; and their purpose being, not to procure partial evidence to promote a decree for the expedition, but to find means (for what would now be a principal object of Alcibiades himself) to prosecute its purpose, they made strict scrutiny.   On their return they reported, that the Egestans could only show thirty talents, between seven and eight thousand pounds sterling, in their treasury, and that, for anything more, their wealth was quite problematical.   Probably none of the generals had relied much upon the wealth of Egesta; yet as it had been seriously proposed as the fund which was to afford

means

means for the first conquests, they were distressed by its deficiency; for the Athenian people were not likely to receive very favorably an immediate application for a supply. The disappointment however did not come single. The Rhegians had been upon the point of yielding to the solicitations and remonstrances of the Athenian generals, who urged them to join their arms to those of their antient allies, for the purpose of restoring their common kinsmen the oppressed Leontines; but they now gave for their decisive answer, ' That they would do ' every office of friendship to the Athenians, within the limits of an ' exact neutrality; but they would ingage in no hostilities, unless in ' concurrence with the Italian states of their alliance.'

This determination of the Rhegians was a disappointment, less on account of the force of land and sea, tho not inconsiderable, which they could have furnished, than for the check it would give to nego-tiation among the Sicilian towns, where the example of Rhegium would be of weight. The Athenian generals found themselves in con-sequence much at a loss. In many places a disposition adverse to the Syracusan supremacy afforded advantageous opportunities: but, through the divisions among the leading men of Athens, and the haste Thucyd. l. 6. of those who promoted the Sicilian expedition to profit from popular c. 44. favor, it had been so neglected that the semibarbarian Egestans upon the verge of ruin through their war with Selinus, and the miserable Leontines, ejected from their city and territory, were the only confederates of Athens beyond the Ionian sea. When therefore it came to be debated what should be the first measures of the arma-ment, the three generals differed, nearly as might be expected from their difference of character; and each had plausible ground for his opinion. Nicias experienced, prudent, from the first little satisfied with his command, and now in ill health, proposed to relieve Egesta, c. 47. which was the primary object of their instructions; and, unless the Egestans could fulfil their ingagement to furnish pay for the whole armament, or readier means should occur, than yet appeared, for re-storing the Leontines, not farther to risk the forces or waste the treasures of the commonwealth. The disposition to assist its allies would be shown in the relief of Egesta; its power would be mani-

fested by the meer circumstance of sending so great an armament
to such a distance, and, satisfied with this, he would return immediately home.

Alcibiades, whose temper was impetuous, but his mind capacious,
and his abilities universal, elated with the extraordinary effects which
his first essay in political intrigue had produced in Peloponnesus, and
not dejected by disappointments for which he was more prepared than
his collegues, had formed his own plan for laying the foundation of
extensive conquest, and persevered in it. 'Such a force,' he said, 'as
' they commanded, ought not to return home without achievement,
' and without honor.   Yet he would not disapprove prudent, or even
' cautious measures.   He would therefore propose that negotiation
' should be tried with all the Grecian cities, except Syracuse and Se-
' linus, and with every barbarian tribe of the iland.   In some places,
' perhaps, zeal in the Syracusan interest might be meerly slackened;
' in others, defection from it might be procured : in some, supplies of
' provisions only might be obtained; in others, auxiliary troops.   The
' beginning should be made with Messena, the most commodious city
' and port of the iland for their principal station, whence to carry on
' the war.   When trial had been duly made what might be done by
' negotiation, when they were fully assured who were determined ene-
' mies, and who were, or might probably be made, friends, then they
' should have a clearer view of the business before them, and Selinus
' and Syracuse must, undoubtedly, be the first objects of their arms.'

Lamachus, much a soldier and little a politician, but experienced in
the captious and greedy temper of the people his soverein, differed
from both his collegues : 'Their whole force,' he said, 'ought imme-
' diately to be directed against Syracuse, while yet in a state of un-
' readiness, and surprize.   If the city could not be taken by a brisk
' effort, which he thought not impossible, the other towns of the ter-
' ritory would however fall into their hands, before the effects in them
' could be removed ; and the produce of the country would of course
' be theirs.   Thus they should acquire means to prosecute the war,
' without the invidious measure of applying to Athens for money.
' But possibly, what of all things was most desirable, the Syracusans

Thucyd. l. 6.
c. 49.

11   ' might

' might thus be provoked to risk a battle; and a victory would in-
' stantly do more toward procuring alliance among the Sicilian cities,
' than negotiation for twenty years. Should the enemy, on the con-
' trary, yield their country without an effort, beside the profit from
' plunder, so decisive an acknowlegement of the superiority of the
' Athenian forces would be highly favorable to any negotiation that
' might be deemed expedient. With regard to Messena, he thought
' it not of so much consequence. The deserted port of Megara, com-
' modiously near to Syracuse, and their own whenever they would
' take possession of it, would be far preferable for their naval station.'

It appears, from what follows in Thucydides, that the opinion of
Lamachus, if conquest was to be sought and the displeasure of the
Athenian people avoided, was not the least judicious; but, being over-
ruled, that general chose to concur with the opinion of Alcibiades, to Thucyd. l. 6.
which Nicias was thus compelled to yield. Alcibiades then undertook c. 50.
himself the business of negotiation with Messena. He could not however prevail so far as to bring the Messenians to join in the war against
Syracuse; but he obtained, what was of some importance, permission for the Athenian armament to contract for provisions throughout their territory. He then went with sixty triremes, Lamachus
accompanying, to Naxus; and he found the people of that city, who
were purely Ionian, and from of old adverse to Syracuse, so much
more favorable to his views, that he ingaged them to join in league,
defensive and offensive, with Athens. Thence he proceeded to
Catana; but the prevalence of the Syracusan party there procured a
refusal even to treat. Still therefore coasting southward, he sent forward ten triremes to Syracuse. Approaching the mouth of the port, a
herald from the deck of one of them proclaimed the intention of the
Athenian commonwealth, ' to restore the oppressed Leontines to their
' just rights, a measure to which it was bound both by ties of blood
' and terms of alliance;' adding, ' that any Leontines would be re-
' ceived as friends by the Athenian armament.' This ceremony being
performed, and such observation made, as circumstances permitted, on
the ports, the city, and the circumjacent ground, the detached
squadron rejoined the fleet, and all together went once more to Catana.

Meanwhile

Meanwhile apprehension, either of the Athenian armament, or of a party among their own people, had so far wrought a change in the minds of the Catanian leaders, that they consented to admit the Athenian generals to declare their proposals to the assembled people. The forces, being landed, were stationed without the walls, while the generals went into the town; and Alcibiades undertook to address the Catanian people. While he was speaking, and the Catanians, collected in the agora, were universally intent upon the harangue, some of the Athenian soldiers observed a small ill-constructed gateway unguarded, through which, in meer wantonness, they made their way into the town; and, finding no opposition, quietly joined the assembly. The sight struck instant alarm into the Syracusan party, who imagined the city betrayed by their opponents. Some of them hastily, but silently, withdrew; and the rest, awed by apprehension of the dreadful calamities usually brought, on the weaker party, by sedition in Grecian cities, concurred in a decree, which was presently proposed, for an alliance defensive and offensive with Athens. Shortly after, the whole fleet moved from Rhegium to Catana, which it was resolved to make the principal naval station.

It soon appeared that the project of Alcibiades to strengthen the Athenian interest by negotiation, and proportionally, of course, to weaken the Syracusan, had been extensively founded. A party in Camarina, incouraged by what had passed at Naxus and Catana, as well as by the reported strength of the Athenian armament, sent to request support in attempting a revolution. The fleet moved thither; but it was found that the innovators had been overhasty in their measures, and the project could not be carried immediately into execution; yet an Athenian party still subsisted in Camarina. In returning, the Athenian commanders debarked a body of forces near Syracuse, and collected considerable booty; but the Syracusan cavalry quickly checked this mode of warfare, cut off some stragglers, and compelled the rest of the maroding troops to seek their ships. The fleet proceeding then to Catana, found there the Salaminian, the ship appropriated to purposes of sacred and solemn office, bearing an order from the Athenian people for the immediate return of Alcibiades and some
other

Thucyd. l. 6. c. 51.

c. 52.

other officers to Athens, to answer accusations preferred against them for mutilating the statues and profaning the mysteries.

Since the armament sailed for Sicily, Athens had been experiencing the worst evils of democratical frenzy. The oligarchal party, unequal to open contention with the democratical, had resolved upon the bold project of making democracy itself their instrument for exciting popular passion, with the hope of directing it to the promotion of their own interest. Instantly after the departure of the fleet, they became sedulous in diffusing rumours and observations, that might excite suspicion and alarm. The power and influence of Alcibiades, his magnificence, his ambition, his unprincipled conduct, and his various extravagancies, were made constant subjects of public conversation. His abilities, at the same time, and even his virtues, were compared to those by which the Peisistratids had acquired the tyranny. The severities which had occasioned the expulsion of those celebrated tyrants were then magnified tenfold; the execration to which their memory had been condemned, by the party which had overborne them, was alledged in proof of their enormities; and the circumstance that the Athenians, unable to effect their own deliverance, had owed it to the Lacedæmonians, was pressed upon public recollection. Shortly every occurrence was made, by some construction, to import a plot for establishing tyranny. Fear, suspicion, and their certain concomitant, a disposition to severity, thus gained complete possession of the public mind. Every one was bent to discover, by any means, the plot and its authors. Officers were appointed, intitled Examiners [6], with full authority for every search and inquiry; and great rewards were offered for any who would indicate anything. The most suspicious and incoherent evidence only was obtained, from slaves and men of the vilest characters. But public alarm, once so excited, was not to be readily quieted. It was deemed better, says Thucydides, that just men should suffer, than that the constitution should be indangered. Many of principal rank and most respectable character were in consequence imprisoned. It appears indeed difficult to discover for whose benefit the Athenian constitution, as it now stood, was calculated. The lower people at least

Isocrat. pro Alcib. p. 138. t. 3.

Thucyd. 1. 6. c. 53.

Thucyd. ut sup. & Andoc. de myst.

[6] Ζητηταὶ.

should

should have had some confidence in protection for innocence, from that government for which they were so anxious, and in which they were, nominally at least, supreme.   But, on the contrary, when Peisander and Charicles, two of the examiners, appointed to that office by

Andoc. de
myst. p. 19.

popular favor, declared their opinion that a plot for overthrowing the democracy was in agitation, and farther inquiry therefore necessary, upon the usual signal for assembling the council, all the people fled from the agora, every one fearful of accusation and imprisonment.

Thucyd. ut
sup.

Nor was this indiscriminating jealousy a humor that had its hour and passed: it held, and grew daily more severe.   Suspicion extended; more persons were imprisoned; and there was no foreseeing where popular rage would stop.

Thucyd. l. 6.
c. 61.

It happened that while suspicion was most rife, yet what or whom to suspect was most uncertain, some movements in Bœotia occasioned the march of a small body of Lacedæmonians to the Corinthian isthmus. This circumstance increased suspicion into imagined certainty, and redoubled every former fear: the business of Bœotia was thought a feint; intrigue with the obnoxious party in Athens, it was supposed, must be the real cause of the movement; and, for one night, the whole people watched in arms.   The panic spred to Argos: designs against the democracy were suspected there; and, tho Alcibiades himself had conducted the removal of the principal Argians who favored oligarchy, and placed them in secure custody, divided among the ilands under the Athenian dominion, yet now the Athenian people gave up those unfortunate men to be put to death by the democratical party in Argos, as if connected in plot with the friends of Alcibiades.

c. 60.
Andoc. de
myst.
Plut. vit.
Alcib.

Alarm and the severities of an alarmed despot were still continuing to extend, when one of the most obnoxious of the imprisoned ('Thucydides has avoided to name him, but we learn from his own extant oration, as well as from Plutarch's account, that it was Andocides) in conversation with one of his fellow-prisoners on their present sufferings and farther danger, yielded to the argument that, guilty or not guilty, it were better to confess something: 'The popular mind,' it was urged to Andocides, 'would evidently not otherwise be appeased; 'and a confession would not only be more likely, than perseverance in

                                                        'asserting

' asserting innocence, to procure his own safety, but would restore
' quiet to the·city; and tho some must be sacrificed, yet numbers
' might so be saved from that mad vengeance, excited by fear, which
' now threatened so indiscriminately and unboundedly.' Information,
thus extorted by the pains of a prison and the fear of death, against
several persons as concerned in the mutilation of the Mercuries, was
received among the people with a childish joy. The dark plot was
supposed completely discovered; the informers were set at liberty,
with all whom they did not accuse; of those whom they did accuse,
tho proof of the facts alledged was utterly defective, yet none escaped
capital condemnation : all who were in prison, or could be taken, suffered death immediately, and public rewards were offered for killing
those who fled from this democratical justice.

To carry the business thus far, little or no deliberation was thought   Thucyd. l.6.
necessary. The difficulty was to bring within reach of the democra-   c. 61.
tical dagger those of the accused who were with the army in Sicily;
and especially Alcibiades himself, now become supremely the object of
terror, as he had before been of favor with the people. His death, as
Thucydides assures, was determined; but it was feared to apprehend,
in the army, the favorite still of the army. It was farther feared lest
the whole armament might be indangered by any tumult which should
come to the knowlege of· the enemy and incourage attack; and the
defection of the Argian and Mantineian auxiliaries, whom the influence
of Alcibiades had obtained for the service, was looked upon as a certain consequence of any severity against him. It was therefore resolved to send heralds in the sacred trireme called the Salaminian, not
to arrest him or any other accused persons in the army, but simply, in
the name of the people, to command their return to Athens. Immediate obedience was paid to this order : Alcibiades followed the Salaminian in his own trireme. In the usual course of the antient navigation, making the Italian coast, they stopped at the friendly town of
Thurium, and there Alcibiades, and all the other accused, absconded
together. The heralds and officers of the Salaminian, having made
search and inquiry for some time to no purpose, returned without their
prisoners;

prisoners; and the Athenian people pronounced sentence of death against them, in what was called a deserted judgement [7].

SECTION IV.

Feeble Conduct of Nicias: Oppression of the Sicels. First Measures against Syracuse. Preparations on both Sides in Winter. Intrigues among the Sicilian Cities. Transactions of the Winter in Greece. Reception of Alcibiades at Sparta. Resolution to renew the War with Athens.

Thucyd. 1. 6. THE soul of political intrigue and extensive enterprize being thus
c. 62. taken from the armament destined for the conquest of Sicily, it re- mained for Nicias, with Lamachus, to decide on measures. The plans of Alcibiades were immediately abandoned; probably indeed nobody remained capable of prosecuting them; and, according to the original proposal of Nicias, not likely nor indeed intended to lead to extensive conquest, it was determined to conduct the armament immediately to- ward Egesta and Selinus. In proceeding westward, they in vain attempted negotiation with Himera, the only Grecian city on the northern coast of the island; but they succeeded in an assault upon Hyccara, a Sicanian town, whose inhabitants they made their own property as slaves, and then gave the place to the Egestans. Little zealous for the objects of his command, and thence apparently waver- ing about measures, Nicias went with a small escort only to Egesta, to demand the supplies promised, or such supplies as the Egestan people were able to furnish; and all he could obtain was thirty talents, between seven and eight thousand pounds sterling. The concluding measures of the campain do him no honor: the prisoners, already ac- quired, were distributed aboard the fleet, which returned by the straits of Messena to its former station at Catana. The army marched for the same place by an inland road, through the country of the Sicels;

[7] Ερήμη Δίκη.

and

and the unhappy barbarians suffered for the false promises of the
Egestans.   They were seized in such numbers that, a market being
opened for the sale of them at Catana, they produced a hundred and
twenty talents, about thirty thousand pounds sterling.   The celebrated
courtezan Laïs is said to have been a Sicel girl, sold on this occasion   Plut. vit.
to a Corinthian merchant.   An unsuccessful attempt upon the Geloän   Nic.
Hýbla was the last operation of the campain.

Perhaps some peevishness, in a command which he originally dis-
liked, in the course of which he met with little but disappointment,
and which nevertheless he could not resign, coöperated with the necessity of his situation, in dictating a measure, to which the mild temper of Nicias, and his generally scrupulous regard for justice, would
otherwise have been averse; tho, among the antients, even the philo-
sophers, to drag barbarians, wherever met with, into slavery, was not
commonly deemed a breach of either justice or humanity.   But apparently Nicias found himself compelled to follow the opinions, and
gratify the wishes, of others, in still prosecuting the scheme of conquest.   Money was absolutely necessary: the expectations of the
Athenian people had met with the disappointment at Egesta, which he
had always foreseen and foretold; and yet probably dared not ask to
have it made good by remittances from Athens.

It was however determined, now after a campain nearly wasted, to   Thucyd. l. 6.
carry war next against Syracuse; and with the beginning of winter pre-   c. 63.
paration was begun for the purpose.   Notwithstanding the vaunts of the
democratical leaders there, the first certain news that the Athenian
armament had crossed the Ionian gulph, excited alarm that went far
to justify the advice of Lamachus.   With every day's delay afterward,
terror abated and confidence grew.   But when, after the recall of Alcibiades, the armament moved away to the farther corner of Sicily, it
began to be held even in contempt and derision; and when, on its return, still no movement was made toward Syracuse, the lower people,
according to the manner of the multitude, as Thucydides remarks,
growing in boldness, demanded of their chiefs to lead them to Catana.
The chiefs were wiser than to comply; but the parties of horse, sent
out to observe, would sometimes approach the Athenian camp, give ill

language, and ask, 'if, instead of restoring the Leontines, the Athe-
' nians intended to settle themselves in Sicily?'

Thucyd. l. 6.
c. 64.
The Athenian army was so deficient in cavalry that it would have
been hazardous, or however troublesome, to have marched through
the open country toward Syracuse, in face of the Syracusan horse.
The generals therefore proposed to profit from the present temper of the
Syracusan people; which, in spite of any prudence in their leaders,
would be likely to lead them to indiscretion. As in most of the Sicilian
towns in the Syracusan interest, there was an Athenian party, so in Catana there was still a Syracusan party. A Catanian was gained, who
had usually communicated with Syracuse. Through him the Syracusans were told, that the Athenian camp was negligently guarded; that
many, both officers and private soldiers, commonly slept in the town;
that, if the Syracusans would attack with their whole force at daybreak, their friends in Catana would rise, and they could not fail of
November.
Thucyd. l. 6.
c. 65.
success. A day was appointed for the attempt, which was accordingly
made. Nicias and Lamachus, meanwhile, accurately informed of
every circumstance, imbarking in the night all their Grecian forces,
with some auxiliary Sicels, sailed for Syracuse; and, debarking totally
unopposed, they seized a situation, opportune for operation against the
city, and for communication with their fleet, and at the same time
secure against the Syracusan horse; on one side defended by walls,
houses, trees, and a pool of water; on the other by precipices:
felled trees, arranged from the camp to the sea and to the village
of Dascon, gave security to the naval station; works were hastily
thrown up where the ground was less strong by nature or accident,
and the bridge over the Anapus was broken.

The first intelligence of this movement filled the Syracusans with
surprize and alarm. They hastily returned to Syracuse, looked at the
Athenian camp, and finding it too strong to be attacked, incamped
themselves for the night. Next morning, the generals little experienced, and the people little practised in military discipline, all imagined that to assault, not to be assaulted, would be theirs, and many
went into the town, which was near. Meanwhile the Athenian generals, having ground now before them on which the enemy's horse would
                                                                       not

not be formidable, drew out of their camp in order of battle.   The Syracusans then also hastily formed; and, however deficient in discipline and skill, Thucydides bears them testimony that they were not
deficient in courage or in patriotic zeal.   A sharp action insued : but
a thunderstorm, with heavy rain, alarmed and disturbed the more inex-
perienced soldiers, and the Syracusan infantry at length everywhere
gave way.   Their horse, however, tho unable to take any considerable
part in the battle, protected their flight, so that little execution was
done in pursuit, and they retired within the city-walls.

This expedition appears to have been in itself very ably conducted
by the Athenian generals ; but it was little connected with any extensive plan of operation.   On the morrow after the battle, having, in Thucyd. l. 6.
consequence of the usual application from the vanquished, restored the c. 71.
enemy's dead, to the number of only two hundred and sixty, they
reïmbarked the whole of their forces, and returned to Catana.   This
flash of victory, however, had its advantageous consequences.   It restored the sullied reputation of the Athenian arms, confirmed the allies, and opened means for farther negotiation within Sicily : it assisted moreover to save, if not to gain credit at home, and tended to
prepare the Athenian people for receiving more favorably any application for supplies and reïnforcement.   The want of cavalry had been
experienced as the great deficiency of the armament.   It was therefore
determined to collect, during the winter, the greatest force of horse
that could by any means be obtained within the iland, and also to apply for a body from home.   A large supply of money was moreover
indispensable ; and it behooved the generals to exert themselves, in solicitation among allies, in rapine against enemies, that they might spare
the Athenian treasury; upon which, nevertheless, some demand was
unavoidable.   The siege of Syracuse was resolved upon for the first
object of the insuing campain.   For the interval, the fleet was laid up,
and the army disposed in quarters, at Naxus and Catana.

Meanwhile among the Syracusans, tho much uneasiness arose from
the late event, which so disappointed the opinion fondly entertained of
their superiority to the Athenians, yet the misfortune was not without
salutary consequences.   The depression of the public mind imposed

silence upon faction, repressed forward ignorance, and gave scope for abilities and patriotism to come forward. The general assembly met, and the people listened with anxious attention, while Hermocrates son of Hermon spoke. ‘ Their late defeat,’ he said, ‘ was no cause for de-
‘ jection such as he saw prevailing. Meer people, as they compara-
‘ tively were, and not formed soldiers, it was much for them to have
‘ shown themselves so nearly equal to select troops, of the first reputa-
‘ tion in Greece. Besides, the very circumstances of the action
‘ pointed out the means of future success. It was not in strength, but
‘ in order and discipline ; not in bravery, but in system of command
‘ and subordination, that they were inferior. The alteration necessary
‘ was obvious ; the chief commanders should be few, but they should
‘ be experienced ; they should be trustworthy, and they should be
‘ trusted. The winter should then be diligently employed in improv-
‘ ing discipline : the force of heavy-armed should be increased, by
‘ giving arms at the public expence to the poor but able-bodied
‘ citizens. Courage and confidence,’ he continued, ‘ will of course
‘ revive, with improved system, improved skill, and increased force ;
‘ and in spring, I doubt not but we may meet the enemy upon equal
‘ terms.’

It were indeed difficult to imagine anything more inconvenient, or more adverse to effectual exertion, than the system of military command which democratical jealousy, inforced by frequent sedition, had established at Syracuse. The supreme military authority was divided among no less than fifteen officers ; and even this numerous board, if the term may be allowed, was, upon all momentous occasions, to take its orders from the people. But the present alarm, and the pressure of evident necessity, gave force to the advice of Hermocrates. The command in chief was committed to Hermocrates himself, with only two collegues, and they were vested with discretionary powers. Measures equally vigorous and judicious immediately followed. The great object, for a town expecting a siege, was to obviate contraval-

Thucyd. l. 6. lation. On the side therefore of the quarters called Temenites, and
c. 75.   Epipolæ, the new generals extended the fortifications of the city ; and they occupied with garrisons two critical posts in the neighbourhood,
                                                                the

the precinct of the temple of Olympieium, to the southward of the city on the farther bank of the river Anapus, and a fort named Megara.   Having thus provided for immediate security, they extended their views.   A watchful eye was kept upon the negotiations of the Athenians among the Sicilian states; and, information being received that the whole Athenian armament was assembled, for the remainder of the winter, at Naxus, an expedition was made, apparently more with a view to revive the drooping spirits of the people, than with the expectation of any other important advantage, to destroy the huts, which the Athenians had left standing, on the ground they had quitted near Catana.

Among the cities in alliance with Syracuse, the fidelity of Camarina, not the least powerful among them, was the most doubted. Tho accounted a Dorian people, the Camarinæans had been from of old adverse: they were the only Sicilian Dorians who had constantly refused to put themselves under the degrading and oppressive protection of the Syracusan commonwealth.   To strengthen themselves in independency, while Laches commanded the Athenian forces in Sicily, they had ingaged in alliance with Athens; but by the general peace among the Sicilian cities, which Hermocrates had procured, without renouncing the Athenian alliance, they became allies also of Syracuse. When the armament under Nicias arrived in Sicily, the Syracusan government required assistance from Camarina; and, the dilatory conduct of the Athenian generals bringing their force into contempt, the Camarinæans, fearful of the resentment of a powerful neighbor, sent a body of auxiliary horse. The late demonstration of the superiority of the Athenian arms, would be likely to make a change in sentiment at Camarina, not favorable to the Syracusan interest; and it was known that the Athenian generals were carrying on negotiation there. To counterwork this, and win the Camarinæans to the Syracusan cause, Hermocrates thought important enough to require that he should go himself at the head of an embassy to Camarina.

As far as the connection with Athens only was to be dissuaded, the business undertaken by Hermocrates was easy. The notorious conduct, and even the avowed principles of the Athenian government,

were

Thucyd. l. 6. c. 75.

were such as could not but give alarm, wherever the Athenian power could be extended. Being admitted to audience by the Camarinæan

Thucyd. l. 6. c. 76. & seq.

people, Hermocrates justly urged, ' that the restoration of the Le-
' ontines, which the Athenians held out as their object in the invasion
' of Sicily, was a shallow prétence. The Leontines indeed were
' Ionians, kinsmen of the Athenians; but what were the Euboïc Chal-
' cidians, the very people from whom the Leontines derived their im-
' mediate origin? Equally kinsmen of the Athenians, they were held
' in strict subjection, and denied the use of arms [8]. Protection to the
' semibarbarian Egestans could, still less than the restoration of the
' Leontines, be the real motive for sending so expensive an armament
' so far. It was in short not dubious that the subjugation equally of
' all the Sicilians was the object of Athenian ambition.' So far the
arguments of Hermocrates were unanswerable. But when he was to
justify the past conduct of Syracuse, and persuade the Camarinæans to
assist the Syracusan cause, whatever fear the power of Athens might
excite, the consideration of the nearer and more obvious danger pre-
ponderated, of servitude to a people of their own iland, their fellow-
colonists; a servitude likely to be more severe, and certainly more
grating. All therefore that could be obtained, by solicitation or remonstrance, urged with all the ability, and supported by the respectable character, of Hermocrates, was a declaration, ' that, being ingaged
' in alliance with both Athens and Syracuse, the Camarinæans could
' take no part, consistently with their oaths, but that of an exact
' neutrality.'

While the Syracusan leaders were thus sedulous, tho not always successful, in negotiation within Sicily, they directed their attention also
to those states in Greece itself, in which they might reasonably expect
a disposition friendly to themselves, and were sure of a disposition hostile to Athens. An embassy was sent first to Corinth, the parent state
of Syracuse. There a disposition was found, if not of the purest kindness to Syracuse, yet of the utmost readiness to oppose Athens. Ministers were appointed to accompany the Syracusan ministers to Lacedæmon, and assist in rousing the usually sluggish counsels of that

---

[8] So Smith translates Ἀπαράσκευος, and I believe properly.

state.

state. The ephors, and others of prevailing power there, were free to incourage by words, and willing even to assist by negotiation, but backward to give that more efficacious assistance which the necessities of Syracuse were likely to require.

But an Athenian was now become the most formidable foe to Athens. Alcibiades had passed in a merchant-ship, from the Thurian territory to the Eleian port of Cyllenë, whence he proceeded to Argos, where his interest, as we have seen, had been powerful. The establishment of his credit now with the democratical party there, would afford the fairest ground for its restoration with the democratical party in Athens; but the diligence of his opponents disappointed him. They procured a decree of the Athenian people for his banishment from Greece, and the mission of ministers to Argos to demand his person. He had hitherto hesitated to accept an invitation from Lacedæmon. A party there favored him : his connection by the claim of hereditary hospitality with the republic, and his services to many individuals, when prisoners in Athens, would recommend him. But he feared the body of the people, who might be apt to recollect, with no friendly mind, the evils which had been suffered, and the greater evils apprehended and risked, from the war excited in Peloponnesus by his ambition, his talents, and his influence ; and he feared not less the prejudice, which could scarcely fail to be entertained against him, on account of his constant connection with the democratical, and opposition to the oligarchal interest, in his own country. The leading men, however, in general, even those otherwise less well disposed to him, aware that he was capable of being no less a useful friend than a pernicious enemy, were in the moment willing to forget every objection to him. He judged it unsafe to remain longer in Argos ; he was therefore ready to go wherever circumstances might afford any prospect of advantage ; and, a safe-conduct being sent to him, he went to Sparta.

On his arrival he found a general disposition in his favor, rather such as he might have wished, than such as could reasonably be expected. The senate assembled, and, the people being summoned to give him audience, all listened with anxious attention, while he communicated

[margin notes:] Thucyd. ut sup. Isocr. pro Alcib. p. 140. t. 3. Ch. 17. s. 3. of this Hist.

Thucyd. l. 6. c. 89.

Thucyd. l. 6.
c. 90. municated information and advice. ' The views of conquest enter-
' tained at Athens,' he said ' were extensive. It was proposed first to
' reduce all Sicily ; then the Grecian possessions in Italy. With the
' inexhaustible supply of ship-timber which Italy afforded, it was in-
' tended so to increase the fleet, that the conquest of Carthage might
' be undertaken. Spain and all the western shores of the Mediter-
' ranean would then be open; whence mercenary troops might be ob-
' tained, in any numbers, and the best of their kind. These would
' be employed against Peloponnesus by land, while the fleet should
' blockade it by sea; and thus it was proposed to complete the subju-
' gation of Greece. The conquered countries, it was expected, each
' as it was reduced, would furnish supplies for farther conquest, with-
' out burthening Athens.

Thucyd. l. 6.
c. 91.   ' And however wild and visionary,' continued Alcibiades, ' these
' vast projects may on first view appear, I, who have long meditated
' upon them, who know the resources of Athens, who have seen the
' deficiencies of the ill-constituted and unconnected commonwealths
' against which its arms are now directed, am confident that success
' is not impossible. The Sicilian Greeks have little military discipline
' or skill. Syracuse, having already suffered a defeat by land, will
' presently be blockaded by land and sea; and, unassisted, must un-
' avoidably fall. Sicily may then be considered as conquered, and
' Italy will not hold long. Thus not Sicily only, but Peloponnesus
' itself, is deeply interested in the event.'

Having by this representation sufficiently alarmed the Lacedæmonians, he proceeded to inform them how the threatened danger might
be averted. ' A fleet,' he said, ' you have not, equal to oppose the
' Athenian ; but troops may be sent to Sicily, making them work their
' own passage, in sufficient number to form, with the Sicilians, a com-
' petent force of regular heavy-armed. But, what I hold of more im-
' portance than any troops you can send, let a Spartan general go to
' Sicily ; who may establish discipline among the Sicilians already
' firm in the cause, and whose authority may bring over, and hold
' united under one command, those not disposed to obey the Syracu-
                                                              ' sans.

' sans. Thus, more than by any other measure, your decided friends
' will be incouraged, and those dubiously affected will be confirmed in
' your interest.

' But it will be neceffary, for the incouragement of the Syracusans
' and the distraction of the Athenians, without reserve to begin hosti-
' lities in Greece. Nothing can be so efficacious, and nothing the
' Athenians so much dread, as your occupying and fortifying a post
' within Attica; and for this purpose the town of Deceleia is to be
' preferred. Thus their country will no longer be theirs but yours;
' no revenue will accrue to them from it; even that from the silver-
' mines of Laureium may be stopped: but, what is still more im-
' portant, nothing will equally superinduce the revolt of those distant
' possessions, whence their principal revenue is derived, as the know-
' lege that they are pressed at home.'

After having thus indicated and advised whatever would most contribute to his country's downfall, Alcibiades thought, for his character's sake, however persecuted by that country, some apology necessary for such conduct. ' I hold that,' he said, ' no longer my Thucyd. l. 6.
' country, which is governed by a set of men who have so injuriously c. 92.
' driven me from it. Nor ought I to be considered as persuading war
' against my country; but rather as endevoring to restore myself to
' the country which was once mine, and to restore that country to its
' due government within itself, and its just situation among the Gre-
' cian republics. I account him a true patriot, not who, being un-
' justly expelled, rests in banishment, but who, still animated by love
' of his country, does his utmost to restore himself. Upon you, Lace-
' dæmonians, I depend for the greatest benefits, to my country not less
' than to myself. You may trust me therefore that there is no danger,
' no hardship, which I am not ready to undergo in your service, and
' that I shall have every satisfaction in coöperating with you, to pull
' down the tyrannical power, now usurped by Athens, and restoring
' Greece to that happy situation, in which you, by common consent,
' and not by violence, presided over it.'

The eloquence of Alcibiades, his advice, but still more the expecta- Thucyd. l. 6.
tion of advantage from the important information which he was un- c. 93.

questionably able to give concerning every circumstance of Athenian affairs, decided the Lacedæmonians, and it was resolved to assist Syracuse, and to renew the war with Athens.

SECTION V.

Measures of the Peloponnesians to relieve Syracuse. Measures of the Athenian Armament in Sicily: Reïnforcement to the Athenian Armament in Sicily: Siege of Syracuse: Capitulation propofed: Arrival of Gylippus and Pythen to the Relief of Syracuse. Official Letter of Nicias to the Athenian People.

THE resolution for war being taken at Lacedæmon, the business of Sicily required the first attention. To command the force to be employed there, Gylippus was appointed, son of Cleändridas, who had been banished, when tutor to the young king Pleistoanax, for misconduct in a former war with Athens, and on suspicion of taking bribes from Pericles. Gylippus was directed to consult, with the leading men of Corinth and Syracuse, about the readiest and best means for transporting troops to Sicily; but those troops were to be collected as they might among the allied states, Lacedæmon furnishing none. A man, however, more qualified than Gylippus, for the business committed to him, could hardly have been selected; and, sparing as Lacedæmon was of troops and treasure, the authority and influence with which he was largely vested, were, as we find by their effects, of extraordinary power. Ordering two Corinthian triremes to attend him immediately at Asinë, he urged the diligent preparation of the rest of the force to be employed under his command.

Thucyd. l. 6. c. 93. Ch. 13. s. 5. of this Hift.

The resolution taken, for renewing war with Athens, might give to expect some restored vigor in the Lacedæmonian councils; but the first operations of the Lacedæmonian arms indicated none. In spring the force of Laconia was assembled, and marched against the Argian territory. On its arrival at Cleonæ, an earthquake, a common circumstance in most parts of Greece, and especially in Laconia, with-

B. C. 414. Ol. 91. 2. P. W. 18. Thucyd. l. 6. c. 95.

out

out doing any considerable mischief, threw all into consternation : superstition saw in it the anger of the gods declared ; the army immediately retreated, and the expedition was given up. Such conduct incouraged and invited the Argians to revenge. Entering the Lacedæmonian territory of Thyreatis, they collected plunder that sold for twenty-five talents, about six thousand pounds sterling ; which was esteemed a large booty, well rewarding the enterprize.

A conspiracy, which about the same time broke out in the little city of Thespiæ in Bœotia, requires mention, as it tends to illustrate the state of Greece. The democratical party rose against their oligarchal magistrates ; the Athenians marched a body of troops to support them. The insurgents were nevertheless overpowered ; some were apprehended (what they suffered we are not informed) and the rest fled to Athens. ^{Thucyd. l. 6, c. 95.}

During winter, the Athenian generals in Sicily had not neglected such measures for promoting their business, as the season would permit. Soon after disposing their troops in quarters they marched with their whole force to Messena, in hope of gaining that city, through intelligence long maintained with a party there : but Alcibiades, who, before his flight, had been privy to the negotiation, gave warning of the danger. The Athenian armament therefore, after suffering in a winter camp for thirteen days, was obliged to return, without effecting anything but the destruction of some of the principal Messenians of their own party, who were seized by their opponents, condemned as traitors, and executed. ^{c. 74.}

Some negotiations among the Sicel tribes had a more fortunate issue. Those of the plains, indeed, habituated to subjection under the Syracusan government, and ready objects of Syracusan resentment, could few of them be persuaded to revolt : but the midland mountaineers, who had always preserved independency, and considered the Syracusans as their natural enemies, were predisposed to the Athenian cause. Most of them readily furnished provisions, and some even paid contributions in money. A small force brought to terms a few who were found adverse, and relieved some others, more favorably inclined, ^{c. 88.}

clined, from the restraint in which they had been held by Syracusan garrisons.

Thucyd. l. 6. Toward the approach of spring the whole Athenian armament moved from Naxus to Catana, to be nearer its principal object; and negotiation was extended as far as Tuscany and Carthage. Overtures had been received from Tuscany, yet the result seems to have been little important, and it does not appear that the negotiation with Carthage produced anything. The generals however succeeded in collecting, within Sicily, horses for a body of cavalry. Iron, bricks, and other materials, neceffary for the proposed contravallation, were prepared, and every disposition was made for undertaking the siege of Syracuse.

B. C. 414.
P. W. 18.
Thucyd. l. 6.
c. 94. Early in spring the army marched. The lands of Megara, which, since the depopulation of the city by Gelon, had been Syracusan property, were ravaged. An attempt upon a fort held by a Syracusan garrison failed; but the vale of the river Tereas was plundered unopposed, the standing corn burnt, and, a small body of Syracusans interfering to check the ravage, some were killed, the rest fled. For this little success a trophy was erected, and the army returned to Catana. After a short time for refreshment, the generals moved again, gained the Sicel town of Centoripa by capitulation, and burnt the corn of the adverse Sicel tribes of Inessa and Hybla. Returning then to Catana, they found the supplies and reinforcements from Athens arrived. For the passion of the Athenian people for conquest in Sicily had not c. 93. abated : the application of the generals had met with favor far beyond their expectation; and all their requests were granted without demur. No addition of infantry had been desired: there were sent two hundred and fifty horse-soldiers, with complete accoutrements, but without horses; three hundred talents in silver, amounting to about seventy-five thousand pounds sterling; and stores of all necessary kinds in abundance.

c. 96. The generals resolved then immediately to lay siege to Syracuse. Nature, art, and a numerous population concurred to make Syracuse strong; and to reduce a place, of but moderate strength, we have seen, in the art of attack of that age, a contravallation always was necessary.

Here

Here two difficulties opposed ; the extent of the town, and the form of a hill, over the skirt of which a suburb extended. The hill, sloping toward the town, was precipitous toward the country ; and the suburb, from its situation, overlooking the town, was called Epipolæ[9]. The Syracusan generals were apprized of the intention of the enemy ; they were not uninformed of the usual mode of conducting sieges ; and they were aware how important it would be to occupy the hill of Epipolæ. But they were new in command ; discipline remained yet to be established among their troops ; and, till danger became pressing, notwithstanding the vote conferring on them discretionary power, the attempt would be hazardous to inforce discipline among those who, by a simple vote, might take away the power they had given. Not therefore till it was known that the Athenians had collected a considerable body of cavalry, and were already prepared to march for Syracuse, Hermocrates and his collegues ventured to take measures for appointing guards and distributing duty. At daybreak they led all the Syracusan citizens, within the age for service, into a meadow on the bank of the Anapus. After a review of arms, they appointed a select body of seven hundred men to be stationed in Epipolæ, as a kind of picket-guard to give assistance wherever danger might press, but to be particularly a protection for that very important post. An Andrian refugee, named Diomilus, versed, as a subject of Athens, in the Athenian discipline, was appointed to the command of the body selected for so critical a service; a circumstance strongly indicating how conscious the Syracusan generals were of the inferior skill and experience of their own officers.

On the very night preceding these measures of the Syracusans, the Athenian generals, imbarking their whole army, had passed, undiscovered, to a place near Syracuse, called Leon, where a body of infantry was hastily debarked, which proceeded immediately to Epipolæ, less than a mile distant and by a pass called Euryelus, mounted the hill unopposed. Information of this surprize being next morning carried to the Syracusans, occupied in the meadow of the Anapus at the distance of three miles, excited great consternation. Courage however did not fail them. With much zeal, but much disorder, all hastened to

Thucyd. l. 6. c. 97.

[9] Nearly synonymous with the English name OVERTON.

repel

repel the invaders. A fierce conflict insued : but tumultuous valor was little efficacious against steddy discipline. The Syracusans were compelled to retreat, with the loss of three hundred heavy-armed, among whom fell Diomilus, the newly appointed commander of the select band. The near refuge of their walls prevented greater slaughter.

Next morning the Athenians drew out into the plain to offer battle : but the temper of the Syracusan people, chastised by the event of the preceding day, no longer disposed them to put violence upon the prudence of their generals, and they did not stir. The Athenians, returning to Epipolæ, applied themselves to construct a fort at Labdalum, among the highest precipices, as a citidel, in which to deposit their military chest and other valuables [10]. While thus employed they were joined by three hundred Egestans, and one hundred Naxian and Sicel cavalry ; and, the Athenian troopers being mounted, the cavalry of the army all together, exclusive of the horse-bowmen, were now six hundred and fifty. The fort being quickly completed, the army descended into the plain, and the work of contravallation was imme--diately begun.

Syracuse was built between two inlets of the sea, called the great port, and the Trogilian port ; and it nearly inclosed a third, called the little, or the Ortygian port, which was separated from the great port only by the little iland of Ortygia, the site of the original city. On the inland side of the town rose the hill of Epipolæ [11]. It was the business

Thucyd. l. 6. c. 98.

[10] Τοῖς τε σκίνοισι καὶ τοῖς χρήμασιν ἀποθήκη.

[11] The site of Syracuse is thus described by a modern traveller : ' The antient city ' of Syracuse was of a triangular form, and ' consisted of five parts or towns ; Ortygia, ' or the iland ; Achradina, that faced the ' sea ; Tychë, joined to Achradina on the ' east ; Neapolis, which lay along the side ' of the great port ; and, at the western ' extremity, Epipolæ. Some lofty rocks, ' crowned with ramparts, formed a strong ' defence all around, except in Neapolis, ' where the walls crossed the low-grounds.

' The circuit, according to Strabo, amounted ' to a hundred and eighty stadia, twenty-two ' English miles and a half ; an account I ' once suspected of exaggeration ; but, after ' spending two days in tracing the ruins, ' and making reasonable allowances for incroachments of the sea, I was convinced ' of the exactness of the measurement.' Swinburne's Travels in the Two Sicilies, p. 327, v. 2.

It will be observed that this writer speaks of Syracuse when it had acquired its greatest extent, some time after the age of the Peloponnesian war. His account of the extensive business of the Athenians to carry their works of contravallation from Epipolæ to the sea on each side; to the Trogilian port on the north, to the great port on the south.   They began on the northern side, and through their superior practice and skill, every possible preparation having been made during winter, the business advanced so rapidly as to astonish not less than it alarmed the Syracusans.   At a loss for measures to oppose to it, their generals resolved to venture a battle, rather than quietly permit the prosecution of works, which threatened, in their completion, the inevitable capture of the city.   They accordingly led out their forces; but, in approaching the enemy, their order became deranged, and deficient discipline among the troops baffled their endevors to restore it.   They had the prudence immediately to command hasty retreat, and were fortunate enough, under the protection of their horse, to get within their walls again with little loss.

This check was salutary to the Syracusans, as it tended to repress that intemperate ardor, which very inconveniently interfered with the authority of the generals; and the genius of Hermocrates soon led him to the measures most proper in the existing circumstances.   The Athenian works would be effectual only if the contravallation were completed.   They were yet confined to the northern side of the town : on the southern side therefore, between Epipolæ and the great port, Her- Thucyd. 1. 6. mocrates carried out a work from the town-wall, cutting the proposed c. 99. line of the enemy's contravallation.   He expected that his work would be interrupted, and perhaps destroyed; but even thus he foresaw considerable advantage from it.   If the enemy assailed it with the whole

---

sive circle of prospect from the summit of Euryelus may deserve notice here:

'Toward the north,' he says, 'the eye wanders over vast plains along a line of coast, to the foot of Etna, whose mighty cone shuts up the horizon with unspeakable majesty.   The mountains of Italy rise like clouds, on each side of it.   Southward the city of Syracuse, now reduced to its original spot, Ortygia, once an iland, but now a peninsula, still containing eighteen thousand inhabitants, seems to float on the bosom of the waters, guarding the entrance of its noble harbour.   The Plemmyrian peninsula locks it on the opposite shore, beyond which an expanse of sea is seen, stretching away to Cape Passaro.   The hills of Noto bound the view to the southward, and the foreground is every where an expanse of rich level plains, thickly planted, and watered by the winding stream of the Anapus,' p. 336.

of

of their forces, he would retire, and he had his end in the interruption of their works ; if with a part, he would oppose with his whole force, and so would probably be superior.   The Athenian generals however

Thucyd. 1. 6.
c. 100.

knew their business : they permitted him to complete his work without disturbance : a guard was placed in it, and the rest of the forces withdrew into the city.   Tho circumstances had occurred powerfully to repress forward rashness among the Syracusans, yet Hermocrates had not yet been able to establish due subordination among those who, having chosen him their commander, retained nevertheless, by the constitution of Syracuse, legal power still to command him.   The Athenians, from the heights of Epipolæ, observed the disorderly negligence of the Syracusan guard ; and, in the heat of mid-day, when part were strayed into the city, and the rest mostly reposing in their huts, a chosen detachment, supported by a strong body, assaulted the fort, while the rest of the army distracted the enemy's attention by a false attack in another quarter.   The guard of the fort immediately fled.   The Athenians and Argians pursuing, entered that quarter of Syracuse called Temenites.   They were however quickly overpowered, and compelled to retire out of the city with some loss ; but they demolished the counterwork, carried off many of the piles, and, in claim of victory, erected their trophy.

c. 101.

On the next morning they began the contravallation on the southern side, from Epipolæ toward the great port.   The Syracusans, urged by their evidently growing danger, notwithstanding their late ill success, began a fresh counterwork, across a marsh lying between the town and the river Anapus, and nearer the sea than their former work.   The Athenian generals, upon this, ordered their fleet from Thapsus, where it had hitherto lain, into the great harbour.   Nicias was at this time confined by illness.   Under the command of Lamachus, therefore, the Athenian forces issued at daybreak from Epipolæ, and making their way across the soft ground of the marsh upon planks, stormed the new work of the Syracusans, and routed the forces which came out of the town for its protection.   The right of those forces easily reached the town again ; but the left made for a bridge over the Anapus.   The Athenians endevored to intercept them ; but the Syracusan

Syracusan horse, of which the greater part was in that wing, facing about
unexpectedly, charged the more advanced of the Athenian troops, repulsed them, and spred confusion through their right wing. Lamachus,
who was in the left, hastening with a small body of bowmen, to
restore order in the right, and imprudently passing a deep ditch, by
which ready assistance was prevented, he was overpowered and killed,
with five or six of those about him. The Athenian left, however,
advancing, the Syracusans retreated again hastily, but carried off with
them the body of the Athenian general, and crossing the river, were
there secure. The momentary success of their comrades, meanwhile, Thucyd. l. 6.
incouraging the Syracusans who had fled into the city, their leaders c. 102.
conceived the bold idëa of assaulting Epipolæ, which they rightly
judged would, upon the present occasion, be left with a small guard.
Accordingly they took and demolished an outwork, and might have
taken the whole, so weak was it left, but for the orders, judiciously
given by Nicias, to the numerous slaves attending the army, to set fire
to the wood, not sparing the machines, which lay before the wall. A
flame was thus quickly raised, which checked the assailants; and, the
Athenian army hastening to the relief of their principal post, while
their fleet was seen entering the great harbour, the Syracusans retreated
within their walls.

All hope of intercepting the contravallation, or by any means pre- c. 103.
venting its completion, was now given up by the besieged; and despondency, and its consequence, discord, began to gain among them. This
became quickly known among the neighboring states; and a general
disposition to abandon the Syracusans, and to fear and flatter the
Athenians, followed. This temper spred as far as the Italian cities:
apprehensions arose that their refusal to furnish a market might draw
on them the vengeance of the conquering commonwealth; and supplies flowed to the Athenian armament from all quarters. Those of the
Sicel tribes also, who had before superciliously rejected invitation from
the Athenians, now solicited their alliance; and from Tuscany three
penteconters joined the fleet.

Meanwhile the Syracusan multitude, impotent against their enemies,
vented their discontent against their generals, and Hermocrates and

his collegues were removed from their office.   One of them, however, Heracleides (unless it was another person of the same name) was restored, and Eucles and Tellias were associated with him in the command.   At the same time suspicion of treachery between party and party, the universal bane of the Grecian commonwealths, especially in adverse circumstances, gained ground.   The lower people were far from being equally apprehensive with their superiors, of the consequences of yielding to the Athenians; capitulation became the subject of frequent debate in the general assembly, and even messages passed to Nicias on the subject: but the terms proposed were not such as that cautious servant of the Athenian people could suppose would satisfy his greedy masters.   Thus nearly however was a great point, and perhaps the most important, carried toward realizing the magnificent visions of the ambition of Alcibiades; and so near was Nicias to gaining, almost against his will, the glory of conqueror of Syracuse and of Sicily, and adding to the dominion of Athens the greatest acquisition ever yet made by Grecian arms.

Gylippus was arrived at Leucas with only two Lacedæmonian and two Corinthian ships, the rest of the squadron to be furnished by Corinth being not yet ready, when intelligence reached him of the ill situation of Syracuse; so exaggerated, that he gave up Sicily for lost, and thought he should do much if he could save the Italian states to the Peloponnesian confederacy.   To this object therefore he determined to direct his efforts.   Taking Pythen, the Corinthian admiral, with him in his small squadron, he went first to Tarentum; where, as a Lacedæmonian colony, he was well received.   He had some hope of gaining Thurium, through family interest there; his father, Cleandridas, having passed his exile at that place, where he was admitted to the rights of citizenship.   Means were thus open for attempting negotiation; but the Athenian interest, supported by the present reputation of the Athenian arms, was not to be overborne, and he could obtain nothing.   In proceeding along the coast, to try negotiation with other towns, a violent storm interrupted his course, and, narrowly escaping shipwreck, he returned to Tarentum.

Some days were necessary for refitting his shattered galleys, and then

Thucyd. ibid.
Di<ol. l. 13.
c. 93.
Plu^t. vit.
Peric. & Nic.

Thucyd. l. 7.
c. 1.

4   he

he proceeded with Pythen to Locri, from whose people, through local interest always adverse to the Athenians, they found a favorable reception. There they gained the first authentic intelligence of the reäl state of things at Syracuse. They learnt that, tho the circumvallation was really extended from Epipolæ to the sea on each side, and so far completed that any attempt upon it, without a very superior force, would be rash, yet over the crags themselves of Epipolæ it might be possible to introduce troops into the city. Learning farther that the strait of Messena was unguarded, they proceeded by sea, along the northern coast of Sicily, to Himera; and with the people of that place they succeeded. Gylippus then immediately determined to lay up his triremes in the port of Himera, and march across the country to Syracuse, with such force as he could collect. He ingaged the Himeræans to send with him a thousand foot, heavy and light, and a hundred horse; and obtaining from them regular armour for those of his crews who were unprovided, he thus made his Peloponnesian heavy-armed seven hundred. He depended upon zealous assistance from the Selinuntines, in whose cause the Syracusans had drawn on themselves the arms of Athens; he had promises from Gela; and an opening offered for negotiation with some of the Sicels, through the recent death of a chief named Archonidas, whose influence principally had decided them to the Athenian interest. In all these negotiations the very name of Lacedæmon, as Thucydides assures us, powerfully seconded the activity and abilities of Gylippus. The Selinuntines indeed, who beyond others owed zeal to the cause, deceived his just expectation, sending only a small body of light-armed: the Geloans also sent only a small body, but it was cavalry; the Sicels joined him with a thousand men. His force all together, with attending slaves, might be about five thousand.

During these transactions in Sicily, the squadron, assembled at Leucas, sailed for the Italian coast, leaving behind Gongylus, one of the Corinthian commanders, who happened not to be ready. This accidental circumstance had most important consequences. Gongylus, as soon as himself and his trireme were prepared, pushing across the gulf, without making the usual circuit of the Italian shore, arrived on the Sicilian coast before the squadron, and entered the harbour of Syracuse

Thucyd. l. 7. c. 2.

Y y 2   unopposed.

unopposed.   For Nicias, thinking success now assured, and holding in
contempt the force which he heard was approaching, kept little watch;
and tho he had not disdained to send four triremes to prevent the passage
of Gylippus through the strait of Messena, yet he sent them too late.
The arrival of Gongylus was most critical.   Summons had been issued
for a general assembly to meet for the declared purpose of debating
concerning terms of capitulation.   Uncertain hope, raised by the arrival
of the Corinthian admiral, gave strength to the party adverse to
the surrender: the question of capitulation was postponed: Gongylus
was allowed to address the people; and the warm assurances he gave of
speedy and effectual succour, not from Corinth only, but from Lacedæmon (for the authority of the Lacedæmonian name, says again Thucydides, was of principal weight) wrought such a turn in the popular
mind, that the chiefs ventured to propose to march out and meet Gylippus, who, from communication which had passed, was known to be
approaching.

It could not be without gross neglect in Nicias, that, with a force of
scarcely two thousand heavy-armed, and those for the most part but
inferior troops, Gylippus shortly after ascended Epipolæ unopposed,
by the same way of Euryelus, by which the Athenians had first obtained
possession of that important post.   The Syracusan forces actually went
out to meet him; and to the astonishment of the Athenian general and
army, busied in the works on the south of the city, the combined forces
made their appearance as if offering battle.   Gylippus however had
the precaution to halt while retreat was still at his option, and he sent
forward a herald with the proposal, 'That if the Athenians would quit
' Sicily in five days with their arms and baggage, he was willing to
' make a truce for the purpose.'   The message was of course received
with disdain, amid their astonishment, by those who thought themselves on the point of becoming conquerors of Syracuse and of Sicily.
Nicias, however, continued motionless, while the herald was simply
ordered to withdraw.   Meantime the able Gylippus had had sufficient
opportunity to observe, that the Syracusan forces were deficient in discipline, to a degree beyond what he had imagined; that they were utterly unable to form on uneven and confined ground; and that the first
thing

Thucyd. 1. 7.
c. 3.

thing necessary for him was to retreat for more space.   Nicias made
no attempt to profit from any of these circumstances, but remained
behind his works.   Gylippus, thus allowed to retire at leisure, chose his
camp for the night on the high ground of Temenites.

Next morning the combined forces appeared again in order of battle,
in front of the Athenian works, and by their position intercluded the
communication of the Athenian general with his fort of Labdalum, and
with his northern lines.   Nicias continued still unaccountably motionless, while Gylippus sent a strong detachment which stormed the
fort, and put the garrison to the sword.   A smaller occurrence on the
same day contributed to raise the spirits of the Syracusans ; an Athenian trireme was taken at the harbour's mouth.

Gylippus having, by this succession of daring but well concerted   Thucyd. l. 7.
measures, in his outset, wholly changed the face of affairs, insomuch   c. 4.
that not only the city was very effectually relieved, but the Athenian
army was now rather in a situation of some danger, prudently checked
the spirit of enterprize, that he might give stability to the advantage
obtained.   Master of Epipolæ through his success against Labdalum,
he began immediately to carry out works to intersect the Athenian
works, using the materials which the Athenians themselves had collected.   Meanwhile Nicias, aware that the moment of opportunity for
that great success with which he had lately had reason to flatter himself, was gone by, and that, however he might still be superior in the
field, to take Syracuse was beyond his present strength, continued
nevertheless to prosecute his southern work toward the sea.   In a
country where all was inimical, to keep his communication open with
his fleet, would be necessary to the subsistence of his army, and might
become necessary even to its safety.   Occupying therefore the headland of Plemmyrium, on the southern side of the entrance of the great
harbour, he raised there three redoubts, in which he placed the greater
part of the baggage and stores of his army, and near them he stationed
his ships of burden and small craft.   This measure, well conceived in
regard to the objects particularly in view, was, however, attended with
great inconveniences.   The soil was swampy and unwholesome; the
water brackish; the Syracusan fort of Olympieium was near, and a
                                                        body

body of horse, stationed there by Gylippus, gave unceasing annoyance;
watching the wood and water-parties, cutting off stragglers, and making it dangerous to stir from the camp, but in powerful bodies.

Thucyd. 1. 7.
c. 5.

It was not long before Gylippus again drew out his forces and offered battle; and Nicias now, at length, did not refuse to meet him.
The field was very narrow, confined between the contravallation and
the city wall.   The Syracusan horse had not space for action, and the
infantry, pressd by the superior discipline of the Athenians, soon retreated within their fortifications.   It seems to have been the purpose
of Gylippus to give practice to the Syracusans, with the least possible
risk, and make them experience the necessity of submitting to the severity of Spartan discipline, if they would hope for the success for which
the Spartan arms were renowned.   Addressing them in assembly, he
took all the blame of the late failure to himself; condemned his mis-
application of their cavalry; praised the valor shown by their infantry;
and flattered them with remarking that, being of the same Dorian origin with the Lacedæmonians, they ought to hold themselves superior
to Ionians and ilanders of the Ægean; and he doubted not but they
would quickly show it, by driving those intruding adventurers out of
their country.

He soon gave them opportunity of trial.   Nicias would rather have
avoided action, but that the Syracusan counterwork from Epipolæ
alarmed him.   Already it barely did not intersect the line of the Athenian contravallation; and if completed would, according to Thucydides, not only prevent the completion of the contravallation, but give
to the Syracusans both the choice when they would ingage, and certain advantage in action.   Gylippus so chose his ground that his
cavalry could attack the Athenian left in flank.   The wing was thus
thrown into a confusion, which spred in some degree through the line,
and Nicias hastily withdrew behind his works.   Having thus established, in his own army, the opinion that they were superior in the
field, Gylippus prosecuted assiduously his projecting work, and it was
quickly carried beyond the Athenian line.   This being effected, says
Thucydides, if the Syracusans should now have the misfortune to be
defeated in battle, and reduced to confine themselves within their
walls,

Thucyd. 1. 7.
c. 6.

walls, it would nevertheless be scarcely possible for the Athenians to complete their contravallation.

But adversity began to pour upon the Athenians. Nicias had sent twenty triremes to the Italian coast to intercept the squadron from Leucas. His army had scarcely recovered 'from the consternation of their late defeat, when they saw the enemy's squadron, consisting of twelve triremes, enter the little harbour of Syracuse. The strength, thus added, gave the city, for the present, complete security. It was therefore resolved to act upon the offensive against the Athenians; and with this view it was proposed to collect a still greater strength, for which the credit of prosperous circumstances and recent success would best give means. Ministers were sent to Lacedæmon and Corinth; and the active Gylippus went himself around the Sicilian cities, to excite the lukewarm, and win the adverse, to exert themselves in the cause of Lacedæmon and of Syracuse, which, he contended, was the cause of liberty, of justice, and of the general interest of Sicily.

What opinion the Athenian general now held of his own situation, we learn from his own account, transmitted by Thucydides. Writing was but beginning to come into common use for ordinary purposes. The dispatches of generals were mostly, or, it rather appears, universally, committed to trusty messengers, who delivered them verbally. Thucydides speaks of Nicias as the first general who made it his practice to transmit his reports home constantly in writing. He had observed, says the historian, that messengers, in delivering verbally to the sovreign people in assembly the reports committed to them, sometimes through inability to express themselves clearly, sometimes through fear of relating the whole of unpleasant truths, sometimes through hope of conciliating favor by exaggerating agreeable circumstances, generally gave an impression wide of the reality. From his first appointment therefore to a command with which he had always been little satisfied, and in which complex operations were to be conducted at a greater distance from home than had been usual for the Athenian arms, he had used the precaution of frequently sending dispatches in writing, with an exact account of every transaction; and these were always formally red to the assembled people, by the

secretary

(marginal notes: Thucyd. l. 7. c. 4.   c. 7.   c. 8.)

secretary of the commonwealth [12].   He had now determined, in consequence of his ill success in the late battle, to remain upon the defensive for the rest of the summer.   For this he thought it necessary to
apologize very particularly in his dispatches to Athens.   He therefore
committed them to officers whom he selected as most competent to
answer any questions that might be put to them, yet he scrupulously
protested that his written dispatches only should be considered as
having his authority.

Thucyd. l. 7.   In these he represented, that, 'After having nearly attained the
c. 11.   'object of the expedition, when Syracuse was already reduced to ex-
'tremity, the arrival of Gylippus, with a considerable reïnforcement,
'partly Peloponnesian and partly collected in Sicily, had changed the
'face of affairs : that he had nevertheless been victorious in the first
'action, but the superiority of the enemy in cavalry and troops of
'missile weapons, was, under able conduct, too much for him to re-
'sist; and, in a second action, he had been constrained to retreat :
'that it was in consequence now become necessary to confine himself
'within his lines, to forego offensive operations, and to consult prin-
'cipally how he might best insure the safety of his army against supe-
'rior numbers; for, instead of besieging, it was rather reduced to the
'condition of a camp besieged : that the superiority of the Syracusan
'cavalry rendered any communication with the country highly dan-
'gerous : that, for increase of evil, he not only apprehended a strong
c. 12.   'alliance within Sicily against the Athenian interest, but was assured
'that additional forces would arrive from Peloponnesus; and that,
'finally, he was threatened with attack, not by land only, but by sea.
'The fleet,' he proceeded to observe, 'had unavoidably gone fast to
'decay; the ships were become leaky; the crews diminished; the
'enemy had not only had more ships, but, secure against attack, they
'could chuse when they would attack him : it was therefore necessary
c. 13.   'for his fleet to be unremittingly watchful : the guard of the naval
'camp, and convoys for the introduction of provisions and stores,
'kept the whole on constant duty : the crews, forced to go far for
'wood and water, were continually suffering from the Syracusan

¹² Ο γραμματεὺς τῆς πόλεως. c. 10.

'horse.

' horse.   Meanwhile not only the slaves deserted in numbers to the
' enemy, but the auxiliaries and mercenaries, who had hoped that
' plunder more than fighting would be their business in Sicily, now
' they saw the Athenian armament declining, and the enemy growing
' in vigor, went home without leave.   Sicily,' continued the unfortunate general, ' is wide; and, wholly to prevent these desertions, is im-
' possible; even to check them is difficult; and of all losses to an   Thucyd. l.7.
' armament, that of able seamen is least easily repaired.   Nor are   c. 14.
' these the only evils that press us: what is to me most distressing,
' both to feel and to complain of, remains yet to be mentioned.   Your
' temper, Athenians, is adverse to subordination.   The army is a part
' of you; a part of that soverein people on whom my power wholly
' depends; and I find my authority insufficient to controul the per-
' verse disposition, and restrain the pernicious conduct, of some under
' my command.   Meanwhile the enemy abound in resources, and we
' are destitute; for Naxus and Catana, our only allies in this part of
' the world, are little able to assist us.   If then, in addition to existing
' evils, the Italian cities, whence our supplies of provisions have been
' principally drawn, should be induced, by the ill state of our affairs
' and your neglect of us, to refuse farther assistance, we should be at
' once undone, and the enemy would have a complete triumph with-
' out the risk of a blow.

    ' I could have sent a more pleasing account, but I could not send
' intelligence which it more imports you to receive.   I know your dis-
' position to be gratified by favorable reports of your affairs; but then
' I know too the change that follows in ·your temper, when the event
' disappoints expectation; and I have therefore thought it best to ex-
' plain to you, without reserve, the real state of things.

    ' Since, then, I can affirm that neither your generals, nor your army, c. 15.
' have deserved blame for their conduct in your service here, since
' Sicily is now united against us, and reinforcements are expected from
' Peloponnesus, I will venture to declare that it is become absolutely
' necessary for you to determine on one of two measures: either your
' forces now here must be immediately recalled; or an additional ar-
' mament, not inferior in either land or naval force to the former, must

' be sent hither: it must be here early in spring, and a large sum of
' money for its use will be indispensable.   For myself, I request that I
' may be superseded in the command, for which ill health disqualifies
' me ; and I hope I may be allowed to claim this as an honourable in-
' dulgence due for my past services.'

The Athenians were not yet practised enough in misfortune to listen
to wise advice thwarting a favorite purpose.   Ambition was a popular
passion, not resting on incitement from Alçibiades.   The pertinacity
indeed and the vehemence with which its objects were pursued, considered together with the near prospect of success, even under the disadvantage of his removal from the execution of the vast projects which
he had conceived, may indeed afford no small amount of apology for
his conduct in directing the effervescence, which apparently none
could still.   The Athenian people would not, on the remonstrances of
Nicias, give up their views of conquest in Sicily : they would not even
allow their infirm and deserving general to retire.   An additional force
was immediately voted ; Nicias was required to remain with the command in chief; Menander and Euthydemus, officers now in Sicily,
were appointed his present assistants in the duty : Demosthenes son
of Alcisthenes, who had already so much distinguished himself by important services, and Eurymedon son of Theocles, who had commanded
at Corcyra, at Pylus, and in Sicily, were named to lead the reïnforcement.   As an earnest of the resolution of the Athenian people to give
the utmost support to their friends in Sicily, Eurymedon was sent forward about midwinter, with ten triremes and twenty talents of silver,
while Demosthenes remained to superintend the equipment of the rest
of the armament.

Thucyd. l.7. c. 16.

SECTION VI.

Deceleia in Attica occupied by the Lacedæmonians. Fresh Reïnforce-
ments for the Athenian Armament in Sicily. Naval Action in the
Harbour of Syracuse. Distress of Athens. Tax upon the States
subject to Athens. Massacre in Bœotia. Naval Action in the
Corinthian Gulph.

WHILE the Athenians were thus madly intent upon distant conquest,
a more serious attack than they had yet experienced, was preparing
against their own country. The success of Gylippus, the prospect of
assistance from the whole force of Sicily, the evident embarrassment of
Athens, the exhortations of Corinth, the advice of Alcibiades, and the
important information and assistance which he was capable of giving,
now all together determined the Lacedæmonians to recommence hosti- Thucyd. l.7.
lities immediately against Athens. They were farther incouraged, says c. 18.
the historian, by the consideration that justice (not simple justice, or
a due consideration of the rights of men, which Grecian religion little
taught to regard, but justice ratified by a solemn appeal to the gods)
was now on their side. Their misfortunes, in the latter years of hostility,
had led them to reflect that the beginning of the war had, on their
part, teemed with injustice, and breach of solemnly plighted faith.
Such were the refusal to submit their disputes with Athens to a judicial determination; the support of the violence committed by the
Thebans against Platæa; and the first invasion of Attica. On the
contrary, since the truce, the Athenians had always refused to submit
matters in dispute to judicial inquiry, which the Lacedæmonians had
frequently demanded. The same transgression, therefore, which they
thought had already brought the vengeance of the gods on themselves,
they concluded would now bring it on the Athenians. The war thus
became popular, and to prosecute hostilities with vigor was determined
with alacrity. It was resolved to carry into execution the long meditated purpose of occupying a post in Attica; and, in pursuance of
z z 2   the

the advice of Alcibiades, Deceleia was the place chosen.   During winter the necessary materials for fortifying it were collected, especially
iron, and preparation was also made for giving effectual assistance to
Sicily.

Thucyd. l. 7.
c. 19.
Ol. 91 ¾.
B. C. 413.
P. W. 19.
About 18
March.

In the beginning of next spring, at a very early season for military
operations, the Lacedæmonians with their allies, under Agis son of
Archidamus, entered Attica; and after extending ravage over the
plain, which had been abandoned to them, applied themselves to fortify Deceleia; a town in sight of Athens, at the distance of about fifteen miles, nearly equally distant from the border of Bœotia, and critically situated for commanding the richest part of Attica.   About the
same time some small reinforcements were sent to Sicily ; six hundred infranchised Helots, under Eccritus, a Spartan; three hundred
Bœotians ; and Corinthians, Sicyonians and Arcadians all together
seven hundred.   The Lacedæmonian reinforcement had no difficulty
in its passage from the Laconian coast, tho a squadron of twenty tri-

Thucyd. l. 7.
c. 17.

remes had been sent from Athens to intercept succours.   To favor the
passage of the others out of the Corinthian gulph, the Corinthians had
prepared a squadron of twenty-five triremes, which took a station overagainst the Attic squadron at Naupactus, consisting of only twenty.

c. 20.

Summer was already begun, and the works at Deceleia were advancing, without any attempt at opposition from Athens, when Demosthenes sailed for Sicily; having under his command sixty Athenian and five Chian triremes, twelve hundred heavy-armed Athenians,
and a greater force of infantry collected from the subject-states.   At
Ægina he met a squadron of thirty Attic triremes, under Charicles,
who, in the circumnavigation of Peloponnesus, was to coöperate with
him in descents on the coast.

c. 21.

Meantime Gylippus was using his wonted activity and skill against
the infirm and desponding Nicias.   From the several Sicilian cities,
who were inclined, or whom he had persuaded, to favor the Syracusan
cause, he had collected a considerable force, with which, about the
time that Demosthenes sailed from Athens, he entered Syracuse.   The
Athenians kept their land-force within their fortifications, which he
thought himself not strong enough to attack, unless he could divide their
strength.

strength. He proposed therefore another measure, which, to some, might appear still bolder: he would man the ships and attack the enemy's fleet. The reputation of the Athenians for naval superiority was so established by their various successes against the Peloponnesians in the beginning of the war, that the Syracusans were startled with the first idea of ingaging them on water. But the influence of Hermocrates powerfully seconded the authority of Gylippus. Together they incouraged the Syracusans, by representing to them, that nothing so daunted an enterprizing people as daring and unexpected enterprize against them. ' The Athenians themselves,' they added, ' had not ' always been a seafaring people: the invading Persians had first forced ' them to become such; nor was there any reason why the Syracusans, ' more prepared for it now than the Athenians then, should not quickly ' even excel them.' Recent good fortune had prepared the Syracusans for incouragement. Having already, under the conduct of Gylippus, succeeded so much beyond their hopes, they were disposed now to carry their hopes high. Accordingly they submitted themselves to his command: thirty-five triremes fit for service lay in the great port, and forty-five in the little port: all were manned by night, while Gylippus led the whole force of infantry toward the Athenian forts at Plemmyrium.

Thucyd. l. 7. c. 22.

At daybreak the stir in the Syracusan fleet became visible to the Athenians, who hastily manned sixty triremes; of which twenty-five were opposed to the thirty-five of the enemy already within the great port, and thirty-five to the forty-five which were advancing to enter it. On the land-side, the watch was so negligent, that the approach of an enemy was neither observed nor looked for, but the whole army made toward the shore to assist the fleet. Gylippus meanwhile, hastening his march, carried the largest of the three forts at the first assault; upon which the other two were immediately abandoned by their garrisons. By this time the fleets were ingaged. Within the great port, the Syracusans had at first the advantage; but their larger division breaking their order in advancing to the attack, were defeated; and then the conquering Athenians, hastening to the relief of their pressed ships,

ships, quickly compelled the other division of the Syracusan fleet to fly.   Eleven Syracusan ships were sunk ; the crews of three were made prisoners ; those of the others, mostly perished.   Three Athenian ships were destroyed.   The Athenians erected a trophy for their naval victory: the Syracusans erected three trophies for the three forts taken.

Thucyd. l. 7. c. 24.

More important tokens of success, however, than any trophies, remained to the Syracusans.   The killed and prisoners in the forts, notwithstanding the numbers that fled, were many : the military chest, all the most valuable effects of the principal officers, large magazines of provisions, most of the stores of both army and fleet, masts for forty triremes, and three complete triremes laid up ashore, were taken.   One of the forts was immediately demolished : garrisons were placed in the other two, and a squadron of triremes was stationed under their protection, to intercept supplies by sea to the Athenian camp ; whither, thenceforward, no vessel could arrive, but by stealth, or by fighting its way.   Notwithstanding therefore their naval victory, the consequences of the late complex action was very seriously disadvantageous to the Athenians ; and while their general, never remarkable for activity, was oppressed with sickness, alarm and despondency began to pervade the armament.

c. 25.

Meanwhile the conduct of the Syracusans, under the able direction of Gylippus and Hermocrates, was all energy.   Twelve triremes, under Agatharchus, a Syracusan, pushing to sea, one went to Peloponnesus with dispatches.   Agatharchus, with the remaining eleven, made the Italian coast, to intercept a fleet of Athenian transports and storeships, of which intelligence had been received, and most of them fell into his hands.   He proceeded then to Caulonia on the Bruttian shore, where he burnt a quantity of navy timber which had been collected for the Athenians.   In his return, meeting at Locri the Thespian auxiliaries destined for Syracuse, he took them aboard his squadron, and made homeward.   One of his triremes was taken by an Athenian squadron stationed at Megara ; the rest arrived safe in the harbour of Syracuse.

Notwithstanding their late naval defeat, Gylippus and Hermocrates

1   resolved

resolved not to give up their purpose of disputing with the Athenians the command of the sea.   Accordingly, to secure their station in the great port, whence they might best annoy the Athenian fleet, they formed before it a kind of rampart of piles.   To prevent the completion of this, and to destroy what was already done, became an important object for the Athenians: The merchantships of the antients, capacious, deep, and firm in the water, like modern vessels for ocean navigation, were much fitter for some purposes of stationary fight than their galleys of war.   A merchantship therefore, of the largest size [13], being fitted with turrets and parapets, was conducted close to the Syracusan rampart; a body of troops aboard annoyed the Syracusan workmen, and drew the attention of the troops appointed to protect them : meanwhile a party in boats fastened ropes about the piles, divers went down and sawed them at the bottom, and thus most of them were hauled up or broken.   To fortify and defend their naval station on one side, and to destroy it on the other, was then for some time the principal object of the two adverse parties; in which, on the side of the Athenians, the skill, activity, and boldness of the people were more observable than the science or vigor of the general.   The Syracusans continued to drive piles, and some in such a manner that, not appearing above water, they were very dangerous to the Athenian boats; yet divers were found, for large rewards, to saw and fasten ropes even to these, so that the labor of the enemy was continually to be renewed; and as the present view of the Athenian general was defence, and to gain time for the arrival of the reinforcement which he expected, his purpose was in a great degree accomplished.

While the Athenian affairs were thus waning in Sicily, Athens itself began to feel severely the consequence of having a Peloponnesian garrison established in the heart of its territory.   In the former invasions a considerable part of the harvest had been consumed or carried off, and the vineyards, orchards, and olive plantations had been destroyed or greatly damaged.   The injury however had not extended over the whole country.   The Lacedæmonian army, for want of magazines, Thucyd. l. 7. c. 27.

[13] Ναῦς μυριοφόρος.

could

could not stay long; and when it was gone, no apprehension remained, during the rest of the year, for what had escaped its ravages: the herds and flocks returned to their pastures, and the owners of the lands might make any use of them that the interval till the next summer would admit. But the garrison of Deceleia kept the whole country, and the city itself, in constant alarm. Its very wants compelled it to exertion: for the troops, little supplied by their cities, were to subsist chiefly by plunder; and the assistance, which they received occasionally from home, was less in money or stores, than in reïnforcements to assist in rapine. The Spartan king Agis, who had led the expedition, and super-intended the construction of the works, remained, after the departure of the rest of the army, as governor of the garrison, and assiduously and ably directed its measures. Not only all produce and revenue from the lands of Attica, with all the herds and flocks which they had maintained, were lost to the Athenians, but more than twenty thou-sand slaves deserted, the greater part mechanics and manufacturers. The Athenian cavalry were to little purpose employed in the endevor to check the ravage and desertion. Many of the horses, the art of shooing that animal being yet unknown, were lamed by unremitted service on rough and rocky ground, some were disabled by wounds, and the rest soon worn down.

Thucyd. l. 7. c. 28.   Among the inconveniencies insuing from the establishment of the enemy in Decéleia, one is mentioned by Thucydides, which marks to a surprising degree the imperfection of antient navigation. The large and fruitful iland of Eubœa was at all times the principal resource to the Athenians for supplying the deficiencies of the scanty and arid soil of Attica. The produce was mostly brought to the port of Oropus,

Chandler's Journey in Greece, and Antonin. Itin.   and thence conveyed by land, along a hilly road of about forty-four miles, to Athens. The nearest, the least hilly, and almost the only practicable road for heavy burdens, passed through Deceleia. The oc-cupying of that post by the enemy therefore made it necessary to carry every thing by sea. With the advantages of modern navigation, this would be incomparably the preferable method; but the cotemporary author assures us that, in that age, the expence of the transport all the

way

way by sea far exceeded that of the old practice[14]. For the rest, we may readily conceive the force and the truth of the concise phrase which Thucydides has used to express the distress of a great city : Instead of a commonwealth, he says, Athens was reduced to the condition of a garrison. Without a territory, it depended upon supplies by sea for subsistence. The whole people were harrassed with military duty, so incessant as to admit little other employment. By day they mounted guard by reliefs ; but for the night, excepting the higher orders who composed the cavalry, none were at any time excused ; those, not immediately wanted for the duty of the ramparts, being required to be in constant readiness with their arms[15]: and this continued through all seasons, during the remainder of the war.

Pressed thus by every inconvenience of a siege at home, such continued to be the zeal of the Athenian people for forein conquest, such the ardor with which they insisted on the prosecution of the siege of Syracuse, a city scarcely inferior to Athens in size or population, that unless it was seen, says the historian, nobody would believe it. Thus indeed, he continues, the expectation of all Greece was strangely disappointed, and the opinion generally entertained, both of the power and of the perseverance of Athens, proved mistaken. The pressure of new evils served but to bring forward new resources. All revenue from Attica, public and private, ceasing, it was necessary to look abroad for augmentation of supplies. A total change was made in the

---

[14] Those less acquainted with the advantages which the arts of modern navigation give to transport by sea, may form some estimate of them from the following circumstances. Much of the trade between London and Canterbury is carried on by water; and Whitstable, six miles from Canterbury, is the port of that city for its communication with the Thames. The passage from London to Whitstable is perhaps eighty miles: but the general charge of carriage is the same for the six miles by land, between Whitstable and Canterbury, as for the eighty by water, between Whitstable and London. Allowance must however be made for the benefit of tides in our narrow seas, which, in the Mediterranean, is little known.

[15] Οἱ μὲν ἐφ᾽ ὅπλοις ποιούμενοι, δι δ᾽ ἐπὶ τοῦ τείχους. The exact value of the phrase ἐφ᾽ ὅπλοις ποιούμενοι, apparently a military phrase of the day, is scarcely now to be ascertained. The explanations attempted by the commentators and translators are very unsatisfactory. For discovering the meaning of Thucydides upon this occasion, the curious reader may however consult another passage of Thucydides, nearly to the same purpose, in the 69th chapter of his eighth book ; and some similar phrases occurring in Xenophon may assist him.

collection of revenue from the subject-states; the antient tribute was abolished, and, instead of it, a tax was imposed, resembling the modern customs; being a twentieth of the value of all imports and exports[16]. Thus light, in comparison of what we have laid upon ourselves, was the heaviest tax, as far as we learn from history, at that time known in the world. _ Yet it caused much discontent among the dependant commonwealths; the arbitrary power by which it was imposed being indeed reasonably execrated, tho the burden itself was comparatively a nothing.

While the Athenians were suffering from the Peloponnesians established in Deceleia, a cruel stroke fell upon their neighbor enemies of Bœotia. The circumstances, little materially connected with the great events of the war, assist however considerably toward a portraiture of the times. Thirteen hundred middle-armed Thracians, hired for the Sicilian expedition, did not arrive till after the fleet under Demosthenes was gone. Means to forward them were not ready, and their pay was burdensome, being an Attic drachma, nearly tenpence sterling ahead, daily. It was resolved therefore to send them home and discharge them; but, by the way, to make any use of them against the enemies of the commonwealth, for which opportunity might offer. The command was committed to Diïtrephes, an Athenian, who, passing through the Euripus, debarked his barbarians on the first hostile shore in his course, that of the Tanagræan territory. Having collected some booty, he hastened to deposit it in the neighboring friendly town of Chalcis in Eubœa, and in the evening again crossed the Euripus

Thucyd.
l. 7. c. 29.

[16] Thucydides, not in the moment aware of the explanation necessary to make this interesting passage clearly intelligible to posterity, for whom professedly he wrote, has expressed himself in his usual close manner, with no other words than these: Τὴν εἰκοσὴν ὑπὸ τὅτον τὸν χρόνον τῶν κατὰ θάλασσαν ἀντὶ τᾅ φόρου τοῖς ὑπακὅοις ἐποίησαν, πλείω νομίζοντες ἄν σφίσι χρήματα ᾅτω προσιέναι. In Duker's edition, the passage is cautiously pointed as it is here given, and neither scholiast nor annotators take any notice of it, farther than to inform of some different readings, which are evidently and grossly bad. The Latin translation runs thus: Per id tempus tributi loco vicessimam mercium, quæ mari vehebantur, populis imperio suo subjectis imperârunt, sperantes se majorem pecuniæ vim hac ratione confecturos. Smith, with whom it is by no means a common fault to be over bold, has ventured, upon this occasion, I think successfully; and tho his authority is not very great, I have been glad to find his support.

for

for farther plunder.   During the night he directed his march toward
Mycalessus, a large and populous Bœotian town, in perfect amity
with Thebes, and at such a distance from the Attic border and from
the sea, that the inhabitants, unaccustomed to fear surprizes, spared
themselves the expence and fatigue both of maintaining complete fortifications, and keeping a regular watch.   Diïtrephes, halting toward
midnight under the shelter of a temple of Mercury, recommenced his
march so as'to reach Mycalessus, only two miles off, about daybreak.
Finding a gate open. and unguarded, his barbarians rushed instantly
to pillage, and massacred as they went, sparing neither sex nor age:
for the Thracians, like most barbarians, says Thucydides, who knew
them from living among them, are commonly bloody-minded in success; insomuch that for sport they would kill even the beasts that fell
in their way.   There was a very large school, in which the boys were
just assembled, when the Thracians broke in, and put every one to
death.   Destruction so unexpected and so complete, continues the
cotemporary historian, scarcely ever fell upon any town.

News of this scene of bloodshed being quickly carried to Thebes, a
body of forces instantly marched; too late to give any relief to the
Mycalessians, but in time to overtake the Thracians.   Those barbarians, who in courage were inferior to none, and in discipline not des-
picable, frequently turning in their retreat, repulsed the Theban cavalry;
and Skirphondas, one of the Bœotarcs, was killed.   They were, however, compelled to abandon all their booty; and when they arrived on
the beach, in the confusion of imbarkation, they suffered greatly;
those unpractised in swimming being indeed without resource; for the
Athenian seamen, little solicitous about such allies, took care to keep
themselves and their vessels out of the reach of the justly inraged
enemy.   About two hundred and fifty Thracians were killed : the rest
were conducted by Diïtrephes to their own country.

Meanwhile Demosthenes, having joined Charicles, was meditating
measures for revenging against Lacedæmon the evils suffered by Athens
from the garrison of Deceleia.   At Nauplia, he took aboard a body of
Argian infantry.   Turning back then upon the Epidaurian coast, he
made a descent and collected some booty.   Having thus ingaged the

Thucyd. l. 7.
c. 30.

c. 26.

3 A 2   enemy's

enemy's attention toward the northern parts of Peloponnesus, he reïmbarked his forces, and proceeding to the Laconian coast, debarked
again overagainst Cythera, as the historian marks the place, where the
temple of Apollo stands. The first business was still plunder, as far as
it could be conveniently extended. A neck of land was then occupied
on which to erect a fort. It was proposed that this should be, on the
eastern side of the country, like Pylus on the western, a place of refuge
for runaway Helots, or any others who might be disposed to live by
rapine on the Laconian lands. Matters being so far settled, Demosthenes proceeded on his voyage. Charicles remained till works
were raised adequate to the protection of a garrison, and then, with
the Argian auxiliaries, returned home.

Demosthenes, arriving at Corcyra, added his personal influence to
the public authority with which he was vested, for collecting reïnforcements among the allies of Athens in western Greece. Naupactus,
Cephallenia, Zacynthus, Alyzia, Anactorium, contributed to strengthen
the armament. At Anactorium he found Eurymedon collecting provisions for Sicily[17], and from him he learnt the unwelcome news that
Plemmyrium was in the hands of the enemy. Nearly at the same time
arrived Conon, now for the first time mentioned in history, who had the
command at Naupactus, and came to request a reïnforcement to his
squadron of eighteen triremes, to inable him to oppose the Corinthian
squadron of twenty-five. The service was thought so important that
ten of the swiftest triremes of the fleet were selected for it, to make his
superiority decisive. Such a request, made by such an officer as Conon,
and granted by such a commander as Demosthenes, shows that the
Athenians had already continued the war too long. Both those officers
were certainly aware that the enemy had improved their naval practice, and that the superiority of the Athenians, experienced in the
actions under Phormion, in the same seas, would be experienced no
more.

[17] Τὰ χρήματα ἄγων τῇ ϛρατιᾶ. Thucyd.
Ἤτοι τα πϱος τϱοφὴν χρήσιμα, καὶ τὰ λοιπὰ
ϲυντείνοντα αὐτοῖς. Schol. This is not the only
occasion on which Thucydides uses the term
χρήματα for necessaries in general. Smith
has translated accordingly; but the Latin
has *pecuniam*, which does not express the
sense intended here.

Demosthenes

Demosthenes and Eurymedon, having prepared everything for the Thucyd. l. 7. c. 33. prosecution of their voyage, crossed the Ionian gulph to the Iapygian promontory. There they stopped to renew the antient alliance of Athens with Artas, a powerful chief of the Iapygian barbarians, through whom they obtained a small reïnforcement of dartmen of the Messapian tribe. From Metapontium, a Grecian town in the neighborhood, three hundred dartmen and two triremes joined them. Proceeding then to Thurium, they found a revolution had taken place there, favorable to their cause: the party friendly to Athens were in possession of the government, and those of their opponents, who had escaped with life, were in banishment. After making such arrangements as they judged most advantageous for the Athenian interest, and obtaining a reïnforcement of seven hundred heavy-armed and three hundred dartmen, they proceeded to the Rhegian port of Petra.

As soon as the Athenian fleet under Demosthenes had clearly quitted c. 34. the Grecian coast, the Corinthian admiral, Polyanthes, resolved upon the bold measure of offering battle, tho with inferior numbers, to the Athenian squadron at Naupactus. He chose his station for the purpose judiciously. It was opposite to Naupactus, in a small bay, on each point of which a body of Peloponnesian infantry was incamped. Thus, in case of being overpowered, his retreat would be short, and protection ready. Nor was this all: Experience had led the Corinthians to improve the construction of their galleys, by strengthening the bows with an addition of timber and metal, which might inable them to resist the destructive shock of the enemy's beak. In the accidental absence, apparently, of Conon, Diphilus commanded the Athenian squadron; and, confident in superior numbers, accepted, perhaps imprudently, the offer of battle thus made by the enemy, on their own coast. After a sharp contest, three Corinthian ships were sunk, but seven Athenian were disabled, through the superior strength of the Corinthian bows. The Corinthians retired, but the Athenians were not in condition for effectual pursuit. The Corinthians therefore erected a trophy; thinking it much, says the historian, not to have been more decisively defeated. The Athenians, on the contrary, tho they remained masters of the wreck, the common criterion of victory, would

erect

erect no trophy; dejected, as by a defeat, not to have been, with superior numbers, more completely victorious.   The enemy's fleet, however, retiring soon after into the harbour of Erineum, and the army
also withdrawing, the Athenians then landed on the Peloponnesian
shore, near the place of action, and erected their trophy.

SECTION   VII.

Affairs in Sicily.   Second Naval Action in the Harbour of Syracuse:
Third Naval Action.   Arrival of Reïnforcement under Demosthenes
and Eurymedon: Attack of Epipolæ: Retreat proposed by Demosthenes,
opposed by Nicias: Secret Negotiation in Syracuse.   Retreat re-
solved: Consequences of an Eclipse of the Moon: Fourth Naval
Action: Distress of the Athenians: Fifth Naval Action.

DURING these transactions in Greece and on the Grecian shores, the
natural consequences of recovered prosperity attended the negotiations,
which Gylippus and Hermocrates were prosecuting in Sicily.   Of the
Grecian cities none remained attached to Athens: Agrigentum alone
persevered in neutrality: even Camarina sent a considerable auxiliary
force to the Syracusans, five hundred heavy-armed, three hundred dartmen, and three hundred bowmen: Gela at the same time furnished
two hundred horse, four hundred dartmen, and two triremes.   Nothing
impeded the march of troops from Camarina and Gela to Syracuse:
but, from the other friendly cities, either the Agrigentine territory
must be traversed, or that of the hostile Sicels; sufferers, or likely to
suffer, on all hands, but readiest in enmity to those with whose
disposition to tyrannize they were most acquainted.   The Agrigentines
resisted all solicitation to allow the passage through their territory: it
was thought unadvisable to exasperate so powerful a people by any
attempt to force the way, and the road through the Sicel country
was therefore taken.   Nicias, informed of what was going forward,
and roused by misfortune and danger, took, upon this occasion, the

Thucyd. l. 7.
c. 32, 33.

                                                       measures

measures which policy would dictate. At his instance the Sicels, forming an ambuscade, attacked the auxiliaries on their march, and killed
eight hundred : fifteen hundred nevertheless reached Syracuse,

Intelligence arriving of the formidable reïnforcement coming from
Athens, under an experienced, enterprizing and successful general,
Gylippus and Hermocrates determined to use the opportunity, yet remaining, for attempting a decisive blow against the decayed, dispirited,
and already half-conquered armament of Nicias. They, like the Corinthians, had learned, from experience, the deficiencies of their triremes,
and of their manner of naval action, and they adopted nearly the same
idea of improvement. The Athenians, confined within the great port,
five or six English miles only in circuit[18], could profit little from
the swiftness of their galleys, and their skill in evolution. They could
not easily find room to attack with the transverse or oblique stroke,
with which they had heretofore been so formidable[19]: under necessity
of meeting prow to prow, the strengthened bows of the Syracusan vessels
would have the advantage. They could not press out to sea, through
the narrow mouth of the harbour, without exposing a part of their fleet
to certain destruction ; and the shore would afford them but scanty
refuge, being mostly occupied by the enemy. The Syracusans, incouraged by these considerations, which were explained by their able
commanders, prepared with new confidence for action. All being
ready, before the fleet moved, Gylippus drew out the landforces. Those
in the city, and those in Olympieium, marched at the same time toward
opposite sides of the Athenian camp, and ingaged the whole attention
of the commanders with a false attack. This feint taking full effect,
the fleet, consisting of eighty triremes, advanced toward the Athenian
naval station. The Athenians, in alarm and confusion, hastily manned

After 16 July.

Thucyd. l. 7. c. 37.

---

[18] Strabo, according to our copies, makes
it eighty stadia; perhaps an error of transcribers. Swinburne calls it rather more
than five miles. Trav. in Sic. p. 343. v. 2.
And another English and a Swiss traveller,
both habituated to accurate observation,
being separately asked, told me they reckoned it, by recollection, between four and six
English miles.

[19] ——Λεπ]ὰ τὰ πρώραθεν ἰχύσας (τὰς τῶι
'Αθηναίων ναῦς) διὰ τὸ μὴ ἀνliπρώροις μᾶλλον
ἀυ]ὺς ἢ ἰκ περίπλου ταῖς ἰμβολαῖς χρῆσθαι.
Thucyd. l. 7. c. 36.

seventy-

seventy-five triremes and met them. The contest was long: two Athenian triremes were sunk; but the fleets parted without any great advantage gained on either side.

Thucyd. l. 7. c. 38.

Next day the Syracusans did not move. But no incouragement arose hence to the Athenians. They felt that they had lost the superiority by sea, as well as by land; and they concluded that the enemy would not long rest satisfied with the progress already made. Nicias therefore directed his principal attention to the security of his fleet. He had already formed a stockade in the water, for the defence of his naval station. In front of this, at convenient distances, he now moored large merchant ships, of the kind called holcades, much loftier as well as deeper than the galleys of war. In these were placed machines bearing instruments of vast weight, called dolphins; so suspended, over the sea, that they might be dropped on any vessel passing near, and with such violence as to sink it. Behind these floating fortresses, any of his ships, pressed in action, might find shelter, with means to return with advantage against an enemy, bold enough to pursue them so far.

c. 39, 40, 41.

The Syracusans did not disappoint the expectation of the Athenian general. The very next morning their land and sea-forces moved at once toward his camp and naval station ; but the serious attack, as before, was on the fleet. As before, also, much of the day was consumed in fruitless contest. At length Ariston, a Corinthian, esteemed the best seaman[20] in the Syracusan fleet, conferring with his collegues in command, advised a measure, judicious in their circumstances, tho, in the authentic description of Thucydides, it marks great deficiency, both in the ships of war of the Greeks, and in their military and naval economy.

Ch. 13. s. 3. of this Hist.

We have heretofore observed a Corinthian fleet, when going to seek an enemy, taking three days provision aboard. But it appears that when immediate action was expected, as on the present occasion, the general practice was to leave everything but their arms in their naval camp; not incumbering themselves ashipboard with a single meal. Toward midday, in pursuance of the advice of Ariston, the Syracusans retreated, but in perfect order, toward their naval

20 "Αριστος ὢν κυβερνήτης.

station

station. The Athenians, fatigued with unavailing contest, did not pursue. The Syracusans, on reaching the shore, found a market of eatables provided. The magistrates, in consequence of notice from the naval commanders, had compelled all persons in the city to send whatever provisions they had ready, and the crews debarking, took hasty refreshment.

Meanwhile the Athenians, retreating to their naval camp, had dispersed, expecting no interruption of leisure for their meal; when suddenly they perceived the Syracusan fleet approaching again in order of battle. With much tumult, and mostly without refreshment, they hastened aboard, and the action was renewed. But it was no longer equally maintained, as before. The strengthened bows of the Syracusan galleys, through management improved by experience, damaged several of the Athenian: the numerous dartmen on the Syracusan decks plied their weapons efficaciously; and practice in that manner of naval ingagement, which the confinement of the port required, had given the Syracusan leaders to imagine a new mode of annoying an enemy, who, like the Athenians, depended chiefly on the skill of their rowers and the shock of the beak. Dartmen in boats, venturing under the quarters, and even under the lateral galleries of the Athenian galleys, gave more annoyance to their seamen than even the dartmen on the decks [21]. Seven Athenian ships being sunk, several others much damaged,

Thucyd. l. 7. c. 40.

[21] Πολὺ δ' ἔτι μεῖζω οἱ ἐν τοῖς λεπτοῖς πλοίοις περιπλέονlες τῶν Συρακυσίων, καί ἔς τε τὲς ταρσὲς ὑποπίπlονlες τῶν πολεμίων νεῶν, καὶ ἐς τα πλάγια παραπλέονlες, καὶ ἐξ αὐlῶν ἐς τὲς ναύτας ακονlίζοντες. This is a passage for which little assistance is to be expected from translators and commentators. An attentive examination of an antique piece of sculpture in the Vatican museum at Rome, mentioned in a former note, assisting the idea furnished by general Melvill, first gave me to imagine I understood it. I doubt however if the version given in the text may carry with it sufficiently its own explanation. I suppose the lateral galleries of the galleys to have been open at bottom, or at most to have had only gratings; their purpose having been, as I imagine, only to give projection and purchase to the upper oars. A parapet, raised on them, protected the rowers in a great degree against missile weapons from the decks of the enemy's galleys, but the open or grated bottom gave passage for weapons from boats underneath.

I am sorry to have to say that Winkelman's description of the piece of sculpture in question, and the ingraving he has given of it, are both very erroneous. Equally the antiquarian and the artist have been evidently ignorant of what a ship or a boat should be or could be. Yet Winkelman flattered himself with the imagination

damaged, and the crews of all weakened with fasting, fatigue, and
wounds, the whole fleet sought the shelter of their floating fortresses,
So far the Syracusans pursued, and three of their ships, elate with success, pushed within them; but two were sunk, and the other was taken
with her whole crew.   The rest retired, satisfied with the success of the
day, and confirmed in opinion that they were now superior, by sea as
well as by land, to that enemy from whom they had so lately apprehended subjugation.   It was therefore unanimously resolved, at the
earliest opportunity, to renew the attack on both elements.

Thucyd. I. 7.
c. 42.
End of July.
In the short and critical interval, between the resolution taken
and the proposed execution, Demosthenes and Eurymedon arrived,
with a fleet of seventy-three triremes, five thousand regular heavy-
armed infantry, and a greater number of bowmen, dartmen, and
slingers; so that, including the attending slaves, the landforce alone
would approach twenty thousand men.   Alarm and astonishment now
returned with double force upon the Syracusans.   They were assured
that Attica itself was in the possession of an enemy; and it appeared
an unaccountable paradox, that, so pressed at home, the Athenians
should send out such a force to make forein conquest; a force in all
points equal to that which Nicias had first led to Sicily.   The power of
Athens, says the historian, thus appeared stupendous, its resources
beyond calculation, and their own danger consequently endless.

Demosthenes, having landed his forces, viewed his ground, and
received the information that Nicias and his officers could give,
formed his opinion of the business before him, and decided on the
measures proper to be taken, with that cool and just judgement, which
might be expected from an officer who, to considerable talents, joined
his extensive experience.   Powerful as the junction with Nicias made
the armament under their command, and much as it struck sudden
terror into the enemy, Demosthenes did not flatter himself with certain
success.   In his younger days he had been enterprizing, even to rash-

that he had discovered, in this monument, or
perhaps in the incorrect drawing of it, which
he contemplated in his closet, a solution of
that difficulty, which the antients, in all
their accounts, have left for us, how their
ships of war were rowed. A man who never
himself pulled an oar, will in such an
attempt hardly avoid absurdity.

ness·

ness.   Now, in mature age, undazzled by the near view of glorious
conquest, unawed by the apprehension of popular rage, neither the hope
of profit, nor the prospect of fame, nor the fear of a tyrannical multitude could move him from what he thought the welfare of his country
required.   The safety of the Sicilian army was not to be staked against
any hope of conquest: the gain would be a precarious advantage to the
commonwealth, the loss almost certain ruin.   His first resolution therefore was to avoid the error of Nicias, losing opportunity by delay: his
next, to fix upon some one undertaking, in which success might be in
some degree decisive, and failure not fatal: and finally he determined,
that should such a first attempt be defeated, it would be improper to
risk farther so large a portion of the strength of the commonwealth,
and, whatever indignation he might incur from the Athenian people,
he would lead the armament home.

Upon this occasion Thucydides sufficiently declares his opinion, that,
with able and spirited conduct in the outset, the conquest of Syracuse
might have been effected by the Athenian arms.   Had Nicias, he says,
instead of wasting almost a year in little enterprize, gone at once against
that city, he might have completed his contravallation.   The Syracusans, at first, confident in their own numbers, did not even think of
desiring assistance from Peloponnesus; and they might have been put
beyond means of relief, before any effectual assistance could arrive.
Circumstances were now very different; but to accomplish the purpose
of the expedition seemed not yet beyond hope.   The Athenian force
was clearly superior in the field.   The principal obstacles to the progress
of the siege were the enemy's counterwork intersecting the line of the
contravallation, and their possession of Epipolæ.   Demosthenes observed that the counterwork was only a single wall, without defence
behind; so that possession of Epipolæ would give him possession of
the counterwork.   He therefore judged that the assault of Epipolæ
would be the best criterion; its success or its failure would best determine, whether the siege of Syracuse should be vigorously prosecuted,
or abandoned without delay.

The account of Thucydides may give to suppose, tho it does not
directly express, that the ideäs of Demosthenes did not exactly meet
3 B 2   those

those of Nicias. The consideration that the reïnforcement had restored superiority in the field, seems to have led to the first measure
taken, which was to ravage the country beyond the Anapus.   In this,
apparently, a double object was proposed.   Possibly the enemy might
be provoked to risk a battle; of all things, perhaps, for the Athenians,
the most desirable.   Should they avoid it, the Athenian army, beside
being gratified with booty, would derive incouragement from the
experienced acknowlegement of their superiority.   Nothing opposed
them : the cavalry and light troops from Olympieium only attempted
some desultory annoyance, with little effect.   The next attempt, which
was against the counterwork, was unfortunate.   The machines were
burned by the enemy, and every attack repelled.   Demosthenes then
insisted that his proposed assault of Epipolæ should be no longer delayed; and Nicias and the other principal officers acceded to the
measure.

Thucyd. l. 7.
c. 43.

Apparently Nicias was at this time too infirm to take any active
part in a business which might require great exertion.   Under the
command therefore of Demosthenes, Eurymedon and Menander, the
whole army, except a small guard for the works, was ordered for the
duty : provisions for five days were carried, and the engineers and artificers attended, to form defences in the instant of getting possession
of the ground.   To attack, however, otherwise than by surprize, so
great a force, in a post so strong by nature and by art, was deemed unadvisable.   Night was therefore chosen for the purpose : the army
moved, as Thucydides describes the hour, about the first sleep.
Ascending by the way of Euryelus, they passed the first Syracusan
post unperceived.   Surprizing then a small outwork, they put part of
the guard to the sword : but the greater part, escaping, alarmed the
camps in Epipolæ.   These were three : the Sicilian allies formed one;
the allies from Greece another; and a third was composed of Syracusans : Gylippus himself commanded.   All was quickly in motion to
oppose the assailants : but the Athenian van, led by Demosthenes, repulsed the first troops they met, and continued mounting the hill, while
those who followed demolished the fort taken.   Attacks were renewed
by Gylippus, but still unsuccessfully : the Athenians pushed forward,
but,

but, in confidence now of success, hastening to complete the acquisition of the enemy's works, they grew more careless of their order.   In this state the Bœotians, who were among the allies of Syracuse, met, and checked them.   Among a large body of men, confined within narrow space, on rough ground, and by night, confusion once arising, spred rapidly.   To communicate commands was difficult; and, tho the moon shone bright, yet when established arrangements were once disturbed, it was no longer easy to distinguish friends from foes.   The repulsed Athenians, meeting those yet advancing, were received with pointed spears   This occasioned frequent and clamorous passing of the word; which thus became known to the enemy, and of course useless or even prejudicial to themselves.   But beyond all things the pæanism, the song or shout of battle, which the Greeks always used in the moment previous to attack, increased the confusion: for that of the allies of Athens of Doric race, Argians, Corcyræans, and others, being the same with the Syracusan, alarmed the Athenians wherever they heard it; and as disorder extended, the troops of the Athenian army, in several parts, fought oneanother.   At length all took to flight.   The only road for retreat was narrow; the fugitives were numerous; and hastening to avoid the pursuers swords, many perished by falling down precipices.   Of the more fortunate, who gained the plain, those who had served under Nicias, acquainted with the country, easily reached their camp or lines; but some of the newly arrived, missing their way, were next day cut off by the Syracusan horse.

The morrow was a day of mourning to the Athenians, as of triumph to the Syracusans.   The dead were restored to the defeated, through the usual ceremonies.   Thucydides does not specify the number[22]; he says it was considerable, but not so great as the number of shields taken would have given to suppose; because those who fled over the precipices disincumbered themselves of their armour; and, tho many perished, some escaped.   The Syracusans erected two trophies; one at

---

[22] Plutarch states it at the round sum of two thousand. Diodorus, always struggling to give celebrity to the deeds of his fellow-countrymen, calls it two thousand five hundred. Later writers however are not likely to have had information. which Thucydides could not obtain.

the

the beginning of the ascent of Epipolæ; the other, on the spot where
the Bœotians made the first effectual resistance.

Every circumstance appeared now to require that the Athenian
generals should quickly enter upon some new plan.   The armament
was sickly, partly from the season, partly from the marshy and unwholesome ground on which it was incamped; and the hope of soon
reducing Syracuse, or indeed of at all reducing it, seemed frustrated.
Demosthenes therefore warmly urged his opinion, before given, that
due experiment having been made and having failed, all purpose of
conquest in Sicily should be at once abandoned, and the armament
conducted home.   Not the necessities of their own situation, he said,
more than the wants and distresses of the commonwealth required the
measure; insomuch that it would be inexcusable farther to risk so
great a portion of the public strength, and continue such waste of the
public revenue, on what was comparatively an unimportant object.
Thucydides very seldom declares, in direct terms, an opinion by which
the character of his cotemporary might be affected.   It is however
easy to perceive that he approved, upon the whole, both the advice
and the conduct of Demosthenes, as, for his country's welfare judicious, for himself disinterested and manly.   It is not equally easy to
discover his opinion of the conduct of Nicias: perhaps he was unable
to determine his own judgement of it.   Nicias positively refused to
lead the armament home.   'The temper of the Athenian people,' he said,
' is well known to me: warm in expectation, and jealous of their
' authority, they will highly resent a measure so disappointing to their
' hopes, unauthorized by their decree.   Our conduct, then, let it be
' recollected, must be submitted to the judgement, and our fate must
' be decided by the vote, not of those who have seen and who know
' what we know, but of those who will be persuaded of anything by
' any eloquent accuser.   Even of those now under our command, of
' those now loudest in complaint of the evils they are suffering, some,
' nay many, will unsay their assertions, blame the abandoning of the
' expedition, impute corruption to their generals, and perhaps become
' our accusers, or at least join in the vote for our condemnation.   I
' therefore, if I am brought to the alternative, will not risk a shameful
      1   ' death

' death from the injustice of my fellowcitizens, to avoid an honorable
' death from the valor of the enemy.   But I think we are not yet so
' straitened.   Ill as the face of our affairs appears, I well know the
' condition of the Syracusaus is worse.   In some points, they are un-
' der great difficulties ; in others, reduced to absolute inability.   They
' are ruined by their expences.   Two thousand talents, already con-
' sumed upon their auxiliary forces and their fleet, have not sufficed:
' they.have besides incurred a large debt.   Their fleet therefore they
' cannot long maintain ; and on the least failure of payment, their
' auxiliaries will abandon them.   We are under no equal difficulty;
' and on these considerations I hold it utterly improper to give up
' the enterprize.'

Such were the sentiments of Nicias, delivered in the council of war.
But, beside his extreme horror of the prospect of living under the
Athenian democracy, with credit so impaired as it must have been by
relinquishing the enterprize, he had reasons for his perseverance which
he did not communicate.   There were among the Syracusans some
who, as their fellowcitizens of the opposite party were to them the most
odious and most dreadful of enemies, wished well to the Athenian
arms.   These communicated secretly with Nicias; they informed him Thucyd. l. 7.
accurately of the state of things in the city ; they urged him to perse- c. 48. & 49.
vere in the siege; and they incouraged him to hope, that the very
distress of the enemy and the zeal of his secret friends, with little exertion on his part, would give him still to return home conqueror of
Syracuse.

Demosthenes, uninformed of this negotiation, was unable to com- c. 49.
prehend the conduct of Nicias; and he strenuously insisted that, if
they must wait for a decree of the people to authorize their return
home, yet the army ought immediately to move from ground so un-
healthy, and still more the fleet from that confined situation, in which
it could not come to action but under the grossest disadvantage.
Eurymedon concurred with him; but Nicias still opposing, deference
to his rank, together with the supposition, and perhaps intimation,
that he might have intelligence unknown to them, occasioned a
suspension of measures, and the armament remained in its station.

Unexpected

Unexpected success had now prepared the Syracusans for any exertion. But Gylippus and Hermocrates would not omit to profit from that credit which grows with prosperity. Information arrived that factions were violent in Agrigentum; and it was hoped that assistance, critically given, might put the party friendly to Syracuse in possession of the government. Accordingly Sicanus was sent thither, with fifteen triremes; but, on his arrival, he found matters accommodated between the contending parties, and the moment of opportunity lost. Gylippus himself was in the mean time more successful in a journey, which he undertook into the Sicel country. Besides collecting a considerable force among the barbarians, he was joined by a body of Peloponnesians, who, to avoid the Athenian fleet, had made the coast of Africa, and thence crossed to Selinus; and he led the whole, without opposition, into Syracuse.

Meanwhile the Athenian armament, dispirited by disappointment, was also weakening daily by sickness. Intelligence, that Gylippus had introduced a powerful reïnforcement within the Syracusan lines, excited new apprehension, and Demosthenes and Eurymedon regretted their concession to their elder college. Nicias at length was persuaded, yet scarcely persuaded, to give the sanction of his consent to the retreat of the armament. He deprecated any public decision of such a measure by that open manner of voting, which, in pursuance of the democratical principle, was the general practice of the Athenian military[23]; and orders were given, with cautious privacy, for the fleet and army to prepare for quitting their station. All was accordingly ready, when the full moon was suddenly darkened. None had then science to foresee the regular return of that phenomenon; few could be persuaded that the cause was in the order of nature. It struck the armament with terror, as a portent boding ill to their purpose: application was made to the generals, deprecating the intended march: the augurs and soothsayers declared that, to bring the heavenly powers

Thucyd. l. 7. c. 46.

c 50.

27 Aug.

---

[23] Μὴ φανερῶς γι ἀξιῶν ψηφίζεσθαι. We want explanation of this phrase, which the commentators and translators do not give. Thucydides has written for those who knew the common forms of proceeding on such occasions in his age, without thinking of the explanation that posterity might need.

again

again to a friendly aspect, required a delay of thrice nine days; and Nicias, more superstitious than the rest, affirmed that, till that period was completed, he would not even consult about removal.

There seems to have been nothing in this omen to persuade the Athenians, more than the Syracusans, that the illboding regarded them.   On the contrary, Plutarch gravely imputes to the augurs ignorance in their profession; they ought, he says, to have known that an eclipse portended rather the favor of the gods to those whose purpose was retreat.   Plutarch apparently must have had a low opinion of the power or of the goodness of the gods, which did not make a signal of favor intelligible, or did not dispose the favored to a just confidence in such a signal.   But omens of undecided import, such is the nature of superstitious fear, commonly were taken as unfavorable by those in adverse circumstances.   On the other hand, the knowlege that the Athenians held themselves to be the objects of the divine displeasure portended, sufficed for the Syracusans to derive incouragement from the portent.   They were confident of superiority by land; they considered the intention of secret retreat as proof of fear to stand a battle.   They resolved therefore not to allow the enemy to establish themselves anywhere in Sicily, by which the war might be drawn into length, but to attack them by sea and land in their present situation, and by their total destruction to deter future invasion.

Plut. vit.
Nic.

Thucyd. l. 7.
c. 51.

Such being the purpose, the able leaders directed their attention, for some days, to exercise their people in whatever they judged most necessary to success in naval action.   Giving then the seamen a day of rest, they led out the infantry, and they gained some small advantage over a body of Athenians, horse and foot, who advanced against them[24]. On the next day they proposed their great attack.   Accordingly

c. 52.

---

[24] Dodwell has been, I think, not successful in the calculation of days from the eclipse forward, and the endevor to assign to each its circumstances.   He has given either not due attention, or not due credit, to the narrative of Thucydides, which, without such minute accuracy, is consistent and clear.   With regard to the delay required by the augurs, whether there has or has not been the corruption of the text of Thucydides supposed by Dodwell, is little important, but Plutarch's account agrees with the common reading.

Vol. II.   3 C   seventy-

seventy-six triremes moved from the naval station, and the whole landforce advanced toward the Athenian lines. The Athenians, superior by
ten triremes, met their fleet. Eurymedon, who commanded the right,
to use that advantage which superiority of numbers gave, stretched
away with a view to surround the left of the enemy. The center spreading, to obviate the danger of too great an interval between the divisions, weakened itself by making the intervals too great between
ship and ship. In this state it was attacked by the enemy in close order,
and presently defeated. The Syracusans then directing their principal
effort against the division of Eurymedon, now cut off from the rest of
the fleet, took, destroyed, or drove aground every ship, and Eurymedon
himself was killed. The left wing, thus wholly without support, fled,
pursued, to the shore. Such is the brief account which Thucydides
gives of this important action; as if feeling too much to relate in
detail a defeat, for its consequences, so deplorable, and the first, of
any importance, which his country ever suffered at sea from an
inferior force. With his usual tenderness for characters, he names
neither Nicias nor Demosthenes; and expresses no opinion, nor imputes
any blame, otherwise than by omission.

Thucyd. l. 7. c. 53. Gylippus, while no part of the landforces were yet ingaged, observed
from the shore the distress of the Athenian fleet, and many of the ships
forced aground beyond the protection of their stockade and their
camp. Immediately he detached a body of infantry to intercept any
of the crews that might fly, and to overpower those who might attempt
to defend their stranded vessels against the victorious Syracusans.
The Tuscan allies were the nearest troops of the Athenian line. The
Syracusan detachment, elate with the success of their fleet, approached
in disorderly haste. The Tuscans, by a vigorous assault, conducted
with regularity, put them to flight. Gylippus sent reinforcement; but
assistance coming also from the Athenian camp, the Athenians finally
prevailed, with some slaughter of the enemy's heavy-armed, and they
saved most of the stranded ships. The Syracusans however took
eighteen, and of these the whole crews perished. An attempt was
made to destroy the Athenian fleet, within its stockade, by a fireship.

1   The

The wind favored the design, but the practised skill of the Athenian Thucyd. l. 7. c. 54.
seamen rendered it ineffectual.   The Syracusan fleet then retired, and
each party erected its trophy : the Syracusans for their naval victory,
the Athenians for their success by land.

But the event of the naval action, so contrary to all hope founded on
former experience, was a disaster so momentous, and so little balanced
by the better fortune of the landforces, that the deepest dejection
pervaded the Athenian armament.   On the other hand, the Syracusans
began to consider themselves no longer as an oppressed people, struggling in the almost hopeless defence of everything dear to them ; they
looked forward to success that might intitle them vanquishers of Athens, c. 56. & 59.
and vindicators of the liberties of Greece.   Accordingly they applied
themselves immediately to blockade the port ; desirous now to prevent
the departure of that force, from which they had expected the worst
evils of subjugation ; and proposing no less than to destroy, or reduce
to the dreadful condition of prisoners at discretion, the whole of that
formidable fleet and army.

Meanwhile not dejection only, from a sense of disgrace, and appre- c. 60.
hension of the swords of their enemies, but the most urgent of wants
pressed the Athenians.   In consequence of the resolution taken to raise
the siege (no suspicion being entertained that the enemy could prevent
their departure by sea) they had forbidden farther supplies of provisions from Catana.   Naval superiority lost, the means of intercourse
with Catana were gone ; and thus the desire to depart was inforced, as
the means were rendered precarious.   A council of war was called to
consider of these untoward circumstances ; and the taxiarcs, officers
nearly of the rank of colonels in our service, were summoned to assist
the generals with their advice.   The result of the deliberation was a
resolution to withdraw the whole armament by sea.   This being determined, the subordinate resolutions followed, to use all possible means
for strengthening the fleet ; and, with this view, to abandon immediately
their extensive line of contravallation, and reduce their works to a
single fort near the naval station, large enough only to contain the
baggage and sick, with a competent garrison.   But naval action now,
far different from that in open sea, where they had been long ac-

3 C 2   customed

customed to a decisive superiority, must be unavoidably similar to that
in which they had already yielded to inferior numbers.   Thus late

Thucyd. 1. 7.
c. 62.
therefore, taught by severe experience, they proposed to prepare accordingly.   Upon this subject the advice of the masters[25] of the triremes
was required.   The lightness of the vessel, a quality necessary to swift-
rowing, and, in open sea, of inestimable advantage within the harbour of
Syracuse would little avail.   On the contrary, to be able to maintain a
stationary fight, as between infantry ashore, was of principal importance.   It was therefore resolved that every man capable of bearing
arms, beyond the necessary garrison of the fort, should be taken aboard;
that numerous bowmen, with the ablest dartmen, particularly the
Acarnanian, should be stationed on the decks; and that, on the prows,
grappling-irons should be fixed, which might at once obviate the shock
of the enemy's stronger bows, and, preventing their retreat, give opportunity for their own numerous heavy-armed to act.   Pursuant to
these resolutions, about a hundred and ten triremes were equipped and

c. 65.
manned.

The bustle of preparation in the Athenian naval camp was observed by
the Syracusans, and intelligence reached them of the grappling-irons with
which the Athenian prows were armed.   Gylippus and Hermocrates,
tho they could not equip eighty triremes, nevertheless determined to pursue the contest, so far successful, for naval superiority.   Against the
new mode of action proposed by the Athenians, they thought it necessary to prepare; but for this it was held sufficient to cover the forecastles
of their triremes with bull-hides, on which the grappling-irons would

c. 69.
not readily take any firm hold.

While the animation of the Syracusans and their confederates seconded
the spirit of their leaders, among the Athenians, notwithstanding the
great superiority of their naval force, a general dejection prevailed.
The discouragement, arising from the late naval defeats, was proportioned
to the former confidence in the opinion, supported by long experience,
of their decided superiority.   But as the spirits of those under his command sunk, the animation, and indeed the whole character of Nicias

[25] Κυβιρνῆται.

seemed

seemed to rise.   His behavior on the occasion was truly great.   Little ambitious, under favoring fortune rather deficient in exertion, and sometimes culpably remiss in his command, his activity and animation increased as evils pressed and dangers threatened.   None was now so warm in exhortation, that might restore the drooping courage of the soldiers and seamen.   The state of his health did not permit him to take the command ashipboard: but he was sedulous in attending the necessary preparation, and directing every arrangement.   When all was ready for the proposed attempt, thinking, says the historian, he had not yet said so much for the incouragement of his officers and people as the singular importance of the occasion demanded, he went around the whole armament; and speaking to each trierarc separately, after mentioning their superiority in numbers, and the measures taken for resisting the enemy's novel mode of attack, he exhorted every one, by his own glory, and by that inherited from his ancestors, to exert himself in the battle to insue.   Leading then the whole to the shore, he there committed them to Demosthenes, Menander, and Euthydemus, under whose orders they embarked, and moved immediately to the harbour's mouth to force the egress.

The enemy, who carefully watched their motions, quickly made toward them, under the Corinthian Python, and Sicanus and Agatharchus, Syracusans; the Corinthian commanding the center, the Syracusans the wings.   With the first shock the Athenians made themselves masters of the vessels that blockaded the mouth of the port, and were hastening to unmoor them and clear the passage, when the Syracusans approached, and a most obstinate battle insued.   Thucyd. l. 7. c. 70.

Meanwhile the Athenian army stood on the shore, observing with the most anxious attention what passed, within such a distance that they could see and hear almost everything.   When therefore after a long contest, with various fortune at times in various parts, the advantage of the Syracusans become decisive, and the whole Athenian fleet fled pursued, then grief, indignation and dismay (says the eloquent historian, at a loss for words equal to the description) rose to the utmost pitch that any circumstances could produce in the human mind, since none could be more hopeless.

Entering

Thucyd. l. 7.
c. 73.
Entering little into detail, and not at all accounting for the event of this disasterous battle, Thucydides proceeds to describe the consequences. The dejection that pervaded the defeated armament was so extreme, and the danger impending so urgent, that the sacred dues of the dead, objects commonly of such anxious attention, were totally neglected ; no herald was sent to request the restitution of the bodies, no care was taken about their burial, but every thought was absorbed in the evils that pressed, and the perils that threatened, the living. Amid the general despair, however, Demosthenes did not lose his usual energy of mind.   Going to Nicias, he proposed what might still have saved the greater part of the forces.   Sixty triremes remained to the Athenians : those of the enemy, tho victorious, were reduced to fifty. He thought it therefore very possible still to force the passage out to sea, if, imbarking that very night, they made the attempt at daybreak. Nicias approved, but the crews absolutely refused.   ' To retreat,' they peevishly remonstrated, ' was áll the generals wanted ; they would go ' anywhere by land, and fight their way, if necessary ; but by sea the ' experience of the past sufficiently proved that they could expect ' nothing but destruction.' The execution of the salutary measure was thus prevented by excess of discouragement.

S E C T I O N   VIII.

Retreat of the Athenians from Syracuse.

c. 73.
GYLIPPUS and the Syracusan chiefs, on considering the advantages which their last success gave them, became more than ever desirous to prevent the departure of the enemy : the Syracusans, by the complete destruction of the invading armament, would deter future invasion ; and Gylippus hoped, in effect, to conquer Athens itself in Sicily. The opinion was general in Syracuse, and it justified the proposal of Demosthenes, that the Athenians would now think only of retreat by land, and it was supposed they would move that very night. But
the

the Syracusan people, wearied with the labor of the day and exhilarated with its success, were more eager to injoy the leisure, which they had so well earned, than solicitous about any future events.   It happened too that the morrow was the festival of Hercules.   Among such an assemblage of people of Dorian race, and on such an occasion, the desire of duly celebrating the day of a hero-god, with whom they esteemed themselves so connected, became irresistible; and nothing could presuade them to quit the religious revel for nocturnal military enterprize. Hermocrates, who had been at'first most urgent for marching immediately to intercept the Athenians, knew his fellowcitizens and mankind too well to attempt, in such circumstances, to force inclination: but his fruitful genius provided still a resource for the attainment of his purpose. In the evening, some persons under his direction went on horseback to the Athenian camp; and approaching enough to be heard, when they could be little distinctly seen, pretended they were of the party which had been accustomed to communicate with Nicias.   Finding credit so far, they charged those whom they had ingaged in conversation, to go and tell the general, ' that the passes were already ' occupied by the Syracusans, and that he would therefore do well not ' to move that night, but wait and concert his measures.'   The fatal Thucyd. l. 7. bait was taken, and the next day was spent by the Athenians in c. 74. various preparation for the march.

But Gylippus and Hermocrates, having yielded in the moment to the wishes of their people, found means, before the morrow ended, to ingage them in their own views.   Their victorious fleet went to the Athenian naval station, and no opposition being attempted, they carried off, or burnt on the spot, every ship there.   The army at the same time marched out, under the conduct of Gylippus, and occupied all the principal passes around the Athenian camp, and in that line of country which the Athenians would probably propose to traverse.

On the next day[26], every thing being prepared, as far as circumstances would permit, orders were issued by the Athenian generals for c. 75.

[26] The third from the naval action, according to the phrase of Thucydides, and the usual manner of reckoning of the Greeks; who counted the day itself of an action first, the next day as second, and so forth.

marching.

marching.   The pen of Thucydides and the language of Athens are wanting, to describe adequately the scene presenting itself upon that occasion; when, in the bitterness of antient warfare, every horror offered itself to expectation, that the human body can suffer or the human mind conceive.   No light distress arose from the reflection, that, instead of fulfilling the lofty hopes of their enterprize, the whole of so powerful a fleet was destroyed; that, through their failure, ruin threatened their country; and that, instead of returning, as they had so lately with reason expected, conquerors of Sicily, an ignominious flight was their only, and that almost a hopeless resource, for avoiding slavery or death.   But, in the circumstances of that flight, many dreadful considerations, many lamentable objects, presented them-selves, striking home to the feelings of every individual.   The dead lay yet unburied; and the recollection, or, in many instances, the sight, of a relation or a friend so neglected, struck not only with grief but with horror.   Yet the voices and the actions of the many living, whom wounds or sickness disabled for the march, their complaints, their ex-postulations, their prayers, their embraces, and the painful, yet fruitless endevors of some to follow their friends, were still more distressing than the compunction which arose from the neglect, impious as it was deemed, but so far excusable as it was unavoidable, of the still and silent dead.   Mutual reproach then, and self-reproach, for that share which any had had in superinducing or inhancing the public calamity, whether by promoting the enterprize, or by obstructing the retreat, occasionally aggravated the bitterness of woe.   Such, in short, says the historian, was the accumulated weight of present misery, that it threw the whole multitude into tears; and, absorbing the apprehension of farther danger, took away almost the desire, and even the power to move.

At length the march commencing, resembled that of a whole city flying from a besieging army.   This is the remark of the cotemporary historian, drawing a comparison from among those circumstances which distinguish antient from modern times.   For the numbers, he continues, including attendants, were not less than forty thousand. Attendants however were of little importance: mostly slaves, they

deserted

deserted openly; and in the instant of the army's moving, the greater part disappeared. Thus even the cavalry and the heavy-armed were reduced to carry their own provisions and necessaries; some being without attendants, some mistrusting those who remained to them: and the small portion of provisions they possessed demanded every care, since it was far from being equal to their probable wants.

Amid the extreme dejection and anguish, not without reason per- Thucyd. l. 7. vading the armament, Nicias wonderfully supported the dignity of c. 76. his character and situation. Individually the distress of the existing circumstances appeared not to affect him; his only anxiety seemed to be to relieve that of others, and to diffuse incouragement among all. The historian's authority for the remarkable words he attributes to him on the occasion, tho not stated, certainly might be good: but whether we consider them as conveying the sentiments of Nicias or of Thucydides, they are highly interesting, as they mark the opinion entertained of the divine providence, by a man of exalted rank, of extensive information and experience, just and religiously disposed, but never taught to consider this life as a state of probation, and to expect, in futurity, the reward of good or the punishment of evil deeds. From the head of the line, according to Thucydides, exerting his voice to the utmost, that he might be heard as extensively as possible, Nicias, with an unruffled countenance, desired the troops to advert to his c. 77. own case: 'I,' he said, 'am in body (you may see indeed the state ' to which sickness has reduced me) very far from being the strongest ' among you. In the blessings of high fortune I was once inferior to ' none: but now I must bear every present evil, I have to apprehend ' every threatened danger, in common with the lowest under my com- ' mand. Such is my lot; who have always been regular and zealous ' in every duty to the gods; and not only, as far as depended simply ' on myself, scrupulously just, but liberally charitable among men. ' Hence I have hope and confidence that our fortune will change for ' the better. The affliction we now suffer is surely beyond our desert; ' the enemy have already been sufficiently fortunate; and if our enter- ' prize against this country has offended any of the gods, it cannot be ' but our present evils are adequate punishment. For we are not the

' first who have drawn our swords in the attempt, unjustifiable be it
' confessed, to subjugate and reduce to slavery our fellow-creatures,
' and seize to ourselves their possessions. In doing thus, doing only
' what is ordinary among men, others have suffered for 'it only what
' men may bear. We therefore have surely reason to hope, that the
' gods will at length moderate their apparent excess of vengeance
' against us ; objects, as we are already become, of pity rather than of
' indignation.

' Confiding thus far then in the divine mercy, let us look to what,
' meer human things considered, our circumstances are, and surely we
' ought not to despond. Such a force as we possess, with so large a
' proportion of regular troops, wherever we establish our abode, we are
' not only a formidable army, we are a commonwealth. Certainly no
' Sicilian state, Syracuse excepted, will easily drive us from any situ-
' ation we may occupy ; or even prevent us from occupying any we
' may desire. To be safe, indeed, we have only to reach the Sicel ter-
' ritory ; for their fear of the Syracusans insures to us the friendship
' of the barbarians. Firm minds and orderly conduct then are
' principally necessary to your welfare ; and not to yours only, but that
' of the Athenian commonwealth ; which, however lamentably fallen
' through our misfortune, it may not be beyond our ability to restore ;
' since the strength of a state consists, not in towns, not in territory,
' not in ships, but in men.'

Thucyd. l. 7.
c. 78.

    Having thus spoken, Nicias led the march, the army being disposed
in two divisions, with the baggage between them ; himself commanding
the van, Demosthenes the rear. The road chosen was not toward their
Grecian friends of Naxus and Catana, but that by which they hoped
most readily to reach the Sicel country ; where soonest they might find
food and safety, with leisure to concert farther measures. At the ford
of the Anapus, very little distant from their camp, they found a body
of Syracusans posted to oppose the passage. These they soon forced
to retire ; but the enemy's horse and light infantry, hanging on their
flanks and rear, gave such continued annoyance, that, after a march of
only five miles, finding a rising ground commodious for the purpose,
they incamped for the night. On the next day they made still less
progress.

progress.   Want of provisions induced them to halt, after a march of only two miles and a half, in a plain where, beside collecting cattle among the farms and villages, they could supply themselves with water, for their progress over the hilly and dry country, which lay next in their way.   But, on the third day, the Syracusan horse and light-armed, in larger force than before, gave so much greater annoyance, that, after many hours wasted in unavailing attempts to repress them, the distressed Athenians returned to the camp they had last occupied. Nor could they profit, as on the preceding day, from their situation: even to obtain water, such was the enemy's superiority in cavalry, was difficult and hazardous.

Errors in conduct, evidently in the opinion of Thucydides, had occurred ; though he has avoided, as usual, the express declaration of any opinion.   Either change of plan, or some greater effort than had yet been made, was clearly indispensable.   On the next morning, there- Thucyd. l. 7. fore, they moved earlier than usual, and pressed their march, with the c. 79. view to occupy the Acræon-lepas, the first narrow at the entrance of the highlands.   But the opportunity lost was not so easily recoverable : their slowness had given the enemy time, both to discover their intended course, and to profit from the knowlege ; and on their arrival at the Acræon-lepas, they found not only an armed force to oppose them, but the natural difficulties of the pass increased by a fortification.   An assault was immediately attempted, which was not in the moment successful.   Meanwhile a storm came on ; such, says the 4 Sept. acc. historian, as in the autumnal season is common ; but, in the present to Chron. wane of the Athenian affairs, and the despondency its consequence, ther about everything was construed as an ill omen, and the generals could not Sep. persuade their troops to renew the attack.   As constant exertion tends to maintain the animation which success has raised, so new and unexpected opposition commonly inhances the depression of the unfortunate.   Gylippus, attentive to every opportunity, and observing the hesitation of the Athenians after their repulse, sent a body of men to raise a fort in their rear, so as to intercept their retreat.   The Athenian generals, however, found no difficulty in checking this purpose.   Their force was indeed yet such as to deter the enemy from giving them

battle;

battle; and accordingly they again chose their camp for the night within the plain.

But on the morrow, when they moved again, still with the view to force the passage of the mountains, they had no sooner quitted their camp, than the Syracusan horse and light-armed were upon their flanks and rear. If they halted to repel the annoyance, the enemy instantly retreated; but the moment they resumed their march, the attack was renewed; and this so repeatedly and efficaciously, that after advancing only one mile through the plain they incamped again. Then the Syracusans also retired to their camp.

Thucyd. l. 7.
c. 80.

The distress of the Athenians was now become very great: while numbers were suffering from wounds received in the many skirmishes, all were in almost total want of provisions and of all necessaries. The generals therefore came to a sudden resolution to break up their camp by night, and take the road toward the sea, the direct contrary to that which they had been hitherto following, and on which the enemy waited to intercept them. For, pursuing along the coast the way to Camarina and Gela, they might still reach the Sicel territory, by a more circuitous course indeed, but through a more level and open country. The usual fires were lighted, to obviate suspicion in the enemy, and then the army was silently assembled and the march begun. Nicias led, with a hasty pace, yet preserving due regularity. Through some unknown fatality, alarm and tumult arose in the division commanded by Demosthenes. Order was after some time restored; but the two divisions were completely separated.

c. 81.

The Syracusans, as soon as day broke, perceiving the Athenian camp deserted, in the usual temper of democratical jealousy, began to criminate Gylippus, as if he had traiterously permitted the enemy to escape. To discover which way so large a body had directed its march, was however not difficult, and shortly all joined in zealous pursuit. Demosthenes, notwithstanding the misfortune which had retarded him, had before daybreak reached the road leading from Syracuse to Elorus. A little farther he found a body of Syracusans raising works to obstruct his passage across the gully, through which flows the brook Cacyparis. These he soon dispersed. According to the plan con-

5   certed

certed with Nicias, he should then have turned up the course of the Cacyparis, to gain the interior country; but, by the advice of his guides, he proceeded, still near the coast, to the brook Erineus; and there the cavalry of the Syracusan army overtook him.

From the first there seems to have been some difference of opinion between the Athenian generals, concerning the manner of conducting the retreat.   Nicias thought the safety of the army depended, beyond all things, upon the rapidity of its march: the insult of assault should therefore be borne, and halts made, to repel attacks, only when they threatened very important injury.   This evidently was what Thucydides approved.   But Demosthenes was more disposed, on every occasion, to revenge with the view to deter annoyance.   No sooner therefore were the Syracusan horse now pressing upon his rear, than he changed that line of march by which he could best gain ground, to form his troops so as to act most efficaciously against the enemy.   The Syracusans saw their opportunity, and pushed by him while he halted. Their infantry quickly came up, and Demosthenes was surrounded. Too late discovering his error, he took the best measure that circumstances would then admit, occupying a walled inclosure near at hand, where the enemy's horse could not reach him, and where he could defy even their heavy-armed infantry.   But repeated sufferings, in the course of this long war, and especially the affair of Pylus, had taught the Lacedæmonians the value of light troops and missile weapons. Gylippus, employing the heavy-armed only in false or in desultory attacks, made principal use of his bowmen, darters, and slingers; and from these, through the remainder of the day, the Athenians had no rest.   In the evening, when many were thus wounded, and all worn with hunger, thirst, and fatigue, he sent a herald with a proclamation, promising liberty to any of the ilanders who would come to the Syracusan camp and surrender their arms.   Not many, even in so hopeless a situation, when all the evils, that the barbarity of antient warfare could inflict, were impending, would forsake their general and their comrades; an instance of fidelity deserving notice the more, as the common conduct of the Athenians would not seem to merit such attachment from their subjects; and while it does honor to themselves.

Thucyd. l. 7. c. 82.

selves and to Demosthenes, it certainly reflects some credit on the government of Athens.   So desperate indeed were the circumstances,
that, in the same evening, Demosthenes capitulated for the rest of his
troops, surrendering himself and them prisoners of war, with no other
stipulation than that none should suffer death, either through violence
or for want of sustenance.   With their arms they gave up all their
money, throwing it into the hollow of shields held to receive it, and
four shields were thus filled with silver.   The prisoners, in number
about six thousand, were immediately conducted to Syracuse.

Meanwhile Nicias, having ascended some way by the course of the
Cacyparis, crossed to the Erineus [27], passed that stream, considerably
above the scene of Demosthenes's fate, and incamped on some high

Thucyd. l.7.   ground near the farther bank.   Early next morning the Syracusan
c. 83.
7 Sep.   army hastened in pursuit, and the horse quickly overtaking him, gave
Chron. Thu.   information of the capitulation made by Demosthenes, and summoned
but rather a
week later.   him to surrender himself and the forces under his command.   Refusing credit to such intelligence so transmitted, he asked a safe-
conduct for a horseman of his own to make the inquiry, which was
granted.   The return of his messenger assuring him of the fact, he
then sent to propose, in the name of the Athenian commonwealth,
reïmbursement to Syracuse of all the expences of the war, upon condition only that the troops under his command might depart in safety;
and for security he would leave Athenian citizens as hostages, one for
every talent that would thus become due.   The proposal was rejected,
and the Athenian army was quickly surrounded by the multitude of
the enemy; who would however neither make nor sustain any regular
attack, but continued, till evening, unceasing annoyance with missile
weapons.

Among the distresses of the Athenians, not the least was the want of
provisions.   Could they have supported the enemy's assaults on their
present ground, they could not have subsisted there.   Nicias therefore, about midnight, called to arms as silently as possible, with intention to pursue his march: but the watchful enemy perceived his motions, and immediately sang the pæan.   Upon this he gave up the

[27] This appears from a comparison of the 80th chapter of Thucydides with the 83d.

design,

design, and remained in his camp; but a body of about three hundred, without his orders, made a successful push at the enemy's line, broke through, and, under favor of the obscurity, quickly got beyond immediate pursuit. Nicias waited for the dawn, and then continued his march. Even then the enemy, under the able conduct of Gylippus and Hermocrates, would come to no regular action, but only infested, as before, with missile weapons and desultory charges of cavalry. Sicily, through the greatest part of its extent, is high land, intersected with numerous valleys, whose sides are commonly steep, and the banks of the streams, flowing through them, often craggy. At no great distance from the camp, which the Athenians had quitted, the river Assinarus has a deep and rocky channel. While extreme thirst urged their steps to its stream, they hoped that, if they could once reach its further bank, they should gain some respite from the annoyance of the enemy's cavalry; and the light-armed would be less formidable, when unsupported by the heavy-armed and horse. But, notwithstanding all the exertion which such motives inforced, when they reached the bank the enemy's heavy-armed were close upon them. Discipline then yielded to the pressure of evil felt and danger threatening. Without any order they hurried down the steep, pushing and trampling on oneanother; and, in the tumult, some were destroyed by the spears of their comrades. The first object of most was to assuage intolerable thirst. Meanwhile the enemy's light-armed, acquainted with all the ways, reached the opposite bank before them, and the whole Athenian army, inclosed in the hollow, was exposed, helpless, to missile weapons on both sides. The Peloponnesians at length led the way for the Syracusans, down into the bottom, to complete the slaughter; while the Athenians, still resisting to the utmost, were so pressed by extreme thirst, that, in the midst of action, many of them would drink the turbid and bloody water, and even fight for it.

Already they were lying dead in heaps in the river, while the horse pursued and cut off any who could escape up the banks, when Nicias, whom nothing could induce to submit to the Syracusans, found opportunity to surrender himself to Gylippus. That general then commanded to give quarter, and was obeyed. Among the rocks, and in

the

Thucyd. 1. 7.
c. 84.
Sept. 8. or
rather about
15.

Thucyd. 1. 7.
c. 85.

the windings of the stream, a large number of the Athenians found opportunity for either concealment or flight: the rest were made prisoners. No capitulation was made, as for the division under Demosthenes: and, prisoners being valuable as slaves, the Syracusan soldiers were diligent in embeziling them as their private property. In this they were so successful, that the prisoners of the Syracusan state remained comparatively few. A detachment was sent after the three hundred who broke through the Syracusan line in the night, and took

Thucyd. l. 7. c. 86. them all. The public prisoners, with what spoil could be collected, were conducted to Syracuse.

It would have been a glorious and a singular triumph, for Gylippus, to have carried the Athenian generals, the two most illustrious men of their time, prisoners to Sparta; one distinguished for his friendly disposition toward the Lacedæmonian people, the other for his successes against them. But the jealous, cruel, and faithless temper of democratical despotism disappointed his just expectation. A decree of the Syracusan people condemned both to death, and they were executed. In the antient democracies, the most worthless individual, touching at any time a chord in consonance with popular passion, could procure the sanction of soverein authority for any villainy. For where neither one person nor a select body was responsible, but the whole people, truly despotic, were the common authors of every public act, the shame of flagitious measures was so divided that it was disregarded. For any one to own himself author of the black decree against Nicias and Demosthenes, the one intitled to the protection of the Spartan general, the other under that of a capitulation solemnly granted in the name of the Syracusan people, appears, for a time at least, to have been avoided. Thucydides says the circumstances immediately leading to the measure were not, in his time, with any certainty known at Athens. It seems likely to have been in the desire of those concerned, to shift the black imputation upon others,

Diod. l. 13. c. 19. Plut. vit. Nic. that it was by some thrown on Gylippus. The party politics of aftertimes led the Sicilian historian Timæus to calumniate Hermocrates. But Diodorus, who, may have had sources of information not open to Thucydides, and who, tho a zealot for democracy and of little judgement
ment

ment, was of much candor, attributes the motion for the flagitious decree positively to Diocles, then a leader of the democratical party, afterward, as we shall see, ruler of the republic, and always the opponent of Hermocrates.   And this well agrees with those circumstances connected with the measure, which Thucydides proceeds to relate, as all he could obtain toward elucidation of it.   The fears, he says, of those who had carried on treasonable correspondence with Nicias, induced them, if not to promote, yet to concur in the vote for putting him to death; and the Corinthians had particular enmity to him, apprehensive, for some cause not explained to us, that his restoration to power in Athens would be injurious to their interest.   All authorities however agree that it was a public and solemn decree of the Syracusan people which consigned the Athenian generals to execution [28].

Meanwhile the miserable remnant of their once flourishing army, the greatest ever sent out by any one Grecian state, was reserved for a still severer lot.   A vast quarry in the hill of Epipolæ, whence the stone had been principally taken for building the city, was judged the most secure and commodious place for the confinement of such a multitude of men, so versed in the use of arms.   Into this the freemen were conducted, to the number of about seven thousand : the slaves were sold by public auction.   But the faith of the Syracusan people, so shamefully broken with the generals, was not very religiously kept with those of inferior rank.   On the contrary, their whole conduct was marked with a spirit of deliberate cruelty, the general vice, it must be confessed, of the fairest days of Greece ; which yet ought not to be attributed to the disposition of the people, since it was the unavoidable result of the political state of the country.   The Syracusans saw, in the Athenian prisoners, not generous enemies, but oppressors, who would have reduced them to the deepest misery.   Tho food therefore was not denied, yet it was given in quantity barely sufficient to support life ; and cruelty was still more shown in the scanty allowance of water,

[28] Plutarch, in his life of Nicias, professes to have taken particular pains to collect and collate whatever remained to his time concerning the expedition against Syracuse; but his account is satisfactory chiefly as it tends to confirm that of Thucydides, without adding scarcely anything of any importance.

No shelter was afforded from the inclemency of the sky; and while the reflected heat of the midday sun, in the open and capacious dungeon, was scarcely tolerable, the chill of autumnal night made an alternacy very injurious to health. No means were given to avoid their own filth; no care was taken of those who sickened; and, when any died, as many did, some of unattended wounds, some of disorder caused by various hardship, the bodies remained to putrefy among their living companions; and the eloquent historian, here as on a former occasion, failing of words to his mind to describe the extreme misery, sums up all with saying, that no suffering could possibly result from so wretched a situation, which was not experienced by the Athenian prisoners. Toward the end of november, after a confinement of about seventy days, the ilanders, and others who were not citizens of Athens, or of some Grecian town of Sicily or Italy, were taken out for the milder lot of being sold to slavery. The Athenians, with the Sicilian and Italian Greeks, remained; and we are not informed that they were ever released.

Thucyd. l. 7. c. 85.

Meanwhile those, of the army under Nicias, who, instead of public prisoners of the Syracusan state, had been made the private property of individuals, suffered variously, according to the condition or temper of the masters, under whom they fell; and, of those who had escaped by flight, few fared better; for, unable to find subsistence, they were mostly reduced to the hard resource of offering themselves, in any town they could reach, to voluntary slavery. Thus, says the historian, all the towns of Sicily abounded with Grecian slaves. A few only had the good fortune to make their way, immediately from the field of action, to the friendly city of Catana, whence they got their passage to Athens; but afterward others found means to fly from bondage to the same asylum.

c. 86.

Plut. vit. Nic.

In the miserable state of servile dependency, to which such numbers of Athenians were reduced, the science, literature, fine taste, and polite manners of Athens are said to have been beneficial to many. Some, who were fortunate enough to meet with masters of liberal disposition, were treated with the respect due to superior accomplishments; some were even presented with their freedom. Since the days of Hieron, the literature of Greece or Ionia had little made its way to

Sicily;

Sicily; and, through defect of materials, copies of books were not yet readily multiplied.   But many of the Athenians retained, by memory, much of the works of Euripides; whose moral and pathetic strains, which they used to sing as the solace of their bondage, singularly touched the Sicilians.   Euripides lived to receive the grateful acknowlegements of some who returned to Athens, and related what kindness they had received in servitude, or what relief in beggary, for the pleasure they gave by speaking, singing, or teaching, his verses.

CHAPTER XIX.

Affairs of GREECE, from the Conclusion of the SICILIAN Expedition till the Return of ALCIBIADES to ATHENS, in the Twenty-fourth Year of the PELOPONNESIAN War.

SECTION I.

Effects at Athens of the News of the Overthrow in Sicily: Effects through Greece of the Overthrow of the Athenians in Sicily. Change in the political System of Lacedæmon. Measures of the Peloponnesian Confederacy for raising a Fleet. Proposals from Eubœa and Lesbos to revolt from the Athenian to the Peloponnesian Confederacy.

Thucyd. l. 8. c. 1.

THE news of the total destruction of the most powerful armament ever sent out by any Grecian state, supposed so far from the danger of such a catastrophë that it was capable of accomplishing almost any conquest, being first brought to Athens by no official messenger, but communicated accidentally in the uncertain way of reports, did

Plut. vit. Nic.

not immediately find credit. Plutarch relates that a foreiner, landing at Peiræus, went into a barber's shop, which, like the modern coffee-house, was the usual resort of idle newsmongers in the Grecian cities (as, we find, afterward in Rome) and spoke of the event as what he supposed would of course be well known there. The barber, with more zeal than discretion, went immediately into the city, and communicated the intelligence to the archons; who, with the natural anxiety of magistrates under the tyranny of a despotic multitude, summoned an assembly of the people, and produced the barber to declare his news. The people, in extreme agitation, demanded his authority. The incautious man could produce none: he had no previous acquaintance with the person from whom he received the information, and knew not

where

where to find him.   The indignant multitude immediately ordered the
barber to the torture of the wheel,(a mode of punishment nowhere exactly
described to us, but which it seems might be borne long[1],) and he was
not released till some of the more fortunate few, who had escaped from
the scene of woe, arriving, confirmed the uncertain intelligence.   Even Thucyd. l. 8.
these, however, were not at first credited for the full extent of the c. 1.
misfortune.   Multiplied concurring testimonies at length removing
every doubt of the magnitude of the calamity, then public anguish B. C. 413
became extreme.   Popular rage began with venting contumely against Ol. 91. 4.
P. W. 19.
the orators who had advised the expedition; as if, says the historian, October.
the people themselves had not directed it; and, in fact, the people in
assembly holding the executive as well as the legislative government,
every one being free to propose, and sometimes a majority with tumultuous clamor commanding measures, there could be no duly responsible minister.   From the orators then the public anger extended to the
soothsayers, augurs, interpreters, any who had contributed to establish
the belief that the gods would favor the project of conquest in Sicily.
But in this excessive irritation of the public mind, fear soon became
the prevailing passion.   Private losses of friends or relations, which
stimulated the first movements, gave way to the consideration, that
the commonwealth had not such another body of citizens, in the prime
of life, as that which had been so rashly committed to destruction, nor
such a fleet, nor naval stores to fit such another, nor funds to supply
the accumulated wants which the conjuncture created: and then it
followed, that nothing less was to be expected then the appearance of
the enemy's victorious navy before Peiræus, and the blockade of Athens
by land and sea.

    In this general consternation, however, there were not wanting either
able heads or magnanimous minds among the Athenians, and the
crisis itself gave them the power to take the lead.   Wise measures
and the most vigorous that circumstances admitted, were accordingly
resolved on; to restore the navy, to collect stores, to raise money, and
to save it, by abridging, not private luxury, which was yet moderate,

----

[1] Ἐς τὸν τρόχον καταδεθεὶς, ἐςρεβλοῦτο πολὺν χρόνον. κ. τ. ι.—Plut. vit. Nic.

                                                                but

but public luxury, which was already immoderate in Athens², and, above all things, to obviate the defection of the allied and subject states, particularly of Eubœa, the most valuable dependency of the commonwealth, and without which the population of Athens could not easily subsist.   But the depth of misfortune, into which their own folly had precipitated them, induced, among the Athenian people, a consciousness that a multitude is unfit to direct executive government. To obviate therefore the extravagancies of unbalanced democracy, a new council of elders was created, whose office was to deliberate on all public measures, previously to their being proposed to the general assembly.   This indeed was providing for the prudence of executive government, but not for vigor, not for secresy, not for dispatch; qualities which could meet in the Athenian administration only when a Themistocles or a Pericles, general at the same time and demagogue, controuled by no council, could first resolve on measures, and then command the approbation of the general assembly.   Never however were the Athenian people so disposed to moderation, order, and attention to wise advice as in the present crisis.   ' It was so resolved ' therefore,' says the cotemporary historian emphatically, ' and it was ' done; and the summer ended.'

Thucyd. l. 8.   Meanwhile the attention of all Greece was excited, and the politics
c. 2.   of every republic put in motion by the blow which Athens had received in Sicily.   Apprehension of the consequence of so great an addition to the power of that ambitious and restles republic, as the conquest of Sicily might have given, had been very general and very serious.   No evil that could befall the aristocracies, which composed the Lacedæmonian confederacy, was so dreadful and so odious as subjugation under the tyrannous rule of the Athenian multitude.   Nor was Lacedæmon itself without alarm ; for tho the conquest of Sparta was not likely soon to be accomplished by the Athenian arms, yet there was no inferior evil which might not be expected, and quickly.   Already the Lacedæmonians beheld, not only many of their dependencies wrested from them,

---

² Duker has a judicious note upon the passage of Thucydides, which I have thus paraphrased.   The fcholiast has undertaken to explain what, for want of better inquiry into the state of Athens at the time, he evidently did not understand:

but

but two garrisons established within their own country, infesting a large part of it with devastation, to which they could neither prescribe bounds nor foresee an end.   At the same time the Athenian fleets so decidedly commanded the seas, that no prospect appeared of means for competition with them on that element; insomuch that not only the Lacedæmonians were unable to extend protection to any allies beyond the ready reach of their landforce, but the extensive line of the Laconian coast must be continually open to insult.   In all these things the catastrophë at Syracuse made a change, that nothing but the mad ambition, or madder jealousy, of a despotic multitude could have produced; and that change was immediate and almost total.   The navy of Athens was no longer formidable; the Peloponnesian fleets now commanded the seas.   The allies of Lacedæmon, therefore, no longer fearing anything from the enemy, became only anxious for exertion, that they might speedily, as they trusted they could easily, complete the purpose of the war, and relieve themselves from burdens under which they had been long uneasy.   The neutral republics, at the same time, thought the moment come for deciding their party, before it was yet too late to claim merit for the decision.   But the principal effect was seen among the subject states of Athens; who, with anadvised eagerness, pressed forward in revolt, taking it for certain that the Athenians would be unable to maintain the war through the insuing summer.   Meanwhile the Lacedæmonians, with the characteristical coolness of their government, injoyed the view of this various fermentation, and prepared to profit from it to the establishment of their own permanent superiority over all Greece, to which they now looked as an acquisition completely within their power.

Among the circumstances of these times, a change in the Lacedæmonian system, which considerably affected the general politics of Greece, will require notice.   The Lacedæmonian kings, who in Lacedæmon, except when presiding at some religious ceremony, were scarcely distinguished from the mass of citizens, being obliged, in all political business, to yield to the tyrannical authority of the ephors, injoyed, in the command of armies abroad, a more truly royal state as well as a more efficacious royal authority.   The interest which they thus

                                                                had

had in leading their country into long and distant wars, had been restrained by' the law of Lycurgus, forbidding such wars; and that law, inforced sometimes by the opposite interest of the ephors, had been much more effectually and constantly inforced by the poverty of the Lacedæmonian commonwealth. Nevertheless, before the Persian war, Cleomenes, by ingaging the state in frequent hostilities, appears to have acquired extraordinary power; and afterward, in the new and vast scene of action which the Persian war opened, Pausanias, tho not king but meerly regent and general of the republic, was able to prosecute ambitious views to a great length. His own imprudence indeed, more than any other obstacle, seems to have ruined his purpose: and the insuing downfall of the power of Sparta checked, for a time, the ambition of its generals and kings. When the Peloponnesian war broke out, Archidamus, a prince advanced in years, and of a character singularly amiable, prudent at the same time and philanthropic, seems to have had no object, in command, but the good of his country and of all Greece. His son Agis, a man of moderate talents, would prehaps not have attempted innovation, if circumstances had not led to it. He succeeded to the throne in an early stage of a most complicated and lasting war. Error in conduct, apparently the consequence of error in judgement, produced, as we have seen, very severe censure upon him from those who, in Lacedæmon, had legal authority to censure and even to punish kings. Afterward, by his success at Mantineia, he acquired some reputation. He was still in the vigor of his age, but of large experience, when the establishment of a standing force in Deceleia gave him, what none of his predecessors ever injoyed, a perennial military command. Here he found himself reälly king: here he was free from the vexatious and degrading controul of the ephors: here he might not only use at discretion the troops immediately under his orders, but he had authority to levy forces, raise contributions, exercise command among the allies of the commonwealth, and treat with forein states. Thus vested with independent power, he was of course respected, and could make himself feared; so that much more deference was paid by the states of the confederacy to Agis, in his garrison at Deceleia, than to any Spartan king at home, or even to the Spartan government itself.

Thucyd. l. 8. c. 5.

i i

The

The residence of his garrison therefore was not unlikely to be preferred to that of his capital.   These were consequences apparently not in the view of the Lacedæmonian administration, when the advice of the Athenian refugee was taken for the permanent occupying of a post in Attica; yet the circumstances of the Lacedæmonian government prevented any effectual effort to check them.

The establishment of a public revenue at Lacedæmon seems to have been a departure from the spirit, at least, of Lycurgus's system.   When such an establishment was first made, we are not informed; but we find Archidamus, in the debates preceding the Peloponnesian war, speaking of it not as a new thing.   The length of that war, and the extent of the scene of action, would make attention to the revenue more than ever necessary; and thus again a new interest was created, intimately connected with that which led the kings to desire war always rather than peace, and any residence rather than that of Sparta. Through the business of the revenue, the leading men at home might have an interest in yielding to the king's wish for forein command; and hence the influence of the king, tho at a distance, might keep together a party in Lacedæmon.   Agis in his command at Deceleia did not neglect this policy.   Thucyd. 1. 8. c. 3.

The Lacedæmonian government now, with serious earnestness, applied themselves to what had been their professed purpose at the beginning of the war, the acquisition of a fleet to rival that of Athens. The project, then wild, was become at length practicable.   Instead of five hundred triremes, originally proposed, one hundred were now required of the confederacy.   The Lacedæmonians themselves undertook for twenty-five.   An equal number was appointed to Bœotia, fifteen only to Corinth, fifteen to Locris and Phocis, ten to Arcadia with Pallenë and Sicyon, and ten to Megara, Trœzen, Epidaurus, and Hermione.   Agis was directed to collect the contributions for the purpose from the northern states.   Accordingly, with such an escort as he judged sufficient, he marched from Deceleia about the beginning of November; and after receiving what had been assessed upon the friendly, he proceeded to increase the sum by taking from the hostile.   Turning   c. 3.

toward the Malian bay, he carried off considerable booty from the
Œtæan vallies; and then, advancing still northward, he compelled the
Phthiot Achaians, with some other tribes subject to the Thessalians, in
Thucyd. l. 8.
c. 4. defiance of the resentment of that people, to deliver hostages and pay
contributions.

Meanwhile the Athenians, recovered in some degree from the first
emotions of grief and alarm, and submitting themselves to able guidance, were taking measures, suited to their reduced circumstances,
for resisting the impending storm.   Their first diligence was directed
to the collection of naval stores, and the building of ships; for on the
possession of a powerful fleet everything depended.   Their next care
was to increase the security of vessels passing betwen Eubœa and Athens;
for without free communication with Eubœa, the city could not easily
be subsisted.   With this view therefore a fort was erected on the promontory of Sunium.   Thus, but especially in the renovation of the fleet,
a large but indispensable expence would be incurred, which would
inforce the necessity of parsimony in matters of inferior moment.   The
garrison was therefore withdrawn from that post in Laconia which had
been occupied by Demosthenes in his way to Sicily, and measures
were taken to reduce unnecessary expences, and establish exact economy
c. 5. in public affairs.   Thus, says the cotemporary historian, in the close
of the nineteenth year of the war, preparations were making on both
sides, as if war was just then beginning.

But it was not possible for any prudence, among the Athenians, to
prevent that consequence of their late misfortune, which they most
apprehended and their enemies most hoped, the defection of their allies
and the revolt of their subjects.   The Eubœans, whose country was so
important to Athens, that a better government would never have left
it in the situation of a subject-state, but would have given its people
one interest with themselves, were foremost to take measures for breaking their dependency.   The residence of the Lacedæmonian king in
their neighborhood offered new opportunity for the intrigues of the
discontented: the consideration of the force that he could command
from the surrounding states, in addition to that constantly under his

1   orders,

orders, gave large incouragement; and, soon after the arrival of the news of the Sicilian defeat, a proposal was communicated to Agis from a strong party in Eubœa, to bring over the whole island to the Lacedæmonian confederacy. Agis gave assurances that the force under his command should be employed in their favor, and in communicating the project to the Lacedæmonian administration, he used his interest to promote their cause. But the cautious government of Lacedæmon, tho unwilling to reject so advantageous a proposal, was nevertheless little disposed to any spirited exertion for assisting it. Three hundred only of those called neodamodes, newly-admitted citizens, were granted for the service; who, under the command of Alcamenes, marched into Attica.

Agis was taking measures for transporting this body into Eubœa, when a deputation from Lesbos, also proposing revolt, reduced him to difficulty. His desire coïncided with the wishes both of the Eubœans and the Lesbians; but neither people could effect their purpose without assistance, and he was unable to give it at the same time to both. He was already ingaged to the Eubœans; and their extensive country almost adjoining to the coast of Bœotia, whether as loss to Athens, or gain to the Peloponnesian confederacy, was far more important than the smaller iland of Lesbos, on the other side of the Ægean. But the Bœotians, the most powerful of the allies of Lacedæmon, had a strong partiality for the Lesbians, whom, as of Æolian race, they considered as kinsmen; while the Lesbians, tho connected by no political interest, revered the Bœotians as the chiefs of their blood. Agis, whether considering the interest of Lacedæmon or his own interest, desirous of gratifying the Bœotians, resolved to postpone the business of Eubœa to that of Lesbos. Accordingly, without any communication with Lacedæmon, he ordered Alcamenes to conduct to Lesbos that very force, which had been sent by the Lacedæmonian government for the express purpose of assisting the revolt in Eubœa.

SECTION II.

*New Implication of Grecian and Persian Interests.   Death of Artax-
erxes and Succession of Darius II. to the Persian Throne.   Effect
of the terrors of an Earthquake.   Congress of the Peloponnesian
Confederacy at Corinth.   Isthmian Games.   Naval success of the
Athenians in the Saronic Gulph.   Influence of Alcibiades in the
Spartan Councils.   A Peloponnesian Fleet sent under Chalcideus, accompanied by Alcibiades, to coöperate with the Satrap of Caria and the
revolted Ionians.   Increased Distress of Athens.   Treaty of Alliance
between Lacedæmon and Persia.*

Not all the sounding vaunts and ingenious panegyrics, of later writers,
mark so strongly the ascendancy which the little commonwealth of Athens
had acquired in the politics of the civilized world, and the degree to
which it had repressed the force, or at least the spirit, of the vast empire
of the east, or display so clearly the superiority, which a few consenting
thousands, ably directed, may acquire over ill-governed millions, as
the cotemporary historian's simple narrative of the consequences of
the Athenian defeat in Sicily.   That event in the west presently set
the east in motion, and the affairs of Greece became in a new way implicated with those of Persia.   Darius had succeeded his father Artaxerxes
in the throne.   Artaxerxes, tho an able prince, and interrupted by no
considerable forein wars, had exerted himself, through a long reign,
with very incomplete success, to restore vigor to the unwieldy mass
of the empire.   While his cares were employed in composing the disorders, which troubles, preceding his accession, had produced in the
central parts, the connection with the distant provinces remained' loose
and imperfect; insomuch that, independently of any effort of the satraps
for the purpose, a more independent power accrued to them, than could
consist with the good government of the whole.   Thus, upon the
appointment of Tissaphernes to the satrapy of Caria, Amorges, natural
son of the late satrap Pissuthnes, was incouraged to revolt; not
                                                                    perhaps

perhaps in professed opposition to the soverein of the empire, but to the new satrap only. Regardless, however, of the mandates of the prince, and in defiance of the arms of his officers, he maintained himself in the Carian mountains.

But the wants of the Persian government pressed upon those to whom its powers were delegated, in proportion as its weakness incouraged opposition to them. The satraps were required to remit from their provinces, not only the accruing tributes, but the arrears. From the time of the victories of Cimon, most of the Grecian towns in Asia had been tributary to Athens, and many of them since those of Xanthippus and Leotychidas. The jealousy of the Athenian government allowed few to remain fortified; yet the terror of the Athenian name kept them secure, as far as history informs us, against any attempts from the Persians, except in one instance, when sedition at Colophon afforded an opportunity, the advantage of which, however, was of short duration. Nevertheless the Persian court affected to consider all those towns as still appendages of the empire, and a tribute assessed upon them was required from the satraps[3]. The wretched policy of Athens, in the government of its dependencies, so far promoted the views of the Persians, that there was in every Asiatic city a party, composed mostly of the higher ranks, who were ready to prefer the more liberal supremacy of a Persian satrap to the oppressive and insulting tyranny of the Athenian people. Under these circumstances it appears difficult to say which was most wonderful, the strength of the little commonwealth of Athens, which could hold such a command, or the weakness of the vast empire of Persia, which could not recover its dominion. The plea of inability from the satraps had at length been allowed at the Persian court, so far that the arrears of tribute due from Tissaphernes, for the Grecian towns within his satrapy, were no longer

Chap. 15. sect. 3. of this Hist.

Thucyd. l. 8. c. 5.

---

[3] What we find from Thucydides upon this subject, in the fifth and sixth chapters of his eighth book, implies the strongest contradiction of the report, transmitted by later writers, of a treaty of peace, by which the court of Persia gave up all claim upon the Grecian towns in Asia, and ingaged that no Persian troops should come within three days march of the western coast. See note 11. sect. 3. ch. 11. of this History.

demanded.

demanded [*]. But at the same time that this indulgence was granted, it was with reason required that a Persian subject should not be al-

Thucyd. l. 8. c. 6.

lowed to maintain himself in rebellion: Tissaphernes was commanded to send Amorges, alive or dead, to Susa. To effect even this, however, either means were deficient or conduct, and Amorges continued to defy the Persian power.

It was very generally supposed that, by the defeat in Sicily, the command of the sea was completely lost to Athens; and, throughout the Asiatic Grecian cities, the aristocratical party were immediately looking out for means of mending their condition by revolt. The Lesbians had begun: the Chians and Erythræans followed: but, diffident of their own strength, their first measure was to communicate with Tissaphernes. The satrap, however, did not think himself able, with his own force, to give them protection; but he gladly united his interest with theirs, and together they sent ministers to Lacedæmon. At the same time Pharnabazus, satrap of the provinces bordering on the Hellespont and the Euxine, with the same view of acquiring revenue from the Grecian cities within his satrapy, was also desirous of forming an alliance with the Lacedæmonians; who would probably rather see those cities tributary to Persia, than sources of revenue to Athens. He employed, for his ministers on this occasion, two refugee Greeks, Calligeitus, a Megarian, and Timagoras, a Cyzicene, who arrived at Lacedæmon about the same time with the ministers from Tissaphernes and from Chios and Erythræ. The Lesbian ministers, who had been negotiating with Agis at Deceleia, also met them there.

The contest which insued, for preference in the Lacedæmonian alliance, gave opportunity for intrigue, in which Alcibiades was likely to enter and likely to be successful. Endius, ephor of the year, was of that Spartan family with which principally his family had had

---

[*] We are little exactly informed of the extent of the several satrapies, or of the powers, privileges, and duties of the satraps. We learn however from Xenophon (Hel. l. 3. c. 1. s. 5. & seq. & c. 2. s. 10.) that Caria was the proper satrapy of Tissa- phernes, and (Anab. l. 1. c. 1. s. 6.) that Ionia was added to his command by the king's particular favor; but his authority, at least in the absence of other officers, was often extended over Sardis and great part of Lydia.

antient

antient hospitality, and Endius was now his particular friend. With Agis he was not upon good terms: it was therefore his purpose to make Endius also the enemy of Agis; and the opposition of interests among those who were contending for the Lacedæmonian alliance, afforded means. Agis favored the pretensions of the Lesbians, whose cause he had already adopted. Alcibiades persuaded Endius to favor the Chians; and grounds were not wanting for giving them the preference: they possessed no less than sixty ships of war: in every circumstance of military strength they were superior to any among the Asian Greeks; and what was perhaps a still more important consideration, their alliance would carry with it that of the powerful satrap who commanded the south-western provinces of Lesser Asia. These motives, urged by the ability of Alcibiades, persuaded Endius, and, with him, a majority of those who directed the councils of Lacedæmon. A treaty was accordingly concluded with the Chians and Erythræans, and forty ships of war were voted, to support them in their proposed revolt. Ten, under Melanchridas, were ordered to sail while it was yet winter; but the superstitious terror which an earthquake inspired, gave some check to the measure. The earthquake apparently was supposed to portend that the command of Melanchridas would be inauspicious; for the Lacedæmonian government immediately appointed Chalcideus to supersede him, and reduced the squadron to five ships.

The part of Sparta being thus taken, and, almost in the same instant, the usual want of energy in her councils demonstrated, the Chians became apprehensive that intelligence of their negotiation would reach Athens, and they might be attacked before succour, sufficient for their protection, would arrive. Toward spring therefore they sent again to Lacedæmon, urging the necessity of early assistance; and the ability of Alcibiades and the power of Endius being united, to promote their cause, it was resolved that the whole fleet in the Corinthian gulph, including the squadron prepared by Agis for the expedition to Lesbos, should be dragged across the isthmus, and proceed for Chios.

Before this was carried into execution, however, it was thought proper to hold a congress of the confederacy; and Corinth was
appointed

Thucyd. l. 8.
c. 7.

B. C. 412.
Ol. $\frac{91}{3\frac{1}{2}}$. $\frac{4}{1}$.
P. W. 20.

Thucyd. l. 8.
c. 8. appointed for the place of meeting.   Agis attended from Deceleia. He had the prudence not to mark any resentment at the interference with his command, or any way to irritate an administration ill disposed to him, by opposing measures on which they had a constitutional right to decide; and yielding thus in part, he carried also a part of his pur- pose.   In conformity to the proposition from Lacedæmon, the congress resolved, that the whole fleet should go first to Chios, under the com- mand of Chalcideus, who was then superintending the equipment of a squadron on the Laconic coast ; that, when the Chians were put in a state of security, Alcamenes, the officer named by Agis, should take the command and proceed to Lesbos ; that, when the business there also was completed, the command should pass to Clearchus, who should conduct the fleet to the Hellespont, and act with Pharnabazus.

The fleet in the gulph consisted of thirty-nine triremes.   Twenty- one were in all haste hauled across the isthmus ; and it was the wish of the congress that these should sail without delay.   Thus, it was hoped, the Athenians, having their attention divided between the division sailing and that remaining to sail, would act effectually against neither.

Thucyd. l. 7.
c. 9. But it happened that the season of the Isthmian games was at hand ; and such was the respected sanctity of the armistice upon that occa- sion, that even the Athenians might come and go and stay in safety. The preparations therefore would become unavoidably notorious ; and even the negotiations, in which so many persons, with various interests, had communicated, would probably not remain long secret.   But the very circumstance of the games, which increased the anxiety of the other confederates for the instant departure of the squadron, deter- mined the Corinthians not to stir.   The force of Athens, they said, was already broken ; and nothing to be apprehended from any dis- covery of the purposes of the confederacy, nor any obstacle that could arise from a little delay, was of importance enough to prevent a large portion of their citizens from partaking in that magnificent and sacred festival, whose period would recur only in the revolution of four years.

The negotiation had indeed been conducted with such care that nothing transpired.   But the movements of the fleet excited suspicion ;
                                                                        the

the persons discovered to be coming and going directed suspicion to its object; and Aristocrates, one of the generals of Athens, was sent to Chios.   His instructions directed him to inform himself of the state of things in the iland, and, as a precaution, to require that the ships, which, according to the terms of the confederacy, the Chians were bound to furnish for the Athenian fleet, should be immediately sent to Peiræus.   The proposed revolt was a measure intirely of the aristocratical party, and not yet communicated to the general assembly, or to any in the democratical interest.   The leaders 'therefore, thus taken unprepared, denied any intention to break their antient connection with Athens, and, in conformity to the requisition, they sent seven ships to join the Athenian fleet.

At the celebration of the Isthmian games many Athenians attended : Thucyd. l. 8. the preparations were seen, the purpose suspected, and measures were c. 10. taken at Athens accordingly.   The festival was no sooner concluded than the twenty-one triremes, already transported across the isthmus, sailed under the command of Alcamenes.   The Athenians attacked them with superior force; the Peloponnesians were defeated; Alcamenes was killed; one trireme was taken; the others reached a desert port of the Corinthian territory on the confines of Epidauria, called Peiræus.   The Athenians followed, but did not think proper to attack c. 11. them there.   According to the usual mode of naval operation in that age, leaving a few triremes to watch them, they withdrew with the rest to a small iland near the coast, where they incamped.

Intelligence of this action occasioned much alarm in Corinth.   The neighboring allies were summoned, and, with such force as could be hastily assembled, the Corinthians marched to protect the defeated armament.   Where soldiers were citizens, not under any regular military command, but having every one a vote in the decision of all public measures, it was often more difficult for the administration to get a service of tedious inconvenience performed, than one of great momentary danger.   Accordingly the first proposal, concerning the ships in the desert harbour of Peiræus, was to burn rather than undertake a lasting guard upon them, in such a situation.   After some deliberation, however, the consideration of the expence and difficulty of

VOL. II.   3 G   repairing

repairing the loss, induced the resolution not to submit to it without a struggle. The ships were therefore hauled ashore, and a considerable body of infantry incamped for their protection. Information of the defeat and death of Alcamenes being in the mean time carried to Lacedæmon, not only the departure of the squadron under Chalcideus was stopped, but it was proposed at once to give up all the great views of advantage, that had been opened on the other side of the Ægean.

The ascendancy of Athenian genius showed itself, even in those circumstances which contributed most to the downfall of the Athenian empire. What the Lacedæmonian administration had neither foresight to plan nor spirit to execute, the illustrious but unprincipled Athenian refugee, participating, through the ephor his friend, in their closest councils, planned and executed for them. He urged that, if

Thucyd. l. 8. c. 12. the small squadron under Chalcideus hastened to Chios, before the news of the disaster on the coast of Peloponnesus arrived there, the acquisition of that iland might yet be effected. He would himself accompany the squadron; he would represent, in proper terms, the weakness of Athens, and the power and zeal of Lacedæmon; and he doubted not of accomplishing the revolt, not only of Chios, but of all Ionia. Such were the inducements which he held out generally. In private he farther stimulated Endius with a display of the credit, which such an acquisition to the Lacedæmonian confederacy would bring to his administration, and of the still more important advantages of an alliance between Lacedæmon and the court of Persia, which would be the ready consequence. In the circumstances of the moment, all was in his own power: if he neglected the opportunity, everything would pass from him to his rival Agis.

Thus incited, Endius became earnest in prosecution of the plans of Alcibiades: they were adopted by the Lacedæmonian administration, and Chalcideus, accompanied by Alcibiades, sailed for Ionia. In their

c. 14. passage, to prevent communication of intelligence, they stopped all merchant-ships they fell in with, compelled them to follow as far as Corycus on the Asiatic coast, and there dismissed them. Deputies from the leaders of the Chian revolt shortly came to Corycus, and the fleet then proceeded for Chios. Its arrival occasioned universal astonishment

nishment and alarm, except among the aristocratical leaders, who were completely prepared.   The council, according to previous concert, was sitting; and Alcibiades and Chalcideus were received by it to make their proposals.   They boldly asserted that a large fleet was on its way from Peloponnésus: fortunately for them not a rumor of the defeat on the Corinthian coast had reached Chios: a decree was proposed for renouncing the Athenian and ingaging in the Peloponnesian confederacy; and, without any material opposition from the democratical party, it was carried.   The Erythræans immediately followed the example; and, three ships only being sent to Clazomenæ, that city also joined in the measure.   Thus, with the small force of only five triremes, Alcibiades struck a greater blow against his country, than the Lacedæmonians and their confederates, after all the great advantage gained in Sicily, had almost dared to meditate.

The affairs of Athens were now in such a situation, that it was judged lawful and necessary to recur to the deposit of a thousand talents, set apart in the beginning of the war for cases of extremest necessity.   No enemy's fleet yet blockaded the harbour of Peiræus (the emergency specified as the requisite justification), yet, on the arrival of intelligence of the revolt of Chios, the danger was thought scarcely less pressing than if Athens were actually invested.   For, the most powerful ally of the commonwealth having set the example of revolt, it was concluded that the other allies and subjects would follow; and thus there would be an end of those resources without which the war could not be supported.   The prohibitory decree therefore was repealed, and a kind of confidential vote passed, directing that every effort should be made for raising a fleet, the most powerful that circumstances would allow, and that the speediest exertion should be used, for saving the dependencies yet remaining to the commonwealth, and recovering, if opportunity should occur, those which had already revolted.

The directors of executive government, thus vested with discretionary powers, sent instant orders for arresting the crews of the Chian ships acting with the fleet on the Corinthian coast.   This was successfully executed: the free were imprisoned, the slaves declared free, and the ships were replaced by an equal number of Athenian ships.   Eight

Thucyd. l. 8. c. 15.

triremes remained equipped in the harbour of Peiræus : they were
dispatched for Asia under the command of Strombichides : twelve,
nearly ready, were ordered to follow under Thrasycles ; and thirty
were put in preparation to be sent after them as soon as possible.

Thucyd. l. 8.
c. 15.

Strombichides hastening to Samos, obtained one Samian ship only to
reïnforce his small squadron.   Receiving then intelligence of a revolt
proposed at Teos, on the Asiatic main, he proceeded thither, and arrived just in time to prevent the immediate effect of a negotiation with
Tissaphernes and the revolted cities of Clazomenæ and Erythræ, supported by a body of troops from each.   He had however scarcely composed [matters, when information reached him that Chalcideus was
approaching with his squadron, now increased, by reïnforcement from
Chios, to twenty-three triremes.   Totally unequal to resist such a
force, which would be assisted by coöperation of the combined army,
he withdrew hastily to Samos.   The Clazomenians and Erythræans
were then admitted into Teos, which became a member of the Peloponnesian confederacy ; but, the Athenian interest being supposed still
prevalent among the lower people, the fortifications on the inland side
of the town were demolished.

c. 17.

Alcibiades had old and hereditary interest in Miletus, and he proposed next to ingage that, the richest and most important of the
Asiatic Grecian cities, in revolt against Athens.   In thus promoting
the Peloponnesian cause, however, it was not possible that he should
have the Peloponnesian interest at heart.   The success of the operations, which had been carried on under his direction, had been so rapid,
so uninterrupted, so important, and so little expected, that he could
not but have great present credit for it.   But one powerful party in
Lacedæmon was already hostile to him, and the moment his services
ceased to be necessary, he would have to apprehend more jealousy
than gratitude among the other.   Moreover, with the insuing annual
change of magistrates there, the ephor his friend would go out of
office, and a new commander-in-chief would supersede Chalcideus ;
whom his friend's interest, and perhaps his own recommendation, had
raised to the command, and who seems to have acted in it constantly
under his influence.   His next measure accordingly seems to show a

5   purpose

purpose adverse to the interest of those in whose service he was ingaged.   Having, together with Chalcideus, pursued Strombichides as
far as Samos, they proceeded to Chios, where they completely changed
their crews, putting the Peloponnesians ashore, to act as heavy-armed
infantry in the guard of the iland, and taking Chian seamen in their
room.   The pretended purpose was to give security to the aristocratical party in Chios, against the democratical, who were less satisfied
with the late change.   But Alcibiades had evidently other views.   In
persuading the Ionian cities to revolt from Athens, it was his purpose
to attach them as much as possible to himself, and as little as possible
to Lacedæmon: an Ionian force would be more manageable in his
hands than a Peloponnesian; and with an Ionian force he might
accomplish what a Peloponnesian would prevent.   Ostensibly, however, he was still the most zealous as well as the ablest promoter of the
Lacedæmonian interest.   Thrasycles, with his squadron of twelve triremes from Attica, had joined Strombichides at Samos.   Apprehensive
for Miletus, they hastened their course thither.   But Alcibiades was so
secret and so rapid in his measures, that, when they anchored off the
iland of Ladë, at the mouth of the harbour, he was already received
into the city, and his friends were in possession of the government.

A new event in Grecian politics followed; a treaty of alliance between Tissaphernes, in the name of the Persian monarch, and Chalcideus, in that of the Lacedæmonian republic.   The terms of this treaty
were perfectly accommodated to promote the purposes of Alcibiades,
but not at all honorable to Lacedæmon or to Chalcideus.   By the first
article a most dangerous concession was made to Persia; for it was
declared in general terms, 'that all the country and all the cities Thucyd. l. 8. c. 18.
' which had belonged to the predecessors of the king should belong
' to the king.'   It was then added, 'that the king, with the Lacedæ-
' monians and their allies, should in common prevent the accruing
' of any revenue, and of any advantage whatsoever, from those cities
' to the Athenians; that the king, with the Lacedæmonians and their
' allies, should carry on war against the Athenians in common; that
' neither party should make peace without the other; that if any sub-
' jects of the king should revolt, they should be held as enemies by
                                                        ' the

' the Lacedæmonians; and that equally if any allies of the Lacedæmo-
' nians should revolt,' (for by that term the renunciation of alliance
with the leading state was described) ' they should be held as enemies
' by the king.'

S E C T I O N   III.

Progress of Revolt against Athens: Exertions of Athens. Siege of
Chios. Battle of Miletus. Service of the Peloponnesian Armament
to the satrap of Caria. Spartan Officers, with the title of Harmost,
placed in the Cities of the Confederacy. Dissatisfaction of the
Peloponnesians with the Satrap. Operations of the adverse Arma-
ments, and Intrigues among the Asiatic Cities. Change in the
Administration of Sparta. Commissioners, sent from Sparta to Ionia,
refuse to confirm the Treaty with the Satrap. Revolt of Rhodes to
the Peloponnesian Confederacy.

Ol. 91. 4. THE riches of Persia being thus by treaty ingaged to assist the military
92, 1.
B. C. 412. force of the Peloponnesian confederacy, the power collected against
P. W. 20. the tottering dominion of Athens might seem more than sufficient to
insure its almost instant downfall. But party divisions and constitutional sluggishness prevailed in Lacedæmon, and the opposite interests
of different commonwealths impeded every measure of the confederacy;
while, the pressure of extreme danger inforcing unanimity in the
Athenian councils, such was the energy of the administration, and
such still the resources of the commonwealth, that Athens was already
again approaching to a superiority at sea.

Thucyd. l. 8.   Diomedon, conducting from Attica a reïnforcement of sixteen ships
c. 19. to the fleet on the Asiatic station, took four Chian triremes, from
which however the crews escaped. The Peloponnesians and their allies
meanwhile obtained the more important advantage of ingaging in revolt
the towns of Lebedus and Eræ on the continent, and afterward the
c. 22. city of Methymnë in Lesbos, the only one of the iland remaining to
Athens. But that wretched system of Grecian policy, which, equally
under

under Lacedæmonian as under Athenian supremacy, kept the higher
and the lower people everywhere at perpetual enmity, afforded opportunity for the Athenians, the moment they could show a force at sea,
to give a turn, in all maritime cities, in favor of the democratical
interest.   Diomedon therefore, proceeding to Teos, where the democratical interest was strong, recovered that city to the Athenian alliance. Thucyd. l. 8.
Meanwhile the body of the higher people of Samos, more depressed c. 21.
than all others since their reduction on their former revolt, were proposing to seize the opportunity that seemed to offer, through the
prevalence of the Peloponnesian arms, for mending their condition.
The lower people, having intelligence of the design, rose upon them, and,
with the assistance of the crews of three Athenian triremes then at Samos,
overpowered them, put to death two hundred, and driving about four
hundred more to seek their personal safety by flight, shared among themselves the property of all.   Nothing could insure to Athens the dominion of that valuable iland equally with this measure, at which humanity
shudders.   But indignation will rise higher at the following conduct
of Athens. The massacre and robbery were rewarded by a decree of
the Athenian people, granting to the perpetrators the independent
administration of the affairs of their iland, which, since the last
rebellion, had been kept under the immediate controul of the Athenian
government.

While success was thus beginning to shine again upon the Athenians,
on the eastern side of the Ægean, they met with an unexpected reverse
nearer home.   The Peloponnesian ships in the Corinthian Peiræus, to c. 20.
the number of twenty, making a sudden attack upon an Athenian squadron of equal force watching them, gained the victory and took four
ships.   Astyochus was then sent from Lacedæmon to conduct the
victorious squadron to Asia, there to assume the command in chief
of the fleet.

The exertions of the Athenian government nevertheless continued
to be efficacious.   Leon, bringing from Attica a fresh reinforcement
of ten ships, proceeded with Diomedon to Lesbos; and, tho Astyochus c. 24.
arrived in time to interfere, yet by their able management, with the coöperation of the democratical party, they recovered the whole of that
                                                    important

important iland. They proceeded to Clazomenæ on the continent,
and that city also renewed its connection with Athens.   Such, in short
had been the energy of the Athenian administration, and such the
supineness of the Peloponnesians, that the Athenian fleet in the Asiatic
seas could now be divided and yet everywhere superior.   The squadron of twenty triremes under Thrasycles and Strombichides had not
moved from Ladë, but watched there for an opportunity of advantage.
Making a descent on the Milesian lands, they defeated the troops
which, under Chalcideus, the Lacedæmonian commander-in-chief,
marched out against them, and Chalcideus himself was killed ; but
their force was insufficient for any attempt against the town of
Miletus.

Naval superiority however being recovered, it was determined to
carry on operations against Chios with a view to the reduction of the
iland ; and the Chians had the mortification to find, contrary not only
to their own expectation but that of all Greece, that their revolt had
been determined on without due precaution and just foresight. Till
the present conjuncture, the affairs of Chios had long been managed
with a steddy prudence, uncommon among the Grecian cities. Moderate in prosperity, blameless toward their neighbours, and using
their increasing wealth and power for no purpose of ambition, but
directing their politics meerly to secure the happiness they injoyed,
their iland, from the time of the Persian war, had never seen an enemy
within its bounds. The Athenians now prepared to attack it on all
sides. They occupied the forts of Sidussa and Pteleus, in the Erythræan
territory, and the little ilands Œnussæ, between Chios and the main,
as naval stations whence to infest the Chian coasts. Debarking troops
then in three several places, they defeated at each the forces which
opposed them; and with such slaughter that the Chians attempted
action in the field no more : giving up the whole of their rich territory
for ravage, they shut themselves within their walls. Under such
circumstances it was likely that the democratical party would be looking for means of accommodation with the Athenians. The leading men,
aware of this, sent information of their apprehensions to Astyochus,
who in consequence came from Erythræ with four ships.

It

It was now toward the end of summer when a fresh and powerful B. C. 412. reinforcement arrived at Samos from Attica; fifteen hundred Athenian heavy-armed, a thousand Argian, and a thousand of the various other allies of Athens, Phrynichus, Onomacles, and Scironidas commanding. From Samos they crossed to the Milesian territory, and landed there. Eight hundred heavy-armed Milesians under Alcibiades, with the Peloponnesians who had been under the orders of Chalcideus, and a force of Asiatic infantry and cavalry, led by the satrap Tissaphernes in person, proceeded to meet them. Both fides being prepared for battle, the Argians in the Athenian army, holding in contempt the Ionians, advanced before their main body hastily and with no good order, as against an enemy who would avoid their onset. But the Milesians, led by Alcibiades, presently routed them, and killed near three hundred. On the other side the Athenians themselves, opposed to the Peloponnesians and Asiatics, attacking the former first, defeated them, and the others immediately fled. Alcibiades, upon this drew off the Milesians; and the Athenians, holding the field of battle, erected their trophy. The event altogether remarkably disappointed common opinion among the Greeks, as well as the superior estimation in which those of Dorian race had been long accustomed to hold themselves ; for on each fide the Ionian troops were victorious over the Dorian.

Ol. 92. 1. P. W. 20. After 3 Sept. Thucyd. l. 8. c. 25.

The Athenians elate with their success, proceeded then immediately to take measures for an assault upon Miletus; but, in the evening of the same day on which the battle was fought, intelligence arrived of the approach of a fleet from Peloponnesus, of fifty-five triremes. Onomacles and Scironidas, anxious to restore the naval reputation of Athens, and perhaps too fearful of the temper of the people, their soverein, to use their judgement with due calmness, proposed to await the enemy's attack. But Phrynichus declared that he would neither be allured by a false opinion of glory, nor yield to unmanly shame : whatever his country's welfare most required, was in his opinion most honorable; and in the present state of the commonwealth, it would ill become them to risk unnecessarily its naval force. Either his arguments or his authority prevailed, and the fleet returned to Samos. The Argians, fretted, Thucydides says, with the disgrace of their own fhare in the late battle, sailed home.

c. 26.

Peloponnesus had not alone sent out the fomidable fleet which thus relieved Miletus. At the instigation principally of Hermocrates son of Hermon, the Dorian Sicilians had generally agreed to take an active part in the war; and Syracuse sent twenty triremes under his command, which had however yet been joined by only two more, furnished by Selinus. The Lacedæmonian Theramenes commanded the fleet in chief. On its reaching the coast of Asia, the Athenian armament being gone, it was to be considered what should be undertaken; and

Thucyd. l. 8. c. 28. the commanders resolved to gratify their new ally the satrap, by directing their first measures against Iasus, the residence of the rebel Persian chief Amorges. The fleet, in its approach to that place, was mistaken for an Attic fleet: the first assault in consequence succeeded; and Amorges being made prisoner, was a grateful present to Tissaphernes, who was thus inabled to obey his soverein's commands, which required him to send the rebel, or at least his head, to Susa. Some Greek troops which Amorges had entertained in his service, being mostly Peloponnesian, were taken as a reinforcement to the army. The other prisoners formed a valuable part of the booty, being made over to Tissaphernes, equally free and slaves, at a certain price a head [5], and the capture all together was among the richest made in the war. Possession of Iasus being made over to the satrap's officers, the Grecian armament returned to Miletus for winter quarters.

In confederacies composed of so many little republics, claiming independency, as those under the lead of Athens and Lacedæmon, to insure any just regularity in business, either military or political, would be hardly possible, without powers to be exercised by the superior, hazardous for the liberties of the inferior people. But the internal divisions of every little state, far more than any consideration for the confederacy at large, induced the subordinate governments not only to admit readily, but often to desire the controuling interference of the imperial people. The Lacedæmonian government accordingly sent superintending officers of their own, with the title of harmost, regulator, to reside in all the cities of their confederacy,

[5] 'The price mentioned by the historian is a Doric stater, the value of which, at the time of the Peloponnesian war, is very uncertainly known.

beyond

beyond proper Greece. The authority of these officers would depend much upon the power of the superintending state at the time, and the weakness of the subordinate, whether the weakness of scanty numbers and property, or weakness superinduced by internal divisions. The harmost, however, generally seems to have been but another name for a governor. Philippus, a Lacedæmonian, was appointed harmost of Miletus. Pædaritus, sent from Sparta to hold the same office at Chios, could not so readily and safely reach his destination. Landing, however, at Miletus, he was escorted by land to Erythræ, and thence found opportunity to make the short passage to Chios, without interruption from the Athenian cruizers.

Early in the winter Tissaphernes visited the Peloponnesian fleet, and, according to agreement with the Lacedæmonians, distributed a month's pay to it, at the rate of an Attic drachma, about tenpence sterling, daily, for each man. He then apologized for proposing to give in future only half a drachma, till he had consulted the king's pleasure; declaring himself desirous, if he could obtain authority for it, to continue the full pay before given. Theramenes, having only a temporary command, for the purpose of conducting the fleet to Astyochus, under whose orders it was to remain, was little disposed to exert himself about its pecuniary interests; but the Syracusan Hermocrates remonstrated warmly ; and Tissaphernes thought it so far of importance to keep his new allies in good-humour, that he at length made an addition to the half drachma, but would not allow the whole.

Thucyd. l. 8. c. 29. After 2d Oct.

In the course of the winter an additional force of thirty-five triremes under Charminus, Strombichides, and Euctemon, joined the Athenian fleet at Samos, which thus acquired again a clear superiority in the Asiatic seas. It was in consequence resolved to push the siege of Chios, and at the same time to blockade the port of Miletus. For the former purpose the greatest part of the landforce was assigned, with a squadron of thirty triremes; for the other, the rest of the fleet, consisting of seventy-four. The commanders drew lots for the services. It fell to Strombichides, Onomacles, and Euctemon, with thirty triremes and a part of the heavy-armed, to act against Chios: the others,

Thucyd. l. 8. c. 30.

3 H 2   with

with seventy-four, commanded the seas about Samos, and prepared for an expedition against Miletus.

Thucyd. l. 8. c. 31. Meanwhile Astyochus, who had gone to Chios to obviate expected revolt, hearing of the reïnforcement brought by Theramenes, from Peloponnesus, but uninformed of the great addition arrived to the enemy's fleet, thought the Peloponnesian interest in the iland sufficiently secure, and crossed to the opposite continent, where opportunity of farther acquisition appeared to invite him. Having however in vain attempted Pteleum and Clazomenæ, he was compelled by tempestuous weather to take refuge in the port of Cuma.

But in all the Grecian towns, through the opposition of interests, and the almost universal attachment of the democratical party to the Athenian cause, and the aristocratical to the Lacedæmonian, intrigues c. 32. were endless. While Astyochus lay with his fleet at Cuma, the aristocratical party in Lesbos sent proposals for bringing that iland again to the Lacedæmonian alliance. Astyochus favored the measure, but the Corinthians were disinclined to it; and the Chians, more apprehensive of their fellowcitizens of the Athenian party than of any other enemy, were extremely averse to any diminution of the friendly force within their own iland. Pædaritus, the Lacedæmonian governor, concurring with them, refused to let any Chian vessels go on the c. 33. service. Astyochus, highly displeased with this opposition to his purpose, declared that the Chians should in vain solicit from him that assistance which they might soon want; and with this threat he departed, to assume his naval command at Miletus.

c. 35. The Peloponnesian cause had continued to gain among the Sicilian and Italian Greeks, and a fresh reïnforcement of ten Thurian triremes, with one Syracusan, had passed to Peloponnesus. The Lacedæmonians, adding one of their own, appointed Hippocrates, a Lacedæmonian, to command the squadron, which they sent to join the fleet at Miletus. Cnidus having lately revolted from Tissaphernes, Hippocrates was sent thither, with orders to watch the town with six of his ships, while the other six took their station at Triopium, a promontory of the iland, for the purpose of intercepting the enemy's merchant-ships from Egypt. Information of this disposition being communicated to the Athenian fleet,

fleet, a squadron was detached, which took the six ships at Triopium, whose crews however escaped ashore.

The loss of six ships to the Peloponnesian confederacy, supported only by its own means, might have been of some consequence, but, with the advantage of the Persian alliance, it was little regarded. Astyochus, on his arrival at Miletus, found the Milesians zealous in the cause, and the armament in high spirits, notwithstanding the reduction of pay, which had occasioned so many murmurs. The pay still given by Tissaphernes was more than the Peloponnesian governments ever had given, or were able to give, and the booty acquired at Iasus was a great gratification. Nevertheless the principal officers could not rest satisfied with the terms of a treaty, which they could so little justify to their people at home, as that made by Chalcideus; and, at length, Tissaphernes was persuaded to allow the objectionable articles to be reconsidered. Theramenes had now the conduct of the business on the part of Lacedæmon, and a new treaty was concluded; in which the sovereinty of the Persian king over the Grecian cities in Asia was rather less explicitly acknowleged, but yet was acknowleged.

The use at this time, made by the Peloponnesians, of the advantages of Persian pay and Asiatic plunder, seems to have been to indulge themselves in the large and wealthy city of Miletus, under the fine sky of Ionia, while their new allies, the Chians, were pressed with danger of the united evils, which faction within, and an enemy without, might bring. Before the winter ended, the Athenians occupied the port and town of Delphinium, not far from the city. The democratical party among the Chians, in itself strong, seeing the Athenian fleets again superior in the Asiatic seas, showed its disposition to the Athenian cause so openly, that Pædaritus and the oligarchal party were in great alarm. They applied to Astyochus at Miletus for succour; but, in conformity to his threat, he refused to give any. Pædaritus sent complaints against him to Lacedæmon; but distress and danger meanwhile continued to press the Chians.

When, among the various applications for the Lacedæmonian alliance, the preference had been given to Tissaphernes and the Ionians, it had not been intended, even by Endius and Alcibiades, to slight the overtures

Thucyd. l. 8. c. 36.

c. 38.

overtures of Pharnabazus. Twenty-seven ships were therefore prepared expressly for the service, in which that satrap desired assistance.
But, in the beginning of winter, the year of magistracy of Endius had
expired, and with it expired, in a great degree, the influence of Alcibiades in the Lacedæmonian administration. A considerable change
of counsels insued. The men in command, and the measures pursuing,
on the Asiatic coast, were looked upon with a jealous eye. The
newly-prepared squadron, placed under the command of Antisthenes,
was ordered, not to the Hellespont or any port of the satrapy of Pharnabazus, but to Miletus, to join the fleet already there; and eleven
commissioners were imbarked in it, to inquire concerning men and
things, and, as a council, to assume in a great degree the direction of
affairs on the Asiatic station. They were particularly authorized to
appoint, if they should see proper, Antisthenes to supersede Astyochus
in the command in chief; and also, at their discretion, to send any
number of ships, with Clearchus for the commander, or not to send
any, to coöperate with Pharnabazus.

Antisthenes, with the eleven commissioners, making Melos, in their
way to the Ionian coast, fell in with ten Athenian triremes. They took
three, but the crews escaped, and the other seven got clear away. This
adventure gave them more alarm than satisfaction. They feared information to the Athenians at Samos, of their approach, and consequent
attack from a superior force. Instead therefore of making farther
their direct course for Ionia, they bore away southward for Crete, and
so on to Caunus in Caria, whence they sent to Miletus intelligence of
their arrival.

Meanwhile Astyochus, notwithstanding his anger against the
Chians, was preparing to attempt their relief, before it should be too
late to save allies so valuable to the confederacy. They were already
severely pressed: a contravallation was nearly completed against the
city: their lands were totally at the enemy's mercy; and their numerous slaves were deserting fast. Astyochus however, upon receiving the advice from Antisthenes, thought it his first duty to give convoy to the council, and his first interest to take care of the reïnforcement; and he accordingly moved with his whole fleet to Caunus. The

2   Athenian

Athenian admiral meanwhile had actually sent a squadron under Charminus, but of twenty ships only, to watch the squadron coming from
Peloponnesus.   Missing this, Charminus fell in with the grand fleet
under Astyochus, dispersed in a fog, and took three ships; but, when Thucyd. l. 8.
the fog cleared, the fleet collecting, he found it necessary to fly for
Halicarnassus, and reached that place, not without losing six ships.
Intelligence of this being carried to the Athenian admirals, they went c. 43.
with their whole force to offer battle to the Peloponnesians, who had
put into the port of Cnidus; but these showing no disposition to stir,
the Athenians returned to Samos.

As soon as the Athenian fleet was gone, the eleven commissioners
from Sparta began the more peculiar business of their mission, the consideration of the Persian treaty; and Tissaphernes thought the occasion important enough to require his presence at Cnidus.   The commissioners, of whom Lichas was the chief, appear to have been friends
of Agis; but, whatever party views they may have had, they conducted themselves in this business with a stern dignity, and with the
appearance at least of an inflexible integrity, becoming the antient reputation of Sparta.   The treaties were certainly very exceptionable.   The
words of the first, yielding to the king of Persia the sovereinty of all
the countries his predecessors had ever commanded; those of the
other, forbidding the Lacedæmonians and their allies from carrying
arms against any of those countries; were an acknowlegement, on the
part of Lacedæmon, of the claim of Persia, not only to all the Asiatic
and Thracian cities, and all the ilands of the Ægean, but to Macedonia,
Thessaly, Locris, and almost the whole north of Greece, including
Attica: so that the Lacedæmonians, instead of supporting their pretensions to be vindicators of Grecian liberty, thus admitted the subjection of near half the nation to the Persian dominion.   The Lacedæmonians did not indeed bind themselves to put Persia in possession of
the countries so in general terms ceded; and, had their leaders been
wily politicians, they might perhaps, after profiting from Persian assistance to serve their own purposes against Athens, have easily prevented
Persia from making any advantage of those articles, which seemed so
to militate with the common cause of Greece.   But Lichas and his collegues

legues would not, for any temporary interest of their country, surrender its honor. They condemned the treaties, both that concluded by Chalcideus, and that by Theramenes, in the strongest manner; they declared that they would on no account ratify them; and they insisted that the troops should receive no more pay from the satrap, unless he would enter into a new treaty upon other terms. Tissaphernes, disgusted with their authoritative tone and unbending manner, went away without concluding anything.

How far the conduct of the commissioners would be approved by the troops, to whom Persian pay had been no small gratification, may be doubted; but a circumstance occurred of a nature to obviate present dissatisfaction. Overtures came to the Peloponnesian commanders from some leading men of the wealthy iland of Rhodes. The fleet, consisting of ninety-four triremes, went thither; Cameirus, one of the principal towns, but unfortified, was taken without resistance: the chief men of the iland were summoned to an assembly, and all the towns were peaceably brought over to the Peloponnesian interest. Intelligence of the motion of the Peloponnesian fleet being conveyed to the Athenian commanders at Samos, they sailed in all haste for Rhodes, but arrived too late for any effectual interposition. The Peloponnesians obtained thirty-two talents from the Rhodians, toward the expences of the war, and, the winter being already advanced, they laid up their fleet in the harbours of the iland.

Thucyd. l. 8. c. 44.

B. C. 411. January.

SECTION IV.

Alcibiades, persecuted by the new Spartan administration; favored by the satrap of Caria; communicates with the Athenian armament at Samos. Plot for changing the constitution of Athens: Synomosies, or Political Clubs at Athens: Breach between Alcibiades and the managers of the plot. New Treaty between Lacedæmon and Persia. Continuation of the siege of Chios, and transactions of the fleets.

WHILE an important acquisition was thus made to the Peloponnesian confederacy, intrigue had been prosecuting, with no inconsiderable effect, in opposition to it. Since the expiration of the magistracy of Endius, the party of Agis had been gaining strength in Lacedæmon; and not only Alcibiades could no longer lead measures, as before, on Thucyd. l. 8. the coast of Asia, but his designs became more and more suspected in c. 45. Peloponnesus. In thwarting Alcibiades, however, the Lacedæmonian administration feared him. What precisely to expect they knew not; but they apprehended some great stroke in politics to their disadvantage; and, according to the concurrent testimony of historians, too unquestionable when Thucydides is in the list, private instructions were sent to Astyochus, to have Alcibiades assassinated. This measure has been attributed by some to the vengeance of Agis: whose bed it is said, Alcibiades had dishonored, and whose queen is reported to have been so shameless, as to boast of her connection with the greatest and handsomest man of the age. Others have ascribed it to the revenge of the queen herself, for a silly declaration of Alcibiades, if he really made it, that no inclination for her person, but meerly the vanity of giving a king to Sparta and an heir to the race of Hercules, induced him to pay her any attention. The cotemporary historian mentions upon the occasion neither Agis nor the queen: his expression rather goes to fix the crime upon the Spartan administration; and, tho the other stories possibly may have originated in that age, they

VOL. II.   3 I   bear

bear much more the character of the taste of following times. Alcibiades however, whether informed of the design, or only suspicious of
the Lacedæmonians, from acquaintance with their principles and consciousness of deserving their enmity, withdrew from their armament
and took his residence with Tissaphernes.

He was not unprepared for the change.   Uneasy, notwithstanding
the favor he found and the attention paid him, in the dependent character of a stranger and a fugitive, it was his object to restore himself
to his country, before that country was reduced so low as to be not
worth returning to.   With this view he had courted the satrap assiduously and successfully.   Neither the interest of the Persian empire,
nor the satrap's interest, were, any more than his own, the same
with that of Lacedæmon or the Peloponnesian confederacy.   An
opening therefore was not wanting, first for insinuations, and then for
advice, that might set the satrap at variance with the Peloponnesians,
and render Alcibiades not only agreeable but necessary to him.   Tissaphernes, pressed for money, both by his court and by the expences of
his government, and at the same time desirous of amassing for himself, listened with ready attention to any suggestion of means to spare
his treasury.   Alcibiades told him, 'that the allowance of pay to the
' Peloponnesian forces was extravagant.   The Athenians,' he said,
' long versed in naval affairs, and highly attentive to them, gave no
' more than half a drachma for daily pay to their seamen; not,' as he
pretended, ' from economical motives, or from any inability to afford
' more, but because they esteemed a larger pay disadvantageous to
' their service.'   Tissaphernes approved the proposal for a reduction,
but dreaded the discontent that would insue.   Alcibiades assured him,
' that he need not apprehend it: a sum of money, judiciously distri-
' buted among the commanders, would quiet all outcry; or, if there
' was a man among them not to be bought, it was only the Syracusan
' Hermocrates.   Representations and remonstrances would probably
' be made: but they might easily be refuted; nor need the satrap
' give himself any trouble about them : he would undertake to answer
' every argument and silence every clamor.   The pretensions indeed
' of most of the Grecian states were extravagant: that of the Chians,
                                                        ' he

' he would not scruple to tell them, was even impudent. The richest
' people of Greece, they were not contented with gaining indepen-
' dency at the expence of the blood and treasure of others, but ex-
' pected to be paid for defending it. Nor were the less wealthy states,
' which had been tributary to Athens, more reasonable. Delivered
' from the burden of tribute, they now grudged an unbought service,
' to preserve the independency and immunity which had been freely
' given them.' Having thus persuaded the satrap that he could obviate clamor, Alcibiades undertook to conciliate favor to him, and
excite zeal in his service: ' He would assert,' he said, 'that the pay
' hitherto given was from the private income of the satrapy; that
' Tissaphernes was laboring to obtain an allowance from the royal
' revenue; and should it be granted, whatever it might be, the whole
' should be distributed to the forces without reserve.' Tissaphernes
approved the proposal, and that reduction of pay, which has been al- Ch. 19. s. 3.
ready noticed, with the insuing discontent, and at length, through of this Hist.
the dexterity of Alcibiades, the compromise, followed.

   Having thus gained the satrap's ear, and recommended himself to
his confidence, Alcibiades proceeded to promote his own views at the
expence of the most important interests of the Peloponnesian confederacy. ' He urged, that both the public interest of the Persian em- Thucyd. l. 8.
' pire, and the private interest of the satrap, required, not speedy nor c. 46.
' complete success to the Peloponnesian cause, but a protraction of
' the war: that the Phenician squadron, which had been promised,
' ought not to be allowed to join the Peloponnesian fleet: that, for
' the same reason, to incourage reïnforcement from Greece, by hold-
' ing out the lure of Persian pay, was impolitic: that the king's in-
' terest clearly required a partition of power among the Greeks: the
' same state should not preponderate by land at the same time and
' by sea; but rather the Athenians should be supported in their
' wonted superiority on one element, and the Lacedæmonians on the
' other. Thus it would always be in the king's power to hold the
' balance between them, or to employ one against the other, as he
' pleased. These being the principles that should regulate the politics
' of Persia toward Greece, it followed that the Athenians were the
' more

' more commodious allies for the king: they had no land-force capable
' of coping with his land-force: they were powerful and rich only by
' holding other states in subjection; and, through their fear of revolts
' and of forein interference, they might be kept always in some degree
' dependent.   At any rate, they would always be glad to share with the
' king and his satraps the tributary cities of Asia.   But, on the con-
' trary, it was the professed purpose, and the known policy, of the
' Lacedæmonians, to emancipate all Grecian states from subjection
' to other Greeks; and they would certainly not rest long, while any
' remained under a forein dominion.   It was therefore the obvious
' interest of Tissaphernes, after having taken from the Athenians what-
' ever he could readily acquire, to break with the Lacedæmonians and
' drive them out of Asia.'

The conduct of the Lacedæmonian commissioners, in the congress
of Cnidus, contributed not a little to give force to these plausible
suggestions; for it went far toward verifying the prediction of Alcibiades,
that, when once the Lacedæmonians had obtained a superiority at sea,
they would not be contented to leave any Grecian cities subject to
Persia. Their disposition having been thus manifested, what followed, on
the part of the satrap, was to be expected; the pay to the armament
was, not indeed immediately stopped, but irregularly issued; and when
the Peloponnesian commanders proposed any exertion with the fleet,
Tissaphernes always objected, ' that the Phenician squadron,' which
he never intended should arrive, ' ought in prudence to be waited
' for.' Astyochus, whether through weakness or corruption, appears
to have deferred to him upon all occasions; and thus, as the historian
remarks, the most powerful fleet ever sent from Peloponnesus, wasted
in inaction.

Thucyd. l. 8.   Alcibiades, having thus far wrought upon the satrap, saw the crisis
c. 47.   approaching that might probably inable him, not only to return to
his country, but to acquire the glory of restoring his country to safety,
and perhaps even to splendor.   The Athenians, in their distress, had
been making great and even wonderful exertions; but those very exertions had nearly exhausted them; and it was evident to all the more
          2   informed

informed among them, that, tho they might still maintain themselves, and perhaps even prosper, against the meer force of the Peloponnesian confederacy, which they knew could not with its own means support its late exertions at sea, yet against that confederacy, supplied by the wealth of Persia, it would be impossible for them long to hold. Alcibiades, well aware both of the weakness of the commonwealth, and of the opinions and dispositions of the people, knew that nothing would give him so much importance as the notoriety of his favor with Tissaphernes. But tho he had risen by the populace, yet as he had also been condemned to death by the populace, he was unwilling again to trust himself under its unlimited authority; and he thought things so much in his power, that he resolved to require a change of government and the establishment of oligarchy, as the condition upon which he would restore his own services to his country, and at the same time bring to it the advantage, in its present circumstances the inestimable advantage, of the alliance of Tissaphernes.

The idea appears bold, even to extravagance; but it was in character for Alcibiades, and the times were singularly favorable. Most of the better sort of people, worn with the capricious tyranny of the multitude, and dreading such other dictators as Cleon and Hyperbolus, desired the change. There were few trierarcs in the fleet who did not desire it, and with these Alcibiades found ready means to communicate. His overtures excited attention: Theramenes, Eratosthenes, Aristocrates, names which will recur to notice, are mentioned among those who went from Samos to confer with him; and the assurances he gave that he would ingage Tissaphernes in the Athenian interest, and through him lead the king himself to an alliance with Athens, were very gladly received by the more powerful and richer men, who suffered most from the war, who were most pressed in consequence of the late public misfortunes, and whose property was principally called upon to supply the increased exigencies of an exhausted treasury. The proposal held out to them the prospect, at the same time, of an advantageous conclusion of the war, and of a change of government, favorable both to the power of those who were ambitious of power, and to the ease of those who only desired ease. Immediately therefore on their return to
Samos,

Thucyd. l. 8. c. 48.
Lys. or. con. Eratosth.

Samos, communicating with their friends, and finding those disposed
to the cause numerous and zealous, they settled the form of an oath
for all who should be admitted to their councils (a precaution common
among the factions of the antient republics) by which they bound
themselves to mutual support and protection.

Body and system being thus given to the party, the leaders ventured
to declare openly their knowlege, that the king would become the
ally of Athens, and furnish money for the expences of the war, provided
Alcibiades were restored, and the government changed to an oligarchy.
Some alarm and indignation at first arose; but the hope of profiting from
Persian pay softened the murmur, and the multitude acquiesced under
the idea of loss of power, when the recompence was to be increase of
both security and profit. Phrynichus however, the commander-in-
chief, known to be vehemently adverse to Alcibiades, was supposed
also zealous in the democratical interest, and the innovators had therefore avoided communication with him. But their measures could not
be intirely concealed from him, and, with such power as he possessed,
he warmly opposed them. Calling together the Athenian citizens of
the armament, he urged the falsehood or futility of the arguments
which had been used to promote the projected change. ' Alcibiades,'
he said, (and Thucydides affirms that he said truly,) ' cared no more
' for oligarchy then democracy, or for anything but for means of his
' own restoration to his country and to power. Nor was it to be
' believed that the Persian king would prefer the Athenian alliance to
' the Peloponnesian;' since the Athenians claimed command over so
' many cities within his country, while the Peloponnesians, whose
' naval strength now balanced that of Athens, formed no such
' invidious pretension. It was equally vain to suppose the promise of
' oligarchal government would allure either the subject-cities which had
' revolted, or those which still remained in obedience. The purpose of
' those cities was, not to be inslaved with an oligarchal rather than a
' democratical constitution, but, under whatsoever government, to be
' independent of forein dominion. Neither was the supposition less
' unfounded, that person and property would be more secure under the
' rule of those called the better people; for those better people, in the
                                                    ' exercise

' exercise of power, commonly sought their own in preference to the
' public benefit.   Nowhere indeed were men in public service so liable
' to oppression of every kind, even to capital punishment without trial,
' as where the power of the people, the refuge of the innocent, and the
' moderator of the excesses of the great, was done away.   That such
' was the opinion, the well-founded opinion, prevailing in most of the
' allied states, he well knew; and, for himself, he could not be satisfied
' with any for the measures now proposed, whether for the return of
' Alcibiades, or whatever besides.'

But in a business of this kind, a political and not a military affair,
the authority of the commander-in-chief availed little.   The associated
party, having a decided majority in the army, resolved immediately
to send a deputation to Athens, to push their purpose there.   Peisander
was appointed first of the deputation, and, notwithstanding any opposition from the commander-in-chief, they sailed for Attica.

Tho all thus far had been conducted peaceably, yet Phrynichus
stood in the situation of a man who, in a rebellion or civil war, has
taken his party.   However he might be inclined to sheath the sword,
he apprehended his opponents would not; he expected they would prevail at Athens ; he feared the consequences to himself, and, to obviate
them, he had recourse to a measure extremely hazardous, but still
more unjustifiable.   Thucydides, on occasion of the retreat from
Miletus, gives Phrynichus the character of an able and prudent man.
We can hardly give him credit for prudence upon this occasion.   He
informed the Lacedæmonian commander, Astyochus, of the divisions
in the armament under his command.   Astyochus, who seems to have
been a weak man, went to Magnesia, and communicated both to the
satrap and to Alcibiades the intelligence he had received.   Alcibiades
immediately sent information, to the principal Athenians in Samos, of
the treachery of their general; insisting that the punishment which
ought to be inflicted for such a crime was death.   Phrynichus, in high
alarm, and indeed in great peril, wrote again to Astyochus, complaining, ' that due secrecy had not been observed about what he had before
' communicated : that the danger insuing to himself was most pressing ;
' the danger of what he most abhorred and deprecated, perishing by
                                                                         ' the

Thucyd. l. 8.
c. 49.

c. 50.

' the hands of his detested domestic foes : that to avoid this there was
' nothing he was not ready to undertake, even to the betraying of the
' whole armament under his command to destruction.'   Nor was this
a difficult undertaking, for Samos was without fortifications; and to
give means of executing it, he added every necessary description and
direction.   Astyochus communicated this also to Alcibiades.

Thucyd. l. 8.
c. 52.
From the dangerous situation in which Phrynichus was thus involved, he extricated himself with singular boldness and dexterity.
Having taken his measures so as to know that Astyochus was still
betraying him, and that fresh communication was upon the point of
arriving from Alcibiades, he called together the army, and told them
he had learnt, by private intelligence, the intention of the enemy to
attack them.   The consideration that Samos was unfortified, and the
observation that part of the fleet was stationed without the port, he
said, induced them to the measure; and he therefore issued immediate
orders for works to be, in all haste, thrown up around the city, and for
every other precaution to be used against the expected attack.   It
had before been intended to fortify Samos; preparations had been made
in consequence; and the business, so as to serve the present need, was
quickly accomplished.   Meanwhile the expected letters arrived from
Alcibiades, indicating that the armament was betrayed by its general,
and that the enemy were preparing to attack it.   The intelligence now
only appeared to confirm that communicated by Phrynichus, and to
justify his measures; so that the accusation accompanying it was
wholly ineffectual, being considered meerly as the scheme of a man,
enough known to be little scrupulous, to ruin a political enemy.

It was a bold undertaking in which meanwhile Peisander and his
collegues were ingaged at Athens ; to propose to a soverein people to
surrender their power, and submit to be governed by the men of superior birth and wealth, over whom they had so long been accustomed
to tyrannize.   But apprehension of the prevalence of the Peloponnesian
arms, supported by the riches of Persia, and of the dreadful vengeance
commonly to be expected in that age from a conquering enemy,
lowered their haughtiness, and, instead of power and wealth, made
them anxiously look for means of secure existence in humbler freedom.

Peisander

Peisander therefore, incouraged by the visible effect of popular fear, Thucyd. l. 8. c. 53.
declared his purpose without reserve: he told the assembled people,
' that they might have the assistance of the king, and thus be not
' only delivered from their apprehensions, but assured of regaining a
' decisive superiority over their enemies, upon two conditions; the
' restoration of Alcibiades, and a change in the form of government.'
Indignant clamor from some, sullen murmurs from others, were excited
by this proposal. The particular enemies of Alcibiades were vociferous:
and they were supported by the sacred families of the Eumolpids and
Ceryces, who urged religion and divine wrath as obstacles to his return.
Those who feared no personal · ill from the restoration of Alcibiades
were less violent. Peisander bore patiently the reproaches of all; and
when opportunity was at length given for him to resume his speech,
addressing himself to the most angry, he observed, ' that the Pelo-
' ponnesians, always more powerful by land, now equal at sea, and
' superior in the number and strength of their allies, were supported
' in the expences of the war by the wealth of Persia;' and he then put
the question, ' What were the means of the commonwealth to resist
' such a combination, or what the hope to escape impending destruc-
' tion?' To this question no answer, or none in any degree satisfactory
to the assembly, was or could be given. ' In such circumstances
' then,' continued Peisander, ' the object for consideration must be,
' not what form of government you would prefer, but under what
' form the commonwealth can exist. And here no choice remains: it
' must be a government placed in such hands, armed with such authority,
' that the king may confide in it, so as to be induced to become your
' ally.' To soften the zealous partizans of democracy, he then added,
' Some among you, I know, think this a great evil. But can you
' hesitate to chuse between certain ruin, and what will at worst be a
' passing evil? since, when peace and safety are restored, nothing
' can prevent the people from restoring, whenever they please, the
' antient form of government.'

Thus exciting at the same time fear and hope, and indeed proving c. 54.
to the people that they had scarcely another chance for safety, notwithstanding the aversion which had so long obtained among them, almost

to an abhorrence, of oligarchy, Peïsander prevailed.   By a decree of
the general assembly, eleven commissioners were appointed, himself
the first, to treat with Tissaphernes and Alcibiades; with full power
to conclude whatever they should judge expedient for the commonwealth.   Orders were then issued for the recall of Phrynichus and his
collegue Scironides; in whose room Diomedon and Leon were appointed
to command the armament.

There were at Athens societies called Synomosies, which bore considerable resemblance to our political clubs; with this difference
principally, that as property, liberty, and life itself were incomparably
less secure there than under the mild firmness of our mixed government, the interests of individuals, which bound them to those societies,
were much more pressing than what commonly lead to any similar
establishments among us.   The sanction of a solemn oath to their
ingagements was therefore always required of the members; whence
the societies obtained their name, signifying sworn brotherhoods[6]:
The objects proposed were principally two; private security, and political power; and for the sake of one or both of these, most men of
rank or substance in Athens were members of some Synomosy.   Against
the oppression of democratical despotism, which was, often, as we shall
see more particularly hereafter, very severely exercised against the
rich, the collected influence of a body of noble and wealthy citizens
might give protection, when the most respectable individual, standing
single on his merits, would be overwhelmed: and the same union of

---

[6] Ξυνωμοσίας ἅπερ ἐτύγχανον πρότερον ἐν τῇ
πόλει ὅσαι ἐπὶ δίκαις καὶ ἀρχαῖς.   Societates
& collegia, quæ prius in urbe erant, & quæ
judiciis & magistratibus præerant.   Vers.
Duker.—*Juntos of the accomplices already
formed in the city, with the view to thrust themselves into the seats of judicature and the great
offices of state.* Smith's Transl. If the word
accomplices, for which there is no sufficient
authority in the original, were omitted, I
should prefer the English translation to the
Latin, which is indeed clearly bad.   The
other, however, is far from satisfactory, and

I know not that this interesting passage, in
which Thucydides speaks of what was familiar in his time, without sufficiently explaining himself for posterity, has been anywhere
duly discussed.   The explanation which I
have ventured to give, is founded on a
comparison of that passage with whatever
has occurred to my notice, anyway bearing
a relation to the subject, in the various
authors whom I have had occasion to consult, and in whose authority I have confidence.

influence

influence which could provide security against oppression, with a little increase of force, would dispose of the principal offices of the state. Peisander addressed himself severally to all these societies, and he seems to have had considerable success in persuading them to concur in his measures. Everything being thus prepared, as well as time and circumstances would permit (for very important interests required his presence on the other side of the Ægean) he hastened his departure with his ten collegues.

Arriving at Samos, they found their cause so prospering that any stay there appeared needless. They proceeded therefore to the Asiatic main, to negotiate with Alcibiades and Tissaphernes; and they were admitted to a conference, at which the satrap attended in person, but which was managed for him by Alcibiades. The conduct of that wily politician, upon this occasion, is not completely accounted for by the cotemporary historian, but the ground of it may be gathered. It could never be his intention to establish at Athens an unbalanced oligarchy; the most adverse of all constitutions, to that supremacy of one person, which he had, like many others before him, injoyed under the democracy, and which it was certainly his purpose to regain. Neither he, nor probably any other, had supposed that the democracy could have been overthrown, and such a government established on its ruin, by so sudden and so quiet a revolution as that managed by Peisander. As he then would be disappointed, so Peisander and his principal associates would be elated; and those terms which he expected to have commanded from the oligarchal and democratical parties balanced, would not be conceded to him by the established oligarchy. Hence apparently it became his purpose now to render the conference abortive, by making demands for the satrap, to which the Athenian commissioners could not consent. Finding them however disposed to yield much, he required the cession of all Ionia, with the adjacent ilands, to the Persian monarch: and, fearing the urgency of their situation would induce them to admit this, he raised new difficulties; a second and third conference were held, and at length he added the requisition, that, along all the coasts of the Athenian dominion, navigation should be free for the king's ships, at all times and in

Thucyd. l. 8. c. 56.

any

any number. Such a demand convincing the commissioners that Alcibiades meant nothing friendly to them or their party, they broke up the conference in some anger, and returned to Samos.

Thucyd. l. 8.
c. 57.
Peisander and his collegues were no sooner gone, than Tissaphernes went to Caunus, in Caria, a situation commodious for communicating with the Peloponnesian commanders, with whom he renewed negotiation. He was now in alarm for the consequences of his refusal of pay to their fleet, which, of three disagreeable things, he foresaw would probably produce one : either the Peloponnesians must fight the Athenians, and would be defeated ; or their crews would desert, and thus the Athenians, without obligation to him and without risk to themselves, would become decisively superior ; or, what he dreaded more than either of these, to supply their pressing necessities they would plunder the territories under his command, and thus weaken the sources of his revenue. In pursuance therefore of his original purpose, to keep the Greeks balanced against oneanother, he invited the Peloponnesian chiefs to a conference at Miletus, which was not refused ; and having then directed the issue of pay as formerly, a new treaty was quickly concluded, which ran thus :

' In the thirteenth year of the reign of Darius, and in the ephoralty ' of Alexippidas in Lacedæmon, a treaty was concluded in the plain ' of the Mæander, between the Lacedæmonians and their allies on one ' part, and Tissaphernes and Hieramenes and the sons of Pharnaces ' on the other part, concerning the affairs of the king and those of the ' Lacedæmonians and their allies.

' Whatever the king possesses in Asia shall be the king's, and the ' king shall direct the affairs of his own country according to his will ' and pleasure. The Lacedæmonians and their allies shall not injure ' any place within the king's dominion ; and if any among the ' Lacedæmonians or their allies shall attempt such injury, the Lace-- ' dæmonians and their allies in common shall prevent it. So also if ' any of the king's subjects shall attempt any injury to the Lacedæmo- ' nians or their allies, the king shall prevent it.

' Tissaphernes shall continue to pay the fleet in the manner here- ' tofore agreed, until the king's fleet shall arrive. After that it shall

4   ' be

' be at the option of the Lacedæmonians and their allies to pay their
' own fleet, or to receive the pay still from Tissaphernes, upon con-
' dition of repaying him when the war shall be concluded.   The fleets,
' when combined, shall carry on operations under the joint direction
' of Tissaphernes, and of the Lacedæmonians and their allies.

  ' No treaty shall be entered into with the Athenians but by mutual
' consent of the contracting parties.'

  Thus the alliance of Lacedæmon with Persia, or at least with the
satrap, was apparently confirmed.

  During these negotiations, Leon and Diomedon, having taken the
command of the Athenian armament from Phrynichus and Scironidas,
had moved to Rhodes with intention to offer battle; but on their
arrival they found the Peloponnesian fleet laid up for the winter.   After
gratifying their crews therefore, with some revenge against the
Rhodians and some profit to themselves, by ravage of a part of the
iland, they took their station at the neighboring iland of Cos, to watch
the enemy's motions.

B. C. 411.
End of Jan.
Thucyd. l. 8.
c. 55.

  While the Peloponnesians were thus inactive, their allies of Chios
were reduced nearly to extremity.   In an unsuccessful sally, Pædaritus,
the Lacedæmonian harmost of Chios, had been killed; the blockade
was completed, and famine began to press the inhabitants and garrison.
In this situation of things opportunity was found to send an officer to
Rhodes, who urged to the Peloponnesian commanders there, that, as
the city was effectually blockaded, its distress was become pressing,
and nothing less than strong effort with the whole fleet could save it.

c. 61.

  Twelve triremes had been left as guardships at Miletus, four of which
were Syracusan, five Thurian, and only one Lacedæmonian; but the
Lacedæmonian commander, Leon, was a man of enterprize.   While
Astyochus hesitated, Leon, taking advantage of the absence of the
Athenian fleet from the neighborhood, conducted his squadron to
Chios.   The Chians, informed of his approach, manned twenty-four
triremes and went out to meet him, while their infantry made a diversion by an attack upon the Athenian works.   Thirty-two Athenian
ships had been left as a guard upon Chios.   With these an obstinate
action insued, in which the Chians were so far successful as to conduct
                                                                  the

the twelve Peloponnesian ships into their harbour, and Leon was received as the person charged with the care of the interests, and with the administration of the authority, of the Lacedæmonian state, in the room of Pædaritus.

The reïnforcement thus acquired was important: it inabled the Chians to obtain some supplies by sea; and occurrences soon after afforded farther opportunity. The renewal of connection with the satrap of Caria did not prevent the Peloponnesians from prosecuting their purpose of extending their alliance to Pharnabazus satrap of the Hellespont.   Early in spring, the twenty-first of the war, Dercylidas, a Spartan, was sent to him. He went by land, with only a small escort: yet, on-his arrival before Abydus, the efficacy of the Spartan name sufficed to induce that city immediately to revolt from the Athenians; and, two days after, Lampsacus followed the example. Strombichides, who commanded the Athenian squadron at Chios, being informed of these circumstances, hastened to the Hellespont with twenty-four triremes. The sea thus was left open for the Chians to receive any relief.

The cautious Astyochus, receiving intelligence that a strong squadron of the enemy was thus called far from the Ionian coast, thought the opportunity favorable for seeking an action with their principal fleet. Upon his moving from Rhodes, Leon and Diomedon quitted Cos, and resumed their station at Samos. Astyochus led his fleet first to Chios, and strengthening himself with the whole naval force there, went to Samos, and offered battle. The Athenians, however, would not stir; and indeed their affairs were in a state, both at Samos and at home, that might have afforded to a more able and active commander than Astyochus, other advantage than that from which he had proposed to profit.

B. C. 411.
Ol. 92. ¼.
P. W. 21.
Mar. 28.
c. 62.

End of April.

Thucyd. l. 8.
c. 63.

SECTION V.

Progress of the plot for a revolution at Athens: Violences of the oligar-
chal party : Proposed new form of government : Establishment of
the new council of administration : Negotiation of the new govern-
ment for peace with Lacedæmon.

PEISANDER and his collegues, returning to Samos from their unsuccessful negotiation with Tissaphernes and Alcibiades, had the gratification to find, not only that their cause had been gaining in the
army, but that the oligarchal party among the Samians themselves
were both disposed and able to effect a change in the government of
their iland. Thus incouraged they determined to pay no more attention to Alcibiades, but, in prosecuting their original purpose of a
change in the Athenian constitution, to rely upon their own strength
for the conduct, both of the domestic affairs of the commonwealth,
and of the business of the war. A large subscription was raised by the
party, for supporting measures upon which now depended, not only
their interest, but their personal safety.

Having established this groundwork for future proceedings, it was
then determined that Peisander, with five of the other commissioners,
should return to Athens to manage the concerns of the party there;
and that the other five should go through the allied and subject-states,
and endevor to bring all under an oligarchal form of government.
Diotrephes was appointed to the superintendancy of the affairs of Thrace.
In his way thither he stopped at Thasus, and succeeded in at once
abolishing the sovereinty of the people there. The consequence, however, was not what Peisander and his collegues intended. Some principal Thasians of the oligarchal party, who had been banished by the
Athenians, had taken refuge with the Peloponnesian armament on the
Asiatic coast. They maintained a correspondence with their friends
remaining in the iland, and had been importunately urging revolt.
Diotrephes did for them the most difficult part of their business, much

better

[right margin notes:]
B. C. 411.
February.
Thucyd. l. 8,
c. 63.

c. 64.

better than they could have done it for themselves. Oligarchy being
established, the Thasians in possession made no longer any difficulty
of preferring the Lacedæmonian to the Athenian connection; the
exiles were restored, and Thasus became a member of the Peloponnesian
confederacy. Meanwhile Peisander and the five who accompanied
him, wherever they touched in their way to Athens, seem to have
found as little difficulty in effecting the change of government they
desired, as Diotrephes at Thasus: but the consequence in most of the
towns (so Thucydides says, without naming them) was the same;
they revolted to Lacedæmon.

Thucyd. l. 8.
c. 65.

c. 64.

By this very circumstance, what otherwise might appear a phenomenon, is explained; how a few citizens of Athens, with self-assumed
authority, could almost instantaneously overturn the constitutions of so
many Grecian republics. Democracy having long principally depended,
throughout Greece, upon the patronage of Athens, when the Athenian
democracy was overthrown and oligarchy substituted, immediately the
prevalence of the oligarchal or aristocratical party was prepared. But
the means by which the oligarchal party at Athens had advanced far in
its purpose, do no honor either to the Athenian government or the
Athenian character. Assassination was largely used; and it seems to
have been chiefly managed by youths of the best families. Androcles,
a man of mean origin, whose influence among the lower people had
contributed much to the condemnation of Alcibiades, and who had
ever since been the most forward champion of democracy, was among
the first taken off. Others, of the most obnoxious to the friends of
Alcibiades and of oligarchy, shared the same fate; for, at Athens, the
causes of Alcibiades and of oligarchy were not yet distinguished.
Inquiry concerning these murders was smothered or deterred, and the
friends of democracy became afraid to show themselves.

c. 66.

c. 65.

The oligarchal party thus finding themselves strong, ventured to
declare openly the kind of change which they proposed to make in the
constitution; in which some consideration was had for established
prejudices, as well as for an appearance of public virtue. There was
to be still an assembly of the people, but in some degree select: it
was to be confined to a body of five thousand, to be chosen among
                                                              those

those most qualified by property and personal ability to serve the commonwealth: and public pay was to be allowed to none but those actually serving in the fleet or army. This, says the cotemporary historian, was something specious and alluring; being not only congenial to the spirit of the antient constitution, but even to modern practice; since so large a number as five thousand citizens scarcely ever met in one assembly; and at the same time it held out to everyone the hope that, if he would concur in the measures proposed, he might be a member of the soverein body.

Thucyd. 1. 8. c. 66.

Meanwhile the general assemblies were regularly held according to antient form, and the council of Five-hundred retained its functions. But assassination was continued; and with so little reserve, and such impossibility of obtaining justice against the perpetrators, that political opposition was deterred. None spoke, either in the assembly or council, but those of the party, and they not without previous communication with the chiefs. The friends of democracy, without equal union among themselves, ignorant of the numbers of the oligarchal party, and supposing them much greater than they really were, scarcely dared complain of enormities practised; every one thinking himself fortunate if, with the utmost caution to avoid offending, he avoided suffering. To this depression of the democratical party nothing so much contributed as the treachery among its reputed friends; for, some of those farthest from previous suspicion having joined the oligarchal party, no one knew any longer in whom he might confide. Thus assassinations continued to pass without inquiry; and, even where proof could be obtained against the perpetrator, nobody ventured to prosecute.

Already things were in this situation, when Peisander returned to Athens. Before his departure, a decree had been made, declaring, in general terms, that the government should be changed: it remained yet to be decided how. An assembly of the people was convened to determine that important question. The oligarchal party had such a superiority, that they might propose, with a certainty of carrying, in the moment, almost anything: but it was not what might be in the moment carried in the assembly at Athens, that would decide the future constitution of the commonwealth, or their own future fate.

c. 67.

Not only turns in the popular mind must be provided against, but great consideration must be had for that large portion of the commonwealth, serving in the armament, on the other side of the Ægean. It was therefore moved, that the consideration of the business should be referred to a committee of ten men, who should make their report on an appointed day; and a decree passed to that effect.

The day being come, the people were summoned to assemble on the hill of Colonus, a little more than a mile from the city. The ten then came forward with the simple proposal of a law, whose aim was nothing more than to obviate illegality in the future measures of the party. It stated, that every Athenian should be free to declare any opinion, in the assembly, upon political topics; and it inflicted heavy penalties upon those who should endevor to abridge this liberty, whether by legal prosecution, according to the antient law, or in any other manner. This being carried, and what before would have been treason thus made legal, some of the party declared their opinion, that the form of the administration of the commonwealth ought to be changed, and that pay and remuneration should no more be issued from the treasury, for any but those employed for the commonwealth on forein service. This also being patiently heard, Peisander then ventured to propose the form of government to be established: ' That five presidents ' should be chosen by the people: that these should elect a hundred, ' and that each of the hundred should elect three: that the council ' of Four-hundred thus formed, should be vested with full power to ' direct the executive government[7]: that the supreme authority in ' last resort should reside in a body of five thousand citizens, to be ' assembled at the discretion of the council[8].'

Thucyd. l. 8.   In this manner it was endevored, by the ablest politician, in the
c. 68.   judgement of Thucydides, at that time in Greece, to remedy the evils
of the Athenian democracy: for Peisander, tho himself able, was but an instrument in the hands of Antiphon; a man, says the historian,

---

[7] Ἄρχειν ὅπη ἀν ἄριϛα γιγνώσκωσιν ἀυτοκρά-   implied, but is not expressed by the his-
τορας.—Thucyd. 7. 67.   torian; nor indeed does it seem to have
  [8] The distinction of the legislative and   been fully and clearly conceived by any of
executive powers appears in some degree   the antient politicians.

                                                              in

in virtue inferior to no Athenian of his age, and in abilities, whether for the closet or the assembly, superior to all. This very superiority exciting jealousy among the people, had prevented the exertion of his talents for the public benefit; a circumstance not uncommon among the antient democracies, and which probably contributed to inhance the aversion of Antiphon to that form of government: but in any private cause, whether in the inferior courts of judicature, or before the assembled people, no man was equally capable of serving his friends, either by his advice or by his eloquence. The second place among the opponents of democracy seems to have been held by Theramenes son of Agnon; a man also of superior powers, both of thought and elocution, and moreover of considerable military experience. But, beside those originally of the oligarchal party, there were some eminent men who had passed over to it from the democratical; and, of these, Phrynichus, the late commander on the Asiatic coast, was the chief. Of a fearless temper, but an unprincipled mind, Phrynichus dreaded, beyond any personal danger, the restoration of Alcibiades to the commonwealth and to power. As soon therefore as the oligarchal party broke with Alcibiades, Phrynichus joined the oligarchal party; and, after the common manner of renegades, exceeded in zeal the most zealous of the original members. A number of superior men, says the cotemporary historian, being thus united in the conduct of the business, it is no great wonder that it succeeded; tho to deprive the Athenian people of liberty, for that is his expression, a hundred years after the recovery of it by the expulsion of the tyrants, during above fifty of which they had been accustomed, not only to obey none, but to command many, was indeed an arduous undertaking.

The decree, directing the new constitution, having passed the assembly of the people, the party managed among themselves the appointment of the new council. But the council of Five-hundred, in whom the old constitution vested the excutive power, had not been consulted concerning any of the measures taken or proposed: they were still in possession of the prytaneium or state-house, in which a part of them, the prytanes, usually resided; and it was apprehended they might not peaceably resign it. When therefore the new council

Thucyd. l. 8. c. 69.

3 L 2

was

was to be introduced, measures were taken, with much forethought, to obviate opposition, which might produce tumult. Since the establishment of a hostile garrison in Deceleia, constant readiness for military duty had been required of the whole people. Daily all appeared in the morning in arms; and the magistrates and officers distributed the duty of the day among them; some to the guard of the works, others to hold themselves in readiness for the field. All who could be spared were then dismissed, with directions only to repair to the general parade at a certain signal. On the day fixed for ejecting the old council, it was provided that the citizens of the democratical interest should be dismissed, and those only retained in arms for the duty of the day, in whom the party could best confide. Among these were a number of Andrian, Tenian and Carystian auxiliaries, with some colonists from Ægina, all brought to Athens for the purpose.

Matters being thus prepared, the Four-hundred went to the prytaneium, armed each with a concealed dagger, and attended by a hundred and twenty youths, who had been accustomed to perform for them the business equally of guards and assassins [9]. They carried with them the arrear of salary due to the counsellors of the bean, as the Five-hundred were called, and making a tender of it, required all to withdraw. The old council, quietly taking their pay, obeyed the requisition, and no stir was made in the city on the occasion. The Four-hundred then proceeded to elect prytanes from their own body by lot; and, with the same ceremonies of prayer and sacrifice, which were prescribed by custom for the antient council, they commenced the execution of their office.

Thus was apparently completed this extraordinary revolution. Athens, and whatever of Attica was not held by the enemy, yielded obedience to the new council, become the supreme power of the commonwealth, through a law made, with all due form, by the assembly of the people, which before held that power. In the general conduct

---

[9] This seems to be the import of the historian's phrase, 'οῖς ἐχρῶντο ἔιτι που δέοι χειρουργῖν. Thucydides calls them Ἕλληνες νεανίσκοι, thus marking that they were different people from the ordinary armed attendants of the Athenian magistracy, who were always barbarians, generally Scythians.

of

of the business, we see something very different from the tumultuous revolutions so numerous among the inferior Grecian republics.
Nowhere else, in the accounts remaining to us, can we discover such
a regard for all the forms of an established constitution : yet, even in
this revolution at Athens, we find strong relics of barbarism, I must
risk the expression, and very defective notions of policy.   None of
those public massacres took place, which were so usual in Grecian
revolutions : public executions, with the pretence of law or popular
judgement, were also avoided : some persons were imprisoned, some
banished ; and, were this all, the duty of the ruling powers to preserve
public tranquility perhaps might have justified it : but many, in the
apprehension of being obnoxious, sought their safety by flight ; for the
horrid and base practice of secret assassination was continued, against
those whom the prevailing party supposed most adverse and most
formidable.

Of the many actually living in banishment, under condemnation
from the assembled people, or the popular tribunals, some the leaders
of the revolution would gladly have restored ; and probably they would
have refused the favor to few, so that, among the number, the historian
Thucydides might have returned to his country.   But the restoration
of Alcibiades, tho he had been the first mover of the revolution, was
looked to by most of the party with no friendly eye.   Some, as Phrynichus, were essentially interested in his exclusion ; and all would be
jealous of the talents, the fame, the popularity, of one who had so long
been the active and successful opponent of the oligarchal interest.
Confident that they no longer needed his assistance, they were no
longer willing to admit that superiority, which must have been yielded
to him ; and therefore, to obviate opportunity for any measures in his
favor, making a merit of supporting the decrees and judgements of the
people, they resolved that none should be restored who had been
banished by the people.

In other points they did not preserve the same respect for the decrees
of the people, or the forms of the antient constitution, or even for
their own declarations concerning the new one.   The appointment of a   Thucyd. l. 8.
supreme assembly of five thousand had been held out only as a lure,   c. 92.

to

to ingage readier acquiescence under the other changes; for such a body would have been perhaps even more difficult to manage, by the Few, who proposed to hold all power in their own hands, than the assembly open to every citizen. But they declared, and they found no small advantage in so doing, not only that the supreme power in last resort was to be vested in such a select, yet numerous body of citizens, but that the selection, though not published, was already made; for thus they kept every man in hopes for himself, and in fear of his neighbor.

The party, being thus completely masters within the city, turned their attention to things without. It was a most important object for

After 27 Feb. them to make peace with Lacedæmon, and they had warm hope of success. Accordingly they sent to Agis, then in Deceleia, representing to him, that he would no longer have a fickle, faithless and arrogant multitude to deal with, but a government more resembling that of Sparta, and which might deserve his confidence. But Agis, considering the probable ferment of men's minds immediately after such a revolution, thought he might possibly find means to command terms instead of treating for them. Declining therefore any negotiation, he sent for a large force from Peloponnesus, with which, added to his troops in Deceleia, he marched to the walls of Athens. The Athenian people, he concluded, would not yet be disposed to pay regular and quiet obedience to their new leaders : the sudden appearance of a

Thucyd. l. 7. hostile army would excite alarm; difference of opinion would pro-
c. 78. bably arise; contention would follow, and perhaps mutiny; and, in the confusion, possibly a well-timed assault might carry the city.

The event justifies the character of ability, which Thucydides gives to the leaders of the oligarchal party in Athens. Nothing happened of what Agis expected. The whole of the Athenian cavalry went out of the city, in good order, accompanied by some light-armed and bowmen, with a body of heavy-armed following to support them. The Peloponnesian army had not a force of cavalry equal to oppose the Athenian. A detachment, advancing very near the walls, was attacked and overpowered, and the Athenians carried off the dead. Agis finding himself thus disappointed, prudently withdrew to Deceleia, and sent back the troops

ı   lately

lately arrived from Peloponnesus. The Athenian ministry were thus encouraged to try again a negotiation, and, fresh overtures to Agis being now favorably received, they made no delay in sending ministers to Lacedæmon.

End of March.

SECTION VI.

Opposition of the fleet and army at Samos to the new government of Athens: Thrasybulus. Dissatisfaction of the Peloponnesian arma-ment with its general. Assistance sent from the Peloponnesian armament to Pharnabazus satrap of the Hellespont. The restoration of Alcibiades decreed by the Athenian armament: Alcibiades elected general by the armament. Fresh discontent of the Peloponnesian armament: Astyochus succeeded in the command by Mindarus. Com-missioners from the new government of Athens to the armament at Samos: Able and beneficial conduct of Alcibiades.

THUS successful in their administration at home, and in train to put an end to war within Greece, difficulties were arising for the oli-garchal leaders, which no wisdom on their part probably could have prevented. Peisander, before he left Samos, had exerted himself among the people of that iland, so far as to persuade many of the democratical party to join the oligarchal; and a society was formed of three hundred friends of oligarchy, who, according to usual practice, bound themselves to oneanother by solemn oaths to support their common measures. Peisander thought the oligarchal interest thus secure among the Samian people, as he hoped it was in the armament. But, after his departure, tumults arose among the Samians: the Athenians of course interfered; and, Charminus, one of the generals, was, with some others, unfortunately killed. In these contests the oligarchal party had the advantage; they depended upon support from the Athenians, among whom they supposed the oligarchal to be now the prevailing interest; and they were proceeding to take farther mea-sures against the supporters of democracy.

B. C. 411.
P. W. 21.
March.

Thucyd. l. 8.
c. 73.

But

But there had always been, among the patrons of democracy, at Athens, some of the first families of the commonwealth : for of these there were always some who could more readily rise to power through the democratical than the oligarchal interest ; and indeed some were considered in a manner hereditary chiefs of the democratical cause. The present generals, Leon and Diomedon, connected as they were with the leaders of the oligarchal party, yet having themselves great interest among the people, were averse to the proposed change of government; and, the democratical Samians soliciting their protection against the oppression of the oligarchal, they readily gave it.

Leon and Diomedon, however, appear to have beeen moderate in party, and not men of commanding characters. There were two younger officers, of inferior rank, Thrasybulus son of Lycus, captain of a trireme, and Thrasyllus, an officer of the heavy-armed, who by their reputation for ability, courage, activity and integrity, were of principal consideration. These were zealous in the democratical cause: they instigated the generals, by whom they were well received; they were sedulous in argument and persuasion among the soldiers and seamen, by whom they were beloved and respected; and thus, while the revolution took place at Athens in favor of oligarchy, the preponderance of the democratical cause was restored in the armament at Samos. The democratical Samians then, obtaining support from the Athenians, prevailed against their opponents. Thirty of the society of three hundred were put to death . three were banished ; and the rest, with a humanity not common in Greek sedition, on submitting to democracy, received a free pardon [10].

Thucyd. l. 8. c. 74.

The revolution at Athens being unknown yet at Samos, Chæreas son of Archestratus, a man of eminence in the Athenian armament, was dispatched in the herald-ship Paralus to report these transactions; not without expectation that he would be the messenger of grateful news to the ruling powers. Information of the extraordinary change that had taken place meeting him on his arival, he

[10] The phrase of Thucydides, singularly concise and singularly expressive, is scarcely to be translated : Τοῖς δ᾽ἄλλοις οὐ μνησικακοῦντες, δημοκρατούμενοι τολοιπὸν ξυνεπολίτευον.

instantly

instantly secreted himself; and the event justified the suspicion which directed that conduct.   Two or three of his officers were thrown into prison : his crew were moved into an ordinary trireme on the Eubœan station ; and the sacred ship was committed to persons more devoted to the ruling party.   Chæreas, waiting only to acquire information, in his concealment, of the circumstances of the revolution, returned in haste to Samos, and reported there, with the usual, or even more than usual exaggeration of party-spirit, the violences of those who held the powers of government at home.   Regardless of truth, he dwelt upon whatever would be likely most to irritate the passions of those serving in the armament.   A few assassinations, if we may judge from the omission of all mention of them upon this occasion by the historian, seem not to have been considered as what would make much impression : the sufferers were probably little connected with the armament, or little esteemed in it : but 'that the Four-hundred inflicted stripes without re-
' serve; that despotic restriction was put upon discourse; that complaint
' was held criminal, and that it was dangerous to open the lip against
' the ruling powers ; that even the wives and children of those on forein
' service were not secure from insult; that it was proposed to confine,
' as hostages, the nearest friends of all those in the armament at Samos,
' who were supposed friends of democracy:' these were the topics on which Chæreas principally insisted.

Such information, from a man of rank, just arrived from Athens, when the armament was already in a ferment, raised an instant flame. In the first moment of alarm and passion, the zealots for democracy were going to turn their swords against those of their comrades who had shown a disposition to favor oligarchy ; and nothing prevented so rash a measure, but the consideration, warmly urged by some of the more prudent among them, that the Peloponnesian armament was near enough to take advantage of such a circumstance, for the destruction of both parties.

Bloodshed being thus prevented, and the commanders-in-chief, as far as appears, passive, Thrasybulus and Thrasyllus took the lead : for it was not now a military business, but the civil interest of the com-

monwealth,

monwealth, which it behooved the armament, a large and almost a
preponderant portion of the commonwealth, to take into consideration.
The first measure was to require an oath from all, with particular
attention to those supposed to favor oligarchy, binding them, in the
most solemn manner, to support democracy, to persevere in the war
against the Peloponnesians, to maintain concord among themselves,
to hold the Four-hundred for enemies, and to admit no treaty with
them. This oath, having been universally taken by the Athenians,
was tendered to the Samians, who also took it universally. Hence-
forward the Samians were admitted to all councils, as men ingaged
in the same cause with the Athenians, and bound by the same interest,
whose assistance was necessary to their welfare, and whose welfare
depended upon their success.

Thucyd. l. 8. c. 76. Matters being thus far settled, the armament would no longer consider the commonwealth as existing at Athens, but took upon themselves to be the commonwealth. The generals Leon and Diomedon,
notwithstanding the degree of concurrence they had thus far given,
were esteemed not sufficiently zealous in the cause. As the general
assembly of Athenian citizens, therefore, the armament assumed authority to depose them, together with every commander of a trireme
whom they thought adverse to democracy; and Thrasybulus and
Thrasyllus were, by the same authority, raised to the command-in-chief.

These measures, in fact declaring a civil war, put equally the armament and the city, both watched by a forein enemy already too powerful,
in a most perilous situation. The armament, however, says the historian, comforted themselves with the considerations, that they were
the strength of the commonwealth; that the oligarchal party, tho in
possession of the city, were comparatively weak: that, the whole fleet
being theirs, the subject-states must also be theirs, together with the
revenue thence arising; the collection of which they possessed means
to inforce, which the oligarchal party were totally without: that, even
for subsistence, those who held Athens were more dependent upon
them than they upon those who were masters of Athens; for not only
they could more command the sea, but they could even more command
2
the

the entrance of the harbour of Peiræus. With regard to a home, Samos, a fine iland with a considerable city, was no contemptible home. Such then being their means, not only of subsistence and security, but even of wealth and power, it was little to be doubted but Alcibiades, ill-treated as he had been by the oligarchal party, would gladly join his interest with theirs; and thus, the king of Persia becoming their ally, there was no kind or degree of success which they might not reasonably hope. But should they finally be deceived, in any or in all their views against their domestic enemies, still, while such a fleet was theirs, retreats would not be wanting, where they might find, not only lands of which to possess themselves, but also cities in which to settle.

The oligarchal party at Athens had always been apprehensive that the nautic multitude, as Thucydides calls them, would not readily acquiesce under the change of government. Immediately therefore after the appointment of the council of Four-hundred, ten commissioners had been dispatched for Samos, with instructions, in giving information of the change, to apologize, soothe and persuade. The commissioners, however, meeting intelligence at Delos of the violent measures of the democratical party in the armament, the deposition of the generals, and the appointment of Thrasybulus and Thrasyllus to the command, feared to proceed.

Fortunately for Athens at this time, there was neither able conduct at the head of the Peloponnesian armament, nor union among the members. Discontent grew so as to threaten mutiny or defection; and in this the Syracusans took the lead. ' It was evident,' they said, ' that the satrap meant no good to their cause. Not only the pay ' which he had ingaged to furnish was reduced, but the reduced ' pay was irregularly and deficiently issued. Under pretence of ' waiting for the Phenician fleet, which he did not intend should ever ' join them, he had prevented action with the enemy when weak in ' numbers. He now continued to prevent it, when they were perhaps ' yet weaker through sedition; and their own commander-in-chief, ' either overreached or bought, yielded to him in everything.'

Urged by fear of sedition among his own people, while he was invited by intelligence of sedition among the Athenians, Astyochus determined

Thucyd. l. 8. c. 72.

B. C. 411. Soon after 27 Feb.

Thucyd. l. 8. c. 77.

c. 78.

Beginning of March. Ann. Thucyd. but rather beg. of April.

Thucyd. l. 8. c. 79.

mined

mined to lead the fleet against the enemy. But, when he arrived off Samos, things were already composed in the Athenian armament under Thrasybulus and Thrasyllus, who were equal to their new command. All was order and vigilance within the harbour : an express was sent to the Hellespont to require the return of Strombichides, who arrived quickly ; and then the Athenian fleet, consisting of a hundred and eight triremes, moved toward the Peloponnesians, who declined the offered battle, and retired into the port of Miletus.

Thucyd. l. 8.
c. 80.
Such, after all the great loss in Sicily, and with faction so raging as to render it doubtful where the government existed, was still the naval power of Athens ; while the Peloponnesians were so far from being able, with their own strength, to support the contest in naval war, that a diminution only of pecuniary assistance from Persia, reduced them immediately to distress. But while Persian policy was successfully employed in fomenting the divisions of Greece, the weakness of the Persian government, and the militating interests of its officers commanding provinces, afforded the Greeks reciprocal advantages. Pharnabazus proposed to profit from the growing dissatisfaction of the Peloponnesians with Tissaphernes. He sent to inform them, 'that if they would bring ' their fleet to the Hellespont, and connect their interests with his, ' he would furnish faithfully and regularly that pay and those supplies, ' which Tissaphernes was evidently no longer disposed to give.' At the same time there arrived from the Byzantines a proposal to revolt, if support could be obtained from the Peloponnesian fleet. These overtures were deemed by the Peloponnesian commanders to require immediate attention. But to make their way to the Hellespont, they must probably fight the Athenian fleet, which the commander-in-chief desired to avoid. Forty ships therefore were sent under Clearchus son of Rhamphias, with direction to take a circuitous course through the open sea, that he might escape observation from the Athenian scouts. His passage was interrupted by a storm. Ten of his triremes only, under Helixus the Megarian commander, made their way good to the Hellespont ; the rest, being dispersed, sought again the port of Miletus, which they were fortunate enough to reach. Clearchus prosecuted his journey by land to take the Hellespontine command,

April.

command, and on his arrival he found Byzantium, through the exertions of Helixus, in concert with the Peloponnesian party there, already a member of the Peloponnesian confederacy.

With this disposition among the dependencies of Athens to revolt, Thrasybulus and Thrasyllus were aware that they had undertaken what, with their own strength, they should scarcely be able to bring to a good conclusion. Whether they had previously held any intelligence with Alcibiades, is not said by the historian, but appears probable. An assembly of the Athenian citizens of the armament was summoned, as if the legal general assembly of the commonwealth. Thrasybulus undertook to explain the advantages to be expected from the restoration of Alcibiades: the assembly assented; and a resolution, in the form of a decree of the Athenian people, declared him restored to the privileges of an Athenian citizen, and no longer liable, for any passed transaction, to either punishment or trial.

This being carried, Thrasybulus, whose measure principally it was, went himself to communicate information of it to Alcibiades, then residing with Tissaphernes. They returned together to Samos: the assembly was again convened, and Alcibiades spoke. After shortly lamenting the calamity of his exile, the injury that had insued to his country, and the misery to himself, he adverted to present circumstances, and dwelt largely on the fair prospect that appeared of future prosperity to Athens, through the benefits which his restoration would bring. ' Nothing,' he said, ' was wanting to induce the satrap to ' take an active part in their favor, but sufficient assurance of steddi- ' ness in the government, and due adherence to ingagements made. ' Nor was it any secret what he would require; for he had repeatedly ' declared, that he would freely treat with Alcibiades, were the affairs ' of the commonwealth again committed to him. In that case, not ' only his revenue should supply the wants of Athens, but the Pheni- ' cian fleet, now at Aspendus, instead of reinforcing the Peloponnesian, ' should join the Athenian against the Peloponnesians.' The assembly were ready to believe what they wished to be true, and the speech of Alcibiades made such impression, that he was upon the spot elected general: those before appointed were continued as his collegues; but

Thucyd. l. 8. c. 82.

the

the chief direction of affairs, with the approbation apparently of Thrasybulus and Thrasyllus, passed immediately into his hands.

Things being so far settled, immoderate joy and thoughtless confidence pervaded the armament. Already they held the Peloponnesians in contempt. Revenge against the Four-hundred was their favorite object; they considered the means as in their hands, and they would sail directly to Peiræus. Alcibiades however had influence, and he did not want prudence, to check the rash design. ' The nearer enemy,' he said, ' must not be so left, to act unopposed against the most va- ' luable possessions of the commonwealth. With regard to himself, ' moreover, it would be utterly improper to run to distant enterprize, ' without going first to communicate personally with the satrap. Their ' interest required that he should show himself in the rank in which ' they had placed him; and, armed with the importance which that rank ' gave, consult concerning the arrangements to be made.' They yielded to these arguments; the assembly was dismissed, and he set off immediately: anxious, says the historian, to show Tissaphernes his power among the Athenians, as to impress the Athenians with an opinion of his influence with Tissaphernes ; and, as he could now be, to both, either a valuable friend or a formidable foe, he awed the Athenians with the name of Tissaphernes, and Tissaphernes with that of the Athenians.

Thucyd. l. 8. c. 83.

Intelligence of these transactions in Samos, being conveyed to the Peloponnesian armament at Miletus, occasioned a violent ferment there. The irregularity and deficiency of the issues of pay, before complained of, had increased since the appearance of the Athenian fleet on the coast, and the refusal of battle by the Lacedæmonian commander. Alcibiades, lately their counsellor, and still the man of most influence with the satrap, was now become commander-in-chief of the enemy. Not only the soldiers and sailors, but the principal officers, openly accused Astyochus of compliance adverse to their interests and that of their country. Weak and mean, they declared, they had always thought it, but they now pronounced it treacherous ; and unless a successful battle was fought, or new measures were taken to procure supplies, the crews, they said, would, and indeed must desert, to find subsistence.

The

The Sicilian force was now no longer guided by the wisdom, the energy, and the influence of Hermocrates, who, in consequence of a change in the Syracusan administration, had been superseded in his command. While then the rest of the armament canvassed matters among themselves, the Syracusan and Thurian seamen, with the licentiousness and arrogance nourished under a democratical government, and either allowed, or not duly controlled, by a democratical commander, went in a body to Astyochus, and, in a tumultuous manner, demanded the pay due to them. Astyochus, who appears to have had no talent for holding authority, reproved them with Spartan haughtiness; and not only threatened Dorieus the Thurian commander[11] (who, improperly enough, accompanied his people, and even spoke for them) but lifted his stick as if to strike him. It is from Thucydides that we have this testimony to the rough manners of a Spartan general; to which the democratical Thurians made the rough return that might be expected. With a nautic shout, they rushed forward to protect and revenge their commanding officer. Fortunately for Astyochus, an altar was near, and he fled to it: the rioters respected the sanctuary, and presently dispersed.

This was not the only wound which the Lacedæmonian commandsuffered. Tissaphernes had taken a strong measure to secure his authority in Miletus; he had built a fort within the walls of the city, and placed a garrison there. In the necessity of the Milesians, on first revolting from Athens, to procure protection, on any terms, against Athenian vengeance, it does not appear that this had occasioned any opposition

Thucyd. l. 8. c. 84.

[11] The scholiast, hastily and carelessly, considering Dorieus as a gentilitious name, interprets it to mean Hermocrates. In recollecting that the Syracusans were a Dorian people, he seems to have forgotten that the Lacedæmonians were so. A Spartan general would scarcely distinguish a Syracusan as *the* Dorian, by way of eminence. In a preceding passage (c. 35. l. 8.) Thucydides particularizes Dorieus son of Diagoras as the commander of the Thurian squadron in the Peloponnesian fleet. Within a few following sentences he mentions Hermocrates as already superseded by an order from Syracuse, and adds circumstances hardly allowing the supposition that he had at all incouraged the offensive conduct of the Sicilians. It may be observed farther that Dorieus son of Diagoras, apparently the same man spoken of by Thucydides, is mentioned by Xenophon, (Hellen. l. 1. c. 1. s. 2.) Nor is this the only instance in which we find Dorieus, like other gentilitious names among the Greeks, taken as the proper name of an individual.

or

or complaint. But, when they thought themselves established members of the Peloponnesian confederacy, they began to consider such a badge of forein servitude with uneasiness; and at length, the spreading discontent against Tissaphernes incouraging, they entered the fort by surprize, with a superior armed force, and compelled the garrison to withdraw. The Lacedæmonian commissioner, Lichas, condemned this violence. Apparently he and his collegues had learned to be more complaisant to the satrap than when they arrived from Sparta. ' Miletus,' he said, "being situated in Asia, was within the king of ' Persia's proper dominion. It became its people therefore to submit ' to Tissaphernes as his officer; and the interest of the confederacy ' required that it should be so.' A majority, however, of the allies in the armament, and, above the rest, the Syracusans, declared openly and vehemently their dissent to the doctrine of Lichas, and their approbation of the conduct of the Milesians. Accordingly the Milesians persisted in excluding the Persian garrison, and asserting their independency, and they manifested, upon all occasions, without scruple or reserve, a warm animosity against the Lacedæmonian commissioner.

Thucyd. l. 8. c. 85.   Things were in this state at Miletus, when Mindarus arrived from Lacedæmon to supersede Astyochus in the command-in-chief. Meanwhile the wary Tissaphernes held to the former advice, and would not change his policy for the present persuasion of Alcibiades. He would hold the balance between the contending parties in Greece; and he could no more be induced now to break with the Lacedæmonians, than he had desired before to give them a decisive superiority. On the contrary Astyochus remained in favor: for the same conduct which had rendered that general obnoxious to many of those under his command, had been gratifying to the satrap. When therefore Astyochus returned home, Tissaphernes sent with him Gauleites, a Carian, who spoke both the Greek and Persian languages, in quality of his minister to Sparta. Gauleites was instructed to apologize for any apparent slackness in Tissaphernes toward the interest of the Peloponnesian confederacy, and to prefer complaints against the Milesians; particularly insisting upon their affronting and injurious conduct in expelling
the

the Persian garrison. The Milesians, informed of this, sent ministers to vindicate themselves; and Hermocrates, reduced to the situation of an individual without office, accompanied them to Sparta.

Such, fortunately for Athens, was the distraction of interests among its enemies, while there was an Athenian commonwealth in Attica and another in Samos, more virulently inimical to each other than to any forein foe. Meanwhile the Four-hundred, through a strange incautiousness, met with a check in their proposed negotiation for peace with Lacedæmon. Their ambassadors imbarked in a trireme, Thucyd. l. 8. manned with those who had been removed from the herald-ship c. 86. Paralus, for their devotion to the democratical party at Samos. In passing the Argolic coast, the crew mutinied, carried the vessel into Nauplia, and delivered the ambassadors prisoners to the Argian admini-stration. No independent Grecian state was so interested in the schism of the Athenian commonwealth as Argos. The revolution had excited great alarm. It was apprehended that the abolition of democracy, at Athens, would be followed by the downfall of the democratical interest throughout Greece. Intelligence of the turn which things had taken, at Samos, was proportionally gratifying: the opportunity to serve the democratical party, by checking the negotiation of their adversaries, was seized with zeal; and, as it was the purpose of the Athenian crew to join the fleet at Samos, the Argians sent with them ministers, com-missioned to assure the democratical party there of their friendship and support

The commissioners, appointed by the Four-hundred to negotiate c. 86. with the fleet and army, meanwhile had ventured to proceed from Delos, and arrived at Samos about the same time with the ministers from Argos. Alcibiades was already returned; an assembly of the Athenian citizens in the armament was summoned, and the commissioners from Athens, and the Argian ministers, were together admitted to audience. Tumult immediately began among the soldiers. ' Those who had ' subverted the democracy,' it was exclaimed, ' should receive capital ' punishment.' The generals used their endevors to restore order, and with some difficulty succeeded. The commissioners then addressed the assembly. Their first solicitude was to discredit the charges, really replete with falsehood, which had been alledged against the Four-hundred by Chæreas. They assured the soldiers and seamen ' that ' their friends and relations at Athens had never received the least ' injury or molestation from the present government.' Thus far they were heard with patience; but when they proceeded to vindicate the change made in the constitution, calling it ' still a democracy, modi-' fied only in such a manner as the present circumstances rendered neces-' sary,' they were interrupted with fresh tumult. When quiet was again restored, still the commissioners could not gain attention: others would speak; various opinions were given, various proposals offered; and at length it appeared the prevailing disposition, and even the decided resolution, to sail immediately for Peiræus, and at once restore the former constitution, and punish those who had overthrown it.

Then, says Thucydides, for the first time, Alcibiades did his country a reäl service, and such a service that perhaps no man ever did a greater. The assembly was on the point of passing the rash decree, and, in the zeal of the moment, it would have been carried into instant execution. Athens thus would have been plunged into the horrors of civil war, and every remaining dependency of the commonwealth in Ionia and on the Hellespont would have passed almost instantaneously into the hands of the enemy. No man certainly, continues the historian, but Alcibiades was able to prevent this; and he did prevent it. He reproved the passion that had been shown in the proceedings, and the people, the armed people, bore his reproof: he demonstrated the destructive ten-dency of what was proposed, and they were alarmed with their own measure: he procured acknowlegement that what had been advised by others was wrong; and, taking upon himself to dictate the answer which should be returned to Athens, they yielded to his authority. ' He did ' not object,' he said, ' to limiting the votes in the general assembly to ' five thousand: but he would require the immediate abolition of the ' council of Four-hundred, and the restoration of the antient council ' of Five-hundred. If the new government had retrenched any super-' fluous expence, so that the forces serving abroad might be more ' certainly and plentifully subsisted, they should have his applause for ' it. He trusted they would not separately make any treaty with the
                                                          ' enemy.

' enemy. With the present strength of the commonwealth intire, there
' was good hope that the enemy might be brought to a reasonable
' accommodation: but, were so large a portion as, either the party now
' prevailing in Samos, or the party now prevailing in Athens, to be
' cut off, there would soon be no commonwealth left for an enemy to
' treat with.' Alcibiades, having thus answered the commissioners, then
addressed the Argian ministers; thanking them in the name of the
assembly for the zeal their commonwealth had manifested, and desiring
they would only hold themselves in readiness to give that assistance,
which might become important, tho in the moment it was not wanted.

This hazardous business being thus fortunately accommodated, it B. C. 411.
became necessary for Alcibiades to attend to the motions of Tissaphernes, P W. 21.
who was gone to Aspendus to visit the Phenician fleet there, and had taken April.
Thucyd. l. 8.
with him the Lacedæmonian commissioner Lichas, with two Pelopon- c. 87.
nesian triremes, under the command of Philippus, the harmost of
Miletus. No less than a hundred and forty-seven ships of war were
actually assembled; a force ample to give the superiority to which-
soever of the belligerent powers the satrap might chuse to favor.
Alcibiades followed him; probably too well acquainted with both his c. 88.
character and his designs, either to fear that he would afford any very
effectual support to the Peloponnesians, or to expect that he would
be diverted from a policy, so congenial to his nature, as that of wearing
out both parties, while he gave hopes to both. Alcibiades knew also that
it was much an object, with the satrap, to gratify his court, by doing
its business with the least possible expence. But he had nevertheless his
end in his journey. He gained the credit, with the Athenians, of
preventing the junction of the Phenician fleet with the Peloponnesians,
and he disturbed the councils and measures of the Peloponnesians, by
giving new force to the jealousy and mistrust they had for some time
entertained of Tissaphernes.

SECTION VII.

Schism in the new government of Athens: Theramenes: a second revolution.

B. C. 411.
Ol. 92. ¾.
P. W. 21.
April.
Thucyd. l. 8.
c. 89.
WHILE, at Samos, the democratical party were held together, and concert was maintained in their proceedings, through the decided superiority of one man at their head, division was growing among the many men of great abilities, but of various tempers, views and interests, who directed the affairs of the oligarchal party at Athens. Aristocrates son of Sicelius, Theramenes one of the generals of the establishment, and some others in high offices, had been for some time dissatisfied with the prospect of their affairs; insomuch that they wanted only
c. 90.
opportunity to disingage themselves from their party. On the contrary Antiphon and Peisander, whose strong measures left no means of retreating, Phrynichus, who dreaded nothing equally with the return of Alcibiades, and Aristarchus, upon principle the most inveterate and vehement of all the enemies of the democracy, together with many other men of considerable weight, remained firm in their purpose of maintaining the oligarchy.

The answer from Alcibiades, and the account, brought by their commissioners, of the state of things in Samos, together with their knowlege of the inclination to secession within their own party, gave much uneasiness, but produced no disposition to yield. Their proposed resource was to make peace with Lacedæmon; and upon any terms, rather than not make peace. With an oligarchal government they trusted they might easily obtain, not peace only, but alliance and certain protection : and indeed they considered the means of connection with Lacedæmonias their only ground of hope, even for personal safety. Their former embassy having been stopped, by the mutiny of the crew of the vessel in which it sailed, Antiphon and Phrynichus now undertook the negotiation. Those who directed the government at home, were in the mean time to take measures for obviating domestic opposition. With this

this view it was judged of much importance to forward the completion of a fort, some time since begun, on a spot called Eetioneia, commanding the entrance of the harbour of Peiræus. It was already so far advanced that they established the public magazine of corn there; and they not only caused all corn imported to be there deposited, but compelled all individuals in the city, who possessed any quantity, to send it thither.

Meanwhile the same answer from Samos, which urged the determined supporters of oligarchy to these strong measures, incouraged the dissentients in their proposed secession. That answer offered them a clear overture for an accommodation. Even in Athens the body of the people was still inclined to democracy ; and, to restore superiority to the democratical party, leaders only were wanting, in whom the body of the people might confide. To obtain their confidence therefore became the object of Theramenes and Aristocrates. This would give them importance with the chiefs of the armament at Samos, and ground on which to open a treaty. ^{Thucyd. l. 8. c. 89.}

Other circumstances followed, still to incourage and incite them. Antiphon and Phrynichus returned from Lacedæmon, without effecting in any degree the purpose of their mission, or however without effecting any purpose that they dared declare. Presently after, intelligence arrived of a fleet assembling in the Laconian ports, to favor the revolt of Eubœa. Appearances gave to suspect that, instead of Eubœa, the fleet was intended for the Attic coast ; and that the fort of Eetioneia was intended to insure the reception of a Peloponnesian fleet, as much as to prevent the entrance of the Athenian into the harbour of Peiræus. Nor was this suspicion, in the opinion of Thucydides, unfounded. The first wish of the oligarchal party, says the historian, was undoubtedly to have the command of the Athenian empire intire: but, if this could not be, they would have been glad to hold the independent dominion of Attica, deprived of the subject-states, yet preserving the fleet and the walls of the city: rather however than submit to the restoration of democracy, which would involve their certain ruin, they would have consented to the demolition of the fortifications of Athens and the surrender of the whole fleet, that their persons and estates only might be secure, under Lacedæmonian protection. The construction of ^{End of April.}

^{Thucyd. l. 8. c. 98.}

the

the fort was therefore prosecuted with the utmost diligence; and, as it arose, the disposition of the gates and sally-ports, says the historian, sufficiently indicated its purpose.

Against these measures, which Thucydides, no friend in general to democracy, reprobates, and which ought to have united, in opposition, every honest hand and heart in Athens, the first signal blow was by assassination; an act in its nature too opposite to all justice, and too subversive of all order, to produce any lasting good, in whatever cause it may be practised. A few days after the return of the ambassadors from Lacedæmon, toward midday, in the full agora, and not far from the state-house, Phrynichus was stabbed by one of the city-guard, and died soon after of the wound. The murderer escaped; but an accomplice, an Argian, was taken, and being put to the torture by the Four-hundred, indicated no name, nor declared anything, but that there had been frequent and numerous meetings in different houses, particularly in that of the commander of the city-guard. No information was obtained, on which any prosecution could be founded: inquiry concerning the murder dropped, the deed being evidently popular; and Theramenes and Aristocrates, whether conscious of the crime or not, were incouraged by the event to proceed in their design[12]. Those of their party, who were of the Four-hundred, meanwhile kept their seats in that council, and Theramenes his office as a general of the establishment.

Things were in this situation when the alarming intelligence arrived, that the Peloponnesian armament, instead of going to Eubœa, had overrun the iland of Ægina, and was now at anchor in the harbour of Epidaurus, as if threatening Athens itself. Theramenes had foretold that this would happen. From the event, thus confirming his prediction, he took occasion farther to animate his party against the party of Antiphon. 'If preventive measures,' he said, 'were not quickly 'taken, the Peloponnesian troops would be admitted into the fort of

Lys. con. Agorat. p. 136. vel. 491. Lycurg. con. Leocrat. p. 217. t. 4. Or. Gr. Reiske.

[12] The orator Lycurgus, in his accusation of Leocrates, relates the murder of Phrynichus differently, in regard to some facts of little consequence; as that it was committed by night without the city, at a fountain near some willowbeds: but he remarkably confirms, what is more important in the account of Thucydides, the popularity of the deed, and the popularity of the principle, that assassination, in the cause of the people, was meritorious.

11

'Eetioneia,

' Eetoineia, and a Lacedæmonian would command in Peiræus.' It
was accordingly resolved to strike the decisive stroke: a large proportion of the heavy-armed were already gained, the taxis' commanded by
Aristocrates, a body nearly correspondent to our battalion, was on
duty at the works of Eetioneia, and Hermon, an officer warm in their
interest, commanded in Munychia.   Under these favoring circumstances, when measures were not yet completely concerted, the soldiers,
in their zeal for the cause, arrested Alexicles, the general commanding
in Peiræus, a man zealous in the oligarchal interest, put him in close
confinement, and then set themselves to demolish the fort of Eetioneia.

Intelligence of this violence passed to Athens while the council was
sitting, and Theramenes present.   The members of the opposite party,
alarmed and indignant, accused Theramenes and his immediate friends,
as instigators of sedition.   Theramenes, with ready coolness, replied
to the charge, and proposed to go himself and release his collegue.
This being incautiously approved, he went instantly, taking with him
one of his collegues present, whose political sentiments he knew to
agree with his own.   Meanwhile alarm spred rapidly, from the state-
house through the city; it was generally supposed that Alexicles was
put to death, and that the democratical party had taken possession of
Peiræus, with intention to maintain themselves there, in opposition to
the existing government.   While therefore Aristarchus, with a small
body of the equestrian order, whom he could collect in the instant,
hastened after Theramenes, all the younger and more zealous of the
oligarchal party ran to arms.   The elder interfered to check the indiscretion of zeal on both sides; and Thucydides of Pharsalus in Thessaly,
a public guest of the commonwealth, particularly distinguished himself
in appeasing the commotion.   Quiet thus was so far restored that,
excepting the few who accompanied Aristarchus, none marched in arms
to Peiræus.

Aristarchus and Theramenes arrived nearly together.   The latter
immediately addressed the soldiers with the authority of general, and
reproved their conduct.   It was however known, by many, that his
words did not perfectly express his sentiments; and, while some attended
to his speech, others continued the demolition of the fort.   Aristarchus,
with

with those of the oligarchal party about him, with much indignation
interfered in vain.   The soldiers, addressing Theramenes, asked, ' If
' he reälly thought it for the public good that the fort should be
' completed, or if the interest of the commonwealth did not rather
' require that it should be destroyed ?'   Having had time then to look
about him, and seeing that he should have sufficient support, he
answered, ' If they were of opinion that it ought to be demolished,
' he could not dissent.'   This sufficed for the soldiers : the whole
body set immediately to work; and the word was passed, or rather a
kind of short proclamation was made through Peiræus, evidently not
a momentary thought of the soldiers themselves, but either preconcerted
among them, or communicated by the leaders of the party ; ' Whoever
' is for the government of the Five-thousand, instead of the tyranny
' of the Four-hundred, let him assist in demolishing the fort.'   To
have named democracy, or the government of the people at large, as
treason against the existing government, would have rendered the
delinquents obnoxious to capital punishment; but an appeal to the
Five-thousand was legal, by the constitution of the Four-hundred
themselves.   Numbers of the inhabitants of Peiræus obeyed the call,
and the demolition of the fort proceeded rapidly.

Thucyd. l. 8.
c. 93.   Next day, the fort being completely destroyed, the soldiers released
their general Alexicles; and then going to the theater of Bacchus,
adjoining to Munychia, there held a regular assembly.   The result of
the debate was a resolution to march into Athens, and take possession
of the Anaceium, the precinct of a temple of Castor and Pollux, as
a place of arms.   The regularity of their proceedings, the appeal to the
Five-thousand, and the care taken to do nothing that a majority among
any five thousand of the citizens might not perhaps approve, alarmed
and distressed the oligarchal leaders, more than if greater violences
had been committed.   The Four-hundred, however, assembling at
their usual hour, sent a committee to confer with the troops. Addressing
themselves more to individuals, and to small parties, than to the assembled body, the committee endevored to conciliate the more moderate,
and to persuade them to use their endevors to pacify the more violent:
' The Five-thousand,' they said, ' should be immediately declared;
' the

' the Four-hundred now in office should lay down their authority in
'. due time; and it should be for the Five-thousand to decide the kind
' of rotation, and the mode of election, by which their successors should
' be appointed.   Meanwhile every dearest interest ought to warn the
' soldiers not, by any violences, to afford those opportunities to an
' enemy at their gates, which might superinduce the destruction of
' the commonwealth.'   These arguments, urged in a conciliating
manner, had their effect: and it was at length agreed that, on a
day named, a general assembly should be held, in the precinct of the
temple of Bacchus, to consider of means for effecting a permanent
reconciliation of parties.

The day appointed being come, the people were already moving Thucyd. l. 8.
toward the temple of Bacchus, when intelligence was communicated, c. 94.
that the Peloponnesian fleet under Hegesandridas, consisting of forty-
two triremes, having crossed the gulph from Epidaurus, and touched
at Megara, was actually off Salamis.   Immediately the whole force of
Athens, of both parties, united for the moment by the fear of a common
enemy, ran down to Peiræus as by consent; and, without waiting,
or, most of them, caring, for orders from the existing government,
each did what the exigency of the moment appeared to him to require:
some went aboard the triremes afloat; others launched those ashore; c. 95.
some took post upon the walls, and some at the mouth of the harbour.
The Peloponnesians however made no attempt upon the Attic coast,
but, doubling the headland of Sunium, proceeded to Oropus.

New alarm then seized the Athenians.   The disposition in Eubœa
to revolt was known.   Already deprived of the produce of Attica by
the garrison of Deceleia, the added loss of Eubœa would nearly deprive
them of means to subsist.   Corn, meat, every article of food came
principally from Eubœa.   Hastily therefore, and under no regular
direction, as in a dissolution of government, they manned some triremes
with such crews as in the moment offered, and, under the command of
Thymochares, the squadron moved immediately for Eretria: some
triremes stationed there made their number thirty-six.   Among the
numerous proofs, in history, of the great defects in the antient system
of naval war, what followed is not in the least remarkable.   Thymochares

landed his crews to get refreshment. The Eretrians, prepared for revolt, had concerted measures with Hegesandridas. No provisions were to be found in the public market; the Athenians could supply themselves only from private houses far from the port, and the crews in consequence dispersed over the town. A signal was given by the Eretrians; the Spartan admiral made across the channel; and the Athenian fleet was attacked, while the crews were in confusion, and before all could be got aboard. After some resistance, therefore, it was compelled to fly. Some of the ships escaped into the harbour of Chalcis; the rest mostly ran upon the Eretrian coast, and the crews fled by land. Those who reached a fort occupied by an Athenian garrison, adjoining to Eretria, were safe; but others, who, confiding in the friendship of the Eretrians, entered the city, were all put to death. Two and twenty triremes fell into the hands of the Peloponnesians; and presently all Eubœa, except Oreus, revolted to them.

Thucyd. l. 8. c. 96.   The consternation at Athens, on receiving the news of the event, was greater than even from the defeat in Sicily. Attica itself was less valuable to Athens than Eubœa; not only as the soil was less fertile, but as the appropriation of the produce was less certain, to a power, hitherto the first upon earth by sea, but inferior to its enemies by land. Nor was this the only distressing consideration; for, had the enemy pushed with their victorious fleet immediately for Peiræus, they might have possessed themselves of the harbour. What precisely might have been the consequence was beyond human foresight; but this, says the cotemporary historian, may be esteemed certain, that nothing less than the return of the fleet from Samos, which would have superinduced the loss of Ionia, the Hellespont, and in short the whole forein dominion, could have saved Athens. It was not however upon this occasion only, he continues, that the Lacedæmonians showed themselves most accommodating enemies to the Athenians; and thus the misfortune, which threatened the ruin of the commonwealth, proved the prelude to its restoration.

Before 24 June.   Twenty triremes remained still in the port of Peiræus, and they were immediately manned. But, in the present state of fermentation, who should undertake the direction of public measures, or who

11   could

could undertake it with effect, was not easy to determine. Probably nothing could prevent the people from assembling wherever public affairs were to be debated.   A proposal hazarded for summoning them to the Pnyx, where, under the democracy, the general assemblies had been most commonly held, met with general approbation and no avowed opposition.   In the Pnyx accordingly the people met; the democratical chiefs found the power in their hands; and a decree proposed was passed, with all the antient forms, declaring, 'That the council of ' Four-hundred should be dissolved; that the supreme authority should ' be immediately vested in Five-thousand; that all, at the time in ' Athens, upon the roll of the heavy-armed should be of the Five-' thousand; that no man in any office under the commonwealth ' should receive any pay.'

This change was no sooner decided, and the party of Theramenes in consequence possessed of a clear superiority, than Peisander, Alexi-cles, Aristarchus, and many others of the principal supporters of oligarchy, quitted Athens, and most of them went to Deceleia.   Aristarchus used the means which his office of general afforded, in abandoning his country, to strike a blow against it.   Œnoë, that town on the Attic border against Bœotia, the ineffectual siege of which, by the army under Archidamus, had, twenty-one years before, been the first object of the Peloponnesian arms in the war, was still held by an Athenian garrison.   The troops passing between Deceleia and Peloponnesus were frequently annoyed from it, and a party of Corinthians had been lately cut off.   The Corinthian government, thus instigated, had invited the Bœotians to join them in reducing the place; and the siege was formed.   When Aristarchus determined to fly, he commanded the attendance of some of the barbarian bowmen in the Athenian service; and selecting for the purpose, according to the historian's phrase, the most barbarian, he went to Œnoë.   Having quickly concerted matters with the besiegers, he told the garrison, that a treaty was made with Lacedæmon, according to which Œnoë must be immediately surrendered to the Bœotians.   The garrison, excluded from other information, gave credit to a man known to be in the office of general of the

Thucyd. l. 8. c. 98.

3 O 2   commonwealth;

commonwealth; and, obtaining from the besieging army a safeconduct, evacuated the place.

Antiphon, with a few oligarchal leaders of less note, ventured to remain in Athens; Antiphon apparently trusting in his policy, his eloquence, his personal influence, and the quiet conduct he had observed; directing the secret councils of the party, but leaving others to be the ostensible conductors of every measure. Upon the flight however of the more active leaders, opposition to Theramenes and his associates had ceased. Many assemblies of the people were successively held, according to the antient forms of the commonwealth, in the Pnyx: the restoration of Alcibiades, and of all who, for the same cause, had absented themselves from their country, was decreed; and the constitution was settled, says the cotemporary historian, upon a better footing than at any time within my memory[13]; a mixed government being established, with the supreme authority judiciously divided between the Few and the Many.

In this concise eulogy is contained the whole of the account, given by Thucydides, of the form of government established by Theramenes; and upon no occasion does he leave us so much to regret the want of explanation and detail. Upon no occasion, however, do we see the historian more strongly marked as the true patriot. Frequently we find him reprobating the extravagancies of an unbalanced democracy so strongly, that we might suspect him of some partiality for oligarchy. But here, as indeed throughout his account of the oligarchy established by Peisander, he shows himself a decided enemy to tyranny in every shape, and the warm partizan only of whatever government might best secure universal freedom through equal and well supported law.

---

[13] 'Επὶ γε ἐμοῦ. *In my opinion*, Smith.— *Meo judicio*, Duker. But Duker adds, in a note, *Acacius ἐπὶ γε ἐμοῦ non malè vertit meâ quidem memoriâ.* I have no doubt in preferring the version of Acacius.

SECTION VIII.

*Transactions of the Peloponnesian fleet under Mindarus, and the
Athenian under Thrasyllus and Thrasybulus.   Naval action near
Abydus.   Wily and treacherous policy of Tissaphernes.   Naval action
near the Trojan shore.   Critical arrival of Alcibiades.   Naval
action near Cyzicus, and capture of the Peloponnesian fleet.   Laconic
official letter.   Liberality of Pharnabazus to the Peloponnesians.
Able conduct and popularity of Hermocrates, the Syracusan
general.*

During these transactions at Athens, the Peloponnesian armament, B. C. 411.
on the Asiatic coast, had been wholly occupied with the distresses, to P. W. 21.
which the want of an adequate revenue of their own, and the failure of Thucyd. l. 8.
the satrap Tissaphernes in his ingagements, had reduced them.   One c. 99.
of the Lacedæmonian commissioners, Philippus, had attended the satrap
to Aspendus : another, Hippocrates, was stationed at Phaselis.   All intelligence, from both, confirmed the opinion, long entertained, of the
satrap's faithlessness, and of his determined purpose to deceive them.
Meanwhile fresh overtures arrived from the satrap of Bithynia, Pharnabazus ; who, having observed the advantage which Tissaphernes
derived from his Grecian connection, the recovery of dominion over
the Grecian towns within his satrapy, and of the tribute from them,
which for a long time had passed to Athens, showed himself disposed
to treat upon terms which, with his more honorable character, might
be inviting.   These united motives induced Mindarus, the new commander-in-chief, to resolve upon moving with the fleet to the Hellespont,
for the sake of readier and surer communication with the Bithynian
satrap.   But the Athenian fleet at Samos was in the most favorable situation to intercept his passage ; and tho his numbers were
superior, he desired to avoid a general action.   Secrecy and caution,
however, he hoped might prevent interruption ; but a storm, coming
upon him in the passage, compelled him to take shelter in the harbour
of Icarus, and remain there five or six days.

During

During this interval, intelligence passed to Samos, that the Peloponnesian fleet had quitted the port of Miletus for the northward.　Thrasyllus, with whom, in the absence of Alcibiades and Thrasybulus, the
chief command rested, in all haste moved with fifty-five triremes for
the Hellespont, anxious to arrive before the Peloponnesians ; but, in
his passage, learning that Mindarus, from Icarus, had gone with his
fleet to Chios, and remained there, he put into Methymnë in Lesbos.
Beside that Methymnë was a commodious station for watching the
Peloponnesian fleet, the affairs of that valuable iland required his attention.　Some men of the first families of Methymnë, exiles on account of their aversion to democracy and the Athenian interest, had
proposed to profit from present circumstances for restoring themselves
to their country ; the Peloponnesian armament being at hand, the two
satraps friendly, and Athens distracted by sedition.　Having accordingly
collected a small force on the continent, in pursuance of the common
prejudice in favor of a leader from the mother-country, they put themselves under the conduct of Anaxarchus, a Theban ; the Bœotians
being esteemed the parent people of the Æolian race, and particularly
of the Lesbians[14].　Their first attempt was a surprize upon Methymnë
itself :

---

[14] 'Αναξάρχου Θηϐαίου, κατὰ τὸ συγγενὲς,
ἡγουμένου.　Hoc Thucydides, 3. 86. 6. 88. &
alibi de populis ejusdem originis & consan-
guineis dicit.　Quænam autem sit Thebano-
rum, & Methymnæorum, vel Cymæorum, si
quis hoc ad eos pertinere putabit, συγγένεια,
nunc non scio, nec vacat quærere.　Duker.
—I own I am better pleased with such direct
confession, than when thofe who undertake
to be commentators, pass by difficult passages, often of much more historical importance, as if there were no difficulty in them.
One cannot, however, but wonder at Duker's
difficulty here, because the consanguinity
of the Lesbians and Bœotians not only is
mentioned by Thucydides in his account of the
Mitylenæan revolt, (b. 3. c. 2.) but the scholiast, commenting upon the passage, explains
it well and clearly thus:—Καὶ παρασκευάζονται

(οἱ Λέσϐιοι) ὥςε ἀπος̃ῆναι, ξυλλαμϐανόν]ων αὐτοῖς
Λακεδαιμονίων καὶ Βοιωτῶν.　Τὸ δὲ ΣΥΓΓΕΝΩΝ
ΟΝΤΩΝ ἐπὶ μόνους τοὺς Βοιωτοὺς ἐνεκτέον· οὗλοι
γὰρ κατὰ τὸ 'Αιολικὸν συγγενεῖς τῶν Λεσϐίων.
The reader, who may desire higher authority
than the scholiast, will find Strabo large on
the subject. I have been induced to say thus
much on this little matter, principally for
the testimony which we here find from Thucydides, in confirmation of Strabo's account
of the origin of the Æolian Greeks of Asia ;
which has been followed in the account given
of the Æolic migration, in the second section
of the fifth chapter of this History.　It is
indeed, not without attention to such little
detached scraps of information, wherever
they can be found among the works of the
most authoritative antient writers, that we
are inabled to collect the scattered members

of

itself: but the vigilance of the Athenian commander in Mitylenë disappointing them, they hastened across the heights which divide the iland, and by a sudden assault took Eresus. Intelligence of these circumstances had called Thrasybulus with five triremes to Lesbos; he found there two Athenian triremes and five Methymnæan, and Thrasyllus now joined him with fifty-five. The heavy-armed were debarked, and preparation was made to attack Eresus by sea and land.

Meanwhile Mindarus, still desirous to avoid action with the Athenian fleet, and considering the business of Eresus as a small concern, left his Methymnæan friends to their fate, and made his course along the Asiatic shore for the Hellespont. Thucydides has thought important enough for notice, what would now appear utterly trifling, except as it marks, more strongly than anything that has yet occurred, the imperfection of the marine of that age. Speed was the object of Mindarus, both for avoiding the Athenians in the passage, and for being before them in the Hellespont: but, as oars were his instruments of motion, intervals of rest were necessary for his crews; and, as we have already had occasion to observe, the construction of a trireme was such, and the crews so numerous for the space, that refreshment could not conveniently be taken aboard. Mindarus therefore landed his crews to dine, at a port of the Phocæan territory, and to sup, at Arginusæ in the Cumæan territory, overagainst Lesbos, where lay the Athenian fleet, which he was so anxious to avoid. Moving again, however, in the night, he dined next day at Harmatous, and, proceeding in the afternoon with the utmost haste, part of his fleet arrived before midnight at Rhœteium, within the Hellespont, and the rest in the harbour of Sigeium at its mouth.   Eighteen Athenian triremes were lying at Sestos.   Firesignals from the Asiatic shore announced to them their danger, and they hastened to get out of the narrow sea. Of four intercepted,[15] one, forced

Thucyd. l. 8. c. 101.

c. 102.

---

of early Grecian history; to detect the supposititious and doubtful among what is related by inferior or later authors; to ascertain and arrange the genuine; and, without the assistance of invention, to form, of parts

so broken and dispersed, something of a harmonizing whole.

[15] Smith gives to suppose, by his translation, that eight were taken; the Latin version more happily imitates all that is dubious

forced ashore near a temple dedicated to Homer's hero Protesilaus, was taken with its crew ; the crews of the other three escaped.

The Athenian commanders had trusted, that the Peloponnesian fleet could not pass Lesbos without being discovered by their scouts.   Receiving intelligence that it was already in the Hellespont, they followed immediately, and in their passage took two Peloponnesian triremes, which had incautiously pushed too far, in pursuing the Athenian squadron from Sestos.   On the second day they arrived at Elæus, upon which place Mindarus had been making an unsuccessful attempt.   His fleet, reinforced with a squadron which he found at Abydus, consisted of

Middle of July.
eighty-six triremes. Thrasybulus and Thrasyllus, with only sixty-eight, resolved to offer him battle[16].   Five days they employed in preparation in the harbour of Elæus, and then moved into the strait, with their line of

Thucyd. l. 8. c. 105.
battle formed ahead.   The Peloponnesians came out of the harbour of Abydus, and formed for action.   The Athenians extending their line, to prevent being taken in flank by the more numerous enemy, weakened their center, which the Peloponnesians in consequence broke ; and, driving fifteen triremes ashore, debarked and destroyed them.   This advantage, however, produced disorder in the Peloponnesian line, from which Thrasybulus, who commanded the right of the Athenian fleet, instantly profited ; and, being quickly well seconded by Thrasyllus,

c. 106.
they put the whole Peloponnesian fleet to flight, and took twenty-one ships : the rest found refuge in the neighboring port of Abydus. The Peloponnesians acknowleged their defeat, by the usual application, through heralds, for the restoration of the dead, and the Athenians erected their trophy on the headland of Cynos-sema.

This victory, gained with inferior numbers, was very opportune

dubious in the original. I think Thucydides meant to speak of only four taken. The matter is not important ; but it may be observed that, as Thucydides never completed his History, the latter chapters, and indeed much of the last book, bear marks of undigested compilation, and in some places, of uncorrected phrase. I should however rather suppose the whole his own unfinished work, than that the concluding part was written

by another, it has been said his daughter, from his materials.

[16] There can be no doubt but Acacius and Hudson are right in their correction of the statement of the numbers of the two fleets in this place. It does not rest on conjecture, or on the authority of Diodorus, but is supported by the clear testimony of Thucydides himself.

                                                        for

for the Athenians.   The depression of the spirits of the seamen, produced by the defeats at Syracuse, was done away, and they no longer
feared the Peloponnesians as their equals in naval action.   A trireme,
sent to Athens with the news, diffused more than common joy.   It
was as the first symptom of recovery from a mortal disease; the more
welcome as the more unexpected.   Leaders and people were equally
incouraged to bear present evils, and exert themselves with good hope,
giving their attention, especially, as the urgency of the moment
required, to the revolt of Euboea, and the disorders occasioned by the
late sedition.

   The advantages, to be expected from a successful battle, followed   Thucyd. l. 8.
the victory of Cynos-sema: the allies and dependants, remaining to   c. 107.
Athens, were confirmed in their fidelity; those who had revolted were
less satisfied with the part they had taken; and means were opened for
new enterprize.   The fleet sailed for Cyzicus; eight Peloponnesian
triremes, returning from Byzantium, were taken by the way; and
Cyzicus, unfortified, surrendering without a blow, paid for its change of
politics by a heavy contribution.   Meanwhile the Peloponnesian commanders, afraid to keep the sea, and apprehensive of losing all they
had gained on the Asiatic and Hellespontine shores, sent for their fleet
from Euboea to reïnforce them.   Alcibiades soon after rejoined the   c. 108.
Athenian fleet with thirteen ships, bringing with him the incouraging
assurance, that he had completely diverted Tissaphernes from his purpose of permitting the Phenician fleet to join the Peloponnesian, and
that he had finally conciliated him to the Athenian interest.   He seems,
however, not to have obtained any pecuniary supply.   To procure
means therefore for subsisting the armament, for which little or no
remittance could be expected from home, he went southward again
with a squadron of twenty-two triremes; levied large contributions at
Halicarnassus, and in the neighboring country; and fixing upon the
iland of Cos as a convenient station, whence to command the Carian
seas and shores, he raised a fort and left a garrison there.

   Tissaphernes, meanwhile, more wily than wise, and true to nothing
but his evervarying opinion of his own interest, was very uneasy at
the departure of the Peloponnesian fleet from Miletus.   He not only
apprehended the loss of advantages derived from his Grecian alliance,

but he envied the probable accession of those advantages to Pharnabazus.   From Aspendus, therefore, he hastened back into Ionia, and
Thucyd. l. 8.
o. 109. on his arrival found fresh cause of dissatisfaction.   The Cnidians, after
the example of the Milesians, had expelled his garrison from their
citadel.   Nor did the evil rest there.   The Greeks under the Persian
dominion, in general perhaps less rigorously treated than under the
Athenian, would yet be more liable, especially in the decay of the
empire, to occasional oppression from the temper of individuals in
c. 108. command.   Arsaces, an officer under Tissaphernes, of a cruel and faithless disposition, had made himself particularly odious, by treacherously
assassinating some of the Delians whom, on their expulsion from
Ch. 16. s. 5.
of this Hist. their iland by the Athenians, the kindness of the satrap Pharnaces had
established in Atramyttcium.   The Antandrians, oppressed by this
man, and fearing farther oppression, had applied to the Peloponnesians
at Abydus; and a body of Peloponnesian heavy-armed, whom they
conducted over the heights of Ida, assisted in expelling the Persian
garrison from their citadel.
c. 109.
Beg. of Aug. Alarmed by all these circumstances, Tissaphernes resolved to go himself
to the Hellespont, to confer and remonstrate with the Peloponnesian
commanders.   Stopping in his way at Ephesus, he performed a sacrifice
to Diana.   Such a compliment to such a religion as the Greek, from
a Persian, tho'a weak man, in the high situation of Tissaphernes, and
whether superstition or policy produced it, appears strong proof that
decay, in various ways, had been making rapid progress in the Persian
empire.   With the mention of this very remarkable fact, the narrative
of Thucydides ends abruptly.

Fortunately for Grecian history and for literature, another cotemporary author, little inferior in abilities, at least equal in acquirements,
and even of more extensive communication among men, has left us a
continuation.   But the narrative of Xenophon begins as abruptly as
that of Thucydides ends; and, tho there appears no material chasm,
nothing important omitted, yet the connection is not complete [17].   The
first

---

[17] It has been disputed, among the learned, off. Unquestionably Xenophon has intended
whether the account of Xenophon begins   a complete continuation; and Dodwell, in
precisely where that of Thucydides breaks   his Xenophontean Chronology, appears to
me

first fact mentioned by Xenophon, in his Grecian annals, is, that Thymochares, the Athenian commander in the unfortunate action near Eretria, arriving with a few ships from Athens, had a second action with the Peloponnesian squadron under Hegesandridas, and was again defeated. Where this action happened, whether still on the Eubœan coast, or whether Hegesandridas obeyed the summons of Mindarus, and Thymochares followed him toward the Hellespont, we are not informed.

Xen. Hel.
l. 1. c. 1.
s. 1.

Soon after this, and a little after the autumnal equinox, the Thurian commander, Dorieus son of Diagoras, coming from Rhodes to the Hellespont with fourteen triremes, notice of his approach was communicated by signals to the Athenian commanders in Sestos, and twenty triremes were sent to intercept them. The Peloponnesian fleet still lay at Abydus: the commander-in-chief, Mindarus, was at the time in the neighboring town of Ilium, on or near the site of antient Troy, performing a sacrifice to Minerva. The situation commanded a view of the strait, and of the adjacent sea; and he saw the movement of the Athenians, and the danger of Dorieus. Hastening to Abydus, he led his whole fleet out of the harbour. The whole Athenian fleet upon this moved, and a general action insued. Through the greatest part of the day it was maintained with various success in different parts of the line; but toward evening eighteen Athenian triremes were seen

B. C. 411.
P. W. 21.
End of Sept.
Xen. Hel.
l. 1. c. 1.
s. 2.
s. 3.

me to have proved satisfactorily that there is no chasm, or next to none, in the narrative. But there is a circumstance, unnoticed, I believe, by the commentators, which very strongly contradicts the notion of a chasm: it is the mention made by Xenophon of the completion of the journey of Tissaphernes, (the beginning of which is related by Thucydides,) stating the time of his arrival at the Hellespont. The Hellenics, or Grecian Annals, are however, evidently enough, a work which has not received the finishing touches of the author: in the very beginning of it he seems rather to have taken some short notes of Thucydides, or to have made some of his own, and left them for future correction, which was never given; and thus, tho all

the principal facts intended for mention are recorded, yet they are neither separately so clearly related, nor is the connection so perspicuous, as might be expected from such a writer. The first paragraph. Μετὰ δὲ ταῦτα ὃν πολλαῖς ἡμέραις ὕστερον, κ. τ. ε. bears all the appearance of an undigested note. Μετὰ ταῦτα has scarcely been intended to relate to the sacrifice of Tissaphernes at Ephesus, with the mention of which the History of Thucydides ends, but rather to something in the course of relating which, had the work received the finishing touches of the author, the place of the insuing action, between the Athenian squadron under Thymochares and the Lacedæmonian under Hegesandridas, would have been stated.

3 P 2   coming

coming into the strait from the southward. They were the squadron of Alcibiades returning from the Carian coast. Then the Peloponnesians fled toward Abydus. But Abydus had no harbour that could protect them : that dubious kind of action between land and water, of which we have already observed many examples, could alone defend their stranded galleys. Fortunately for them, the satrap Pharnabazus was at hand with a considerable landforce. Of widely different character from the deceitful and timid Tissaphernes, Pharnabazus rode at the head of his cavalry, as far as his horse would carry him, into the sea, to relieve his distressed allies. Through the protection thus afforded, the crews mostly escaped ; but the Athenians carried off thirty triremes. Thrasyllus was dispatched to Athens to announce the victory, and desire reïnforcement ; and Alcibiades, judging forty ships now sufficient for the station at Sestos, sent the rest of the fleet various ways, to collect contributions which might supply immediate need.

Nothing farther of importance had occurred, when Tissaphernes arrived at the Hellespont[18]. Alcibiades went to wait upon him, expecting a reception more favorable than formerly, in proportion as his own circumstances were improved, as he had less need of personal assistance, and more power to serve or injure. He did not however neglect to carry presents, both such as Grecian hospitality prescribed, and such as the eastern great were wont to expect, or be gratified with[19] ; but he found himself greatly deceived. The faithless satrap, alledging orders from the king to consider the Athenians as enemies, caused him to be arrested and sent prisoner to Sardis. After a confinement of about a month, however, he escaped to Clazomenæ, a city of the Athenian alliance ; whence, with six ships[20], which he found there, he returned to his fleet in the Hellespont.

While Alcibiades was thus absent, and the Athenian fleet scattered,

Xen. Hel.
l. 1. c. 1.
s. 4.

s. 5.

s. 6.

B. C. 410.
Ol. 92. 2.
P. W. 22.
March.

---

[18] Ες Ἑλλήσποντον.

[19] Thus I suppose the ξίνια' τε καὶ δῶρα of Xenophon may be interpreted, the former word relating to Grecian customs, the latter to Persian.

[20] Σὺν πέντε τριήρισι καὶ ἰπακτρίδι. Cum quinque triremibus et una navi actuaria.

Xenophon seems afterward to reckon the ιπακτρὶς among the ναῦς. I do not recollect that Thucydides ever gives the title of ναῦς to any but ships of war, except once to a merchant-ship of very large size, ναῦς μυριοφόρος, in the harbour of Syracuse, l. 7. c. 25.

Mindarus

Mindarus having received reinforcements which made his fleet sixty triremes, proposed to attack the forty which lay at Sestos ; but timely intelligence of his intention coming to the commanders they withdrew by night to Cardia, at the bottom of the gulph on the other side of the Chersonese. Alcibiades joined them there ; but he joined them with other hopes than he had given, both the armament and the people at home, to entertain. All the expectations, which he had raised so high, of assistance from the great king through the satrap, the coöperation of the Phenician fleet, and, what was still more important to the commonwealth, and what would be incomparably more felt by the armament, the pay which would never fail, were at an end. Deprived of Ionia, of the Hellespontine cities, of the Thracian colonies, of Attica itself, and retaining but a precarious dominion over a part of Eubœa, the sources of that revenue, by which the commonwealth had hitherto been powerful, were gone ; and the pay of Persia, promised by Alcibiades, was what both the armament abroad and the people at home had depended upon, for means to recover their losses, and to support even a defensive war.

In these circumstances Alcibiades saw that daring measures, and quick decision, were necessary, both for himself and for the commonwealth. Mindarus, disappointed of his purpose against the fleet at Sestos, by its retreat to Cardia, had moved to Cyzicus ; and, Pharnabazus meeting him with his land-forces, that defenceless town was compelled again to receive its law from the enemies of Athens. Alcibiades resolved, tho with a force considerably inferior, to seek them there. From Cardia he moved to Sestos ; and every preparation being made that circumstances admitted, orders were already issued for proceeding up the Propontis, when Theramenes arrived from Macedonia, and Thrasybulus from Thasus, each with twenty triremes. This fortunate reinforcement made new consideration necessary : it was important to conceal from the enemy the increased numbers of the fleet. On arriving therefore at the iland of Prœconnesus, a proclamation was issued, denouncing capital punishment against any who should be taken in the attempt to cross to the Asiatic shore. The soldiers and

Xen. He.l
l. 1. c. 1.
s. 9.

s. 8.

s. 10.

seamen

seamen were then summoned, as to a popular assembly; and Alcibiades, addressing them, ventured to declare, without reserve, the
necessities of their situation. ' Supplies,' he said, ' to the amount
' that the prosecution of the war would require, were not within their
' present power to obtain, or within the means of the commonwealth
' to afford : the enemy, on the contrary, supported by the wealth of
' Persia, knew no want.   Vigorous exertion and quick decision were
' therefore indispensable: they must prepare for action both by sea and
' land ; and by land both in the field, and in the attack of fortifica-
' tions.'   Past success, superiority of present strength, and an opinion
of their general's ability, gave confidence, and the speech of Alcibiades

Xen. Hel.
l. 1. c. 1.
s. 11.
was received with applause ; the assembly was dismissed, all were
ordered aboard, and the fleet, consisting of eighty-six ships, got under
way.

A heavy rain presently came on, which favored the purpose of surprizing the enemy.   As the fleet approached Cyzicus, the weather
cleared, and the enemy's fleet, of sixty triremes, was seen exercising, at
such a distance from the port that its return was already intercepted.
The Peloponnesians, discovering the Athenian fleet so much stronger
than they had expected, were in great consternation.   They had no hope
of success in naval action, and the enemy was between them and their
port.   The resource, which the nature of the antient marine afforded,
was to make for the nearest shore, and depend upon the assistance of

s. 12.
their land-force for the protection of their stranded ships.   Alcibiades,
aware of their intention, passing with twenty ships beyond their line,
debarked his people.   Mindarus, seeing this, also debarked, met
Alcibiades, was defeated, and himself slain.   The crews of the whole Peloponnesian fleet then fled ; and, except the Syracusan squadron, burnt

s. 13.
by its own people, every ship was carried off by the Athenians.   Cyzicus
was abandoned, both by the Peloponnesians and by the satrap ; and
next day, the Athenian fleet approaching, the inhabitants immediately
surrendered.

This important success, which left the enemy in a moment without
a fleet, would of course go far to restore the animation of the armament,
and the popularity of the commander.   But the situation of Alcibiades

was

was still of extreme difficulty.   The government at home could not
yet the more for his victory supply his armament.   Instead therefore
of prosecuting operations against the enemy, his first attention was necessarily still to be given to providing subsistence for his own people.
Remaining twenty days at Cyzicus, he raised large contributions there.
The historian remarks that the Cyzicenes experienced no other Xen. Hel.
severity ; as if he thought another general might not have been so l. 1. c. 1.
indulgent : tho in the defenceless state of their town, to have avoided s. 13.
contending with the united force of the Peloponnesians and the satrap,
it should seem, could not very reasonably be imputed to them as a
crime.   The fleet then went to Perinthus and Selymbria, where contri- s. 14.
butions were also raised.   Proceeding thence to Chrysopolis in the
Chalcedonian territory, near the entrance of the Euxine, Alcibiades
caused that place to be fortified, and established there a custom-
house for levying a duty of a tenth in value of all cargoes passing
the strait.   This mode of collecting a revenue requiring force, he
left, beside a garrison, thirty ships there, with Theramenes and
Eubulus to command.   With the rest of the fleet he returned to the
Hellespont.

While Alcibiades was thus profiting from victory, the Peloponnesians s. 15.
were suffering distress, of which a very remarkable picture remains, in
the letter written to the Spartan government by Hippocrates. to whom
the command-in-chief devolved on the death of Mindarus.   It was intercepted by the Athenians, and, being reported in the original dialect
by Xenophon, is among the most curious and authentic specimens of
Laconic writing.   In any change of language it must suffer, but it ran
nearly thus : ' Success hath turned against us : Mindarus is slain : the
' men hunger : what to do we know not.'   These four short sentences
made the whole of the dispatch.

The Peloponnesians, however, found an able and generous friend in s. 16.
the satrap Pharnabazus, who not only relieved their wants but soothed
their feelings : ' Their loss in men,' he said, ' had not been great, and
' the meer loss of ships ought not to dispirit them : the king's domi-
' nions abounded with materials ; and they should soon have another
' fleet.'

' fleet.'   Distributing then to every man of the armament a garment,

Xen. Hel.
l. 1.   c. 1.
s. 17.

and subsistence for two months, he sent the generals [21] and commanders of triremes to Antandrus, at the southern foot of Mount Ida, where timber abounded, to superintend the construction of a fleet ; directing, that as many vessels should be built, for every state of the confederacy, as had been lost by each in the late action.   That the seamen might not in the mean time be totally idle or useless, furnishing them with heavy armour, which was a gratification, inasmuch as an idea of superior honor was attached to the service of the heavy-armed, he appointed them to the guard of the maritime territory.

While the Peloponnesians were employed in building a fleet at Antandrus, the Antandrians themselves were busied in raising walls for the defence of their town.   But among the numbers of the Peloponnesian armament, in this unavoidable intermission of military enterprize, some would have times of total leisure ; and some, notwithstanding the endevors of Pharnabazus to obviate the evil, would be likely to abuse that leisure.   In these circumstances none, among the various people who composed the armament, behaved so unexceptionably toward the inhabitants as the Syracusans : and this was the more remarkable, as discipline was much less inforced by law among them than among any of the Peloponnesian forces, or even the Athenian ; the Syracusan democracy being a constitution far less well regulated than the Athenian.

s. 21.

B. C. 410.

But Hermocrates had been restored to the command of the Syracusan squadron ; and he not only himself possessed the confidence of all under him, but he taught the superior officers to acquire the confidence of the inferior, and these that of the multitude.   Thus a gradation of influence supplied the place of subordination inforced by penalty, and a strict discipline was founded upon reverence and affection.   To effect this requires the most capacious mind united with the most refined temper, and is indeed among the most exalted efforts of

[21] Military and naval command were constantly, among the antients, united in the same person, whence they had but one title for the commanders-in-chief in the two services. The complete separation of the two commands, with us, has produced distinct titles ; and hence we are without a word to express the office which united the two, as the antient languages are without terms to express the distinction. The term General here is not accurate, but we have none more so.

human

human genius. The benevolence of Hermocrates led the way for those under his command to be benevolent, and the leisure of the Syracusans was employed in assisting the Antandrians in the construction of their fortifications. In gratitude for this kindness, a decree of the Antandrian people gave the freedom of their city to all the people of Syracuse.

Meanwhile Syracuse, led by faction, was preparing a most ungrateful return for its meritorious officers. Hermocrates and his collegues, for he had not been intrusted alone with the chief command, were not only superseded, but, without a trial, without an opportunity to speak for themselves, and while they were ignorant even that they were accused, banishment was decreed against all.   The news of their being deprived of the rights of citizens, in their own country, reached them just as their good deeds had procured an extension of the rights of citizenship to every one of their fellowcountrymen; a privilege indeed little likely to be very advantageous to many individuals, but honorable to the commonwealth, as well as to the generals and army for whose sake it was given. The troops and seamen were called together, and Hermocrates spoke, for himself and his collegues. ' Irregular as the proceedings against them,' he said, ' had been, ' and unjust as the condemnation, they should nevertheless submit to ' the voice of their country; and, as their legal authority was abrogated, ' and their appointed successors not arrived, it would be proper for the ' armament to elect their own commanders for the interval.'

His speech was answered with shouts from the soldiers and seamen, declaring their approbation of the conduct of their present generals, and their indignation at the illegal sentence against them. The principal officers not only declined to offer themselves for the command, but, in the name of the whole armament, desired that Hermocrates and his collegues would hold it till the new generals should arrive. These, in reply, admonished to -avoid whatever might bear any appearance of sedition. ' The time will come,' they said, ' when, in a constitutional ' manner, we shall desire your honest support to us against a malicious ' prosecution. You will then declare how many battles you have ' fought, how many ships you have taken, what general success has ' attended you under our command; and you will relate the testimony

Xen. Hel. l. 1. c. 1. s. 18.

s. 19.

Xen. Hel.
l. 1. c. 1.
s. 20.

' of the whole confederate armament to your merit and ours, manifested
' in the post of honor which has been constantly assigned to us, upon
' all occasions, by sea and land.' The admonition had the full effect
proposed from it. Nothing disorderly insued. A unanimous declaration only was made, that the generals were without blame, and the request
was persisted in, that they would hold the command till their appointed
successors arrived. Soon afterward Demarchus, Myscon, and Potames
came from Syracuse, and the command passed into their hands without
any commotion. The armament however showed that they would not
have suffered any violence to the persons of their former generals ; and
most of the trierarcs entered into an agreement, upon oath, to exert
themselves, on returning to Syracuse, for procuring their restoration
to their country.

History affords few examples of so warm an attachment, in an
armament, to the persons of their generals, united with so just a consideration of the welfare of the country, and of the constitutional
authority of those to whose party principles they were adverse, and
with whose measures they were highly and justly dissatisfied. Hermocrates, dismissed from his command, was still capable of serving the
common cause, and of promoting those measures for ruining the power

s. 22.

of Athens, for which he had long been zealous. He went to Lacedæmon,
where he was honorably received, and he explained to the government
there the state of things in Asia; particularly the conduct, the character,
and the designs of the Persian satraps, the frank generosity of
Pharnabazus, and the crafty interestedness of Tissaphernes[21] Having
thus confirmed the resolution to carry on the war, and opened views
to the means, and at the same time strengthened his own interest
among the principal men of Lacedæmon, which might be important
toward the promotion of his views at Syracuse, he returned to Asia,
where Pharnabazus received him with distinguished friendship. Not
waiting for solicitation, the generous Persian was forward to relieve

---

[21] In consequence of the defective connection, already noticed, of the beginning of
the narrative of Xenophon with the end of
that of Thucydides, it seems not perfectly
clear whether a second journey of Hermocrates to Lacedæmon is here intended, or
the account r lates only to that before noticed from Thucydides.

his

his wants and promote his wishes; especially giving money unasked. Hermocrates, thus furnished with means, prepared triremes and hired seamen, to assist the common cause in which already he had shown so much zeal and ability; and to assist afterward, if occasion should be, the party with which he was connected in his own country, and promote his restoration.

SECTION IX.

Effects of the naval successes of the Athenians.   Reinforcement under Thrasyllus: His transactions on the Ionian coast.   Winter campain of Alcibiades.   Defeat of Pharnabazus.   Weakness of the Lacedæmonian administration.

THE affairs of Lacedæmon were at this time ill administered; while Athens, so lately supposed ruined in Sicily, and since upon the point of bringing destruction upon herself, was again raised toward a superiority over the Peloponnesian confederacy, tho the Peloponnesian confederacy was supported by the wealth of Persia.   The effects of returning prosperity spred: a party in Thasus, in the Athenian interest, rose upon the Lacedæmonian harmost, and expelled him, together with those citizens who principally favored the Peloponnesian cause. Pasippidas, who had been sent from Lacedæmon to take the command-in-chief on the Asiatic station, and had collected a small squadron at Chios, was accused of being privy to the revolt, induced by bribes from Tissaphernes.   What interest of Tissaphernes this measure was to promote, does not appear; but the accusation so far had credit at Sparta, that Pasippidas was recalled and banished, and Cratesippidas was sent to succeed him in the command.

B. C. $\frac{410}{409}$.
Ol. 91. 2.
Winter.

Xen. Hel.
l. 1. c. 2,
s. 23.

About the same time an occurrence within Attica itself, otherwise little important, contributed to raise the spirits of the Athenian people, and to confirm the hope, which had begun to revive among them, that they should be finally superior in the war.   Agis, marching out of Deceleia for plunder, approached Athens.   Thrasyllus, taking the command as a general of the establishment, led out the whole force of the city, and

s. 24.

3 Q 2   formed

formed for battle near the gymnasium of the Lyceium. Agis had apparently not expected such a measure, only because in the whole course of the war the Athenians had hitherto avoided it. Being probably now not strong enough prudently to meet their numbers, he withdrew hastily; and the Athenian light-armed, following his retreat, made some slaughter of his rear. Great credit was given to Thrasyllus for his conduct on this occasion. The reinforcement for the armament in the Hellespont, which it was his principal business in Athens to request, was voted with alacrity; a thousand heavy-armed, a hundred horse, and fifty triremes; and he was authorized to select the heavy-armed from among the citizens inrolled for that service. To give more security then to the communication by sea from Athens eastward, particularly with Eubœa, and perhaps to afford some protection to the silvermines of Laureium, Thoricum, near the Suniad promontory, was fortified, and a garrison established there.

Agis, not a prince of shining abilities, had however the merit of diligence in his command. On his first appointment, he seems to have been highly satisfied with it; but the late turn in the fortune of war, in favor of Athens, was likely to render it less agreeable. Hitherto he had had a decided superiority: all Attica was either under his orders, or liable to the terror of his arms; and even the glory of conqueror of Athens seemed within his hope. But should the Athenians acquire a decided superiority in the Hellespont and on the Asiatic coast; should Alcibiades then return with his powerful fleet and troops flushed with conquest; and should the Persian satrap not furnish money to inable the Lacedæmonians to maintain, together with a powerful fleet, such a force through the year in Deceleia, as the supplies to be obtained from their own confederacy certainly would not inable them to maintain; he might be reduced to act on the defensive, and risk even to be without means to defend himself. Urged by these considerations, he sent a remonstrance to the government at home. It was to little purpose, he observed, that he and the army with him, had been so long using their diligence, by land, to deprive Athens of the produce of Attica, if the sea could furnish the city with that plenty, which, before his eyes, was continually passing into the

Xen. Hel.
l. i. c. i.
s. 25.

harbour

harbour of Peiræus.   He therefore proposed that a squadron should
be stationed at Byzantium and Chalcedon, to intercept the vessels
from the Euxine (for it was from the fertile shores of that sea that
Greece had long been accustomed to supply the deficiency of its
produce in corn) and he recommended Cleärchus son of Rhamphias,
a public guest of the Byzantines, for the command.   The proposal was
approved; fifteen, ships were collected from the allied states, mostly
from Megara, for there were none in the ports of Laconia; and, under
the Spartan Cleärchus, they sailed for their destination.   In passing
the Hellespont, three were taken by the nine Athenian guardships always
stationed there: with the remaining twelve, Cleärchus was fortunate
enough to reach Byzantium.

Herod. l. 7.
c. 147.

    In spring the armament under Thrasyllus sailed from Peiræus.   It
was resolved that, before it joined the fleet under Alcibiades, something
should be undertaken in Ionia.   Possibly, while Alcibiades occupied
the attention of Pharnabazus and the Peloponnesian commanders,
some part of that rich country might be recovered to the Athenian
dominion..   But if no lasting acquisition could be made, contributions
might be levied; and, by hostile incursions those supplies might be
taken from the territories acknowleging the authority of Tissaphernes,
which were no longer to be expected from that satrap's friendship..
Thrasyllus, to give more efficacy to the force he commanded, armed
five thousand of his seamen as targeteers.   Usually they carried only
light armor; but he proposed to make them act with his regular
middle-armed.   Having touched at Samos, he proceeded to the Milesian

Xen. Hel.
l. 1. c. 2.
s. 1, 2.
B. C. 409.
Ol. 92. $\frac{1}{2}$.[23]
P. W. 23.

---

[23] This date is Dodwell's.   Xenophon is
far from being equally accurate with Thu-
cydidès in marking times and seasons; but
he has specified the year, here intended, as
an Olympic year, and, unless interpolation
is to be suspected, as that of the ninety-
third Olympiad; which, according to the
chronologers was the year 408 before the
Christian æra.   I am utterly unsatisfied with
Dodwell's correction, in which he has followed Diodorus: I much rather give credit
to Xenophon for knowing what happened in

the year of the ninety-third Olympiad.   But,
doing so, I am unable to divide the years of
the Peloponnesian war, from the time when
the narrative of Thucydides ends, so that
Xenophon and Thucydides may agree.   Dodwell's boast may perhaps suffice for my apology: Intelliget autem operis a nobis sus-
cepti difficultatem, qui expenderit quid viri
maximi tentarint in primis Xenophontis
annis, Petavius et Petitus, nec tamen operam
nostram supervacuam fecerint.   Dodw. Ann.
Xen. in ann. Bel. Pel. 21.

coast,

coast, and, debarking near Pygela, ravaged the country.   A body of
Milesians coming to assist the Pygelians in the protection of their property, fell upon the Athenian light-armed, scattered in quest of booty,
and put them to flight.   But the numerous targeteers of the Athenian
armament were at hand; and supported by only two lochi of heavy-
armed, they attacked the pursuing Milesians, and routed them with
considerable slaughter.   Two hundred shields were taken, and the
success was thought important enough to warrant the erection of a
trophy [24].

Thrasyllus, however, did not follow the blow; whether he found the
strength of Miletus too great, or any intelligence induced him to
turn his arms another way.   On the day following the action, reïmbarking his forces, he proceeded to Notium, an Athenian colony; and
marching thence to the neighboring city of Colophon, where a strong
party favored the Athenian interest, he gained admission, and Colophon
was restored to the Athenian alliance.   On the next night he entered
Lydia, burnt many villages, and collected much booty, chiefly money
and slaves.   Stages, a Persian who commanded in the neighborhood,
interfered with a body of horse, but with little effect.

Xen. Hel.
l. 1. c. 2.
s. 3.

s. 4.

Thus far successful, Thrasyllus resolved next upon a more important
enterprize; but he seems to have been too long and too open in preparation.   It became evident that he had a design upon Ephesus; and
against Grecian arms Tissaphernes invoked efficaciously the aid of
Grecian superstition; to which, as we have seen, he had been paying
compliments, that, from a Persian of his high rank, appear extraordinary.
He sent through the towns of his satrapy, urging that Diana was
threatened, and it behooved all Greeks to exert themselves in her
defence.   It was not till the seventeenth day after the invasion of
Lydia that Thrasyllus arrived off Ephesus.   He debarked his forces in
two divisions; the heavy-armed near mount Coressus; the horse, who
would be but few, with the targeteers and light-armed, on the other
side of the city, near the marsh.

July.

[24] The SHIELD, ἀσπὶς, always implies a
heavy-armed soldier. Two hundred targets,
πέλται, taken, would by no means have been
of equal consequence, and two hundred light-
armed slain would scarcely have been
thought worth mention.

Tissaphernes

Tissaphernes had already collected a large army at Ephesus. The Xen. Hel. l. 1. c. 2. s. 5. Asian Greeks were numerous. The Syracusans, from the twenty ships destroyed near Cyzicus, and from five lately arrived from Syracuse, with the Selinuntines from two ships, were together perhaps five thousand men. The satrap himself headed a body of horse; and to all this were added the numerous population of the city. Such a force would not wait to be besieged by the small army of Thrasyllus. Taking advantage of his apparently faulty arrangement, in dividing his strength, they quickly overpowered his heavy-armed, pursued to the ships, and killed about a hundred. They proceeded then against the other division, s. 7. less likely to make effectual resistance, and killed three hundred. For this double success they erected two trophies, and they decreed the aristeia to the Syracusans and Selinuntines. The sum given upon the occasion was considerable, and presents were besides made to individuals who had distinguished themselves.

The spirit of Hermocrates seemed still to animate the Sicilian forces. Their conduct altogether was so acceptable to the Ephesians, that a perpetual immunity from taxes (probably those assessed upon strangers) was granted to all Syracusans of the armament, who might at any time reside in Ephesus: and the Selinuntines, having lately lost their home (for Selinus had been taken by the Carthaginians) were presented universally with the freedom of the city.

Thrasyllus, after his defeat, proceeded toward the Hellespont. s. 8. While he stopped at Methymnë in Lesbos, the Syracusan squadron of twenty-five triremes (the munificence of Pharnabazus, seconded by the diligence of the Syracusan officers, having already repaired the loss at Cyzicus) was seen passing from Ephesus. Thrasyllus took four with their crews: the rest escaped back to the port whence they came. Among the prisoners one was remarkable: he was the first-cousin of the general Alcibiades, and of the same name. He had accompanied his kinsman in his flight, when persecuted for the business of the Mercuries; but, instead of the Lacedæmonian, had ingaged in the Syracusan service; and, apparently satisfied with it, under the admirable regularity which Hermocrates had established, he continued to fight against his country. Thrasyllus nevertheless gave him his liberty. The other prisoners, being sent to Athens, were put

into

Xen. Hel.
l. 1. c. 2.
s. 9.
into the stone-quarries of Peiræus, in retaliation for the confinement of the Athenian prisoners in the quarries of Syracuse. They were, however, less carefully guarded, or the prison was less secure; for, in the following winter, digging a passage through the rock, and flying by night, all escaped, some finding their way to Deceleia, and the rest to Megara.

The successes of Thrasyllus seem to have been very inferior to the expectation formed of his expedition ; and the delay in the junction with Alcibiades, appears to have prevented that active general from undertaking anything of consequence against the enemy. Thirty triremes being stationed at the entrance of the Euxine, on the indispensable duty of collecting revenue, his force remaining in the Hellespont was unequal to great enterprize ; and the occupation to which he was himself obliged principally to direct his attention, was the maintenance of his forces. The summer was far advanced when he was joined by Thrasyllus at Sestos. He appears however to have had, then ready, a plan for winter operations. He conducted the whole fleet

s. 10.
End of Sept.
to Lampsacus on the Asiatic shore. There the ships were as usual laid up. The town being without defence, he employed the troops in raising fortifications. But a point of honor occasioned some disturbance : those who had been serving under Alcibiades refused to rank with those newly arrived under Thrasyllus : they had been always conquerors ; those under Thrasyllus were tainted with the disgrace of defeat. Alcibiades seems not to have opposed a prejudice, dangerous only under weak command, and from which, on the contrary, abilities might derive advantage. He quartered them separately, and employed them separately on the fortifications.

From Lampsacus an extent of territory, subject to Persia, was open to inroad ; but, in the neighboring city of Abydus, Pharnabazus had his winter residence, attended by a large force of cavalry. Alcibiades led his army toward Abydus, purposely to invite a battle. The satrap unadvisedly met him ; was defeated, and, being pursued by the small body of Athenian cavalry, led by Alcibiades, was saved only by the swiftness of his horse and the darkness of supervening night. After this action, in which the soldiers under Thrasyllus had their equal share, the rest of the army saluted them as cleared from dishonor, and no
longer

longer refused to join them in arms in the field, or associate with them in quarters. The victory deterring opposition from the enemy, several incursions were made into the country during the winter, with some profit to the Athenians, and extensive injury to those whom the power of the Persian empire ought to have protected.

Meanwhile the Lacedæmonian government was distracted by domestic disturbance. A rebellion had taken place among the Helots; a large body of whom, getting possession of some strong posts among the mountains, toward the Malean promontory, defended themselves with such successful obstinacy, that a capitulation was at length granted, allowing them to go and settle themselves anywhere out of the Lacedæmonian territory. While such was the derangement at home, able attention to distant concerns could hardly be. The pride of command, however, and the jealousy of their prerogative over the republics of their confederacy, did not cease among the Lacedæmonians. Little as they were able to support their colony of the Trachinian Heracleia, they were dissatisfied with that interference of the Thebans, which had probably saved it from utter ruin. They sent thither a new governor, who, in conjunction with the Thessalian Achaians, led the whole force of the colony against the Œtæans, its perpetual enemies. The Achaians betrayed their allies, the governor was killed with seven hundred of his people, and the colony was thus reduced to a weaker state than when the Thebans interfered for its preservation.

Xen. Hel.
l. 1. c. 2.
s. 12.

SECTION X.

Important successes of Alcibiades. Friendly communication opened with the satrap Pharnabazus. Ambassies to the king of Persia. Return of Alcibiades to Athens.

The successes of Thrasybulus and Alcibiades having restored superiority to the Athenian arms, the next, and a most important object, was to restore to the commonwealth a revenue equal to the expences of a

war, which, long as it had lasted, was not yet likely to be soon concluded.   Through the measures already taken, something accrued
from the trade of the Euxine: but, to secure this, a large force must
be constantly employed at great expence, and yet the enemy, from
Byzantium and Chalcedon, could interrupt the collectors and
share the profit.   Alcibiades therefore resolved to direct his next
measures against those two towns.   They being recovered, the whole
revenue from the trade of the Euxine would accrue to Athens, and her
dominion, on the shores of the Propontis and Hellespont, would be
restored to nearly its former extent.   A decisive superiority on the
Hellespontine coasts might induce Pharnazabus to treat; Tissaphernes
would become alarmed for his Ionian towns, naturally the next objects
for the Athenian arms; and thus an opening might be gained for
counterworking the negotiations of Lacedæmon, and stopping those
supplies from Persia, which alone inabled the Peloponnesian confederacy to maintain its fleet.

With these views, in the twenty-fourth spring of the war [24], Alcibiades led his whole force to the iland of Prœconnesus.   The Chalcedonians had suspected that attack would soon approach them, and this
movement confirmed the suspicion.   Immediately they stripped their
country of every moveable of value; which, however, they would not
trust within their city, but committed all to the care of their neighbors the Bithynians, a Thracian hord.   Intelligence of this being
carried to Alcibiades, he put himself immediately at the head of his
cavalry, directed a select body of heavy-armed infantry to follow, and
the fleet at the same time to attend his motions; and, going to the
Bithynian frontier, he threatened fire and sword to the country, if all
the Chalcedonian property was not surrendered to him, together with
hostages and pledges to insure peaceful conduct from the Bithynians
themselves.   His demands were complied with, and he then directly
formed the siege of Chalcedon.

B. C. 408.
Ol. $\frac{92}{93}$. $\frac{4}{1}$.
P. W. 24.
After 25th
March.
Xen. Hel.
l. 1. c. 3.
s. 1.

[24] Or the twenty-fifth; as observed in a   on the matter noticed in the twenty-third
marginal reading of Leunclavius, in the   note of this chapter.
Paris edition of 1625, which seems founded

Hippocrates,

Hippocrates, a Lacedæmonian, commanded in that city.   He had Xen. Hel. l. 1. c. 3. s. 4, 5, 6. sent information of his danger to Pharnabazus, who hastened to his relief with an army strong in cavalry ; but the Athenians were so rapid with their works that they completed a contravallation, from sea to sea, except where a river interfered.   Nevertheless Hippocrates, aware of the satrap's approach, sallied with the whole garrison, while the Persians endevored to force a passage through the works, by the bed of the river.   Thrasyllus opposed Hippocrates, and a fierce conflict was long equally maintained between them.   Alcibiades in the meantime compelled Pharnazabus to retire, and then led his cavalry, with a small body of heavy-armed, to the assistance of Thrasyllus.   Hippocrates was thus overpowered, himself killed, and his surviving troops fled into the town.

After this successful action, Alcibiades committed the conduct of s. 7. the siege to the generals under him, and passed himself to the Hellespont, to prepare for other enterprize, and at the same time to promote that business which was unceasingly requiring his attention, often to the interruption of enterprize, the collection of supplies.   Meanwhile Pharnabazus, finding himself unable to relieve Chalcedon, sent proposals to the generals commanding the siege.   His connection with the Peloponnesians had not answered his expectation : they had been defeated in every action they had attempted ; several of the Grecian towns which acknowleged his dominion and their alliance, were already taken ; the fate of Chalcedon was sure, if not prevented by a treaty ; if the maritime towns of Æolis should next be attacked, he was unable to protect them ; and to judge of the future by the past, the Lacedæmonians were equally unable.   His overtures were accepted by the Athenian generals, and an accommodation was shortly concluded on the following terms ; ' that Pharnabzus should pay twenty talents, ' about four thousand pounds, as ransom for Chalcedon : that the ' Chalcedonians should in future pay tribute to Athens as formerly, and ' should also pay all the arrears of tribute : that Pharnabazus should ' conduct ambassadors from Athens to the king : that till the return of ' the ambassadors, the Athenians should commit no hostilities against ' the Chalcedonians.'   Apparently Chalcedon was to be considered still

within

within the satrapy and under the protection of Pharnabazus; as formerly we have seen Potidæa tributary to Athens, while under the sovereinty of Corinth.

Xen. Hel.
l. 1. c. 3.
s. 8.

Meanwhile Alcibiades, having assembled the whole Grecian military force of the Chersonese, and a body of Thracian foot, with between three and four hundred horse, (for he had property in the Chersonese, and great personal interest among both Greeks and Thracians there) he made himself master of Selymbria, on the northern coast of the Propontis, and was taking measures to form the siege of Byzantium. Pharnabazus, informed of his approach, sent to require his ratification of the agreement concerning Chalcedon. That agreement seems to have corresponded with the views of Alcibiades; but he nevertheless refused to confirm it by his oath, unless the satrap would enter into reciprocal obligation with the same ceremony; meaning, apparently, to assert his claim to equal rank. Pharnabazus however consenting, he crossed to Chrysopolis; where two Persians, Metrobates and Arnapes, attended to receive the oath from him, while Euryptolemus and Diotimus waited upon the satrap for the same purpose in Chalcedon. This public ceremony being concluded, private compliments and mutual assurances passed, that might form the foundation of an intercourse of friendship.

s. 9.

The next business to be arranged was that of the embassy to the Persian court. Euryptolemus and four other Athenians were appointed, together with two Argians. Intelligence of this being communicated to the Lacedæmonian generals at the Hellespont, excited considerable jealousy there. An embassy from Sparta was already at Susa; but application was nevertheless made to Pharnabazus, that other ministers might go at the same time with the Athenian and Argian, which he readily granted. Of no great abilities, but of an open generous disposition, averse to wily policy, the satrap seems to have meant equal friendship to both parties, and to have proposed no advantage to himself but what might arise from general esteem. Pasippidas, the commander-in-chief, put himself at the head of the Lacedæmonian embassy; Hermocrates the Syracusan, and his brother, Proxenus, still

exiles

exiles from their country, accompanied him. Cyzicus was the appointed place of meeting for all, and Pharnabazus in person undertook to be their common conductor.

Matters being thus settled for the country on the Asiatic side of the Hellespont, so that his satrapy was in peace, Pharnabazus appears not to have concerned himself about Byzantium. The Lacedæmonian, Cleärchus, commanded there. In addition to the inhabitants, he had some troops from old Greece, a small body of Lacedæmonians of those called Periœcians and Neodamodes, some Megarians under Helixus, and some Bœotians under Cyratadas. The Athenians attempted all the modes of assault, known in that age, without success; but they completed a contravallation, and the place was soon pressed by famine.

Xen. Hel. l. 1. c. 3. s. 10, 11, 12.

Thus reduced to distress, while the Peloponnesian commanders, who should have endevored to relieve him, were passive, Cleärchus formed the bold project of going himself to infuse vigor into their counsels, and collect a fleet with which to make a diversion, such as might compel the Athenians to raise the siege. He depended upon money from Pharnabazus. There were some triremes in the Hellespont, which Pasippidas had stationed for the protection of the maritime towns; some were just completed at Antandrus; Hegesippidas commanded a squadron on the Thracian coast. All these he proposed to assemble, and to promote the building of more. But Cleärchus, tho an able man, wanted the policy of Brasidas. Thucydides informs us, that the fame of the conciliating and liberal conduct of Brasidas was extensively serviceable to the Lacedæmonian cause, long after his death: Brasidas was considered as an example of the Lacedæmonian character; generally to the grievous disappointment of the people who allied themselves with Lacedæmon; for the governors or superintendants, placed in every city with the modest title of Harmostes, Regulator, assumed almost universally a despotic authority. Cleärchus was not less despotic than the rest. When provisions began to fail in Byzantium, his soldiers from old Greece were still supplied; the Byzantine people were disregarded. General discontent insued: an Athenian party had always existed in the city; it now gained strength, and the absence of

s. 13.

Cleärchus

Cleärchus added incouragement. While famine grew more and more pressing, communication was managed with Alcibiades; a gate was opened for him by night; the Athenian troops entered; and Helixus and Cyratadas, to whom the command had been committed by Cleärchus, after some resistance, were compelled to surrender themselves prisoners.

The services which, by the reduction of Byzantium, Alcibiades had completed for his country, less brilliant than some, were yet perhaps, in importance, equal, and, by the union of ability and vigor displayed in an extensive and complicated command, even superior to what any Athenian or any Greek had ever before performed. When the forces first placed him at their head, Athens scarcely commanded more territory than its walls inclosed; revenue was gone, and the commonwealth depended for existence upon its fleet, which was at the same time dispirited and mutinous. He had restored loyalty to the fleet; he had restored dominion to the commonwealth; he had destroyed the enemy's fleet; and, under his conduct, the navy of Athens again commanded the seas: and, what was not least among the services, his successes and his reputation, without solicitation or intrigue, had conciliated the adverse satrap Pharnabazus, and opened probable means for checking those sources of supply to the enemy, the failure of which would restore to Athens certain superiority in the war. In this state of things he thought he might with advantage revisit his country, whence he had been absent six years; and he proposed at the same time, as winter was approaching, to gratify the greater part of his forces with means of seeing their friends, and attending to their domestic concerns.

Xen. Hel.
l. 1. c. 4.
s. 4.

These being his purposes, after he had settled the affairs of Byzantium, and the other dependencies of the commonwealth on the Propontis and the Hellespont, he led the armament to Samos. Thence he sent Thrasybulus with thirty ships to the Thracian coast; and, the restored reputation of the Athenian arms seconding the measures of that active and able officer and statesman, all the cities which had lately revolted were quickly recovered. Alcibiades went himself with twenty ships to the Carian coast; and, in tribute or contribution, collected a hundred talents, about twenty thousand pounds, for the public treasury. On his return to

s. 5.

Samos,

Samos, reserving twenty ships, he sent the rest, under the conduct of Thrasyllus, to Attica. There was yet a strong party in Athens so inveterately inimical to him, tho since the last revolution it had less dared to show itself, that he would not venture thither till the temper of the people should be more completely manifested, in the reception of the returning fleet.   Meanwhile he went with his squadron to the coast of Laconia, under pretence of gaining intelligence of the enemy's designs, and of observing what was going forward in the port of Gythium.

Information from his confidential friends reached him at sea, that he had been elected general of the commonwealth, and that Thrasybulus, who was also absent, and Conon alone of officers present, were appointed his collegues.   Upon this he made immediately for Attica. It happened that he entered the harbour of Peiræus on the day of the Plynteria, a kind of mourning religious ceremony, when the statue of Minerva was veiled; and, tho to any other Greek, such was Grecian superstition, not esteemed unlucky, on that day no Athenian dared transact any important business.   Many people, as the cotemporary historian tells us, considered this as an ill omen, both to Alcibiades and to the commonwealth.

Xen. Hel. l. 1. c. 4. s. 4.

s. 5.

25 Sept.

Nevertheless, the approach of Alcibiades being announced, a vast croud attracted by curiosity, both from Peiræus and from the city, assembled about the port.   The general language was, ' that Alcibiades ' was the most meritorious of citizens: that his condemnation had ' been the wicked measure of a conspiracy of men, who scrupled nothing ' to promote their own interest: that his abilities were transcendent; ' his liberality unbounded: his opposition to his country had been ' forced; his eagerness to return to its service proved his patriotic ' inclination.   As for danger to the democracy, men like him had no ' temptation to innovate; the favor of the people gave him all the ' power and preëminence he could wish for.   Accordingly he had ' never oppressed any: whereas his opponents had destroyed by assas- ' sination the most deserving citizens; and, if ever they appeared to ' possess any popular confidence, it was only when the death or exile of ' all better men left them without competitors for the leading situa-
                                                                    ' tions

Xen. Hel. l. 1. c. 4. s. 6.

' tions in the commonwealth²⁵.' While these were the sentiments
sounded by the general voice, a few were heard to say less loudly,
' that Alcibiades had alone been the cause of all the past misfortunes,
' and it was to be feared he would still be the promoter of measures
' dangerous to the commonwealth.'   He was not yet so assured
of the prevalence of sentiments in his favor, but that he approached
the shore with apprehension.   He even hesitated to quit his galley, till
from the deck he saw his cousin-german Euryptolemus son of
Peisianax, with others of his relations and confidential friends.
Nor did even they trust intirely in the protection which the etablished
government, hardly indeed yet established, could or would afford.
They came prepared to resist any attempt that might be made
against his person ; and, surrounded by them, he proceeded to
the city.

Xen. Hel.
l. 1. c. 4.
s. 8.

His first business, in regular course, was to attend the council of
Five-hundred ; his next to address the general assembly.   Before both
he took occasion to assert his innocence of the sacrilegious profana-
tions, of which he had been accused, to apologize for his conduct
during his banishment, and to criminate his prosecutors.   Many after
him spoke strongly to the same purposes ; and the current of popular
favor became so evident, that not a word was heard in opposition to
him; for the people, says Xenophon, would not have borne it.   He
was chosen, with a title apparently new, governor-general, or commander-in-chief with supreme authority ²⁶, as the only person capable
of restoring the former power and splendor of the commonwealth.   So
nearly allied we commonly find democracy with absolute monarchy;
and not in effect only, but often in form also.

s. 8.

Soon after he was vested with this high dignity, opportunity
occurred for Alcibiades to gratify the people who conferred it, and to
acquire

---

²⁵ 'Αυτοὺς δὲ μόνους λειφθένlας, δι' αὐlὸ τοῦτο
ἀγαπᾶσθαι ὑπὸ τῶν πολιτῶν, ὅτι ἑτέροις βελτίοσιν
ὀυκ ἔχον γρῆσθαι. This expression of Xenophon strongly marks the distinction of

ranks, yet existing in public opinion, among
the Athenian people, when legal distinction
was most exploded.

²⁶ Απάντων ἡγεμὼν αὐτοκράτωρ. The title
of

acquire at the same time, at an easy rate, no small addition to his renown through Greece. Since Deceleia had been occupied by a Lacedæmonian garrison, the Athenians had never dared to make the mysterious procession of Ceres to Eleusis, according to the customary forms, along that called the Sacred Way: they had always passed by sea, and many of the prescribed ceremonies were necessarily omitted, or imperfectly executed. Alcibiades, with the forces from Asia, added to the former strength of the city, undertook to conduct the procession by land, and protect it in the fullest performance of every accustomed rite. He was completely successful: the train went and returned, escorted by the army, without an attempt from the enemy to give any disturbance.

With the new glory and new favor, acquired in this mixture of military and religious pageantry, Alcibiades proceeded to direct the inrolment of the forces and the equipment of the fleet, with which he proposed again to cross the Ægean.

Xen. Hel. l. 1. c. 4. s. 9.

of the generals of the Athenian ordinary establishment was not Ἡγεμὼν, but Στρατηγὸς. Ἀυτοκράτωρ was the term by which the Greeks afterward rendered the Roman title *Dictator*. What was the kind and degree of power committed to Alcibiades, with the title of Ἡγεμὼν ἀυτοκράτωρ, does not clearly appear; but, as the Στρατηγὸς, the chief of the board of general officers, had, through his privilege of summoning at pleasure the general assembly, and of acting as representative of the commonwealth in communication with forein states, large civil authority in addition to his military command, the Ἡγεμὼν ἀπάντων ἀυτοκράτωρ would of course have all those powers, and some besides which the Στρατηγὸς did not possess.

CHAPTER XX.

Affairs of GREECE, from the Return of ALCIBIADES to ATHENS, till the Conclusion of the PELOPONNESIAN War.

SECTION I.

State of the Persian empire: Cyrus, younger son of Darius II. appointed viceroy of the provinces west of the river Halys. Lysander commander-in-chief of the Peloponnesian fleet: Seafight of Notium, and its consequences.

WHILE prosperity was restored to the Athenian arms, under the conduct of Thrasybulus and Alcibiades, the Lacedæmonians had succeeded in negotiation, which might overbalance many victories. We have little authentic information of the detail of transactions in the interior of the Persian empire: but we learn that troubles, frequently recurring, principally caused that weakness of the government, and failure of the extension of its energy to the distant provinces, whence, among other inconveniencies, the satraps of Asia minor were reduced to the necessity of courting the Greeks, that, by assistance from one party among them, they might be enabled to withstand oppression from another. The rich kingdom of Media, we find, had revolted; but in the year preceding the return of Alcibiades, through the exertions of Darius in person, it had been reduced to submission. Apparently, in the ideä that his empire was too extensive and unwieldy to be duly and securely administered under a single government, Darius seems then to have had in view to divide it. Detaching a portion, as an appanage for Cyrus, his younger son, which, under able conduct, might form a very powerful kingdom, he could still leave, for his eldest son, Artaxerxes, an empire scarcely less powerful, inasmuch as it would be more compact and manageable, than what himself commanded.

Xen. Hel. l. 3. c. 2. s. 12.

manded. After the recovery of Media, the provinces bordering on the
Grecian seas principally demanded his attention. But, growing infirm
as he advanced in years, he found repugnance to undertake the
troublesome task of regulating matters duly in regard to that nation of
little military republics, by which, for near a century, himself and his
predecessors had been constantly troubled, and sometimes materially
injured. He therefore resolved to commit the business to Cyrus; a
youth of great hopes; who seems to have wanted only a better education to have made him a great prince; but whose active and ambitious
temper, never duly either restrained or directed, gave disturbance and
excited jealousy in the seat of government.

Such nearly was the state of things in the Persian court, when a Xen. Hel.
Lacedæmonian embassy arrived there; having made the journey appa- l. 1. c. 2.
rently through the assistance of Tissaphernes. The political circum- s. 1.
stances of the empire had prepared a good reception for them. Being
then uncontradicted probably in their assertions, as without competition in their solicitation, and paying their court ably and successfully to the young prince who was going to assume the command of
the western provinces, they obtained the declared favor of the monarch
to their confederacy; and particularly to Lacedæmon, in opposition
to Athens. This important point being gained, they set out on their
return to the coast of Lesser Asia.

Meanwhile Pharnabazus, with those ambassadors, Athenian and Pelo- B. C. 408.
ponnesian, whom he had undertaken to conduct to Susa, had proceeded P. W. 24.
in autumn as far as Gordium in Phrygia, where he passed the winter.
In spring he was proposing to prosecute the journey, when the other B. C. 497.
ambassadors arrived on their return, accompanied by Persian officers P. W. 25.
commissioned to announce the approach of Cyrus, to take the command of the western provinces. This stopped Pharnabazus. Cyrus
arriving soon after, the Athenian ministers applied themselves to win
the favor of that prince, and ingage him to their country's cause; but
finding him immoveably attached to the Peloponnesians, they desired
to prosecute their journey to the Persian court. Pharnabazus would
still have assisted them, but Cyrus interfered: refusing them permission either to proceed on their embassy, or to return home, he

required

required that they should be delivered to him. The upright satrap. considering himself as their sworn protector, would not give them up; but it was long before he could obtain leave to send them home '.

Xen. Hel. l. 1. c. 2. s. 5.

It was a rule, jealously observed by the Lacedæmonian government (perhaps the treason of Pausanias might have given occasion for it) that none should hold the command-in-chief of the fleet beyond a year; and perhaps it was from a congenial principle, that the command of the fleet was not committed to the kings. After a long dearth of eminent men in Lacedæmon, some were now coming forward, likely to give new vigor to her councils, and new energy to her arms. Lysander, who succeeded Cratesippidas in the important command of the Asiatic station, was little of the antient Spartan; but he was formed to advance himself and his country in a polished and corrupt age, when the simplicity of antient manners had no longer its former esteem, and the simplicity of antient policy no longer its former efficacy.

B. C. 408. P. W. 24. l. 1. c. 5. s. 1.

Receiving his appointment early in winter, he passed to Rhodes; and, taking the command of a squadron which lay there, he proceeded to Cos and Miletus, and thence to Ephesus; where, with the ships he had collected by the way, he found himself at the head of a fleet of seventy triremes.

B. C. 407. P. W. 25.

Xen. Hel. l. 1. c. 5. s. 2.

As soon as he heard that Cyrus was arrived at Sardis, he hastened, in company with the ambassadors newly returned from Susa, to pay his court there; and he found a most favorable reception. The prince told him, ' that it was equally his father's command and his own ' inclination, to join the Lacedæmonians in zealous prosecution of the ' war against Athens; that he had brought with him five hundred ' talents, about a hundred and twenty-five thousand pounds sterling, ' for the particular purpose; and he would not spare his own revenue ' in the same cause;' adding, in the warmth of youthful zeal, and in the hyperbolical manner of the east, ' that he would cut up the throne ' on which he sat,' (which was of solid silver and gold,) ' rather than

s. 3 & 4.

' means for prosecuting the war should fail.' In the treaty concluded

' Our copies of Xenophon say three years; but archbishop Usher has supposed years to have been put for months by the carelessness of transcribers.

4   with

with the Persian court, it was stipulated, that the king should allow
thirty Attic mines for the monthly pay of every trireme; which made
three oboli, not quite fourpence sterling, for each man daily [2]. Incouraged by the prince's free promise, and not yet accustomed to the
extravagance of oriental diction, Lysander proposed, that an Attic
drachma, which was eight oboli, nearly tenpence sterling, should be
allowed for daily pay to every seaman. ' The increase of expence,' he
said, ' tho it might on a hasty view appear profuse, would in the end be
' found economical; inasmuch as the desertion that would insue among
' the enemy's seamen would, beyond all things, accelerate a happy con-
' clusion of the war.' Cyrus, who had not expected that such advantage
would be taken of his warmth of expression, answered nevertheless,
with much politeness, ' that he doubted not the proposal was founded
' on a just view of things, but he could not exceed the king's command.'
Lysander, with the complacency of a courtier already formed, implicitly assented; and the prince, satisfied altogether with his behavior,
invited him to supper. Wine usually circulated freely at a Persian Xen. Anab.
entertainment, and Cyrus did not always stint himself to moderation.
Lysander's manner and conversation were insinuating; the prince's spirits
were elevated ; and, drinking to Lysander after the Persian manner, Xen. Hel.
he asked ' what he could do for him that would give him most satis- ut sup.
' faction ?' Lysander answered, ' that nothing would gratify him equally
' with the addition of a single obolus to the seamen's daily wages.'
Pleased with the apparent disinterestedness and generosity of the Spartan
general, the prince consented, and the pay was augmented accordingly.
The armament was of course highly gratified; and, whether his influence
with the prince was considered, or his generous preference of the common welfare to his private emolument, for which such an opportunity
seemed offered, very great credit accrued to Lysander.

The people of Athens were not apprized of the acquisition of the Xen. Hel.
alliance of Persia by the Peloponnesian confederacy, when Alcibiades, l. 1. c. 4.
in the third month after his return, sailed again from Peiræus. His s. 9.

---

[2] This, if all were paid alike, would give
two hundred and sixty-six men to every
trireme. Commonly we find, in the Grecian service, the pay of inferior officers and
privates the same, and that of superior
officers only double.

armament

armament consisted of fifteen hundred heavy-armed foot, a hundred and fifty horse, and a hundred triremes.   Aristocrates and Adeimantus were appointed generals of the landforces under him.   He directed his course first to Andros, which had revolted.   The ilanders, assisted by a small body of Lacedæmonians, were rash enough to meet him in the field.   They were defeated with some loss ; but Alcibiades, finding their walls too strong to be readily forced, satisfied himself, for the present, with erecting a trophy for the little success obtained, and proceeded with his armament to Samos.

Xen. Hel. l. 1. c. 4. s. 10.

c. 5. s. 5.   The intelligence, which greeted him on his arrival, of the treaty concluded by Lacedæmon with Persia, the treatment of the Athenian ministers, and the favor of the young prince toward the Lacedæmonians, was highly unwelcome, and threw a damp on the spirits of the whole armament.   It was not the military force, but the wealth of Persia, that was dreaded, as it would give efficacy to the military force of the Peloponnesian confederacy ; and a greater portion than before of that wealth was now likely to be ready, for purposes of hostility to Athens. The active mind of Alcibiades was immediately turned to counter-work the effect of the Lacedæmonian negotiation, and circumstances affording hope occurred.   According to the antient policy of the Persian empire, the satraps, within the extensive country which was put under the command of the prince, retained still a share of independent authority in their respective satrapies.   Nevertheless Tissaphernes, in a manner eclipsed by the prince's superior rank and power, and the greater splendor of his court, fell comparatively into neglect and contempt, particularly with the Lacedæmonians.   Hence, notwithstanding his late injurious treatment of Alcibiades, it was thought interest might now possibly reünite him with the Athenians, and through him means might be obtained for negotiation, from which some advantage might be drawn.   Tissaphernes was actually gained ; but he was in no favor with Cyrus, and all his endevors to procure a reception for Athenian ministers were ineffectual.

This turn of things greatly injured Alcibiades both with the armament at Samos and with the people at home.   His promises of Persian assistance, which he, and he only, could procure, had first and principally

pally led to his restoration. That assistance alone, he had said, and his confidential friends had always maintained, could save the commonwealth. Not only these promises had totally failed, but that important assistance had accrued to the enemy; and in a greater degree than he could ever promise it to Athens. He felt these circumstances, and was hurt by the temper of the armament which followed. His naval force was yet superior to that of the enemy; but quick decision alone probably could either secure his own situation in command, or avert impending ruin from the commonwealth. He led his fleet therefore to Notium, on the Asiatic shore, within view of Ephesus, where Lysander lay. Information came to him that Thrasybulus, who had wintered with his squadron in the Hellespont, was employed in fortifying Phocæa on the Æolian coast. Possibly Alcibiades thought it might be advantageous to withdraw himself, till the moment offered for important action. He left his fleet, however, to go and concert measures with Thrasybulus, intrusting the command to Antiochus, but with strict orders to avoid a general ingagement.

Xen. Hel. l. 1. c. 5. s. 6, 7.

During his absence, Antiochus, whether actuated by honest but injudicious zeal, or coveting a glory to which he could not honestly aspire, went with a few triremes to the harbour of Ephesus, as if to explore; but passed by the very prows of some of the enemy's fleet, as if to provoke pursuit. Lysander, who had now ninety triremes, was yet employed in improving the strength and condition of his fleet, without meaning to seek an action. The conduct of Antiochus induced him to order a few galleys to be hastily launched and manned, and to pursue. Notium was so near that this movement could be seen there, and a superior force presently advanced to relieve Antiochus. Lysander being prepared, led out his whole fleet. The Athenians, not equally prepared, hastily, and as they could, in the exigency of the moment, put all their ships in motion. Lysander began the action with his fleet regularly formed. The Athenians, one after another endevoring to get into the line, maintained the fight for some time, in a confused and scattered manner, but at length fled for Samos. Fifteen of their ships were taken, but most of the men escaped: a few were made prisoners;

Antiochus

Antiochus was among the killed.   Lysander erected his trophy upon
the headland of Notium, and carried his prizes to Ephesus.

Xen. Hel.
1. 1. c. 5.
s. 9.

This was a most mortifying event for Alcibiades.   He hastened back
to his fleet, and, highly anxious to repair its disgrace, he went to the
mouth of the harbour of Ephesus, and offered battle.   Lysander however, being considerably inferior in force, would not move, and Alcibiades returned to Samos.

Plut. vit.
Alcib.

Pausan.
1. 10. c. 9.
s. 818.

The policy of the Lacedæmonian government seems to have met the
vanity of Lysander, in the endevor to give more than its due splendor
to the victory of Notium.   Nine statues were dedicated at Delphi on
the occasion, the effigies of Lysander himself, of Hermon the master
of his ship, and of Abas his soothsayer, with those of Castor, Pollux,
Juno, Apollo, Diana, and Neptune.   That victory, little in itself, became important, as Plutarch justly observes, by its political consequences.   The credit of Alcibiades had already received injury among
the ill-judging multitude of Athens.   They held that he ought not to
have left the revolted iland of Andros unsubdued: yet there can be
no doubt but he would have been inexcusable in wasting the time of
his powerful armament upon that little object, when concerns of importance so beyond comparison greater to the commonwealth, called
him to the Asiatic coast.   His commission excused him from that
constant communication with the people, usually required of Athenian
generals : but it might nevertheless be not difficult to persuade the
people, that the neglect of such communication was disrespectful, and
marked an unbecoming arrogance : nor is it indeed improbable that
Alcibiades may sometimes have used the ample powers committed
to him, in a more lordly style than prudence would justify.   But, as
Plutarch continues to observe, his very glory injured him : the people
expected that nothing should resist the man to whom, whether serving
or opposing his country, all had seemed hitherto to yield.   When information came that he had quitted Andros without subduing it, they

Xen. Hel.
1. 1. c. 5.
s. 10.

bore the immediate disappointment ; but it was with the daily expectation of intelligence that Chios and all Ionia were conquered. When
therefore the news arrived that the fleet had fled, before an inferior
                                                          force

force, with the loss of fifteen ships, Athens was in uproar. Intelligence of a much more threatening misfortune, the alliance of Persia with Lacedæmon, communicated at the same time, made no comparable impression. The enemies of Alcibiades took immediate advantage of the popular temper; and those in the city were assisted by some who came from the fleet for the purpose. Of these Thrasybulus son of Thrason, mentioned on this occasion only in history, principally distinguished himself. An assembly of the people being convened, and curiosity eager for the detail of an unexpected and alarming event, Thrasybulus mounted the bema, and exclaimed vehemently against the commander-in-chief: ' His pride,' he said, ' was intolerable, and ' his negligence of the public service shameful. IIis abilities indeed ' were great, but he was continually quitting the fleet: and while he ' pretended to be employed in raising contributions for public service, ' his time was spent among Ionian courtezans, in the indulgence of ' the most extravagant luxury. In a station in view of the enemy's ' fleet, he had intrusted a command, involving the being of the ' commonwealth, to men who had no merit, but that of flattering his ' pride and ministering to his desires. The late ignominious disaster ' had had no other source. As for any regard for Athens or the Athe- ' nian people, it was evident he had none; and if, in consequence of ' a better knowlege of him, their partiality toward him should cease, ' he was prepared to do without them. While vested with so great ' a command, his attention had been more given to his estate in the ' Thracian Chersonese than to their service. A castle, which he had ' built there, was already prepared to receive him, in that second banish- ' ment which he so well deserved, and which he evidently expected.'

Plut. vit. Alcib.

Some mixture of known truths, with the falsehood and malignity of this accusation, probably assisted to give it efficacy. There seems to have been no ground for the imputation of negligence. Indeed some of those points, in the character of Alcibiades, which were most exceptionable in his youth, appear to have been improved with increasing years and increasing experience; and, as passion cooled, and reason strengthened, and adversity instructed, the lessons of Socrates were remembered and had their effect. In his conduct since his restoration, whether in military or political business, neither rashness shows itself, nor dishonesty.   On the contrary, all his projects appear to have been formed with singular prudence, as they were executed with singular vigor.   However he may have failed in regard to the person to whom he intrusted the command of the fleet, during that short absence which proved so unfortunate, in every other instance his choice of assistants and deputies in command was judicious, liberal, and happy.   The confidence which he continued always to give to Thrasybulus son of Lycus, and to Thrasyllus, at the same time conferred and reflected honor.   But these considerations escaped the Athenian people; called upon, in a moment of indignation and anxiety, to decide upon a matter of the utmost consequence, and plied by the eloquence of interested men, while the information necessary for due discussion of the question was not before them.   Without waiting to know how their general might apologize for his conduct, or what necessity, or what view of public service might have directed it, the multitude, whose momentary will decided, without controul, the most important measures of executive government, passed the fatal decree. Thrasybulus was involved with Alcibiades; and thus the two men who were by experience, added to singular gifts of nature, beyond all others perhaps then in the world, qualified to relieve the commonwealth, in its almost desperate circumstances, were dismissed from their employments.   Ten generals were appointed in their room, and the long list requires notice: they were Conon, Diomedon, Leon, Pericles, Erasinides, Aristocrates, Archestratus, Protomachus, Thrasyllus, Aristogenes.

How that balance in the powers of government at Athens, which Thucydides mentions to have been so judiciously established, when the council of Four-hundred was abolished, had already been completely deranged, Xenophon gives no direct information; but, in the circumstances related by both writers, it remains suggested. Alcibiades, disappointed in his first great political purpose, of leading the aristocratical interest in Athens, and, through his antient family connection with Lacedæmon, extending his influence over Greece, threw himself at once on the democratical interest; with the extraor-

1   dinary

dinary success, followed by the rapid reverse, which we have seen. When his country, through the evils which he principally brought on it, was prepared to make terms with him, he preferred an aristocratical or oligarchal party for his future support.   But, finding himself presently deceived by the persons actually leading those interests in Athens, so that democracy was his only resource, it was an unbalanced democracy only that could answer his purpose; because an unbalanced democracy only would give him that plenitude of authority, which-could inable him to overbear the aristocratical and oligarchal parties, so warmly disposed to oppose him.   Having reëstablished himself then on the ground of the democratical interest, yet, in the necessity of absenting himself on command abroad, his power failed for controlling the movements of faction at·home. How parties there were at the time divided, and how little, notwithstanding the rash vote for the deposition of Alcibiades and Thrasybulus, any held a clear superiority, is indicated in the composition of the new board of generals.   Pericles was a near kinsman of Alcibiades; Aristocrates had been his general of infantry in his last command; Thrasyllus one· of his most active partizans, and among those whom, as an officer, he had most favored and trusted.   But Conon, the first of the ten, a man of superior qualifications, appears to have been not his friend.   Meanwhile Epigenes, Diophanes and Cleisthenes, men of high birth, but in no office, led the mob, and led it to the most despotic measures : on the vague accusation of being unfriendly to the multitude[3], some, who had taken part with the Four-hundred, were condemned without trial, by a single vote of the general assembly, and executed ; many suffered confiscation of their property, some were banished, some incapacitated for honors and public employments; some were compelled to purchase their safety.   In this state of things, Alcibiades, not indeed being actually summoned, but of course to give an account of his conduct, if he appeared, and probably to defend himself against impeachment, not unreasonably avoided, to trust his fate to such a judicature as the assembled Athenian people.   Thrasybulus,

Lys. Δῆμ
καταλύς.
Apolog.
p. 74. 1.
vel 778.

Xen. Hel.
l. 1. c. 5.
s. 10.

---

[3] Οὐκ ἰυνους τῷ πλήθει.

less

less obnoxious to the jealousy of party, seems to have remained with the fleet, retaining the command of his trireme.   Alcibiades retired to his estate in the Thracian Chersonese.

SECTION II.

Conon commander-in-chief of the Athenian fleet: Callicratidas of the Peloponnesian.   Mitylenë besieged by Callicratidas.   Seafight of Arginusæ.

B. C. 407.   Conon, at the time of his appointment to be one of the new generals-
P. W. 25.   in-chief, was absent, being employed in the siege of Andros, where he
Xen. Hel.
l. 1. c. 5.   commanded.   A decree of the people directed him to go immediately,
s. 11.   with the squadron of twenty ships under his orders, and take the com-
mand of the fleet at Samos.   It was already late in the year, and, on his arrival at Samos, he found a dejection in the armament, not inviting to great undertakings.   Fortunately the enemy's fleet was not yet so strong as to incourage them to enterprize.   His first measure then, and apparently a measure of absolute necessity, was precisely that which had been so objected to Alcibiades, as to be made a ground of his impeachment.   Selecting seventy triremes, and strengthening the crews by drafts from above thirty more, Conon divided them into squadrons, which were sent various ways; and they were successful in executing his orders to collect contributions and plunder, in several parts of the coast of Asia and the neighboring ilands, which acknow-leged the dominion of Persia or the alliance of Lacedæmon.

c. 6. s. 1.   In the insuing winter, Callicratidas was sent from Sparta, to take the
2. 3.   command-in-chief of the Peloponnesian fleet.   Callicratidas, widely different from Lysander, was one of the purest models of the old Spartan character; a zealous and sincere disciple of the school of Lycurgus [*].

On

___

[*] Barthelemi has not scrupled (c. 42.   clearest terms, to affirm that Callicratidas,
p. 103, vol. 4. ed. 8vo.) on the authority of   Lysander, and Gylippus, were all born in
so late a writer as Ælian, given also in not the   that class of freemen of Lacedæmon, which

was

On his arrival at Ephesus, Lysander told him, that he resigned to him a victorious fleet which commanded the seas. Callicratidas replied, ' Pass ' then with your fleet to the westward of Samos, and deliver up the ' command to me in the harbour of Miletus.' The Athenian fleet lay at Samos, and passing to the westward of that iland would put a general action in the choice of the Athenian admiral. Lysander excused himself by alledging, that in so doing he should go beyond his duty, since the officer appointed to supersede him was arrived. Callicratidas, gratified with the implied acknowlegement that the fleet was not strong enough to meet the enemy, made it his first business to increase its force. He sent to Chios, Rhodes, and other states of the confederacy; and, having thus collected fifty triremes, which made his number all together a hundred and forty, he then proposed without delay to seek a battle.

The condescending politeness of Lysander, so different from what was usually experienced in Spartan commanders, his apparent disinterestedness, and his attention to the welfare of those under him, together with the ability he had shown in every kind of business, had rendered him highly acceptable to the armament and to the allied cities. Callicratidas had not been long in his command, before he discovered that some of the principal officers, devoted to his predecessor, were forming a party against him. They not only obeyed negligently and reluctantly, but endevored to excite discontent in the armament and among the allies. ' The Lacedæmonian system,' they said, ' was most impolitic. Such continual change of the person at ' the head of things must produce immoderate inconvenience. A

---

was of acknowleged servile origin; and he adds, ' that they obtained the full rights of ' citizens only as the reward of signal ex-' ploits,' for which he seems to have had no warrant whatever. He appears to have forgotten that Gylippus was son of Cleandridas, who held the high station of regent during the minority of Pleistoanax son of Pausanias, and that it was the clear dignity of a Spartan, which, according to Thucydides, made him a fit person for the Sicilian command. If we may trust Plutarch, whose authority is at least as good as Ælian's, and whose assertion incomparably more probable, Lysander was of the Heracleid family, esteemed the first in Greece. But Herodotus, Thucydides and Xenophon, all make it sufficiently evident that, in their time, no men of servile, or any other neodamode families, as they were called, could reach those high situations, under the Spartan government, which Gylippus, Lysander and Callicratidas held.

' most

' most important naval command thus fell into the hands of men
' unversed in naval affairs ; and those, who had had no communication
' among the allies, were to preside over the interests of the allies.
' The consequences would be ruinous, both to the allies and to the
' fleet.'

The measure taken by Callicratidas to obviate this dangerous cabal,
as it stands reported by the cotemporary historian, strongly marks his
Xen. Hel.
l. 1. c. 6.
s. 5.
character.   Calling together the Lacedæmonians of the armament, he
spoke to them in the following style of Laconic eloquence : ' I could
' be very well contented to stay at home ; and if either Lysander, or
' any other, pretends to more skill in naval command, I shall not gainsay
' it.   Being however, by the appointment of the Lacedæmonian govern-
' ment, admiral of the fleet, it is my business to act in that situation to
' the best of my ability.   I therefore now require your advice.   You
' know, as well as I, what the purpose of the government is, which I am
' anxious to have duly performed.   Will it then be better for me to
' remain here ; in which case you will give me your zealous coöpera-
' tion ; or shall I go home and relate the state of things ?'   This speech
s. 6.
had in a great degree the desired effect.   All were anxious to obviate
accusation at Sparta ; and all were in consequence forward to demon-
strate, both by word and deed, that they meant no resistance to the
legal commands of the Lacedæmonian admiral, and no backwardness
in the service of the confederacy.

The difficulties of Callicratidas, however, did not end here.   His
rough manners, ill accommodated to relieve, on the contrary irritated
the regret of his predecessor in resigning a very high situation ; and his
simple and unsuspicious honesty did not conceive any political necessity for condescending communication with the man whom he came
to supersede, not for any pleasure of his own, but for the service of his
country.   Lysander had a large sum of money remaining, of what had
been committed to him by Cyrus for the pay of the fleet.   No way desirous of gratifying Callicratidas, he would not make it over to him,
but, to earn credit with the prince by a display of his economy, returned
the whole into the Persian treasury.   Callicratidas immediately found
himself in want.   He made, however, no difficulty of going to the court
of

of Sardis, to ask for a supply, which he supposed was to be issued of course: but to provide for a favorable reception by any previous intrigue or any ceremonious compliment, or to obviate any ill impression that Lysander or the friends of Lysander might have made, did not come within his imagination. On arriving at Sardis, he applied for an audience. He was answered, that he must wait two days. Patience was a Spartan virtue, and he did not immediately feel the affront. But, on going according to the appointment, he met still with procrastination; and as he repeated his fruitless attendance in the antichambers, everything he saw, the pomp, the insolence, the servility, which struck his first notice, and the faithlessness and venality which soon became evident, all excited his indignation. At length, in complete disgust, he departed without having seen the prince, and with his business in no part done; exclaiming ' that the Greeks were indeed wretched who would so truckle ' to barbarians for money! He saw,' he said, ' what would be the con- ' sequence of their quarrels among oneanother; and, if he lived to ' return home, he would do his utmost to reconcile Lacedæmon with ' Athens.'

On arriving at Ephesus, his first care was to move his fleet from a place so near Sardis, and so immediately under the controul of Persia. He conducted it to Miletus, whose people preserved more independency. Thence he sent a small squadron home for a supply of money. For intermediate need he obtained a loan from the Milesians and Chians, and he then proceeded to employ the force he had collected, his fleet consisting of a hundred and seventy triremes. Methymnë in Lesbos was his first object, and he took that city by assault. All the effects were given up for plunder, and the flaves were collected in the market-place, to be sold for the benefit of the armament. The allies proposed the sale of the Methymnæan citizens; but Callicratidas, with a spirit of liberal patriotism, of which instances are rare in Grecian history, declared that, ' where he commanded, no ' Greek should be made a slave.'

While Callicratidas had been so increasing his fleet, Conon adhered to the different system which, on first taking the command, he

had

Xen. Hel. l. 1. c. 6. s. 7, 8.

s. 9.

had adopted, reducing the number of his triremes, to have more select crews. If we may guess at the purpose, of which we are not positively informed, he was urged by the same deficiency of supplies from home, which had not a little interrupted the operations even of Alcibiades, and, beside a strict parsimony, made every attention to the collection of contributions necessary. With select ships, and select crews, he could be quicker in his motions, make sudden attacks upon defenceless places, pursue merchant-ships or small squadrons, and avoid an enemy too strong to be opposed: and hence apparently the expression which Xenophon reports of Callicratidas, ' that ' he would stop Conon's adultery with the sea⁵;' implying, that it was not by a fair superiority, but through a furtive kind of success, that Conon had appeared in some degree to command that element.

Xen. Hel.
l. 1. c. 6.
s. 10.

The Peloponnesian fleet was lying at Methymnë, when Conon was seen passing with seventy triremes. Callicratidas pursuing, endevored to intercept the retreat of the Athenians to Samos. Conon fled for Mitylenë; but the Peloponnesian rowers exerted themselves with such vigor, that Callicratidas entered the harbour with him. Compelled thus to fight against numbers so superior, the Athenians lost thirty triremes, the men however escaping. The other forty triremes they secured by hauling them under the town-wall, so as to be protected from the battlements. Callicratidas, stationing his fleet in the harbour, and sending for infantry from Methymnë and Chios, formed the siege of Mitylenë by sea and land. After these successes, unasked supplies came to him from Cyrus.

s. 11.

s. 12.

The situation of Conon meanwhile was highly distressing. The city was populous and unprovided; and not only he was without means to procure supplies, but he was at a loss for means even to send information of his distress. To attempt this however was necessary. For the defence of his triremes, lying on the beach, a guard from his landforces was placed in each. From two of them of known swiftness, he moved the soldiers⁶ before day, and put, in their stead, crews of his best rowers, who gave place again to the soldiers after dark. This was

s. 13.

---

⁵ Κόνωνι δὲ εἶπεν, ὅτι παύσει αὐτὸν μοιχῶντα τὴν θάλασσαν.   ⁶ Τοὺς ἐπιβάτας. Xen. Hel. l. 1. c. 6. s. 14.

repeated

repeated four days.   On the fifth, at noon, the apparent inattention of Xen. Hel.
l. 1.   c. 6.
s. 13.
the enemy, while their crews were ashore at their dinner, seemed to
afford the wished-for opportunity : the two triremes pushed out of the
port ; and, according to orders, one directed its course westward, immediately for Athens, the other northward toward the Hellespont.   This
however could not be done unseen by the enemy.   In some confusion,
cutting the cables[7] of some of their ships, they were quickly in pursuit ; s. 15.
and one of the Athenian triremes was taken about sunset the same s. 16.
day : the other reached Athens.

The exertion which the Athenian commonwealth was still able to
make, after all its losses and all its internal troubles, shows extraordinary
vigor in the system, which owed its origin to the daring genius of Themistocles, and its improvement and permanence to the wisdom of Pericles ;
yet which perhaps could never have existed, or could not have lasted, but
for the well-constructed foundation, which the wisdom of Solon had prepared.   The circumstances required every effort. A hundred and ten tri- s. 17.
remes were equipped and manned : but, for this, not only every Athenian
citizen, within age for forein service, of the two lower orders, but many
of the order of knights, who on all common occasions were exempt from
naval service, imbarked; and, all being insufficient, numerous slaves
were added, to complete the crews.   The whole number wanted would
not be so few as twenty thousand.   In thirty days, however, this numerous fleet was ready for sea : the generals, before appointed, were
directed, as admirals, to take the command (for, in speaking of the
Greek naval service, we have continual difficulty to chuse between
these titles), and under the orders of those who were at the time
in Athens, it proceeded to Samos.   Ten Samian triremes reinforced it s. 18.
there; and, requisition being sent to the other allied and subject states,
for the utmost naval force that they could furnish, allowing no able-
bodied citizens to avoid the service[8], an addition was thus collected
which made the whole upward of a hundred and fifty : its course was
then directed toward Lesbos.

At the time of Conon's defeat, Diomedon, another of the ten ge- s. 16.
nerals, was cruizing with a separate squadron of twelve ships.   Receiving

---

[7] Τὰς ἀγκύρας ἀποκόπϊοντις.   [8] Ἐσβαίνειν ἀναγκάσαντες ἁπάνϊας.

information of his collegue's distress, he made an effort, apparently with more zeal than judgement, to relieve it.   Callicratidas took ten of his ships : Diomedon himself escaped with the other two.

Xen Hel. l. 1. c. 6. s. 19.
The Spartan admiral was yet with his whole force at Mitylenë, when intelligence reached him, that a powerful fleet from Attica was arrived at Samos.   Leaving then fifty triremes, under Eteonicus, to continue the blockade, he went with a hundred and twenty to meet the enemy. The same evening putting his people ashore, according to the usual prac-
s. 20.
tice, upon the headland of Malea in Lesbos, for their supper, as night came on he discovered the fires of a naval camp on the little ilands of Arginusæ, between Lesbos and the main : and, soon after, information was brought him that the Athenian fleet was there.   About midnight he weighed, proposing a surprise ; but, a thunder-storm coming on, compelled him to wait for day.

s. 21.
Early in the morning the approach of the enemy became known to the Athenian commanders, who immediately imbarked their crews, steered southward for the open sea, and formed their order of battle. Eight of the ten generals of the commonwealth were aboard the fleet.
s. 22.
Xenophon informs us, but without accounting for it, that the Peloponnesian ships were at this time generally swifter than the Athenian ; so that, since the first years of the war, the circumstances of naval action were inverted, the Lacedæmonians proposing to profit from rapid evolution, while the Athenians directed their principal care to guard against it.   The Lacedæmonian fleet therefore was formed in a single line. The Athenian order of battle was remarkable : each of the eight generals commanded a squadron of fifteen ships ; and the eight squadrons, in two lines, formed the wings of the fleet.   The allies held the center, in a single line ;
s. 25.
and with them were posted thirteen Athenian captains ; Thrasybulus, Theramenes, and another, not named, who had all formerly commanded as admirals, and ten who held the rank of taxiarc in the land service, which seems to have been superior to that of trierarc in the navy. The attention to rank, here marked by Xenophon, deserves notice, as it was less to be expected in a democracy, and as it accounts for the regularity with which the Athenian military service was conducted, while, in some of the Grecian democracies, subordination was very defective.
s. 23.
Xenophon seems to have thought the disposition of the Athenian
fleet

fleet judicious, and the master of the Spartan admiral's ship, Hernon, a Megarian, apparently saw that it was.   More experienced probably, in naval affairs, than his commander, he augured ill of the approaching battle, and advised retreat from superior numbers.   Callicratidas answered, with the spirit of a disciple of Lycurgus, but not with the judgement which the great command intrusted to him required, 'that ' his death would be a small loss to Sparta, but flight would be dis- ' graceful.'

The fleets met, and the action was long disputed in line.   Various exertions then broke the regularity of order, and still the fight was maintained for some time with much equality.   At length Callicratidas, who commanded in the right wing of his fleet, in the shock of his galley striking an enemy with the beak, fell overboard and perished. About the same time the Athenian right, commanded by Protomachus, made an impression upon the Peloponnesian left: confusion spred to the right, no longer directed by the orders, or animated by the exertion, of the commander-in-chief; and shortly the whole fled.   Above seventy triremes were either destroyed or taken : of the Lacedæmonian squadron, consisting of ten, only one escaped.   Twenty-five [3] Athenian ships were sunk or disabled.

Xen. Hel. l. 1. c. 6. s. 24.

When pursuit ended, the Athenian admirals held a council of war to consider of measures next to be taken.   To collect the wreck and the dead, but more especially to relieve the living, who might be floating on the ruins of galleys, or endevoring to save themselves by swimming, was commonly an important business after naval action.   Diomedon proposed that this should be the first concern of the whole fleet.   Erasinides, on the contrary, was for proceeding immediately with the whole fleet to the relief of Conon, the primary object of their instructions.   The enemy's fleet under Eteonicus, he said, were due diligence used, might be taken intire; the destruction

s. 25. & c. 7. s. 3 & 10.

---

[3] In Xenophon's account of the battle, twenty-five is the number of ships mentioned as lost, together with their crews.   In a following passage (c. 7. s. 10.) twelve only are stated to have been lost; and the context proves that in the latter passage there has been no error in transcription. Unable more satisfactorily to reconcile the contradiction, I have stated the twenty-five as sunk or disabled.

of

of their navy would thus be nearly complete; and the exigencies of the commonwealth required that such an opportunity should not be lost, in the endevor to save the wrecked, which the growing roughness of the weather would render utterly unavailing.   Thrasyllus differed from both: he insisted that, as the fleet was equal to both services, neither the relief of the wrecked should be neglected, nor assistance to Conon delayed.   His opinion prevailed; and it was resolved that forty-six ships should remain to collect the wreck, while the rest of the fleet proceeded to Mitylenë.

There is in this affair, which had important consequences, some mystery, of which, whether party-spirit or private friendship or whatever may have caused the reserve, it may be suspected that Xenophon knew more than he has chosen to unfold.   None of the generals took the command of the large squadron appointed to the relief of the wrecked: it was committed to Theramenes and Thrasybulus, who both had held high naval commands, but were then only in the situation of captains of triremes.   To make the appointment more respectable, some of the taxiarcs were ordered upon the duty with them.   All the generals were in the mean time to go, with the main body of the fleet, to Mitylenë.   Neither measure however could be executed.   The increasing violence of the storm compelled all to seek the shelter which the Arginusan ilands afforded; and the unfortunate crews of twelve ships, wrecked in the battle, were thus left to perish.

In the night, nevertheless, one of those small light vessels called keletes, which had attended the Peloponnesian fleet for the purpose of carrying intelligence or orders, reached Mitylenë with news of its disaster.   Eteonicus, who commanded the blockade, ordered the captain to go immediately to sea again, observing the most careful secrecy, and to return into the harbour by broad daylight, with his crew wearing chaplets, as was usual for the messengers of victory, and proclaiming that Callicratidas had destroyed the Athenian fleet.   This was punctually executed.   Eteonicus then, assembling his troops in sight of the Mitylenæan ramparts, performed the evangelian sacrifice, the thanks-offering for good news, and, at the conclusion of the ceremony, or-

Xen. Hel.
l. 1, c. 6.
s. 25.

s. 24, 25, 26.

s. 7.

11

dered

dered that all should immediately take their supper. Meantime he caused his principal stores to be imbarked in the vessels of burden attending his fleet: the crews of the triremes were then hastened aboard; and, the wind being favorable, all sailed for Chios, while, after setting fire to his camp, he led the infantry to Methymnë.

These unexpected motions of the besieging armament, which were so ably conducted as to give no opportunity for advantage against it, first intimated to Conon the defeat of Callicratidas. Hastening to launch his triremes, he met the victorious fleet already approaching from Arginusæ, and himself communicated the information that his deliverance was already complete. The fleet then went to Chios; but, no opportunity offering for any blow against the enemy, it proceeded to Samos, the usual station.

Xen. Hel. l. 1. c. 5. s. 28.

SECTION III.

Impeachment of the generals who commanded at the battle of Arginusæ.

THE victory of Arginusæ, the greatest obtained by the Athenians during the war, in which, with above seventy ships, more than ten thousand men must have been lost by the enemy, might have gone far to procure final success to Athens, had Athens had a government capable of any steddiness, or even secure against acts of madness. Fruitful of superior men, she never had more citizens equal to the conduct of the greatest affairs than at this time. At least three, Alcibiades, Thrasybulus, and Conon, already of large experience in great commands, and yet in the prime of life, were scarcely inferior to any known in her annals. But, since the restoration of democracy, the people, frantic with the wild joy of recovered power, and not less mad with jealousy of superior men, were more than ever dupes to the arts of designing orators: and, like a weak and fickle tyrant, whose passion is his only law, tho no single tyrant can reälly be so lawless, were led as the flattery, or the stimulation, most in consonance with the passion of the moment pointed the way.

Hence

Xen. Hel.
l. 1. c.7.
c. 7. s. 1.

Hence followed one of the most extraordinary, most disgraceful, and most fatal strokes of faction recorded in history. Of the eight generals who commanded at the battle of Arginusæ, Protomachus and Aristogenes only remained with Conon at Samos: Diomedon; Pericles, Lysias, Aristocrates, Erasinides and Thrasyllus went home; little expecting what was to meet them there. Matters had been prepared by intrigues, which are known to us only by their effects. A decree of the people had deprived all the generals of their command, Conon only excepted, to whom Adeimantus and Philocles were given for new collegues. As soon as the six arrived, Erasinides was arrested. Archedemus, then the popular orator, and considered as head of the democratical interest, had preferred an accusation against him, for embeziling public effects out of ships in their passage from the Hellespont, and for other misconduct in his command; and the court [9], before which the charge was exhibited, ordered the victorious general to prison. It remained then for the other five to give, before the council, an account of transactions under their orders. At the conclusion it was moved by Timocrates, that all should be put in safe custody, to answer before the people for their conduct. The council accordingly ordered all the five into confinement.

When the assembly of the people met, Theramenes came forward as the principal accuser; Theramenes, to whom, with Thrasybulus, when in the situation of simple trierarcs, the accused generals had intrusted the command of a fleet of forty-six triremes, with the charge of saving those wrecked in the battle of Arginusæ; yet the crime now alledged against the generals was the neglect of that very duty. Xenophon has not accounted for this apparent contradiction [10]. The council, however, was evidently guilty of the grossest and most tyrannical oppression. The accused were not allowed to conduct their defence in the usual form: advantages which the law positively pre-

s. 3.

---

[9] Τὸ Δικαςήριον.

[10] The account of Diodorus, differing in some small circumstances from Xenophon's, agrees in the result. It assists indeed little to explain; but it tends to establish the fairness of Xenophon, who, as a cotemporary, acquainted with some of the persons concerned, and interested in the event, might otherwise be supposed liable to some partiality.

scribed

scribed were denied them: and each was permitted only to make a short speech to the people.

Thus restricted, all made nearly the same apology. ' After a most ' glorious victory,' they said, ' they had taken upon themselves a very ' important and urgent duty, the pursuit of the enemy, and the relief ' of the besieged armament. In the mean time the care of the wrecked, ' as far as depended on them, had not been omitted or slighted : it had ' been intrusted to officers whom none would deny to be competent ' for such a duty, to officers who had distinguished themselves in great ' commands and arduous enterprizes. If then there had been a failure, ' those alone were fairly accountable, to whom the execution had been ' committed. It was, however, not their purpose to accuse: injurious ' treatment should not provoke them to be unjust: they imputed to ' none any failure in duty; well knowing that the violence of the ' supervening storm rendered the saving of the wrecked impossible. ' For this there was no want of respectable witnesses : every master of ' the fleet would bear testimony to it: and many persons actually saved ' from the wrecked ships knew it; among whom was one of the gene- ' rals, included in the present accusation.'

A short speech to this purpose having been made severally by each of the generals, the question was put. It was evident that the majority of the assembly was for the acquittal of the accused. But the party, which had resolved on their destruction, had on their side the presidents and a majority of the council. Their resource therefore was to procure a declaration from the presidents, ' That in the dusk of evening, ' then advanced, the number of hands could not be distinguished, ' and that the decision must be referred to the next assembly.' Ac- quiescence under this determination seems to have incouraged them to push their point, and they proceeded to move, ' That, in the in- ' terval, the council should consider and determine, in what manner, in ' the next assembly, the trial should be conducted.' To move any question, when it had been already decided that the assembly could not proceed to a division, seems a strange incongruity; but the motion made shows that they depended upon the passions, and not upon the reason of the people. It was no less than a proposal for authorizing the council

Xen. Hel. l. 1. c. 7. s. 4.

council to dispense with the forms, established by the constitution, for the security of the subject in cases of criminal accusation. But the party was strong, and the body of the people thoughtless and impatient: the friends of the accused were apparently surprized, and perhaps fearful of irritating the hasty and unwary: the question was carried without a division, and the assembly was dismised.

Having thus obviated the acquittal of the unfortunate generals, which, according to Xenophon, a majority of the assembly had actually pronounced, and which wanted **only** the declaration of the presidents to give it effect; having procured authority for the council to substitute, at their pleasure, any mode of trial instead of that prescribed by law, the party were still apprehensive that they might fail of their purpose; and the consequence of failure, in so violent an effort of faction, would probably be ruin to themselves. Recourse was therefore had to a kind of oratory, suited to excite that popular passion which would favor their views. It was the season of the Apaturia, a festival derived from patriarchal times, in which families assembled, and the chief of each received a kind of homage from its members. A number of persons, clothed in black, and with their heads and beards close shaven, as was customary in mourning, were procured to show themselves about the city, as relations of those lost in the storm, after the battle of Arginusæ. This artifice was not without effect among the lower people. Meanwhile, in the council, the business was managed by Callixenus, who was a member, and who succeeded to the utmost wish of his party.

When the assembly was held, to decide the fate of the generals, Callixenus came forward to report the resolution of the council, which was to guide the proceedings. The resolution, as it stands reported by Xenophon, ran thus: ' The accusation of the generals ' having been heard in the assembly, together with their defence, the ' council hath decreed, " That the people shall proceed immediately " to ballot by wards: that there shall be for each ward two vases: " that proclamation shall be made by the herald, informing the " people, That whoever deems the generals criminal, in neglecting to " save from the waves those who were conquerors in the battle, must

" put

" put-his die into the first vase; whoever deems them innocent, into
" the second: that the punishment, in case of condemnation, shall be
" death, to be inflicted by the Eleven" (magistrates whose office bore
some analogy to that of our sheriff) " with confiscation of all property,
" a tenth to the goddess, the rest to the commonwealth."

In the whole of these proceedings the oppression of the individuals
accused was so flagrant, and the violation of the constitution of so
dangerous a kind, that the party thought something might be still
wanting, to inflame passion sufficiently among the people, and stifle
just consideration. Their resources however seem to have been, according to the account of Xenophon, such that we cannot but wonder Xen. Hel.
at their success. A man was produced who declared before the assembly, s. 7. l. 1. c. 7.
' that, having been in one of the wrecked ships, he had saved himself
' on a flour-barrel; and that his drowning comrades had conjured him,
' if he should escape that fate which for them was inevitable, not to
' let it pass unknown to the Athenian people, how the generals had
' abandoned those who had deserved so well of their country.'

Athens was not yet without a constitution, and laws, as well for
the security of the constitution itself, as for the assurance of justice to
individuals; tho faction, supported by a majority in the assembly, might
sometimes violate both.   The friends of the generals therefore did not s. 8.
yet give up their defence, in which Euryptolemus son of Peisianax took
the leading part.   Nor was there wanting a considerable body among
the people disposed to support him, when he remonstrated against the
violation of the constitution, attempted by the decree of the council,
and declared that he would cite Callixenus to answer, according to law,
as the proposer.   The resource of the opposite party was still in popular
passion.   They directed their rhetoric to the jealous temper of democracy: ' It was intolerable,' they said, ' for an individual to presume
' to set limits to the authority of the people;' and immediately an angry
multitude vociferated, ' that it was intolerable for an individual to
' prescribe bounds to the will of the people.'   Thus incouraged,
Lyciscus, one of the leading men, declared, ' that whoever should
' presume to check the authority of the assembly, he would move that
' his fate should be decided by the same ballot with that of the generals.

The assembly upon this was again in uproar. Euryptolemus feared, by irritating the multitude, to injure the cause he meant to defend, and, retracting his proposed citation of Callixenus, declared his submission to the will of the people.

Xen. Hel.
l. 1. c. 7.
s. 9.
This legal impediment being thus violently overborne, still opposition occurred to the purpose of the prosecutors. The prytanes had the virtue to declare, that they would not put the question for a decree subversive of the constitution, and which the law forbad.   Callixenus, imboldened by the support he had already found, and dreading the consequences of defeat in his measure, again mounted the bema, and, addressing the people, accused the prytanes of refusing their duty.   The multitude, with renewed jealousy of their ill-conceived and undefined rights, indignantly called for those to appear, who resisted the orders of the people.   The virtue which had incited to oppose a measure so destructive of the constitution, and so iniquitous toward individuals, then yielded to fear; and the prytanes, with only one very remarkable exception,

s. 9, & mem.
Socr. l. 1.
c. 1 s. 18.
Plat. apol.
Socr. p. 32.
obeyed the tyrannical command.   The son of Sophroniscus, Socrates, who was of their number, persisted in declaring, that nothing should move him to act otherwise than according to law.   But his collegues consenting to propose the question, the ballot was taken according to the resolution of the council.

Xen. Hel.
l. 1. c. 7.
s. 10.
This point being thus decided, Euryptolemus ventured again to ascend the bema; no longer to oppose the resolution of the council, but to speak in favor of the accused, as the law authorized, what the people might yet bear to hear.   Fearful, however, of exciting outcry, he began with cautiously declaring, ' That his intention was partly ' to accuse, as well as partly to defend, Pericles his near relation and ' Diomedon his intimate friend; and at the same time to advise the ' assembly what, in his opinion, the public good required.' Observing then no disinclination to hear him, he proceeded: ' I accuse them of a ' misdemeanor in their command, inasmuch as they dissuaded what ' ought to have been done, and what their collegues otherwise would ' have done, sending information in their dispatches to the council ' and to you, that the duty of relieving the wrecked had been com- ' mitted to Theramenes and Thrasybulus, and had not been performed.
' This

' This was their crime only, yet their collegues are involved in the
' accusation: a crime against the public it must be confessed, tho not
' of a very hainous nature; it was an act of benevolence toward those
' very officers, who are now requiting the charity by a capital prosecu-
' tion, conducted in a new and unheard of form of severity, against
' their benefactors.'

Having stated his accusation and his defence, he proceeded to his
advice, which marks strongly the state of the Athenian government at
the time.   Frequent experience of being misled by designing men, into
measures which they found occasion severely to repent, made the
antient democracies generally jealous of advice given by their orators,
unless it flattered some passion, which in the moment swayed the popular
mind.   ' In what I have to recommend,' said therefore Euryptolemus,
' neither I nor any man can lead you into any dangerous error.   For
' it must always be in your power to inforce against offenders, equally
' whether many be involved in one common judgement, or each be
' allowed a separate trial, any punishment at your pleasure.   I there-
' fore most earnestly wish and recommend, that you would allow each
' of the accused generals at least one day for his separate defence: and
' I most anxiously deprecate your giving confidence to those who'
' would persuade you, that it can be dangerous to take time, for such
' deliberation as may produce a reasonable conviction in your own
' minds, and that it is safer to trust others than yourselves.

' The decree of Canonus, that powerful sanction of the democratical
' authority, is well known to you all[11].   It declares, ' That if any
' shall injure the Athenian people, he shall answer before the people
' in bonds: if he is found guilty, he shall be punished with death ; his
' body shall be thrown into the Barathrum ; and all his property shall
' be forfeited ; a tenth to the goddess, the rest to the commonwealth.'
' I desire no other, Athenians, than that the generals be tried according
' to the provisions of that severe law ; and, if you think proper, let
' Pericles, my near kinsman, be the first to abide your sentence.

[11] Τὸ Κανώνου ψήφισμα.   If there is anywhere any farther account of this remarkable
law, than what we have here from Xenophon,
it has escaped me.   I think it is not noticed
by either Petit or Potter.

' The

' The crimes held most atrocious, among men, are sacrilege, and
' high-treason. The generals before you are accused of none such.
' But if the decree of Canonus is, in your opinion, too mild for them,
' let the law against sacrilege and treason be your guide. Even so,
' each will have his separate trial; a day for each will be divided into
' three parts: in the first you will inquire and determine whether there
' is cause for putting the accused upon trial; the second will be allotted
' to the accusation; the third to the defence. Let it be recollected
' how lately Aristarchus, the most obnoxious of those who overthrew
' the democracy, and who afterward, in his flight from Athens, per-
' formed the signal treachery of betraying Œnoë to the Thebans, even
' Aristarchus was allowed his day, and even to chuse his day, for his
' defence. Will you then, Athenians, who were so scrupulously just
' to one whose treason was so notorious, and whose conduct so grossly
' injurious, will you deny the common benefit of the laws to those who
' have so signally served their country? Will you break down the bar-
' riers of that constitution by which, hitherto, individuals have been
' safe, and by which the commonwealth has become great, to deliver
' to the executioner your meritorious generals, covered with the recent
' glory of the most important victory that has been gained in a war of
' twenty-six years? If you would consult the justice, the honor, or
' the safety of the commonwealth, you will rather reward them with
' crowns, their due as conquerors, than, yielding to the malicious
' arguments of wicked men, condemn them to an ignominious death.
' To what therefore I have at present to propose, I trust you cannot
' but assent: it is, ' That each of the generals be separately tried,
' according to the provisions of the decree of Canonus.'

Xen. Hel.
l. 1. c. 7.
s. 11.

According to the forms of the Athenian assembly, the question was
at the same time put upon the motion of Euryptolemus and that of
Callixenus. The majority was declared for the motion of Euryptolemus;
but, at the requisition of Menecles, the holding up of hands being
repeated [12], it was declared for that of Callixenus. The resolution of
the council being thus confirmed, in conformity to that resolution
the people proceeded to ballot. The fatal vase pronounced sentence

[12] Ὑπομοσαμένου δὲ Μενεκλέους, καὶ πάλιν διαχειροτονίας γενομένης.

of

of death against the eight generals, and the six present were executed [13].

Plutarch relates of Alcibiades, that when, on his recall from Sicily, he avoided returning to Athens, being asked, ' If he could not trust his country? ' he replied, ' Yes; for everything else: but in a trial ' for life, not my mother; lest by mistake she should put a black ball ' for a white one.'   Whatever authority there may have been for this anecdote, it contains a very just reproof of the Athenian mode of giving judgement on life and death, by a secret ballot; which, without preventing corruption, admits mistake, excludes responsibility, and covers shame.

But while, under the security of our own admirable constitution, we wonder at the defective polity of a people whom we find so many causes to admire, it is not a little advantageous, for the writer of Grecian history, that circumstances have been occurring, in a nation calling itself the most polished of the most polished age of the world, which not only render all the atrocious, and before scarcely credible, violences of faction among the Greeks, probable, but almost make them appear moderate.   At the same time it may not be digressing improperly to remark, that, as what has been passing in France may tend to illustrate Grecian history, and to exculpate the Grecian character from any innate atrocity, beyond what is common among other nations, there occurs also, in Grecian history, what may inable to form a juster estimate of the French character, than a view of the late enormities, compared only with what has at any time passed in our own country, might lead us to conceive: and, if the inability of wise and worthy men, such as undoubtedly must have existed in France, to hold their just influence among the people, and prevent those disgraceful proceedings, appears itself a disgrace both to themselves and to the nation, Grecian history, and the extant writings of the ablest Grecian politicians, will perhaps furnish their fairest apology.

For, so many men of the brightest talents and highest acquirements, as in Greece turned their thoughts, with the closest attention, to a

[13] Lysias mentions this transaction in his oration against Eratosthenes, (p. 123. vel 406.) and his account, as far as it goes, confirms that of Xenophon.

subject

subject so universally and deeply interesting, not one seems to have been able even to imagine a form of government which might, in a great nation, reconcile the jarring pretensions arising from that variety of rank among men, without which even small societies cannot subsist. Our own writers, through meer familiarity with the object, as foreiners from unacquaintance with it, have very much overlooked what, in importance, is perhaps not inferior to any one circumstance in the singular constitution of our government. It was not till after the troubles in France began, that a refugee, who had been in situations inabling him to see and compelling him to observe, discovered, what, but for those troubles, would perhaps never have occurred to his notice; that 'nowhere else, in the world, such harmony subsists, between the several 'ranks of citizens, as in England.'

Lettre au
Roi par M.
de Calonne.

This harmony is indeed the foundation, the firm foundation, on which the proud superstructure of the British constitution rests. Ranks vary, as much, or perhaps more than elsewhere. But no one rank has that gigantic preëminence, which can inable it to trample upon its next inferior. In the scale of subordination, the distance from top to bottom is great; but the gradation is scarcely perceptible, and the connection intimate. Each rank, moreover, is interested in the support of its next superior: none are excluded from the hope of rising; and, of all the various ranks, the highest is most interested in the support of all. We cannot consider without wonder, that an order of things, apparently the most natural, as well as the most beneficial, never subsisted in any country but our own.

It has not always perhaps been duly recollected, by speculative politicians, that, among the antient republics, no such order of citizens existed as that which, in Paris, after the first revolution, assumed, or, for nefarious purposes, was complimented with, despotic power; and, while the representatives of the nation were deliberating on the rights of man, trampled under foot all rights. The functions of that order of citizens were, in Athens, performed by slaves; and, without keeping this circumstance constantly in mind, we cannot but be liable to the grossest error, in applying the rules of antient policy to modern times. Those writers, who would infer that formerly the lower people in England were not free, because the lowest rank were

actually

actually slaves, attempt a fallacy upon their readers.   In treating of Athens, Lacedæmon, or Rome, they would have distinguished, as they ought, slaves from citizens.   It is unquestionable that, from the Anglosaxon conquest downward, the constitution of this country has been always free: and tho, in unsettled times, and especially under the first Norman kings, law might be overborne by the violence of accidental power, yet both the law, and the established mode of administering the law, never were otherwise than highly, and even singularly, favorable to the freedom and property of even the lowest citizens [14].

Montesquieu has undertaken to foretel the fall of the English Constitution; and a credit has been given him, proportioned rather to the merit of the prophet than of the prophecy.   Montesquieu, evidently, had not duly adverted to that peculiar amalgamation of ranks in England, through which all coälesce; or, if it may be so expressed, to that concatenation, by which the lowest end of a long chain is as firmly connected with the highest, as the intermediate links with oneanother. Through this advantageous constitution, England has always avoided, and it may well be hoped will continue to avoid, that violence of internal fermentation, which continually disordered, and at length destroyed the governments of Athens and Rome; and hence she has been inabled to resist the contagion of French politics, so alluring in distant prospect, so hideous in near approach, which perhaps no other

[14] It seems to deserve more notice, than I think it has yet met with, that the monarchs to whom our constitution is most indebted, Alfred, Henry II. and Edward I. were conquerors. It is certainly a most unworthy slander upon those uncommon great men, as well as upon the parliaments, from Edward the first, till the time when Fortescue wrote under Henry the sixth, to assert, as often has been done, that England had no valuable constitution, and no true freedom, till the opposition to the Stuarts, or the expulsion of the Stuarts, procured them. The debates on occasion of the King's ilness, in 1788, brought forward records of Parliament, not only proving that the constitution was as well understood, in the reigns of Henry the fourth and Henry the sixth, as at any time since, to this day, but affording precedents for most difficult and delicate circumstances, such as the wisest, of any age, might rejoice to find established by the wisdom of their forefathers. These records, and most of the important historical matter they relate to, had escaped the notice of all our historians.

Europeän

Europeän government, whose mildness would allow it equal admission, could, without forein assistance, have withstood.

Nor is it, I apprehend, as some political writers have asserted, of no importance to trace the freedom of the constitution of this country beyond the civil war in the reign of Charles the first. For the purpose indeed of establishing the right of the British people to freedom, it is utterly unnecessary. But, toward a clear comprehension of the constitution itself; toward a certain knowlege of the broad and deep foundation on which it rests; toward a ready and just perception of the manner in which it may be affected, through the various changes to which all human things are liable, and through some which we have already seen; extension of dominion, influx of riches, increase of population, increase of revenue, immoderate debt, and the possible reduction of that debt; toward a just judgement how far any of these changes are beneficial, and how far injurious, and when alteration or remedy may be wanting, and what, in any given circumstances, will be the probable effect of any alteration or remedy proposed; toward all these an acquaintance with the history of our constitution, from earliest times, is of great importance.

If then it is to ourselves important to know the history of our constitution from earliest times, it will also be not a little important to other nations, if any such there are, who would form a constitution on the model of ours, or who would improve the constitution they possess, after our example. Nor will it be less important to those who, without any good foundation to build on, and without any valuable experience within their own country, would raise, with the airy materials of theory, a constitution more perfect than the most perfect that has yet existed upon earth. For want of attention to the breadth and antique firmness of the basis on which our envied and truly enviable government rests, the singular manner in which the materials of the superstructure are adapted to each other, and how they are held together by their natural fitness to coälesce, the complexion of Europe seems to threaten many new and memorable lessons in politics; lessons for every order that can exist in a state separately, and lessons for nations united. Happy then those, who, gathering wisdom from the

sufferings

sufferings and dangers of others, can avoid the miseries which many will probably feel.

Such were the sentiments occurring on what appeared the readiest probable consequences of the state of things, in Europe, when this part of the history was first offered to the public. The extraordinary revolution, which has insued, was, rather for the wonderful rapidity of its progress, than for its character, then less within reasonable expectation. And, in digressing thus far, I trust I have not over-stepped the limits within which the writer of Grecian history may claim, not an exclusive, but a common right. A Grecian history, and indeed any history perfectly written (these volumes pretend to no such merit) but especially a Grecian history perfectly written, should be a political institute for all nations [15].

[15] As M. de Calonne's letter, referred to in the text, tho printed, was, I believe, never published, it may not be superfluous to give here, in its original language, the passage where the observation noticed occurs.

J'ignorois, lorsque j'ai commencé cette lettre, à quel point la division éclatoit déja entre la Noblesse et le tiers Etat, dans les différentes provinces de votre royaume: depuis que je l'ai appris, j'en frémis. Vu la situation où les choses ont été amenées, il n'y a pas lieu d'espérer que la concorde puisse se rétablir d'elle-meme, et sans qu'on ait extirpé les germes de dissention qu'on n'a que trop fomentés. Il faut donc y pourvoir par quelque moyen nouveau, puissant, et efficace. Celui que je propose est éprouvé. C'est par lui qu'il existe en Angleterre, entre les Grands et le Peuple, plus d'accord qu'il n'y en a, je pense, dans aucune autre nation; nulle part ailleurs l'ésprit public n'est aussi marqué; nulle part l'intéret n'a plus d'empire pour réunir tous les Etats.

Or il est constant que rien n'y contribue davantage que l'institution d'une Chambre Haute et d'une Chambre Basse dans le Parlement; ainsi que leur composition respective, les distinctions qui les séparent, et les rapports qui les unissent. Plus on étudie cet ensemble, plus on trouve à l'admirer: Les Lords qui forment la Chambre Haute,

et qui tous sont titrés (ce sont les seuls qui le soient en Angleterre) partagent dans une meme association, sans préjudice néanmoins à leurs qualifications distinctives, l'honneur de la Pairie; et c'est, sans contredit, le premier corps de l'Etat. Leur prérogative n'est jamais contestée ni enviée par les Communes, qui ont parmi leurs Membres les fils, les frères, les parens, de ces memes Lords, et des plus grandes maisons du royaume. C'est ce mélange, cette transfusion, si je le puis dire, de la plus haute Noblesse dans le corps representatif du peuple, qui entretient l'harmonie entre l'un et l'autre, et qui resserre le nœud de leur union; c'est ce qui fait que les deux Chambres fraternisent sans se confondre, qu'elles se contrebalancent sans se rivaliser, que l'une empeche l'autre d'empiéter, et que toutes deux concourent également au maintien de la prérogative royale et à la conservation des droits nationaux. Lettre addressée au Roi, par M. de Calonne, le 9. Fevrier, 1789, p. 67, 68.

The very great advantage, to a free constitution, of having a hereditary first magistrate, the depositary of the supreme executive power, so distinguished by superior rank as to exclude all idea of competition, has been very well explained by De Lolme; but the benefit of that singular amalgamation of various rank among the people,

SECTION IV.

Sedition at Chios. Lysander reäppointed commander-in-chief of the Peloponnesian fleet; in favor with Cyrus. Unsteddiness of the Athenian government. Measures of the fleets: Battle of Aigospotami.

B. C. 407.
P. W. 25.

WHILE Athens, by a violent exertion of power in the soverein assembly, overthrowing the barriers of the constitution, and trampling on law and justice, was preparing her own downfall, there occurred, on the Peloponnesian side, what will deserve notice, as it affords additional proof how little all Greece was prepared to receive a constitution, that could establish peace throughout her confines, and give security to all, or to any,

people, which prevails in England, has, I think, nowhere been duly noticed. In no court of Europe, I believe, is rank so exactly regulated, among the highest orders, as in England; and yet there is no rank perfectly insulated; all are in some way implicated with those about them. To begin even with the heir apparent; as a subject, he communicates in rank with all other subjects. The king's younger sons rank next to the elder, but their rank is liable to reduction: their elder brother's younger sons, if he succeeds to the crown, will rank before them. The Archbishops and the Chancellor, and the great officers of state, rank above Dukes not of royal blood; but their rank is that of office only: the Dukes, in family rank, are commonly much above the Archbishops and Chancellor. Thus far our rule, I believe, differs little from that of other Europeän courts. What follows is peculiar to ourselves. The peers, all equal in legal, differ in ceremonial rank. The sons of peers, of the higher orders, rank above the peers themselves of the lower orders; but, superior thus in ceremonial rank, they are in legal rank inferior. For the sons

of all peers, even of the royal blood, being commoners, while in ceremonial rank they may be above many of the peers, in legal rank they are only peers with the commoners. This implication of the peerage with the body of the people is the advantageous circumstance, which has particularly struck Mr. de Calonne. But there is another thing which perhaps not less strongly marks the wise moderation of our ancestors, to whom we owe the present order of things. No distinction, between subjects, can be reälly more essential than the being or not being members of the legislative body; yet the rank of a member of parliament is known neither to the law, nor to the ceremonial of the country. Among untitled commoners there is no distinction of rank, that can be very exactly defined; and yet a distinction always subsists, in public opinion; decided partly, and perhaps sometimes too much, by wealth, partly by consideration given to birth, connections or character; which, upon the whole, perhaps more than under any other government, preserves the subordination necessary to the well-being of large societies.

1

of

of her people.   After the defeat of the Peloponnesian fleet, in the battle of Arginusæ, the Peloponnesian cause seems to have been neglected by Cyrus.   The squadron, which had escaped from Mitylenë, remained at Chios; where its commander Eteonicus joined it from Methymnë, but without money to pay it.   Accustomed as the Greeks were to subsist on military service by their own means, this gave at first no great uneasiness.   In so rich an iland, the industrious found opportunity to earn something, by working for hire; and wild fruits, or those cheaply bought, were resources for the less handy or more idle; so that, in the joy of recent escape, ,and with the hope of speedy relief, the wants that occurred, during summer, were patiently borne.   But when, in advancing autumn, clothes became ragged, shoos worn out, wants of all kinds increased, while means of earning lessened, and, as the stormy season approached, the hope of relief grew fainter, reflection began then to excite the most serious apprehensions.   In this state of things the comparison of their own circumstances, with those of the wealthy Chians, was obvious to remark; and the transition was ready to the observation, that, having arms in their hands, it depended only upon themselves to change situations.   A conspiracy was in consequence formed, for making themselves masters of the iland; and it was agreed that, for distinction, every associate should carry a reed. *Xen. Hel. l. 2. c. 1. s. 1.*

Intelligence of this plot did not reach Eteonicus, till the number of associates was so great, that to oppose it by open force would have been highly hazardous.   If we may judge from the expression of Xenophon, upon the occasion, compared with so many of Thucydides, Plato, and other writers, which show how widely it was held, among the Greeks, that might made right, and that the useful was the measure of the honest, Eteonicus would not much have regarded the robbery of his allies, even with the massacre that must probably have attended, if disadvantageous consequences had not been to be apprehended to his commonwealth, and blame on that account to himself.   The fear of a general alienation from the Lacedæmonian cause, according to Xenophon, determined his opposition to the conspiracy; and rather an arbitrary power, conceded on the necessity of the case to military commanders, than any defined and constitutional authority, inabled him to oppose it with effect.   Selecting fifteen confidential persons, *s. 2.* *s. 3.*

and arming them with daggers, he went through the streets of Chios. The first person observed, bearing a reed, was a man with disordered eyes, coming out of a surgeon's shop, and he was instantly put to death.   A crowd presently assembled about the body : and, inquiry being anxiously made, answer was, in pursuance of direction from Eteonicus, freely given, ' that the man was killed for carrying a reed.' Information of these circumstances was communicated quickly through the city. The conspirators, themselves unprepared, were ignorant what preparation might have been made against them ; and every one, as the report reached him, hastened to put away his reed. Eteonicus,

Xen. Hel.
l. 2. c. 1.
s. 4.

who watched the event, without giving time for recovery from surprize, ordered all aboard. The mark of distinction was gone ; none of the conspirators any longer knew whom to trust ; all became anxious to avoid crimination ; ready obedience would be the first proof of innocence : and presently not a man, of either land or sea forces, remained ashore.

Eteonicus then assembled the Chian magistrates, informed them what a danger they had escaped, and represented the necessity of providing for the present wants of the armament. A supply was instantly given him, with which he repaired to the fleet, and distributed a month's pay for each man. In doing this he passed through every ship, and spoke to all the soldiers and seamen of their several duties, and particularly of the probable business of the insuing campain, as if he had known nothing of the conspiracy. All were happy to receive this tacit assurance that they were free from danger ; all became anxious to show themselves zealous in the public cause : and thus, with only the death of one man, not the most guilty perhaps, but certainly connected with the guilty, a mutiny was completely smothered, which, under a hesitating commander, might not have been quelled without shedding many times more blood, and not being quelled, would have spred havoc over the richest and most populous iland of the Ægean.

s. 5.

It was about the time when this dangerous business was so fortunately settled, that a congress of the Peloponnesian confederacy was held at Ephesus. The Chians, and probably all the Asian Greeks of the confederacy, sent their deputies particularly commissioned for the purpose. For the European states, the principal officers of their respective forces

mostly

mostly acted as representatives.   What had been passing in Athens was unknown, or imperfectly known; and the same wisdom and spirit in council at home, the same ability and energy in operation abroad, which had so wonderfully restored the Athenian commonwealth from agony to vigor and victory, were expected still to continue.   It was therefore a question of most serious concern, not only how the war should be conducted, but who should direct operations.   Much would depend on the good-will and ready assistance of the Persian prince, and with him it was therefore deemed proper to communicate.   The result of the deliberations was a resolution to send ministers to Lacedæmon, in the joint names of the prince, the armament, and the allies, with information of the state of things, and a request that Lysander might be reäppointed to the command-in-chief.

No Spartan, Brasidas alone excepted, had ever so conciliated the allied cities as Lysander; no Spartan knew equally how to render himself agreeable to a Persian prince : his military as well as his political conduct had been able, and his success against the Athenian fleet at Notium had gained him fame.   At another season, nevertheless, the Lacedæmonian government might perhaps not have been persuaded to contravene a rule, esteemed important, never to commit the command-in-chief of the fleet twice to the same person.   But the consideration of the great defeat they had received, and of their utter inability to support their Asiatic allies, or to dispute the command of the seas with the Athenians, without the aid of Persian money, disposed them to relax a little.   Nominally however they still adhered to their principle, while, by a subterfuge, they gratified the Persian prince and their Grecian confederates : Aracus was appointed navarc, admiral of the fleet, for the year: but Lysander was sent to command in Asia, with the title of epistoleus [16], vice-admiral.

Lysander, arriving at Ephesus when winter was not yet far advanced, made it his first concern to provide that, in spring, he might have a fleet

B. C. 407.
P. W. 25.

---

[16] The word seems to have meant originally an officer *sent* by a superior officer to command for him; but it appears to have become the usual title for the second in command in the Lacedæmonian service.   See Xen. Hel. l.1. c.1. s.15.   It is pretty exactly rendered by the Roman title Legatus.

able

Xen. Hel.
l. 2.   c. 1.
s. 7 & 9.
able to meet that of Athens.   The squadron under Eteonicus at Chios,
and all other detached ships, were sent for to Ephesus, examined, and
the necessary repairs directed.   Measures were at the same time taken
to hasten the completion of the triremes building at Antandrus; and
when this business was duly put forward, Lysander hastened to pay his
compliments personally to the Persian prince at Sardis.   He had the
satisfaction to find that absence had not diminished his interest there:
he was received with distinguished attention, and treated as a confidential friend.   Cyrus showed him a particular account of the sums
issued for the pay of the fleet; remarked that they much exceeded
what the king had given him for the purpose; but added, ' that as the
' country, which the king had put under his command, afforded a great
' revenue, and his good inclination to Lysander and the Lacedæmo-
' nians remained perfect, money should not be wanting for the prose-
s. 8.
' cution of the war.'   Lysander, returning to Ephesus with an ample
supply, paid the armament all the arrears due, according to the rate
before established; and, with goodwill thus conciliated toward himself,
B. C. 405.
P. W. 26.
and zeal for the service apparent among all ranks, he was proceeding to
make arrangements for opening the campain, when a message arrived
from Cyrus, desiring his presence again at Sardis.

Condescendingly as the Persian prince conducted himself toward
the Greeks, his haughtiness among his own people was extravagant.
Assuming the tone of soverein, he required those marks of servile respect,
which custom had appropriated to the monarch of the empire.   The
Xen. Hel.
l. 2. c. 1.
s. 6.
court-dress of Persia had sleeves so long that, when unfolded, they
covered the hand; and the ceremonial required, of those who approached
the royal presence, to inwrap the hands, so as to render them helpless[17].
Two youths, nearly related to the royal family, refusing this mark of
extreme subordination to Cyrus, were, in pursuance of an arbitrary
command from that prince, put to death.   Complaint was made at

---

[17] In the East fashions change little, and
the strange one here mentioned, it seems, is
retained to this day. ' The beneesh,' says
one of the most intelligent and exact of modern travellers, ' is the ceremonial dress of
' the Mamalukes. It covers very completely
' the whole body, even the fingers' ends,
' which it is held very indecent to show be-
' fore the great.' Volney's Travels in Egypt.

Susa,

Susa, by their unhappy parents, and indignation was loud and general against the cruel and dangerous pride of Cyrus. Darius, an indulgent father, desirous of repressing the evil, but tender about the means, sent a message, mentioning only, that he was laboring under a severe ilness, and therefore wished to see his son. Cyrus did not refuse obedience to the paternal summons; but, before he would leave Sardis, he sent for Lysander. The Spartan general, hastening to the call, was received with distinction, even more flattering than before. Cyrus expressed the warmest interest in the Lacedæmonian cause; anxiously dissuaded risking a general action at sea, without a decided superiority; remarked that, with the wealth of Persia, such a superiority might certainly be acquired; showed an account of the revenue, arising from the countries under his own command; and, directing a very large sum to be put into the hands of the Spartan general, for the expences of the war, parted with this kind exhortation, ' be mindful ' of my friendship for Lacedæmon and for yourself.'

Xen. Hel. l. 2. c. 1. s. 9.

Lysander, returning to Ephesus thus abundantly supplied, gave a new flow to the already high spirits of his forces by another issue of pay. In the mean time, such had been the effect of his well-directed attention, seconded by an unfailing treasury, that the fleet was already equal in strength to the Athenian. He proposed therefore to proceed upon offensive operation; but not to risk the uncertain event of a general ingagement, which no necessity of his circumstances required. His view was directed less immediately against the fleet, than against the subject dependencies of Athens, the sources of the revenue by which the fleet was supported. Accordingly he led his armament first to the Carian coast, where he took the town of Cedreia by assault. His troops shared the plunder; among which ere reckoned the inhabitants, a mixed race, Greek and barbarian, who were sold for slaves.

In every one of the towns on the Hellespont and Propontis, which the successes of Alcibiades and Thrasybulus had restored to the dominion of Athens, a Lacedæmonian party remained. In giving efficacy to the efforts, which such a party might be able to make, two very important objects might be at once accomplished, the checking of the revenue which supported the Athenian fleet, and the recovery of the trade

trade with the Euxine, which furnished the best supplies of corn.
The Hellespont was therefore the point, to which Lysander proposed
to direct his principal attention; having apparently no immediate
view beyond the objects abovementioned.   Desirous to avoid the
Athenian fleet in the passage, he made his way close along the friendly
shore of Asia, and, without interruption, reached Abydus.   Of all
the towns on the shores of the Hellespont and Propontis, which the
defeat in Sicily had given to the Lacedæmonian confederacy, Abydus
alone had not been retaken.   The harbour of Abydus therefore
was made the station of the fleet.   The city was populous ; its force
of infantry was added to the infantry of the armament, and all
put under the command of Thorax, a Lacedæmonian.   The neighboring city of Lampsacus, being then attacked by land and sea, was
taken by assault.   The plunder, which was considerable (for Lampsacus
was rich, and large store of provisions had been collected there) was
given to the troops and seamen, but the free inhabitants were not
molested in their persons.

Xen. Hel.
l. 2. c. 1.
s. 11, 12.

The government of Athens, after that violent struggle of faction which
produced the condemnation of the generals, appears not to have recovered its former consistency.   It was not long after (so Xenophon says,
without mentioning how long) that the Athenian people, repenting,
directed their anger against those who had misled them to the atrocious
deed; and Callixenus, and four others, were compelled to find sureties
for their appearance before the same tremendous tribunal, which had
consigned the victorious generals to the executioner.   At the same time
opportunity was taken to procure the recall of the banished, and the
restoration of the dishonored; while the people, brought to their
senses, (such is the expression even of the democratical Lysias,
confirming the account of Xenophon,) more gladly directed their
vengeance against those who had promoted prosecutions, for interest or
malice, under the democracy, than against those who had ruled in the
oligarchy.   Xenophon proceeds, with evident satisfaction, to relate,
that Callixenus, who found opportunity to fly, and afterward found
means to make his peace and return, lived nevertheless universally
hated and avoided, and, among those public distresses which will
hereafter occur to notice, was starved to death.

Xen. Hel.
l. 1. c. 7.
s. 12.

Lys. Δημ.
καταλ. απολ.

It

It was however vainly attempted, by an oath of concord, taken by Xen. & Lys. ut. sup. the whole people, to put an end to the ferment of party. Administration was weak, and democratical jealousy interfered in every measure. The command-in-chief of the fleet was already divided between three officers, Conon, Adeimantus, and Philocles. Three more were now added, with equal powers, Menander, Tydeus, and Cephisodotus. For Xen. Hel. l. 2. c. 1. s. 11. subsistence, the armament depended upon itself. It was indeed able to collect the tribute, assessed upon the subject-states of Asia and Thrace, and it could sometimes raise contributions from the enemy's country: but this business unavoidably ingaged the attention of the generals, to the hindrance of that enterprize, which was necessary toward final success in the war; while the Peloponnesian commanders, having all their pecuniary wants supplied by the wealth of Persia, could chuse their measures.

The fleet, which the Peloponnesians were thus inabled to raise and maintain in energy, far greater than had ever formerly been seen in wars between the Greeks, made it necessary for the Athenians to assemble their whole naval force in one point; and that decisive action, which it was the obvious policy of the Peloponnesians to avoid, was possibly to the Athenians necessary. In ability for command, perhaps, Conon did not yield to Lysander; and his fleet, at s. 13. least equal in number, for it consisted of a hundred and eighty triremes, and probably superior in the proportion of practised seamen among the crews, was inferior only by the division of the supreme authority. Confident therefore in strength, and elate with recent victory, the Athenians passed from Samos to the Asiatic coast, and s. 11. plundered the country acknowleging the sovereinty of Persia. They moved then for Ephesus, to offer battle to the enemy; but, in their way, they received intelligence that Lysander had already passed northward. In alarm for the dependencies of the commonwealth on s. 13. the Hellespont, they hastened after him. Arriving at Eleus, they were informed that Lampsacus was already taken, and the enemy's fleet there. Stopping therefore only while they took refreshment, they proceeded to Sestos, where they procured provisions for the night, and arrived the same evening at Aigospotami, directly overagainst

Lampsacus. The historian, describing their progress, particularizes, what deserves notice as it marks the manner of antient naval operations, that they dined at Eleus and supped at Aigospotami, where they formed their naval camp.

The strait between Lampsacus and Aigospotami being scarcely two miles wide, the arrival of the Athenian fleet was instantly known to Lysander, and his plan almost as instantly formed. On the same night his orders were issued. By daybreak next morning his crews had taken their meal, and went immediately aboard. All was completely prepared for action, but no movement made. By sunrise the Athenian fleet was off the harbour of Lampsacus in order of battle. The Peloponnesians remained motionless: the Athenians waited till evening, and then returned to Aigospotami. As the Athenian fleet

Xen. Hel.
l. 2. c. 1.
s. 15.

withdrew, Lysander ordered some of his swiftest galleys to follow them, with instruction to the commanders to approach the opposite shore enough to see the enemy debark, and form some judgment of their immediate intentions, and then hasten back with the information. This was punctually executed. Lysander meanwhile kept his fleet in readiness for action; and, not till he was assured that the enemy's motions indicated no enterprize, he dismissed his crews for their refreshment. On the morrow these movements were exactly repeated, and so for the two following days.

Xen. Hel.
l. 1. c. 5.
s. 10.
l. 2. c. 1.
s. 16.

Since the battle of Notium, Alcibiades had resided in his castle in the Thracian Chersonese. The two fleets in his neighbourhood of course attracted his attention, and he was at least so far sensible to the welfare of his country as to be uneasy at what he saw. Aigospotami had neither town nor defensible harbour, but only a beach on which the galleys might be hauled, or near which, in the shelter of the strait, they might safely ride at anchor. The ground was commodious for incamping; but, in the defective military system of that age, the seamen and soldiers went to Sestos, two miles off, for a market. The enemy meanwhile, at Lampsacus, had the security of a harbour for their fleet, with a town for their people, where, always in

Xen. ut sup.
Plut. vit.
Alcib. &
Lysand.

readiness for every duty, they could procure necessaries. Alcibiades went to the Athenian camp, and communicated with the generals on

these

these circumstances; observing that, if they moved only to Sestos, they, equally with the enemy, would have the benefit of a town with a harbour, and equally, as from their present situation, might fight when they pleased; with the advantage, which in their present situation they could not command, of fighting only when they pleased. This admonition, slighted by the other generals, was treated by Tydeus and Menander with unmannerly disdain, and Alcibiades withdrew.

Lysander, meanwhile, had observed that every day's experience of his inaction increased the confidence and negligence of the Athenians, Not confining themselves to the market of Sestos, they wandered wide about the country, to seek provisions, or on pretence of seeking them. Still they continued in the morning to offer battle, returning in the afternoon to their camp. On the fifth day, he directed the commanders of his exploring ships, if the Athenians debarked and dispersed as usual, to hasten their return, and communicate notice to him, by the way, by elevating a shield. The whole armament was kept in readiness, the landforces under Thorax were aboard, the expected signal was made, and the fleet moved across the strait. Xen. Hel. l. 2. c. 1. s. 17.

Conon alone, of the Athenian generals, was in any state of prepa- ration. As soon as he saw the enemy in motion, he ordered the call to arms, and the signal for all to go aboard: but soldiers and seamen were equally dispersed; some of the triremes were wholly without hands; and the distance was so small, that the Peloponnesians were upon them long before any effectual measures for defence could be taken. Conon's trireme, with seven others of his division and the sacred ship Paralus, had their complete crews aboard; and these pushed off from the shore. All the rest were seized by the enemy, at anchor or upon the beach. No effort, within the power of nine ships, could have any other effect than adding the loss of those nine to that of the rest of the fleet. While therefore the enemy were intent upon their great capture, made without a blow, but still to be secured against the Athenian landforce, Conon fled unpursued; not unmindful, however, of such service as his strength might accomplish. Sails were an incumbrance to the antient galleys in action. Within so narrow a strait therefore, and with his port at hand, Lysander had left those of s. 18. s. 19.

his

his fleet ashore.   Conon had intelligence that the store was not within the walls of Lampsacus, but at the point of Abarmis.   Accordingly landing there, he carried off all the mainsails [18], and then hastening to the mouth of the Hellespont, escaped to sea.

Meanwhile Lysander, having secured possession of the Athenian ships, to the number of a hundred and seventy, directed his attention to the scattered crews and troops.   Some of these found refuge in the neighboring towns and fortresses [19]; but the greater part, together with all the generals [20], were made prisoners.   In the evening of the same day on which the fleet was taken, Lysander sent away an account of

Xen. Hel.
l. 1. c. 1.
s. 20.

his extraordinary success.   A Milesian privateer [21] was chosen to convey it; and the captain, Theopompus, used such diligence, that on the third day he reached Lacedæmon.

s. 21.

The prisoners in the mean time being conveyed to Lampsacus, it became matter of very serious consideration how to dispose of numbers, so beyond all common example of battles among the Greeks.   The allies were assembled for consultation; and that animosity appeared among them, which the antient manner of warfare was likely to excite. Many accusations were urged against the Athenians, of what they had done, and what they had proposed to do.   Of two triremes, a Corinthian and an Andrian, lately taken, the crews by order of the Athenian general Philocles, had been put to death by being thrown down a precipice. It was averred, and Xenophon seems to acknowlege it as a truth, that the Athenians, in a council of war, had determined to cut off the right hand of every prisoner to be made in the action which they were seeking.   Adeimantus alone, of the generals, is said to have opposed this inhuman resolution.   Many other enormities were alledged; and

s. 22.

the council resolved, that all the prisoners who were Athenian citizens, except Adeimantus, should be put to death.   Lysander, after reproaching Philocles with setting the first example, among the Greeks, of a most cruel violation of the law of war (which however, as in the

---

[18] Τὰ μεγάλα ἰςία.

[19] Τὰ τειχύδρια al. χίιδρια.

[20] So I think Xenophon must be understood; and the expression of Plutarch, in

his life of Lysander, tho rather loose, tends to confirm the interpretation.

[21] Μιλήσιος λῃσὴν.

course

course of this History we have had too much occasion to observe, was neither. the first nor peculiar to the Athenians) began the execution, for so much the expression of Xenophon seems to assert, by killing that general with his own hand. The Athenian citizens, who fell victims to the vengeance of the allies, and perhaps in some measure to the convenience of the Spartan general, were, according to Plutarch, three thousand. Plut. vit. Lys.

Adeimantus, alone saved from this bloody execution, did not escape with his character clear: it was asserted that, being corrupted by Lysander with Persian gold, he had betrayed the fleet. The charge, however, was never proved; nor does it appear how Adeimantus could have commanded the circumstances which put the fleet into the enemy's hands[22]; and the execution of the other generals, who indeed seem never to have been. accused, appears proof of their innocence. Not that the narrative of Xenophon gives all the information we might desire. The conduct, however, of the Athenian commanders altogether seems to have been totally inexcusable; tho in what degree any one was separately blameworthy does not appear. While the command of gold, which Lysander possessed, excites one kind of suspicion, the haste and the extent of the execution, together with the little scrupulousness usual among the Greeks, may excite another. At the same time it is possible that the misconduct, in the Athenian armament, may have arisen from division of command and violence of party. To carry any steddy authority may have been impossible; and, while none could confide in the government at home, all would fear it; not for their misdeeds, but for the prevalence of a faction, adverse to the faction with which they were connected. Xen. Hel. ut. sup.

Athens, the trap and grave of her victorious generals, would not be the place where, in the present disasterous circumstances, Conon would expect refuge for himself, or where nine ships could probably be of

[22] We find, in the Grecian services, where a command was committed to many, it was common for each to take his day in turn (Herod. l. 6. c. 110. et Thucyd. l. 6. c. 91.); but the historian does not say that the day of the action was the day of Adeimantus's command, or that, till the attack made by Lysander (except, in the negligence of the Athenians, which had increased gradually) the circumstances of that day differed from those of the four preceding.

any

any important service to the public.   As soon therefore as he was
beyond danger of pursuit, he dispatched the sacred ship Paralus alone
to bear the news of a defeat, which could be scarcely less than the
stroke of death to the commonwealth.   For himself, fortunately having
friendship with Evagoras, who ruled the Grecian city of Salamis in
Cyprus, he directed his course thither, with his remaining squadron,
and was kindly received.

SECTION V.

*Consequences of the battle of Aigospotami.   Siege of Athens.   Con-
clusion of the Peloponnesian war.*

THE ruin of the Athenian marine, effected at Aigospotami, put all the
dependencies of the commonwealth at once into the power of the
enemy : Lysander had only to direct the course of his victorious fleet,
and take possession.   The command of the strait, communicating with
the Euxine sea, was his first object.   As soon as he appeared between
Byzantium and Chalcedon, both those important places desired to
capitulate.   The Athenian garrisons were allowed to depart in safety;
but policy prompted this apparent lenity.   Lysander already looked
forward to the conquest of Athens; and, against the uncommon strength
of the fortifications of that city, famine would be the only weapon of
certain efficacy.   As therefore any augmentation of the numbers within
would promote his purpose, he permitted all Athenian citizens to go
to Athens, but to Athens only.   Those Byzantines who had taken a
leading part in delivering their city to Alcibiades, apprehensive perhaps more of their fellowcitizens than of Lysander, retired into Pontus.
Meanwhile the Paralus, arriving by night at Peiræus, communicated
intelligence, such as no crew perhaps of the unfortunate fleet, not
protected by the sacred character of the ship, would have dared to carry.
Alarm and lamention, beginning immediately about the harbor, were
rapidly communicated through the town of Peiræus, and then passing
from mouth to mouth, by the long walls, up to the city, the consterna-
12   tion

tion became universal; and that night, says the cotemporary historian, no person slept in Athens. Grief for the numerous slain, the best part of the Athenian youth, among whom everyone had some relation or friend to mourn, was not the prevailing passion; it was overborne by the dread, which pervaded all, of that fate to themselves, which, however individuals might be innocent, the Athenian people as a body were conscious of deserving, for the many bloody massacres perpetrated at their command. The treatment of the Histiæans, Scionæans, Toronæans, Æginetans, and many other Grecian people (it is still the cotemporary Attic historian who speaks) but, above all, of the Melians, a Lacedæmonian colony, recurred to every memory, and haunted every imagination.

Athens was not even now without able men, capable of directing public affairs in any ordinary storm. But, beside that the remaining strength of the commonwealth was utterly unequal to the force that would be brought against it, the lasting strife of faction, and the violence of intestine tumult, had nearly destroyed all coherence in the constituent parts of the government. Nothing remained of that public confidence, which, after the Sicilian overthrow, had inabled those who took the lead to surprize all Greece with new exertion, and even to recover superiority in the war. The leader of the soverein many was Cleophon, by trade a musical-instrument-maker, who, treading in the steps of Cleon and Hyperbolus, had acquired power even superior to what they had formerly held. Such was his confidence in his ascendancy, that he did not scruple, in scorn of democratical equality, to assume the distinctions and pomp of command. To have a residence suited to his new dignity, he used opportunity offered by the banishment of Andocides, chief of one of the most antient and eminent families, to occupy his house. But public agony and fear inforced, for the moment, sober conduct, and a disposition to listen to those fittest to advise. On the morrow after the arrival of the fatal news, a general assembly being held, such measures were resolved on as the exigency of the moment most required. Immediate siege by land and sea was expected. To raise a fleet able to oppose that of the enemy was no longer possible. It was therefore determined to block up all

the

Isocr. de pace, p. 218. t. 2. Æsch. de legat. p. 254.

Andoc. de myst.

the ports except one, to repair the walls, to appoint guards, and prepare every way to sustain a siege.

Xen. Hel.
l. 2. c. 2.
s. 3.

Meanwhile Lysander, after receiving the submission of the Hellespontine cities, sailed to Lesbos, where Mitylenë immediately surrendered to him. He sent Eteonicus, with only ten ships, to the Thracian coast, and all the Athenian dependencies there acceded to the Lacedæmonian terms. All the ilands hastened to follow the example, Samos alone excepted. The Samians, in the savage fury of democracy, answered the summons by a massacre of the men of rank[23] among their citizens, and prepared for defence.

s. 4.

Means to punish this insulting barbarity were not likely to be wanting: at present a greater object called Lysander. He sent information, at the same time to Lacedæmon and Deceleia, that he was ready to sail for Peiræus with two hundred triremes. The Lacedæmonian government determined upon a strong exertion, to put a speedy end to a war which had lasted, with scarcely any perfect intermission, twenty-six years. The Peloponnesian allies were summoned to arms, consisting now of all the states of the peninsula except Argos. The whole force of Laconia was at the same time ordered to march: the king, Pausanias, son of the regent who won the battle of Platæa, commanded in chief. With the powerful army thus assembled, Pausanias entered Attica: Agis joined him with his troops from Deceleia; and they fixed their head-quarters together in the celebrated gymnasium of Academia, close to Athens.

s. 5.

The interval of leisure for the fleet, during the preparation for the march of the army, was employed by Lysander in an act of justice and charity, likely to bring great credit to himself, and popularity to the Lacedæmonian name. There were, wandering about Greece, some Melians and Æginetans, who, by accidental absence, or some other lucky chance, had escaped the general massacre of their people by the Athenians. These Lysander collected and reïnstated in their ilands. From Ægina he proceeded to Salamis, which he plundered; and then, with a hundred and fifty triremes, took his station at the mouth of the harbour of Peiræus, to prevent supplies to Athens by sea.

[23] Τῶν γνωρίμων.

Without

Without an ally, without a fleet, without stores, and blockaded by Xen. Hel.
l. 2. c. 2.
s. 6. sea and land, the Athenians made no proposal to their victorious enemies : in sullen despondency they prepared, to the best of their ability, for defence, without a reasonable view but to procrastinate their final doom, and certain to suffer in the interval. But the consideration, for the cotemporary historian dwells upon that point, that without even revenge for a pretence, in meer wantonness of power [24], they had doomed to massacre and extirpation so many Grecian states, whose only crime was alliance with those who had now obtained such a superiority in arms, incited to stubborn resistance and deterred intreaty. Not that there was unanimity on this subject within the walls of Athens. On the contrary, the party which had established the Lys. adv.
Agor. &
Eratosth. government of the Fourhundred, of which a relic was still considerable, far from viewing the approach of the Lacedæmonians with the same apprehensions as the democratical chiefs, looked to it rather as what might afford them relief, and even be turned to their advantage. But hence the democratical party had only the more jealousy, not wholly an unreasonable jealousy, of any treaty to be managed under their direction; and, between the two, the moderate and worthy had difficulty to interfere at all in public affairs.

Meanwhile the operations of the besiegers tended meerly to blockade : no assault was attempted : the purpose was to make the effect of famine sure; and before long it was severely felt by the Athenians. Not however till many had died of hunger did they even talk of capitulation. Xen. Hel.
l. 2. c. 2.
s. 7. At length a deputation was sent to king Agis, for he appears to have remained alone to command the blockade, offering alliance offensive and defensive with Lacedæmon, which, in the language of Grecian politics, implied political subjection, but stipulating for the preservation of their fortifications and their harbor. Agis gave for answer, ' that ' he had no power to treat; proposals must be addressed to the admi- ' nistration at Lacedæmon.' Ministers were then sent into Pelopon- s. 8. nesus : but at Sellasia, on the border of Laconia, a haughty message from the ephors commanded their immediate return; informing them,

---

[24] 'Ου τιμωρούμενοι—ἀλλὰ διὰ τὴν ὕϐριν ἠδίκουν.

' that the terms they brought were known at Lacedæmon ; and, if they
' desired peace, they must come better instructed.'

This answer, communicated at Athens, filled the city with despair.
Condemnation of the Athenian people to slavery was the least evil
now expected from the revenge of a conquering enemy ; and, before
even another deputation could bring an answer from Lacedæmon,
many must perish of hunger. In this nearly-threatening wreck of

Lys. adv.
Eratosth.
p. 428.

the commonwealth, the council of Areiopagus, still holding a dignified
existence, tho with curtailed authority, endevored to mediate between
the contending factions, and proposed to undertake that negotiation,
for preserving the ruins of the falling state, which the enemy refused
to enter into with one party, and the people pertinaciously refused to
commit to the other. But popular jealousy prevented the salutary
measure. The Many were taught to fear that the Areiopagus would

Xen. Hel.
1. 2. c. 2.
s. 9.
Lys. adv.
Eratosth.
p. 412.
& adv. Agor.
p. 451, 453.
Xen. ut sup.

join the oligarchal party, and make terms for their exclusive advantage. It was understood that the Lacedæmonians, among other things,
required the demolition of the long walls for the space of ten furlongs.
Archestratus, a member of the council, only declaring his opinion, in
his place, that such a requisition ought not to prevent a treaty, which
might save the wretched remains of the commonwealth, was imprisoned ;
and a decree of the people passed, forbidding even to consult about
such an article.

But, in holding out the requisition to demolish the walls, no assurance having been given that slavery should not be the common doom,
the dread of this made the people so untractable, that the leading men
seem to have been at a loss to know what safely they might even propose,
in so pressing an exigency. Cleophon himself could no longer either
command or appease the popular mind. His opponents used the opportunity for preferring a capital accusation against him. Examples of
what might be done, by ably using critical emergencies, abounded in
the annals of the Athenian government. Cleon, when nearly the
despotic tyrant of Athens, had been fined ; Hyperbolus banished by
ostracism : Cleophon was condemned to death and executed. If

Lys. in. Ni-
com. p. 849.
ed. Reiske.

Lysias, speaking as a pleader, should be trusted, a fraud, of most
dangerous tendency, was used by his opponents : the real law not warranting

ranting a capital sentence, they made an interpolation in the code of
Solon, in pursuance of which condemnation was pronounced. That
some of the party adverse to Cleophon were not very scrupulous, we
have sufficient assurance; but what credit may be due to the story told
by Lysias, no information on the subject remaining from the cotemporary historian, seems not easy now to judge.

The execution of Cleon however was evidently the removal of a
principal obstacle to accommodation. Theramenes, becoming more
a leading man, ventured to undertake that, if he might be commissioned to go to Lysander, as well as to Lacedæmon, he would bring
certain information whether there was a serious intention to reduce the
Athenian people to slavery, or whether the demolition of the walls was
required only to insure political subjection. The people in assembly
gave their approbation, and Theramenes went; but it seems implied,
by Xenophon, that he did not execute his commission with perfect
good faith. He remained with Lysander more than three months.
What his difficulties really were, is nowhere clearly indicated; but the
appearance rather is, that he waited for the time when the total failure
of provisions, among the Athenian people, should inforce patient attention to any advice, by which their immediate destruction might be
obviated.

*Xen. ibid. &
Lys. adv.
Agor. p.451.*

How the Athenians were inabled to support themselves so long, after
mortality from famine was begun among them, the historian has
omitted to mention: but some incidental information, remaining from
Isocrates, considered together with Xenophon's account of the circumstances of the siege, in some degree explains it. The Peloponnesians, masters of Attica, and commanding the seas, trusted that they
could starve the city into submission, without the great labor and
expence of a contravallation, such as the circuit of Athens and Peiræus,
and the walls connecting them, would require; and, more completely
to deter the introduction of provisions, they denounced, by proclamation, immediate death against any who should be taken in the
attempt. But the pressure of want, and the dread of captivity, coin-
ciding with the passion for distinction, strong in Athenian breasts,
excited to daring action; and the Peloponnesian army could not

completely guard the extensive circuit of the walls, nor the fleet, in
all weathers, perfectly block the harbours.   In these circumstances
the captain of the Paralus (the same who had been sent by Conon
with the news of the defeat at Aigospotami) distinguished himself by
successful adventure.   His name is unknown to us; but, through the
incident that Isocrates afterward pleaded a cause for him, we learn
that he, together with his brother, found means, not only to introduce provisions into the harbour of Peiræus, but sometimes even to
intercept vessels bringing provisions for the Peloponnesian fleet; and
that they were rewarded with crowns, and with the public thanks of
the Athenian people, solemnly pronounced before the statues of the
heroes, styled the eponymian, standing near the prytaneium, from
whom the wards of Attica were named.

But notwithstanding these occasional supplies, want, and the apprehension of want, grew more and more pressing in Athens.   Theramenes
therefore, in the fourth month after his departure, trusting that the
ferocity of the democratical spirit might be sufficiently tamed, ventured to return, without having performed what he had undertaken.
To the anxious multitude, assembled in haste to learn the result of
his tedious negotiation, he excused himself, by imputing his detention
to Lysander; who dismissed him, he said, at last, with a declaration,
' that he had no authority, either to grant terms, or to say what the
' Lacedæmonian government would require; and that application to
' any purpose could only be made to the ephors.'   It was no longer
time for hesitation.   An embassy, consisting of ten persons, with
Theramenes at the head, was immediately appointed to go to Lacedæmon, with the fullest authority to treat concerning the fate of
Athens, and save the miserable remains of the commonwealth, if
they could.

The sacred character of ambassadors procured free passage for
Theramenes and his collegues, as far as Sellasia.   There, as the former
embassy, they were met by an officer from the ephors, who would not
permit them to proceed, until they had given satisfactory assurance
of the fulness of their powers.   On their arrival at Lacedæmon, an
assembly of the deputies of the Lacedæmonian confederacy was held,

in

in which the fate of Athens was to be decided   The Corinthian and
Theban deputies contended vehemently 'that no terms should be Xen. ibid.
Isocr. de
Pacæ. p. 220.
t.2.& Plataic.
p. 44. t. 3.
' granted : the Athenian commonwealth, the enemy of the common
' liberties of Greece, so nearly successful in the horrid attempt to
' inslave or exterminate the whole nation, ought to be annihilated :
' the people should be sold for slaves, and the site of the city should
' be made a sheepwalk, like the Crisæan plain.'   Many of the other
deputies supported these opinions: but the Lacedæmonians, whose
administration was little subject to passionate counsels or hasty decision, seem to have predetermined otherwise.   Deprived of its navy
and of the revenue and power derived from transmarine dependencies,
Athens, under oligarchal government, they thought might be a valuable
dependency of Lacedæmon; and perhaps the recollection of what had
happened but a few years before, when almost all Peloponnesus had
been united in war against them, might give to apprehend that, at
some future period, they might want a balancing power against
Corinth, Thebes, or Argos.   They declared therefore, with ostentation
of regard for the common welfare and glory of Greece, that it would
not become the Peloponnesian confederacy, and least of all the Lacedæmonians, to reduce to slavery a Grecian people, to whom the nation
was beholden for the most important services, in the greatest danger
that ever threatened it.   Accordingly, they proposed, and it was resolved, that the conditions, upon which the Athenians should be permitted to exist in civil freedom, should be these: 'That all ships of
' war should be surrendered, except twelve; that the long walls, and
' the fortifications of Peiræus, should be destroyed; that all exiles and
' fugitives should be restored to the rights of the city; that the
' Athenians should hold for friends and enemies all other people, as
' they were friends or enemies to Lacedæmon; that the Athenian
' forces should go wherever Lacedæmon might command, by land
' and sea.'

With these terms Theramenes and his collegues hastened back to Xen. Hel.
l. 2. c. 2.
s. 13.
Athens.   Already such numbers had perished for want, that to hold
many days longer was impossible.   The arrival of the ambassadors
therefore was no sooner announced, than the people from all parts of
                                                      the

the city crowded about them, in the most painful anxiety, lest an irresistible enemy should still have refused to treat, and no choice should remain but to die of hunger, or surrender to the mercy of those from whom they had scarcely a pretence to ask mercy. Information, that a treaty was concluded, gave, for the night, general relief. On the morrow an assembly of the people was held. Theramenes declared the terms, which, he said, were the best that himself and his collegues had been able to obtain, and such as, in his opinion, the people, in the present most unfortunate state of things, would do well to accept. A considerable body, nevertheless, even now, affirmed pertinaciously, that they would not consent to the demolition of the walls. A large majority however, yielding to the pressure of extreme want, carried a decree, ratifying the treaty concluded by their ambassadors.

Xen. Hel.
l. 2. c. 2.
s. 14.
The acceptance of the offered terms being notified to the besieging armament, Agis took possession of the walls, and Lysander entered the harbour of Peiræus with his fleet. The demolition of the walls
5 May.
B. C. 405.
Ol. 93. ¼.
Ann. Thu.
was a principal circumstance of triumph for the Peloponnesians. It was begun by the army, with much parade, to the sound of military music, and with an alacrity, says the cotemporary Athenian historian, natural to those who considered that day as the era of restored freedom to Greece. Notices were then sent to the exiles and fugitives, mostly men of the best families of Athens, to whom this sad reverse in the fortune of their country would alone give the means of returning to it, and recovering their property. Their presence was necessary toward the probable permanence of the next measure, the change of the
Xen. Hel.
l. 2. c. 3.
s. 1, 2.
government to an oligarchy. The popular assembly was abolished, and the supreme authority was committed, for the present, to a council of thirty, among whom Theramenes found a place. They were directed to consider of a new form of political administration, such as Lacedæmon should approve, preserving the antient laws and civil govern-
s. 3.
ment of the commonwealth, as far as might consist with oligarchy.

Things being so far settled in Athens, Agis led away the Peloponnesian army, including the garrison of Deceleia; and all Attica, but Attica only, became once more the quiet possession of the Athenians. Lysander conducted the fleet to Samos. The people of that iland,

l   after

after sustaining a siege for some time, capitulated; and the terms granted were milder than their conduct had intitled them to expect: they were permitted to depart in safety, whither they pleased; carrying, however, only the clothes they wore. The lands, houses, slaves, cattle, the whole iland in short, with all it contained, were given to their fellowcitizens of the aristocratical party. After having settled this business, Lysander dismissed the ships of the allies, and with the Lacedæmonian squadron sailed for Laconia.

So ended the Peloponnesian war, in its twenty-seventh year; and so Lacedæmon, now in alliance with Persia, became again decidedly the leading power of Greece; and the aristocratical, or rather the oligarchal, triumphed over the democratical interest, in almost every commonwealth of the nation.

END OF THE SECOND VOLUME.

Lightning Source UK Ltd.
Milton Keynes UK
16 October 2010

161404UK00001B/19/P